I WAS WRONG

JIM BAKKER

with KEN ABRAHAM

THOMAS NELSON PUBLISHERS
NASHVILLE • ATLANTA • LONDON • VANCOUVER

Published in Nashville, Tennessee, by Thomas Nelson, Inc., and distributed in Canada by Word Communications, Ltd., Richmond, British Columbia, and in the United Kingdom by Word (UK), Ltd., Milton Keynes, England.

Unless otherwise noted, Scripture quotations are from THE NEW KING JAMES VERSION of the Bible. Copyright © 1979, 1980, 1982, Thomas Nelson, Inc., Publishers.

Scripture quotations noted KJV are from The Holy Bible, KING JAMES VERSION.

Scripture quotations noted NIV are from The Holy Bible: NEW INTERNATIONAL VERSION. Copyright © 1978 by the New York International Bible Society. Used by permission of Zondervan Bible Publishers.

Scripture quotations noted TLB are from THE LIVING BIBLE (Wheaton, Illinois: Tyndale House Publishers, 1971) and are used by permission.

Heritage USA photographs taken by PTL staff photographers. © Regent Carolina Corp. Used by permission.

ISBN 0-7852-7425-1 (hardcover)

ISBN 0-7852-7136-8 (paperback)

Printed in the United States of America

4 5 6 7 — 02 01 00 99 98 97

To my two wonderful children,

Tammy Sue and Jamie Charles,

who never wavered in their love and support

and who gave me a reason to go on when

all hope was gone.

Contents

Acknowledgments

To Tammy Sue and Doug, for giving me the best gift a grandfather can receive—two wonderful grandchildren, my namesake, James Martin, and Jonathan Douglas Chapman.

To my mother and father, sister Donna and brother Norman, who never wavered in their love and support of me.

To my beloved Grandma Irwin, who gave me and taught me unconditional love.

To Dr. Ruth Westrick, a truly great lady and a compassionate, unsung hero of the prison system who fought to give me self-respect.

To all those faithful friends who wrote to me in prison and those who visited me.

To my PTL Partners, who prayed for and supported me throughout the years.

To Tammy Faye, for all she gave to me, especially our two fabulous children.

To all those I hurt and disappointed. Since I can't speak to each of you personally, please consider this my heartfelt apology.

To Dr. Dan Foster, who helped change my life and guided me through the valley of the shadow of death.

To my fellow inmates, who will always be my brothers.

To Paul Olson, Owen Carr, Dave Roever, C. M. Ward, Larry Wright, Bob Gass, and especially Pastor Phil Shaw, who went beyond the call of duty to keep me alive.

To Alan Dershowitz, for winning my appeal, and to the judges who granted it, and to Susan and Jim Toms, for never giving up!

To Professor Jim Albert, his students, and Ben Malcolm for their invaluable work on my case.

To the Honorable Judge Graham Mullen, for reducing my forty-five-year sentence to eight years. I will be eternally grateful.

To the entire Paulk family; and to Carlene Julian, Mike Young, and Bo Foutch; Molly and Bob D'Andrea; Tommy Barnett; and Mike and Heather Wall, for being an extended family to my son when I could not be there.

To all those God used in my life-changing journey, including the journalists, judges, prosecutors, lawyers, and those who testified in my trials.

To Roger, for teaching me so much, especially how to catch a ball.

To the kind guards, who helped make life a little better, and the unkind guards, who drove me closer to God.

To Shirley Fulbright, for all her hard work on this book and for standing with and helping our family for two decades.

To Sam Moore, Byron Williamson, Rolf Zettersten, Rick Nash, Ted Squires, Melanee Bandy, Bob Bubnis, and the team at Thomas Nelson Publishers, for believing in this book.

To Lonnie Hull Dupont, whose tenacious editorial skills were like those of a kind surgeon, wielded with charm, wit, and compassion.

To Doc, for teaching me how to clean toilets and for being a good friend when I needed one desperately.

To Billy and Ruth Graham, who demonstrated God's love to me, giving me dignity when my self-worth was zero.

To Franklin Graham, who risked so much to reach out and minister to me.

To the unknown guard.

To Ken Abraham, my patient, kind, long-suffering, gentle friend who used his skills to craft this book and tell my story.

Most of all, to my best friend, who never left me . . . Jesus!

Introduction

THE WORDS "I WAS WRONG" DO NOT COME EASILY TO ME.

For most of my life I believed that my understanding of God and how He wants us to live was not only correct but worth exporting to the world. One reason I have risked putting my heart into print is to tell you that my previous philosophy of life, out of which my attitudes and actions flowed, was fundamentally flawed. God does not promise that we will all be rich and prosperous, as I once preached. When I really studied the Bible while in prison, it became clear to me that not one man or woman—not even prophets of God—led a life without pain. God does promise that He will never leave us or forsake us, no matter what trial or pain we must go through . . . whether it be loss of reputation, loss of position or power, financial calamity, addiction, separation, divorce, or imprisonment.

It is important to understand that some people who have played key roles in my life have described events and circumstances discussed within these pages in radically different terms. Both friends and foes have written books and given interviews to the media, and a few have even given sworn testimony before judges. In doing so, they have presented their stories from their perspectives. That is their prerogative. This book is written from my point of view and represents how I saw events transpire that toppled me from the pinnacle of PTL power and eventually put me in prison.

Admittedly, I would have been much happier to skip some of the information within this book. I had no desire to relive many of these experiences. Dredging up and facing for the first time many of the things that were said and done during the pivotal days of PTL's demise was extremely difficult for me. Yet that was nothing compared to the torturous task of going back through the emotional breakdown during my trial and my first frightening experiences inside prison walls.

At several points during the writing of this book, I was ready to quit. I don't need to write a book. I do not have any axes to grind with anyone. What is in the past is over and done, and I am ready to move on with my life. Only the conviction that I owed this book to my family, friends, and the many dedicated former PTL staff members and PTL Partners, along with the confidence that God could use this volume for good, kept me going.

I hope that when you have finished reading these pages, you will have a better understanding of how and why I did things at PTL, in prison, and beyond prison's gates. More importantly, I hope that the lessons I have learned the hard way will be helpful to you. I trust too that my story will be preventive medicine for some. The mistakes I made are still being perpetuated in ministries, churches, businesses, marriages, and families. The temptation to have more, do more, earn more, build bigger, emphasize material things rather than spiritual, protect the image regardless of the cost, look the other way rather than confront wrong—these are just a few of the areas in which I have a new mindset, which I hope will be helpful to you.

I did not want to sugarcoat my story, but in some instances, with the help of the editorial team at Thomas Nelson Publishers, I have purposely sanitized certain parts of the account to avoid unnecessarily offending anyone. It is impossible to overemphasize the horror I felt when I was placed in an asylum after my collapse during my trial in 1989 or the dehumanization that I experienced in prison. Similarly, the lifelong impact and the fear of exposure I felt as a result of being molested as a child cannot be told too emphatically. While I have tried to stay within the realms of decency and discretion, please know that one's worst nightmares frequently become reality in prison, and I can give you only a shrouded glimpse into what I experienced.

To be sure, certain information in this book has been culled from other sources. Facts relating to my emotional breakdown, for example, obviously were supplied to me by the doctors, media personnel, and other witnesses. I was in no condition to chronicle anything, and to this day, many of the details remain hidden from me, embedded somewhere in the corners of my brain. Similarly, information regarding what happened at PTL after my resignation in 1987 was supplied to me in massive doses by friends, family members, and former employees. In all cases, any facts to which I could not personally attest veracity were corroborated by at least two credible sources, and usually three or more. My editorial team and I have meticulously researched any information that was not firsthand. This is an accurate story insofar as it can be told without destroying more lives.

To prevent further pain, some names of people who are not public figures have been changed. In other cases, to shield the identities of real individuals, I have purposely created composite characters. Be assured, however, that these are stories of real people; the events recorded within these pages actually happened.

In many ways I have written this book with much trepidation, because in it I have attempted to tell the true story without violating the principles of forgiveness. It took nearly five years in prison for me to fully forgive others and to accept forgiveness for myself. I have no desire to uncover what God has laid to rest. Yet I have felt compelled to write this story to show you that, in the darkest moments of my life, God was there, even when I thought He had abandoned me. And I know that if God did not leave me in my time of trouble, He will not leave you when you walk through your deepest valleys.

I have been branded for life by the events you will read about in this book. Strangely, perhaps, I would not have it any other way. Through it all I have come to trust God more than ever before. By no means do I feel that because of my experiences I have arrived. On the contrary, I am in process; my restoration continues on an ongoing basis. I am a fellow struggler, living one day at a time, along with the millions of other people in the world whose lives have been decimated and who are now involved in the various stages of healing and rebuilding. For that reason, in this book I offer no simplistic solutions to difficult problems. Instead, what you will find is an irrepressible confidence that no matter how dark your day might be, you can make it, because God loves you. He really does.

1

Judgment Day

JUST BEFORE THREE O'CLOCK ON OCTOBER 24, 1989—THE day of my sentencing—Judge Robert Potter furrowed his brow and bowed his head slightly as he lowered his voice to a mumble. The crowd in the U.S. district courthouse in Charlotte, North Carolina, collectively leaned forward in an attempt to hear the judge's words. Judge Potter was known in the Carolina court system as "Maximum Bob," a nickname he had earned for his tendency to hand down the longest sentences allowed by law. Few in the courtroom that day expected him to deviate from his normal pattern.

It had already been a difficult afternoon. The sentencing procedures had begun promptly at 2:00 p.m., but by the time my lawyer, Harold Bender, and the Federal prosecutors, Deborah Smith and Jerry Miller, had completed their final presentations, it was 2:55 p.m. Now, after two and a half years of uncertainty concerning my future, it all came down to one man's opinion of what should be done with me.

It had been a tempestuous trial that received more pretrial publicity than any trial in Charlotte's history. Judge Potter had personally seated a jury for the case in one day. Once under way, one witness fell off the stand and was thought to have died. I collapsed the following day, and the judge shipped me off for psychiatric evaluation. When the trial resumed, it was interrupted again, this time by Hurricane Hugo, which ripped into the Atlantic coastline at Charleston, South Carolina, and struck nearly two hundred miles inland, all the way to Charlotte, a rare meteorological phenomenon. The hurricane was one of the worst in history, devastating thousands of homes and damaging millions of dollars' worth of property. In Charlotte, my trial was postponed for several days.

I had been charged with fraud and conspiring to commit fraud for allegedly receiving $158 million from 152,903 PTL Lifetime Partners during my tenure as president of Heritage USA, a four-square-mile Christian retreat center operated by Heritage Village Church and Missionary Fellowship in Fort Mill, South Carolina. Heritage USA was intended to be a modern version of the old-time camp-meeting grounds that had so profoundly shaped America's heritage during the eighteenth and nineteenth centuries. The primary means of presenting the ministry and message of Heritage USA to the world was our television program, variously known as *The PTL Club, The Jim and Tammy Show*, and other names. From its meager beginnings in a storefront studio in downtown Charlotte, *The PTL Club* grew to become the flagship program of the Inspirational Television Network, a satellite network which, at its peak, aired in more than fourteen million homes in the USA and around the world.

If *The PTL Club* was the inspirational mouthpiece of the ministry, the PTL Lifetime Partners were the spiritual and financial backbone of Heritage USA and the Inspirational Television Network. Nearly all the ministries at PTL, including the television programs, were funded primarily by donations from the viewers. Anyone who donated any gift at all to our nonprofit, tax-exempt organization was known as a "partner" in ministry with us. Absolutely no legal obligations or connotations were connected to the term *partner*. It was simply our term for what another charitable organization might call a financial donor or a contributor.

The PTL Lifetime Partners, however, were a group of people who wanted to do more to support the ministry than send an occasional contribution. They wanted to be "partners" in our ministry for the remainder of their lives; many of them wanted to come to Fort Mill and be on the grounds to enjoy and become involved in the ministry, and they expressed that desire in a tangible way.

Most of the PTL Lifetime Partners donated a one-time gift of one thousand dollars to PTL. Those who did were offered lodging free of charge for four days and three nights at the Heritage Grand Hotel, the gorgeous five-hundred-room luxury hotel constructed in 1984 on the grounds of Heritage USA. It was this program (which I will explain in greater detail later in this book) that eventually led to the government's charges of fraud against me and conspiracy to commit fraud along with one of my top executives.

2

The government purported that I had knowingly "overbooked" the lodging space at Heritage USA by continuing to encourage people to become Lifetime Partners beyond the point at which we were able to accommodate them. The government maintained that we were trying to dupe some of our most loyal financial supporters out of their money. Because I had promoted the program on television, I was charged with wire fraud. Because I had promoted the program through our brochures, newsletters, and other written materials that had been sent through the mail, I was charged with mail fraud. Since I had ostensibly done these things with the mutual consent and knowledge of my senior executive officer, he and I were charged with conspiracy to commit fraud.

Much of the case, however, revolved around my lifestyle. The government took three weeks to build their case against me, calling ninety-one witnesses, twenty-two of whom did not even speak to the issue of fraud, but who were apparently on the stand simply because I had made an "extravagant purchase" from them. When it was the defense's turn, however, Judge Potter complained, "It's getting ridiculous now," after two days of testimony on my behalf.

I felt that my lawyers did little to defend me against the government's charges. They spent most of their time trying to discredit the prosecution's witnesses, showing to the jury that the PTL Lifetime Partners trusted me. One juror later stated that throughout the trial, she kept waiting to hear my defense. It never came.

In a last-ditch effort I took the stand on my own behalf, hoping to convince the jury that just as I had said over the air and through the mail, we were in fact building enough facilities to house the Lifetime Partners. I had pinned most of my hope on a chart that I had made myself, which depicted the progressive growth of the Lifetime Partners program and facilities. I had planned to present the exhibit to the jury, but the judge ruled that I could not present it because substantiated facts and evidence must precede the introduction of a chart to the jury. I had submitted the required substantiating evidence, including PTL newspapers, blueprints, and promotional literature, which would have shown the progression of the Lifetime Partnership program and that the PTL Partners had been well informed concerning it. Unfortunately, my lawyers had placed the materials into evidence without reading it to the jury during the trial. Therefore my chart depicting the information was inadmissible as an exhibit.

Judge Potter allowed me to place my chart out of the sight of the jurors, at my feet, so I could refer to it as long as the jurors could not see it. I presented the information, looking down at the chart, rather than at the jurors. My efforts to communicate were totally ineffective.

Ironically, my one last glimmer of hope was that the prosecutors would vigorously cross-examine me. I was ready for them. I knew what I had done and not done at PTL. But after only a few inquiries, the prosecutors announced, "No further questions."

My heart sank. I knew that I had not gotten my story across at all. At that moment, I felt certain I had lost the case. Few people were surprised when on October 6, 1989, the jury foreman announced "Guilty as charged" to all twenty-four counts.

Then, a mere nineteen days later, I was back in court to receive my sentence. Prior to pronouncing my sentence, Judge Potter commented on my character. I felt that he had shown contempt toward me throughout the trial, and in his concluding remarks, the judge said, "He had no thought whatever about his victims, and those of us who do have a religion are ridiculed as being saps from moneygrubbing preachers or priests." Although Judge Potter's comment would come back to haunt him later, at that moment, it sliced deeply into my heart and the hearts of my friends and family members who were in the courtroom that day. Looking back today and considering the information Judge Potter had before him, if I had been the judge, I would not have liked Jim Bakker either.

I was instructed to rise by my lawyer, and as I did, Harold Bender draped his arm around my shoulder. Terry Wilkinson, Harold's paralegal, placed her arm around the small of my back. It was as though my lawyers were trying to brace me for what was coming.

Judge Potter paused, looked down from his bench, and then in his usual muffled, gravel-toned voice began reading my sentence. The entire courtroom seemed to strain forward to hear what he was saying. Even standing only a few feet in front of the judge, I could not discern what he said.

The judge rattled off my sentences with machine-gun rapidity. "On counts One and Two, I sentence you to five years to be served concurrently. On counts Three and Four, I sentence you to five years to be served concurrently. Counts Five and Six, five years concurrent. Counts Seven and Eight, five years concurrent. Counts Nine through Eleven, five years concurrent. Counts Twelve through Fourteen, five years concurrent. Counts Fifteen through Seventeen, five years concurrent. Counts Eighteen through Twenty-three, five years concurrent. Count Twenty-four, five years."

In a matter of seconds, it was done; the judge's words were on record, words that began my prison years . . . years that would bring the greatest pain, fear, and loneliness I have ever known.

Judge Potter stopped the proceedings long enough to allow reporters to exit the courtroom if they wanted to leave. Thirty-eight of the forty-member press corps bolted out the door. Hundreds of other members of the press, forced to wait outside due to the space limitations, screamed for information from the reporters tearing from the building.

Inside the courtroom, I still did not understand what had happened. I turned to my lawyer and asked what the judge's words meant.

My lawyer replied in what seemed to me a matter-of-fact manner. "Forty-five years."

Forty-five years! I was stunned. I felt as though a huge wrecking ball had dropped on top of me. Every bone in my body felt like it had been pulverized, yet I continued to stand expressionless before the judge. I thought I might collapse right there in the front of the courtroom. The emotional pain was so intense, my body slipped into a state of shock.

My daughter, Tammy Sue, was seated in the first row beyond a railing right behind me. I heard Tammy Sue gasp; she let out a loud cry and then began to sob uncontrollably.

Judge Potter rapped his gavel several times and called out, "Order in the court! If there is not silence in the courtroom, or if there are any more outbursts, I will have the entire courtroom cleared."

To avoid antagonizing Judge Potter further, Gene Kennett, a minister friend of mine sitting next to Tammy Sue, attempted to quell the sounds of her sobbing by pulling my daughter toward him so her face was buried in his shoulder. She continued to cry.

I wanted to hold her and tell her everything was going to be all right as I had done so many times when she was a little girl. But I had to let my daughter pour her grief onto the shoulder of a person she barely knew. I wished it were still earlier that day, when Tammy Sue had hugged me and told me she loved me as we walked into the courthouse together.

Tammy Faye, my wife of thirty years, was not in the courtroom during my sentencing; she was in Orlando trying to keep our fledgling ministry alive. The stress and strain of the past three years had taken a severe toll on Tammy Faye, and by this time, she was unable to handle much more. My thirteen-year-old son, Jamie Charles, now grown-up enough to wear my clothes when he had come to be with me during the trial, also stayed home to take care of his mother. We were all emotionally exhausted.

I had planned to stay in a Charlotte hotel room near the courthouse the night before my sentencing. Tammy Sue decided she didn't want me to spend the night alone, so she, her husband Doug, and their nine-month-old baby James—my grandson and namesake—all moved into my one room at the hotel near the courthouse. I was glad for their company.

Baby James especially helped me to keep my mind off the ensuing sentencing. I fed James his bottles throughout the night and took him from his crib and held him close to me all night long. My first grandchild was a bright spot in my rapidly darkening world.

The following morning I carried James in my arms as I stopped at my lawyer's office on my way to court. I was so attached to my grandbaby, I did not want to let go of him. I wanted to take him with Tammy Sue and me to the sentencing, but my lawyer said, "It would be very offensive to the court to have a baby in the courtroom."

On Tuesday afternoon, just after Tammy Sue and I entered the federal courthouse, a rainbow appeared in the sky. Journalists and the crowd of onlookers awaiting Judge Potter's sentence stared and pointed at the unusual sight. *The Charlotte Observer* later described the rainbow as "a multicolored halo," forming a quarter of a circle around the sun.[1]

The rainbow remained in the sky from the time I went inside the courthouse until shortly after Judge Potter passed down my sentence. However, I never saw it.

Now the judge was ready to entertain further motions. Attorney Harold Bender immediately announced that we would be filing an appeal and asked Judge Potter to release me on bail, pending our appeal. Bender insisted that I was not a flight risk, that it would be highly unlikely that I would try to escape incarceration because I was so recognizable nationwide. Furthermore, the media reporters were already watching my home twenty-four hours a day.

Throughout the trial, the prosecution, on the other hand, had painted a picture of me as a menace to society and to myself. The prosecution persisted in characterizing my friends and especially the PTL Partners, people who had supported PTL with their prayers and donations, as mindless, easily manipulated cult members who might attempt to spirit me out of the country. On the day my verdict had been read, Potter himself expressed an opinion that the supporters who had testified on my behalf in court were so zealous in my defense that they had what he described as a "Jim Jones mentality."

To counteract that impression, at the sentencing hearing, Harold Bender had called several character witnesses to speak on my behalf, including my brother Norman, who had attended nearly all six weeks of my trial. Norman and the others had spoken lovingly, making their case as to why I should be released on bail pending my appeal.

But Judge Potter would have none of it and abruptly broke off all further comments. I was stunned by the realization that the forty-five-year sentence I had received, when added to my current age of forty-nine, was essentially a life sentence—but to me it felt more like a death sentence.

Now Judge Potter said, "Mr. Bakker, I order you to report to Federal prison immediately. Marshals, take the defendant to lockup until you can arrange to transport him."

It suddenly hit me: I was going to prison! Not someday, not next month after I had been allowed time to set my affairs in order, as is often permitted in white-collar cases. I was going to prison *today*. Right now!

I turned to reach out to the apple of my eye, to hug my little girl. Of course, Tammy Sue was no longer a little girl, but a grown, beautiful woman with her own husband and baby. But at this moment, she looked so fragile. Tears streamed down her face, yet I felt helpless to take her pain away. The dad who was always able to make things happen was being pulled away by a Federal marshal and could do nothing to help his daughter.

I quickly removed my watch and placed it in Tammy Sue's hand. "I love you, Susie!" I whispered. "I have to go now."

"I love you, Daddy." I could still hear her crying as the marshals led me from the courtroom.

The marshals escorted me down the hall, through several doorways, and finally into a room with a series of steel-barred cells. They unlocked a small, narrow cell with benches lining both sides. A strange looking exposed metal commode, with a sink atop the bowl where the water tank should have been, sat at the rear of the room. I walked inside the cell and sat down.

One of the marshals passed my travel clothes through the bars and instructed me to change. My attorney had warned me prior to my sentencing that there was a possibility I could be going to prison and suggested I bring a change of comfortable clothing to court. Although I decided to heed his advice and pack an outfit of clothing, I never dreamed that I would need them. I figured that even if the judge sentenced me to prison, he would surely allow me to return home to say good-bye to my family.

I had entered the courtroom on October 24 wearing one of my favorite, well-tailored suits. Little did I know that this would be the last day for years I would wear a fine suit of clothes.

Deep within the recesses of the Federal courthouse, I took off my tie and coat and changed into my blue jeans and a casual, deep blue shirt. I slipped on my favorite tennis shoes. Finally, I put on a bright royal blue corduroy jacket with squared shoulders. The jacket was one of my favorites. In selecting my wardrobe for that day, I had unconsciously chosen familiar, favorite clothing for a sense of security.

About that time the marshals came and unlocked my cell and took me across the hall to a small, closetlike room where I spent a few minutes talking to my lawyer, who could now only converse with me through a tiny opening from the other side of a glass window.

Harold tried to be encouraging. "Don't worry, Jim," he spoke quietly. "We're going to appeal this. We'll get you out of there. You won't be gone long. I'll come visit you soon and let you know how things are going."

I stared back at Harold Bender. Any hope was quickly slipping away. Harold seemed to me as nonchalant as he might have been had I been going off on a vacation. But I was leaving to begin a forty-five-year prison sentence! Perhaps he was simply trying to cheer me up.

The officers then took me down to the end of the small cell block where there was a camera and equipment for fingerprinting. A marshal there took my hand and placed my fingers, one at a time, onto a black ink pad, and then rolled each finger onto the appropriate square on a card. He did the same with both of my palms.

Another marshal ordered me to stand against the wall to be photographed. I made a conscious commitment to smile in every picture anyone ever took of me in prison. Even though my heart was breaking, I was determined that I would smile for the record. And I did! While serving my sentence, I did time in ten separate prisons, jails, and holding units. Most of these facilities took pictures of me upon entering their institution. I smiled in every single picture. Occasionally I would hear an officer say, "Take a few extra shots." I'm not sure what they did with the extra copies, but I suspect they will show up someday.

The marshals at Charlotte Federal Courthouse took my photograph with the numbers that would accompany me everywhere I went within the prison system. In a matter of moments, I had ceased to be Jim Bakker; I was now Inmate 07407-058.

I was entering a whole new society, with its own hierarchy, rules, and even vocabulary. Nobody prepared me for what I was to face in prison.

The marshals returned me to my cell where I sat for nearly two hours, staring at the bars. Suddenly I could hear the sound of rattling chains.

They were for me.

An officer fastened the chains around my waist; my hands were handcuffed and fastened to the chain. My feet were cuffed with manacles and chained together. The marshals opened my cell and led me, shuffling as fast as I could move, down a corridor and out several doors until we stepped outside into the fresh air. The courthouse had at one time been a post office, with a large loading dock in the rear of the building. Whether it was standard procedure or to avoid publicity and commotion, the marshals had decided to take me out by way of the loading dock.

The word had already gotten out that the marshals would be bringing me out the back way. The area behind the courthouse was actually twenty-five to thirty feet below street level with sidewalks above surrounding the huge pit in the ground, creating a crude amphitheater-like setting. Our "getaway car" was parked at the bottom of the amphitheater, flanked in front and back by police cars.

As soon as I came out the door, I looked up and saw people standing all around the ledge above the amphitheater. Members of the press with their cameras crowded in next to the railings, trying to get one last picture of me in what appeared to be total defeat.

I recognized several faces as I scanned the crowd. I saw many curious onlookers, a few hostile faces, but mostly I saw friendly faces. Some of the people waved at me and called out words of encouragement. I tried to wave back, but my chains prevented me from doing so. I smiled and nodded at them; that was all I could do.

The marshals led me down the steps from the loading dock to the car and then guided me into the rear seat. As the marshals' car climbed the ramp to the street level, I caught a glimpse of one of my longtime employees, a dear, motherly sort of friend, who was standing by herself along the rail weeping. I tried to wave good-bye but could not stretch my chained hands to the window level. She was the last supportive human being I saw as I left Charlotte.

The police escorted us out to the interstate highway. The last time I had received a police escort in Charlotte, our PTL television program had just won a Dove Award from the Gospel Music Association in Nashville. Upon returning to Charlotte, the plane on which Tammy Faye and I were traveling was running late. We were trying to get to our live TV broadcast on time and the Charlotte police escorted us from the airport to our studio.

As the police escort led the way, I tried not to think about the painful parallels between the better days at PTL and what I was experiencing now. Hardly had I made that determination when I noticed we were passing a road sign indicating the route to McAdenville, North Carolina.

McAdenville is a wonderful little town with a big Christmas spirit that had contributed to my inspiration to develop "Christmas City" at Heritage USA. Each year during the Christmas season, the people of McAdenville decorate their homes, stores, and trees with thousands of Christmas lights. This beautiful spectacle attracts thousands of appreciative sightseers.

As I passed the sign, I could not help recalling that about this time in previous years, our creative "Christmas City" staff at PTL would have been putting the finishing touches on our decorations. The trees throughout Heritage USA were adorned with 1,250,000 lights. Besides the celebration of lights, our staff created dramatic productions such as a "Living Nativity," featuring Mary and Joseph, the wise men, and baby Jesus, as well as live sheep, goats, horses, and even three camels!

We also created "Angel Boulevard," an amazing display of angels depicted in lights all the way down the road behind the five-hundred-room Heritage Grand Hotel and the almost completed five-hundred-room Heritage Grand Tower. A huge lighted Christmas tree sat atop the twenty-one-story Tower. According to a national bus-tour association, Christmas City became one of the top Christmas attractions in the United States. The Heritage USA security department recorded over one million visitors during the 1986 Christmas season alone.

Memories of Christmas City only served to exacerbate the darkness that was enveloping my soul. Everything within me wanted to scream.

All my life I had dreamed of building a center of inspiration that became PTL. Now, however, I honestly wondered if in fact it had not all been a colossal mirage. Was it real or had I merely imagined that I had once been the president of a worldwide ministry known as PTL? Maybe I had never implemented any ministry at all. Had I really been the host of a television program seen in all fifty states and many foreign countries? With the help of my dedicated staff and thousands of other people, had I truly spearheaded the building of a twenty-four-hour-a-day Inspirational Network?

And what of Fort Hope, a community designed to welcome homeless people; the more than nine hundred "People That Love" centers that fed hungry people every day in various parts of the world; and the Heritage House, a home for unwed mothers that provided a viable alternative to having an abortion; or the "Upper Room" prayer ministry, which had pastors available at any hour of the day or night to pray and counsel with hurting people? Maybe it was all an illusion. My brain continued to play tricks on me as I struggled in the back seat of a squad car to assemble the pieces of my broken heart, my dreams, and my life.

I had always believed that God loved me. He had literally granted me every desire of my heart, and I believed that His favor was upon me. Granted, anyone who knew my family and me also was well aware that we had gone through many personal problems and spiritual battles. Yet almost everything I had ever attempted to do in God's name prospered. Now I wasn't even sure where God was in my life, or if He loved me at all. I felt as though God had turned His back on me. Rejected and alone in the back seat of the squad car, questions ripped through my heart and mind. Was God punishing me for my sins? Was I really a "cancer upon the Body of Christ" as I had been labeled by one prominent Christian leader? Was I the evil person that the prosecutors in my trial and the media had presented to the world? Did I deserve to go to prison? Did I deserve to live . . . or did I deserve to die?

Deeper and deeper I plummeted into my own pit of depression. No answers were forthcoming from heaven. I heard no divine voice, only the sound of the police car's engine and the monotonous drone of tires on the pavement, taking me ever closer to prison.

How did I get into this mess?

2

Opening the Door to Destruction

THERE ARE MANY ANSWERS TO THE QUESTION "WHERE did things go wrong?" and one answer is my much-publicized encounter with Jessica Hahn. I knew I was wrong the moment I stepped into room 538 at the Sheraton Sand Key Resort in Clearwater Beach, Florida, on December 6, 1980. I never dreamed, however, how much trouble opening that door would cause. Inside that room, I met for the first and only time in my life, a twenty-one-year-old woman named Jessica Hahn.

Earlier that afternoon, I had been relaxing on the beach with my ten-year-old-daughter, Tammy Sue, and my administrative assistant, David Taggart. We were in Clearwater, along with several other PTL television production people, to do a fund-raising telethon on our affiliate station, WCLF, Channel 22.

I glanced up and noticed John Wesley Fletcher, a frequent guest on our PTL programs, walking toward us. He was wearing street clothes and a broad smile. "Jim! I need to talk to you right away in private," he said, still smiling. "Why don't we take a little walk?"

I turned to Tammy Sue. "I'll be right back, honey." I got up, slipped on a pair of beach sandals, and followed John down the sidewalk toward the hotel. He had someone he wanted me to meet, he told me as we walked.

"My friend from Long Island that I was telling you about is here," he said. "I want you to come up and meet her."

"No, I am not comfortable with that," I replied.

"She really wants to meet you."

"Well, have her come down, and we can take a walk on the beach," I suggested.

"Oh, no! You can't do that! You're Jim Bakker. You can't be seen with a woman on the beach, unless it's your wife."

"Why not? I'm seen with people of all ages all the time. Everywhere I go, people come up to talk to me."

"Oh, just come up and see her. You don't have to do anything; just come up and say hello."

"I'm just not comfortable with that," I reiterated.

"Okay, I'm going to have her come out on the balcony and wave to you. That's the room, right up there," he said, pointing to a balcony of the hotel. Fletcher disappeared and in a few moments he and a young woman appeared on the balcony. They both smiled and waved to me.

In a few minutes, John was back. "Now you've met her. Come on up. She really wants to meet you."

By 1977 the fire had begun to flicker and wane in Tammy Faye's and my marriage. Although we were candid about our problems, often discussing them on the set of our live television show, many viewers refused to accept that we were anything other than the ideal Christian couple with no more than a normal complement of marital woes. Many viewers actually took comfort in our troubles because they could identify with our problems. By admitting that we were struggling, Tammy Faye and I were giving the audience permission to acknowledge their own marital tensions. Few in our audience, or even among our staff members, really knew how close Tammy's and my marriage was to total dissolution.

Ironically, as PTL grew larger, so too did the rift in our relationship. Most of our arguments centered around my obsession to build Heritage USA. I felt that I had a vision and a commission from God to build PTL and eventually Heritage USA. Tammy Faye felt no such mandate. On the contrary, at times she even said she hated Heritage USA. She frequently referred to it, both privately and publicly, as my "mistress." Although Tammy loved being on television and genuinely loved the people who surrounded our lives as a result, she nonetheless resented the long hours I worked and the constant pressures of the ministry. I was home with her almost every night and lavished her with gifts and attention, but it was never enough. Our basic natures were very different. To Tammy, life was supposed to be fun, fun, fun, not work, work, work. She and I shared a passion since college to reach the world with the gospel message. We were convinced the means were through the medium of Christian television.

Tammy expressed her faith more comfortably through her music. Consequently, while I threw myself into building Heritage USA, she worked at recording Christian music, much of which we used on our *PTL* programs. I encouraged Tammy to use her God-given talents; with Tammy's singing and my preaching, I had always thought we were a great one-two punch. About that same time, one of the guests on our show was a Nashville record producer named Gary S. Paxton. Gary's skills in the recording studio were legendary, dating back to his own pop records in the 1950s and '60s with songs such as "Cherry Pie," "Alley-Oop," and "Monster Mash." He produced hit records such as "Cherish" for The Association, and "Sweet Pea" for Tommy Roe. He had written country hits for Glen Campbell and Roy Clark, and one of his songs, "Woman, Sensuous Woman," recorded by Don Gibson, was a country classic.

In 1971, after a life of wild living, Gary S. Paxton became a Christian— and a gospel singer. He became an instant "Christian star," so it was only a matter of time before Paxton wound up on the set of *PTL*.

Before long he was using his skills to produce music for us at *PTL*, including the *PTL* theme song, "Praise the Lord," which we used to open every program for several years. Gary also produced albums of my preaching and Tammy's music.

In the late seventies, Tammy began spending more and more time with Gary Paxton in his recording studio in Nashville. One of the reasons Paxton was such a successful music producer was his ability to bring the best out of people by providing just the right balance of encouragement and uplifting advice. It was the kind of positive feedback Tammy Faye longed for; Paxton encouraged Tammy and made her feel important.

In 1978, Paxton wrote the foreword for Tammy's book, *Run to the Roar*. About that same time, I embarked on a round-the-world trip to visit the growing number of mission projects sponsored by PTL, including numerous foreign versions of our *PTL* television program. Tammy Faye hated to fly, so she opted to stay at home to host the show while I was away. She invited Gary Paxton to cohost with her.

Any time that I traveled, I called home nearly every night. Usually Tammy wanted to talk, in her perky, chatty way telling me about everything from important issues to mundane matters. But now Tammy could hardly wait to get off the phone. I called from places all around the world, and she gave me the bum's rush, hastily concluding every conversation.

Somehow or other, I could not bring myself to believe that she was merely being frugal. A man knows when his wife is brushing him off.

I sent Tammy Faye gifts from all over the world. Nothing seemed to make an impact. I knew we had not been communicating well lately, but I was nonetheless surprised and panic-stricken to sense my wife slipping into the arms of another man. My fears were not unfounded. Tammy Faye had indeed fallen in love with Gary Paxton. She later told me that she had not engaged in sexual intercourse with Gary, but they had spent long hours talking, hugging, and kissing. Consummated or not, in my mind, Tammy's and Gary's relationship amounted to an affair, even though both Tammy Faye and Gary insist to this day that they had "only" an "affair of the heart."

By summer of 1980, Gary and his wife would be getting divorced, and Tammy Faye and I would be close to it. Our marriage may not have survived the year had it not been for the outstanding help of a group of counselors at Palmdale Hospital, northwest of Los Angeles. The 123-bed hospital was owned and directed by Dr. Lester Nichols and his wife, June, both of whom were dedicated Christians. Many of the hospital staff members were Christians as well. In their professional counseling, the Palmdale team headed by Dr. Fred Gross, Palmdale's Chief of Psychology, used biblical principles and prayer along with psychological tests and psychiatric treatments. I had been extremely fascinated when I had interviewed Dr. Gross on *PTL* about his "psychospiritual" approach to counseling.

In 1980, I scheduled a physical examination at the Palmdale Hospital. During the course of my stay, I talked with Dr. Gross and told him that I felt sure Tammy was involved with another man. Dr. Gross was flabbergasted. He suggested that I send for Tammy immediately.

Tammy reluctantly flew from Charlotte to California—with the help of the tranquilizer Ativan to help calm her fear of flying. We spent the next two weeks meeting daily with Dr. Gross and his team of counselors. During that time, we laid some of our fears and frustrations with each other on the table for the first time. The counselors were extremely straightforward with both of us. They told me point-blank that I had better adjust my work schedule to allow more time to be with Tammy Faye.

As for Gary Paxton, when Tammy and I returned from Palmdale, I called Gary in Nashville and accused him of sleeping with Tammy Faye.

"No, Jim. I did not," Gary told me. "Just the opposite. I could have, but I didn't." Then Paxton attempted to turn the tables on me. "It's your fault, you know. You really should spend more time with your wife."

Gary S. Paxton never again appeared on any *PTL* television programs.

15

Tammy Faye and I returned to PTL, determined to patch up our marriage, though I was more enthusiastic about our reconciliation than was Tammy. I committed myself to spending more time with Tammy—no easy task, since we had just begun building the Barn, a $2 million, 2,000-seat auditorium and state-of-the-art television studio, from which we eventually began broadcasting our daily programs.

But before long, I was back to the regular grind, coming home exhausted. For a while, it looked as though the Barn might not get built. PTL simply did not have the money on hand. Construction at Heritage USA ground to a halt, and I lapsed into depression as I saw my dreams beginning to disintegrate. Both the Barn and our headquarters building, the World Outreach Center, stood hollow and empty, monuments to defeat. For more than a year, the projects remained idle. I sulked and despaired, trying to find a way to get the projects moving again. During that time, not surprisingly, Tammy saw me as a moody and discouraged man rather than as someone to run to for comfort and security.

In an effort to please Tammy Faye, I asked her to join me on the television set as the regular cohost of *The PTL Club*. I already had a cohost, our longtime friend and coworker, "Uncle" Henry Harrison. Although only fifty-two years of age as compared to my forty years, Uncle Henry evoked a grandfatherly image, parking on the couch to my right, laughing boisterously, and fawning over my guests and me. I hoped Henry understood why I needed to replace him with Tammy Faye. He did remain on our show, but in a lesser role.

Throughout the summer of 1980, Tammy's and my marriage remained strained. In an interview with *The Saturday Evening Post,* Tammy acknowledged our marital problems while giving the impression that our problems were in the past. "Thank God we've straightened them out," she told *The Saturday Evening Post*'s writer. "You've got to talk. Even if you're screaming at each other, you've got to get it out." Tammy attempted to encourage struggling marriage partners by saying that too many "see an easy way out and they take it. You've got to work at a marriage. If you don't, it will fail."[1]

To make matters worse, I was so obsessed with getting the construction projects at Heritage USA back on track that I moved our family from our home onto the grounds of Heritage USA. We lived in a small log cabin chalet, so I could more readily oversee the projects. I vowed that we would not move back home until the Barn auditorium was completed.

I worked feverishly trying to get the Barn open in time for our announced Fourth of July dedication. This was the first of many projects at PTL for which I would publicly declare an unrealistic completion date, making an already difficult job tougher than it had to be. In a way, setting such lofty goals caused all of us to expand our faith in God, and we completed projects in record time. Besides, like me, many of the young and idealistic staff members at PTL enjoyed a challenge. Just the thought that something couldn't be done was motivation enough for us. Although Tammy lent tacit public support to my efforts to build Heritage USA, inside she was unhappy about my growing obsession. Eventually, the projects were completed, but it would be years before the rift those buildings had created in our relationship could be healed.

Besides the toll my workaholic schedule took on my family and me, I remained suspicious of Tammy Faye. I was not convinced that she had broken off her relationship with Gary Paxton. By her actions and demeanor, I felt strongly that Tammy was still seeing him.

She wasn't.

There was someone else.

Despite our troubles, I loved Tammy Faye. She was my wife of nearly twenty years and she was the mother of my children. I realized that I was losing her, yet I refused to give up on her. I determined in my heart that I would do anything to get her back.

I tried more material gifts, but the presents had little impact on Tammy Faye. I took her, along with our two children, to Acapulco for a vacation. My secretary at the time, Ruth Egert, and her husband, Phil, accompanied us. Tammy Faye was still unhappy. We left Mexico and flew to Los Angeles. Tammy complained that I never took her anywhere without an entourage, our bodyguards, and other PTL staff members who were always available to help me handle the myriad responsibilities of PTL. I recognized that she was probably right about our never going anywhere alone, so I took her on vacation to the Bahamas—just the two of us. We enjoyed a brief respite from our day-to-day haggling, and for a few days, our love flourished. Once back at Heritage USA, however, we quickly slipped back into our destructive patterns.

I was clueless, and I was exhausted. All my attempts to woo Tammy back from her mystery lover and make her happy proved futile. I did not know what else to do.

One day during a casual conversation with John Wesley Fletcher, I flippantly said that I ought to have an affair to make Tammy jealous. "I have tried everything else to win Tammy Faye back. Just think, I could say to Tammy Faye, 'I had an affair, too, Baby.' I'd be fighting fire with fire!"

"Really?" he asked. "Do you think that would help?"

17

"Well, you know how jealous Tammy Faye is. She would go nuts if she thought that I was even attracted to another woman."

"Hmmm," Fletcher answered thoughtfully.

Over the next few weeks, Fletcher and I occasionally joked about my having an affair to make Tammy Faye jealous.

I did not really want to have an affair. As a highly visible television personality, and as president of Heritage USA, had I desired to have a relationship with another woman, it would have been relatively easy to do so. But Tammy Faye was the only woman I wanted. She was the woman I loved.

Nevertheless, my foolish, male-ego-driven statement soon took on a life of its own, fueled by the hurt in my heart and by John's questionable motives.

I cannot say that I was surprised when John showed up in Florida with a woman in tow. I followed him inside the hotel, up the elevator, and down the hallway to room 538. I knew it was wrong; my conscience screamed at me every step of the way. But I stupidly determined to make my wife jealous and get back at her, and that is the truth. It was an adulterous act of the first degree. I stifled the screaming voice in my head and heart and stepped inside the room.

3

Crossing the Line

THE FIRST TIME I SAW JESSICA HAHN SHE WAS WEARING A plum-colored wraparound dress, which she quickly removed. Beneath the demure-looking dress she wore black lace. I had never before seen Jessica Hahn; nor had she been my secretary, as some people later mistakenly proclaimed, nor had she ever been employed at PTL.

Jessica Hahn, I learned seven years later, had grown up in Massapequa, New York, as a Catholic, but since the age of fourteen had been attending a Pentecostal church pastored by Eugene Profeta, a flamboyant, well-known, Brooklyn-born cleric. Immediately after graduating high school in 1977, Jessica Hahn went to work as Profeta's church secretary, a position she held the day I met her, and where she remained employed until 1987 when she resigned after becoming a household name.

Jessica Hahn and I never had a love affair. We had a fifteen- to twenty-minute sexual encounter. We had no ongoing relationship, although our brief meeting intertwined our lives more than either one of us ever dreamed possible as we sized each other up that fateful afternoon.

We conversed very little. I may have uttered a total of six sentences to her. We did not drink wine, as was reported later. Nor did I imply that by having sex with me she was serving God somehow. Most of all, *I did not rape Jessica Hahn.* Foolish and sinful as it was, the sexual encounter for which we are both now infamous was completely consensual.

As I said, I knew I was wrong the moment I entered the hotel room. I should have run out of that place. Nobody forced me into the room or to stay once I was there. Yet I rationalized the situation: I was feeling rejected by my wife; I knew that Tammy Faye was seeing another man; I was wondering whether I was much of a man at all. Suddenly, I felt as though I were an adolescent boy who had to prove he was a man by having sex. I willfully crossed the line and went through with it.

At first, I was so nervous I could not even function sexually. I knew that what I was doing went directly against everything I believed as a Christian; I had never cheated on my wife in all our years of marriage. Jessica Hahn, however, seemed quite comfortable with the situation. When she recognized my problem, she aroused me to the point where I simply abandoned myself to the moment. We did not make love; we had sex.

When it was over, I quickly left the room, and in a daze, hurried to the elevator and pressed the button marking the eighth floor. The winter afternoon sun was already on the horizon as I stepped inside my room.

I was horrified. *Oh, God! What have I done?* I had not considered the consequences of my absurd attempt to make Tammy Faye jealous. I had not even paused to think of the potential ramifications of my actions while I was giving in to the temptation of having sex with a woman other than my wife. I had simply reacted.

I had opened the door to attack on the ministry I headed, my family, and me personally. Worse yet, the devil had not made me do any of it; I had done it of my own stubborn will.

I disrobed and immediately stepped into the shower, turning the water on as hot as I could stand it. I never felt so dirty in all my life. *Maybe if I make the water hotter, it will wash it all away*, I thought.

Eventually I realized I had to get out of the shower and get dressed. It was almost time to go to the telethon at Channel 22, my reason for being in Florida in the first place. I thought seriously about canceling my appearance on the program that night. I felt that I had nothing to say to the audience, that I had somehow squandered away my credibility and my "right to be heard" as a result of my sexual sin that afternoon. On the other hand, I knew that my friends at the Clearwater affiliate were counting on me to help them meet their telethon goals. They were depending on my high profile to attract viewers and convince the audience to help support the very valid ministry of Channel 22. I went to the telethon and tried to put on a happy face, but it was a false face. I was anything but happy. I felt as if the television cameras could see right through me, boring into my soul and exposing my sin to the world. I carried on, doing my duties as the special guest through sheer enthusiasm and religious hype. Inside, however, I felt dead; I knew that I was wrong.

That night following the telethon, I was in no mood for conversations. I returned to my room around eleven o'clock and tumbled into bed. I felt exhausted in every way, yet sleep eluded me. I stared at the ceiling. I replayed the events of the day in my mind again and again. *Why did I ever allow things to get to this point?* I tossed and turned all night long.

I arose at the first ray of sunshine. Although it was Sunday, I chose not to attend morning worship services at a local church. I could not get away fast enough. By midmorning, Tammy Sue and I, along with several other members of our staff, were on our way back to Charlotte.

On Monday, I called for Dr. Fred Gross, the clinical psychologist from Palmdale Hospital who was at PTL that week conducting marriage seminars. Dr. Gross had developed a Christian therapy program at PTL that had already helped hundreds of married couples renew and revive their marriages. I felt I could unburden my heart to Dr. Gross, and he would have both the spiritual and the psychological wisdom to help me.

If Dr. Gross was surprised that I called him to my office that Monday, he did not let on. He greeted me cheerfully but quickly realized that I was deeply troubled about something. We went back into the private dressing room next to my office and sat down. I didn't know where to start. Finally, I sat down and slowly began to tell him about my sin with Jessica Hahn the past weekend in Clearwater. As I spoke, I could feel my body beginning to quake. I was acutely aware of the enormity of my sin.

Dr. Gross did not attempt to counsel me. He did not allow me to rationalize that Tammy Faye was being unfaithful. Dr. Gross knew that the only way I would find emotional health and spiritual freedom was by seeking forgiveness from God, forgiveness from Jessica Hahn, and forgiveness from myself.

Together, Dr. Gross and I knelt down on the floor and began to pray. I cried out to God for forgiveness. I literally lay face-first on the floor, prostrate before God. Then, in a sense, Dr. Gross placed himself in the position of a priest to me and declared, "Now I tell you before God, Jim Bakker, that you have been forgiven of God."

That same day, I talked to Jessica Hahn by telephone and immediately asked her to forgive me. She invited me to meet her again in Long Island. I said, "We must not get together again. What we did was wrong, and we need to ask God for forgiveness." That was the last conversation I had with Jessica Hahn.

I do not blame Jessica Hahn. If she has not already done so, I hope she will one day find it within her heart to forgive me. Before she and I ever met, she had been used and hurt by men who purported to represent God, but that does not lessen my responsibility or absolve me of the fact that I was wrong to have had sexual intercourse with her. I will always be grieved that I added more hurt to her already damaged heart.

At this point, I had sought and received the forgiveness of God, confessed to my spiritual "elder," and had attempted to seek forgiveness from the party I had offended. *Now I must tell Tammy Faye*, I thought.

No longer did I want to flaunt the fact that I'd had an affair too. Now, I genuinely wanted to confess to her and seek her forgiveness. I could only hope that she would be willing to forgive and give me another chance.

When I asked Dr. Gross about how I should break the news to Tammy Faye, he was adamant that I not tell her. "I am not sure Tammy Faye can handle this, Jim," Dr. Gross said to me. "The way your relationship has been floundering the past few months, this will destroy any incentive Tammy Faye has for trying to work things out between the two of you. She is looking for any excuse to end the marriage already, and this news will just push her over the edge."

"I think she can handle it, Dr. Gross. Tammy Faye is a tough woman. She cries easily, but inside she has quite a bit of courage and stamina."

Dr. Gross remained unconvinced. "It's not worth the risk. Right now, from what I know and have seen of Tammy Faye, I don't think she could handle it. When the time is right to tell her about this incident, you'll know it, but in my professional opinion, that time is not now."

I was surprised that Dr. Gross would instruct me to keep my sexual sin a secret from my spouse. Nevertheless, I respected him immensely. He had been instrumental in helping hundreds of married couples restore their marriages, so I felt he knew what was best in this sort of situation.

In retrospect, I now believe that it would have been much easier—and the right thing to do—to have confessed to Tammy Faye right after it happened and accepted the consequences. I believe she could have handled it, and we would have been able to work through it. But I decided the doctor knew best. I kept quiet.

Over the next six years, as Tammy Faye and I tried to put our marriage back together, she often lamented her moral failures. Frequently, Tammy commented about how sorry she was and how guilty she felt about her own past. Usually, when she went on one of those guilt trips, I tried to console her by saying, "Honey, I am just as guilty as you are. I have failed you too." The burden of my guilt was almost more than I could bear.

But I never told Tammy Faye about Jessica Hahn . . . not until March 1987.

CHAPTER

4

Strange Bedfellows

"TAM, I NEED TO TALK WITH YOU. PLEASE COME SIT DOWN with me," I said as I guided Tammy Faye toward the sitting area of our bedroom. Tammy could tell by the expression on my face that this was to be no ordinary conversation. Although the morning sunshine streamed through the windows, brightly lighting the Spanish architecture and natural desert wood of our vacation home in Palm Springs, California, this was to be one of the darkest days of our lives.

"Jim, what's wrong?" Tammy asked.

"I just talked to Reverend Dortch. He's coming out here tomorrow, and I need to tell you something before he gets here."

I had talked with my executive vice president, Richard Dortch, earlier that day, and he informed me that *The Charlotte Observer* had learned of my 1980 sexual encounter with Jessica Hahn. The paper was preparing to expose the matter to the world. Everyone involved recognized that the news of my moral failure could ruin me as a minister and possibly trigger the beginning of the end for PTL.

I had confessed to Dr. Fred Gross and had apologized to Jessica Hahn in 1980 the same weekend that the encounter had taken place. Dr. Gross assured me that since I had repented and sought forgiveness for the wrong that I had done, there was nothing more I could or should do. I went back to my work at PTL with a new vigor, thinking that the situation was over and done with.

I was wrong.

In December 1984, *The Charlotte Observer* and the executive offices at PTL both received a series of telephone calls from a distraught woman claiming I had raped her. Journalist Charles Shepard fielded the calls at the newspaper, and Richard Dortch handled the calls at our offices. Reverend Dortch maintains today that he did not believe the woman's story—he had received crank calls at PTL before—but he, along with Aimee Cortese, a PTL Board member and pastor in Brooklyn, arranged to meet with the woman in New York. There Richard Dortch met Jessica Hahn. Accompanied by a female paralegal, Jessica Hahn repeated her accusations to Reverend Dortch and Aimee Cortese. Hahn indicated that she had suffered emotional distress as a result of the encounter and needed money for medical bills and psychiatric help. At the close of their meeting, Reverend Dortch did what he now admits in his book was a tragic mistake—he gave the pastor two thousand dollars of his own money to give to Jessica Hahn to cover counseling or medical expenses.[1] Upon his return to PTL, Reverend Dortch felt that the matter had been resolved.

Reverend Dortch says he did not believe Jessica Hahn's story. Perhaps that's why in an almost offhand manner he said to me, "Oh, by the way, I have been dealing with a woman who says that you raped her."

No doubt Richard Dortch was not prepared for my response. I told him that I had never raped anyone, but I let him know that I had had a sexual encounter with Jessica Hahn. I suggested Reverend Dortch talk to Dr. Gross about what had transpired in Clearwater in 1980. Reverend Dortch talked first to Dr. Gross, and then he returned to my office with Vi Azvedo, one of our top counselors and the head of the PTL pastoral staff. They asked me to tell them in exact detail what had happened between Jessica Hahn and me. I told them the truth and answered their questions. I asked, "What should I do now?"

They were all in agreement that I should have no further contact with Jessica Hahn, not even a telephone conversation. Richard Dortch assured me that he would handle the matter from that point. At that time, to our best knowledge, the issue was settled. Looking back, however, I now see what an untenable position in which I was placing Dortch.

According to Richard Dortch and others in our executive offices, at this point, Jessica Hahn began calling repeatedly. Then PTL received a legal-sounding letter, apparently written by Hahn's paralegal friend. The letter, documented by both Richard Dortch and Charles Shepard in their books, again listed a number of accusations against me and stated, "We're giving you the opportunity to settle this matter justly and privately, according to what you perceive to be a rightful settlement. $100,000.00 (one hundred thousand dollars) is not excessive in view of what happened here."[2]

Had we been wise, we would have turned the matter over to the FBI at that point. But in an effort to avoid the negative publicity, and to protect the ministry and my reputation, Reverend Dortch decided on a wait-and-see course of action.

About the same time, Jessica Hahn began calling *The Charlotte Observer.* She repeated her story to Charles Shepard, referring to the same document her paralegal friend had sent to PTL, only skipping the part of the letter asking for $100,000 in return for her silence.[3] Charles Shepard smelled blood. He began chasing the story from coast to coast.

In January 1985 a package containing several legal-looking documents arrived at Richard Dortch's office. One, an eight-page document, was from Paul Roper, a California law student and a self-appointed watchdog of Christian ministries. Roper's watchdog group was known as Operation Anti-Christ.

Roper had enlisted the help of John Stewart, a fellow law student as well as a part-time pastor who eventually became a law professor and a popular Christian radio talk-show host. Nearing the completion of his law studies and preparing for his bar exam, Stewart found time to research and prepare a draft lawsuit—not an actual suit, but a formal complaint—outlining Jessica Hahn's charges against PTL and me and five other potential defendants. The complaint stated clearly that the potential "punitive damages" liability for me and the other defendants now totaled $12.3 million. The cover letter from Roper and Stewart, dated January 14, 1985, demanded a response by 8:00 a.m. on January 21, 1985—one week later—or "the documents would be sent to an attorney in an appropriate jurisdiction for possible litigation."[4] The letter included a phone number to call if a representative of PTL wanted to contact Roper before the matter became a bona fide "filed lawsuit and a public record."[5]

Richard Dortch met with Paul Roper in early February. According to Shepard and Stewart, Roper suggested a conciliation panel, made up of one person selected by Reverend Dortch, one person selected by Paul Roper, and one mutually acceptable person. The panel then could decide whether Jessica Hahn's claims and demands were valid and to what extent.

Richard Dortch took a different tack. He hired Los Angeles attorney Howard Weitzman to settle with Roper and Hahn out of court. By February 19, Weitzman and Roper had come to an agreement. A detailed document was drawn up and agreed to in the presence of now retired Superior Court Judge Charles Woodmansee on February 27, 1985. In addition to the judge, Jessica Hahn, Paul Roper, and Scott Furstman,

Howard Weitzman's partner, signed the agreement. It was agreed before the judge that Jessica Hahn and her representatives should receive an immediate payment of $115,000, of which Jessica Hahn would receive $20,000. Paul Roper, the Christian watchdog, reportedly received $90,000, of which he paid John Stewart $15,000. Another $150,000 was placed in a trust fund for twenty years. In signing the document, Jessica Hahn agreed "not to discuss or otherwise disseminate to the public any information" regarding her claims. She also agreed not to contact or harass PTL or file further legal actions regarding this case. If she held true to her word, at the end of twenty years, the $150,000 was hers. In the meantime, she received the annual interest the trust fund accrued. If Hahn violated the agreement by going public, the trust fund was to return to PTL.[6]

Richard Dortch returned to Heritage USA with the task of coming up with $265,000.

Dortch considered who had the most to lose if there were any kind of reversal of PTL's growth. He determined it would be the contractor of the buildings, the developer of Heritage USA, Roe Messner.[7]

Roe put up the money to pay the Jessica Hahn out-of-court settlement. I did not know that at the time and didn't want to know. Reverend Dortch simply said that a concerned businessman had come to our aid.

Looking back, I now recognize that I should have handled the matter of my sin with Jessica Hahn differently in the first place. I should have admitted my moral failure to the presbyters of the Assemblies of God, my lifelong denominational affiliation. As a minister who committed adultery but who sought forgiveness and restoration, I could have defused the entire matter by submitting to my spiritual elders and accepting whatever discipline they decided to mete out. I knew the rules, however, and recognized that my admission of the tryst would most likely result in my ministerial credentials being rescinded for a two-year period. More disconcerting, I would probably be banned from the pulpit and from our television programs for at least a year. Moreover, if I had simply resigned my credentials with the Assemblies, it was likely that all of the Assemblies of God ministers on our PTL staff would have had to follow suit or give up their jobs at PTL.

In light of the staggering consequences, the possible ramifications in so many lives, I did not inform the Assemblies of God hierarchy of the matter. By March 1987, I felt that the Jessica Hahn matter had been adequately resolved by Richard Dortch in the best legal and spiritual manner possible, considering the awkward circumstances.

I was wrong.

Secret agreements rarely remain so for long. By late 1985, stories of my sexual indiscretion were already circulating in hushed tones. John Stewart, who had done the research for Paul Roper's original draft lawsuit, had contacted reporter Charles Shepard at *The Charlotte Observer*, seeking information concerning where the Hahn settlement money had come from. In the process, he discovered that Shepard knew about Hahn, and Shepard found a willing source of information. The two remained in contact.

Nevertheless, Shepard had been unable to confirm enough of his allegations to satisfy his editor's concerns over accuracy and potential lawsuits. Charles Shepard may well have continued to stumble in the dark had he not found some allies in the Christian broadcasting ranks. In 1987, the National Religious Broadcasters' convention was held in Washington, D.C., the first week in February. It was there that John Stewart met John Ankerberg, and John Ankerberg met Jimmy Swaggart.

Both Ankerberg and Swaggart had television programs on our satellite network, the Inspirational Network that we had recently canceled. Ankerberg frequently attacked other ministries, organizations, and people by name, something the Board of Directors and I did not feel was appropriate. Rather than building up fellow Christians, I felt Ankerberg spent most of his program tearing the church world apart. After he met with Ankerberg at Heritage USA, Richard Dortch reported that Ankerberg's attitude was inconsistent with what we wanted to air on the Inspirational Network. The Board voted unanimously not to renew his contract. PTL had a wide variety of programs on our Inspirational Network, and we never told any of them what to preach or not to preach. We did not, however, want one program we aired to be firing bullets at another program or preacher on our network, Hatfield-and-McCoy-style.

In the mid-1980s Jimmy Swaggart was one of the most popular evangelists on television. His program aired fifteen times per week on the Inspirational Network. One of his time slots was 9:00 A.M., Monday through Friday. Tammy Faye's and my show, the flagship program of the Inspirational Network, aired at eleven o'clock each morning. Swaggart had been publicly attacking PTL in writing and on his television programs, which aired on our network! Jimmy Swaggart did not approve of much at PTL and he was extremely vocal about saying so. It seemed as though he did not like Christians having as much fun as we were having at Heritage USA. Nor did he like much of the music we aired, some of which was more contemporary than Swaggart's gospel style. He was most critical of us having Hollywood celebrities on our program who came to give their Christian testimonies. Jimmy Swaggart was particularly opposed to Christian psychologists and Christian counseling, which we at PTL felt could be a valuable asset to many Christian families and individuals. At that time, Jimmy Swaggart had never stepped foot on the grounds of

Heritage USA. Yet he spoke out loudly and often, denouncing almost everything we were doing at PTL. That was his prerogative as a Christian and his right as an American. But we did not have to provide him air time to do it!

In addition to PTL, Jimmy often castigated Roman Catholics and other denominations. When Swaggart and his guests started lambasting fellow ministers by name, such as Robert Schuller and Kenneth Copeland, men whom I respected and considered to be friends, he crossed a line. The PTL Board of Directors and I had a firm policy that nobody on our network could criticize another ministry by name. I asked Reverend Dortch to discuss this matter with Swaggart.

Richard Dortch made the decision to remove Swaggart's morning show from our network lineup. Our Board of Directors and I unanimously backed Reverend Dortch's decision. Initially, we continued to air Jimmy's program at other times of the day, but the morning show was his bread and butter.

Consequently, when John Stewart encountered Ankerberg and Swaggart at the 1987 NRB convention, he found two men who were extremely angry at PTL in general, and at me in particular. Not surprisingly, the three soon traded information back and forth, fanning the rumor flames even further. Ankerberg also discussed his "concerns" about me with Jerry Falwell, and before long a comradeship was formed between Ankerberg, Swaggart, and Falwell, with John Stewart serving as the willing liaison between the ministers and *The Charlotte Observer*.

On Thursday, March 12, 1987, Charles Shepard and John Stewart talked by telephone. In the course of their conversation, Shepard told Stewart that he had a story about Jessica Hahn, the money, and me almost ready to print.[8] Stewart immediately contacted Ankerberg, who asked the lawyer to write a letter to me on behalf of Ankerberg, Swaggart, and Falwell, ostensibly to confront me in the spirit of Matthew 18—Jesus' instructions for confronting a fellow believer—about the sexual episode with Jessica Hahn that had taken place seven years earlier. Stewart wrote the letter, but when Ankerberg faxed it to Swaggart and Falwell, the television preachers' response was less than enthusiastic. In a fax back to Ankerberg, a copy of which I have in my files to this day, Swaggart expressed his reservations about being associated with the letter. Falwell, too, shied away from the letter, saying he wanted to have his lawyer examine it before lending his name to it.

That same afternoon, Richard Dortch was in the Tampa Bay area when he received a call from his secretary, Leslie Jones. Leslie told Reverend Dortch that several members of Jerry Falwell's staff were trying to contact him. Reverend Dortch recognized the name of one of the men, Warren Marcus, who had once worked at the Christian Broadcasting Network. The other two men were Jerry Nims, a leader in Falwell's political action group, The Moral Majority, and Mark DeMoss, son of the famous philanthropist, Arthur DeMoss.

When Richard Dortch contacted Warren, the Falwell assistant told him, "We've learned there is a problem at PTL, and we want to help if we can."[9]

The Falwell representatives urged Reverend Dortch to meet them at the Tampa Airport executive aircraft area at eleven o'clock that very night! This was obviously serious.

When the men arrived on Jerry Falwell's jet, Jerry Nims got straight to the point. "John Ankerberg called us and told us he and Jimmy Swaggart know about the Jessica Hahn incident."[10] Nims showed Reverend Dortch the fax Jerry Falwell had received from John Ankerberg and a copy of the Swaggart reply.

Reverend Dortch had met with Jimmy Swaggart in a stormy meeting in Baton Rouge earlier in the year, but he was still shocked as he read Swaggart's response to Ankerberg.[11]

Swaggart's letter insinuated that it was only a matter of time before my sexual encounter with Jessica Hahn would be exposed, I would be brought down, and PTL would be vulnerable. He assured Ankerberg that *The Charlotte Obersver* would do its part, as would the Assemblies of God.

As Reverend Dortch read Swaggart's words, he immediately was reminded of the recurring rumors hinting that Jimmy Swaggart wanted to take over the PTL Inspirational Network. What Richard Dortch knew that the Falwell aides may not have known at that time was that I was the president of PTL for life. Written into our corporate bylaws was a stipulation that said if for any reason I could not serve as the president, the entire ministry was to be placed into the hands of the Assemblies of God. With me disgraced, Jimmy Swaggart could easily lay claim to PTL on the logical basis that he was the leading television preacher associated with the Assemblies of God denomination.

Consequently, the information that the Falwell aides provided about Swaggart rang true in Dortch's mind. Reverend Dortch remained reticent.

As a former presbyter in the Assemblies of God national office, Reverend Dortch recognized that the Falwell camp and the Bakker camp were poles apart on a theological spectrum. Falwell, a Baptist, preached a more traditional approach to Christianity. Those in "charismatic" circles such as PTL and the Assemblies of God believe that the "gifts of the Spirit"—such as speaking in tongues and prophecy—are still operative in the world today. Charismatics characteristically have a more upbeat, "God can work in the now" approach to life. Questions concerning spiritual gifts and how they are relevant to Christianity today often created a "Y" in the road when charismatic and noncharismatic Christians discussed these issues. It was highly unusual that Jerry Falwell and his staff, people who held such opposite views of the Christian life from ours, would rally to our assistance in what appeared to be a growing conflict between two charismatic ministries, Jimmy Swaggart and PTL. Consequently, Dortch's first questions to the aides were, "Why are you telling us these things? Why have you gotten involved in this matter?"

The Falwell aides were ready for Richard Dortch's questions. Jerry Nims answered, "Jerry Falwell is convinced, and we're convinced, that if Jimmy Swaggart brings you down, he would certainly bring us down, too. He's probably out to get us also. We need to stand with you to stop Jimmy Swaggart from trying to tear up your ministry."[12]

The Falwell aides went on to tell Richard Dortch that they had evidence that Jimmy Swaggart had obtained enough people to bring a class-action suit against PTL in regard to the PTL Lifetime Partnership program. Nims had suggested that such a case could put PTL into receivership and eventually shut down the ministry. (Ironically, the same ideas would surface less than a year later, only it would not be Jimmy Swaggart promoting the idea.) Nims also informed Richard Dortch that Jimmy Swaggart had a "plant, a spy, in your organization who keeps him informed of everything going on at PTL."[13] The idea seemed plausible to Reverend Dortch, especially in light of the fact that Nims accurately told him of a check written by PTL to a specific organization in recent weeks, a check that only someone inside PTL's offices would know about.

Reverend Dortch and Jerry Falwell's men talked into the wee hours of the following morning. Throughout the conversation, it appeared to Dortch that two points were continually and emphatically made: Swaggart is out to get you, and Jerry Falwell can help you. Before the long meeting had concluded, Reverend Dortch had confirmed that certain parts of the Jessica Hahn story were true. He did not go into details at that time.

Jerry Nims reassured Reverend Dortch of Jerry Falwell's ability to assist in dealing with the negative fallout that was sure to come once the story became public. Nims told Reverend Dortch, "Dr. Falwell has helped others in this situation. There was a church in Maine whose pastor had a moral failure. Jerry Falwell took the church over for a period of time and helped them. Then he returned the church to its pastor."[14]

The obvious implication was that Jerry Falwell could and would do something similar for me. Reverend Dortch finally agreed to broach the subject of Jerry Falwell's help with me.

The meeting concluded around 2:00 A.M., after which Reverend Dortch immediately telephoned me in Palm Springs and gave me a full report. He faxed copies of the Swaggart letter and other materials the Falwell men had given to him. He told me that *The Charlotte Observer* was definitely planning to proceed with the story. It was not a matter of *if* the story would run, but *when* the story would hit.

As I listened to Reverend Dortch's voice on the phone, it was as though someone were punching me in the stomach with every word. I thought again and again, *This can't be happening!* But Reverend Dortch's report repeatedly assured me that it was happening and we needed to get ready for it. Falwell's men had advised him to call New York lawyer Norman Roy Grutman, a hard-boiled attorney who might be able to get the story stopped temporarily. Grutman had represented Jerry Falwell when Jerry had sued *Hustler* magazine for printing a derogatory parody of the preacher. Grutman won the case and a judgment of $200,000 for Falwell, although the case was later overturned by the U.S. Supreme Court.

Reverend Dortch said that the Falwell aides had suggested that the controversial lawyer might be able to stop the impending article and wrangle us enough time to get our heads together. Reverend Dortch then contacted Jerry Nims about securing the services of Norman Roy Grutman.

As I hung up the phone, I sat quietly by myself, playing and replaying the possible scenarios in my mind. Even if Grutman could convince *The Charlotte Observer* to hold the article exposing the tryst with Jessica Hahn and the out-of-court settlement that had been arranged with her, Swaggart and Ankerberg now knew about it as well. Exposure was inevitable.

I worried, *What will our PTL partners think? How will the news affect the Church?* The press was always looking for a real-life Elmer Gantry-type story. Now, they were going to have one—me! I buried my face in my hands and grieved deeply. I kept thinking, *There are so many people who could be hurt by this—my staff and fellow ministers, my elderly mom and dad, and my children, seventeen-year-old Tammy Sue and ten-year-old Jamie Charles.*

And then there was Tammy Faye.

"Oh, God," I cried. "How am I going to explain this to Tammy Faye?"

5

Betty Ford

FRIDAY, MARCH 13, 1987, DAWNED ANOTHER GORGEOUS California day, but I did not want to open my eyes. I languished around the house in a deep depression. I did not want to go anywhere; I did not want to see anyone. I did not want to stray too far from a phone, because Richard Dortch had said that he would be calling to let me know about Grutman and Falwell's possible help.

Norman Roy Grutman was already at work. He contacted *The Charlotte Observer* and threatened the paper with a lawsuit if they ran the Hahn story that weekend. The paper pulled the story and we all thought Norman Roy Grutman was a hero. Actually, as I learned much later, the paper's editors had already decided to hold the story. Rich Oppel, editor of the paper, and in particular Mark Ethridge and the paper's legal counsel, Jon Buchan, felt Charles Shepard's story was not bulletproof. They had already killed the story for the weekend papers, the *Observer's* best-selling editions.[1]

Regardless, I was glad to know that the immediate pressure was off. Had I known, however, that the paper had pulled the story for lack of solid evidence, that Jessica Hahn had retracted much of her story, and that several key players had refused to be named publicly, it would have definitely influenced the way I responded to Jerry Falwell's overtures offering help and intervention. Thinking that Grutman had been influential in getting the paper to pull the plug on the article, I was open to accepting many other disingenuous Grutman moves in the following week.

When Richard Dortch asked me if I wanted to meet with Jerry Falwell, I told him that I would but that I did not want to leave Tammy Faye at that time. However, Falwell was welcome to come to Palm Springs.

Reverend Dortch forwarded that message to Jerry Nims and Mark DeMoss. They in turn took it to Jerry Falwell.

The reason Tammy Faye and I were in California in the first place was to get her well. While the tumultuous events were happening back east, Tammy Faye and I had been going through a twelve-step, Alcoholics Anonymous-type program at the Betty Ford Center to help Tammy overcome her addiction to over-the-counter drugs. Both of our children went to special classes for family members at Betty Ford.

The crisis began in the late fall of 1986. Tammy Faye was always medicating herself and had a dangerous habit of mixing over-the-counter and prescription drugs. She carried plenty of pills in her purse. It was a standard joke among many of our close friends that Tammy Faye's purse was like a mobile drugstore. If someone had a headache, Tammy was always quick to pipe up, "I have a pill for that." If someone had a sinus problem, Tammy had a pill for that. Arthritis pain? There was a pill in Tammy's purse for that too. Aspirin, nasal sprays, and allergy medications filled Tammy Faye's medicine chest at home and her purse and travel bags when we were on the road.

Tammy seemed to be getting sick before Christmas, and the many holiday activities we worked on at Heritage USA exacerbated her already weak condition. We had established a tradition of spending Christmas with the thousands of PTL partners who came to Heritage USA each year. We had special programs in the Heritage Grand, and our staff wrapped hundreds of presents for all of our guests. Christmas at Heritage USA was always the best of times and worst of times due to the huge crowds, the many Christmas parties, and other responsibilities of the season in addition to the usual pressures of doing a daily television program and keeping a huge ministry functioning. It was a festive but exhausting time.

As usual, we hosted a large Christmas party for the PTL management team. Tammy had not been feeling well but she was able to function enough to be a gracious and gregarious hostess to our guests. Upon entering our Tega Cay home, each person attending the party had his or her photograph taken with Tammy Faye and me. Despite being sick, Tammy Faye smiled happily in every picture.

The Christmas party was one of our best ever. PTL had enjoyed a wonderful time of growth and ministry during 1986. Our eighty-six services a week were instrumental in changing thousands of lives. Our Lifetime Partnership program was expanding as work continued on the Towers, and financially, PTL was enjoying its best year ever. PTL was clearly working. We had much for which to give thanks. We closed the party with prayer and our usual singing of Christmas carols.

Tammy struggled through the following week, but by the time we hosted our all-night gospel sing on New Year's Eve, she was extremely weak. As was our custom, we had planned our annual vacation after all the frenzied holiday activities—we usually needed a vacation simply to recover from Christmas week! We had purchased a getaway home in Palm Desert in 1984. Unfortunately, we rarely were able to spend much time there, so we had already decided to sell that home. We had purchased a new home in the mountains of Gatlinburg, Tennessee, which was much closer to Heritage USA and easily accessible by car from the Charlotte area. We decided to spend our vacation there this year.

Before departing for the mountains, however, on my forty-seventh birthday, January 2, I presided over the groundbreaking ceremonies for what I considered to be one of the most fabulous projects ever begun at Heritage USA—the construction of the Heritage Crystal Palace. The Crystal Palace Ministry Center was to be the largest church building in the world. Once completed, the auditorium was designed to seat as many as thirty thousand people, with electronic, moveable dividers that could be configured for a wide variety of smaller crowds. The Crystal Palace would house a five-thousand-seat television studio with state-of-the-art equipment. The huge structure would enclose 1.25 million square feet in glass and would have exhibition facilities large enough to accommodate large conventions such as the Christian Booksellers Association Convention. A unique and highly functional feature of the building was the planned underground loading dock in which the many tractor-trailer rigs used to service such conventions could unload their materials and have them hoisted by elevator directly to the exhibition floor.

I was convinced that the Crystal Palace would pay for itself by selling time-share units in the adjoining thirty-story Crystal Tower. Contrary to misinformation that would soon be widely propagated, our hotel space at the Heritage Grand was not used as time-share units, nor were the five hundred rooms in the nearly completed twenty-one-story Heritage Grand Tower. Those lodging facilities were included in our no-ownership, Lifetime Partnership program as well as open to the general public. The

Crystal Tower, however, would be built and paid for strictly with Partner-owned time-shares in mind.

With a special choir singing "The Hallelujah Chorus" from Handel's *Messiah* and a crowd of dignitaries looking on, I was ecstatic as the PTL Board of Directors and I pushed our shovels down into the soft ground and turned over the dirt. I looked up as the cameras flashed and said, "This is the best day of my life!"

I had envisioned the massive project for more than a year now, and I was thrilled to get started on it. My projected completion date was three years from groundbreaking. Little could I guess that the groundbreaking ceremony would be my last official, public act at Heritage USA. Nor could I have ever dreamed that I would not be celebrating my fiftieth birthday surrounded by friends and family in a glass superstructure, but instead surrounded by strangers, some of whom were dangerous, and confined by a razor-wire fence.

Tammy Faye, Jamie, and I left for Gatlinburg after the groundbreaking ceremonies. Tammy Sue stayed behind to visit with some of her friends. I was looking forward to a bit of rest and relaxation, but it was not to be.

Tammy Faye's condition worsened. She said, "My throat feels like razor blades are cutting it!" By our second week in Tennessee, she was so sick that she consented to go to a local doctor, a rare concession on her part. I drove Tammy Faye down the mountain, and up the road to the small town of Sevierville, where we were able to get an appointment with a doctor. The doctor prescribed some medicine for her flulike conditions, and I found a drugstore nearby where the medicine could be obtained.

With a prescription drug in her possession and her usual battery of over-the-counter medications at her disposal, Tammy Faye grew increasingly delusional and irrational. She eventually got to the point that she did not remember what medications she had taken or when. All she knew was that she was not feeling better, so she continued to take more and more.

On January 12, I was scheduled to present a long-term master plan of our vision for Heritage USA to the York County Commissioners, the local authority governing our growth and development. Although Heritage USA maintained its own facilities, roads, water towers and water lines, underground electric lines, and telephone system, the commissioners were still concerned about how our future expansion plans would fit in with the community. It was an important meeting and I dared not miss it.

At the same time, I felt that it would be unconscionable for me to leave Tammy Faye without an adult to help her, even though I planned to be gone for one day only. I asked Vi Azvedo to come from Heritage to Gatlinburg (about a five-hour drive) to stay with Tammy Faye until I returned. I drove back to Heritage the day before my meeting with the local commissioners.

The meeting with the commissioners was held at Heritage USA. I gave them a tour of our current facilities, showed them the progress on the Towers, and showed them the site where we had just broken ground for the new Crystal Palace. After that, I took them back to the Heritage Grand for lunch and showed the commissioners the master plan and drawings for our future plans, including a retirement village, the re-creation of "Old Jerusalem," and numerous new hotels, camping areas, lakes, and the long-range development of our back acreage where we planned to construct a Christian theme park based on the lives of great characters and stories from the Bible.

The commissioners were more supportive than I could ever have expected. Heritage USA was the largest employer in the Fort Mill area, providing more than two thousand people with jobs. We were also one of the largest sources of local tax revenue. Our school taxes alone for one year were over $600,000, not to mention sales taxes from our shops and other property taxes paid by Heritage USA on those parts of the property not used directly in ministry purposes. Perhaps the commissioners hoped for even more tax revenue from our expansion plans.

While I was still with the commissioners, Vi Azvedo telephoned PTL from Gatlinburg with the news that Tammy Faye had gotten worse rather than better. The night before, Tammy had washed her hair and gone out into the snow on the deck. Vi brought her back inside and asked her not to do such things. Tammy went into the bathroom, locked the door, and washed her hair again. She was running a temperature of 103 degrees.

That night Vi slept on the couch in the living room, and ten-year-old Jamie slept in the same room with Tammy Faye. In the middle of the night, Tammy Faye awakened and started screaming. She yelled to Jamie, "There's a giant elephant in the room!"

Young Jamie had been around enough deliverance ministries that he felt he knew what to do. He called out in the direction where Tammy had indicated the elephant, "In the name of Jesus, get out of here!"

When Vi called and explained to me what was happening, I immediately asked her to contact our friend, Dr. Lester Nichols, a California physician, and the former owner of Palmdale Hospital. Dr. Nichols had treated Tammy previously, and I knew she would be more comfortable with him than a new doctor, especially under the circumstances. Vi called Dr. Nichols, who answered the call from his car, where he was driving on the freeway in Los Angeles. Vi urged him to come to Tennessee immediately.

"I have no clothes for a trip," the doctor said. "I will go home and pack and catch the first flight I can."

"No! No!" Vi protested. "There is no time. You must come now!"

"I'll be right there." Dr. Nichols changed his course, headed to the airport, and caught the first flight to Knoxville.

When Dr. Nichols arrived at our house in Gatlinburg, he was extremely concerned about Tammy's condition. He called me and told me she needed to get to a hospital—fast. We wasted no time in arranging to get Tammy into Eisenhower Medical Center, near our California home. Eisenhower was a top-quality hospital where our good friend Dr. Marvin Brooks served on the staff. Eisenhower was also accustomed to dealing with high-profile personalities who needed to have their privacy protected.

By that time, no commercial flights were available from the mountains of Tennessee to Los Angeles, and more importantly, Tammy Faye was in no physical condition to get onto an airplane with a crowd of strangers. Back at PTL, arrangements were made for a private aircraft to pick up Tammy Faye, Jamie, Vi, and Dr. Nichols and get them to California as fast as possible. Meanwhile, after completing my presentation to the county commissioners, I would catch a flight out of Charlotte the following day.

Before leaving the Gatlinburg house, Vi Azvedo went around the house and collected all the various medications Tammy was ingesting. She gathered enough medicine to fill half a grocery bag. Tammy had been taking megadoses of aspirin, so much that her hearing became temporarily impaired.

She also had been taking allergy medicine, Aspergum to soothe her sore throat, throat and nasal sprays, and the antibiotics the local doctor had prescribed. One container was conspicuously low—Tammy's supply of Ativan, a tranquilizer. The children and I could always tell when Tammy had taken the Ativan. Her system was on supercharged overdrive . . . for a day. Walking down the street or through a mall, it was difficult to keep stride with her. The following day, she moved in slow motion. The difference in her demeanor when she took the Ativan was like that of a strobe light one day, and a slow . . . slow . . . slow . . . neon flashing light the next.

Tammy's trip to California was a virtual nightmare for her and everybody with her. Dr. Nichols and Vi tried to make Tammy Faye comfortable, but it was a futile attempt. During the drive to the airport, Tammy talked nonsense. As the car passed a man standing in front of a small store, Tammy told Jamie, "Go tell that man, ashes to ashes, dust to dust; then he will know that you are Jim and Tammy's son." Jamie had no idea what his mom was talking about. When they passed a fire hydrant, she said to Jamie, "Look at that cute little girl over there!"

On the plane, Tammy began hallucinating uncontrollably. She said she saw an orchestra playing outside on the airplane's wings and people dancing on the wings. She cried out to Jamie to get off the floor because he was covered with bugs. She also mistook the safety lights for giant bugs. She saw a cat sitting on the wing as the plane flew through the sky.

At one point, Tammy Faye tried to open the door to get out of the plane. Dr. Nichols and Vi had to restrain her to keep her from killing them all as the executive jet flying at high altitude and high speed whisked them across the country.

It was midnight by the time the plane landed on the West Coast. Dr. Marvin Brooks and a specialist in internal medicine met the group at the hospital. Tammy checked in under a pseudonym . . . or so everyone thought. The name may have been real to her just then.

Dr. Brooks and other doctors examined her immediately. The doctors were concerned that Tammy might go into shock at any moment. Their first task, they determined, was to get her off the medications she was on, but they had to bring her down slowly. To do so, they loaded her system with Valium. Valium had little effect on Tammy. They gave her more and more, and still she could not calm down enough to sleep. A doctor later said to me, "We gave her enough Valium to kill a truck driver." Dr. Nichols called me at 4:00 A.M. North Carolina time to let me know that they had finally succeeded in getting Tammy to sleep.

As I left Heritage USA the morning of January 13, 1987, little did I realize that it was the last time I would ever be there as president, C.E.O., and chairman of the board. I caught the first flight to California. By the time I arrived at Eisenhower hospital later that morning, Tammy Faye was resting comfortably. I was shown Tammy's X rays; she had pneumonia in her lungs. The doctors at Eisenhower also told me something I had feared to be true for some time—that Tammy Faye was addicted to drugs.

The combination of the pneumonia and the drugs could have permanently impaired Tammy Faye physically, the doctors told me, or possibly left her mentally incapacitated for life. More likely, one doctor told me, had we not gotten her into the hospital, within twenty-four hours, she would have been dead.

I listened in horror as the doctors described Tammy's condition. I knew she had been sick, and her moods ran the gamut from superplayful to almost dazed, but I never dreamed it was that serious!

The doctors explained to me that the drugs Tammy Faye had taken were not illegal—Tammy Faye never took illegal drugs—but she had unwittingly taken over-the-counter and prescription drugs that were in the same pharmaceutical family. This compounded their effects and created a powerful chemical dependency. The doctors attributed a major part of Tammy's day-to-day emotional instability to the fact that the drugs she took were not quite enough to give her a "high" such as one might get from heroin or cocaine, but because she took them so frequently, she lived a large part of her life in a constant state of withdrawal. Just as one medication was wearing off, she'd take another, prolonging the withdrawal symptoms, causing her to have extreme mood swings. The doctor's treatment plan was to slowly wean Tammy away from the drugs. They then recommended that when she was healthy enough to do so, she should go through the drug-dependency program at the Betty Ford Center, located right behind the Eisenhower hospital.

I agreed with the doctors and committed in my heart and mind that I would stick with Tammy Faye for the duration, whatever it took to help my wife get a fresh, clean start in life. In the past, I had not always been there for her when she needed me most. For instance, when Tammy was about to give birth to Jamie Charles, I took her to the hospital early in the morning, at the first sign of her contractions. When we got to the hospital, the doctor told us that, in all probability, Tammy would not be giving birth until much later that day. "Go ahead and do the television show, Jim," Tammy told me. "I'll be fine."

"Are you sure?" I asked. "I don't want to leave you, Tam."

"Yes, I'm sure. I'll be okay."

I left and did our television program, and while I was there, Tammy developed a complication of toxemia, which caused her blood pressure to skyrocket. Because Tammy Faye had experienced problems in giving birth to Tammy Sue, requiring a long labor period, the doctors decided not to take chances. For the sake of Tammy's life and that of the baby, they performed an immediate cesarean section. While I was still on the set of our live television broadcast, a staff member handed me a note, informing me that I was the father of a beautiful baby boy. We announced it on the air and made a big deal about it, and I was genuinely thrilled. Nevertheless, there was a deep regret in my heart because I had not been there with Tammy through that crisis time. Although I would not find out until 1980, when Tammy and I went through marriage counseling, she resented my not being there with her when Jamie Charles was born.

At Eisenhower it took three weeks for the doctors to detoxify Tammy Faye. When they felt she was able to function without drugs, they released her from the hospital and immediately checked her in at the Betty Ford Center. On February 20, the first night she was there, staying in a room by herself, Tammy fell apart. She could not stand being cooped up. She screamed and cried throughout the night. In the early hours of the morning, she called and cried into the phone, "Jim, please come and get me out of this place!"

The next day, we arranged for Tammy to take the Betty Ford program as an outpatient. She made me a promise that if I would allow her to stay at home, she would do everything required by the Betty Ford program. And Tammy held true to her word. Days, we were free to rest, relax, shop. After dinner each evening, the Bakker family headed off to the Betty Ford Center. The doctors indicated that not only should Tammy be in the program but the entire family and those friends closest to her. Each evening, Tammy Faye stood by her chair in front of the others in her twelve-step group as she introduced herself, "My name is Tammy Faye, and I am addicted to over-the-counter drugs." About the same time, I was in a different group dealing with codependent issues.

Due to Tammy Faye's illness, we reconsidered our plan to leave the desert. We moved to a house in Palm Springs, a beautiful, old, Spanish-style house, once owned by the Florsheim family. The property included a large swimming pool and a guest cottage and was completely surrounded by citrus trees and a high privacy wall—which would soon come in handy.

That's where we were when I received Richard Dortch's phone call informing me that Jerry Falwell wanted to see me. Falwell would meet me in Palm Springs since I had made the decision that I would not go back to Heritage USA until Tammy was completely well. I could not possibly have imagined the full ramifications of that commitment.

CHAPTER

6

Beginning of the End

WHEN MY TELEPHONE RANG EARLY SUNDAY MORNING, IT was the call from Richard Dortch that I had been awaiting.

"The Hahn story did not run in today's paper," he told me. "Roy Grutman succeeded in stopping the story from running in *The Charlotte Observer*."

I breathed a huge sigh of relief.

"But. . . ." Reverend Dortch paused.

"But?" I asked nervously.

"But Grutman says that he can't hold them off much longer."

My heart sank. We were back where we started from, the story was going to run, and the world was going to learn about my sin in the worst possible light. I knew I had to tell Tammy soon.

"Jim, Jerry Falwell has offered to help us with damage control," said Reverend Dortch. "Falwell and his people have offered to fly out there to meet with you. I will come with them. We can be there as early as Monday night. Time is of the essence."

I didn't say a word.

"Jim, I think we should let them help us."

"All right," I said reluctantly. "Tell them to come on."

I hung up the phone, and the plan that would change my life forever was set in motion. The next day Jerry Falwell and his aides flew out to see me. Mark DeMoss, Jerry Falwell's young spokesman, later explained to the press why Jerry Falwell came to Palm Springs without John Ankerberg and Jimmy Swaggart—who apparently were left out of the loop. Mark DeMoss said, "Dr. Falwell went to Palm Springs at Reverend Bakker's request, as a Christian brother and pastor."

Technically, I suppose that is true. I did indeed acquiesce to Richard Dortch's insistence that I allow Jerry Falwell to come meet with me . . . after Falwell's representatives had approached him and emphatically offered to do so.

Before the arrival of Falwell and his entourage, I sat down with Tammy Faye on the sofa in the sitting room of our bedroom at the Palm Springs house. I knew Tammy was much stronger than most people gave her credit for, but suddenly she looked so terribly fragile to me.

"Tam, I love you. You know that, don't you?"

"Of course, Jim. What's wrong? Just tell me. It can't be that bad after all we have been through. . . ."

How does one tell his wife that he has been unfaithful? And as a result, every facet of her existence is about to be blown apart, landing on newspapers, radios, and television screens around the world?

"Tam," I slowly started again, "I just got off the phone with Reverend Dortch. He's coming out to see us tomorrow."

"Why is he going to do that? Jim, tell me what is wrong!"

"*The Charlotte Observer* is going to print an article in the next few days and I want to tell you about it before it comes out. Tam, the article is going to expose the fact that seven years ago, when we were going through a tough time in our marriage . . . remember?"

Tammy nodded but remained quiet.

"When we were going through a hard time in our marriage . . . the article is going to say . . . that I had an affair. . . . And it is true. I had an affair, if that is what you want to call it."

Tammy slumped against the back of the sofa as though somebody had just knocked the wind out of her. I guess somebody had. At first, the color drained from her face. Then just as quickly, she burst into tears. She didn't yell. She didn't scream. She just cried. And cried.

I tried to hold her in my arms but she would not let me. She continued to weep. I never felt so low in all my life.

I told Tammy exactly what I did, that I had had a one-time sexual encounter in Florida with a woman named Jessica Hahn. I emphasized that it had happened that one time only. I was not in love with the woman; I had been foolishly trying to make Tammy jealous. I told Tammy that Reverend Dortch and Reverend Jerry Falwell were coming the next day to help us figure out what to do next.

"Jerry Falwell?" Tammy asked as the tears streamed down her face. "What does he have to do with us?"

"I don't know, Tam," I replied. "All I know is that Reverend Dortch says that he has offered to help us deal with all of this. You know I trust Reverend Dortch completely."

Tammy nodded. She was taking this much better than I had expected. I now realize she was like someone whose house had burst into flames. It was time to put out the fire and assess blame later. For now, Falwell and Dortch were coming. We needed to get ready.

We spent most of the day in uneasy silence. Occasionally, Tammy would break out in tears. I was concerned for her emotional well-being. It had been a tough month already. Not only was Tammy Faye in recovery, about a week or so before Reverend Dortch's call, our seventeen-year-old daughter Tammy Sue had run away from home. Tammy Sue had hosted our television program, along with Richard Dortch and others, during the month of January. On the air one day, Tammy Sue introduced her boyfriend, Doug. A few weeks later, with no advance warning to her mother and me, they were engaged to be married. Tammy and I felt our daughter needed to give the relationship some time, so we had Don Hardister, our chief of security, bring Tammy Sue to California to stay with us. Tammy Sue was not happy. When she ran off in March, we had a fairly good idea of where she might be going. Within a month, she and Doug were husband and wife. The untimely marriage ripped our hearts out, as it would most parents. But our relationship with our daughter would not be the only thing wrenched away from us this week.

Monday afternoon, March 16, Richard Dortch flew to Lynchburg, Virginia, to meet Roy Grutman and Jerry Falwell. Dortch had met Falwell previously but was meeting Grutman for the first time. Together the men, along with Falwell aides Jerry Nims and Mark DeMoss, boarded Falwell's private jet and took off for Palm Springs.

Jerry Falwell had first met Norman Roy Grutman as his adversary in a courtroom. At that time, Grutman was representing Robert Guccione, publisher of Penthouse magazine, and Falwell was suing Penthouse for printing what he claimed was a bogus interview. So impressed was Falwell by Grutman that after the trial he said, "Counselor, if I ever get in serious trouble, be assured I will call you first." Mr. Grutman replied, "It will be my great honor to represent you, Doctor."[1]

Even before the plane took flight, Jerry Falwell began questioning Reverend Dortch regarding the Jessica Hahn matter and the overall operating structure of PTL. Reverend Dortch answered Falwell's questions cautiously, avoiding any discussion of the details concerning PTL's out-of-court settlement with Jessica Hahn.

After dinner, Reverend Dortch asked Roy Grutman to go to the front of the plane so he could speak privately to the lawyer. The previous Friday, during a phone conversation between the two men, Grutman had agreed to represent PTL. "I will be your lawyer," he promised Reverend Dortch.

Now, aboard Jerry Falwell's jet, Reverend Dortch asked Roy Grutman, "Can I tell you some things confidentially?"

Grutman assured Dortch that he could speak openly, with complete lawyer-client confidentiality. At that point, Reverend Dortch told Roy Grutman everything he knew concerning the out-of-court settlement, the money that was paid to Jessica Hahn, and how it was paid. Before the plane landed in Palm Springs on Monday afternoon, Grutman was privy to all the intimate details of my sexual indiscretion.[2]

I have often wondered how much of that Dortch-Grutman conversation was known to Jerry Falwell on Tuesday, March 17. Although I did not know it at the time, PTL had already paid Roy Grutman a fifty thousand dollar retainer to represent us. Besides violating Richard Dortch's confidentiality, Roy Grutman conveniently ignored this conversation—and the retainer—when a month later Jerry Falwell appointed a committee to investigate the financial settlement with Jessica Hahn. The committee was comprised of two new PTL board members . . . and Roy Grutman.[3]

Reverend Dortch and the Lynchburg group were met by Vi Azvedo's husband, Eddie. En route to the hotel, the group's discussion centered completely around the upcoming presidential election and Vice President Bush's campaign. The Falwell troupe checked in at Maxim's Hotel in Palm Springs and Reverend Dortch came straight to see Tammy and me.

I was glad to see Richard Dortch. I had known Richard since 1977, when he had already earned a reputation within our denomination as a pastor to pastors. At the time of his first appearance on our *PTL* program, Reverend Dortch was serving as the Illinois state superintendent of the Assemblies of God and as one of our denomination's thirteen national presbyters. In 1978, as PTL was beginning to grow exponentially, I sensed the need for a strong, pastoral influence on our Board of Directors. I asked Richard Dortch to consider the position, and he accepted.

By the fall of 1983, PTL had taken on a life of its own. We had a huge budget, hundreds of employees, and an exhausting schedule of television productions and growing ministries. I knew I was in over my head trying to run an organization this large. Although I had read many business, customer-service, and people-management books in an attempt to be a good manager, I had no formal business training. I was an ideas person; I could look at a lot covered by weeds, rocks, and trees, and see a vision of a Grand Hotel. But when it came to poring over financial statements or confronting staff members, I was gladly willing to let other people handle that.

Nevertheless, I was the president of our organization and it was my responsibility to find good people to deal with the myriad details of taking care of the business and personnel matters. That is how I came to hire Richard Dortch. Not only was he a trusted PTL board member, but I figured that anyone who knew how to manage hundreds of ministers and churches, plus the Illinois state office staff and radio stations, could handle the financial and personnel pressures at PTL. Richard came on staff full-time as our senior executive vice president, corporate executive director, and my copastor of Heritage Village and Missionary Fellowship Church.

I hired Richard Dortch to be my general manager, to be the executive at PTL that I was not. I was the visionary, the dreamer, the builder. I was happy to let Richard handle the details. Unfortunately, television is heady work, and Richard was soon drawn away from the reason I brought him on board.

Richard Dortch put it this way:

> The fascinating aura surrounding television can suck you in like quicksand if you let it. Almost every time I went to PTL for a board meeting, I made a television appearance. It didn't take long for me to be captivated and enchanted by the experience. Surrounded by cameramen and sound people who focused on my every word and movement, I enjoyed the exposure and attention of television—not realizing its dangers.[4]

Reverend Dortch's admitted fascination with the spotlight of television and his intense desire to protect and maintain the ministry of PTL most likely colored some of his decisions and advice that third week in March. I will never know.

I do know that when Reverend Dortch visited with Tammy and me on Monday evening, March 16, there was no man in the world I trusted more than him. He gave me a glowing report of PTL's progress during the first few months of 1987 and then reluctantly told me that he had slowed construction on our building projects almost to a standstill until more money came in. I was not happy to hear that, and Reverend Dortch knew it. But that was not the reason he was in Palm Springs.

Speaking quietly but emphatically, he told Tammy and me the same information he had given me by phone. Reverend Dortch seemed convinced that Jerry Falwell's help was the only way to stave off an attempt by

Jimmy Swaggart to destroy our ministry. Beyond that, Falwell was a highly visible, credible television preacher himself, and his vast influence would help us defray some of the certain fallout if and when *The Charlotte Observer* story went to press.

It seemed to make sense.

The next day Tammy Faye and I again met Richard Dortch at his hotel room around 8:30 A.M. on Tuesday, March 17. We talked briefly and then prayed before going to meet Jerry Falwell and his group in a suite at Maxim's Hotel around 9:00 A.M. When we arrived, Jerry Nims, Mark DeMoss, and Norman Roy Grutman met us there. Jerry Falwell invited Tammy and me into an adjoining room in the suite. He closed the door and came over to where we were standing. He stepped between Tammy and me and put his big arms around us, forming a small huddle.

"Jim and Tammy, I want to help you," he said, sounding like a compassionate father. "I love you and I want to help you," he repeated. "First of all, I need to know the facts. I want you to tell me everything that happened seven years ago in Florida with the Hahn woman."

Still huddled together with Falwell like a big bear holding his cubs, I told the story in specific detail, right in front of Tammy, emphasizing that it was not an ongoing affair, but a foolish, fifteen- to twenty-minute sexual encounter, and that I definitely did not rape the woman. Next we talked briefly about the potential Swaggart attack on PTL. Then Falwell encouraged Tammy to go back home. He and I would remain to discuss how things should best be handled. As Tammy left the room, Jerry called after her, telling her that he would be praying for her. Tammy did not answer.

Once Tammy was gone, Jerry closed the door, and he and I sat down and began to discuss the attempts of Jimmy Swaggart to take over the ministry of PTL. We discussed Jimmy Swaggart's letter to John Ankerberg, indicating that *The Charlotte Observer* would do its part, and the Assemblies of God would do its part to excoriate me. Jerry implied that he felt it was a conspiracy to bring me down. He also made it sound as though his motives for getting involved were not totally altruistic, but that he was concerned about Swaggart's designs on his own ministry. "Jim, if we don't stop Swaggart at your place, he will eventually be at our door."

My suspicions of Jerry Falwell's motives for wanting to help us began to break down. I wanted to believe the man, and the fact that he seemed so open and sincere about wanting to protect his own interests rather than trying to convince me that he was concerned about mine lent credibility to what he was saying. I had been suspicious of Jerry because it was common knowledge that he regarded charismatics as doctrinally unsound. He had often joked that charismatics were people who had eaten too much pizza and thus their propensity to speak in tongues. But because Jerry was expressing his own self-interest and his concern for self-preservation, he came across to me as believable.

Falwell indicated that he could help me fend off Swaggart's attempts and deal with the Hahn fallout. He was willing.

"But you must ask me to help you, Jim," Jerry said.

"Well, of course, I'd be glad for your help," I replied.

Jerry was extremely specific and emphatic. "I want to help you, Jim, but you must ask me."

I thought it rather strange that Jerry was stressing the point that I had to ask him, but I thought it might be necessary because his denominational affiliation was so different from my own.

Again he said, "You must ask me, Jim."

"Okay, I'm asking you," I said. "Will you please help me?"

Jerry Falwell smiled broadly. "Why certainly, I will help you, Jim. Let me tell you what we need to do. . . ."

For the next hour, Jerry Falwell outlined how I should resign from all three of my positions at PTL, as president, chairman of the board, and pastor of the church. After thirty to ninety days, when the furor over the Hahn disclosure would have dissipated, I could then return to my positions. He told me how he had once helped a church in Bangor, Maine, when its pastor committed adultery. Jerry told me that he had stepped in and "helped," and now the church and pastor were both doing fine. He felt in his heart, he said, that we could see similar results at PTL.

Jerry then suggested that we should have the current board members resign as an act of good faith and a willingness to show that PTL was making a fresh start. We could replace them with a new Board, all friends of mine whom I respected and trusted—pastors and people such as Pat Boone and Dale Evans Rogers. We agreed that Richard Dortch would serve as the new president in the interim and as host of the television program.

"You stay here and take care of getting Tammy Faye completely well," Falwell said. "You'll still be in charge of the ministry. We'll work to protect you and save PTL from Jimmy Swaggart." He then outlined how he would take a group of leaders, including Billy Graham, to meet with Jimmy Swaggart and try to persuade him to back off from his destructive plan for the Body of Christ's sake. That idea sounded good to me, but I was still hesitant to resign from the organization to which I had given birth.

"Is this okay with you, Jim?" Jerry asked.

47

"Well, I don't know. . . . I guess as long as Richard Dortch is the president and the host of the show . . . and as long as I choose any new board members. . . ."

"You must make up your mind, Jim. We don't have much time. Do you want my help?"

"Yes, I do."

"Okay, I'll have Roy Grutman come in and explain how we can do all of this. Excuse me just a minute," Jerry Falwell said. He stepped outside the conference room and I buried my head in my hands at the table.

Jerry Falwell closed the door. He spoke to Grutman within the hearing of the others. "Roy, Jim wants to talk to you."

Falwell then walked over to where Richard Dortch was sitting. He looked down at Reverend Dortch and according to Dortch spoke firmly, "Jim has just turned the PTL ministry over to me, provided that you are the president and the host of the show. I've agreed to that. So you and I need to get to work to decide who we want on the new board of directors, because Jim wants to approve who the new board will be."[5] Falwell went on to tell Dortch that "within six months to a year, we'll give the ministry back to Jim."[6]

I was shell-shocked. Perhaps because of that, I violated several of my own personal principles during my meeting with Jerry Falwell. For one thing, in all my business dealings, I made it a practice never to meet with anyone alone. I always wanted someone else as a witness for all my dealings. I wanted to avoid the "my word against your word" syndrome. But for some reason, possibly because I knew that we would be discussing the sensitive matter of Jessica Hahn, I did not invite Richard Dortch or anyone else into the conference room that day. That was a mistake. Once Tammy was gone, I had nobody to corroborate what was said in the meeting that morning. To this day, Jerry Falwell and I recall the words and intent of that meeting differently.

Roy Grutman came in and talked to me, and while Falwell talked to Dortch, Grutman kept reiterating, "This is like a play, Jim. You have to play dead for a while. If you don't, Swaggart is going to destroy you. You'll only have to play dead for thirty to ninety days and you will be back at PTL."

I was concerned about how Tammy was going to take all this and I told Grutman so. I wanted to trust Norman Roy Grutman, and his authoritative eloquence engendered my confidence; he said that he would represent me and I believed him. Grutman suggested that he and I go over to my house and tell Tammy what was going on so he and the other members of Falwell's group could get back east as soon as possible to put the plan into action. Compliantly, I agreed.

My head was in a whirl as Grutman and I walked out of that room. But I was still surprised when I heard the bombastic lawyer announce to the other men, "Jim and I are going over to the Bakkers' house to tell Tammy about the decision to turn the ministry over to Jerry Falwell."

I had not turned the ministry over to Jerry Falwell. I *never* turned the ministry over to Jerry Falwell! I had agreed to turn my presidency and television responsibilities over to Richard Dortch for a period of thirty to ninety days, after which I would return to my own posts. Richard Dortch was already the general manager of PTL, so I felt safe in doing so. Jerry Falwell had assured me that he himself would remain in the background as one of the men working to save the ministry. "Jim, I'll never even go to PTL!" he told me.

Norman Roy Grutman and I drove back to my home to tell Tammy. It was one of the longest drives of my life. Along the way, Grutman continued to emphasize that my resignation was the only way to defuse the powder keg that was about to explode with *The Charlotte Observer*'s disclosure of my sin with Jessica Hahn. Grutman implied that the best way to take the attention away from that story was to make a bigger headline with my resignation. He also spoke in threatening terms of how Ankerberg and Swaggart in their efforts to take over PTL might instigate the PTL Partners to initiate a class-action lawsuit in an effort to take over PTL. Grutman seemed fond of using the term "hostile takeover" to describe what he said Jimmy Swaggart was trying to do. I was aware of some of the articles Jimmy had written in his magazines concerning certain ministries that had theme parks (I wonder whom he meant!) and some of the comments he had made concerning me in recent meetings with Assemblies of God leaders. According to the reports I received, Jimmy's words about me, as well as his actions and attitude, were virulent. Consequently, Grutman's constant warnings of a "hostile takeover" attempt seemed plausible.

By the time we arrived at my home in Palm Springs, my stomach was tied up in what felt like a million knots. Tammy was not happy to see me coming through the door with Roy Grutman in tow.

"Tam, we need to talk to you," I told her. Grutman took it from there. He told Tammy in detail the reasons why I had to resign. We walked outside in our garden as Grutman laid out the scenario. "Jim needs to appoint this blue-ribbon panel to the board to lead the ministry for thirty to ninety days and get you well while you finish your outpatient program at Betty Ford. We'll take care of everything. Richard Dortch will be president and, of course, Reverend Falwell will help. You and Jim can choose the board of directors."

Tammy smelled a rat. She distrusted Jerry Falwell's motives and she was not buying Grutman's story at all. She was especially reluctant to have me resign my position on the board. She could almost handle why I might have to stay off the air for a while; that wasn't a major change since I had not been hosting our show for almost three months anyhow. She could also understand the need for me to stay out of the pulpit for a while. Tammy was aware of how the Assemblies of God normally handle moral failures. But she could not see why I had to step down from the PTL Board of Directors.

Outside in our yard, she adamantly insisted that I not resign. Grutman seemed to sense that although he was the master orator, Tammy Faye's instinctive intuition was swaying my position.

"Look, Mrs. Bakker, if it makes you feel any better, we will have each member of the new board, including Reverend Falwell, sign resignations before they even come on." Grutman looked squarely at me as he continued speaking. "We will place those signed resignations in your hands, and that way, any time you are ready to return, you just turn in those resignations of the new board, and you can bring back your old board members or do as you please. It will be your prerogative."

I looked at Tammy. In my nervous, embarrassed condition, the arrangement was sounding better to me, but I could tell by Tammy's facial expression she was unconvinced.

"I don't feel good about this," Tammy said.

"Oh, everything will be fine," Grutman assured her. "You have been through quite a lot lately. You need to just relax and take your mind off this situation. We'll take care of everything. Go relax and read a book."

Later that day, Grutman sent a thick romance novel to Tammy. Tammy Faye may have been through a lot, but she was beginning to resurface stronger than ever. Our marriage was flourishing despite the recent revelations of my infidelity. Tammy had forgiven me, and we were starting to fall in love all over again. We had nearly completed our aftercare program at Betty Ford, and would have, in all probability, returned to PTL within weeks had not these new developments occurred. Tammy was ready for a fight, but I was not. She saw through the sham that was being perpetrated in the name of God; I did not. She felt that my resigning was an inappropriate way to handle the situation. As the events unfolded in the weeks to come, it became increasingly clear that she was right and I was wrong.

Grutman seemed in a big hurry to get going. "We must make haste and get back to the plane," he kept saying. "We must hurry."

I have often been asked since that day, "Why didn't you take some time to think things over before making such an important decision?"

That is exactly what I should have done, but I did not, and I was wrong. Years before, when I was just starting out as a young preacher, the words of another speaker at a charismatic Lutheran conference in Minneapolis left an indelible impression upon my heart and mind. He said, "Beware voices of haste."

It was excellent advice that unfortunately I disregarded. Both Falwell and Grutman, as well as the others in their group, emphasized that I must make up my mind quickly. We had to act quickly to stave off the "hostile takeover." We had to act quickly to thwart the impact of *The Charlotte Observer*'s ensuing article. Everything had to happen now. Fast. Hurry.

In retrospect, I firmly believe that had I taken just twenty-four hours to think about the Falwell-Grutman proposal I would have rejected it out of hand. If I were going to implement any part of what they had suggested, I would have done it under the careful watch of men with whom I had worked over the years and trusted to have the ministry's and my best interests at heart. Unfortunately, I did not take time even to consult the usual battery of PTL lawyers and financial advisors concerning Jerry Falwell's offer. Had I simply stopped long enough to think, to seek God's direction, to surround myself with a group of wise counselors as the Bible instructs, I would not have allowed a group of men, many of whom I barely knew, to take the reins of PTL. Unfortunately, because of my concern for Tammy's recovery, the impending Hahn article, and my own fears and foolishness, I allowed Heritage USA to be stolen from the PTL Partners and me while I looked on. Because of my haste, within twenty-four hours I lost my ministry, my life's work, and my will to live. Overnight, I went from having a worldwide ministry with several thousand employees to having no ministry at all and being an unemployed pariah.

Back home on Tuesday night, our houseguests, Doug and Laura Lee Oldham, assured me that I could trust Jerry Falwell. Doug had worked in ministry with Jerry for many years, long before he ever came to PTL. When I confided to Doug some of the details of the day's meeting, my friend repeated again and again, "Jim, Jerry Falwell would never hurt you."

7

The Hostile Takeover

ON WEDNESDAY, MARCH 18, RICHARD DORTCH CALLED A special emergency meeting of the PTL Board of Directors. After a brief explanation of the purpose of the meeting by Reverend Dortch, Roy Grutman informed the board members that they were being asked to resign. Grutman took special care to emphasize that there could be legal and financial problems for the members if they did not comply with Jerry Falwell's request. Several of the board members later told me that they felt they were being threatened.

Before the board resigned, however, they annulled the official board resolution of December 10, 1980, which had placed PTL in the hands of the Assemblies of God if for any reason I could no longer serve as president of PTL. Thus, in one fell swoop, all threats that Jimmy Swaggart could legally exercise a "hostile takeover" of PTL through the Assemblies of God were removed. Nobody on our board had yet figured out that the hostile takeover was not being orchestrated in Swaggart's office.

Grutman had arranged for me to talk to the board over a speakerphone. Embarrassed that I had failed my faithful friends and coworkers on the PTL board, I sat at a desk in an enclosed outer veranda of our home, waiting for Grutman's call. It rang at about 7:00 P.M. Pacific time. With his usual loquacious flair, Grutman took us on a meandering journey of words before turning the phone over to me. In a simple, brief statement, I resigned as president of PTL, as the chief executive officer, and as chairman of the board. I did not invite any questions and none were asked. The dedicated board members all promised that they would be praying for me. One of the most crushing events of my life to date had taken only a few minutes. It was over. I hung up the phone and wanted to die.

Back at PTL, Jerry Falwell, who was also connected to the meeting by phone was elected as the new chairman of the board. He accepted the position over the phone, and then continued to listen as one by one, the board members stepped down and were replaced with selections made by Jerry Falwell and his aides. Pat Boone, Dale Evans Rogers, and most of the other well-known charismatic leaders whom I had chosen to serve on the new board were not asked. Nor was I given opportunity to approve those who were asked to serve on the new board, one of the fundamental aspects of Jerry Falwell's and my discussion little more than thirty-six hours earlier.

In addition to Richard Dortch, two men of charismatic persuasion were elected to the new Falwell board: James Watt, former U.S. Secretary of the Interior, and Rex Humbard, pastor of the Cathedral of Tomorrow, near Akron, Ohio, and a frequent guest on our programs. The remainder of the new board were noncharismatics: Jerry Nims, one of Falwell's close associates; Ben Armstrong, executive director of the National Religious Broadcasters; and Sam Moore, president of Thomas Nelson Publishers. Pastor Charles Stanley of First Baptist Church, Atlanta, was extended an invitation to serve on the new Falwell board, but he declined the offer. Bailey Smith, former president of the Southern Baptist Convention, eventually received that seat around the table.

Grutman never produced the signed resignations of the new board members. When Shirley Fulbright raised the question of the whereabouts of the missing signed resignations, she was told by Reverend Dortch to keep quiet. The subject never came up in any official meeting ever again.

On Thursday afternoon, March 19, at about 2:30 P.M., in a conference call arranged by Norman Roy Grutman, I went on the phone line to do the interview Grutman had promised *The Charlotte Observer* the weekend before if they would hold the Hahn article, which they had already decided to kill. Because of the potential for lawsuits, it is highly debatable that the editors would have run the story the next week, or ever, had it not been for us providing them with a scoop better than they dreamed.

Earlier that day, I called several of my key staff members and told them what was about to happen. I did not go into detail; I just wanted them to know before the rest of the world knew. I told them that I planned to be back within thirty to ninety days, and I pleaded with them to do their best to hold PTL together. Reverend Dortch had already scheduled a staff meeting for later that day when he and Norman Roy Grutman could break the news of my resignation to the rest of the staff.

The editors of the local paper were not sure what to expect when they learned that I would be talking to them from my home in Palm Springs. Grutman had promised them a front-page scoop, though, so they knew something big was in the air. *The Charlotte Observer*'s editorial offices, I later learned, looked like a war room that day, with tape recorders set to record my interview, reporters ready to write the story, and the paper's top brass and lawyer ready to call any shots necessary.

The newspaper people must have been shocked when they learned that our "interview" would be a statement by me. Norman Roy Grutman had written my formal resignation, taking kernels of the truth and twisting them together with his own interpretations. He faxed it to me shortly before I was to read it publicly. The resignation sounded much more like Grutman than me. I thought back to when I had come out of my meeting with Falwell. I asked Reverend Dortch, "Is this what I should do?"

Dortch looked back at me and said, "There are no other alternatives. This is what must be done."

I had no other option. I had to resign. I fumbled with the fax in front of me. I didn't want to read it. Tammy Faye would not even listen.

I began to speak.

> Thank you. As you know, for many years, Tammy Faye and I and our ministries have been subjected to constant harassment and pressures by various groups and forces whose objective has been to undermine and to destroy us. I cannot deny that the personal toll that these pressures have exerted on me and my wife and family have been more than we can bear.
>
> In fact, as our friends are all too well aware, my and Tammy's physical and emotional resources have been so overwhelmed that we are presently under full-time therapy at a treatment center in California. We want to express our gratitude for the support and encouragement we've received from so many of our friends and partners. I have decided that for the good of my family, the church, and of all of our related ministries that I should resign and step down immediately from PTL.
>
> I have also today resigned from the Assemblies of God. I am not able to muster the resources needed to combat a new wave of attack that I have learned is about to be launched against us by *The Charlotte Observer*, which has attacked us incessantly for the past twelve years.

54

Although I did not mention Hahn's name, I went on to admit that I had been guilty of adultery. Grutman wrote it more ambiguously:

> . . . I categorically deny that I've ever sexually assaulted or harassed anyone. I sorrowfully acknowledge that seven years ago, in an isolated incident, I was wickedly manipulated by treacherous former friends and then colleagues who victimized me with the aid of a female confederate. They conspired to betray me into a sexual encounter at a time of great stress in my marital life. Vulnerable as I was at the time, I was set up as part of a scheme to co-opt me and obtain some advantage for themselves over me in connection with their hope for position in the ministry.
>
> I have sought and gratefully received the loving forgiveness of our Savior who forgives us of our sins. I have told Tammy everything and Tammy, of course, has forgiven me, and our love for each other is greater and stronger than it has ever been.
>
> Now, seven years later, this one time mistake is seized upon by my enemies to humiliate and degrade me to gratify their envious and selfish motives. They have falsified, distorted, and exaggerated the facts so as to make the occurrence appear many times worse than it ever was. Anyone who knows Jim Bakker knows that I never physically assaulted anyone in my life.
>
> In retrospect, it was poor judgment to have succumbed to blackmail. But when extortionist overtures were made, I was concerned to protect and spare the ministry and my family. Unfortunately, money was paid in order to avoid further suffering or hurt to anyone, to appease these persons who were determined to destroy this ministry.
>
> I now, in hindsight, realize payment should have been resisted, and we ought to have exposed the blackmailers to the penalties of the law. I'm truly sorry for all this that has happened in the past or any harm that may have occurred.
>
> I bear no malice to anyone. I forgive those who have borne false witness against me.
>
> I cannot undo the past, but must now address the future. I have no doubt God has a redemptive plan for PTL and for Jim and Tammy.
>
> I fervently pray for the future of PTL and Heritage USA. It is my life to preserve, to protect those cherished values which it embodies.

I had difficulty reading the next section of the resignation letter. First of all, Grutman had intimated that Jerry Falwell and I were friends, which could only have been said in the loosest sense of the word. Prior to our Tuesday meeting, I could remember exchanging only a few words with Jerry in my entire life, usually at conventions. Anyone who knew me well knew that Jerry and I were not "friends."

> I've asked my friend, Jerry Falwell, to help me in my crisis.
> The PTL board of directors has accepted my resignation, and
> appointed Jerry Falwell as chairman of our board of directors,
> requesting him to designate a new board of directors. He has done
> this and the old board has accordingly resigned.
>
> I ask the prayerful support of our friends and foes for the
> preservation and advancement of God's work and the future of
> PTL. God bless you and good-bye.[1]

Like a zombie I had read the whole thing just as it had been written, saying things I knew were not true. How foolish! I was lying. I was not really resigning. It was a "play act," Grutman had said. I knew things were not happening the way Falwell, Grutman, and I had discussed. Most importantly, Jerry Falwell had selected a new board, without consulting me. Nevertheless, I went along with the play, thinking I was saving the PTL ministry and everything I held dear.

I was wrong to do so. I was a fool to go along with such a hoax.

According to Grutman's instructions, I quickly hung up the phone to avoid answering any questions. Grutman continued the interview and answered *The Charlotte Observer's* questions. He then introduced Jerry Falwell, who came on the line from Lynchburg. Falwell's comments were telling: "They [the new board members] all have promised to continue in prayer for the complete healing and restoration of Jim and Tammy Bakker and with the prayer that God somewhere down the road has another fruitful and effective ministry in store for them somewhere."[2]

The editors at *The Charlotte Observer* were skeptical. The paper and I had had a running battle for years, and they could not imagine that I would give up so easily. In an attempt to allay their suspicions, Grutman lied to the reporters and emphasized to them that my resignation was for real. "There are no conditions," he said. "It is not a sham, word is that he has resigned and stepped down. Period. End of report."[3]

The Charlotte Observer's reporters rushed the story to press. So, too, did most major news outlets. Almost immediately, our Palm Springs home came under a media siege with reporters and satellite trucks.

The Charlotte Observer sold more papers the next day than at any other time except the death of Elvis Presley. They had to restart their presses three times on Friday to keep newspapers in the racks.

Within hours of my resignation becoming public, my telephone began ringing. One of the first to call was Dr. Billy Graham. He let me know that he and his family were praying for me. Bill Bright, president of Campus Crusade for Christ, called soon after. So did Oral Roberts.

One of the most unsettling early calls I received was from Dr. Robert Schuller. First, Dr. Schuller assured me of his love and prayers. As we talked longer, however, Dr. Schuller warned me not to resign hastily.

I cringed. "It's too late. It's already been done."

A few days later, as the media uproar about a "holy war" began to explode, Robert Schuller called again, offering Tammy and me his ministerial retreat center in Hawaii if we wanted to escape the crowds for a while. Again Dr. Schuller reiterated the concerns he had expressed in his previous call. I thanked Robert for his kind offer but felt that I needed to stay in Palm Springs and finish Tammy's aftercare program.

Several people whom I had never expected to respond to our hurt called almost immediately, offering everything from financial help to invitations to spend time in the privacy of their homes. Richard Simmons, the fitness guru who had appeared with Tammy Faye on her show, called within hours, offering to help. Singer Elton John, whom I had never met, reportedly invited us to his home. I wasn't sure if the call was real or a hoax.

For the next few days, I simply curled up on the couch for hours on end, racking my brain over what I had done, wondering, *Could I have handled it differently?* I drew blanks every way I turned.

One night on television I watched an interviewer ask both Jimmy Swaggart and Jerry Falwell about rumors of a "hostile takeover." Swaggart denied having designs on PTL and called me "a cancer that needed to be excised from the Body of Christ." When the interviewer pressed Falwell on the question of a hostile takeover of PTL, Jerry Falwell looked into the camera and said, "I do not know anything about a hostile takeover."[4]

At that moment, I knew I had been deceived. Jerry Falwell was the man who had informed *me* of the hostile takeover threat!

He later reiterated his on-air comment. "I . . . at this moment, do not feel anyone attempted a hostile takeover." He covered himself by adding, "I did not say the Reverend Bakker did not think that. . . . He may have hard evidence to prove that."[5]

A letter was sent to the PTL Partners. The letter was not written by me but went out under my name saying that I was resigning, but PTL would be going on to higher heights than ever before, and the partners could trust this group of good men!

A week or so after my resignation, Tammy and I taped a video segment from our home in California that was to be run on PTL. The purpose of the segment was to give our side of the story to our PTL audience and partners. I apologized for my sins and the hurt I had caused the Body of Christ. Tammy, too, expressed the fact that she had forgiven me and was willing and ready to move on with our lives. Tammy Faye then sang a song, "The Sun Will Shine Again," from the porch of our guest house.

When I saw the edited tape, I was appalled. Specific, crucial details had been edited. For example, on the original tape, I confessed to our audience that I had had a fifteen- to twenty-minute affair seven years ago. The words "fifteen- to twenty-minute" were deleted, making my statement, "I had an affair seven years ago," implying an ongoing relationship.

Despite the edits, something connected with the audience at PTL that day. The studio audience responded to the videotape with a standing ovation. The PTL phone lines lit up with callers saying, "We love Jim and Tammy. We want them to return."

I was ready and willing to return, but the Falwell troupe firmly resisted that idea and even some of my closest coworkers, Richard Dortch, David Taggart, and Shirley Fulbright, assured me that everything was working out as planned. I telephoned my friends saying, "Something is not right. I think we have been had!" They in turn went to Jerry Falwell with my concerns. Jerry said, "Oh, no. We're right on schedule."

I called Jerry Falwell and expressed my concerns to him personally. Again Jerry replied, "The plan is working perfectly. Just stay calm. This is like a play. You have to play dead or PTL will be destroyed."

Within hours, Jerry Falwell sent David Taggart and Shirley Fulbright to Palm Springs on a private jet to allay my concerns. "Just stay calm and lie low," they told me. "Falwell is taking care of everything."

Over the next few weeks, even Richard Dortch slowly began to change his tone. I told him, "Reverend Dortch, I have to come back to PTL." Reverend Dortch was aware of the plan for me to return from the beginning of my discussions with Falwell and Grutman. Nevertheless he replied, "Oh, no, Jim! You can't come back. The Assemblies of God rehabilitation program requires that you must be gone for a year or two." Ironically, both Richard Dortch and I had resigned from the Assemblies of God when my sin became news.

I never went back to my office at PTL again. I was not even given the opportunity to clean out my desk or gather my personal possessions and pictures in the room. It was suddenly as though I had never existed.

I spent much of those early days in seclusion behind the walls of our home. When I wasn't curled in a ball on the couch, I occasionally went out to our swimming pool, dodging the helicopters that hovered over our house and the reporters attempting to get photos over the walls. It got to be almost like a game. Every time a helicopter came by, I'd jump up from where I was sitting and run back under the large eaves of our house. One day I was sitting on a chaise lounge at our pool. Scott Ross, with whom I had worked at CBN, and Tammy Faye were in the water, only inches away. Next to me, Scott's wife Nedra was stretched out on another chaise. Unknown to us, a full block away a photographer was perched atop a local hospital and, with a high-powered lens, was shooting pictures of us. The following day, a photo of Nedra and me appeared with Scott and Tammy Faye cropped out of the frame. The picture ran in papers across America. The caption blared: *Jim Bakker and Unidentified Woman!*

Tammy and I completed our aftercare program at Betty Ford. After that, when we attempted to go out for dinner, we were always followed by a parade of press cars and vans.

It was due to Tammy's urgings that we went out to eat at all; had it been up to me, I would have been happy to eat at home to avoid the press. Not so with Tammy. We dined mostly at Sonny Bono's restaurant in Palm Springs. Sonny was kind enough to arrange a table behind some plants in an alcove. During those early days, with our names and photos splattered all over the world, Sonny often came and talked with Tammy and me about his own hurt when his former wife Cher left him. He told me how it had taken time to pick up the pieces. Sonny was encouraging us not to give up when some of our closest friends were no longer calling. In his own way, Sonny Bono ministered to Tammy and me and helped us through some of the most difficult days of our lives.

By Wednesday, April 22, Jerry Falwell and others seemed extremely concerned that I was going to make a bid to return to Heritage USA. They were not far wrong, but I knew that the first step toward my eventual return, pastoral rehabilitation, and restoration must be to get PTL back into the hands of a group of leaders who might be sensitive to those issues. By telephone, I dictated a letter to Shirley Fulbright. When Shirley completed the letter, she walked to the fax machine and inserted the letter.

"What are you doing?" Shirley heard Richard Dortch's voice behind her.

"I am sending this letter from Reverend Bakker to Reverend Falwell," she replied in her best formal executive assistant's voice.

"You can't do that!"

"Oh, yes I can." Shirley hit the button and the letter curled through the fax machine, over the phone lines, and into the office of Jerry Falwell.

The letter read:

Tammy and I have tried many times to reach you by telephone so I decided to send you this message.

Due to the unrest in the Charismatic world and also among the Charismatic leadership, I feel that it is time now for you to turn the PTL Ministry over to Charismatics, appointing James Watt as Chairman of the board, with Rex Humbard and Richard Dortch remaining. Others will be added.

I am recommending that a strong COO [Chief Operating Officer] be appointed by this Charismatic board.

As you committed to me at our meeting in Palm Springs when you brought me the information that you believed that Jimmy Swaggart was plotting a hostile takeover of PTL, promising to save the Ministry from this hostile takeover, you were going to hold the Ministry and, when I asked, you would turn it back. I am asking that you turn it over to this group of Charismatics. I am going to submit to a large group of elders in the Charismatic church world and I will return to PTL when they feel it is God's time.

I have been in touch with major leaders of the Charismatic world. Jerry, I will not fight you if you ignore my wishes but I must let you know that what you are embarking on will truly start what the press has labeled a "holy war." Please let brotherly love continue and control what we do, and let us not allow the world to have any more opportunity to wag their tongues at the cause of Christ. Let us get back to our first love and calling, winning souls for the Kingdom. . . .

I have given to one of the most outstanding Christian journalists in the world all the documentation on what is being done on both sides of this issue and I have also given the documentation to a journalist in the secular media. I have sworn them to secrecy unless something happens. No matter what happens to me, they will write the true, documented story of this unprecedented event . . .[6]

I received no response from Jerry Falwell concerning my letter.

That same day, Jerry Falwell and Jerry Nims met in a Nashville hotel with John Ankerberg and four men who claimed to have damaging information about me in regard to alleged homosexual actions. Ankerberg declared that he was going to accuse me of homosexuality on the talk show Larry King Live, airing on CNN later that week.[7]

When Ankerberg's interview aired, I was at Little Bear Lake, not far from Palm Springs, with my son Jamie and our longtime security guard, Don Hardister. Unknown to me, Don had shifted his allegiance from me to Jerry Falwell. In fairness to Don, he had been told by the new leaders at PTL that if he wanted to keep his job, he must keep a close watch on me and keep my family and me away from Heritage USA. Consequently, even on a trip for Jamie and me to have some father-and-son time together, Don came along. I had taken Jamie to the mountain lake area to protect him from the awful things he was hearing said about Tammy and me every day on television. We had been gone only a day or so when Hardister called home. Tammy Faye told Don to have me call her right away.

Don brought the message to me just as Jamie and I were about to go fishing. I went to a pay phone and dialed our number. When Tammy came on the line, she was furious. She informed me of Ankerberg's accusations of homosexuality not only on Larry King's program, but repeated that same night on ABC's *Nightline* with Ted Koppel.

My heart sank. Like Ankerberg and Falwell, I knew that an accusation of homosexual conduct was one of the most damaging charges that could be leveled at an evangelical minister. That is why of all the things said about me during the weeks following my resignation from PTL, Ankerberg's accusations were the most painful. Not only were they the death knell of my reputation, they signaled the end of my ministry, I felt sure.

I tried always to avoid even the appearance of evil, so much so that in my early evangelistic years when praying for a woman, I had Tammy put her hands on the woman, and I put my hands on Tammy's. I would not hire a female masseuse for the same reason. Nor would I ever go to a massage parlor, which I had been accused of. All of the massages I received were given by a male masseur. I never considered this type of contact as a homosexual act.

The nightmare of everything that was happening wrapped itself more tightly around my neck. For the first time in my life, I seriously contemplated suicide. Fortunately, Jamie and Don Hardister were with me, or I might not have returned from the lake. Thoughts of suicide became a regular part of my mental contemplation for several months to come. In a strange way, thoughts of suicide kept me alive. I had lost all other control over my life; I had lost my position, my possessions, my ministry, and now my reputation. The only thing I felt that I could control was my existence—that I could kill myself and escape if the pain got too bad. I even believed my family would be better off without me. Only thoughts of hell and eternal damnation kept me from killing myself—those, and the hand of God.

On a day when I had actually planned out how, when, and where I was going to commit suicide, Pastor Ty and Jeannette Beeson and some friends drove all the way from the Palmdale area, about three hours away, to our home at Palm Springs. They said, "We feel God sent us here to minister to you." They literally helped pack our clothes and insisted that Tammy and I go with them to church and stay with them for the weekend.

I have often wondered whether I would have followed through on my suicide plans had not those friends shown up. I would like to think that I might have resisted the urge for spiritual reasons or out of respect for my family. Yet my depression was so deep, only God knows what I might have done. Thanks to some friends who were sensitive to the Lord and who loved Tammy and me, I never had to make that choice.

Many people wondered aloud how and why Jerry Falwell, an avowed anticharismatic, could become involved in PTL, a leading charismatic-oriented ministry. Certainly supporters of PTL were confused, but Falwell's friends were equally frustrated in their attempts to make sense of Falwell's actions. One pastor was Dr. Bob Gray, a close friend of Jerry Falwell's, pastor of Trinity Baptist Church and president of Trinity Bible College in Jacksonville, Florida. Dr. Gray could not understand what Falwell was doing. Addressing this issue with his congregation in a regularly scheduled service, Dr. Gray first emphasized his close affinity to Jerry Falwell:

> While I was in Germany for the month of March doing missionary work, the news broke on the immorality of the sponsor and emcee of the PTL television club. When I got back, I tried to read as much I could on the news magazines and the papers to find out exactly what happened. It's a tragic mess, and of course, the thing that perhaps shocks you and shocked me the most was that Dr. Jerry Falwell, who is a very dear personal friend and has been a friend of our church down through the years, took over this ministry and became the chairman of its board. . . .
>
> Let me say, first of all, that Dr. Falwell has been a friend to [our] ministry like few other preachers of our acquaintance. We love him; we thank God for him. . . .
>
> However, when I learned that he had taken over the chairmanship of [PTL's] board, I was, frankly, shocked. I could not comprehend what was going on. . . . So, I got one of the letters that he sent out to everybody on his mailing list, asking for money to save the PTL Club.

Several of you had told me that you had seen a televised news conference where he was answering questions from the press. I did not see it, but I take your word for it. You said that on that news conference he said that there would be no change in the format of the PTL Club, which meant that the charismatic influence and program would go right on. Well, that shocked me also. So then when I got this letter pleading for money, I felt like that was just absolutely as far as I could go without making an inquiry. I flew to Lynchburg on Thursday. Dr. Falwell gave me an appointment, and I met with him, and I will give you the essence of our conversation. . . .

I said, "Realize that I am only saying this as your friend, I'm not trying to tell you what to do, and I'm not trying to tell you how to conduct your ministry, but as your friend, I think you've made the biggest mistake you've ever made in your life and your ministry by identifying favorably with the PTL format." I said, "I know that you're not charismatic, and unless you've changed since the last time we've talked, in your doctrine, I know that you certainly have not changed to embrace the charismatic position."

He said, "You're absolutely right. I haven't changed one iota. I've always been against it, and I still am. Let me explain to you what my motive is and where I am going.

"When I received word that this was about to happen, I determined that if at all possible I would try to get the PTL network for *The Old Time Gospel Hour,* and this is the only way that I felt like I could do it."

I said, "Well, I personally don't agree with your methods, and I don't agree with your philosophy. But that's between you and the Lord. But I do feel that it was wrong for you to identify with this movement."

He said, "My whole purpose—I don't care what happens to the country club down at Charlotte and all of the jamboree stuff that goes on there. I'm only interested in the PTL cable network. It's the largest Christian cable network in the nation, and I'd like to get that for *The Old Time Gospel Hour.*"

I said, "Well, I feel that you have placed your friends in an indefensible position, and I'm one of them. I am 100 percent opposed to PTL, and when I got your letter asking for money to save it, my first reaction was, why not go ahead and bury it, and everybody would be a lot better off. I've never felt that God was in it from the beginning. If that offends you, I'm sorry, but that's my honest conviction. I think it's been the biggest charade on television that's ever been telecast, and I've been 100 percent against the charismatic movement. . . . "

Then he said, "I think that you would also like to know that this coming Tuesday I'm having a press conference, and at that time we plan to expose Jim Bakker, not only for immorality with a woman, but homosexual immorality. Not only him, but Dortch, and all of those in a leadership position on PTL. I plan to fire 1,600 workers on Tuesday, and probably it will be in bankruptcy before too long, and the sooner the better. All I want out of it is the cable network for the Lord."

I said, "Well, that's between you and the Lord, but again, I do not agree with your philosophy of getting it. I do not agree with what you had to do to get it. Millions of people across this nation are confused and wonder what in the world is going on, and why would you suddenly identify with a movement that you've always been in opposition to." And he has. For example, on the application blanks for Liberty University, this question is clearly asked: "Do you believe in speaking in tongues, and have you ever spoken in tongues?" And if a person says "yes" they don't get enrolled in Liberty University. That's how strong of a stand he's taken in the past. And that stand, he says, will continue.

He also said that he thinks the sooner the organization goes bankrupt, the better off it will be because the assets will then be auctioned and disposed and the network will then be free for purchase, and they hope to purchase it and go on from there. . . .[8]

Events leading to the demise of PTL proceeded rapidly after Ankerberg's television appearances. On April 28, amidst rumors that he might resign, Jerry Falwell announced at a PTL board meeting that he was staying on "for the duration."

He then turned to Roy Grutman, who accused Reverend Dortch of using PTL funds to pay off Jessica Hahn. He also asserted that Reverend Dortch knew that the Lifetime Partners programs were actually timeshares, which they were not. Mr. Grutman apparently conveniently forgot that he represented Reverend Dortch, PTL, and me. Instead, he suddenly turned coats and became the ministry's antagonist. Ironically, within little more than a month after Reverend Dortch and I first met Norman Roy Grutman, he was paid a half million dollars from PTL funds for his role in decimating the ministry, almost half as much as I had been paid the entire year before to build it! Just then, Bailey Smith moved that Richard Dortch be terminated or allowed to resign as president of PTL. The motion was seconded and Falwell called for a vote.

Rex Humbard stood up and announced, "I will not be a part of what is taking place here." He walked out of the room and off the board.

Sam Moore, Ben Armstrong, and James Watt voted against the motion to fire Reverend Dortch. The Lynchburg group voted to dismiss Dortch or allow him to resign.

Overnight, PTL became something out of a George Orwell novel. Armed Pinkerton guards took control of the PTL headquarters building. The guards permitted no one to leave the building without being searched. Women's purses especially were searched for documents and other PTL materials. Firings of employees were taking place hourly. Weeping could be heard all over the building as faithful employees, many of whom had come to PTL to fulfill what they felt was God's call upon their lives, were summarily terminated. Those who remained employed were required to sign a loyalty oath to Jerry Falwell.

One senior executive said that suddenly a piece of Christian paradise was turned into somthing like a totalitarian government. Each level of middle-management employees was made to fire the level below them. Then the next level fired the managers who had just been responsible for terminating the jobs of the people on the level below them. Whoever perpetrated the plan must have studied the Nazis.

Toward the end of May, Jerry Falwell sent Roe Messner to visit Tammy and me and to deliver a curious message: "Jerry Falwell wants to continue your salary at or about the same level you were receiving when you resigned. He wants you to have a house, a car, a maid, and a secretary."

From the beginning Falwell had said publicly, "PTL would not be here without Jim and Tammy Bakker. It would be less than Christian to terminate and cut off the life supply for the persons responsible for this ministry."[9] Then during the press conference following the termination of Reverend Dortch, Falwell announced that PTL would no longer offer lifetime partnerships to be sold (they were never sold in the first place!), and that Tammy and I would no longer be paid. The Bakkers' "ministry here has ceased," he told 270 members of the press.[10]

Now nearly two months later, Falwell had suddenly taken an interest in paying us. Roe seemed pleased that Falwell had apparently had a change of heart. Roe reported that Jerry Falwell had instructed us to make up a list of what we needed to continue life as we normally would if we were at PTL. "Don't be afraid to make it a little extravagant," Roe told us that Falwell had said. "These are simply negotiating points, and we will establish the final package from here."

Tammy Faye wrote an exaggerated "wishlist" on her stationery of things we thought we might need to maintain life as it had been. It was not a formal request or a presentation of any kind. Roe took the wrinkled piece of Tammy Faye's stationery, just as it was, back to Jerry Falwell.

Imagine our horror and embarrassment when at a news conference on May 27, 1987, Jerry held up the list, written on Tammy Faye's personal stationery, and declared, "I don't see any repentance there. I don't see any concern for the welfare of this ministry in that kind of request. I see the greed. I see the self-centeredness. I see the avarice that brought them down."[11] I could not believe my ears! We had done exactly what Jerry had asked us to do, and most of the things on the list were items he had suggested we should have. Roe Messner and I had been merely business associates and coworkers before that incident, but after Roe saw that news conference we became close friends.

Tammy and I were scheduled to appear live on ABC's *Nightline* that night. How coincidental that Jerry would hold up the "wishlist" that very afternoon.

Tammy's and my appearance on *Nightline* was historic, not for us, but for ABC. The show that night received the highest ratings in its history. As of this writing, the Nielsen record set that night still stands.

The interview with Ted Koppel went well, so well in fact that Tammy and I decided to go back to PTL for a visit to explore return possibilities. We also had to pack up all our things from the Tega Cay house, since we had been ordered to get our possessions out of there. The house was owned by the ministry; we had no choice but to comply. On June 10, 1987, we returned to the Carolinas. When we visited Heritage USA a few days later, we were greeted by a crowd. We weren't sure initially whether the throng was friendly or hostile. As we pulled up right in front of the Heritage Grand, people mobbed our car. Don Hardister bolted from the car, leaving us at the mercy of the clamoring crowd. Don had once told me, "Jim, I would take a bullet for you if I had to." Now that his job was to keep me away from PTL, he did not want to be seen with me. Years later, Don apologized for his actions.

Fortunately, the crowd was, for the most part, excited to see us back. They started clapping their hands, shouting, "Jim and Tammy, we love you! Welcome back!"

Tammy and I got out of the car and greeted the people and basked in the warm reception. We walked into the hotel and down "Main Street" and back out to our car. A few days later we were invited to a reception at "Kevin's House," the home we had built for handicapped children. Hundreds of people formed lines snaking down the driveway. People literally walked through a muddy field to get to where Tammy and I were greeting and hugging everyone. It was a reception I will never forget.

That same week, Jerry Falwell and his board of PTL directors voted to seek bankruptcy protection. Things moved quickly from that point. After months of badgering by insiders of the new PTL regime, a federal grand jury was convened in Charlotte on September 21, 1987, to investigate PTL in general, and me in particular. South Carolina officials had refused to get involved in the case, so the pressure was shifted to a North Carolina jurisdiction because technically some of Heritage USA was located across the border. Somebody had given the government the impression that our Lifetime Partnership program had been illegally operated with the PTL Partners not receiving the benefits they had been promised. Interestingly, the first witness called was Jessica Hahn.

The government spent thousands of dollars over the next sixteen months going through a mountain of materials, including personal letters and private files that had been flung wide open and made available by the Falwell team to the press and to government investigators. Grand-jury members heard testimony from everyone who had anything negative to say about PTL, whether they were credible witnesses or not.

On October 8, 1987, after a judge refused Jerry Falwell's reorganization plan for PTL and allowed the PTL Partners and creditors to present a separate plan, Falwell abruptly resigned. Adapting a line from Jimmy Swaggart, Falwell referred to me as "probably the greatest scab and cancer on the face of Christianity in two thousand years of church history."[12] I felt that PTL had been placed in bankruptcy for one main reason—to keep me from coming back. PTL and Heritage USA were now in the hands and complete control of the government.

Little did I know that I would have such a long time to think about it. On December 5, 1988, I was indicted by a federal grand jury. The judge said that if I was convicted I might be going to prison for as many as 120 years.

CHAPTER

8

The Collapse

NOW, LESS THAN A YEAR LATER, I HAD BEEN TRIED, CONVICTED, and sentenced to forty-five years in prison. The marshals' car carrying me closer to incarceration sped south along Interstate 85 toward Atlanta on our way to Talladega, a small town approximately sixty miles away from Birmingham, Alabama. The trip was almost 350 miles long and would take about six hours. The marshals accompanying me were kind and occasionally spoke to me, but for the most part, I sat silently in the back seat, watching the daylight fade to blackness. Along with thoughts of my past, impressions of what prison life might be like began to pummel their way into my brain. Fearful images of scenes from old Jimmy Cagney prison movies, of prison riots, rapes, and murders filled my mind. I felt stark terror.

Although I had visited prisons as a minister, my only other knowledge of what incarceration might be like related to a horrifying experience I had recently undergone during my trial. The trial began in mid-August 1989. Approximately two weeks into the ordeal, on Wednesday, August 30, Steve Nelson, a former PTL employee, was testifying as a government witness against me. As I sat listening to Steve's testimony, I believed that some of the information he was relaying to the court was inaccurate.

During his cross-examination of Steve, my lawyer rigorously grilled him on the details he was purporting to be true. Steve answered haltingly, and his face turned ashen in color. It soon became obvious that he was in trouble. Steve suddenly keeled over and literally fell off the witness stand!

Pandemonium swept through the courtroom. Judge Potter sprang to his feet and peered down at the body. Marshals quickly converged on the courtroom floor. Nobody knew whether Steve Nelson was dead or alive.

In the midst of the confusion, one of the jurors, a nurse, left the jury box, ran to Steve Nelson, and began attending to him. Her actions violated a cardinal courtroom rule, that a jury member is not to have any contact with a witness, but at that point nobody seemed too concerned about it. She took Nelson's pulse and announced, "This man has fainted!"

Steve Nelson had been a part of my staff for several years, so naturally I was deeply concerned for his well-being despite the fact that he had been testifying against me. As Steve's former boss and former pastor, my first inclination at the sight of him lying on the floor was to pray for him. My lawyers asked Judge Potter for permission for me to pray for my former employee. The judge reluctantly granted the request.

I stepped up to Steve, knelt down near him, and placed my hands on his foot as I prayed and asked God to touch him and heal him. Almost immediately, he revived. Nelson's fortuitous revival prompted some people to later proclaim that I had raised the man from the dead, which, of course, I had not.

Steve Nelson was taken to a local hospital for examination. His collapse was later blamed on a case of the flu and the fact that he had not eaten breakfast that morning.

Back in the courtroom, Judge Potter regained order just long enough to announce a recess until the following day.

A marshal noticed that I too looked as though I was close to collapsing. He offered to help me escape the onslaught of questions from people in the courtroom by exiting through a side door. I nodded my head and whispered, "Yes, I would appreciate that."

Following the marshal's lead, I made my way out of the courtroom through the side door and into a conference room across the hall. The cumulative emotional strain of the case was overwhelming me. The pressure of almost three years of unprecedented publicity and public disgrace, the loss of my life's work, and the deep pain my family and friends were going through were more than I could bear. I slumped into a chair and simply began to weep. I wept and wept and could not stop.

Someone sent for my father, who had been in attendance at the trial that day. Dad came into the room and attempted to console me. I appreciated Dad's kind words, but I still could not contain my emotions.

That afternoon, one of my lawyers called Dr. Basil Jackson, a good friend and highly respected psychiatrist from Milwaukee who had made several appearances on our television shows. Dr. Jackson had been trained as a psychiatrist by a variety of academic institutions, including the Menninger Clinic in Topeka, Kansas. He now directed a psychiatric clinic with a large staff at Milwaukee's St. Francis Hospital.

When Dr. Jackson learned of my condition, he caught the first flight to Charlotte. He came directly to the apartment where I was staying during the trial. As soon as he saw me, he knew I was in bad shape.

Dr. Jackson examined me thoroughly and we talked about the extreme stress I had been experiencing. I told the doctor that I anticipated that I was going to have a difficult time sleeping that night. He gave me a small dose of a popular antianxiety medication known as Xanax, which he said would help me sleep, yet allow me to function normally. He assured me that the dosage of the drug he was giving me was extremely small, less than half of the lowest dose he normally prescribed for most of his patients. The usual dosage of Xanax prescribed by most doctors is one to two milligrams. The tablet I was prescribed was only .125 milligrams, and Dr. Jackson suggested that I begin by taking only half of that amount.

"Try taking this dosage every four hours," my doctor ordered me. Since he was prescribing such a low dosage, Dr. Jackson suggested that if I had trouble sleeping, I could take the medicine more frequently.

What the doctor did not tell me, however, was that Xanax is a tranquilizer. Unfortunately, in my deeply distraught state, I failed to inform the doctor that my body reacts violently to tranquilizers of any kind. While they produce a calming effect in most people, for some reason tranquilizers produce the opposite effect in me. Tranquilizers make me hyper and cause me to feel like I'm out of touch with reality.

Certain that my good friend, Dr. Jackson, would never knowingly give me any medication that would be harmful to me, I followed his instructions. Every few hours the night of August 30, I swallowed another Xanax.

On Thursday, August 31, I got up early and dressed in a new suit. I had gained weight since leaving Heritage USA in 1987, and few of the clothes I had worn prior to the fall of '89 would now fit me. Despite publicized reports to the contrary, my financial resources had already been depleted. Consequently, my sister Donna went out and bought me a new outfit.

I had already taken several Xanax tablets throughout the night, but I gobbled down another before Herb Moore, the elderly friend with whom I was staying, and I set out for Harold Bender's law office, located downtown near the courthouse. Considering Herb's feeble physical condition and my drug-induced lethargy, it is a miracle either of us could drive. To this day, I am not sure who actually sat behind the wheel that morning.

By the time Herb and I arrived at my lawyer's office, I could hardly move, let alone walk. My entire system was on autopilot. We parked our car and walked up the stairs of the beautifully renovated Victorian-style home that served as Harold Bender's office. We walked across the spacious wraparound porch to the front door and on into the reception area. Herb and I turned to the left and walked past several desks where Harold's paralegals were busily at work. The room was buzzing with activity, just as it was every morning of my trial. Like two drunks, Herb and I wove our way through the clatter and entered Harold's private office.

Harold took one look at me and knew immediately that something was wrong. My body had become bloated, I had a dazed look on my face, my speech was slurred, and I was making ridiculous, erratic statements. It was as though my body was shutting down.

In addition to Harold Bender, Dr. Jackson had already arrived at the office. The doctor was extremely concerned, and he quizzed me thoroughly about how I was feeling. Early on, he recognized that I was distraught and anxious. As the time approached for us to head for the courtroom, Dr. Jackson noticed that I was becoming increasingly agitated.

Also in the office that morning was my other lead lawyer, George Davis, a feisty eighty-four-year-old criminal law specialist who had earned his reputation by winning numerous murder trials on the basis of establishing reasonable doubt in the minds of jury members. I had secured George's services through the help of Herb Moore.

Although I had been indicted by a federal grand jury on December 5, 1988, I totally underestimated the seriousness of the charges against me. I knew in my heart that I was not guilty of trying to defraud anyone, and I was confident that any lawyer who had passed the bar exam could convince a jury of my peers. Besides that, I often told my friends, "I would rather trust God than the best lawyers in the world!"

Herb Moore, a former PTL executive and a longtime friend and confidant, was not so passive about my legal representation. Herb kept prodding me, "Jim, you better hire a lawyer."

Finally, I said, "Okay, do you have any idea who is good at this sort of thing?"

"No, I don't," Herb replied, "but I know someone who does." Herb called a good friend of his, well-known prison minister "Chaplain Ray" Hoekstra. "If anyone knows criminal lawyers, Chaplain Ray does," Herb assured me. Chaplain Ray suggested that we contact George Davis, one of the most famous trial lawyers of his time.

I hired George, and George hired Harold Bender, and my legal team was in place. Because of his age and reputation, George pulled no punches with anyone, least of all me. The morning of August 31, George said straightforwardly, "Jim, you are in no condition to go to court today."

"I agree," said Harold quickly.

"I have to go!" I replied desperately. Even though I had lost control of many of my mental faculties, I nonetheless knew that the last thing I wanted to do was to make the judge and jury angry at me. Already during the trial, I had been publicly castigated, mocked, and derided as everything from a pampered emperor to a self-aggrandizing, manipulating madman. I did not care to give people any more ammunition they could use against me.

I could feel that I was losing touch with reality, so while everyone else moved to the outer office, I slipped into Harold's private office to pray. I knelt down at a couch with my knees on the floor and my elbows on the sofa cushions and literally began to cry out to God. At some point—I have no recollection when—my nervous system collapsed. Harold told me later that when he came looking for me, he found me hiding beneath his sofa with my face on the floor and my knees tucked up against my chin. The sofa stood on arched wooden legs, providing an open space of less than twenty inches between the floor and the bottom of the cushion area. Dressed in my new suit, I somehow had managed to crawl into the narrow cavern. I lay there sobbing and babbling unintelligibly.

Harold immediately ran out of the office to get Dr. Jackson. When the doctor entered the room, he took one look and got right down beside me on the floor. Dr. Jackson spoke to me very softly and compassionately. He quickly determined that I was "decompensating," a fancy psychological term for "flaking out." I had no clue as to what was going on. Dr. Jackson saw that I had regressed to the point that I was curled up like a baby in a fetal position and that my nasal secretions were running down my face.

With great anxiety and trepidation, I began to tell Dr. Jackson about the giant bugs that were coming at me. He soon realized that the "bugs" to which I was referring were stimulated by the thick maze of television cameras, microphones, aerials, and antennae through which I had to tread a path each day on my way into the courtroom. He concluded that in some way, I was experiencing the media equipment as fearful menaces. How ironic that the same technology that had helped make my face familiar to millions of people now struck terror into my heart and mind.

Dr. Jackson attempted to reassure me. "Jim, you are not feeling well. You do not need to go to the courthouse today. Your lawyers can take care of it. They can explain to the judge what has happened and I will go with them to vouch for your medical condition. You just need to rest." He then left the room to speak to Harold Bender. The doctor emphatically told

Harold that I was incapable of attending the court proceedings that day. Harold certainly was already convinced of that.

Dr. Jackson wanted to have me hospitalized as soon as possible, but he knew that because I was on trial, to have me admitted he would need a second professional medical opinion. He immediately set about the task of telephoning other psychiatrists to find someone who could corroborate his opinion. Finally, he called Charter Psychiatric Hospital in Charlotte. The resident doctor on duty that day was Dr. Kevin M. Denny—whom I had never met. He agreed to come that morning.

Once Denny arrived, Dr. Jackson went with my lawyers to inform the court concerning my condition. The doctor testified to the court that I was in a severe state of panic, precipitated by the stress under which I was living at that point. Unfortunately, Judge Potter refused to accept my friend's word or his highly regarded professional opinion that I required immediate hospitalization. The judge gave little credence to Dr. Jackson's emphatic appeals that my mental state was so precarious that I should be admitted to a private psychiatric facility that morning.

Instead he ordered me to be sent to Butner Federal Penitentiary for evaluation to see if I was mentally competent to continue standing trial.

Dr. Jackson warned that I might never recover if the judge ordered me to be committed to a prison psychiatric hospital. "I believe that to commit him to a state hospital at this time would produce a definite aggravation in his psychiatric condition," he told Judge Potter.

The judge disregarded Dr. Jackson's testimony and ordered the marshals to go to Harold Bender's office to get me. It was about 10:30 A.M.

Dr. Jackson left the courthouse to return to check on me at Bender's office. On the way to the car, a film crew from CNN stopped Dr. Jackson and questioned him about my condition. The doctor replied, "Mr. Bakker is completely broken because of the tremendous stress to which he has been subjected."[1] Some of the reporters followed the doctor back to my lawyer's office and set up their cameras on the front yard.

When Dr. Jackson got back inside Bender's office, he quickly closed and locked the door. Dr. Denny confirmed Dr. Jackson's diagnosis completely. I had talked with the new doctor freely from my secure place under the sofa, but I have virtually no recall of what I said to him. Eventually, he too left the room, but I remained where I was, lying under the sofa in a fetal position.

Dr. Jackson rightly assumed that he did not have much time to get me ready to leave for the federal prison facility. He finally coaxed me out from beneath the sofa and had me lie down on it instead. He tried to gently break the news to me that the marshals would soon be coming to take me

73

to a facility for evaluation. My mind was so agitated, however, that my friend could not get through to me.

Less than ten minutes after Harold and George had returned, the marshals were pounding on the front door of Harold's law office. The door was still locked and the marshals demanded that it be opened immediately.

"Just wait a minute," Dr. Jackson called through the door. He then came back to the inner office to get me. As he and Harold Bender slowly walked me to the front door, he again tried to explain what was happening.

I kept asking him, "Where am I? What's going on? Where are they taking me?" But Harold's and Dr. Jackson's answers never sank into my brain.

When Harold opened the front door, the marshals burst into the office foyer and quickly placed shackles on my hands and feet. It became obvious that one of the other marshals was upset. Dr. Jackson later found out that the marshal was a kind Christian gentleman who despised placing me in custody in my condition.

The marshals escorted me out the door and onto the porch, with Dr. Jackson slightly behind me, helping to support me. My body was bloated; my hair and clothes were disheveled. One of the marshals placed my new suit coat over my cuffed hands as we slowly made our way toward their car. I was disoriented and weeping uncontrollably. My nose was dripping profusely, but since my hands were shackled, I had no way to wipe it.

As we shuffled down the porch stairs, I cried out, "Please, don't do this to me!" But the marshals continued to drag me to their car.

Adding to my humiliation were the incessant questions being hurled at me by the throng of reporters as well as the much quieter but far more debilitating sounds for me of clicking cameras and rolling videotape. One of the most humiliating moments of my life was splattered across television screens and newspapers around the world.

Both Dr. Jackson and Dr. Denny later said that I was the first and only patient ever seized from their hands in the midst of treatment. Moreover, Dr. Denny later commented in the press that what was done to me sent mental health care back to the Dark Ages.[2]

In no way do I blame the marshals for what happened to me. To a man, they were always kind, polite, and professional in carrying out their orders. In the years since that day, many people have told me they thought the marshals were being cruel when they pushed my head down to get me into the car. Actually, they were being kind. If I had tried to get into the police car while handcuffed and shackled, I would have smashed my head against the door frame of the car as I fell into the back seat.

Even with the marshals' help, I still fell over when they placed me in the car that day. I didn't care. It was almost a relief simply to be away from the prying eyes of the cameras. I had landed on my side; my hands were raised up toward my head as far as the chains would allow, and my knees were drawn up toward my chest.

The marshals drove me to the courthouse. I was taken to a holding cell, where I waited in silence for the next two and a half hours while a decision was being made about where I would be taken. Finally the federal marshals came and led me out a rear door and down the steps of the loading dock. Again they helped me into the back seat of the car. I sat upright for a few moments, and then slumped across the seat as the car drove off. I stayed in that same fetal position for the next three hours as I was driven to a place I thought I heard the marshals refer to as *Butler*. In my foggy state of mind, the name reminded me of the animal hospital where, in better days, my family and I had often taken our pets.

Surely they are not taking me to an animal hospital! I thought. I had no idea where I was going. I lost track of time. After what seemed like several hours had passed, my kidneys felt as though they were going to explode. I was in real pain, needing to use the rest room, but I refused to ask the marshals to stop. I was in a nightmare, like a caged animal being transported to a zoo.

At last, the car stopped. I tried to raise my head to look around.

Oh, God; where am I?

9

The Asylum

IT WAS LATE AFTERNOON, ALMOST 4:00 P.M., BY THE TIME we arrived in Butner, North Carolina, a small town northeast of the city of Durham. I had not moved or spoken during the three-hour trip. I could see an ominous, massive complex of buildings looming in front of me. At first I thought it might be a hospital, but I soon learned that Butner was no hospital—it was a federal psychiatric penitentiary. Butner Correctional Institute is a medium-security prison, completely surrounded by chain-link fence with razor barbed wire scrolled across the top.

The marshals opened the car door. My nose was still running, but I could do nothing about it. Wet mucus smeared on my face as the marshals carefully pulled me from the vehicle. Everything seemed shrouded in darkness. The lights had all been turned down. My world was literally getting darker and darker.

Six years later, Dr. Basil Jackson would explain to me that I had, in fact, suffered a nervous breakdown that morning. The darkness was my brain's way of "dissociating," a process in which the brain begins to blot out aspects of one's consciousness that are too difficult for that person to handle, shutting down as a means of emotional and physical self-preservation. When a person's body can take no more, the brain says, "Switch off." Dr. Jackson had often seen the same sort of reaction when he served as director of a U.S. Veterans Administration Psychiatric Hospital during the Vietnam War. Some Vietnam veterans' dissociation shattered them so completely, they literally went insane. For many others, their minds are unable to fully return to reality. When they try to recall the acutely stressful conditions they went through, their minds fade to blackness. That was what I was experiencing.

Members of the media had beaten us to Butner and were already entrenched on both sides of a sidewalk leading from the parking lot to the building, camera flashes blazing, videotape rolling, and microphones stretched toward me. To my eyes squinting through the glare, the parallel rows of reporters reminded me of a royal honor guard pointing their swords high above their heads, the microphone boom extensions forming a peak above the center of the sidewalk. But this was no honor guard—to me they were the *dishonor* guard, ready to record every detail of my dehumanizing circumstances. My blurred mind marveled, *The photographers aim and shoot, but I do not die.* I wished I could have.

Unaccustomed to moving in manacles, I had difficulty walking. Furthermore, my legs had remained motionless for several hours and now they did not want to function. Consequently, the two marshals held me, one on each arm, and helped me walk, virtually having to drag me each step of the way. My beautiful new suit, my sister's sacrificial gift to me, now looked wrinkled and sloppy, as though I had rolled it into a ball, tossed it into a clothes hamper, and then put it on again the next day. I still wore the white shirt and tie that I wore when I left the apartment that morning. My hair looked as though I had been sleeping in the streets for months. And the interminable snot hung from my nose. I felt that I was no longer a human being.

It was as if I were being pulled into a long, dark tunnel. Each step doused a little more light from my eyes. Every inch of the way, the tunnel's sides constricted, getting tighter and tighter . . . and suddenly everything went black. The protective pain shield had closed over my brain.

The next thing I remember is being in a dismal-looking room about the size of a large elevator. I was seated on a backless bench in the middle of the room. The cubicle seemed to be filled with people, most of whom appeared to be doing nothing other than watching me.

One man was sitting on the bench to my left and was rifling through my wallet. He took out my money and counted it. He took out my credit cards and pictures, examining each one carefully. I saw him flip past the picture in my wallet of baby James. Something stirred within me.

"Please!" I cried, reaching toward the man. My hands had been unshackled, a sign, I later came to understand, that I was now deep within the bowels of prison with no chance of escape. "Please, let me keep a picture of my grandson, baby James," I pleaded.

The man stared at me hard, then down at the picture of James, then back at me. "I'll see about it," he replied with cool detachment.

The officers ordered me to take off all my clothes, including my underwear. Slowly I began to strip. I fumbled with my expensive tie that I had so carefully knotted that morning, which now seemed like a lifetime ago. Eventually I got the tie off and laid it neatly on the bench behind me. I began unbuttoning my shirt.

"Hurry it up!" someone growled.

Nervous beyond description, I could barely force my fingers to push the buttons through the buttonholes. At last the shirt fell open and I struggled to pull it off my back.

I laid my shirt next to the tie, removed my shoes, then began pulling at the belt on my trousers. My captors never took their eyes off me. I have always been a shy person off camera or away from the pulpit, so the idea of pulling my pants down in the middle of a room full of strangers made me extremely uncomfortable. I hesitated. . . .

"Come on, let's go, Bakker," a coarse voice commanded.

I stepped out of my pants, took off my socks, and hesitated once again. I glanced around the room at my captors. There was no point in prolonging this exercise. I removed my underwear and placed it in the pile on the bench. For a long moment, I simply stood there. I was stark naked in a room filled with people, and everybody was looking at me.

My God! What is happening to me? I could not understand how my dear friend, Dr. Jackson, and my lawyers, Harold and George, could possibly have allowed these people to do these things to me! I felt betrayed by my friends. I was not a convicted criminal! This was happening in the middle of my trial—the trial in which I had been confident some portion of my integrity would be restored. Whatever happened to the concept of "innocent until proven guilty"?

Was I not an American citizen? Did I not have rights guaranteed by the Constitution? Or, was I now in some Communist country? I had grown up hearing horror stories from behind the Iron Curtain, tales of how the Communist secret police had stormed in on an unsuspecting citizen and hauled him or her off to prison with not so much as a chance to say good-bye, let alone a bona fide trial. No United States citizen should have to be subjected to such treatment as I was being given, I thought. My mind, sluggish as it was, flashed such thoughts on and off, much like a slow-blinking strobe light.

It got worse.

An officer handed me an orange prison jumpsuit and a pair of under-pants. "Put them on," he ordered.

The guards led me out of the small room into another slightly larger room. It appeared to be some sort of clinic.

"Take off your clothes," commanded a man wearing a white medical smock.

It seemed useless to remind the man that I had just put on the prison clothes. Whatever they wanted me to do, I'd do it. I slowly peeled off the jumpsuit and underwear and stood before them, nude once again.

Two or more individuals inspected every cavity of my body—they felt or looked inside my mouth, ears, navel, rectum, under my arms, between my legs, everywhere. Perhaps they were doctors; I had no idea what they were looking for, but whatever it was, the men were not subtle about trying to find it. Finally, they were finished. "Put it back on," a prison official said as he nodded in the direction of the jumpsuit.

After I had put my jumpsuit back on, another faceless guard—in my condition they all looked faceless—escorted me out into the prison compound. The heat of the late summer evening hit me as I came out into the open air. The guard started leading me across the empty prison yard when suddenly from someplace high and to the right of me, I heard a voice shouting my name.

"Jim! Jim! Don't let them break you!"

I turned and looked up, but all I could see were large buildings with narrow horizontal slits for windows.

There it was again! "Jim, don't let them break you!"

I heard it more distinctly this time, but was not coherent enough to get a fix on which window hid my secret encourager. *What does he mean?* Whatever it was, my benefactor was too late. I was already broken.

The guard steered me across the prison yard and into a room in another building. I was told to take off my clothes for the third time in less than an hour. One of the officers took out a Polaroid-type camera. They were going to photograph me in the nude, but a man who must have been a senior official called out, "Let him leave his underpants on!"

The officers took several pictures of me standing in my underwear. No explanation was offered why the photos were necessary. When the photo session was completed, the guards ordered me to get dressed again. They led me into another room and gave the pictures to two ladies, a white woman and a black woman, who were seated at a large, heavy, wooden table outside of an office. I later learned that the white woman was Dr. Sally Johnson, the chief of psychiatric services at that prison. The women were cordial and asked me to sit down while they filled out some forms.

Following my interrogation by the two women, the guards began leading me toward my cell. I say "began" because paranoia had so completely taken over in my body, I was too fearful to take normal-sized steps. I had to take baby steps as if walking on eggshells, slowly, tentatively, with my eyes glued to the ground. The guards had to drag me along, step by step. In my mind, I felt as though I were picking my way along a rugged, steep cliff. I didn't dare get too close to the precipice because I knew if I fell over the edge, I would tumble into a huge gorge, hundreds of times the depth of the Grand Canyon. I was tiptoeing along the very edge of the earth, and I was scared to death.

For the next six years I would live with the fear that became instilled in my mind during that initial trip down the Butner prison corridor. I awakened every single morning terrorized by the image of the guards coming to pull me out of my bed, fearing that I would crack my head on the cement, my skull would split open, and my blood would gush out.

I was completely unprepared for what happened next. I had never been in prison before except as a visitor, but as the guards led me into the cell block, even though my mind was terror-stricken and numb, I immediately recognized that I was in no ordinary jail. This was a high-security facility! Everywhere I looked, I saw wild eyes peering through the slots in the solid steel doors where the prisoners' food is passed into the cells. The slots were only about four inches high and eighteen inches wide—just large enough to get a tray and small cup through—and were positioned in the doors about thirty inches up from the floor. For a person to see out those slots, he would have to sit or kneel next to the door and place his head up against the open slot. Only the eyes could be seen to passersby.

As I proceeded into the cell block, the guards nudged me to make a right turn down a corridor. Just as we were about to make the turn, I was able to see, because of the way my head was cocked, straight into a food slot on a corner cell. As I passed by, I caught a glimpse of the man's eyes, not merely empty, hopeless eyes; these were the eyes of a man possessed, the most demonic, crazed eyes I had ever seen. I was already stepping precariously close to the edge of insanity, but seeing the eyes of that man and the others I passed nearly sealed my doom.

The place was a madhouse. Some prisoners were screaming incessantly at the tops of their lungs. Others were talking gibberish. Many were groaning or whining. If a person was not mentally ill upon entering this cell block at Butner Federal Prison, the sheer cacophony of the place was enough to drive him insane.

When the guards pulled me past the next-to-last cell on the right, I heard a man singing—if that is what you could call it. He sounded like an old 45 rpm phonograph recording on which the needle had gotten stuck and was continually skipping back to the same notes. He sang three notes over and over: la . . . la . . . la; LA . . . LA . . . LA; *LA . . . LA . . . LA!*

As I reached the end of the corridor, the guard indicated that I was to enter the last cell on the right. Just as I turned into the cell, I paused long enough to look back up the row. The awful sights, sounds, and smells struck my senses full force. I suddenly realized that I was not simply in prison—I was in an insane asylum!

Looking into my tiny cell from the doorway, I could see that on the right-hand side of the back wall was a hard slab with a one-inch-thick plastic pad on which to sleep. No pillow was allowed. I later learned that pillows were not permitted in this solitary confinement cell due to the potential suicide risk to prisoners who might use the pillow to smother themselves. Above the middle of the slab, a narrow, vertical window about as wide as a book provided my view—a bird's-eye view of another cement block wall of an adjacent building. Only inches from the front of the bed, along the right wall, sat a commode and a sink. Toward the back left corner was an exposed shower, with no curtain. The door, with its slot, was on the left side of the front wall of my cell. To the right of the door was an observation window, approximately three square feet in size. I stepped across the threshold of my cell, and the guard slammed the door behind me. I will never forget the terrible thud that door made as it closed. The sound sealed my tomb, sucking away the last remnant of what little freedom I felt.

Right outside my cell was a guard's station, a desk that was occupied at all times by a guard, who could view me through the observation window in my cell. I was to be watched twenty-four hours a day. The guards had plenty of help, though. At night, every time I glanced at the narrow window above my bed, I saw the reflection of another set of eyes peering in at me through the observation window. Every employee of that prison must have come to look at me that night. Everyone wanted to see Jim Bakker.

The curious onlookers kept coming all night long, and every new set of eyes I saw reflected in my window magnified the fear that continued to build in my mind.

I slept very little that night. I tried, but the sleep simply would not come. Then in what seemed like the middle of the night—I could not yet see any daylight through the window in the wall above my bed—prison medics came and injected me with needle after needle. Apparently they were drawing vials of blood, but in my darkness, I had no way to be sure. My blurry mind wondered if they were drawing blood out of me or putting something into me.

Why did the government want me so badly? I asked myself throughout the night. *And if they did want me, surely there must be a better way, an easier way.*

It was during those early hours in Butner that I learned to fear the sound of rattling keys. Most prison workers wear large rings of keys on their belts. The keys jingle when the guards walk. I quickly learned that the sound of the keys coming in my direction meant they were coming to stick me with more needles. Like Pavlov's dogs, I responded reflexively to the sound. My stomach began churning every time I heard the keys.

At some point during that first night, my picture of baby James was returned to me. The guard must have thought he had given me a million dollars; in fact, he had given me much more. He had given me a reason to survive. I curled up on my bunk, faced the wall, and held that picture close to my face.

I tried to block out the surreal world around me, but it was impossible. The inmate in the next cell continued singing his three-note song over and over. Periodically the guards pushed food through the door slot to me. They never opened the door to bring in a tray of food. It was always pushed through the slot.

It didn't matter to me. Any appetite I might have had was obliterated by the obscene conditions in which I was expected to eat. For meals, I had to sit on the edge of the slab and place my food tray on the bed, right next to the commode. Consequently, if I attempted to eat, I had to do so while gazing directly into the toilet.

My cell neighbor's toilet plumbing was connected to mine. The poor man not only sang incessantly, but he was desperately sick. He could keep nothing inside him for long; anything he ate landed in the commode either as vomit or diarrhea.

Besides the awful sounds emanating from the cell next to mine, it did not take me long to discover that the plumbing system at Butner was not functioning properly. When my sick neighbor flushed his commode, it came up in my toilet. Often, he would flush while I was sitting on my slab, staring into the commode, with a tray of food on my lap, as I was trying to eat. Overeating at Butner was not a problem for me.

I wanted to make a phone call to let my family and lawyers know what the doctors were doing to me. Every time the guard started to bring a phone to me, the doctors would show up, saying it was time for more testing. I felt isolated and rejected, as though no one knew what was happening to me, or nobody cared. The constant, horrendous din of the place was driving me over the edge. Again and again, I wondered, *Is this a nightmare or have I gone completely mad?*

I finally got to the place where I could take no more. I decided to allow myself to go insane. I dropped to the floor in the corner of the cell, close to the door. It was the one spot in the room where no eyes could see me. Just as I was letting go of my will to go on, a voice called out my name.

"Jim . . . God loves you!"

I stopped short, like a deer caught in an automobile's headlights. I thought, *Now I am hearing things.* Then I heard the voice again.

"Jim . . . God loves you!"

"But I think I'm going crazy," I responded aloud.

The voice answered, "No! No, you are not. God loves you!"

Had God sent an angel? I looked up and saw two eyes filled with compassion looking at me through the slot in the door. The voice belonged to the guard who was on duty. He spoke again, and he offered to pray with me. I wasn't sure I could pray; I was confused and close to being convinced that the God I thought I knew had abandoned me, but I accepted the guard's offer. He began to pray, he on one side of the steel door, and me huddled on the floor on the other side. The guard prayed quietly but fervently, with incredible faith in his voice. When he finished praying, I knew there was a God in prison, even if I could not sense His presence in my own life just then.

After he prayed, the guard talked quietly with me for a few more minutes. He told me that he was a lay pastor in his church. Nevertheless, he asked me not to tell anyone about our time of prayer; if anyone found out he had prayed with me, he could be fired.

I shall never forget that servant of God who risked his livelihood to save my life, for whether he knew it or not, that is exactly what he did. Years later, Dr. Basil Jackson confirmed to me that I was indeed at the point of willing myself into either insanity or death. It was over for me. All hope was gone. But a courageous prison guard allowed himself to be a vehicle through whom the Lord could reach out to me with His message of love and hope. Like the Good Samaritan in the Bible, he decided to cross the line to reach a dying man. It would have been much easier, and far less risky, for the guard to have looked the other way. But if he had, I might not have lived to tell you this story. I will be eternally grateful to my nameless "angel." I hope God lets me meet him here on earth someday. If not, I know I will meet him one day in heaven.

Days blended into nights at Butner, so it is difficult to know on what days certain events took place. My days were consumed by batteries of psychological tests, including the Minnesota Multiphasic Personality Inventory, the Wechsler intelligence test, and a Rorschach test. Interestingly, many of the questions I was asked had religious connotations. The questions subtly implied that anyone who talked with God, believed that Jesus would return, had spiritual dreams or visions, or had experienced any sort of ecstatic religious phenomena must be considered suspect. Of course, I qualified.

My head was still in a fog, but I was becoming increasingly aware of my environment. I could hardly believe the way I was being treated at that facility. I could get no personal messages out, so I decided to draw a picture of what my cell looked like. I hoped to give it to Tammy Faye when she came to visit me. But I had nothing with which to write. I sat down on the floor and spoke into the slot in the door and asked if I could have paper and a pencil.

A short time later, through the slot in the door, several sheets of paper and a pencil were slipped into my cell. To prevent it from being a potential weapon, the pencil was ground down to a meager two inches long, but I was glad to get it, nonetheless. My grade-school art course on perspective came in handy as I set about drawing my cell.

Tammy Faye first heard about my collapse from the news media. During the early part of my trial, Tammy had stayed behind in Orlando, Florida. On Thursday afternoon, a gaggle of reporters was encamped around our home. When Tammy learned the news, her first concern was for thirteen-year-old Jamie Charles, who was expected home from school shortly. Tammy did not want Jamie subjected to another media blitz. She decided to make a deal with the press.

She went outside our house and was immediately inundated with shouts from reporters. Tammy boldly told members of the media that she would agree to talk with them, if, and only if, the reporters would leave before Jamie got home. The members of the media agreed to abide by Tammy Faye's conditions—which they did, for the most part.

Tammy Faye gave a brief but emotionally charged statement about what had happened to me, outlining the details as best she could considering she was relying completely on secondhand information. She then answered the reporters' questions. She concluded her statement by saying, "If you came to see me cry, you got your wish."

Tammy Sue was living in Fort Mill, South Carolina, near Heritage USA, when she heard about my collapse. She watched the newscasts of me in chains and cuffs. It was devastating to my daughter.

Tammy Sue called her mother, who confirmed the details as much as she knew them. Tammy Faye said that she was going to leave for Butner in the morning. "What you need to do is bring baby James, and you and

Doug and I will go see Daddy tomorrow." Tammy Sue agreed and they continued talking briefly about meeting in Butner on Friday.

On Friday evening, the officers said that I should get ready for a visit. My wife was coming to see me! She had been driving all day to North Carolina from Orlando. My sister Donna and our good friend Fran Moore accompanied her. Tammy Sue arrived earlier and waited at a nearby motel along with Shirley Fulbright.

The women were extremely tired after traveling all day. Tammy Faye had not been informed about standard protocol concerning visitation procedures. No information had been given to her concerning my condition. When the women finally arrived at the prison, Tammy was shocked to learn that the facility was not a hospital, but a prison.

Inside the facility, I attempted to make myself presentable for my wife. I asked the guard for a razor with which to shave, and then I stepped into the shower in my cell. While I was showering in ice-cold water, Tammy Faye was getting an even colder reception at the entrance to the prison. Thinking that she could simply identify herself to the supervisor and she would be swept in to see me, she was surprised to discover that she, too, in some ways, was at the mercy of the prison officials.

The prison officials asked Tammy Faye for two pieces of identification, one of which needed to be a photo ID. Such irony! On that day in history, Tammy Faye's face was one of the most familiar in the world, yet the prison officials demanded formal identification. Another of the requirements for entering the prison was that every visitor must register, which included listing each person's Social Security number. Tammy Faye was at a loss. She could not remember her Social Security number!

The prison officials refused to allow Tammy to enter the prison without registering. She was becoming more unnerved by the minute. Through a series of phone calls, Tammy was able to track down her number and after completing numerous forms she was ready to come see me.

Back in my cell, I was still having an extremely difficult time walking. I felt the same sort of fear that I had experienced on Thursday evening when the guards first accompanied me to my cell. Again, I was like a man walking on the edge of a high cliff, totally possessed with fear. Slowly picking my way up the same corridor I had entered, I tentatively made my way to my waiting loved ones. As I shuffled along, the guards informed me of the rules governing my visit. For instance, I was allowed to hug my wife when I greeted her, and we were allowed one kiss. After that, no touching was permitted until the visitors were ready to leave, when we could repeat the routine. No gifts or food were allowed.

The guards pointed the way into a narrow, makeshift visiting room. A guard sat inside the entrance.

When I walked into the room, I hugged and kissed my wife, and sister. I was overjoyed to see my family. To them I looked frightened.

We sat down in institutional-type chairs facing the guard. Tammy attempted to comfort me. She assured me that God would use even this for good.

I had no sooner sat down when I started pouring out my story to Tammy and Donna. I was agitated and nervous as I told the women about the conditions in which I had been living. I spoke softly, not daring to let the guard hear me talking about the prison, yet emphatically telling my wife and sister all the gruesome details my semiblurred mind allowed my lips to blurt. Concerned that I was so upset, Donna attempted to rub my neck. I jumped back in stark terror.

"Prison rules say 'no touching whatsoever in the visiting room'!" I shrieked. Donna recoiled as though she had been snakebitten. After a while, Donna left the room to allow Tammy Faye and me a few minutes of privacy. I talked and talked, faster and faster, knowing that our visit could end at any moment or at the whim of the guards. But the more I talked, the more upset Tammy Faye became.

All too soon, the guard indicated to me that it was time for our visit to end. That was hard enough. Worse yet, it was time to go back to my cage.

I had hoped that Tammy Faye might be able to tell somebody about my awful conditions at Butner. She didn't let me down. From the moment Tammy Faye and the other two women had pulled into the prison parking lot several hours earlier, members of the press were after them every minute. Tammy tried to avoid answering their questions as best she could. After visiting with me, however, Tammy wanted to talk to the media. I'm sure I had not yet reached my cell before an emotional Tammy was outside the prison talking with reporters who were awaiting her exit.

She told reporters, "I'm really upset tonight. As I walked in, I didn't realize that I would be coming to a prison." Tammy went on to describe the way I had been treated. She was especially irate that I had been strip-searched. Little did she know that even as she spoke, the guards were strip-searching me again, which was standard procedure after a visit.

I slept very little that night. I simply lay on the hard slab with my face to the wall. At every sound of jangling keys, my heart jumped.

The next morning, I took more tests. Then a guard informed me that my mother, my father, Tammy Faye, Donna, Tammy Sue, and my brother Norm were all coming to see me. I was glad to see them.

After I had been in Butner for several days, one of the staff members gave me an encouraging word. "Tomorrow," the counselor said, "if all goes well, you may be able to go outside for some exercise."

I was so excited! Outside! I could hardly wait. To me, being allowed to go outside was a ray of hope that perhaps I would be released soon.

True to the counselor's word, the next day, I was allowed to go outside for some exercise. A guard came to my cell door and, speaking through the slot, he ordered me to turn around with my back to the door, then stick my hands through the slot. As soon as I did so, he slapped a pair of heavy steel handcuffs on my wrists. "Now, pull your hands back through the slot," he instructed me.

When I had my cuffed hands back inside the cell, the guard opened the door and allowed me to come out. "Come on, you get to go outside today," he told me. He led me through the corridors and out a side door.

Fresh air! A small sense of freedom began to grow inside me.

"You will be over here," the guard informed me. With my hands behind my back he led me to a chain-link cage a few feet away from the building. The cage was about the size of a small office; it was not much larger than my cell inside. The guard instructed me to step inside the cage, after which he closed and locked the cage behind me. The officer told me to stand with my back to the slot in the cage door and stick my hands out through it. I did as I was told, once again. He removed the handcuffs. The guard stayed there and watched me.

I couldn't believe it! Some exercise. I went over and stood in a corner of the cage. When added to all the demeaning treatment I had received, this insult was totally dehumanizing. I had not even been convicted of a crime, yet I was being treated as an animal.

After about five minutes of standing in the corner, I told the guard that I had finished "exercising." He recuffed me and took me back to my cell inside. Although I later learned that the cage is standard procedure for prisoners who are in solitary confinement, the false hope of increased freedom only served to plunge me deeper into depression.

My being taken to Butner Correctional Institute raised serious concerns about whether I would be able to return to stand trial. Many trial observers predicted that Judge Potter might declare a mistrial because of the events leading up to my incarceration at Butner. It is highly unlikely that the judge ever considered that possibility. On the other hand, he seemed quite interested in getting me back into court as soon as possible.

When I was first admitted to Butner, Dr. Sally Johnson, chief of psychiatric services at the facility, told reporters that normally evaluations such as mine take at least thirty to forty-five days and longer. Instead of four to six weeks, I was ordered to return to court after six days at Butner. Believe me, I was not complaining!

It is interesting to note, however, that when the assistant to the warden was asked whether he was pressured to expedite my evaluations, he would only say, "A judge has to request . . . an accelerated study."[1]

Dr. Johnson's team determined that I had indeed suffered from a stress-induced panic attack. (I could have told them that much!) "He is not going crazy," she said. "Our evaluation did not find Mr. Bakker was suffering a severe mental disease or defect. He does not have a psychotic disorder. He is in the midst of a serious trial and a life-changing circumstance. That is the source of the stress that got him to our doorstep."[2] Johnson's report got me out of Butner, but it sent me right back to court.

The guards awakened me early on Wednesday morning, September 7; it was moving day. At 6:15 A.M. the marshals from Charlotte, acting under Judge Potter's direct orders, arrived at Butner Correctional Institute to take me back to court for a competency hearing later that same morning. I left Butner wearing a pair of gray prison work pants and a bright, open-necked prison shirt. Two and a half hours later, I arrived at the federal courthouse much the way I had left six days previously—rumpled and unkempt, manacled and handcuffed, and lying prone in the back seat of a marshal's car. The marshals wasted no time; they whisked me into the courthouse, past the usual throng of reporters.

In front of the courthouse, local deejays Billy James and John Boy Isley of WRFX-FM did their radio show on location from a couch. They offered a special feature: Anyone who wanted an album by Tammy Faye Bakker could have one for free. All a person had to do to get a free album was drop by the boys' show and stick his or her head under the couch.

Street vendors were hawking food, drinks, pictures, pins, bumper stickers, T-shirts, and all sorts of paraphernalia. One man was doing brisk business selling cassette tapes of songs making fun of Heritage USA, our PTL television program, and of course, Tammy Faye and me. It was a circus, and I was their clown.

The marshals escorted me to a holding cell, took off my shackles, and told me I needed to get ready to go back into the courtroom as soon as Judge Potter called for me. Tammy Faye arrived at the courthouse about twenty minutes after I did. She brought a clean gray suit, a white shirt, black shoes and socks, a blue tie, and a shaving kit. By the time the competency hearing began later that morning, I was beginning to look like a human being again, but it would be years before I felt whole again.

Judge Potter must have anticipated the outcome of my competency hearing before it began. He had already instructed the jury to return at 2:00 P.M. The hearing itself lasted two and a half hours. For most of it, I sat slumped in my seat. I never heard most of the speakers.

I did hear Judge Potter, however, when he asked me if I thought I could understand the charges against me and assist in my own defense.

I answered slowly, "I am very tired, but I believe I can, sir." As for understanding the charges, I never quite understood the charges in the first place. How could nearly a week in Butner's snake pit change that? Five weeks later, when Judge Potter sentenced me to forty-five years in prison, I still did not understand how I could possibly be on trial.

The trial was now over, and I was a convicted criminal in the back seat of a marshal's car on my way to Talladega Federal Prison to begin serving a forty-five-year sentence. The horrors of Butner, fresh in my mind, colored every thought as I contemplated what new terrors I might encounter at Talladega. I was about to enter the shadowy, unknown world of prison where, without the grace of God, I would most likely die.

CHAPTER

10

Talladega

AS THE CAR I WAS IN MOVED CLOSER AND CLOSER TO Talladega, I was moving deeper and deeper into my personal twilight zone. Approximately sixty miles away from Birmingham, the marshal driving the car turned off Interstate 20 and pointed the vehicle southwest down State Road 21, a desolate two-lane stretch of road. Darkness had fallen, but at least there had been lights along the roadside. Now, however, the headlights of a passing car only occasionally pierced the darkness. I sat upright on the back seat, staring out into blackness.

I kept thinking, *How can this be? I am in chains on my way to spending the rest of my life in prison. This can't really be happening!*

But it was.

The marshals in the front seat were talking on their police radio with officers at Talladega Federal Prison, making preparations for my arrival.

In the distance, I could see a glow of light. I wondered if the lights emanated from my new abode. As we drew closer to the glow, I saw an old, country-style general store with gas pumps out in front of it. A few other buildings hugged the intersection, and that was the extent of the town. The entire area seemed to be bathed in an ethereal, amber light. The few people I saw seemed eerily untouchable, as though if I reached out to them, they would disappear, or if I called out to them, they would not have answered. The scene reminded me of a movie I had seen many years ago in which aliens had landed on earth and taken over a small town.

I was still dressed in the same clothes I was wearing when I had left the federal courthouse in Charlotte—my casual shirt, jeans, tennis shoes, and my bright blue jacket. The marshals had offered to stop at a McDonald's along the way so that I could get something to eat. I declined. My stomach was churning too much to put anything into it. The marshals spoke kindly to me, but when I tried to talk, the words would not come out.

I remembered several years earlier when actor Burt Reynolds had invited Tammy Faye and me to attend a rehearsal of a play Burt was producing. The play was written by Bill C. Davis and starred Charles Durning. The full cast was in rehearsal at Burt's estate in Florida. The plot was a religious topic, so Burt was interested in our opinion.

The play included a powerful scene of a young priest presenting one of his first sermons. The young man told of a day when he had awakened to find all his tropical fish floating on the top of the water in their tank. Apparently, the thermostat had malfunctioned and the water had gotten hotter and hotter, killing every fish in the aquarium.

The young priest wondered if his fish had begun to scream—a scream nobody could hear—as the tank got hotter and hotter. The priest paused and said, "I wish I had ears that could hear fish scream, I wanted to save them so much." Then he drove home his point, that many people are screaming a silent scream, and no one hears them.

I felt like one of those fish. Every cell in my body was in pain, my entire being was screaming for help, but no one could hear me.

As we pulled into the Talladega prison, my brain began to close down just as it had when I had entered Butner prison.

At the front of the prison, the marshals helped me out of the car, and we began shuffling toward a two-story, cement-block building about a half a city block away. There the marshals turned me over to the prison authorities, and I was escorted into a narrow cell with benches all around the walls. More benches lined the middle of the room. A television hung near the ceiling at the far corner of the room. Twenty-five to thirty men were crammed into the cell, and most of them were talking loudly, all at the same time. The cell grew quiet as I entered. After a few seconds, the noise level increased again, and I was sure the men were talking about me.

For years I had heard of the crowded living conditions in prisons, and since this was the first time I was being checked in as a convicted felon, I could only assume that this room so chock full of flesh was to be my "home" for the rest of my life. I was horrified!

I sat down on a bench against the wall. Trying to be inconspicuous— as if I would not stand out!—I kept my gaze on the floor. I was scared to death. Once I dared a furtive glance at a couple of tough-looking men and immediately the thought hit me, *Bakker, you are a dead man.* Horror stories I had heard about prison flooded my mind.

A guard entered and gave me a health form to fill out, which asked if I had ever had any communicable diseases. I became aware that the room was buzzing with whispers of my name. Finally someone asked me, "Hey, are you Jim Bakker?" I hesitated for a moment. I was not happy to be Jim Bakker just then. Of course, it never crossed my mind to deny my identity, and it would have been futile anyhow. My picture had been all over the television newscasts throughout the day, and most prisoners watch a lot of TV. Probably everyone in the room knew who I was the moment they saw me. Besides that, when there is a highly publicized trial, speculation runs rampant among the prison population that the convicted person will land in their particular prison. Most of the inmates at Talladega probably knew I was coming there before I did.

I acknowledged, "Yes, I'm Jim Bakker."

"Alriiiiighhht," I heard someone say.

A number of the men tried to talk to me, but I was not very talkative. I certainly did not want to offend anyone during my first encounter as an inmate, but I answered so briefly and quietly the men soon left me alone and moved on to other subjects in their conversations.

We waited for what seemed like over an hour before a guard came in and barked out our processing orders. "Step this way," he said, pointing to the door exiting the room, "and line up in a straight line outside in the cell block. Let's move it."

The men began moving toward the door. Several guards awaited us outside the room and helped herd us along into a single file. I stepped out into the cavernous cell block and caught a good look at it for the first time. It was a huge, open space, two stories high, with cells on upper and lower levels. A single, open, steel staircase connected the two stories in the middle of the cell block. Each cell was a self-contained, walled-in room made from cement blocks, with cement floors and a heavy metal door. The entire cell block was painted stark white. Each cell door had a small window, approximately twelve inches square, with wire mesh inside double-paned glass. All sounds in the room seemed to have a half-life longer than that of nuclear waste. As the sounds reverberated from one cement wall off another, it was as if no sound ever truly died.

At one end of the cell block was a recreation area housing a number of Ping-Pong tables and small card tables. At the opposite end of the cell block was a shower and toilet area, behind opaque glass.

"No talking, and keep the line tight!" I heard a guard bellow like a Marine drill sergeant. He pointed to a row of metal folding chairs lined up outside the processing room. "Move as far down the line as you can and sit down on a chair. Keep the line tight, no empty chairs. Let's go, keep it moving, all the way down."

When the line of chairs was completely filled, one of the guards began going man to man, passing out small brown bags to each new inmate.

"Thank you," I said as he handed me a bag.

The guard did not reply. He simply looked at me as though I had just dropped into the prison from another planet.

I opened my brown bag and found a cheese sandwich and an apple in it. Although I had not eaten since early that morning, I did not feel hungry. My stomach was swirling and I simply had no appetite for food.

The other guard kept yelling, "Tighten up that line!"

As I looked up the row of men jammed against each other, I felt as if we were a line of cattle on our way to a slaughterhouse. Although it was late at night, and the prisoners who lived at Talladega were all locked down until morning, I noticed that many of the inmates were peering out their small windows at the line of men with which I was sitting.

"Fresh meat," someone said.

The men nearest the processing room were ordered to remove their street clothes and hand them to the guard inside the door. "You cannot have any article that you brought in here with you," the guard informed us. When each man neared the processing room door, he stripped naked out in the open cell block.

The line stretched down the cell block, where five or six men at the end of the line stood naked waiting to enter the processing room. As one man entered, the man on the last chair got up, took off his clothes, and took his place standing, while all the rest of us slid down the line from chair to chair.

"Keep the line tight!" a guard repeatedly barked.

When at last it was my turn to enter the processing room, I stepped inside. I gave the guard my name and number, and he wrote the information on a bag and tossed my personal clothing items into it. He then tossed the bag into a large canvas cart. The processing guard assured me that my street clothes would be sent back to my home address.

Bereft of our clothing, about fifteen men at a time stood in line inside the room for a superficial medical examination. Then the prison medical personnel conducted a strip search. "Hold your hands up in the air. Okay, turn your hands back and forth, palms in, palms out. Let's have a look behind your ears. Pull your ears down. Rub your hands through your hair. Open your mouth, please. Lift up your tongue. Pull up your privates. Turn around. Bend over and pull your buns apart. Okay, fine. You're done. Move down the line. Next!"

Grateful that the indignities of my physical exam were over, I stepped into the next room where I was issued something to wear—prison underwear, socks, shoes, and a bright orange jumpsuit. I had started out the day of October 24, 1989, wearing a fine-tailored suit, and now I was finishing the day dressed in a much-too-big, wrinkled, orange jumpsuit.

Just before I walked out of the processing room, a guard handed me a set of sheets and a blanket for my bunk. I exited the processing room and took my place on the first vacant chair at the other end of the constantly moving line.

"Keep the line tight!" I heard again.

When we had all been processed, one by one, the men at the end of the line were escorted to their cells. As the line got shorter and shorter, and I knew my time was approaching, I became increasingly nervous.

What will my cell be like? I wondered. My only reference point was the cell in which I had been confined at Butner. *Oh, God, please don't let it be like that!* I begged. I thought back to the tough-looking group of men I had initially encountered. *Which of them would be confined with me in a small room?* The more I thought about it, the more anxious I became.

"Bakker, let's go," a voice broke in on my thoughts.

Moving like a robot, I stood to my feet and began to follow the guard. We walked to the cells on the opposite wall, facing the processing room. A little more than midway down the row of doors, the guard stopped. He fumbled with his large ring of keys and finally picked out a single key and inserted it into a cell door. The door swung open, and the guard stepped aside for me to enter.

As the big, steel door closed behind me, I heard the guard turn down the lock. I was in my cell. . . . This was my "home away from home" for the next forty-five years, as far as I knew.

In the dim light, I saw a man move. An inmate was already in my cell. He looked as though he was waiting for me.

11

The Colombian Connection

"HI, I'M DAVID SINGLETON," MY NEW CELLMATE SAID AMIABLY. He held out his hand as he spoke.

"Hello, I'm Jim Bakker," I replied, reaching out to shake hands with the man. The stranger standing before me looked nothing like a stereotypical convict. David looked like a clean-cut, successful, young businessman in his late thirties or early forties.

"Come on in. Welcome to our home; have a seat," David said as though he were welcoming me to a visit at a posh country home.

David said that he had been airborne to a prison camp at Eglin Air Force Base, near Pensacola, Florida. In midair, a prison official sat down next to him and asked David if he would be willing to be my cellmate for a while and help orient me to prison life.

Eglin, the prison to which David Singleton was en route when he was approached about being my cellmate, was a minimum-security prison camp. Although there is no such thing as a "safe" prison, the degrees of risk at Talladega and Eglin were like night and day. For David to willingly choose to put himself into jeopardy merely to help me become acclimated to prison life was a tremendous act of kindness.

David told me that part of the reason he accepted the assignment of helping me adapt to prison life was because of the culture shock he had experienced when he was first processed as a prisoner. Due to David's crime, he had been allowed to return home for a few weeks following his sentencing. For him the shock of going from the life of a successful attorney to prison life was nearly overwhelming.

"I made a comfortable living, Jim," he told me, "and the night before I went to prison, I was eating a delicious dinner off fine china and drinking from crystal stemware. The next night, I was in prison, eating prison hash with a plastic fork and spoon. One night I slept in a soft, warm bed with my wife; the next night, I was sleeping alone, on a steel bunk bed in the hell of a prison cell."

David allowed me to have the bottom bunk. As I made the bed, David began to explain some basics of prison survival. He emphasized that prison was a dangerous place that had its own code of ethics. One major mistake could be fatal. "I am not trying to frighten you, but you must understand these things."

In a straightforward manner David informed me, "Trouble often takes place in the TV rooms in prison. Guys have gotten into serious fights over something as simple as changing the channel on the set. My advice is to stay out of the TV room as much as possible."

"TV room?" I asked. "Where's the TV room?"

David burst out laughing. "Why, you were in it, Jim! The first room they brought you into tonight, up the corridor, near the processing room. That is the TV room."

"It is? I had thought that was going to be my cell," I said sheepishly.

David convulsed in laughter again. "No way, man! Next to the chow hall, that's the most popular room in the place." Then David turned serious again. "It is also one of the most dangerous."

David continued. "Don't ever get involved in an argument or a fight in the chow hall. If you do, the prison officials will give you a major 'shot'—a dose of punishment. All prison offenses are given a number indicating the severity of the offense and the shot that you will receive as punishment in return. For example, you can slug someone in your cell, and that might be considered a lesser offense. But if you slug the same guy in the chow hall, they consider it inciting a riot. The prison officials will give you a long stay in the 'hole,' solitary confinement with no privileges. Or, if you accumulate a certain number of demerits, they'll put you in the hole."

I had finished making my bed, so I sat down and listened intently as David went on. "Snitches and child molesters are hated in prison. Don't ever snitch on anyone, if you know what is good for you. Obey all the prison rules, whether or not you think they are fair. Make your bed by 7:30 A.M. every day or you will get a shot."

"When can I call my wife?" I asked.

96

"If you want to use the telephone in this facility, you have to get out of your cell first thing in the morning and sign up for a fifteen-minute time slot on the call sheet, which is out in the cell block near the window where you get your clean sheets and clean clothes. If there are any other time slots left open, you might be able to get a second calling time."

David yawned—it was getting late. "Tomorrow, I'll fill you in on some more important details of prison life," he promised as he climbed into the top bunk. "Right now, you better get some sleep. You've had a long day."

I rolled into the bottom bunk and stared at the bunk above me. As I lay there thinking about the events of the day, the denial process began to pound away at my brain again. *This can't be happening to me.*

But I *was* in prison, and a quick glance around the sparsely furnished cell, with the open commode and sink next to the wall, the desk, and a small storage cabinet, confirmed my whereabouts. After a while I allowed my eyes to close and I tried to sleep.

Clang! Crash! Clank! A loud sound scared me half to death and I bounded out of bed and stumbled toward the door in the dark. I heard loud voices outside my cell door, so I looked out the window into the main cell block. I saw dozens of inmates, all handcuffed and shackled, coming into the prison cell block to be processed. They went through the same entry routine I had experienced several hours earlier, with one exception— their chains. A guard was unlocking each man's cuffs, shackles, and chains as he went through the line. The chains were thrown onto the cement floor, where another guard came along and tossed them into a bag made of heavy material. The noise from the chains clanging and banging was ear piercing.

I watched the scene repeated again and again. Finally, when I could stay awake no longer, I tumbled into my bunk and fell into a troubled sleep for a few hours.

I awakened just as the guards were opening our cells; I looked around and wondered, *Where am I?* Before long, reality began to set in and I recalled what had happened yesterday. I realized that not only was I in prison, I was going to be in prison for the remainder of my life. I wanted to roll over, shut my eyes, go to sleep, and never wake up.

David, however, was already up, dressed, and was making up his bunk. "Come on, Jim," he said kindly, but firmly. "It's time to get up. You must have your bunk made up by 7:30 A.M."

Reluctantly I rolled out of bed, put on my jumpsuit, and walked over to the sink. I brushed my teeth and shaved. My top priority for the morning was to get my name on that telephone registration list so I could call

Tammy Faye. I wanted to find the list, but I was extremely afraid of doing something wrong and getting into trouble either with other inmates or with the prison officials. I decided I better stick with David.

The noise of the awakening prison population was staggering. As I stepped out of our cell into the open cell block, the din was nearly deafening. It seemed to be growing louder every minute as more men poured out of their cells into the cell block. I had never heard such a roar. As more men struggled to be heard, everyone tried to talk louder than the next person until the decibel level in the white echo chamber was so high I thought my eardrums were going to explode. I quickly realized that the leader in this environment was the man who could talk the loudest.

I wanted to find the telephone sign-up sheet, but David said it would be out after breakfast; right now I should follow him closely. This was my first experience in a prison chow line, and I was not prepared for the cattle-call atmosphere. Almost all of the inmates were already lined up by the door, so David and I got in the back of the line and awaited our cell block's turn to go eat breakfast. Talladega Federal Prison houses hundreds of prisoners, so only some of the inmates can eat at one time. Prisoners from each separate cell block must eat together, then leave the chow hall "mainline," as it is known in prison, as a group.

As we exited our building, the guards were yelling at us repeatedly, "Keep in double lines and don't move out of formation." We were marched outside to the edge of the sidewalk and told to halt until we were given further orders. As I stood there in the light of day, getting my first real look at the huge prison compound, I noticed a large group of inmates to my left. Their hands and feet were cuffed and manacled, and the men were chained together in a line. I had never before seen human beings treated like this, and the sight was nearly overwhelming for me.

Someone gave the signal that it was our cell block's time to eat. We were marched across the compound to the chow hall. We entered the building just as the men from the previous building exited. Once inside, the men spread out, filing through the several lines in which inmates were dishing out the food military style. I was still in the back of the line. I didn't really mind. Breakfast had never been my favorite meal, and besides, the grits, eggs, and other food being dished out of giant rectangular pans did not look very appetizing.

Nevertheless, I did not want to stick out of the crowd, so I went through the chow-line routine, picking up my plastic spoon and fork and a plastic plate full of food just as everyone else did. As I went through the line I could hear guys whispering my name. Many men openly stared at me, making no effort to divert their gaze if I happened to see them. I hastily took my tray and tried to find a seat.

I had no sooner sat down than the guard said, "Let's go! Time's up. Breakfast is over." I couldn't believe it. I had not even taken a bite, and the guard was saying it was time to get out of the chow hall. The next group was already lined outside in front of their cell block, waiting for their signal to get into the chow hall. I dumped my food in the garbage. We marched back to our block. Once inside the cell block, the men scattered in all directions. Some went to the showers; some gathered around the Ping-Pong tables; many started playing dominoes. I never dreamed that dominoes could make so much noise as they were slapped down onto the tables. Other men went to the laundry lineup to get fresh clothes to wear or clean sheets for their bunks.

By far the most popular place in our cell block was the phone sign-up line. The line of men waiting to use the phone was already long by the time I got there. I waited my turn to place my name on that important sheet of paper. I had to talk to my precious wife. I scheduled my fifteen-minute segment for that afternoon. Later that day, I was also able to secure another fifteen-minute block for that evening.

I turned to go back to my cell, and as I did, I saw a man approaching me. He was headed right for me. I stopped cold, paralyzed with fear, not knowing what to expect. As the man got closer, he stuck out his hand and broke into a broad smile. He introduced himself to me as John and told me that he had been in prison most of his adult life. John offered to advise me on prison "etiquette."

I started to thank him and to let him know that I was already receiving some helpful instructions, but before I had a chance to get out a sentence, we were suddenly surrounded by guys coming from everywhere. A group of men gathered around me and began asking me all sorts of questions. They were not belligerent; they seemed honestly interested in me, Heritage USA, my trial, and what had happened to me.

One man was particularly interested in the "million-dollar, air-conditioned doghouse" he had read about in the papers, flaunted as proof of my extravagant life at PTL. The men all laughed when I told them the doghouse had cost me about four hundred dollars and that it was nothing more than a big shed built out of rough lumber. My family loved animals, so the shed was large enough to provide shelter for all six of our dogs.

"Six dogs!" one of the men behind me exclaimed.

Before I knew it, I started telling my fellow inmates the entire story. "Yes, six dogs," I repeated. "Tammy Faye loves dogs. I used to tease her, saying that she loved animals more than people."

The inmates roared in laughter at that. "I'll say!" one of them chipped in. "You can trust them a lot more!"

The guys all cracked up again.

"Well, we were out of town back in the winter of 1986 when a bad cold spell hit the Carolinas. Tammy Faye was worried that our pets would freeze to death, so I called our security department at Heritage USA and asked them to find one of the old window-mounted air-conditioner units that would also blow heat and put it into the doghouse to keep the animals from freezing. Our chief of security at PTL couldn't find a unit in the warehouse, so he took an air conditioner out of our little backyard cottage. He cut a hole in the side of the dog shed to fit the air conditioner inside so it would blow heat and keep the dogs warm. The dogs never used the shed, but it made Tammy Faye feel better.

"After I left PTL, the new managers had a truckload of men go over to our home and lift up the doghouse to take it back to PTL to be sold at an auction. You may have seen the picture in the magazines of a bunch of guys carrying that shed. The people who bought the doghouse at the auction took it around to shopping centers, hoping the public would pay money to see it. But people who saw our 'luxurious' doghouse wanted their money back from the people who were putting it on display. They were disappointed that it was nothing more than a shed. So that's it. That's the real story about the famous doghouse."

Again, the inmates seemed to truly enjoy getting the inside story on something they had seen on TV or had read about in the magazines.

"Well, let me tell you the real story 'bout this place," one of the men said. "We're mighty glad you were sent here."

"Really?" I asked.

"Yep. From the moment everyone found out 'bout you coming to Talladega, our food has gotten ten times better."

"Yeah," another man piped up, "and they pulled a lot of the men out of here, so we aren't sleeping on mats on the floor anymore. 'Fore you got here, Jim, we were sleeping two guys on bunks and one on a mattress on the floor in just about every cell."

"And you prob'ly noticed the paint job. Did it in one day. They painted the whole place here. Guess the government boys wanted everything to look pretty for the cameras that might be followin' you around."

"Now that you mention it, I did notice the paint smell in the air," I said. "I just thought somebody was painting something somewhere."

"They were!" one man said to the laughter of all the others. "See all this clean, white paint around here? You didn't think these walls looked like that last week, did ya?" The men roared with laughter once again.

"Well, I . . . I don't know. . . ."

"Hey, Jim, it's all right. We're glad you came. Best cleanup job we've had 'round here in a long time." I wasn't sure whether the men were exaggerating or not, but they made me feel like a hero rather than a heel.

A number of the fellows came up to me and began asking me for autographs. Many wanted me to sign things for their moms or their grandmothers.

After a few minutes, my new friend John, the seasoned inmate, invited me to come down to his cell, which was two cells down from mine. I said, "Sure," and we walked under the steel staircase together toward his cell. Several of the men followed us.

When I got outside John's cell, I was surprised to see that John had a game table and some chairs. No other cell that I had seen so far had such a table or chairs. John obviously had connections. We talked some more, with John and the other men offering me advice on how to survive in prison. Then John pulled out his personal address book.

"I'd like you to sign my book," John requested with a laugh. "But I want you to sign it, 'To John, my best road dog.'" By then John's cell was filled with inmates and they all burst out laughing.

I had no idea what John meant by *road dog*. I was so paranoid after my trial, I did not want to be signing my name to anything that I did not understand.

I said, "John, I'll be glad to sign your book, but I can't sign it that way because I don't know what that means."

"Oh, go on. Just sign it," John said, and the other men broke out laughing again.

I looked around at the other men in the room. They were obviously having a good time at the expense of my ignorance, but they did not look mean spirited. They were just having fun. I asked in a lighthearted way, "Are you guys sure that it's not something dirty, or something wrong?"

Gales of laughter filled the room again.

I felt that I better not take a chance. I signed John's phone book, but I did not sign "To my road dog."

Later, someone informed me that the term "road dog" was actually quite a compliment, especially in the culture from which John had come. A dog is your good friend. A road dog is one who travels the same road with you, who "hangs out" with you. Basically, what John was asking me to do was to sign, "To John, from your best friend, Jim Bakker." John was a bit disappointed with a simple signature and "God bless you," but he remained my good friend while I was at Talladega.

Suddenly a guard showed up in the doorway and announced, "You have too many men in that cell!" The officer then walked on.

I was petrified that I was breaking a prison rule, something David had told me never to do, so I made a move toward the door to leave.

"Sit down, Jim," John said with a laugh. "If that cop was really concerned, he would have moved us out of here right now." I marveled at John's prison savvy. The guy even knew when the guards were serious and when they were not.

Although I was still shell-shocked as a result of all I had experienced in the past two and a half years (especially the past thirty-six hours), I was beginning to feel a strange sense of acceptance and camaraderie in my new environment. At Talladega we had men from diverse racial and ethnic backgrounds. One of the fellows who was laughing with us in John's cell was from Colombia. His name was Carlos and he was built like stone, with muscular legs and arms on a finely chiseled, athletic body.

As we were all laughing in John's cell, someone said that it was almost time to line up for recreation time. In front of all the other men, Carlos looked straight at me and, in a thick Latin-American accent, said, "Hey, Mr. Jim. We are playing soccer today. You come. Be on our team."

I paused a long time before answering. This was the first time in my life I could remember anyone asking me to be on a sports team. As a child, I was extremely small and shy. Nobody ever picked Jim Bakker to be on their team. Consequently, I had never played sports. I had no clue how to play soccer. Nevertheless, to my surprise, I heard myself answering Carlos, "Yes, I'll play. But I don't know how to play soccer."

Without a moment of hesitation, Carlos replied, "No problem. Just stick with me; just do what I do. I won't let you get hurt."

Actually, at that moment, I felt it would be a blessing if I were to get killed on the soccer field. I had no fear of dying, although I *was* a bit concerned about making a fool of myself. But then I realized that I no longer had any reputation to protect. I thought, *What do I have to lose?*

Carlos left to remind his fellow Colombian inmates about the big soccer game coming up at rec time. Meanwhile, David guided me to where the guys were lining up in double columns waiting for the guards to march us out to the recreational fields, a distance of about a city block.

When we arrived at the rec area, the men fanned out to various activity areas such as the basketball courts and the running track. Some of the older men simply sat at picnic tables and philosophized. Some of the younger men—jailhouse lawyers—sat around debating their cases. I fell in step with a group of men headed toward the running track and the soccer field beyond that. I wasn't convinced Carlos wanted me to play. But as I neared the end of the track, Carlos came running up to me and shouted, "Come on, Jim. We're ready to go."

"Okay," I replied nervously, as though I were heading for my execution.

Carlos positioned me right next to him and ran interference for me. Occasionally he would feed the ball to me so I got an opportunity to kick it. I knew immediately that these men were not amateurs. They were skilled soccer players. They played with passion and a strong competitive spirit. Most of the men were in their twenties and in excellent physical condition. I later learned that many of these players were in fact semiprofessional soccer players. Even those who were not semipros were highly skilled. Soccer was their national pastime.

Carlos and his Colombian inmates treated me like a guest star rather than a disgraced minister. They deferred to me, spoke respectfully to me, and protected me, attempting to make sure that I was not kicked unnecessarily. I was surprised. This was not the perception of hardened inmates that I had imagined prior to entering prison.

During a break in the action, Carlos told me it was my turn to play goalie. From being brought up in Michigan, I was vaguely familiar with ice hockey. I knew the goalie position was a highly important spot on the team. I was scared stiff! Besides the possibility of getting smeared, these boys took their soccer seriously. I did not want to make any mistakes that might cost our team the game.

As it turned out, I was goalie in name only because Carlos always stayed a few feet in front of me, deflecting the shots that came near the goal. God knows I tried! When the game was over, I knew I had not contributed much to our team, but all of my teammates acted as though I had. Several of them told me that they were going to write to their family members to tell them that they had played soccer with Jim Bakker.

I honestly do not remember who won the soccer game that day, but I know I came away from it feeling like a winner. For the first time in a long while, I felt a part of a team. I had felt acceptance, concern, and compassion from my Colombian soccer players that caused me to remember that I was still a human being.

It was almost time for my phone call home. I could hardly wait to talk to Tammy Faye. When I arrived back at my cell block, I was dirty, hot, and sweaty. A guard told me that my lawyer had come to visit, so I hurriedly picked up my soap and towel and went down to the end of the cell block where the showers were located. The shower stall was made of opaque glass and had a door that could be shut, providing some semblance of privacy, even though the guards and others could see someone in the stall. I hastily showered and informed the guard that I was ready to receive my visitor.

One of the guards escorted me to the room where Harold Bender was waiting for me. When Harold had arrived, he could not believe that he had to wait because his client was out playing soccer with the Colombians. Harold probably had expected to see me depressed and cowering in the corner of a dark cell. Actually, I was extremely depressed, but the active prison community in which I was now living allowed little time for introspection. . . . That time would come later.

Harold informed me that he had filed an appeal concerning my case. He also told me something about a "Rule 35" by which I could have my sentence reconsidered and possibly reduced. I listened to Harold rattle off his legalese, but I had little faith left in the justice system and even less confidence in lawyers. Harold's visit brought me face-to-face again with the harsh reality that I was facing forty-five years in prison. Any euphoria I had been feeling after surviving my soccer experience was squelched by my lawyer's offers of what I considered to be false hope. It was easy for Harold to speak optimistically about the time it might take for the appeal process. He wasn't living in a prison cell.

I ended my meeting with Harold abruptly when I noticed the time on his wristwatch. "I have to go, Harold. It's almost time for my phone call."

The guard escorted me back to the cell block and I made a beeline for the telephone. The phone was located about shoulder high in the open cell block, next to the laundry room. An industrial-sized clock hung directly above the phone, so there could be no mistaking when a prisoner's allotted time began and ended. There was no phone booth to provide privacy. Anyone nearby could eavesdrop on anyone's phone conversation if he wanted to do so. Many did.

When I arrived at the telephone, several men were standing in line, hoping someone would give up his time. Another man was on the phone, finishing his call. He actually ran a bit over his time, but I was reluctant to say anything. Finally it was my turn.

All calls by inmates had to be placed collect. Tammy Faye had been anxiously waiting to hear from me, so she could hardly wait to accept the charges.

"Yes, yes, yes!" she said before the operator had even completed her spiel. We had not talked to each other directly since before my sentencing. I told her how much I loved her and tried to inform her about everything that had happened in the past forty-eight hours. It was difficult to squeeze all the details into a fifteen-minute phone call.

Tammy Faye was worried sick. She had no idea where the authorities had taken me until she had seen it on television. She told me that she was going to do everything in her power to get me out of prison. I was glad to hear that but even more excited because my wife said she would be coming to visit me. Tammy said she would leave for Talladega first thing in the morning. I told her to be sure to give my love to Jamie and Tammy Sue. Tammy Faye said Jamie had been mocked in school because of me. Although Jamie has always been extremely polite and well-mannered, he would not stand by and let kids say horrible things about his dad. Jamie nearly slugged one boy who had made a remark, but Jamie's friends grabbed his arms until the boy could escape.

The clock on the wall alerted me that our time was almost up. Not only that, a man in the line behind me was noisily letting me know that if I went a second past my time, I would regret it.

I hated to hang up, but I quickly said, "I love you, Baby. I have to go. My fifteen minutes are up and the other guys are waiting."

"I love you, Jim. Don't worry, honey. We've made it through other things. We'll make it through this too."

I had barely hung the receiver in the phone's cradle when another man had it up to his ear and was already dialing a number.

Just as she promised, Tammy Faye was at the prison the following evening in time for the beginning of visiting hours. She, Donna, and Fran Moore had driven from Orlando to Talladega. My brother Norman also drove from Charlotte. That evening I heard my name called out by a prison guard, using my new title for the first time:

"*Inmate Bakker!* You have a visitor."

A guard accompanied me to the visitation building, where Tammy Faye was waiting for me. I had been briefed on prison policy of one hug and one kiss upon meeting, so when I saw Tammy Faye I gave her an extra long hug before I kissed her. It was as though I was trying to absorb her warmth, her scent, and her vibrant energy. Tears filled our eyes, tears of joy at seeing one another and tears of sadness at our circumstances. I was nervous and physically depleted, but just having Tammy Faye in my presence lifted my spirits. We had quite a reunion that night. I told them, in as much detail as I could remember, what had happened to me since I had last been seen publicly in Judge Potter's courtroom.

My family stayed for several days and visited me every night. Tammy Faye, Donna, and Fran checked into a motel near the prison. They were constantly hounded by reporters wanting to interview them. Reporters booked rooms on both sides of theirs and watched for the women to come out so they could interview them. Some reporters stooped to hiding in the shrubbery near the motel, trying to get candid photographs of the women when they came out of their room. One evening, the reporters from a tabloid paper followed the women to their room, where one man stuck his foot in their door and absolutely insisted that Tammy Faye talk to him. Donna fought the man off, then hurried to call the front desk for help. The person answering the call said that there was nothing that could be done.

The next day, while my family members were visiting me in the prison visiting room, a warm, friendly family introduced themselves to us. The father and mother were there visiting their son at the time. The family members asked if they could have a photo taken with Tammy Faye and me. We wanted to be cordial, so we agreed. The photograph later turned up in a tabloid newspaper. I hated to see Saturday come. Tammy Faye had to return to Orlando to be at the church where we had been pastoring prior to my incarceration. For our final visit together, an inmate who had become a friend did a special favor for me—a fresh, clean, *blue* jumpsuit from the laundry room where he worked. It felt so good to be wearing something other than an orange prison jumpsuit.

Tammy Faye and I ate our prison-visit lunch consisting of stale vending-machine sandwiches. We talked as long as the guards would allow and had an emotional visit. And then it was time for her to go.

"Wrap it up. Visiting time is over," the guard announced.

Tammy Faye and I hugged and kissed our legal limit. I held her in my arms, not wanting to let her go.

"I'll see you next week, Jim," she said as cheerily as possible.

Little did we know that by this time next week, I would be thousands of miles away.

CHAPTER

12

Crying in the Chapel

THE NEXT DAY I WAS IN THE CHOW HALL, GOING THROUGH the line as usual. As I picked up my tray, I saw the vaguely familiar face of a man outside looking in the window. The man was waving at me. I looked around to see if he had been trying to get someone else's attention. He waved at me again.

The man was mouthing words to me through the window. "Blackwood," he seemed to be saying.

Blackwood? The only Blackwoods I knew were singers who used to appear on my television program at PTL.

The man held a Bible up in the window. Then suddenly, he was gone. I went on eating my food, unaware of the drama that began unfolding outside the window. A guard outside had seen Ron Blackwood looking into the chow-hall window and waving a Bible. The officer was one of the toughest guards on the compound. He had a reputation for sending prisoners to the hole, even for minor infractions.

The guard yelled at the prisoner, "Blackwood, what are you doing?"

"I'm trying to get this Bible to Jim Bakker," Ron replied.

The guard began cursing at Blackwood. The guard got right in Ron's face and screamed, "What are you trying to do?"

Ignoring his fear, Ron said, "Sir, let me tell you something. That man needs this Bible because it is a comfort to him. It won't cost you a thing to give it to him."

The guard stared back at Ron Blackwood and didn't say a word for the longest time. Finally, the guard reached down and grabbed the Bible out of Ron's hand. He brought it into the chow hall, and gave it to one of the officers on duty. When an officer gave me the Bible, it was like someone had given me the greatest gift in the world. Inside, I found Ron's name and prison number written on a page near the front of the Bible.

One day a prisoner who had been to the chapel told me that Ron Blackwood, the chapel choir director, had invited me to attend the chapel service on Sunday. Finally, I recognized Ron's name! Ron's dad was one of the original Blackwood Brothers and had died in a plane crash. Ron and his famous family of singers had appeared on the *PTL* television show. His uncle, James Blackwood, was a good friend of mine and had appeared on our show along with Cecil Blackwood and the world-renowned Blackwood Brothers Quartet. All of the Blackwoods continued to support Tammy Faye and me long after we had departed PTL and had started a new ministry in Florida. I will always be indebted to the Blackwood family.

I was surprised, however, to learn that Ron was in prison. Apparently, he had gotten in trouble over a tax problem. I made up my mind that although it might be awkward, I would go to chapel Sunday morning.

Chapel was held at 10:00 A.M. in a small room in a concrete multipurpose building. The chapel could comfortably seat about fifty or sixty inmates. To the left was a room where a Muslim group met.

As we walked into the service, I tried to ascertain whether I was welcome there. After all, the media blitz that had made my name a household name in America had also made my name infamous. I felt that many religious leaders might not be happy to have me in their services.

I sat down about halfway back next to the aisle. I no sooner sat down when the prison chapel choir began singing "You Can Make It," a song written by Mike Murdock and popularized by Tammy Faye, who sang it on our *PTL* television program. I was overwhelmed! This was the theme song of my television ministry for years, sung almost every day by my wife. Hearing it in prison, at first, was almost like an indictment. My own words were being thrown back into my face, a message I had given to millions of people at the close of almost every television program, but had by now forgotten myself.

When I saw Ron Blackwood up close in the chapel, I recognized him immediately. He had aged a bit since coming to prison, but he was still vibrant. An inmate informed me that prior to my arrival at chapel, the prison chaplain had instructed the other prisoners to stay away from me, not to communicate with me in any way, not even to talk with me at chapel. He said that I was coming to chapel to worship like everyone else and that I should be left alone. Ron Blackwood, however, had arranged to sit next to me, and Ron talked with me throughout the service. Ron talked so much that I feared the guards were going to get angry. Ron told me that he had been at Talladega for over a year. He wanted to encourage me; he could tell that I was a beaten, traumatized human being.

Ironically, most of the songs Ron taught the members of his choir were songs he had first heard sung on the *PTL* television program. What they did not know about music they made up for with enthusiasm. Ron got up to introduce "Don't Give Up on the Brink of a Miracle." He looked directly at me and said, "Jim, I want to dedicate this song to you this morning. This is your song."

As soon as Ron and the choir began singing the song, tears began to flow from my eyes. The song's message said "don't give up," yet I knew that I had already given up. I wrapped my arms around myself. Tears surged down my face.

Ron cried all the way through the song as well. When Ron returned to sit back down with me, I leaned over and told him that "Don't Give Up on the Brink of a Miracle" had been written for Tammy Faye and me by Mike Adkins. Ron said that was the reason he had selected that particular song for the choir to sing that morning. He said that as soon as he saw me, he could tell that I was extremely distraught. He wanted to do all he could to help lift my spirits. It would be many years before I was able to fully realize the miracle of that morning. Only God could have arranged for a prison choir to sing on the first Sunday I was incarcerated two of my favorite songs written by two of my best friends, directed by a member of a family I respected and loved, a man who risked all to get a Bible to me.

It would be years before a mutual friend would tell me about the high price Ron Blackwood had paid to get that Bible to me. About a month after I left Talladega, three officers approached Ron Blackwood on the prison compound. One of the men was holding the Bible Ron had given to me. I had been afraid to take it with me for fear of breaking prison rules. He asked Ron, "Is this yours?"

Ron hesitated. "Does it have my name in it?" he asked.

"Yes," the guard replied.

"Well, then I guess it's mine."

They put Ron Blackwood in the hole for thirty days. His offense? Giving me a Bible. The guards said that Ron had given me contraband, that prisoners were not allowed to give each other personal items, even though the Bible Ron had given to me was one that he had gotten from the prison's government-issue supply.

Every day during my first week at Talladega, I met with a prison counselor. He seemed genuinely interested in how I was acclimating to prison life. One day he told me that I would not be staying in Talladega for much longer. Fear gripped me all over again. I begged the counselor to please keep me from being exposed to the media and to more public ridicule. I knew I was breaking a vow I had made to myself that I would never ask for any special treatment while I was in prison, but I found myself shaking over the mere thought of more public humiliation.

A few days later, I was called back to the counselor's office. He informed me that within a few hours, probably early the next morning, I would be transferred to Rochester, Minnesota, where I would be incarcerated at the Rochester Federal Prison, known officially as the Rochester Federal Medical Center. I was just starting to become familiar with my surroundings at Talladega. Now the fear of the unknown came back with all its fury as I faced going to the far northern part of the United States while most of my family was living and working in Florida. I felt the prison system was conspiring to separate me as far from my family as possible. Actually, I learned later, they were putting me in a place where I could receive attention if I were to suffer another nervous breakdown.

I appreciated the opportunity to telephone Tammy Faye and let her know that I was being transferred. She had already planned another trip to Talladega for that week. Had she shown up and I'd been gone, she would have been frantic.

I went through the usual exit process. Take off your clothes. Strip search. Chains. I was given khaki travel clothes to wear with dark blue canvas shoes. No jacket. Driven in a van to an airport, I was surprised to find that I would be traveling to Minnesota in a Lear jet. One of the marshals told me that this plane had been confiscated from a drug smuggler.

I sat down in the plush leather seat on the back right side of the plane next to a telephone. I had flown in many private jets over the years. At one time, our ministry had owned a jet with almost the exact same cabin configuration, and I had always sat in exactly the same spot to which I was assigned today. Here I was sitting in the multimillion-dollar Lear aircraft wearing handcuffs, chains, and shackles. The irony was not lost on me.

What sort of place was Rochester Prison going to be? I wondered. I was about to find out.

110

13

F. M. C. Rochester

IT WAS SNOWING WHEN I ARRIVED IN ROCHESTER, Minnesota. Since I was sitting in the back of the plane, I was the last person to exit. When I popped my head out the door, several snowflakes lingered on my eyebrows before melting. With my hands cuffed and chained, it was impossible to brush the chilly flakes away.

The first thing that struck me in Minnesota was how awfully cold it was! I had spent my first days in prison in Alabama, where it was still pleasant, shirtsleeves weather. I left Talladega wearing my lightweight prison clothes, a collarless pullover shirt with a scooped neck and short sleeves, and lightweight khaki prison pants, held up by only a thin piece of elastic.

Now, here I was in Minnesota—a beautiful state, especially if you are a fan of winter—and where any temperature above zero from October to April is considered a heat wave!

I stepped off the plane. I could see no signs of Minnesota's lush, green parks and its pristine lakes. I had attended Bible school many years before in Minneapolis—it was where I had met Tammy Faye—so I knew the state. But on this day, the place looked gray and barren.

Inside the prison, the men were watching my arrival on television. Both local and national news teams had assembled at the airport to cover my arrival. Fortunately for me, as standard policy, prison officials refuse to allow the press to get too close to a runway when prisoners are being transferred. The cameramen had to use telephoto lenses and shoot from a distance at least a city block away to even capture my photo. The lenses so

111

magnified the snow that one reporter stated that I had arrived in the midst of a bad blizzard. In fact, it was merely a light snow.

Guards stood on the runway with automatic rifles at the ready as the other prisoners and I clambered out of the plane. We were herded toward a prison van the moment our feet touched the pavement.

When the van pulled out and we made our way from the tiny airport toward the town of Rochester, daylight was waning. I was still able to make out the images of drab, squat homes—houses built to take the weather. I would wonder for years what downtown Rochester looked like.

We approached the front gate of the prison. I saw an electric fence with three-foot-high spirals of razor wire at the top, enclosing the entire perimeter of the prison. Another electric fence with the identical type of razor wire enclosed the inside perimeter. About fifteen feet separated the two fences. Two white pickups carrying armed guards perpetually patrolled the no-man's-land outside the two fences. One of the inmates told me that the fence had sensors all over it, so if a person even touched the fence with his hand, an alarm went off and a sensor in the monitoring room showed exactly where the infraction took place. "No escaping over that fence," the inmate lamented. "It will cut you to shreds." Me, I wasn't planning any attempted escapes; I was simply hoping to survive.

The van pulled into the prison parking lot and up to the gatehouse. Even the gatehouse had rolls of razor wire spiraling across its roof. Every person who entered Rochester prison—guards, doctors, visitors, and prisoners—all had to pass this way. We got out of the van and walked into the gatehouse. Again, guards with guns watched our every move. Once inside, sliding bars opened in front of us. We stepped inside a small space where a guard sat behind a window, checking everyone in or out. Then another set of bars opened and we entered the main part of the prison compound. We turned right, escorted by officers, and walked into "R & D"—Receiving and Discharge.

The guards took my cuffs, chains, and shackles off. I was processed by myself. I was photographed and fingerprinted. I completed more health forms. The Rochester officials appeared slightly keyed up about me being there and acted as though they were in a hurry to get me settled.

It was time for my reentry strip search. Any time a prisoner leaves or enters a prison, every cavity of his body is inspected for drugs, concealed weapons, or other contraband he might be trying to smuggle into the prison. I didn't think I would ever grow accustomed to the strip searches.

After the search, I was given a fresh set of clothes, better and warmer clothes than those in which I had traveled. They resembled military clothing without the epaulets. I was learning that fresh clothes are also standard procedure when entering a prison. A prisoner is never permitted to enter a prison compound in the clothing he was wearing outside the prison compound, even if he just came from another prison. Again, it is a precaution against the smuggling of contraband. For some reason, however, the guards checking me in allowed me to keep my blue travel shoes. I later wished that the guards would have taken those shoes away from me right then and there.

Rochester Federal Prison was comprised of many large buildings inside the razor-wire fences. Building One was the mental hospital, housing inmates who were mentally ill or those being evaluated for the courts, as I was at Butner. Building Two housed the general prison population. In addition, many inmates were confined to the hospital and the outpatient facilities, which were also inside the prison compound.

A team of guards escorted me to Building One. We went upstairs and turned left into an office. The office was warm and homey, with plants in the windows and family pictures on the desk. Indian art pieces decorated the walls. Other pieces of art—made by inmates, I later learned—were placed around the room.

A sophisticated-looking woman sat behind a desk. She exuded strength yet had a frail, almost grandmotherly quality that reminded me of my Grandmother Bakker who had died when I was a little boy.

The woman rose to meet me, extended her hand, and said, in a crisp, aristocratic tone, "Hello, Mr. Bakker. I am Dr. Westrick." I could not help wondering what such a charming and dignified woman was doing in this place. Dr. Westrick turned toward a tall man standing off to the side of her desk. "And this is Dr. Foster," she said. Dr. Foster leaned over toward me like a towering oak bending in the wind and stretched his hand toward me. He said in a deep but gentle voice, "Hello, Jim. I'm glad to meet you. Have a seat." Dr. Foster motioned toward a chair. I gratefully sensed that there was something different about this man.

I sat down. Dr. Westrick welcomed me to the medical center and told me of their commitment to treating me—and all people—with dignity and to protecting my privacy and well-being in the best way they could. She assured me of her and Dr. Foster's support. She also explained that it was their policy not to judge me because I was incarcerated but to assist me in any way they could to sustain a healthy quality of life and my personal integrity. Dr. Westrick and Dr. Foster then asked some basic questions concerning my mental health. The prison at Butner had already sent them a large report on my test results there, my I.Q., and my mental competency, so Dr. Westrick and Dr. Foster already knew a great deal about me. But it was obvious that they were probing for something that was not in the written file. Finally, I realized they were trying to assess whether or not I was suicidal.

After a short while, Dr. Westrick stood up and extended her hand again. "I have asked Dr. Foster to make himself available to you. I will be seeing you again soon," she said. I felt a tinge of personal dignity.

Dr. Foster rose as well and nodded toward the door. "Right this way, Jim." Dr. Foster escorted me to his office where he continued to talk quietly to me. I was surprised when Dr. Foster began listing the names of numerous people we knew in common. Although I did not know it at the time, Dr. Daniel V. Foster was one of many "coincidences" that I would experience in prison. He had been serving in the Federal Bureau of Prisons for over a decade when I was sent to prison. At the Federal Medical Center, he was the chief of psychological services.

What made Dr. Foster such a gift to me was that in addition to outstanding academic qualifications, he also had been raised in the same church denomination as I had been. He had spent many years counseling ministers, missionaries, and their families. Dr. Foster was uniquely qualified to understand where I was coming from, and how I could best adjust to spending the rest of my life in prison.

My initial interviews with Dr. Westrick and Dr. Foster were relatively short but extremely important. Although I did not know it at the time, the doctors had to decide if I was mentally competent to live in the general prison population. Had they assessed me as suicidal or mentally unstable, I would have been placed in Unit One, a unit where inmates with mental problems were incarcerated.

I was taken to Building Two, which was a large, two-story structure that housed the general prison population. Once inside, I was escorted up a stairwell to the second floor. At the top of the stairs, I saw a guard station. The officials led me down the corridor to what I would come to know as "my wing."

The prison official ushered me into the office of a man named Sam Houston, the unit manager, the ultimate authority in Building Two. He was a big man who wore glasses and smiled easily, but despite his jovial demeanor, it was clear that he was not a man to be tangled with. He greeted me warmly and then in a businesslike manner said, "Sit down, Jim. I want to talk to you." Mr. Houston then proceeded to give me a talk concerning survival at Rochester. His advice was as close to being a fatherly lecture as one ever gets in prison. He instructed me to beware of predatory individuals. "There are people here who will try to take advantage of you in every way imaginable," he warned.

I could tell by talking to Sam Houston that he was a man who went strictly by the rules, but he also let me know that if I played by the rules, he would protect me as he would any man in his unit. I appreciated Sam's wisdom and advice, but I was still in a traumatized state and not functioning normally, so I simply sat silently in his office, my shoulders hunched over, awaiting my next order.

Finally, Mr. Houston said, "Come on, Jim. I'll introduce you to your cellmates." Mr. Houston had already selected my cell, across from the shower and right around the corner from his office. We walked out of Sam's office and turned the corner. Just then, we nearly banged into an inmate who was hurrying up the hall in the opposite direction. The man was wearing shorts, T-shirt, and tennis shoes. He looked like an athlete on his way to a game. In one lithe movement, he steered his body out of the path of Sam Houston and me. "Excuse me, sir," he said in Houston's general direction. But he was looking at me as he spoke. "Hi!" he called enthusiastically.

"That is Tom Brandon," Houston explained. "I'll introduce you to him more formally tomorrow. It might be good for the two of you to get to know one another."

The cell was a narrow room about the size of my walk-in closet at home. It was originally designed to house one human being, but now four men were living in that small space. In addition to the two sets of bunk beds, it had a small desk, a commode, and a tall clothes closet with room enough for two or three outfits per person. The cell was so small that if all four men in the cell stood up at once, they would bump heads. Sam Houston explained to me that all new arrivals at Rochester are placed in a four-man cell. Through good behavior, in two years, an inmate could earn the privilege of being in a two-man cell.

Houston introduced me to my "cellies"—my three new cellmates. One of the men, Bob Grayson, was a pharmacist and owned a drugstore. He looked to be about my age.

Shawn was a "good ole boy," a down-home, country fellow in his early twenties. The third man, Billy B., was a young, heavy-set, good-natured fellow. They were a friendly bunch of guys.

When I first entered the room, we immediately began making small talk, just getting to know one another. One of the men was from Minnesota, so I said, "Well, do you know where International Falls is? That's where my wife, Tammy Faye, was born and grew up."

The man replied, "Oh, yeah, of course I know where International Falls is. I grew up not far from there. International Falls is the icebox of the nation. It gets to forty below zero there in the winter."

I told him, "I know what you mean. Once I pulled Tammy Faye on a sled and almost burned my lungs out from sucking in the frigid air." The guys laughed good-naturedly.

The farm boy talked about Minnesota's short growing season. "My dad always said, 'Summer comes on the Fourth of July; it also leaves on the Fourth of July.'"

I told the men, "When I used to introduce Tammy Faye in churches I told the congregations that the reason Tammy Faye was so short was because they had such a short growing season in International Falls!" The guys really cracked up at that.

"Hey, Bakker," one of the guys called. "I saw you on TV tonight. I watched you get out of the plane."

"Oh, really? I didn't see any cameras."

"Yep. They were there. It looked like they must have been bouncing around a lot."

"They must have been shooting from far away." I explained, "When you use a telephoto lens from a distance, it is hard to hold the camera still enough. The distance magnifies even the slightest move of the camera."

"It must be nice to have all that attention," the younger fellow piped up. "I'd like to get on TV."

"Not me," I mumbled.

"Yeah, we were kinda expecting you," the heavy-set kid said. "Matter of fact, we knew even before you were found guilty that you were coming here!" The room erupted in laughter at that.

All three of my cellmates smoked in our cell. I had been assigned an upper bunk, and as I lay in my bed that night, cigarette smoke curled up all around me. I have never used tobacco products, and my system is extremely sensitive to smoke. Yet I didn't want to complain. I understood that I was in a far different environment than the one with which I was accustomed. For the most part Heritage USA was a smoke-free environment. Now it was extremely difficult for me to breathe in a room that looked as though it had been socked in by a dense London fog.

Even more irritating than the smoke surrounding me was the language that permeated the prison air. Almost every other word I heard was obscene. I am not implying that the language was merely offensive—it was a cesspool. I had never in my life heard such talk. The most crushing curses were those that incorporated the name of Jesus Christ. Growing up in a Christian family as I did, my dad once literally washed my mouth out with Palmolive soap for saying "Gee whiz." Dad always said that "Gee" was a short way of saying "Jesus," and we should never use the name of Jesus without respect.

In prison, hearing the Lord's name used as a curse word bruised my soul. I could hardly stand it. Any time I heard someone use the Lord's name in a derogatory manner, I silently prayed, "Oh, Jesus. Please forgive us." Even in the sluggish mental condition in which I was living, the name of Jesus retained all its beauty, majesty, and power. Although I was emotionally battered to the point that I had begun doubting God's love for me, somewhere deep in my heart I still believed that Jesus was as good as His word. He had promised never to leave me or forsake me, and I knew Jesus was not above going into prison to be with me.

Most of my life I had been surrounded by people who did not use profane language. Rarely did I hear anyone using Jesus' name as a curse, or using vile terms for excrement, sexual intercourse, or disparaging comments about someone's parentage.

Men in prison were not purposely being crude. Many of them spoke respectfully around me, and those who frequented our cell often apologized when they swore in front of me, especially if they used the name of Christ. For many prisoners, using vulgar language was not a conscious choice; profanity was simply the vocabulary of prison and the streets.

Nevertheless, as I lay on my bunk that first night in Rochester prison with the swirling smoke enveloping me and the sludge of language inundating me, I thought, *I must be in hell.*

I had been traveling all day and was feeling sweaty and soiled so I decided to take a shower. I hopped down from my bunk, removed my clothes, and wrapped a towel around my waist. I started walking barefoot across the hallway toward the shower room when suddenly a huge black man roared at me, "Stop! Stop! You can't do that!"

I whirled around in terror, thinking, *Oh, no! What did I do wrong?*

The man walked up to me and pointed at my feet. "You can't take a shower in your bare feet."

"Why not?"

"You'll get the worst case of athlete's feet you've ever seen, and who knows what else!"

"I don't have any shower shoes." All I had were the clothes that were given to me when I checked into the prison and the blue canvas shoes.

"Wait a minute. I have an extra pair." Before I had time to point out the obvious disparity between our shoe sizes, the man bounded down the hallway toward his cell. He returned in a minute or so, carrying a pair of used shower shoes . . . size humongous! I ordinarily wear a size seven-and-a-half shoe. This man must have worn at least a size fourteen!

"Here, give these a try," he said. "They're a little big, but they'll keep you from getting some sort of disease. You can keep them."

A little big? I slid my toes up toward the thong. I still had room for another person's foot on the back of the flip-flop!

I was grateful for the man's kindness, and I told him so, as I flipped and flopped toward the shower stalls, my feet sounding like a seal.

The Minnesota prison had private shower stalls with white rubber curtains that could be pulled shut in each stall. The stalls allowed more privacy than those I had used in Talladega. I stepped inside the stall and turned the water on full blast, as hot as I could stand it. I stood for a long time in the stall. I did not want to get out.

After my shower, I walked back to my cell. Bob the pharmacist was reading a book and smoking. Billy B. was lying on his bunk, listening to some music on a radio with a headset in his ears. Federal prison rules did not allow cassette or CD players, phonographs, televisions, personal computers, or any other electronic equipment. The only link to the outside world we were allowed to have in our cells was a small, battery-operated radio like the one Billy B. was using. There were no blaring boom boxes in the prison. The radios could only be used with headsets.

"Where did you get that?" I asked Billy, wondering if it was legal.

"In the commissary," Billy B. answered loudly since he had not removed his headset. I determined that I wanted to get one of those radios as soon as possible.

"But I have no money," I yelled so Billy could hear me.

"Get it from your old lady!" Billy replied.

"Can we have money in here?"

Billy lifted the headset off one ear, still listening to the music as he spoke to me. "No, but you can have it sent to your commissary account."

"I didn't know I had a commissary account."

Billy B. explained: "You need to go get your picture taken over at R & D, and they'll give you a card that looks like a credit card. You can't even buy a candy bar here without that card. Then you get a commissary slip that will list what items you are able to buy. You turn that in at the commissary window and they'll deduct your purchases from your account. You can shop at the commissary once a week on your assigned day. If you miss your time, you won't be able to get anything until the next week."

"Thanks, Billy. It sure seems like a lot of trouble just to buy a radio."

Billy nodded, already lost again in his music.

Later Tom Brandon, the man I had nearly bumped into in the hall with Sam Houston earlier that day, stopped by to see me in my cell. "How do you like the place so far?" he quipped, with a sparkle in his eye.

"I'm not sure," I answered glumly. "My head feels like I'm in a fog."

"Yeah, we've all known that feeling," Tom tried to reassure me. "Anything you need?" Tom glanced around the room. "Well, let me put it this way, is there anything you *don't* need?"

I liked Tom instantly. His upbeat attitude and his sardonic sense of humor piqued my interest. I would never have guessed that he was a former medical doctor and a recovering alcoholic who had lost his practice and wound up in prison in one fell swoop.

"Well, I could use some stamps. But I don't have any money. Is there anywhere I can get some stamps around here?"

"I don't think so. Not without money," Tom laughed. "They don't give you anything here. You have to earn it. But don't worry. I think I have some stamps in my cell. I'll be right back."

Tom returned a few minutes later with a book of stamps. "I'll loan you these till you get some," he said with a smile. "Here, take these too." Tom handed me a pair of blue tennis shorts. "I noticed that you don't have any clothes yet. Have you told your little sweetie to send you two outfits? Otherwise you'll be wearing prison khakis day and night. During the day, the prison requires us to wear khakis, but they let us wear our own clothes at night around here. Anyhow, you can have these shorts to get you started. Wear 'em with a T-shirt and you will be right in style."

I went to bed early that night and every night during the early weeks of my prison life. I wanted to anesthetize myself, maybe sleep away my troubles. Our room was in such an active area of the wing, though, it was difficult to get any sleep. Right outside my door, guys were running numbers and devising sports pools. Not wanting to get into trouble, I soon learned to block out any overheard conversations. I did not want to guess who was doing what when it came to illegal activities. Nor did I try to match voices heard in the hall with those I heard elsewhere. I just wanted to ignore anything or anybody that might be a potential "con."

Sometimes it was impossible to avoid hearing about covert activities. Once when I was trying to get some rest, I overheard a conversation several guys were having about new bank alarms and supposedly burglar-proof systems. They had already figured how to circumvent the complicated wiring and tripping devices in the alarms. One man sounded as though he could easily have been a college professor as he instructed the others how to defeat the supposedly fail-safe alarm systems. I had always heard that prisons were "schools of crime," and now I understood why.

I hated to do it, but I knew I needed to call Tammy Faye for some money. I needed to buy stamps, toiletries, pens, paper, food items, and shower shoes . . . and I definitely wanted one of those radios like Billy's. This was the first time in thirty years of marriage that I had been forced to ask Tammy to help me financially. The last time I had asked Tammy for money was when I had borrowed the money from her to make the down payment on her engagement ring.

Now as I contemplated calling and asking her to send money when she had so little to support herself, our struggling ministry, and our son, I really despised myself. I thought, *Jim Bakker, you have really sunk a long way.*

I called Tammy Faye the next day and told her where I was and what it was like at the Rochester prison. I explained to her why I needed some money. I asked her to send my blue jeans and my favorite jeans shirt, a pair of black slacks, a pair of black dress shoes, my tennis shoes, a sweat suit, and the shirt and sweater that Fran and Herb Moore had given me. That was the limit of personal clothing allowed by the prison. Tammy assured me that she would send the clothes and the money as soon as she received the necessary paperwork from the prison.

From then on, we talked by telephone every day for about an hour throughout the first two years of my prison experience. Tammy Faye's love, prayers, and optimistic attitude helped carry me through the tough transition period. She was always upbeat and cheerful when she talked to me, even when she was exhausted and emotionally drained, as she was during that first phone call from Rochester.

I would soon have a job inside the prison. My starting pay would be eleven cents an hour. It was not an accident, I now believe, that the job would involve Tom Brandon.

Sam Houston called me into his office. We talked briefly about how I was adapting to my new surroundings. Then he called Tom Brandon into his office.

"Doc," he said, "I want you to teach Jim Bakker how to clean toilets."

Officially, Sam Houston assigned me the job of being an orderly, a part of the support staff who helped keep the entire medical and prison facility functioning. Specifically, Tom's and my duties were to clean all the public toilets, sinks, and showers on our wing of the second floor of Building Two. Tom did not really have to teach me much about toilet cleaning. It is not exactly rocket science, after all. Moreover, I had been an orderly while working at North Central Bible College when I had been a student there. Cleaning the bathrooms in the dormitory was part of my job.

I did not have to clean any toilets in inmates' cells. Those were the responsibility of the inmates living in their cells. But the bathrooms and showers that we all used in common were my responsibility. And I went after it with a vengeance. In Tom's inimitable way, he bragged, "Why, our toilets are so clean you could eat a Caesar's salad out of them!"

Word leaked out quickly that Jim Bakker, former president of PTL, was now cleaning toilets in prison. Many people took strange delight in the image of me doing one of the most demeaning jobs on earth.

Actually, I didn't really mind cleaning toilets. To me, it was not a degrading job—messy, but not degrading. Someone had to do it. Beyond that, there was at least one valuable fringe benefit. Every morning after the men on our floor left for their various work duties—every prisoner who can physically function works in prison—I could do my job well and still have plenty of time for reading, writing, or doing whatever I wanted before the rest of the guys returned after lunch. Tom Brandon and I often joked that we were not simply toilet cleaners, we were "porcelain experts"!

Having a friend like Tom really helped. I was beginning to settle into my new environment—nobody ever gets used to prison—but I was still waking up every morning in despair and denial. I simply could not understand what I was doing in prison. Beyond that, I was living in constant apprehension, never knowing whom I could trust. Who were the "good guys" and who were the "bad guys" in this place? I was about to meet one of the bad guys . . . and he was not an inmate.

14

Miracle in the Airwaves

I COULD HARDLY WAIT TO GET TO THE OFFICER'S STATION to get my commissary slips. Securing a radio similar to Billy's had become almost an obsession. My clothes, shoes, and money from home had not arrived yet, but I wanted to be ready to go to the commissary as soon as I could. After all, Billy B. had said if I missed my assigned time, I would have to wait another week to get the items I needed.

I had changed out of my khakis into a white prison T-shirt and socks, the tennis shorts that Tom had given me, and my blue canvas shoes.

I had gotten my commissary slips and was walking back toward my cell when I heard a guard's booming voice. "Bakker! Come here!"

We were not allowed to run in prison but I came close to it as I scurried back to the officer's station.

"What are you doing with those shoes on?" he screamed at me.

"Well, they gave them to me. . . . "

"You're not allowed to have those shoes in here," he bellowed.

"Well," I stammered, "they gave them to me at Talla—"

"Give me your shoes," he demanded. Another guard seated next to the one talking smirked as though he was trying to keep from laughing.

I took off my shoes and held them in my hand.

"Throw them here," he ordered. I tossed the shoes onto the table.

The guard crossed his arms over his chest as he glowered at me standing there in my socks. Finally he said, "Don't you have any other shoes?"

"Yes, sir. I have a pair of black, high-top, work shoes." The steel-toed high-tops were given to me on my first day of work duty.

"Go put them on," he ordered. "Put these shoes back on, go get your work shoes, and bring these blue ones back to me."

I was petrified! I was committed to being a model prisoner. I did not want to get into trouble about anything. This was prison, after all, a strange, hostile environment in which I had already been stripped of my sense of self-worth and personal security. I was scared that the guards would put me in the hole, and memories of Butner still gave me nightmares.

I hurried back to my cell, put on my black work shoes, and returned to the officer's station carrying my blue canvas shoes. The officers were laughing when I reached their desk. They quickly wiped the smiles off their faces as the guard turned to talk to me again.

"Throw the blue shoes right over here," he nodded toward the table. I tossed the shoes onto the table. "Now get out of here," he roared.

I am still hard pressed to explain why I was so traumatized by this incident. To some people it may seem to have been an insignificant event, but to me, in a fragile condition, having just undergone a nervous breakdown a few weeks before, and now facing forty-five years of prison, the officer's head game could easily have sent me over the brink.

I walked back to my cell, literally shaking. I climbed into my bunk and turned my face toward the wall. I could not help thinking that just a few years ago I had employed almost three thousand people and had an annual budget of well over $150 million, and now I was being humiliated by a prison guard over a pair of cheap shoes. I began to realize that this episode was all about power.

Officer Jack Ensley personified the worst aspects of prison life. He became my personal bogeyman, popping up in my life and always intent on messing with my mind. One day, I was moving from one cell to another and had a pile of books and other possessions stacked on a cart. Officer Ensley was not even the guard on duty in our wing but happened to walk by just as I was pushing the cart out of my cell.

"Hold it!" he shouted. "Bakker has too many personal belongings there. You better do an inventory count on him," he called to the guard on duty. Ensley glowered at me.

I did not have too many personal belongings, but there was no use in protesting. No doubt Officer Ensley would have been delighted to find an excuse to throw me in the hole. When the guard on duty arrived, he bowed to Ensley's bluster and consented to do an inventory of my belongings. As soon as Officer Ensley went on his way, the guard on duty turned to me and whispered, "Forget it, Bakker."

Another day, I was walking back to my cell and I saw Officer Ensley and a work cadre of four or five inmates working in the hallway. I tried to walk by inconspicuously, but Ensley spied me. "Bakker!" he bellowed. "Come over here and clean these panels." I walked back to where the officer was standing. He was pointing to a stack of stainless-steel panels that had been removed from the interior of the prison phone booths in our hallway and were now spread out on the floor. The backsides of the panels looked as though they had not been cleaned in decades.

The prison phone booths represented one of the few areas of semiprivacy in prison, and it was known that inmates often masturbated in the booths during phone calls with their wives or girlfriends. Although the outsides of the panels were cleaned regularly, the inside panels were covered with filth and grime, spittle, and dried semen that had apparently caked on them for years. I nearly gagged. Nevertheless, I maintained my composure, went over to my mop closet, gathered my cleaning materials, and put on a pair of rubber gloves.

I took the panels into the bathroom and started scrubbing. I used every kind of disinfectant available. I made a conscious effort to accept this demeaning job and do it as unto the Lord. I forced myself to concentrate on Christ rather than Officer Ensley. I scrubbed and scrubbed. And when I was done, the stainless-steel panels shone like mirrors. I took the panels back to Officer Ensley and lined them up against the wall.

Ensley stared at the shining panels in disbelief. Then he looked back at me and said gruffly, "Bakker, that's all."

From that day on, anytime I saw Officer Ensley walking across the prison compound, I turned and went in the opposite direction.

"Jim. Jim! Come on, little buddy. It's time to get up. I can't clean these toilets without you." I rolled over and pulled the covers higher over my face. I hated it when Tom Brandon called me "little buddy."

"Let's go, little buddy. We're going to be late," Tom called again as he pulled the covers off me. I reluctantly rolled off my bunk. "Come on," said Tom. "If we can get our work done quickly enough, we can go over to the recreation building to see if your money has come in yet. There is a machine in the hall outside the commissary door. You can put your commissary card into the machine and it will tell you how much you have in your account. Even though the commissary is closed right now, the machine will tell you if something has come into your account. I've been wanting to show you around over there anyhow. The rec building has a workout room, a library, a place to do leather crafts and ceramics. You can sign up for college courses, all sorts of things."

Tom and I hurried through our toilet-cleaning responsibilities and got to the commissary by midmorning. I ran my card through the scanner, and to my delight, my account showed that I had one hundred dollars in it!

Later that evening, I skipped going to mainline for chow because I was so excited about getting my radio at the commissary. I thought I would be first in line, but by the time I got there, at least fifty men were ahead of me.

The commissary was like a small grocery store. It stocked toiletries, postage stamps, socks, tennis shoes, T-shirts and running shorts, tobacco products, inexpensive watches, cans of tuna fish, rice, picante sauce, corn chips and potato chips, fruit, powdered milk, oatmeal, soft drinks, cookies, and a wide variety of other products. The commissary had queue lines that reminded me of the way Disney World lines people up to get into the attractions. Back and forth, back and forth, until you finally got on the ride.

As I got to the entrance, I noticed something unusual. A large window separated the inmates from the products that were for sale. The inmates turned in their grocery lists by inserting them through a narrow slot. Inmates working inside the commissary retrieved the lists and then filled the orders, which were delivered out a chute where each prisoner bagged his groceries with his bag, usually a laundry bag. We were allowed to "buy" one roll of quarters, one roll of dimes, and one roll of nickels to be used in the vending machines on our wing and in the visiting room. The bill was deducted from our commissary accounts.

On my first visit to the commissary, I purchased some stamps, enough for myself and enough to repay Tom. I also bought a pair of shower shoes in my size, some oatmeal, food snacks, and the main object of my shopping spree—the battery-operated radio, batteries sold separately.

As soon as I got the radio back to my cell, I put the batteries in it, placed the headset in my ears, and turned it on. I was stunned! Suddenly my ears were filled with rapturous sound! On the one hand, hearing the music made me realize how bleak my existence had become in such a short time. On the other hand, it was like finding a rose in the midst of hell. Inside the fences, everyone played the same sour note, the music of prison life, the sound of the living dead.

That night, as required by prison rules, one of my cellmates turned the ceiling lights out at ten o'clock as usual. I climbed up onto my top bunk and awaited the ten o'clock count, one of the five daily, mandatory, counts of inmates conducted by prison personnel to make sure all prisoners were still present. Other counts took place at midnight, 2:00 A.M., 5:00 A.M., and 4:00 P.M.

At the Rochester prison, there was no official time when prisoners had to go to bed. An inmate could stay up all night if he so desired, as long as he was in his cell for the counts. But for many inmates the workday began at 7:30 A.M., so as soon as the main lights went down at ten o'clock, it was a signal for many prisoners that it was time to start getting ready for bed, especially since for the ten o'clock count, it was not necessary to stand, or even to be awake.

On the other hand, at four o'clock each day, every prisoner in the federal prison system across the United States must stand up next to his or her bed to be counted. The four o'clock "holy count" is the only one of the five counts for which all prisoners must be in their cells, awake, and standing. At least once a day, the federal prison system wants to know that all of the men and women confined within its walls are still alive.

Although the overhead lights were out, my three cellmates had small gooseneck reading lights attached to their beds so they could continue reading without disturbing their cellies. The reading lights were legal and available in the commissary, but I had been so interested in securing my radio, I hadn't given a thought to how I was going to see it in the dark. Now alone with my thoughts, I lay on my side, faced the wall, and cupped the tiny radio in my hands as though it were a priceless treasure.

The man in the bunk below me was smoking and scouring a newspaper, looking for sports scores. The pale glow of his reading light and the rising smoke shrouded my bunk.

Soon a guard checked to see that my cellmates and I were still there, all prisoners present and accounted for. The heavy cell door made a *whooosh!* sound as the guard closed it behind him. I hated that sound. It was as though all the air was being sucked out of the closet-sized room.

The closed door had become a symbol of my life. As I lay there that night, I felt as though all the life had been drained out of me. I didn't know if God cared about me anymore; I could not feel His presence in my life. I wondered if He had written me off, if He had simply said good-bye to me. At my lowest times, I even doubted that God existed.

Oh, sure, somewhere deep within the recesses of my heart and mind, I knew that God was still alive and well. But wherever He was, I could not find Him. Whatever He was saying, if anything at all, I could not hear His voice. I honestly did not know where God was.

I began to think, *Maybe one of the things that have been said about me are true. Maybe the well-known preacher was right when he had proclaimed, "Jim Bakker is through. He will never preach again."*

In the semidarkness of the room—which seemed bright when compared to the complete darkness of my soul—I fumbled with the dial to my transistorized treasure chest. I put on the headset and began turning the dial back and forth, scanning the frequencies. The little radio was emitting nothing but static. I began to wonder if perhaps the radio was defective when suddenly the static cleared and I heard a familiar tune. And then I heard a familiar voice!

It was the voice of my wife, Tammy Faye! And she was singing the song we had used as our theme song at PTL, the same song that Ron Blackwood and the prison choir had sung in the Talladega Prison chapel service—"You Can Make It."

In stunned silence, I lay on my prison bunk bed and listened as my wife sang these words:

> You may face some of life's toughest trials.
> You may walk some long, lonely miles,
> But trav'lin' with you, you will find a friend,
> And there won't be a battle you and God can't win.
>
> If there's someone who has crushed your dreams,
> The things you want may never seem to happen, it seems.
> Every single doubt your Father will dispel.
> You're His child, there's no way He'll let you fail.
>
> You can make it. You can make it.
> This trial you're going through,
> God's gonna show ya just what to do.
> You can make it. You can make it.
> I don't care what's going wrong.
> God won't let it last too long.
> You're not in this thing alone;
> You can make it.[1]

Amazingly, as the last refrain of the song finished, the radio station faded out. I tried my best to tune it in again—I wanted to know where this music was coming from—but to no avail. For the remainder of the night, I heard nothing but static at that location on the radio dial.

To some people, this event might seem to have been mere coincidence. To me it was a miracle. I had experienced many miracles over the years. I used to laughingly say that I needed a miracle every day just to keep the PTL television ministry alive. But since the loss of PTL and Heritage USA, it seemed that all miracles in my life had ceased and God had turned

His back on me. Looking back, I now realize that hearing Tammy Faye's song on the radio was one of the more significant miracles in my life.

Few if any radio stations were playing Tammy Faye's albums at that time. She and I were outcasts on the religious airwaves and the subjects of ridicule on secular broadcasting systems. It had been more than two and a half years since our departure from PTL, and most of Tammy's records had long since been confiscated by the new "caretakers" of the ministry. And "You Can Make It" was not exactly on heavy rotation at most radio stations.

Yet out of the static, all the way from a station I later discovered was located somewhere in Georgia, as I lay in my prison bunk in Rochester, Minnesota, I heard the message, "You can make it." To me, it was as though God was saying, "You are going to make it, Jim. I will never leave you or forsake you. And here's a little miracle to help remind you." Sadly, in my emotional pain and devastation, I did not perceive the full impact of this miracle until nearly six years later.

I could hardly believe what I had heard. I sat up in bed and excitedly told my cellmates, "I just heard my wife singing on the radio!"

"Oh, yeah? That's great," one of the men replied. The men responded politely but indifferently. Their lack of enthusiasm doused my excitement over hearing Tammy Faye singing the song. Hearing Tammy Faye's voice so clearly in my headset reminded me that I was not at home in our bed with Tammy with our children sleeping down the hall. I was in a smoke-filled prison cell with three other inmates. I had little hope of ever spending another night at home with my family. I was no longer a man of faith and power; I was a man of utter despair and hopelessness. At that moment, I felt like a scared little boy.

But things were about to change.

15

Surprises

I SPENT MUCH OF THE MONTH OF NOVEMBER 1989 GETTING acclimated to my new surroundings and lifestyle at the Rochester Federal Medical Center. Each day my routine was basically the same—up early, skip breakfast or eat something purchased from the commissary, then clean the rest rooms shortly after 7:30 A.M. when the 192 men who lived on our floor left for their work assignments. Once I completed my chore of cleaning up after the men had used the rest rooms and showers, I was on call to the guard on duty to do whatever jobs needed done on our floor.

During those first evenings, I did a lot of talking with inmates who dropped by my cell. Many of my visitors had some sort of spiritual background and some were genuine Christians. Some men wanted to know about my experiences at PTL. Others wanted to talk theology. I tried to enter into the conversations as wholeheartedly as possible. These were, after all, my new neighbors, and I did not want to be rude.

Throughout my life I have always been an extremely shy, private person. Because people saw me on television, they assumed that I was a gregarious, outgoing, spontaneous personality. Nothing could be further from the truth. In prison, my shyness, coupled with my extremely low self-esteem, often caused men to think that I was aloof and unfriendly.

Many men tried their best to involve me in the warp and woof of prison life. Tom Brandon kept telling me that the guys really wanted to be my friends. I could not believe anyone wanted to associate with Jim

Bakker, the man they had read and heard so many negative things about, a man even church leaders had castigated and declared as no good.

The highlight of my day was my daily telephone conversation with Tammy Faye. I would call her in the morning after I had finished my work. Tammy Faye always answered my collect phone calls in her perky voice no matter what sort of difficulty she was encountering herself. She was a tremendous encouragement to me.

We were not only marriage partners, we were best friends, so we talked about all sorts of things. Every day I described for her in as much detail as I could all the things that I was doing, the men I had met, and the concerns I had. She told me about the church and her responsibilities as the pastor of the congregation in Orlando. Frequently she would tell me what she was planning to speak about in church on Sunday and we would discuss the sermon on the phone. The spiritual insights we shared were a source of inspiration to me at that time.

I asked Tammy Faye to send what I called my "Crisis Bible," the one I had used in the two years after I had lost PTL up to the time I had gone to prison. Unfortunately, in the flurry of activity surrounding my hasty departure from the federal courthouse in Charlotte, the Bible had been misplaced, and Tammy Faye could not find it. She promised to send me a *PTL Parallel Bible*, a dual translation Bible, the same as those we had sent out to many of our supporters during our best days at Heritage.

In order to receive anything from the outside, I had to have permission from the prison authorities. I went to Sam Houston and asked him what I needed to do to have a Bible sent in by my wife.

"You must have a written permission form signed by the chaplain," Mr. Houston informed me.

The next day during my free time, I went to visit the chaplain. We talked briefly and I told him my desire to have a Bible sent in from home. He readily agreed to sign the form. He explained that the Bible had to be sent through the prison chapel. In the meantime, he gave me a prison Bible to use.

We talked a bit further, and he stammered uneasily, "I'm always here if you need me, Jim." Slowly but surely, it began to sink in to me that the man did not want me to attend the chapel services. "It would be better if you did not come around the chapel," he suggested. I got the message.

Several years later, I learned that he had been given specific orders by his superiors to make sure that Jim Bakker did not do any preaching in prison. He was afraid that if I became involved in the chapel program, eventually I might take advantage of an opportunity to speak, and then both of us would be in trouble. The best way he knew to avoid the problem was to keep me away from the chapel.

In my current state of depression, I was not all that enthused about attending chapel services anyhow. I still loved the Lord, and my heart was tender toward God, but I felt that because some ministers had worked so hard to discredit me, I really wanted no part of organized religion.

True to his word, the chaplain received my Bible from Tammy Faye and made sure I got it. He called me to his office, and there on his desk was the *PTL Parallel Bible*. It was like being reunited with a dear, old friend. To this day that prison Bible is my most prized earthly possession.

In 1989, the American public was becoming much more concerned and aware of the health hazards associated with using tobacco products. And many government agencies pressed for restrictions on smoking in all federally operated buildings, including federal prisons.

Since my arrival at Rochester, I had been living with three cellmates who smoked almost constantly. I never complained, but it bothered me, and my friend Tom Brandon knew it. "We have to get you out of that cell before you choke to death," Doc often said, only half-joking.

One evening as I was resting in my smoke-filled cell, Tom came rushing in to see me. "I need you outside in the hall right away."

Once out in the hall and away from my cell, Tom began talking excitedly. "We have just found out that there is going to be an open bunk in our cell. One of my cellies is getting transferred tomorrow. As soon as he is out the door, you need to be in Sam Houston's office, requesting a transfer to a room with nonsmokers, our room to be exact."

"Can I do that?" I asked Tom in amazement.

"Sure you can," Tom replied. "It's the new nonsmoking rule coming down out of Washington. Prison policies are going to be changing and the prison officials know it. If you request to be put in a room with nonsmokers, the prison will comply if it is possible. Get your room-transfer request into Mr. Houston's office. These bunks do not stay open long."

The next day, as soon as Tom's former cellie had vacated the room, I was knocking on Mr. Houston's office door. Sam Houston was happy to transfer me to Dr. Brandon's cell. By the end of the day, I was bunking with Tom and two other nonsmokers.

One of the first inmates to welcome me to my new smoke-free environment was a jolly, rotund man named Gleason West.

Gleason stopped by our cell almost every day. He was always asking me to sign things for him, pictures, news articles about me that he had salvaged from newspapers and magazines, or anything else that was loosely associated with me. Gleason was especially fond of bringing me the more outlandish tabloid papers that often contained fabricated articles about me.

Some of the stories, although they were total fabrications, still hurt. For instance, from the first day I went to prison, the tabloids ran stories "reporting" that Tammy and I were divorcing. We were not. I loved Tammy Faye, and we talked by phone every day.

One article said that my mother and dad had no place to live and were out begging in the streets because of me. In reality, Tammy's mother and my parents were living in homes that we had purchased for them while we were still at Heritage USA.

Another article defamed my dear daughter by "reporting" that to help finance my legal appeal, Tammy Sue had agreed to pose nude in *Playboy*. Anyone who knows my daughter knows that she would never consent to such a thing regardless of the reason or the amount of money offered.

In a strange sort of way, inside the prison the rags actually tended to give me more credibility with the inmates. In many cases, the men read the articles and knew for a fact that what they were reading were out-and-out lies. For instance, one popular tabloid ran headlines: "Jim Bakker Escape Plot Foiled." In a two-page spread, the article purported that a Colombian drug cartel had attempted a daring escape plot that had helicopters landing at the Rochester prison in hopes of sweeping me off into the sunset. The article included sketches of the prison walls, complete with gun turrets at each end.

The inmates howled with laughter. Not only did they know that no such helicopter raid had ever taken place, they were quick to point out that the Rochester prison does not even have gun turrets.

Another article that got a big response declared that Jim Bakker was standing on his bunk, preaching to inmates. Considering that I had the top bunk and the ceiling was only three or four feet above my head, that would have been quite an accomplishment!

Most of the inmates at Rochester tried to protect me from such inane articles. They often hid the tabloids when I was around or tried to keep me from seeing them. They recognized that even though I knew the articles were ridiculous, they often sent me into prolonged states of depression.

In contrast to most of the inmates who attempted to shield me from the rag mags, Gleason would bring them to my cell and want me to sign them! I signed some of the articles and pictures he brought—no doubt they will turn up again somewhere—but I refused to sign the more salacious articles. Nor would I sign the *Playboy* photos of Jessica Hahn that Gleason and other men brought to my cell for me to sign.

It was Gleason who introduced me to one of the true "delicacies" of prison life—prison pizza. Actually it is not a delicacy, nor is it really pizza. It is more like deluxe nachos, and while the recipe may vary from prison to prison, some basic ingredients are usually included.

The pizza was prepared in a cardboard box—the biggest box that would fit inside the microwave oven. The base of the pizza was a layer of tortilla chips. On top of that we spread whatever was available from the prison commissary at the time—tomatoes, green peppers, and any sort of meat we could obtain. Occasionally we were able to get actual pepperoni, making the pizza taste almost normal. For the weight conscious, I often made my prison pizza with pieces of canned chicken. We doused the entire conglomeration with picante sauce.

Atop the growing mountain of ingredients, we placed plenty of cheese, whatever type was available from the commissary. String cheese was our favorite because it could be pulled apart in strips and melted down over the other ingredients. We often used jalapeno cheese.

Once all the ingredients were included, another row of chips was added and the process began again. The prison pizza recipe was constantly in flux; it changed with the resources that could be obtained by the person making the concoction. Once the mountain of ingredients was near the top of the box, a final layer of cheese was spread across. The pizza was then inserted into the microwave and usually took about twenty minutes to cook.

A much quicker, though less tasty, way of producing a prison pizza was to throw all the ingredients into a large plastic garbage bag. We then melted gobs of cheese in the microwave oven, and simply poured the hot cheese into the sack and shook it. Voila! Instant prison pizza!

Much of the "social life" of prison as well as any special celebrations or going-away parties revolved around prison pizza. Just as people outside of prison might have a dinner party and invite some friends over for a meal, inmates invited their friends over to their cells for a pizza party.

To my surprise, soon after my arrival at Rochester, I began to receive an unusually large amount of mail. Some of the cards and letters I received were merely addressed to "Jim Bakker, Minnesota." One letter was addressed "Jim Bakker, Federal Pen." The most amazing delivery was a letter addressed simply to "Jim Bakker." The postal system obviously knew where to find me. Daily mail call was at 4:30 P.M.

It was not necessary to open our mail. The prison staff had already done so, searching for contraband and removing any money that might have been sent to us. When I received a greeting card or letter that had included money, the prison staff took the money out, deposited it in my commissary account, and issued me a yellow slip, notifying me that the deposit had been made. Prisoners were never allowed to receive directly any checks, paper money, or coins.

Immediately after mail call, I went to my cell, climbed into my bunk, and began to read my mail. Even though we talked on the phone every day, I always found a familiar pink, Estee Lauder-perfume-scented envelope from Tammy Faye. I saved my wife's letters to read last, sometimes tucking them under my pillow to read later when things were quiet.

Many of the letters I received were kind and encouraging, but I also received a few vile letters. The hate mail jolted me, especially during my first weeks in prison. I had thought that my enemies would be satisfied that I would probably die in prison. Perhaps some people felt they could say anything they wanted to a convicted prisoner who was locked away.

More than one person wrote to me: "I hope you die in prison."

One wrote, "I hope you get raped by the biggest black man in prison."

Some of the oddest mail I received came from individuals who felt compelled to shred me into tiny pieces and then sign their letters "In Christian love."

The cruelest mail I received came from the same person. This person wrote such vulgar filth in his letters to me, I dare not attempt to describe them. The letters continued throughout my entire stay in prison.

Even though the hate mail was not even 1 percent of the total mail I was receiving, it left the most indelible impression. No matter how many beautiful rabbits you may have, one skunk can leave a lasting impression.

In stark contrast to the hate mail were the hundreds of letters of encouragement and support I began to receive. Many people said they were praying for me. Some even went so far as to express their faith that through some miracle I might be released from prison and restored to Christian ministry. My correspondents had much more faith than I had.

During my phone conversations with Tammy Faye throughout the month of November, she expressed her intention to come to visit me for Thanksgiving. I was elated, but I was also concerned. The media blitz that had surrounded us for the past three years had not yet diminished. For a while it seemed as though I had to report to the warden's office nearly every day to respond to interview requests from around the world. I refused every interview opportunity. I knew, however, that if Tammy Faye showed up at Rochester, the media would follow her every move.

More disconcerting than that, she would be alone, far from home, with no friends or family nearby. I worried about Tammy Faye's safety as well as about where she would stay and how she would get around.

About that time I received a letter from Phil Shaw, a local pastor with the Assemblies of God. The pastor had seen my arrival at Rochester Federal Medical Center on television. I had never met the man in my life. Pastor Shaw wrote kindly and compassionately, "Dear Jim, I am a brother in the Lord. How can I help you?" Pastor Shaw added, "I am an Assemblies of God pastor," and he included his phone number.

My recent experiences with "men of God" caused me to be cautious. Yet as I lay awake in my prison bunk, pondering how I could possibly handle all the details pertaining to Tammy's upcoming visit at Thanksgiving, feelings of helplessness continued to plague my mind. I had always taken care of everything for Tammy and my family. If I couldn't do it myself, I hired someone else to do whatever needed to be done around our home. But now I was unable to help my family at all.

I didn't know where they could stay. I didn't know the city of Rochester, I didn't know the airport or the hotels, and I certainly didn't have an enclave of friends in the area upon which I could call. I did know that everywhere Tammy and the children had gone in recent months, an onslaught of press people soon followed, badgering them for interviews and photographs.

My mind kept turning back to Phil Shaw's letter. Pastor Shaw had offered to help. I wondered if he really meant it. Finally, in desperation about a week before Tammy's planned visit, I decided to call Pastor Shaw. Telephoning the pastor was humiliating in itself since I had to place the call collect because of prison regulations.

When Pastor Shaw spoke into the phone, his voice took me by surprise. He was soft-spoken, articulate, and most of all, extremely kind. I immediately began apologizing to Pastor Shaw for calling him collect.

"Oh, Jim, call anytime; don't worry about calling collect."

I must have sounded like a scared rabbit, because several times in our conversation, Pastor Shaw encouraged me, "Don't hang up on me, Jim. What can I do for you?"

I told him that Tammy was planning to come to Rochester to visit me at Thanksgiving, and I expressed my concern about how she would deal with the media mayhem, where she should stay, how she would get through the airport and into the hotel, and a host of other details.

Pastor Shaw instantly replied, "Don't worry about a thing. I will take care of it."

"Well, if you are too busy, if you could just point me in the right direction. . . ."

"I'll take care of everything. I wouldn't have it any other way. You just relax and let me help you."

Pastor Shaw was so humble and kind. He did not sound the least bit judgmental. Many pastors, some of them quite famous who used to appear regularly on the PTL television network, did not dare to associate with me now that I was a convicted felon. Many of my closest associates and peers had not spoken to me since the day I had lost the PTL television ministry. But Pastor Shaw seemed genuinely interested in helping my family and me. I sensed that the pastor truly had a servant's heart.

I gave Phil Shaw a phone number where he could reach Tammy Faye. The pastor assured me that he would call her the following day and make any necessary arrangements, which he did. Phil arranged for Tammy to stay at the Kahler Hotel, a fine, stately hotel right across from the Mayo Clinic. He visited with the hotel security personnel prior to Tammy's arrival and made special arrangements to get Tammy Faye into her room safely without having to deal with a deluge of media.

Pastor Shaw recruited a group of friends from his church to accompany him in a van to the airport. When Tammy Faye showed up accompanied by Jamie and my sister Donna, the media were waiting for them at the airport. Tammy responded graciously to the press, then Pastor Shaw and his friends quickly ushered my family members into the van and drove them to the hotel. Tammy Faye, Donna, and Jamie stayed in the same room at the Kahler to save money, but also to be able to present a united front to the press if necessary.

On Thursday, November 23, 1989, Phil Shaw drove Tammy Faye, Jamie, and Donna to the prison around 8:30 A.M.

The visitors were searched upon their arrival. The visiting room itself had all the warmth of the mental institution for which it once served. The floor was covered with indoor-outdoor carpet. Video cameras in the ceiling behind dark glass recorded every move anyone made in the room. Approximately twenty low Formica tables lined the room. Four to six white plastic chairs surrounded each table. Adjoining the main visiting room was another room, this one with vending machines. If we wanted anything from the vending area, we had to get our food early in the day and hold on to it until we were ready to eat. Otherwise the vending machines would sell out before visitation time was over.

A microwave oven for heating our vending-machine delicacies and a water fountain sat along the wall opposite the machines. A television was mounted high in the corner at the front of the room. In the far back right corner was a cubicle with a large window so the guards could see inside it. This room was used for legal visits in which inmates and their lawyers could have some measure of privacy within the visitation area.

Outside the two visiting rooms was a paved walking area for inmates and visitors. The walking "yard" was enclosed by a high wooden fence.

The night before, I pressed my clothes with extra care. I wanted to look my best for my wife and family. The last time I had seen Tammy Faye had been at Talladega Prison, several weeks earlier. I could hardly wait to see her again. I was excited to see Jamie and Donna as well.

When I walked through the door, I spotted my family members immediately. I wanted to race to them and embrace them, but I knew I had to check in with a guard first. I walked over to his desk and said, "Inmate Bakker, sir: 07407-058."

He wrote my name and number on his clipboard and nodded. I quickly walked toward the table where Tammy Faye, Jamie, and Donna were waiting for me. They rose to their feet as I approached and we met and embraced in the aisle. It felt so wonderful to kiss and hold my wife. It seemed like an eternity had passed since we had last been together. Other than that, no touching was allowed during visits. When inmates or their family members dared to violate the rules, a guard was quick to remind them that if they wanted to continue to have the privilege of visitation, they had better abide by the regulations. Of course, for the inmates themselves, the threat of "the hole" always loomed large in their minds.

My family members and I spent the next six hours together talking. Tammy Faye tried hard to encourage me. "We're going to lick this thing," she kept saying. Our Thanksgiving dinner consisted of food purchased from the vending machines in the visitation room.

Throughout our visit the room was constantly buzzing around us as family members of other inmates approached us to ask for autographs. Often someone would say to me, "Would you please sign this for my grandmother? She just loves you." Tammy Faye and I signed numerous autographs. I felt rather strange doing it, but most of the people were extremely nice, so I complied. At times, family members of inmates wanted to talk further with Tammy and me, but the guards reminded us that it was against the rules to talk with anyone not on my own visitor list.

Our Thanksgiving visit was the first of many heartrending marathon visits by Tammy Faye and other family members and friends. I was always glad to see them come, but after a few hours together with nothing to do but talk, with no place to go, and no privacy, the visits often were as draining as they were refreshing. I would challenge any husband and wife or parent and child to turn off the television set for a weekend, and do nothing but stay in the same room with each other and talk for six straight hours, three straight days!

Tammy Faye stayed through the Thanksgiving weekend before heading back to Orlando. The moment she stepped outside of the prison, reporters were waiting for her. "How is your husband doing?" one reporter asked.

Tammy Faye replied in her usual upbeat tone, "As well as can be expected. He's a tough man."

I wasn't feeling so tough just then. While Tammy Faye was talking to the media, a guard had ordered me into a small room between the hall and the visiting room.

"Take your clothes off, Bakker," the guard said to me. I peeled off my khakis and prepared for yet another strip search.

It would be Christmas before I would see Tammy Faye again.

CHAPTER

16

The First Christmas

"INMATE BAKKER! COME TO THE OFFICERS' STATION," I heard a guard command.

I immediately dropped my cleaning materials and briskly walked up the hall to where the guard was waiting.

"Decorate this Christmas tree here in the sitting area," he ordered as he pointed to a shabby box containing an artificial Christmas tree and shoved a box of ornaments in my direction. Although I did not say a word and would not have disobeyed his command, I must have shown my reluctance. The guard noticed my pained expression and mellowed just a little. "Do the best you can," he said quietly.

I looked at the box of ornaments—a few colored lights, one short straggly garland, and beat-up ornaments that most people would have given up on years before and put in the garbage. These ornaments were worse than ragtag—they were the ragtag ends of nothing.

The scrawny artificial Christmas tree was worse yet. It was actually an assortment of parts from two separate trees. I began working on it, carefully removing the dilapidated branches from the box and laying them out on the floor, trying to determine where each one went on the tree. It was like putting together a puzzle in which a large number of the pieces were either broken or missing. I assembled the three-legged base, forced the warped pole into the hole, and screwed the pieces together as tightly as I could. The tree was truly pitiful.

I started to string the Christmas lights around the tree. Some of the lights were burnt out, but being the new style lights, the others continued to work. As I wrapped the tree in the shabby lights, I could not help thinking, *God, are You trying to beat me up? Is this some kind of trick You are playing on me? Is this rubbing it in, God?*

The point was not lost on me that our Christmas decorations at Heritage USA had been spectacular. We had won great acclaim and had been listed as one of the top Christmas destinations in America. I remembered the hundreds of trees and their more than a million lights all across the property. The Grand Tree in the lobby of the Grand Hotel was nearly three stories tall. The tree on Main Street had been decorated with elaborate, moving characters.

Now, here I was trying to decorate this poor excuse for a tree with these pathetic lights, many of which did not work. It was like a sadistic joke was being played on me.

The guard ordered another inmate to help me decorate the tree. While I was trying my best to make something decent of the miserable tree, my helper was totally unconcerned about it. He could not understand why I kept trying to find a place where our one garland would look the best. He just wanted to slap the few decorations on the tree and be done with it as soon as possible, but I continued moving the ornaments around, hoping to create a better look, repositioning the bulbs, stretching the garland as far as it would go.

Several of the inmates passed by and cursed. "What are you doin', Bakker, puttin' that tree up like that?" several asked bitterly. More than a few told me in no uncertain terms where I should shove that tree. I was shocked! I could not understand why the men would not welcome any semblance of the joy of Christmas in prison.

I was a person who had always loved everything about Christmas, but suddenly I was confronted with the darker side of my favorite holiday. Of course I was aware that the Thanksgiving and Christmas seasons were hard times for some families and individuals, but in prison I began to realize in a profound way that for many people, the season was not one of rejoicing but one of despair.

Not long after I arrived at Rochester, I received a letter from a woman whose boyfriend was serving a life sentence in prison for committing murder. In an effort to familiarize Tammy Faye and me with the prison mindset, the woman predicted that we would soon start telling the time by Christmases instead of months, days, or years. She was correct. If you were to ask a prisoner who had been incarcerated for fifteen years, "How long have you been in here?" most likely he would respond, "Fifteen Christmases."

For this reason and others, many of the inmates hated that tree and all that it symbolized. They didn't want it there and would have preferred that it be tossed out. Many long-term prisoners have not received a gift or a Christmas card from the outside in years. Others remember their wives and children and what used to be, and they do not want to be reminded of Christmases past. They would prefer to ignore Christmas altogether, which, of course, is impossible, even in prison. The men see and hear Christmas advertisements on the television and radio or see ads in the newspapers and magazines. They cannot escape Christmas, yet for many it is too painful to celebrate the holiday.

I was about to find out why.

I was so excited on Christmas Eve! My new friend Phil Shaw had picked up my family members at the airport and they were planning to visit me on Christmas Day. It was one of the few times Tammy Sue, her husband Doug, and little baby James could come all the way to Minnesota to see me. I had not seen Tammy Sue and her family since I had been escorted out of the federal courthouse in Charlotte. It seemed like ages ago when I had last held baby James in my arms. Ironically, I felt a bit nervous at seeing my family members; it was almost like going on a date when I was a teenager.

Christmas Eve had always been a special time at the Bakker home, but in prison it was just another night. I made it special by preparing for my family's much-anticipated Christmas Day visit. I went to the guard station and exchanged my commissary card for the privilege of borrowing one of the two irons and ironing boards available to the men on our floor. I took the ironing board and iron back to my cell, where I meticulously pressed every wrinkle out of my clothes and ironed creases in my pants and shirt. After I returned the ironing equipment, I went back to my cell and began shining my high-top boots. I wanted to look my best when I "hosted" my family for Christmas dinner tomorrow.

Tammy Faye, Donna, and our children were staying at the beautiful Kahler Hotel, the same place where they had stayed during their Thanksgiving visit. By now, our funds had been thoroughly depleted and Tammy was concerned that the fine hotel was out of her price range. She approached the front desk and asked to speak to the manager. "Do you have any fifty-dollar rooms?" she ventured.

The manager recognized Tammy and smiled kindly. "Well, er . . . let me see what we can do." The manager began punching up something on his computer screen at the registration desk. He scowled momentarily, pushed some more keys, and a broad smile spread across his face. "Yes, this will be just right," he said aloud.

He turned back to Tammy Faye and handed her a key to a large room with two double beds and a roll-away bed for Jamie. "You are welcome here anytime, Mrs. Bakker, at this same rate."

"Oh, thank you very much," Tammy Faye gushed. "God bless you!" From then on, every time Tammy and our family members came to visit me in Rochester, they stayed at the Kahler . . . at the greatly reduced rate.

By the time my family members got into their rooms at the Kahler on Christmas Eve, all the stores were closed. Only the Webber and Judd drugstore in the lobby of the hotel remained open. My family members went to the drugstore late at night and purchased small presents for each other. The drugstore manager gave them some leftover gift wrap and they went back upstairs to wrap their presents. A friend of our family had sent a basket of flowers to their room, so they placed their presents around the basket as though it were a Christmas tree. Tammy Sue made a tray from a box, covered it with a bath towel, and arranged it with cookies and candies. Then my wife, my children, and my sister opened their simple presents to each other. It was a far cry from the many wonderful Christmas Eves we had known together with presents strewn around our gorgeously decorated tree in our home in South Carolina.

I awakened early on Christmas morning. I couldn't wait to see my family, but other than the childlike excitement I was feeling, it was difficult to tell that it was Christmas. No music filled the air. Nobody was hurrying to get the last present wrapped before the children awakened. No warm sounds and smells of Christmas breakfast; only the everyday sameness of prison life could be seen and heard. The only distinction this day had over any other was that the inmates did not have to go to work and, those fortunate enough to have visitors could eat Christmas dinner with their family members.

Around 6:00 A.M. on Christmas morning, Pastor Phil Shaw drove my family members to the prison gates. Phil said that he would be back to pick them up at the end of visiting hours, later that day.

Then came the long waiting game. Inside my cell, I waited to be called to the visiting room, while my family members stood outside in the cold, waiting for the gatehouse doors to open at around 8:30 A.M. Once inside the gates, they endured the arduous process of getting into the prison visiting area.

After the visitors went through the x-ray machine, the guards searched everything—even Tammy Sue's tube of lipstick and baby James's diaper bag.

Finally, the call came for me. "Inmate Bakker to the visiting room."

I hurried across the compound from Building Two. As soon as I stepped inside the doors, I spotted my family members through the crowd. I quickly made my way to them and kissed and hugged each one. Tammy Sue hugged me for so long I was afraid the guards were going to reprimand us.

I was so happy to see everyone. Our emotions were running at a high pitch, and we were all on the verge of tears. We spent several hours visiting together in the hot and stuffy room packed with visitors. It was difficult to hear one another, and we were unable to express our feelings well, but we were together as a family.

Eventually, the visitation room became so crowded the guards announced that they were going to move us to the basement of the chapel, where we could continue our visit until it was time for Christmas dinner. The prisoners were moved to the chapel basement first, and then the family members were escorted across the compound. Soon we were reunited in the chapel basement in a large multipurpose room that could seat about one hundred people at round tables. The crowd of people in the room quickly swelled to the point where people were crammed in back-to-back. My family and I stayed in the noisy basement for several more hours.

The crowd of prisoners and their families was too large for everyone to eat Christmas dinner together, so we had to eat in shifts. Somehow my family and I were assigned to the last group to enter the chow hall. My family went through the chow-hall lines with me, just as though it was any other day. On this day, however, we had a wide variety of foods to select from—ham, turkey, all sorts of vegetables, and pumpkin pie. We even had a visit from Santa Claus, one of the inmates dressed in a Santa's outfit.

It was getting near three o'clock and the guards had already warned our group that we were not going to have much time to eat together. It was imperative that all inmates be back in their cells in time for the four o'clock count, even on Christmas Day.

We quickly placed some food on our trays and hurried to a table where we could all sit together. It was the Bakker family Christmas dinner, prison style. Tammy Faye and I sat on one side of the table, and Jamie, Tammy Sue, Doug, and baby James sat across from us. I prayed a hasty prayer, thanking God for the food and for our special time together. We had barely begun to eat when a prison official announced, "Wrap it up."

Sadly, we dumped most of our Christmas dinner in the trash. It was not the lack of food that wrenched our stomachs, it was the total loss of our freedom to celebrate anything sacred, holy, or personal about Christmas. We were not able to read the Christmas story or exchange gifts. We sang no carols about the true meaning of Christmas.

"Wrap it up," the prison official again said matter-of-factly.

My family and I looked at each other in disbelief and disappointment. This was to be the extent of our long-awaited Christmas dinner. It was over before it had really gotten started, and now it was time for my family to leave. It was almost impossible to hold back the tears. We all hugged and kissed one more time. As Jamie, who had just turned fourteen, hugged and said good-bye to me, he started to sob. Everyone had been trying so desperately to remain stoic and strong throughout the exasperating day, but now the emotion was more than Jamie and Tammy Sue could contain. Susie burst out crying. Tammy Faye followed suit. She pulled us closely together as a family and put her arms around us. Standing right there in the chow hall of a federal prison with other prisoners and their family members looking on, we experienced one of the worst moments in our family history. It was a moment none of us will ever forget.

Then it was time for Tammy Faye and the children to go. Once again, our family was being torn apart.

I was not allowed to accompany my family outside, so I remained in the chow hall, watching out a window as my family followed the guards out the door and started walking across the prison yard. It was a cold, dreary, Minnesota winter afternoon. The skies had already started to darken. Just as my family began to walk across the compound, it was as though a cloud exploded and the snow came pouring down. It was the sort of snow songwriters and poets write about, and people dream about when they think of a white Christmas—large, soft flakes falling to the ground. But who cared?

My entire family was crying openly by now. They did not speak to each other; they walked, Jamie and Doug supporting Tammy Sue and the baby, and they cried. Only Susie looked back and waved. Tammy Faye later told me that she was crying too hard to look back.

I pressed my hands and face against the cold glass, the hot tears streaming down my face and mixing with the condensation on the window. I was straining for every last, longing look as my family trudged through the blizzard and then disappeared inside the gatehouse.

I had never felt so utterly alone in all my life. I stood there staring out that window as the snow quickly covered the tracks of my family. In a few minutes, it would be hard to tell that they had ever been there.

"Merry Christmas," I said sarcastically to myself.

The Christmas dinner had run late. It was almost 4:00, so rather than strip-searching us in private, all the prisoners in the last group through the chow line were herded into an open room and made to strip off our clothes. Like a bunch of naked cattle, we stood there in a row. We were quickly examined for drugs or other contraband.

"Open up your mouths, men," one of the guards commanded. "Hurry up. We don't have much time. Run your fingers through your hair. Pull your ears down. Lift up your privates. All right, turn around, lift up your feet. Bend over and spread 'em."

I kept thinking that since it was Christmas, the guards would be kinder and more compassionate in their search. No such luck. I should not have been surprised. Nor could I blame the guards. They had an unpleasant job to get done in a hurry, as the sacred four o'clock count was looming. No one dared violate the four o'clock count, not even for Christmas.

Finally we were ordered to reclothe and were hurriedly marched to our cell block. As I made my way back to my cell, passing numerous men already in their cells, I realized that the majority of the inmates had not had any Christmas visitors. I could tell by the reaction of my fellow inmates that many of them envied me. I knew that I was blessed to have my family visit, but the pain of the day had blurred the reality of the blessing.

I arrived back at my cell just in time for the count. I stood at my bed until the guard passed by and I heard the words, "Count clear!" Afterward, I climbed up into my bunk and collapsed. I thought, *My family needs me now more than ever, and there is nothing I can do to help them.* I felt helpless, worthless, and emotionally exhausted. I lay there for the longest time, wondering, *Are we going to have to go through this sort of emotional devastation every Christmas for the next forty-five years? How long can my family stand the gut-wrenching trauma of being pulled apart like this? Will this nightmare ever end?*

In a deep depression, I fell asleep, hoping against hope that the new year would somehow be better than the past year.

CHAPTER

17

God, Where Are You?

I DIDN'T FEEL MUCH LIKE CELEBRATING ON NEW YEAR'S Eve. My family had gone back home, and since I didn't have to work on the holiday, I spent most of New Year's Day in bed. Nor did I feel like facing my fiftieth birthday on January 2. I spent most of that day, as well, hunkering down in my bunk. My depression was so deep I did not even bother to eat. I felt that life had come to an end. My appeal to a higher court was stalled and seemed to be going nowhere, so I was rapidly losing hope of any sort of action concerning my sentence.

Around seven o' clock, my perpetually jovial friend, Gleason, stopped by my cell to see me and to ask me to sign a clipping of a press report about Tammy Faye's recent visit to Rochester. Because it was a legitimate news article, I signed it for him. "Be sure to date it," Gleason reminded me. Gleason was convinced his collection of signed memorabilia would be more valuable one day if it was dated. We talked briefly, and Gleason recognized that I was having a rough time dealing with things, so he said, "Jim, come on down to my cell. I just made a big pizza and you look as though you could use some food. Come help me eat it."

"No thanks, Gleason," I replied.

"Oh, come on, Jim," Gleason chided me as he started gently urging me toward the door.

"No, thank you, Gleason, I think I'll just stay here."

But Gleason would not take no for an answer.

"Oh, all right," I finally acquiesced. "But only for a few minutes."

As we walked down the hall closer to Gleason's cell, I began to notice a number of men hanging around outside his door. We weaved our way through the crowded hallway and stepped inside Gleason's cell. The ceiling light was out, but the desk lights were on, creating a warm and inviting look.

To my surprise, the cell was filled with men, some of whom I knew, many of whom I did not. Huge trays of food, all sorts of food—crackers with tuna fish, chicken salad, cheese, hors d'oeuvres, and, of course, prison pizza—were spread all over the bunks. A mop bucket lined with a plastic bag was full of cans of soda pop packed in ice.

"Happy Birthday, Jim!" the men called out to me.

I could not believe it. As I stood there in the doorway, I was so emotionally moved I almost burst into tears. I was absolutely amazed that these men would do something like this for me!

The fellows broke into a discordant but enthusiastic rendition of "Happy Birthday." It wasn't the most melodious version of the song I had ever heard, but it was one of the best. Over the years, I had experienced some wonderful birthday parties. Especially during my years at PTL, my birthday became an occasion on which my staff loved to play "Can You Top This?" They outdid themselves every year in pulling off a birthday party that verged on an extravaganza. We sometimes planned special events around my birthday party. On my last birthday at PTL, for example, we broke ground for the Crystal Palace Church and Conference Center.

I was always deeply appreciative of the friends and family members who made my birthday parties so special at Heritage USA. But I had never experienced a more meaningful party than the one these prisoners had worked to put together from nothing. At a time when I was feeling totally worthless and not caring whether I lived another day, the inmates reminded me that every day of life is special. Even the day you turn fifty.

Throughout the early part of 1990 I continued to ride an emotional roller-coaster, occasionally having an up day and then plunging headlong into another stomach-wrenching period of despair.

Often when I was alone in my cell, I would lie with my head against the wall, groaning from deep within. It was more than a physical or emotional pain; it was a soul pain. "Oh, God, where are You?" I cried. "Have I offended You so badly that You will not even speak to me anymore?" I feared, *I must have done something terrible that God would turn His back on me.* I thought God must be punishing me for every sin I ever committed.

Beyond my own troubles, Tammy Faye told me that my eighty-four-year-old mother, who still lived at Heritage USA, was in the hospital again.

Mother had been devastated by my departure from PTL and her emotional hurt was taking a physical toll as well. She had fainted one day at home, so Daddy and my brother Norm picked her up off the floor and rushed her to the hospital. She was hemorrhaging by the time they got there. The doctors discovered the problem was related to my mother's kidneys not functioning properly. Her condition was exacerbated by the fact that she had injured her spine as a young girl, and by now she could hardly straighten up enough to walk.

I felt awful that my mother was in the hospital, yet it was impossible for me to do anything to help her. Since all prisoners were required to call collect, and I could not reverse the charges when calling the hospital, I asked for, and received, special permission to call my mom from a prison office. I tried my best to encourage her. Mother appreciated my call, but she was sharp enough to recognize that there was a hollowness to my words that had never been there before.

Back in Florida, Tammy Faye was having problems of her own. Lacking sufficient financial support, she had reluctantly stopped doing our television show altogether. The show had never really regained its popularity after we left PTL, but it aired on more than two dozen television and cable stations around the country and was a sort of lifeline to us and our friends. Now, that too was gone. Tammy concentrated her efforts on trying desperately to hold our church together.

Prior to my imprisonment, our church fellowship, New Covenant Church, had been meeting in a large shopping plaza near what is now Universal Studios in Orlando. The land on which the church was located is now a vacant lot, overgrown with weeds and mangroves. Only a billboard stands on the grounds, advertising "ValuJet—Now with 20 Destinations."

I had high hopes for the property. Besides providing plenty of meeting space, offices, and potential television studios, the plaza could also be occupied by Christian-oriented businesses and shops. I had actually received verbal commitments from numerous shop owners who were ready to move their businesses to our new location. But because the former owners of the shopping plaza had gone bankrupt, our plans were delayed. Looking back, it was probably providential that we were not able to complete our plans rapidly. We had been having difficulty raising enough money to rent the shopping plaza even before I went to prison. Once I was out of the picture, the plaza became an albatross around the neck of the church.

Early in 1990, while trying to get into a permanent church building, and in an attempt to reduce costs, Tammy Faye and the congregation

I'm sitting on my father's lap next to my mother in this early 40s family photo. My brother Norman is on the far left, my older brother Bob is in the middle, and my sister Donna is standing next to my mother.

Lucky was my best friend for 12 years.

This picture was taken in 1961 on a train trip to introduce Tammy Faye to my parents. A few months later we left Bible College to get married.

Oh, to be nineteen again!

Tammy and I pictured in the mid-Sixties on the first set that I built by hand for our fledgling children's TV program. It was produced at Pat Robertson's Channel 27 at Portsmouth, VA, and as far as I know, it was the first live daily Christian programming specifically for children in America.

Our daughter Tammy Sue was almost born on television; she was raised in front of the camera. She's pictured here on the last and more sophisticated set built for "The Jim and Tammy Show" in the early 70s.

Our puppet family. During the early 1960s Tammy and I felt our ministry was reaching out to everyone except children, so we created this family of puppets called the "Susie Moppet" family. The puppets were the original reason Pat Robertson invited us to join CBN, his pioneering Christian television ministry.

Tammy Faye and I were invited to appear with Paul Harvey at the Hampton Roads Coliseum during our years at CBN. This appearance almost three decades later would be the theme of one of Paul Harvey's "Rest of the Story" segments.

After leaving CBN, Tammy and I journeyed to Southern California, where we helped pioneer the Trinity Broadcasting Network with my former youth pastors, Paul and Jan Crouch. I'm pictured hosting one of the first PTL programs from the original studio in Santa Ana, CA.

Jamie Charles, Tammy Faye, and I clowning around in happier days.

In the mid-Seventies, I resigned my presidency at TBN and moved to Charlotte, NC, where Tammy and I began the PTL Television Network in an abandoned furniture store. Here we are presenting our newborn son Jamie Charles to our television audience.

This is one of the pictures of my son, Jamie, that I had on my prison bulletin board.

Three generations of Bakkers. My father, Jamie, and I in a rare, quiet moment backstage at the PTL studio located at Heritage USA.

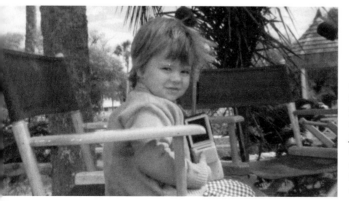

Both of our children grew up on the sets of our television programs, and often cameramen and directors became their best friends. Here's Jamie Charles on the set of PTL while we were on location at Gerald Derstine's Christian Retreat in Bradenton, FL.

Tammy Faye pictured with her beloved Grandmother Fairchild, her mother Rachel Grover, and our daughter Tammy Sue in the early 70s.

Tammy Sue, the sweetest little girl who ever lived, pictured with her new pet.

Tammy Sue, on an archaeological expedition we had sponsored in Jerusalem. Times like these, spent with my children, were some of my happiest.

Tammy Sue at her "Sweet Sixteen" party at our home in Palm Desert, CA. She had just released her first singing album, simply called "Sixteen."

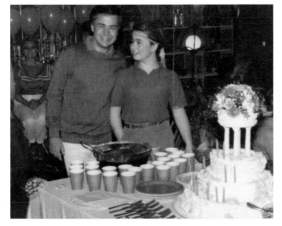

I always tried to do something unusual for Tammy Sue's birthday. One time we even celebrated in a sultan's tent I had erected in our driveway. This time we celebrated in our playroom at the Tega Cay home.

Our family on the set of PTL.

Our family "on location" with Uncle Henry in Hawaii

Our family posing for a Christmas card picture.

Our family pictured with Patti and Gavin MacLeod at our Palm Desert home. I think the kids were in the swimming pool.

This is my favorite picture taken of Tammy Faye in the office I had built for her next to mine. This picture was taken without any artificial light, just the ambient light coming in her office.

Tammy Faye pictured with her little dog Tuppins II which I purchased after the death of her beloved dog Tuppins I.

Tammy Faye not only hosted her own program, Tammy Faye's House Party, *she also co-hosted and often hosted our* PTL *program. Pictured here, she's interviewing Mickey Rooney and his wife Jan.*

Art Linkletter dominated the television scene during my formative years, and it was always a thrill to have him on TV with me. Here I am introducing him to my son.

Every time Tammy and I visited Israel, Prime Minister Menachem Begin took time from his busy schedule to meet with us. He always gave me a carte blanche letter giving full access to all archaeological sites, including those under the Temple Mount.

Over the years, I had the privilege of visiting with Ronald Reagan in his home, at his Beverly Hills office, and several times in the White House. The most treasured moments came when we were able to spend hours just sitting around in our shirt sleeves, discussing his beliefs with a small group of friends.

One of the greatest, true Christian gentlemen to ever occupy the White House in my estimation was Jimmy Carter. I had the privilege of not only having breakfast with him in the White House and receiving a dual humanitarian award presented to his wife and me, but I also had the privilege of flying and praying with him on Air Force One.

I felt honored when George Bush asked for me to have lunch and meet with him privately and discuss his deep faith and belief in the fact that Jesus Christ was and is the Son of God.

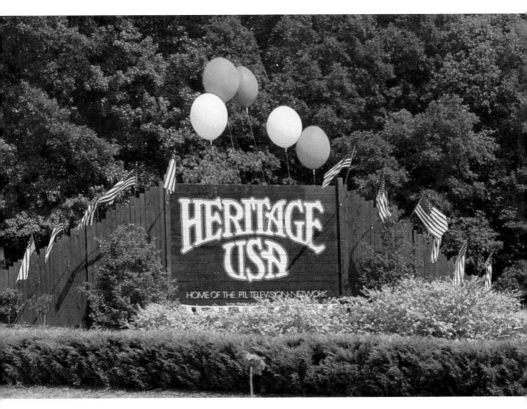

The original sign marking the entrance to Heritage USA.

Heritage USA was just a rugged landscape when construction began. Pictured above, staff member Bob Daniel and I discuss plans for the first stage of the development of Heritage USA.

When we opened the first phase of Heritage USA, which included the Fort Heritage Campground, instead of cutting a ribbon, I used a chain saw and cut a log.

One of the biggest undertakings of my life was the building of the Heritage Grand Partner and Ministry Center, consisting of 500 lodging rooms, shops, restaurants, and beautiful meeting facilities.

This is one of the 500 beautiful guest rooms utilized by PTL and lifetime partners. This shows a standard room in the Heritage Grand.

Fort Heritage Campground at Heritage USA featured almost 500 campsites.

In Phase 2 of the lifetime partnership program, I added the beautiful facilities of the Heritage Inn.

One of the most popular places at Heritage USA was the fellowship lobby. Surveys showed that the number one reason people came to Heritage USA was for Christian fellowship.

The exciting Main Street Heritage USA located in the beautiful Heritage Grand Partner Center housed a variety of shops, restaurants, and activities with well-appointed hotel suites and rooms located above the shops.

The Heritage Island was the nation's only inspirational water park, which provided water fun, recreation, live Christian music, Bible teaching on the beach, refreshments, and fellowship in a wholesome family atmosphere.

moved out of the shopping plaza. The church began meeting in a piano store, which the owner, Dale Griner, allowed the congregation to use free of charge. Before each service, members of the congregation had to move the pianos out of the way for the people to be seated!

On a family level, we had recently discovered that our son Jamie suffered from dyslexia, an impairment in the brain that made written communication difficult for him. In one sense, we were thankful to find out the cause of Jamie's learning difficulties. We knew he was an extremely intelligent boy, yet he continually had trouble with his subjects at school. No wonder! The pressure on Tammy during this time was immense and, although she tried to be encouraging to me during our conversations on the phone, I could hear the stress beginning to gnaw at her stamina. I wondered how long she could take it.

Tammy Sue and her family had moved back to South Carolina, where they were now living in a mobile home not far from Heritage USA. Susie and her husband, Doug, were struggling financially, like most young couples with a new baby. Their phone had been disconnected and the electric company was threatening to turn off their power. They had been having yard sales, selling their possessions in an attempt to pay their bills. When Tammy Sue dared to venture from her home into the community, she was often accosted by people who felt compelled to make snide and often lewd remarks about me. The caustic comments seared my daughter's sensitive heart.

Tammy Sue plunged into a severe depression. For about six months she refused to come out of the house unless absolutely necessary. She became so reclusive she was almost as much a prisoner as I was. Being the daughter of Jim Bakker was not exactly a plus for Susie at that point.

Night after night, as I turned my face against the wall next to my bunk, I could not escape the thought, *My entire family is in some sort of turmoil because of me, and I am buried alive in prison unable to help. Oh, God, where are You?*

To make matters worse, about this same time the NBC television network began to produce a movie about my family, PTL, and me. The movie starred Bernadette Peters as Tammy Faye and Kevin Spacey as me. The inmates in prison scoffed up every tidbit of news about the movie and brought it to my attention. I didn't want to see the articles, and I didn't really want to talk about the movie. To my new friends in prison, it was a big deal that somebody they knew was the subject of a movie. But to me it was just more dredging up slime and slapping it onto a caricature of parts of my life.

Besides, I had already read the script.

A scriptwriter for the project, Ken Trevey, and an NBC researcher had spent four days interviewing Tammy and me in early 1988. Tammy and I answered their questions as thoroughly as possible. When the writers left our home, we felt that we might have a shot at seeing a fair representation of what happened at PTL come to the screen. Later when the original script was shown to us, we still believed the same. We should have known better.

Before the movie went into production, the script was rewritten and revised several times. Referring to the new script, Trevey said he wrote what he called "a newer, tougher one that was more balanced and dramatic".[1] When Tammy and I read the new script, the one the network decided to use, we were very unhappy. The script only vaguely represented the information we had shared with our interviewers.

Not surprisingly, throughout the filming of the movie, crew members made fun of things Tammy and I held sacred. Filming took place in Pasadena in a Presbyterian church. On February 28, 1990, an earthquake hit Pasadena—right in the middle of Bernadette Peters's rendition of one of Tammy's songs. The "gospel choir" backing up the singer quickly scampered off a cross-shaped portable stage, and crew members immediately scurried out of the church. I honestly have to say that I was tickled by this report.

In prison, I was longing to hear Tammy Faye sing again. Each night as I went to sleep, I turned on my battery operated radio and scanned the dial, searching for the gospel station from Georgia that had played Tammy during my first week in Rochester. One night, when I was in a deep depression, I was sure I had found it. A station was broadcasting gospel music, but I could not get a clear signal. The sound kept fading in and out. Finally, I fell asleep with my radio headphones still on.

I don't know how long I slept, but suddenly I awakened. Strangely, I didn't know where I was. I thought for a moment, *Maybe I have died and gone to heaven!* A wonderful peace filled the prison cell. That's when I noticed the sound in my ears. I was still wearing my radio headset. I strained to hear the sound again. The radio signal cleared of static, and I could hear plainly the voice of Tammy Faye singing:

Don't give up on the brink of a miracle,
Don't give in, God is still on the throne;
Don't give up on the brink of a miracle,
Don't give up, remember you're not alone.

When Satan would have you look at the trials of life that surround you
And he tries to appear and brings doubt and fear all around you.

150

Don't look with the eye, or listen with your ear,
Just cry out to God, He is always near;
In your darkest hour, your miracle is here.
The devil is a thief and he sends those troubles to confound you
And he lies and says, This time there's no way you can find to make it
    through.
Remember God's true Word, the battle is the Lord's,
Don't give in to fear, think on things that are pure.
And praise the Lord, your miracle is here.[2]

I could hardly believe my ears! Twice now, right at a time when I was feeling totally overwhelmed by my own circumstances and the problems others I loved were facing largely because of me, God sent this special message to me over the airwaves. As before, it was not just any song; it was a song written by Mike Adkins, a dear friend of Tammy's and mine, who had appeared on our television programs many times. Nor was it just any voice; it was Tammy Faye singing a message that reached directly into my heart. Although my spiritual senses were numb and my emotional system was running on overload to the point that I walked around the prison compound most of the time looking like a scared rabbit, I could not escape the fact that God was showing me something. But what? What did it all mean? Surely God must have some concern for me. Otherwise, why would He set up such an unusual set of circumstances? Yet if I had any value to God, why would He allow me to be publicly disgraced, humiliated, and dumped into this prison in the first place?

The next day I could hardly wait to tell Tammy about hearing her singing "Don't Give Up On the Brink of a Miracle" on my radio. Tammy was excited and believed that God was showing me that He was going to do something really special.

In at least one sense, Tammy was absolutely right. God was about to perform a series of miracles in my life, but I was not ready to receive them yet.

CHAPTER

18

Clubs in the Fed

I HURLED MYSELF INTO KEEPING BUSY INSIDE THE PRISON. In addition to my daily responsibilities cleaning, I joined any organization in the prison that expressed an interest in having me.

One of the first groups with which I became involved was the prison Jaycees. The Jaycees' primary fund-raiser and service within the prison was taking prisoners' photographs, which the inmates could send home. Other than pictures taken in the visiting room, all photos were required to be taken in one location, in the recreational building in front of a wall mural depicting a picturesque Minnesota lake and river rippling through a lushly forested area. The prison did not allow us to take a camera anywhere on the compound or to take shots of the cubicles in which we lived.

In the early part of 1990, I spent a great deal of time working with the Jaycees, so much so that I became the executive secretary of the group. Much of our work had to do with the Jaycees' photo program. Each week, the inmates could purchase tickets from the commissary to be given to the Jaycees as payment to have their pictures taken. The tickets were then redeemed by the Jaycees to purchase more film and used to pay for special events, such as the annual Inmate Family Christmas Dinner, including gifts for inmates' children who visited at Christmas time, and the Fourth of July Inmate Family Picnic. The Jaycees also paid for pay-per-view sports events and movies in the television room and other programs.

I also joined the Growth Awareness & Development Association (GADA), a club that had replaced the NAACP club in the prison. All of the members of GADA were black except for two—Lyndon LaRouche, the Libertarian Party presidential candidate, and me. I had met Lyndon in the visiting room prior to joining GADA. Lyndon was a brilliant man, even if he was perhaps a bit eccentric, and an articulate spokesmen for all sorts of causes. It was no surprise to see his white face in a group dedicated to promoting issues relating to black people. Little did I know that this controversial man would soon be my cellmate.

The guys in GADA voted me in as the religious coordinator of the club. My job was to arrange for guest speakers at our meetings. One of the highlights on GADA's schedule was the Martin Luther King Day celebration. It was an entire day of special speakers, music, and seminars.

The members of GADA asked me to pray the opening prayer of the day's events. Knowing how sensitive the prison officials were about me being involved in any kind of religious service inside prison, I said, "I'll be glad to do the prayer, but we better get permission first."

The answer came back a categorical "No! Jim Bakker is not to lead any religious activities in prison. And that includes prayer!" The members of GADA were upset by this decision. I assured them that it was no problem to me, and I did all that I could to defuse the situation.

Another group I joined in my efforts to fill the void in my life was the Vietnam Veterans. The Veterans sold greeting cards in the prison, and I was one of the group's best customers. I received an avalanche of mail, and I tried to answer as many of the cards and letters I received as possible. To do so, I would often send a nice greeting card. The Hallmark company donated thousands of first-rate greeting cards to the federal prison system, cards that were in perfect condition but for some reason had not been sold. A certain number of these cards were available to each prison and were given to the chapel for distribution to any inmate who wanted them, free of charge.

Each week after I had exhausted my allotment of Hallmark cards, I spent a portion of my commissary money on cards I purchased from the Vietnam Veterans. One day, one of the vets invited me to join the organization. "But I'm not even a veteran," I said.

"That's okay," the vet said. "Our organization is open to anyone. If you have a concern for the Vietnam vets, you are welcome."

I was so surprised and overwhelmed that men would actually want me as part of their groups—especially in light of the public humiliation I had recently experienced. I readily accepted the invitation to join the Vietnam Veterans. Before long, the guys asked me to be the chaplain of the group.

I developed a deep empathy for the soldiers who had served in Southeast Asia. And I learned a lot too. One of our guest speakers said that more Vietnam veterans have committed suicide than any other group of soldiers, and that more Vietnam vets have committed suicide since the war than the number of American soldiers who died in the war. Another statistic he presented startled me as well: Of all the single-auto accidents in America, the highest percentage of drivers have been Vietnam veterans. One of the best things I was able to do as part of this group was to help get Dave Roever to come in to the prison to speak. Dave is a Vietnam vet whose face was nearly blown off by a hand grenade during the war. It's tough to feel sorry for yourself when you look at Dave and hear his heart-wrenching but inspiring story.

Later in my prison experience, I also joined the Toastmasters, a group designed to encourage a person to speak in public. Ironically, as a man once accustomed to speaking to millions of people on television and to thousands of people at our regular church services at Heritage USA, now I was having trouble talking to a small group of inmates and our sponsors. Nevertheless, I served in almost every Toastmaster position, including table chairman, the guy who was supposed to keep the talk going and encourage the other members of the group to speak in public.

My joining various groups was not lost on Dr. Westrick and Dr. Foster. Dr. Ruth Westrick, the psychiatrist who was assistant warden in charge of mental health at the Federal Medical Center in Rochester, also served on the board of directors at the Mayo Clinic. At five feet, four inches tall, Dr. Westrick was anything but diminutive. She was on a first-name basis with numerous heads of state. A bright woman of German descent who looked to be in her early sixties, Dr. Westrick was the "Mother Teresa" of the Department of Prisons. I found her to be a deeply compassionate woman who was dedicated to helping humanity. She oversaw the mental health status of inmates as well as the Chemical Dependency Program at the Rochester prison. Dr. Westrick always found the time to listen to an inmate's problems. She had checked on me at regular intervals since my arrival and kept, through Dr. Foster, close tabs on my mental condition.

More than anyone else, Dr. Westrick and Dr. Foster realized how far I had fallen in a short period of time. Beyond losing my position at PTL, my reputation, my friends, and most of my material possessions of any value, I was feeling as though I had been abandoned by God. Consequently, I was burying myself in busywork. Good work, but a poor solution for the awful sense of loneliness and loss I felt deep within my soul.

Dr. Westrick and Dr. Foster noticed my silent cry for a reason to live. In January 1990 Dr. Westrick broached an idea to my cellmate Tom Brandon. Because of new federal regulations coming to the prison system in the years ahead concerning smoking in a government-run facility,

Dr. Westrick wanted Tom and me to create and teach a smoking cessation class to any inmates who wanted to break the smoking habit. Dr. Westrick was hoping Tom and I could devise a program that would be successful.

When Tom told me about Dr. Westrick's ideas, I was excited yet reticent. After all, trying to convince inmates to stop smoking is a formidable task. At the time more than 80 percent of the prison population smoked. Many of the inmates incarcerated at Rochester were serving long-term prison sentences. To prolong their lives meant only that they would spend that much more time in prison, even if the quality of their lives improved. What a challenge! Then, too, can you imagine telling a bank robber, a professional hit man, or a Mafia kingpin that he can stop smoking and that you can help him to do it? The program better work!

Dr. Westrick called Tom and me to her office to discuss the details of the program. She was convinced we were the perfect combination to develop and teach a program that would be effective. With Tom's medical background, plus his own battle with alcoholism, and my background in motivating people to work toward a cause, she felt certain we could succeed where others had failed. I wasn't so sure, but I was willing to try. In addition to the other clubs and organizations with which I had become involved, I threw myself into the job of gathering resource material Tom and I could use in our smoking cessation class.

Tom waxed downright philosophical about our serendipitous selection. "What are the odds of two men with our backgrounds and specialized skills ending up as roommates in the federal prison system and getting the chance to teach a smoking cessation program to the most difficult group of nicotine addicts imaginable—federal prisoners?"

Best of all, because the smoking cessation class would be taught as an all-day seminar for a month, Dr. Westrick had hinted that Tom and I might get out of cleaning toilets for a while. "Just think, maybe I can even start biting my fingernails again!" Tom quipped.

Of all the groups I joined in my attempts to bury myself in work, the one that grabbed my heart the most was my work as a hospice volunteer. My job would be to sit with a dying man at the prison hospital and help him to express his feelings, overcome his loneliness, realize that his life was not lived in vain, maintain some degree of control over his last dying days, and basically come to grips with death.

Although I was already keeping extremely busy, I could not pass an opportunity to be involved in such a program. The first patient to whom I was assigned was a heavy-set man named Cecil. Cecil was dying of cancer.

155

Cecil told me that while serving time in another prison, he had developed a pain in his hip. Eventually, the prison officials sent Cecil to have surgery in Florida. The doctors there operated on him and released him after saying that he should have no further problems with the hip.

The pain in Cecil's hip persisted. His condition worsened to the point that he could no longer move. That's when the prison system sent Cecil to the Federal Medical Center in Rochester. The doctors at F.M.C. discovered a cancerous tumor that had been punctured during surgery. Like a leaking water pipe, the cancer had slowly but surely leaked from that tumor, spreading to various parts of Cecil's body.

By the time I met Cecil, he was going to die. All I could do for Cecil was to be there for him. I sat by his bedside every day for several hours. I searched the Bible and found every Scripture about heaven that I could, and I read those Scriptures again and again to Cecil. He loved to hear the Scriptures describing how God would one day wipe away all our tears and that there would be no more pain. Eventually, I introduced Cecil to Jesus Christ. Cecil became a bona fide born-again Christian. Although he was dying, maybe because he was dying, he quickly developed a love for the things of God. Not long after I had signed on as a hospice volunteer and had begun to strike up a friendship with Cecil, Officer Ensley was transferred to the hospital, on the same floor where Cecil was located. One day when Officer Ensley saw Cecil reading a Bible that Tammy Faye had sent him, he came over to Cecil's bed and ripped the Bible out of his hands. "You can't have that!" Officer Ensley roared.

Officer Ensley's desk was located near the nurses' station in an area enclosed by glass, right inside the door through which I entered every day when I came in to see Cecil. Prior to Officer Ensley's arrival on the ward, I had always walked up the stairs onto the hospital's intensive-care floor and down the hallway past the guard station. With all the other guards, I merely waved as I walked by the glass enclosed area. I was a registered hospice volunteer, approved through proper procedures to be there, so when the guards saw me they simply put my name on the list and waved me on.

Not so with Officer Ensley. He demanded that the hospice workers go inside the enclosed area and stand in front of his desk to report to him. It was almost as if he wanted the prisoners to pay homage to him. Each day, I had to say, "I am Inmate Bakker, 07407-058, checking in to the hospice unit." This was not optional with Ensley. He demanded it.

One day, as I was reporting for hospice service, I was thinking about Cecil and not concentrating completely on my check-in routine. I simply stood in front of Officer Ensley's desk and said, "I'm Mr. Bakker, checking in."

I had seen many faces gawking and glowering at me during my trial and sentencing. Yet never in my life had another human being looked at me with the disdain that Officer Ensley did just then. He curled his lip and snarled, "You mean *Inmate* Bakker?"

I bowed my head and said, "Yes, Inmate Bakker, 07407-058."

In a single sentence, Officer Ensley destroyed all the dignity and respect that Dr. Westrick and Dr. Foster were trying to rebuild in me. I felt like an ant being crushed beneath a jack boot.

One day when I arrived for my hospice service, I was surprised to see Cecil extremely angry. I asked, "Cecil, what's wrong? Why are you so upset?"

"Oh," he said, "I'm just so mad at God. I thought for sure that God would take me home last night. But He didn't. I didn't die."

I said, "Cecil! You're my friend. Do you mean you want to leave me?"

"I just want to die," he repeated.

In his final days, I helped Cecil plan his funeral. I helped him say good-bye to friends and family. I helped him write to an old girlfriend.

Cecil had a wish that dominated his thoughts during his last days. He wanted to be buried next to his father back home in the family cemetery plot rather than in a nondescript prison cemetery plot without even a headstone. I was able to help contact his mother and sister who arranged to have his body sent back home for burial. By the time Cecil was losing his grip on life, the chaplain and Cecil's family had made all the funeral arrangements.

One night when I went to see Cecil, I could tell he would not be with us much longer. The cancer had been working its way through his body, eating through his internal organs. He could no longer talk. He merely made gestures. I could do little for him other than sit and talk to him and read Scriptures. After a while, I got ready to go back to my cell for ten o'clock count. Before I left his room, I leaned over Cecil, took his hand, and prayed. Then I said softly, "Cecil, I'll see you tomorrow."

Cecil roused slightly and shook his head no.

The next morning when I went back to see Cecil, his room was empty. All his things had been removed and his room had been cleaned. Cecil was gone, and it was as though he had never existed.

But I knew he existed. And I know he is in heaven waiting for me. Over the years, well-intentioned people had lavished praise on me for the huge number of people I had led to have a relationship with Jesus. I wasn't sure anymore how many people I had actually helped get to heaven. Only eternity will reveal the truth about that. But I know I led at least one person to heaven, because I walked him right to the gate.

A few days later I received a note from Cecil's sister: "Cecil was buried on Wednesday morning aside his father at Pleasant Lawn. . . ."

157

CHAPTER

19

Tega Cay

EARLY IN 1990, I BECAME IMMERSED IN CERAMICS AND painting. I enjoyed it, and it kept my mind busy. Often, I would stay up for hours at night, painting pictures for my family and friends.

For Tammy Faye's birthday on March 7, I stayed up until midnight painting a watercolor picture of her beloved little Yorkshire terrier, Tuppins. Actually, my painting was of Tuppins II. Tammy's first Yorky had been a faithful companion to her all the way through the frenzied, emotion-packed days following our departure from PTL. Then in 1988 Tuppins died of a brain disease. The veterinarian said that by rights, Tuppins should have died months earlier, and the only reason Tuppins stayed alive was because the dog sensed that Tammy Faye needed her.

I desperately wanted to get Tammy Faye another dog when Tuppins died, but by this time, our financial resources were gone. We had sold nearly everything except our furniture and clothing. We had even sold our car to make ends meet, so "Doc" Boyd, a dear friend who owned the Chrysler dealership near Heritage USA, loaned us a new car to drive. We certainly did not have any extra money for an expensive little puppy.

Nevertheless, I knew how much Tuppins had meant to Tammy Faye and I found a way to get her another dog.

Tammy dubbed the new Yorky Tuppins as well, and before long, it was as though the first Tuppins had never died. When I went to prison in 1989, Tuppins II became Tammy's constant companion.

I wanted to paint the picture of Tuppins for Tammy's birthday. To express to Tammy how I was feeling about missing her birthday, I painted in two tears falling from Tuppins's eye. On the back of the painting, I wrote:

This is how I feel tonight. I miss being with you. It's the first birthday of yours I missed in 29 years. I will make it up to you someday. Hope you like the picture. It is watercolor; they do not allow oil paints in the prison. Happy Birthday!

Tammy Faye wrote back:

I love the little Tuppins picture, only it makes me cry when I look at it. Someday you will be able to paint over that tear! I know that "great joy" is ahead for you and me and our family.

Our attorney Mr. Bender called today. Attorney Allen Dershowitz is anxious to meet with you, but he is very busy right now on Leona Helmsly's case. I'm glad that he is going to take part in your appeal. He assured Harold Bender that he will meet with you soon. Harold has great confidence in him.

Yesterday I got a sideways look at Jamie standing out by the car with a bunch of kids and I thought it was YOU! He looks more like you everyday. Everyone says so. It's unbelievable!

I *never* stop thinking about you. From the minute I get up in the morning, until I go to bed at night. You are always on my mind! This nightmare will be over one of these days, Honey. Hold on, be strong!

On Friday, March 9, I had just begun another painting, this one for Tammy Sue. I had become so absorbed with the painting that I suddenly realized I would have to hurry to make it through the chow line.

I rushed to the chow hall. I had just picked up my tray when a young inmate came up behind me and said with a heavy foreign accent, "Jim, I hear your home at Teka Bay just burned down!"

"What?" I said. "What are you talking about?"

"Yes, it's true. I see on the television. Teka Bay. All burned down."

The inmate was mispronouncing Tega Cay, the location of my family's former home. More than any other place my family and I had ever lived, the Tega Cay house was the place that instantly came to mind when we thought of "home." We had lived there for nearly a decade while we were at PTL. It was where Tammy and I had raised our children.

I hurriedly gulped down my food and headed back to my building. When I returned to my cell, I received a message from the guard on duty to report to the warden's office. The warden confirmed the news. Our former home at Tega Cay had been gutted by fire. Only remnants of the structure remained standing.

As I walked back to my building again, I was concerned about how Tammy Faye and the children would take the news. As soon as I was able, I called Tammy Faye. Yes, she had seen the newscast and had seen our home in flames. So had Jamie and Tammy Sue. I started to cry right there on the telephone. I had never before cried over losing a material possession. But this was different. My heart was broken over that house. Though my family and I had been forced to vacate the property when I resigned as president of PTL in 1987, I had secretly hoped to buy the house back someday and restore it to my family.

To me the house represented so much. It was the house where we put our marriage back together.

In the late 1970s it was no secret that Tammy Faye and I were having marriage problems. Anyone who watched our program for long could witness Tammy and me airing our dirty laundry on television. As we went through our problems, rather than trying to hide them, we talked about them on our programs, often bringing a guest on the show who could address the issues. At times watching our program was like watching a soap opera in which the audience could vicariously experience someone else's problems through the television. Actually many marriages were helped as people realized that they weren't the only ones who had trouble in their relationships. Although our show was thriving on the chaos of our lives, our own marriage was falling apart.

As I said before, after Gary Paxton I suspected there was another man in Tammy Faye's life, and by 1980 I was sure of it. In December, we took our television show to Hawaii to do a series of programs from Waikiki. We also held our international conference at this time, so we brought in our hosts from the various *PTL* programs around the world. At that time we were on the air in fifty-two nations.

Every show from Hawaii was spectacular. With Diamond Head in the background and the help of graceful Hawaiian dancers and singers, we probably did some of our most beautiful programs ever. Tammy and I dressed in Hawaiian outfits; our children were with us so Tammy Faye and Tammy Sue dressed in matching clothes and Jamie and I did the same. All week long, every time we were on camera, we were the picture of an ideal, loving family, even if we did look a bit hokey.

Our friends and television audiences did not know, however, that Tammy Faye and I had agreed to separate at the end of that week. During one of our first days in Hawaii, Tammy and I were walking along Waikiki beach when she suddenly said, "Jim, I don't love you anymore."

I was devastated. Her words confirmed my worst fears. I felt strongly that Tammy had been seeing someone else. I would later discover that I had paid for him to accompany us to Hawaii as part of our staff!

I smiled through every show that week despite knowing that when we were done, Tammy Faye was going to fly off to California where she planned to get a job. At the conclusion of the week, we held a traditional Hawaiian luau. On the way to the luau, Tammy and I argued; she refused to get out of the car when we arrived. She said she didn't feel well enough to sing that night and went back to the hotel.

At the close of the luau, as I stood alone on the stage to thank the people for coming and to say good-bye, I began to weep uncontrollably. I had held up well through all the shows and all the convention meetings, but now the thought of Tammy leaving was overwhelming to me. I walked away from the microphone, across the stage, and sat down on the back steps, sobbing.

The following day, Tammy Faye boarded a plane to California, and Tammy Sue, Jamie, and I boarded a plane and flew back to Charlotte. When we got home, the kids and I moved out of our home in downtown Charlotte near South Park and put it up for sale. We moved into a double-wide mobile home next to the church, better known as "The Barn" on the property of Heritage USA. The trailer had previously been used as a dressing room and extra office space.

I continued to do the television show without Tammy, which was not unusual during those days. Tammy had often been absent from the show. She had been sick frequently, so nobody gave it much thought that she did not show up after the shows from Hawaii. "Uncle" Henry Harrison, my faithful cohost, was there, and between Henry and our many guests, the show perked right along, without missing a beat.

But I missed Tammy horribly. So did Tammy Sue and Jamie. Although Tammy Sue was only ten years old, she seemed to be keenly aware of the void in my life. Every time she saw me she said, "Daddy, I love you." Her love helped carry me through those difficult days.

Since Jamie Charles was too young to go to school, I took him with me everywhere I went, even to the office. Jamie loved it. One day, however, Jamie crawled into a cardboard box in my outer office and was saying over and over, "I hate my mommy, and my mommy hates me!" Jamie

Charles loved his mother; he just couldn't understand why she had gone away and left him.

My children needed their mother, and I wanted my wife back. I prayed, "God, You have to show me what this is all about."

I sensed the Lord urging me to go out to our house at River Hills. This was a small house we were trying to sell on the lake. Before we had gone to Hawaii, Tammy Faye had been spending a lot of time there. I felt strongly that God was guiding me to go there. I got in the car and made the twenty-minute drive. When I arrived at the house, it was deserted. I went inside and began to look around, not really knowing what I was looking for.

As strange as it seemed, I felt certain that the Lord was directing me to look in the garbage can. I dumped the contents of the can onto the floor. Then I saw it. At the bottom of the garbage were some shreds of paper with writing on them . . . Tammy Faye's handwriting.

I began slowly putting the paper shreds together on the dining-room table. I found a small roll of tape and I began taping the puzzle together. My heart was pounding as I began to realize that I was reading a letter from Tammy Faye to her lover. Tammy had apparently decided not to mail it and had instead ripped it up and thrown it in the garbage.

It took me hours to piece that letter together—it was several pages long. I ran out of tape long before I got the final pieces in place. Not until I had reassembled the last pieces of the letter did the shreds reveal the identity of the person to whom it was addressed. I stared out the window in disbelief. The person was one of my most trusted associates.

I drove back to Heritage USA in a daze. At that point in the history of PTL, I rarely did any of the hiring of personnel, so I was not in the habit of personally firing anyone, either. But in this case, I decided to make an exception. Normally I am a good-natured person, I'd go the second, third, or umpteenth mile with anyone in our employment.

But the one unwritten policy I would not violate was: "You cannot fool around with my wife and stay on my payroll!"

I confronted Tammy's lover—and my coworker . . . and fired him.

I still loved Tammy and was committed to trying to win her back. I began courting her as though we had just started dating. At the same time, however, I had to do a live daily television program. How could I woo Tammy and keep the show going at the same time?

A local businessman came to the rescue. He had an airplane that he was willing to rent. It was a small jet aircraft, and the businessman allowed me to take out some of the seats so I could lie down in the plane. Back and forth across the United States I flew, spending a few precious hours with Tammy on the West Coast, then flying back all night to be on the East Coast in time to do the morning television program. I maintained this routine for several weeks.

When Tammy and I were together, away from the pressures of PTL and building Heritage USA, it was like old times. We went out for quiet dinners. We talked. We laughed. We had fun together. We went to church.

One Sunday we went to church together in Van Nuys, California, at The Church on the Way. The sermon that morning sounded as though it had been prepared with Tammy and me in mind. The message hit us right between the eyes and discussed in detail many of the problem areas Tammy and I were experiencing in our marriage.

The following week, Tammy began to seek God in earnest. She opened her Bible and it seemed as though God was speaking directly to her. She told the Lord that she was willing to go back home to the children and to me. Within ten minutes of Tammy's prayer, I called her on the telephone. Tammy agreed to come back home. My heart leaped for joy!

By the time Tammy Faye and I returned to South Carolina, our house in Charlotte had sold and the new occupants were ready to move in within thirty days. The children and I had been living in the double-wide trailer, so as soon as Tammy Faye came back, we began house hunting.

Nothing seemed suitable or within our price range. As a last resort, I suggested that we look at Tega Cay, a then problem-riddled subdivision on Lake Wylie, about a fifteen- to twenty-minute drive from Heritage USA. Along the way, our children led us in singing a takeoff of the song, "This Is the Day (That the Lord Has Made)." "This is the way; this is the way to Tega Cay! We will rejoice; we will rejoice at Tega Cay!" We all sang at the top of our voices. It felt so good to be back together again as a family.

We went to the real-estate office on the property. The man there showed us around the development, but nothing seemed to be right. We were about to leave when the real-estate agent said, "Well, you know, there is a doctor living here and his house is not up for sale, but he has told us that he might be interested in selling his house sometime soon."

We drove around the lake and as soon as we turned the corner, I saw the house perched on the cliff overlooking the edge of the lake. It was a strange but marvelous-looking Polynesian cedar wood house with pagoda roofs. It looked a bit old and run down, but the moment I saw it, I said, "This is it! This is it!" We hadn't even seen inside the house, and we were not sure whether it was for sale. The doctor and his wife who owned the home were not there at the time, so we made an appointment to return.

I couldn't wait! Once I stepped inside the house, I knew we were home. The living room was two stories high with dry, unvarnished mahogany paneling. It had a large fireplace and plenty of room. Out back was a kidney-shaped swimming pool visible from the windows on the side of the house facing the lake. I noticed a number of places where the roof had obviously been leaking, but all in all, the big, sprawling, split-level house was a one-of-a-kind dream house to me.

We decided to make the owners an offer. We did not make an exorbitant offer of money, but worse yet, we told the couple we had to be in the house within thirty days! Amazingly, the couple accepted our offer and within thirty days, we were living at Tega Cay.

Immediately Tammy Faye and I set about remodeling the house. I had noticed that some of the happiest times in our marriage had been when we were working on putting a house together, so I attacked the house at Tega Cay with every bit of energy I could muster. Over the years that we lived at Tega Cay we practically remodeled the entire dwelling. The house was big to start with, but by the time we would leave in 1987, it would grow to over ten thousand square feet.

The house was more than a piece of property; it was a haven, a place of respite in our frenetic lives. It was a place where we could relax, let our hair down, and just be a family rather than television personalities. Beyond that, to Tammy and me, the house was a symbol of our marriage. We took an existing structure, removed what was decayed or rotten, rebuilt on what was good and salvageable, and replaced what was not with airy new rooms. We were doing something similar in our relationship.

But the best thing about the house is that it was where Jamie Charles and Tammy Sue grew up. Our next-door neighbors, Judy and Dr. Blair Bycura, had two sons, Ryan and Darren, who were close to our children's ages. The Bycura boys and the Bakker children became best buddies and played together constantly. Dr. Bycura took an approach to fatherhood similar to my own. Because we were both so busy with our work, when we were home and could play with our children, we went all out. For instance, our kids wanted us to build them a tree house, so we weren't satisfied to build just any old tree house. Dr. Bycura and I built a two-story tree house for our children. The kids loved it. They often spent the night in it and had many real and imaginary adventures there.

One hot summer Saturday morning, our children were out back playing between the Bycuras' house and our house. The kids had brought home a long sheet of plastic and were pouring water on it with a hose, then sliding down the plastic. Before long, Dr. Bycura and I were right in there with the kids, pouring water on the plastic and sliding down the hillside toward the lake.

Suddenly I got an idea. *If it is such great fun to simply slide a few feet down the hill in the water, what would it be like to slide all the way down the hill to the lake?* We were all soaking wet and covered with mud anyhow, so we started digging out a trench down the hill toward the lake. As we did, we lined the trench with plastic, ran water down it and slid our way down the hill toward the water. Once as I slid down the makeshift waterslide, I hit my ankle on a tree root that was sticking out of the ground and ripped open a gash. But I didn't care. We were having a ball!

Call it the builder in me, but later, after we had all cleaned up and dried off, I began to talk with Dr. Bycura about building a real waterslide in our backyard down the hill to the lake. After all, we had the trench practically dug! Excitedly, we made plans. We ordered pipe and began construction of our backyard waterslide, but a neighbor in our subdivision complained. Soon inspectors came to see our project, and they refused to allow us to continue. They said, "You can't build something like that in a residential community." We reluctantly abandoned our idea, but I never forgot the sound of our children squealing in delight as they slid down that muddy hillside. *Someday*, I thought.

Perhaps more than anything, the Tega Cay house established some semblance of stability in the life of our family. From the time Tammy and I married on April 1, 1961, to the day we moved in at Tega Cay, we had lived in over twenty homes. In the early years, Tammy and I had ministered as traveling evangelists, so we were always moving around. Even after our children were born, we continued to move quite frequently. At one point during the mid-seventies, Tammy and I moved several times in a single year. It was almost as though every time we had another problem in our marriage, we moved to a new house and started fixing it up. Working together on those houses brought us together in a common cause.

When we finally settled at Tega Cay, my children, my wife, and I had a place we could call home.

The news commentator's detached voice brought me back to my present reality in prison. I had made my way to one of the television rooms at the end of the hall where some of the older inmates gathered to watch the news. Most of the televisions in prison are tuned in to "escape from reality" types of shows, but there is usually one set that is kept on a news channel throughout the day. Because I rarely went near the TV room during my first months in prison, I had to search to find the room where the news

165

was on. In the TV room closest to my cell, the inmates had on CNN's *Headline News.* I didn't have to wait long.

The newscaster described the details of how sometime around 2:00 A.M. on Friday, March 9, the house had caught fire. I watched in horror as the screen filled with flaming images of our former home. The house was a virtual inferno, with flames twenty to thirty feet high.

I cried out loud, "Oh, my God, no!" Some of the guys who were standing around in the room stopped and stared at me. I didn't care.

The newscaster was talking about gold faucets and a black marble fireplace, although the fireplace was made of man-made stone and the faucets were actually made of brass. At that point, however, I could have cared less about misrepresentation of the facts. There was one incontestable truth right there on the screen—our family home was engulfed in flames and burning to ashes. The reporter went on to say that the fire seemed to have a suspicious origin, and investigators were already on the scene.

I later learned that it had taken fifty firefighters nearly two hours to extinguish the blaze. The house was completely gutted; the entire rear of the home collapsed, leaving only the entryway, part of the garage, and part of a chimney still standing. An agent with the South Carolina Arson Investigation unit commented wryly, "We're looking at all possibilities and talking with everyone who knows anything. But one thing's for sure— Bakker's alibi is solid."[1]

Sitting in that prison TV room watching my former home crumble in flames was one of the most traumatic times of my life. The house was a part of me. It was a tangible expression of my love for my family. Now it was gone. It was the end of an era. Although it was impractical and improbable, I had always dreamed that someday we could go back there. Now there was nothing left to go back to. Prison or no prison, I could not hold back the tears.

The inmates watched in respectful silence as I got up and walked back to my cell. I climbed into my bunk and shut my eyes. *Oh, God! I thought. Why did You allow this to happen? What are You doing to me? I have already lost everything I owned. My ministry is gone. My reputation is gone. I am locked up, facing a forty-five-year sentence, and I can't get out, and I sit here in prison and watch my family home burn down! God, is this some sort of cruel trick? God, where are You? What are You doing to me?*

CHAPTER

20

Love at First Sight

PEOPLE DEAL WITH TRAGEDIES IN DIFFERENT WAYS. THE night I watched our family's former home at Tega Cay burning on television, I went back to my cell and began to paint.

I painted furiously, as though I were a man on a mission. *I must rebuild our home at Tega Cay*, I thought, *at least, on paper.* As I reconstructed with paints our family's home, each section I painted brought back special memories. With less than an hour or so before dawn, I finally finished the painting. When it dried, I wrote the date on the back of it, along with a message to Tammy.

Tammy's response was characteristically upbeat:

> I miss you so much tonight. Some nights get so bad that at
> times I can hardly stand it without you. Sometimes I want to strike
> out at the whole world! But, I think a quiet trust in the Lord will
> eventually pay off for you and me.
>
> I love the paintings (the one of Tuppins and the one of the
> house). They both make me cry! We had so many wonderful times
> there, raising our kids. But I guess God wants us to move ahead . . .

I also received a constant flow of encouraging mail from Tammy Sue. Each of Susie's letters was bittersweet. I loved reading about my grandson's first steps, his first words, his first experience playing in the sandbox, the first time he went to the park, and the day he ate his first orange. Yet with every "first" that Tammy Sue shared with me, it drove home the truths that I was missing the joy of watching my grandbaby grow up and that James himself would be my present age before I had served the complete forty-five-year prison term.

One of the most poignant cards I received in prison came from my son Jamie. More than ever before, I now understood how difficult it was for him to write to me because of his dyslexia. Yet Jamie picked out a special card. On the front of it was a sort of red rubber blob with white eyes and a large mouth. The blob was funny looking in one sense and sad in another. Jamie had written on the front of the card around the blob, "Hi, Dad. We will get you home." Then around the remainder of the blob, he wrote, "This is my latest picture (with an arrow pointing at the red face), Your son, Me." On the inside of the card he had written, "I miss you and I want to see you. So try to have fun. I know you will be home soon. I love you Dad. Jamie."

Another letter I received about this time was from Roe Messner. When I went to prison, PTL still owed Roe's company millions of dollars for work he had done or was in the process of doing at the time of my departure. PTL's collapse directly affected Roe and his business. Ironically, during my imprisonment, Roe Messner, the man who personally lost more money at PTL's demise than any other person in the world, became one of my best friends. In a letter dated March 8, 1990, he wrote:

> I want to encourage you to keep a good, positive attitude and keep
> believing God for a miracle. You have tens of thousands of people pray-
> ing for you. . . . I want to make you aware of a recent development in
> my situation. I filed Chapter 11 Monday, March 5, 1990, to protect my
> personal assets until the PTL bankruptcy is finalized. I know the Lord
> has a purpose in all this and will work it out for His glory. . . . Is there
> anything I can do to help Tammy or Jamie?

Tammy Faye continued to write every day, even though we talked by phone each day. Although Tammy Faye always tried to present a positive impression, the loneliness began to show. She wrote:

> I can hardly look up at the moon. I always think, "That same moon is
> shining on Jim." I get so terribly lonely for you. I remember how good
> it felt to just lean against you on our last visit. For a few moments I felt
> secure again—whole again. I'm just *nothing* without you, baby!

Another day Tammy Faye expressed:

> I miss you an extra lot today. Some days are so much worse than others. Today is one of those "worse" days. I need your hugs so *bad*! I need you to take care of me. I'm not very good by myself. Sometimes I miss you so bad that I get physically sick. I guess I'm going to have to come see you soon. But then that's worse than ever!

I sent a card to Tammy Faye every day. I conveyed my love to her and hope for a future together, although I knew it would not be soon.

Tammy replied: "I love the cards you send me! I look at them and read them over and over again. They make me feel close to you. I miss not being with you. I miss your hugs—our talks—I miss you lying next to me in our bed. I'm so terribly lonely for you. . . ."

It was April 1, 1990—our twenty-ninth wedding anniversary—before Tammy Faye was able to return to see me in Minnesota. She, Jamie Charles, my sister Donna, and our friend Vivian Keller drove ten hours a day for three days to get from Orlando to Rochester. We had not seen each other since Christmas. That three-month period of time was the longest we had ever been apart since we had met thirty years earlier.

I first met Tammy Faye when we were both students at North Central Bible College in Minneapolis, Minnesota. It was love at first sight on my part. The first time I saw her, Tammy Faye LaValley was wearing a lavender argyle sweater, and a deep purple, pleated skirt, with white tennis shoes and white bobby socks. She had the brightest blue eyes and wore no makeup. Her hair was long, and at four feet, ten inches, she was the cutest girl I had ever seen. Unfortunately, Tammy Faye was engaged to be married to the son of the pastor of her hometown church.

Midway through our first term, Tammy Faye broke up with her fiancé. That was exciting news to me!

I worked as the night door monitor at the front entrance to the dormitory in which Tammy lived. My job was to keep the riffraff out and to sign out the students when they went out at night and to check them back in as they returned to the dorm. Tammy Faye had to pass by me on her way out and back into the dorm every night. I certainly knew when Tammy came by. Once, she teasingly gave me a little bell that had fallen off one of her ice skates. I put that bell in my pocket and carried it with me everywhere I went.

One night after Tammy had broken up with her boyfriend, she went out bowling with a group of about ten guys, all Bible college students. To

Tammy, hanging out with ten guys seemed quite natural, since she was one of eight children in her family. To Tammy Faye, the college students were all simply "brothers and sisters in the Lord." I didn't see it that way, but then, I was interested in dating Tammy myself.

That night, when Tammy Faye walked into the dorm, I looked at her and said, "Little girl, you are going to ruin your reputation if you keep going out with all those guys." Tammy looked back at me as if she had no idea what I was talking about—which, I later discovered, she did not.

I had already fallen head over heels in love with Tammy.

I worked up my nerve and asked Tammy to go to church with me. For our first date, one cold winter evening we went to church at Minneapolis Evangelistic Auditorium, located at Nicholette and 14th Street, and pastored by Pastor Russell and Fern Olson. I did not own a car in those days, so we had to walk from the Bible College to the church, a distance of more than a mile.

On the way back, I suddenly stopped and said, "Tammy, kiss me!" Although Tammy later told me that she had never before kissed a fellow on the first date, she did kiss me.

On our second date, I asked Tammy Faye to go steady with me. On our third date, I asked her to marry me. Three months later, on April 1, 1961, we were married after a church service at Minneapolis Evangelistic Auditorium in the prayer room. We did not have the money to have a big wedding. We did not even have enough money for a wedding gown and tuxedo, so Tammy wore a mint-green dress and I wore my favorite black blazer and gray slacks. Pastor Olson conducted the ceremony as his wife Fern looked on. My college roommate and my sister Donna were the only other people to attend our wedding. My mother and father were opposed to Tammy and me getting married while we were in college. Tammy Faye's mom gave us her reluctant blessing the night before the wedding.

Tammy and I held hands throughout the ceremony, with Tammy Faye giggling and me looking stoically ahead. Tammy had just turned eighteen years old and I was twenty-one. Because of the Bible school's policy prohibiting students from marrying during the academic year, we had to drop out of North Central Bible College. We were in love! To us that was all that mattered. Tammy Faye had a job at Woolworth's department store, and I worked as a busboy in the Fountain Room Restaurant at Rothchild's Young-Quinlin, an aristocratic department store in downtown Minneapolis. We volunteered our spare time at Pastor Olson's church and worked with the youth group. I preached my first sermons to this youth group.

One of the guest speakers visiting in our church was Pastor Aubrey Sara from Burlington, North Carolina. He took an interest in Tammy and me and invited us to hold a series of meetings in his church in which Tammy sang and I preached. We had never preached a revival before, but Pastor Sara had so much confidence in us, he convinced us we could do it. When we concluded the meetings at Pastor Sara's church, with his continued guidance and support, we struck out on our own as traveling evangelists. Tammy Faye sang and played the piano and accordion, and I did the preaching.

In the early days of our marriage, we lived in a third-floor, walk-up apartment. We bought our furniture at the Salvation Army store. We decorated the apartment ourselves . . . and it definitely needed redecorating! Some fellows had lived there before us, and the apartment looked like a pigpen. The bathroom decor was bright red with pictures of naked women hung on the walls.

We used anything we could find to transform that first tiny apartment into a home. Even though we had little in terms of material possessions, we were richer than at any other time in our lives. Years later, when we had money in the bank and lovely possessions in our homes, I often longed to return to those days when our poverty drove us to creativity and each other.

Although Tammy Faye and I were not able to go on a honeymoon, we were passionate young lovers and "honeymooned" most every day. Tammy's and my walk-up apartment truly became a "love nest" in every sense of the term.

Throughout our first twenty-nine years of marriage, although we were stressed and strained in many ways, our physical expressions of love for each other remained an intense, integral part of our relationship. When reporters insinuated that Tammy's and my love life was cold or nonexistent because of my obsession with building Heritage USA, at first we flinched, and then we had to laugh. Nothing could have been farther from the truth. In the best of times and in the worst of times, Tammy and I made love. We always took time with each other. We did not merely have sex; we made love.

Now, on our anniversary, as I waited to hear my name over the prison intercom, the memories of anniversaries past caused desire for my wife to build within me. In expectation of Tammy Faye's visit, I had gotten new prison khakis, then pressed them in crisp military-style pleats.

When the call finally came—"Inmate Bakker, report to the visiting room"—I raced across the compound as fast as I could go without running. When I was finally able to enter the visitation room, I was so excited to see Tammy Faye. I walked straight to her. I embraced her hungrily, kissing her much longer than prison rules deemed appropriate.

"Happy anniversary, honey," I whispered in her ear. "Thank you so much for coming! I have missed you so badly."

I had not been intimate with Tammy Faye in over six months. I desperately missed the closeness we had always shared in our marriage. It was so wonderful to be able to hold her close to me.

I greeted my sister Donna and our dear family friend Fran. We pulled our plastic chairs around the tiny table and wiped the tears from our eyes. It was wonderful to see everybody! We got some food from the vending machines and sat for hours, catching up on what was going on in each other's lives.

After a while, I wanted to spend some time "alone" with my wife on our anniversary. While the others remained at the table, I offered to show Tammy Faye the recreation field. I guided her toward the back visitation room, to the window near the end of the line of vending machines. From that vantage point, I stood behind Tammy Faye, reaching around her and pointing out the various areas on the recreation area.

"And over there is the softball field," I said, pointing past her shoulder.

Tammy Faye leaned over slightly to look out the window and as she did, I could feel the warmth of her body next to mine.

"And there's the track that we walk around," I said, trying to sound nonchalant.

I stepped forward slightly, reaching around Tammy Faye and pointing to the right side of the recreation area. When I did, our bodies pressed fully against each other for a few seconds. It was like electricity shot through me. I wanted to be a husband to my wife in a complete sense, to express physically the love I felt for her, as I had thousands of times before, and to experience one more of those intimate times that seemed to temporarily heal so many of our hurts. Tammy Faye's hand brushed my leg. We were a married couple, celebrating our twenty-ninth year of marriage on this day, yet we furtively concealed our touch like two teenagers stealing a kiss outside the front door.

We were jolted back to reality by a man who loudly asked, "Hey, Jim and Tammy! How about an autograph?" Our intimate moment was over. Tammy Faye and I stepped away from each other as I reached out to sign an autograph on the man's paper. The man thanked me and handed the paper to Tammy for her signature. I tried not to resent his intrusion into the first intimate moment Tammy and I had been able to share in over half a year.

"Wrap it up!" The guard's order signifying the end of visitation time came all too soon. "Inmates to the front, visitors to the back."

"Don't give up, honey," Tammy Faye said as we kissed good-bye in a much more perfunctory embrace than our previous kiss that day. "We can make it," she said. As I waved good-bye and started toward the strip-search room, I heard Tammy Faye say to Jamie, "Don't look back." None of us wanted to let go of each other, yet none of us wanted the pain of that last look before going out our respective doors—my family going out the door to freedom, and me going through the door to be strip-searched once again. I thought of my family on their way back to Florida. The old saying was right: "You don't know what you have until it's gone."

21

Dying Embers

"DADDY, I THINK I'M PREGNANT."

When I first read the words in Tammy Sue's letter, my heart leaped for joy at the thought of another grandchild. Then the reality of the situation set in. Susie and Doug were struggling to make it financially. Doug was out of work, and the family had no health insurance. Beyond that, Tammy Sue was still dealing with her own depression. She and Doug were not in an ideal condition to bring another baby into the world.

Tammy Sue sounded almost apologetic in her letter. I knew that she would be a great mom to her baby, just as she already was to baby James. Nevertheless, I worried. Where was she going to get the money for proper nutrition, for herself and for the new life growing within her? Would she find a doctor who would take adequate care of her? How would she ever pay a hospital bill? Again, my inability to help my family in their time of need smacked me right in the face.

Concern over Tammy Sue's pregnancy, combined with the sense of loss I was feeling since Tammy Faye's anniversary visit and the Tega Cay house fire sent me spiraling downward into my own trough of despair.

During the week following Tammy's visit, in my ceramics class I had made a vase. I kiln fired the vase on April 7, 1990. Again, as part of my futile attempt to re-create the burned-out house, I painted a picture of the Tega Cay house on the vase. I fired it in the kiln again. The vase came out beautifully. I was going to send it to Tammy Faye, but then I discovered something.

Dr. Tom Brandon and I had been preparing for several months now to teach our smoking cessation class. We were receiving a deluge of information, as part of our research for the class. I came across some interesting comparisons between giving up smoking and other losses people experience, such as the death of a loved one, divorce, loss of property, or the loss of position or prestige. As one of the first major steps toward healing, one had to quit living in denial and stop pretending that nothing has happened. Accept it, begin to deal with it, and get on with your life.

I grabbed the vase on which I had painted a lovely rendering of our house at Tega Cay. I spattered black and red paint all over the vase in an attempt to portray the house on fire. When the paint dried, I placed the vase in the kiln again. When the vase cooled, and I removed it from the kiln, I was flabbergasted. The black and red ceramics paint had spread over the house, creating an eerie sense of fire, smoke, and darkness. In a real way, seeing the vase with the house on fire helped me to come out of denial, to admit that the house was gone, and to accept the fact that I must move on with my life.

Because Tom had been a medical doctor, he still received more than twenty medical publications each month. He had also joined the American Society of Addiction Medicine before I had moved into his cell. Consequently, Tom received a wealth of current medical information pertaining to smoking and nicotine addiction.

At the same time, Tom and I scoured newspapers, magazines, and religious periodicals for information we could use in teaching our class. Tom handled the medical material, and I prepared the motivational material.

I devoured dozens of books on the psychology of motivation, self-worth, and a positive mental attitude. I read books by Zig Ziglar, Og Mandino, Robert Schuller, and a host of other spiritually based authors. Additionally, I studied information from the Hazelden Addiction Center.

I had one big problem. How was I to stand in front of a group of inmates and help motivate them to stop smoking without referring to God, the Bible, or my faith (weak as it was at this point)? The prison administrative officials were adamant that I not be involved in anything that gave me access to a pulpit. Moreover, the warden and his assistants did not want me in a position of leadership. It was only through Dr. Westrick's significant influence that I was allowed to do anything other than clean toilets.

"I can see the headlines in the tabloids now," Tom quipped. "Bakker Faith-Healing Inmate Smokers!"

I was informed that I was not permitted to do any preaching in the smoking cessation class. I could talk about a "higher power" but references to Jesus Christ, the Bible, or to prayer all had to be avoided. The prison had used a smoking cessation program once before, and the material that was used in that course was approved for my use. I was required to confine any Scripture references or spiritual information to the material that had already passed government censorship. To my delight, when I examined some of the material that had been used previously, I found that the accepted program was the "Breathe Free Plan to Stop Smoking," which included some of the most effective materials in the world for dealing with addictions, and was prepared by the Seventh-Day Adventists, a group that based their instruction on biblical principles.

Tom and I didn't know what to expect when we stood before a roomful of inmates for our first session. Twenty-four men had enrolled in our first course. We had arranged for a special mixture of orange and grapefruit juice to be available to the men who enrolled in our class. The juices actually change the acid content in the person's body who is trying to quit cigarettes "cold turkey." It decreases the rate of nicotine excretion and lessens the withdrawal effects.

Sunflower seeds were distributed to the inmates to munch on during class. Part of the cessation process involved keeping the addicted person's hands occupied. We had discovered that handling the cigarette was part of the total addiction. For our first class, the prison supplied most of our juices and seeds. After that, Tom and I purchased the seeds with our commissary funds.

I was extremely nervous. I hadn't spoken in front of a group in a long time. My own feelings of worthlessness only exacerbated my insecurity. As I looked into the faces of the men attending that first session, I thought, *This has to be the toughest audience I have ever seen!* Dr. Westrick introduced the program and told the men that this class was one of the most important that any inmate who smoked could take. She added some complimentary statements about Tom and me, and then she left. Her confidence in us was astounding.

Tom began the first session by giving the men a brief history of smoking in America. Then Tom gave the men some of the hard-hitting facts about smoking. He told them, "Smokers die (on the average) eighteen years sooner than nonsmokers."

Tom went on to provide the inmates with a wealth of current, accurate medical information concerning the damaging effects of smoking. One of Tom's one-liners about smoking was: "Once you get lung cancer, you might as well send your shirts to the laundry one at a time."

Tom then outlined the reasons why this program would work for the inmates and why they should quit smoking immediately. He emphasized the fact that he and I did not think we were know-it-alls, but that we had done our homework and the men could be confident that the methods and techniques we were going to teach them had worked for fourteen million other people who had used the "Breathe Free" program to quit smoking.

When it was my turn to speak, my first session was on the subject "You Are Valuable." I knew that if I was going to help these men kick the nicotine habit, they must be convinced of their value as people.

"You are incredibly valuable," I said. "According to calculations by Professor Harold Morowitz of Yale University, your body is worth $245.54 per gram of dry weight. This means that a 168-pound man is worth $6 million in chemicals alone."

I gave the Judeo-Christian background to the idea that the men had value. I was able to quote the Bible at this point because the previously approved program had done so. I explained to the men that they had the right in our program to believe in God or not to believe, and they could take from the program what helped them and leave the rest. I reminded the guys, however, that the most successful addiction cessation programs had a "faith factor." Such groups as Alcoholics Anonymous, Teen Challenge, and D.A.R.E. all had at their core a firm belief in the power of faith in God. "Addiction is bigger than the individual," I said, "so it takes something bigger than the individual to cure it."

As I spoke, it was becoming clear to the men that this message was about much more than merely learning how to quit smoking. It was about learning how to develop an entirely new mind-set about life.

I closed my session that morning by telling the men, "Believe you are worth it. Believe you are a valuable human being, accept yourself as a worthwhile person. Be nice to yourself."

Outside, as we were leaving, an inmate who had attended the sessions walked up to me and said, "Thank you for your speech. It was really good." He paused and looked me in the eye, and said, "You are the first person who ever told me that I am worth anything."

Ironically, the message I was presenting to the men that morning was one I desperately needed to hear myself. Although I did not realize it at the time, now I can see that every lesson I taught the men, God wanted me to learn.

For instance, my second session was on the subject of "Your Self-Image." I was standing up teaching the men how to raise their self-esteem when my own self-esteem was nonexistent. I felt lower than a worm.

Yet I told the men, "Your self-image controls you. Everything you do—your actions, feelings, and behavior patterns—is consistent with the image you hold of yourself. If you think you are shy, you will act shy. If you see yourself as a smoker, you will be a smoker."

I went on to say, "Don't let others paint a bad self-image for you. Label a man a loser, and he will start acting like a loser." I did not recognize it then, but that was exactly what I was doing to myself. I was allowing the words of men who had engineered my departure from PTL to influence the way I was thinking about myself.

Even when I turned the message around in a positive sense, I still did not yet see it as applying to myself. I told the men, "Your self-image is not permanent. You can change. You can design your own mental blueprint. You can hold a good picture in your mind, and your outward behavior will fall into line."

The very messages I needed somebody to tell me, I was telling myself.

The process continued with my third session, which was on "Positive Mental Attitude." I started by comparing a positive mental attitude to what I called a "prison mental attitude."

As an example, I said, "Some inmates say, 'Hey, man! Why are you working so hard cleaning toilets? You're just working for the guards.' I always answer, 'The guards don't use these toilets. You use them and I use them.'"

I went on to say, "Whenever you do a job less than you are capable of doing, you are cheating yourself. You are stealing from yourself. The biggest thief steals your dreams."

On day five of our eight-day crash course, I taught the men about the stages of loss or grief, using the pattern established by Dr. Elisabeth Kübler-Ross, and showing how smokers who give up their nicotine go through similar emotional stages as a person who has lost a loved one, a job, a friend, or has lost a spouse through divorce. Research done by a group in Minnesota discovered that smokers consider their cigarette a "buddy," but "it is a buddy that will always let you down," I told the men. When that buddy is gone, the grieving process sets in.

"Although there is no orderly flow to the grieving process, the first stage is often denial," I told the class. "Denial is a psychological buffer that protects us from feelings we are not yet ready to deal with mentally, emotionally, or spiritually. Many smokers live in denial, denying that they are addicted, denying that they can't quit, or trying to deny the validity of information concerning smoking-related diseases and deaths."

Although I didn't realize it at the time, part of the reason I had painted the Tega Cay house and reproduced it on the vase was an effort to deny in my mind that it had been destroyed. I did not want to accept the fact that it was gone, that a precious portion of my life was obliterated forever. Moreover, for the first few years after losing PTL I lived in denial. I had lost so much, not simply materially or in terms of personal power and prestige, but in terms of emotional and spiritual losses as well. I did not want to admit to myself that it was gone.

Now here I was trying to help other inmates, and by digging out the materials to teach the men, I was finding the tools I needed to dig out of my own quagmire.

What an amazing, wonderful trick God played on me! Until I wrote this book, I truly never realized that as I was teaching others how to escape the stranglehold of their addiction, I was in fact learning what I needed to know for the rest of my life. Not only was God going to use this material to help pull me out of my own doldrums, He was also preparing me for the tough days ahead.

CHAPTER

22

Through the Valley of Loneliness

I HAD BEEN MAKING NEW FRIENDS. THOUGH SOME OF them were of dubious backgrounds, I had discovered an unusually high level of friendship, compassion, and camaraderie in prison. I had also been hearing from friends I never knew I had. One day, for example, I received a warm letter from U.S. Senator Mark Hatfield of Oregon. The senator sent me a devotional book he thought might be of help to me. He wrote:

> The enclosed came to me from a friend and, in turn, I am sending it to you with the thought that perhaps it will serve to comfort and inspire you. While I am sure that the past months have been difficult, I hope that your faith in God has sustained you and I wanted you to know that. . . . You are in my prayers each day.

I greatly appreciated Senator Hatfield's note, and the book he sent to me was helpful. More than that, I appreciated his support and prayers.

Roe Messner wrote to me regularly while I was in prison. The man who had lost so much money because of my demise at PTL still cared enough to go to bat for me. By the spring of 1990, Tammy Faye and I could not afford to hire a dream team of lawyers to handle the appeal of my case. We could barely afford a nightmare team of lawyers. Even though his own business was being dragged into bankruptcy largely because of us, Roe had become personally involved in the negotiations with appeals attorney Alan

Dershowitz, hoping to secure the services of the famous lawyer to help make my case.

Roe's willingness to help was overwhelming to me. The one man who had lost more "real" money than any other person when PTL fell apart was willing to put up still more of his own money in the effort to get me out of prison.

Another friend who surfaced quickly when the tide was rolling out was Bob Gass, a popular pastor and evangelist. With his quick wit and charming Irish brogue, Bob endeared himself to our PTL television audiences and appeared on numerous programs over the years. Early in my prison experience, Bob wrote me a powerful letter. In it he said:

> In the past week I talked with . . . Malcolm Smith and Jamie
> Buckingham. They all said the same thing . . . that you are going to
> come out of there a new man, with a message you have never had
> before, to touch people you could never identify with.

As I read Bob's letter, I was deeply touched by his concern for me, but I did not understand then how deeply I would be affected by the truths he shared with me—that out of my deep sense of loneliness I would learn things that would change my life and the lives of many others.

Another dear friend who wrote early and often was C. M. Ward, a pioneer in Christian broadcasting, the inimitable voice of *Revivaltime*, the official worldwide radio program of the Assemblies of God.

"Make no mistake about it," he said in one of his early letters, "Dorothy and I remain your friends. To me 'steadfastness' is the essence of the Gospel." C. M. Ward never failed to include a gift in the form of a money order to help me pay for stamps and commissary items.

One of the first friends to come visit me in prison was Kenneth Copeland, the renowned faith teacher. He did not simply stop in to say hello, he stayed with me for five hours and ministered to me amid the noise and confusion of the prison visitation room.

Kenneth told me that his Native American heritage taught him the power of an earthly blood covenant. If a man is an Indian blood brother to another man, he would dedicate his life to the defense and protection of the other. The brothers would die for one another. How much more should we as Christians stand together in covenant, Kenneth encouraged me. When I lost PTL many of my longtime friends and employees switched loyalties faster than I could keep up with them. I realized then that for some, PTL had been little more than a paycheck. We had few covenant relationships.

On the other hand, in the midst of the 1987 scandal revelations, Kenneth and Gloria Copeland had invited Tammy Faye and me to their Believers Conference in Los Angeles, California. At a time when our names were being besmirched in every conceivable way, the Copelands put us up in a lovely hotel and arranged for us to sit right on the front row during the services. They knew Tammy and I were hurting, so they invited the ministers at the conference to come to our hotel room to pray for us privately. I will always be indebted to Kenneth and Gloria Copeland for their kindness and compassion.

Others who visited me during the early days of my imprisonment included Reverend Owen Carr, the founder of the first full-powered Christian television station in Chicago. Owen wrote numerous letters to me and almost made me cry when in one of his early letters he wrote, "I was your friend before you went to prison. I am your friend while you are in prison. I will be your friend after you leave prison."

Paul Olson was also a regular visitor in the early days of my incarceration at Rochester. Paul is the son of Pastor Russell Olson, the pastor of the church Tammy and I attended before we were married. Paul is now a powerful evangelist in his own right, crisscrossing the world in his travels, yet he always found time in his busy schedule to stop long enough to see me. In almost all of Paul's services around the world, he asked his audience to pray for me.

The mail continued to pour in, and along with it came the usual assortment of encouraging letters as well as the hate mail. Several of the photographs for which I had posed with people in the visiting room were now showing up in tabloid newspapers, accompanied by the wildest of headlines and stories. One of the signed photos of my family and me appeared in a tabloid under the headline, "Jim Bakker Cowers in Cell—Terrified He'll Be Raped by Fellow Inmates." The story went on to describe how I never went anywhere in prison without my protective cell-mate known as "Big Doc." Tom Brandon got quite a charge out of that one! It was a made-up story. *No one would try to rape me in this prison, would they?* I thought. Although I was still on edge, I was beginning to relax and feel a little more secure.

I also received numerous books, magazines, and articles from people around the world. One book, *Through the Wilderness of Loneliness*, by Tim Hansel, was literally life-changing to me. The book came at the exact moment I needed it.

Tim told of a time when he had been speaking to a large crowd. They had clapped their hands and cheered him as a great and entertaining speaker. But when the auditorium was empty, Tim walked out alone and drove back to his hotel room, where he had intentionally left the lights on so the room would not seem so dark and lonely when he returned.

The light didn't help.

Tim Hansel wrote in his journal words that God used to begin prying open the ever-thickening shell I was building around my heart. Tim wrote, "The loneliness was so bad tonight that it sucked all the oxygen out of the room. It was so intense it felt like it could peel the paint off the walls."[1]

Whoooom! Tim's words exactly described what I had been feeling since coming to prison.

Tim continued, "Lately I have experienced a loneliness so deep that I feel as though I need a second heart to contain all the pain."[2]

Yes! I wanted to shout. *That's how I have been feeling.*

Tim suggested that part of the reason God allows us to walk through the valleys in our lives is so we will learn to depend on Him in new ways.

But I can't even hear God's voice anymore! I talked back to the pages. *I feel like God has abandoned me.*

No, Tim wrote, "Loneliness is not a time of abandonment . . . it just feels that way. It's actually a time of encounter at new levels with the only One who can fill that empty place in our hearts."[3]

I had been reading Aleksandr Solzhenitsyn's books about the same time as I had received Tim's. I had even written in the front of my Bible one of the statements the brilliant Russian writer had penned while in prison: "When you have robbed a man of everything, he is no longer in your power. He is free again." I felt like I had lost everything, but I in no way felt free . . . yet.

Through the combined impact of Hansel's and Solzhenitsyn's books, I caught the first dim glimpse of what God might be doing in my life. Tim drove home the message:

> Perhaps one of the main reasons we fall into loneliness and despair is
> that we are so preoccupied with ourselves, so invested in our own egos.
> We're so concerned with how we are doing that we can't seem to get a
> clear focus on what God is doing in us and around us.[4]

Could it be? I wondered. *Could it possibly be true that I was in prison by the very design of God? Was there really a larger purpose behind my imprisonment, as some of my friends had implied?*

Tim Hansel taught me how to turn my loneliness into solitude with God.

At this point in my life *Through the Wilderness of Loneliness* impacted me second only to the Bible. No other book has been more useful to me. The transformation did not come quickly or easily for me. I still felt as though I had not heard from God in several years.

In early 1980, I had sinned seriously, but when I repented and sought God's forgiveness, I knew He was there. I knew He forgave me, whether other people chose to believe that or not, or whether they chose to forgive me or not. God continued to use my life and seemed to bless everything I set out to do in His name. The ministry kept getting bigger and bigger. Then, after the disclosure of my sin and my subsequent departure from PTL, nothing I tried to do in God's name bore any fruit. I tried to start another television program in Charlotte. It didn't work. I tried to begin again in Florida; that also soon fell apart. Everything I tried turned to dung. What do you do when God doesn't hear you?

As I read Hansel's book, I renewed my cries to God. "God, please talk to me! Show me something, anything, just please let me know that You haven't given up on me."

Then one night, I had a dream unlike any dream I had ever experienced before. The colors in the dream were so vivid; it was like dreaming in blazing Technicolor! In this dream, I was sitting next to Jesus. He was dressed in white and blue and He seemed to have a brilliance and depth like diamonds—yet like nothing I had ever seen in my life!

As I was sitting there, Jesus reached up and pulled out a slice of His own eye. It looked like a contact lens. He reached over and gently put the thin slice of His eye into mine and said, "I want you to see everything and everyone through My eyes."

I woke up. I knew that something supernatural had happened. And I felt it was the first time in several years that God was speaking to me in an overt way. But what did it mean?

I began to ask, as much to myself as to God, "How can I see everything and everybody through the eyes of Jesus?"

The answer, whether from God or my conscience or my own mind, was crystal clear: *I must read every word Jesus said, because if I know Him and His words, then I can see everything through His eyes.*

Instead of reading my usual two motivational or inspirational books each day, I began reading the Gospels every day. I got a red-letter edition of the Bible from the chapel library, the words in red indicating the words of Jesus. I literally wrote down every word Christ spoke as recorded in the Scriptures. Then I wrote a condensed version of the verses to help me remember them. For instance, "Love your neighbor." "Love God." "Do not sin." I began to see things in the Bible that I had never seen before. I made up my mind then that I was going to ask God all the difficult questions I'd skirted over in my busy years. The first question I asked God was, "Why are there so many dying people here, and why can't I help them? What can I do?"

I was surprised at the answer I heard from God: "You are arrogant. You think that you are the only person I have in this prison. I have many others here. I am God." And then God said to me, "I did not bring you to prison to minister. I brought you here to get to know Me."

185

CHAPTER

23

Power Plays

BETWEEN 1987 AND 1989, TAMMY FAYE'S AND MY FINANCIAL
resources had been depleted except for the salary we received from New
Covenant Church in Orlando, so we had little money to go lawyer shopping. Most of our salable possessions were long gone.

Even my retirement funds were gone. PTL had established a retirement fund for Tammy and me through my denomination, the Assemblies
of God. By the time I went to trial in 1989, our retirement fund had grown
to nearly $1 million. Shortly after I went to prison, our retirement savings
were divided by the Internal Revenue Service and my lawyers as payment
for their legal representation in the original charges brought against me. It
was only through the kindness of people who had generously contributed
to a legal defense fund we had established that we were able to mount any
defense at all. Yet despite the sacrificial gifts of many friends and family,
when it came time to hire lawyers who would appeal my case, our options
were few. Roger McDuff, a singer who had appeared on our PTL television programs, recommended to Tammy a legal team within our price
range headed by an attorney from Houston, Texas. Although he had done
none of the work on our original case, we hired him. Not long after that,
we were able to secure the services of Harvard law professor Dr. Alan
Dershowitz to handle a part of our appeal as well.

Professor Dershowitz is known as one of the leading appeals lawyers
in the world. His clients had included millionaire Claus von Bulow, who
had been accused of trying to murder his wife; kidnapped newspaper

heiress Patty Hearst; New York hotel owner Leona Helmsley; and Wall Street's Michael Milken. The fact that Alan Dershowitz would even take my case gave me a ray of hope for the first time. He was convinced that my appeal had validity since several points of law had been violated in my trial. I wanted to believe Dershowitz's optimistic outlook, but I kept remembering the prison adage, "You ain't got nothin' comin'."

The appeal process was scheduled to begin on May 25, 1990, but was delayed while the courts prepared the transcripts of my trial. The transcripts did not come cheaply; it cost in excess of fifteen thousand dollars simply to obtain the written record of my trial. On June 15, 1990, my written appeal was filed before the Fourth Circuit Court of Appeals in Richmond, Virginia. The prosecutors then had time to file their legal briefs reasoning why the trial had been fair. Throughout the summer of 1990, the process ground along.

The NBC-TV movie *Fall from Grace*, the supposed "balanced and dramatic" portrayal of Jim and Tammy Bakker and PTL, aired early in May. The movie riveted prisoners to the set in the TV room. I went to my cell and crawled into my bunk. One inmate after another called into my cell, "Come on, Jim! Don't you want to see yourself in a movie?" No, I did not. I could hardly remember who the real Jim Bakker was. In my counseling sessions with prison psychologist Dr. Foster, we were trying to separate the real me from the images of me as "Jim Bakker, television personality" and to discover what God expected of me. At that moment I was not interested in seeing a Hollywood caricature of myself.

I kept busy throughout the spring and summer of 1990 by immersing myself in teaching the smoking cessation course, even though at times I was so depressed I did not want to get out of bed. Often my only motivation to do anything at all was the knowledge that Tom and I had committed ourselves to helping the inmates who attended our classes kick the smoking habit. The class provided me with a sense of being needed.

Each week, my meetings with Dr. Foster were becoming more and more helpful in acclimating me to prison life. I had just begun an upturn on my emotional roller-coaster ride when I learned that a deal had been accepted by U.S. Bankruptcy Judge Thurmond Bishop to sell Heritage USA to California-based evangelist Morris Cerullo for $52 million, about ten cents on the dollar of what the total ministry was worth at the time I resigned as president of PTL. Morris had been a guest on our television program and hosted his own TV show as well. At the time the judge accepted Cerullo's offer, the evangelist placed $7 million in an escrow account to secure the purchase of the Inspirational Satellite Network, the prize plum at Heritage USA. Morris had until November 2, 1990, to come up with the other $45 million.

Morris Cerullo was not the first to have designs on Heritage USA and the powerful satellite network the PTL supporters and I had assembled there. Jerry Falwell (and others) claimed that Jimmy Swaggart wanted it, a rumor Swaggart vehemently denies to this day. Jerry Falwell took control of it and eventually realized that he had to get away from it. Within a few months after Jerry had encouraged my resignation, he and his associates took Heritage USA and the Inspirational Satellite Network into bankruptcy.

After Jerry Falwell and his friends left Heritage USA, Dr. David Clark, an employee of the Christian Broadcasting Network, became the trustee of PTL. David Clark remained in control of PTL from late 1987 through the summer of 1988. Sam Johnson, a former employee of mine, who had been appointed by Jerry Fallwell as pastor of Heritage Church, did his best to spearhead a reorganizational plan to save Heritage USA and the television ministry, but his plan never got off the ground. At a 1988 meeting with James Robison serving as a neutral party between us, I pleaded with Sam to allow me to return to help pull the ministry back together, but he said that because I was under disciplinary action by the Assemblies of God, he felt that he could not allow me to come back.

I had offered to meet with Reverend Roland Blount, the district superintendent of the South Carolina Assemblies of God, under whose jurisdiction the church now functioned. Reverend Blount had agreed without reservation to a meeting with his district board and me concerning my possible restoration. But then I received a letter from him stating that I had already had plenty of opportunity to appear before the North Carolina presbytery, the district with which I was ordained and under which the church had originally been established at Heritage Village in Charlotte. Therefore, my request for a meeting to discuss reconciliation was denied. The possibility of my returning to Heritage USA with any sort of blessing from my denomination was a dead issue. Along with the letter, the South Carolina presbytery sent me copies of a batch of letters.

As I looked at the letters, I could hardly believe my eyes. They were letters that had been sent to me via registered mail at PTL, requesting me to appear before the North Carolina Board of Presbyters. These letters were from North Carolina District Superintendent Charles Cookman and they were warm and kind and held out the possibility of pursuing a restoration process. But because I had not responded to the letters, the Assemblies of God leadership had assumed that I was not interested in working with them any longer.

Not only had I not received the original letters, I did not recognize the name of a single person who had signed for the registered mail. I began to piece together what had happened. The letters had been sent to PTL while I was still in California in the months immediately after the news of my resignation had been made public. They were clearly addressed to me personally, but not a single one of the original letters was ever forwarded to me. I would never have known the letters existed had not the copies been sent to me by Reverend Blount more than a year later.

In September 1988, I had hoped to buy Heritage USA and return it to the PTL Partners—whom I considered to be the rightful owners—but I was unable to obtain the necessary funds. That same month, Stephen Mernick, a Jewish real-estate investor from Toronto, backed out of his $65 million offer. By late 1989 a number of people, including billionaire David Murdock, owner of Cannon Village in Kannapolis, South Carolina, and the Christian Broadcasting Network's founder, and my former boss, Pat Robertson, had their sights set on PTL assets. According to the Charlotte Observer, Pat and CBN actually submitted a bid to purchase the PTL satellite network.[1]

My friend and the chief building contractor of PTL, Roe Messner, also let it be known that he intended to offer over $50 million for Heritage USA. George Shinn, owner of the NBA basketball team the Charlotte Hornets, and Cy Bahakel, owner of a group of television stations including one in Charlotte, also expressed an interest in the property. Oral Roberts and his son Richard announced their intentions to purchase the television network in July of 1990.

But by August 5, 1990, the top bidder was Morris Cerullo, thanks to the financial backing of a group of Malaysian Christian businessmen. Cerullo's offer was accepted by the bankruptcy judge.

Cerullo emphasized to the press that Tammy Faye and I would not be offered roles in his new ministry, which he dubbed "New Heritage USA" and the "New Inspirational Satellite Network." He did say that we were welcome to visit whenever we might like. Concerning Tammy and me, Cerullo said, "We're not looking for their endorsement. We're not looking for them to have any role. They'll be welcome on the property, just as anyone would be welcome on the property."

From my vantage point, it seemed doubtful that I would be visiting Heritage USA anytime soon.

In prison, I learned of the proceedings at PTL with mixed emotions. I felt as though people were fighting over my own child. Although I had always known Heritage USA belonged to the PTL Partners and ultimately to God, the Lord had used me to give birth to the place. At the 1979 groundbreaking for Heritage USA, when we had dedicated the property to God, I prayed a prayer like I had never prayed before. I said, "God, I dedicate this property, Heritage USA, to You today. If it ever be used for anything other than the gospel of Jesus Christ, let it be accursed." Years later, someone showed me a transcript of the dedication ceremony, and I was shocked to see my prayer in print. I had never before prayed a curse on anything or anybody, nor have I since.

I had numerous visitors during the spring and summer of 1990, Jerry and Sandy Barnard visited from San Diego where Jerry was pastoring at the time. Herman Rohde, an executive with the Minnesota Assemblies of God, also visited. My cousin, Marge Klages, sort of the matriarch of my family, visited shortly after I learned of the sale of Heritage USA. Marge and her sister Beverly Halgren greatly lifted my spirits by talking about our childhood days, growing up in Muskegon, Michigan.

Other visitors that summer included Don Argue, president of North Central Bible College and now president of the National Association of Evangelicals.

The month of September was a big month at F.M.C. Rochester. It was the time when inmates who had completed their Adult Basic Education, GED, or any other educational program went through formal graduation ceremonies, complete with cap and gown. The warden and other prison officials handed out the diplomas as the inmates filed by in the chapel. Besides the recognition that accompanied graduation, the graduates were allowed to stuff themselves with good food and all the cookies they could eat following the ceremonies. That in itself made graduation a big deal.

Dr. Westrick insisted that all the men who had completed Tom's and my smoking cessation course be honored along with the other graduates by going through the formal ceremonies. That was fine with Tom and me; it meant we could go to the ceremony and eat some good food too! It was rewarding, however, to watch our course participants traipsing across the platform to receive their "Nonsmoking" certificates from the warden.

On September 24, 1990, Tammy Sue gave birth to a six-pound, ten-ounce baby boy, Jonathan Douglas. Tammy Faye drove up from Orlando to visit her new grandbaby for a few days, and each night during her stay, I called from prison to talk to members of the family. Tammy Faye said it was almost like we were a family again . . . except that I was not there in person. As I talked to the family members by phone, I knew I was missing so much. I couldn't wait to see my new grandson, but he would be more than a year old before I ever saw him face-to-face.

Near the end of September, I learned of a difficult development in the life of someone I had once considered to be one of my best friends, Doug Wead. Doug had been a frequent guest on our television programs. He was a tremendous inspirational speaker and was a favorite among our audiences. In the mid-1980s Doug left the ranks of professional motivational speaking and writing, where he had carved a comfortable niche, and threw himself headlong into the Bush campaign organization. His desire to see George Bush in the White House became an obsession. For several years, Doug worked full-time for the campaign; in the process he lost a lot of money and a lot of friends.

Another friend who had become politically involved in the mid-1980s was Pat Robertson, host of *The 700 Club*. His political clout and his campaign war chest were growing on an almost daily basis. In 1986, Pat came to visit me at Heritage USA. I had not talked with him personally about his political aspirations. Tammy and I had hosted many daily programs on CBN and after almost eight years had resigned. Pat and I were never close after that. Nevertheless, when I learned that he wanted to stop by Heritage USA, I welcomed him with open arms. Following our visit, a guest on my television show brought up the subject of politics and a Christian's role in the political arena. Without endorsing Pat or any other candidate, I emphatically supported Pat's right to run for president of the United States. Just because Pat was a Christian minister, I contended, he should not be excluded from an opportunity to seek a role of political leadership if he were elected to it. I made a generic statement supporting Pat's right to run; I could have just as easily made the statement about a member of the ACLU or a Buddhist or any other citizen. I believed in the American Constitution that provides this freedom for all.

As the host of a daily talk show seen by millions of people, I wielded some measure of influence, and I had been courted by politicians of all sorts. I had been to the White House on several occasions and had flown in *Air Force One* with Jimmy Carter. I had been a guest of President and Mrs. Reagan at the White House as well as at their home in California. During one of my visits to Washington, I met then Vice President George Bush. On another visit, Barbara Bush invited Tammy Faye to her upstairs sitting room at the vice presidential residence to look at some of her needlepoint. I was not an enemy of the Bush presidential campaign.

Nor, however, was I a card-carrying member of the Moral Majority in the 1970s and 1980s. I have always been opposed to preachers publicly throwing their spiritual influence after a political candidate, regardless of the person's party affiliation. I have felt that as a private citizen, preachers have a responsibility to vote and to be involved in the political process as well as to help their congregations recognize their responsibility as citizens to do the same. But beyond that, it always seemed like a step down for a preacher to publicly endorse a particular person for political office. More important, I felt a minister should not alienate any group, but be able to minister to "whosoever will." My policy had always been if the president or any other leader called for prayer or spiritual help whether he be Democrat, Republican, or Independent, I would be there.

When George Bush came to Charlotte for a speech in 1986, I received an invitation to have lunch with the vice president privately in his downtown Charlotte hotel room. I gladly accepted. By this time, Doug Wead had become one of George Bush's closest advisers, especially in regard to religious issues and specifically those concerns of the Christian community that made up a large voting bloc in our nation.

Consequently, I was not surprised when, shortly after our lunch began, the vice president brought up the subject of Christianity. I quickly realized that the future presidential candidate was interested in how he might make inroads with the evangelical Christian voters. In the presence of only his personal aide and my assistant, George Bush probed, "Jim, I believe in God, but I am just not comfortable with the term 'born again.' That is not a term we use in our church tradition."

"Well, do you believe the Bible is the inspired Word of God?" I asked. "Yes, I do."

"Do you believe that Jesus Christ is the Son of God, that He was born of a virgin, and that He died on the cross for our sins? Do you accept Him as your Lord and Savior?" I asked the vice president.

"Yes, yes, I do," George Bush replied.

"Well, that's what being born again is all about."

The vice president and I went on to talk about prayer, and he emphatically declared that a day never went by when he did not ask for God's help and wisdom in dealing with his responsibilities.

Perhaps one reason the vice president asked me to lunch was so that I would support his efforts to become president and use my influence in any way I could to that end. But because of my past association with Pat Robertson and my recent support of his right to run for president, some members of the vice president's staff were not sure whose side I would be on in the coming primary elections. One of those people was my good friend Doug Wead.

By the time the election campaigns had begun in earnest in 1987, my problems had already become national news. Doug was a key player in the Bush campaign, still advising the vice president as to how he could best win the hearts and votes of the Christian voters. That is why, no doubt, Doug advised George Bush at this point to stay away from me. Doug later confessed to me that in the midst of my troubles, before I was ever even brought before a grand jury, much less indicted for a crime, George Bush asked Doug, "Should I intervene to help Jim Bakker?"

Doug replied, "Don't get involved. It could hurt you politically."

Doug Wead rode the Bush political bandwagon all the way to the top. He helped coalesce the evangelical community behind George Bush and in 1988 even wrote Bush's biography, *George Bush: Man of Integrity*, in an effort to convince conservative evangelicals that the candidate was "one of them." As a result, George Bush received a higher percentage of the evangelical vote in the 1988 election than he did any other single voting bloc. Once in the White House, Doug continued to serve as President Bush's liaison to the conservative religious community.

Doug's demise came in July of 1990 after President Bush's staff members began inviting liberal and left-wing leaders to White House events. Among the groups invited to various bill signings and other events in the spring and summer of 1990 were representatives from The National Gay & Lesbian Task Force, the ACLU, *Playboy* magazine, and the gay newspaper *The Washington Blade*. Conservative groups criticized the president. In an effort at damage control, Doug Wead wrote a letter that strongly reaffirmed the president's commitment to traditional family values. Doug further stated that the president's staff had not served him well by inviting such groups. Within weeks, on Friday, July 13, Doug Wead was fired. As often happens in the political arena, when a problem occurs, a scapegoat must be found and fired. Doug Wead became such a political sacrifice.

Tammy Faye sent me a news article describing Doug Wead's undoing. The man reflected in the article was not the man I knew, a man whose children had grown up with mine. I never knew Doug to be intolerant; in fact, I felt he was often liberal in his dealings with others.

As I read of Doug's termination, I was reminded of the fickleness of politics and the corrupting influence of power.

24

Lyndon LaRouche

AS I WALKED TOWARD MY CELL ONE AFTERNOON IN October 1990, I could not help noticing the large, imposing figure standing next to a pushcart in front of the cell. The cart was loaded with books, a few personal items, and prison-issued clothing. The man turned his head, and I immediately recognized Lyndon LaRouche. I had first met Lyndon months before and had talked with him briefly in the visitation room. Now, as I got closer to my cell, I realized Lyndon LaRouche was moving into my cell!

Lyndon was a political extremist and a five-time presidential candidate, although even the best political analysts could not pinpoint his positions on most issues. At various times LaRouche had been labeled as being on the extreme left, and sometimes the extreme right.

Lyndon was approaching seventy years of age and had deteriorating health. Despite this, Lyndon's mind was still sharp. His greatest pleasure came from engaging in combatant dialogues with any inmate who dared match wits with him. Most of Lyndon's dialogues quickly slid into diatribes, with Lyndon exercising his masterful grasp of the English language.

When one of our cellmates was transferred, the prison officials decided to house Lyndon with Tom and me since we were older and supposedly more stable inmates.

Tom thought it was extremely interesting that the prison now had two of its more notorious inmates—Lyndon LaRouche and Jim Bakker—living together in the same cell, something most press reports incidentally said would never happen when I was first incarcerated.

I actually enjoyed living with Lyndon—he certainly made prison life more interesting. Sometimes I tested Lyndon's knowledge just for the fun of it. As I lay on my bunk below Lyndon's, I would open my Bible dictionary or some other theological book and pick out the most remote word or subject I could find, something I knew little about. Then I would call up to Lyndon, "Hey, Lyndon, tell me about this subject." Lyndon would launch into an explanation of the subject that often matched the material in the book almost word for word.

Besides being an expert on every topic from virology to classical music, Lyndon knew every subject from its inception. Tom was convinced that Lyndon could not give a guy directions how to get to the rest room without going back to the time of Rome to explain it.

Although Lyndon had never been elected to any office that I knew of, the man was well connected to high-level information sources. While most inmates were still struggling to be awake at 6:00 A.M., Lyndon received a daily news briefing by phone that kept him up to date on world issues. He also received daily, lengthy, computer-generated intelligence reports through the mail. At times Lyndon's reports told of major news events halfway around the world several days in advance of their happening! Tom and I would often listen in awe as Lyndon would ramble German on his long-distance phone calls. We couldn't understand a word the man said, but he sure sounded impressive! Of course, many said that about Lyndon when he was speaking in English.

LaRouche was always upbeat, even when other inmates made fun of him, which they often did. And he always had plenty of jokes to tell. The only problem with his humor was that he was the only one who could understand most of his jokes. But I laughed along with him, because Lyndon's telling of the story was hilarious, regardless of the punch line.

To say that Lyndon was slightly paranoid would be like saying the Titanic had a bit of a leak. He was convinced that our cell was bugged by the prison officials. I never saw any evidence of it. But my friend Gleason introduced me to another inmate who worked on electronic systems for the prison. The inmate reported that the prison had recently received a shipment of small electronic listening devices. The electronic worker said that he had actually installed the bugs, but not usually in prisoners' cells. He had been ordered to install the bugs in locations where the prison officials could listen in on one another. That was all Lyndon needed to hear. He was convinced we were living in a virtual recording studio.

During the Gulf War, Lyndon's intelligence reports increased in frequency. Fascinated, I read some of the reports and then went to the television to watch the war reports on TV. Again and again, what I had read in Lyndon's reports was reflected on the screen . . . sometimes as much as a day or two later.

Perhaps because Tom and Lyndon were constantly haggling over some political issue or current event, Tom approached Dr. Westrick with the suggestion that it might be a good idea to have a weekly current-affairs group. The idea was to provide a setting in which inmates who were interested in such things could express their thoughts and opinions in a give-and-take atmosphere without fear of reprisal. Lyndon especially loved the idea. Dr. Westrick approved, and we initiated a Friday night meeting. The group included several Wall Street stockbrokers, bankers, lawyers, Dr. Tom Brandon, me, and of course, Lyndon.

In no time at all, our current-affairs discussion group turned into *The Lyndon LaRouche Hour.* It was interesting just to watch Lyndon "wow" the unsuspecting listeners who did not know him as he attempted to explain the current Persian Gulf crisis by reviewing history as far back as the ancient Roman Empire. Newcomers to the group did not want to appear ignorant, so they often simply sat there nodding their heads in agreement as they listened to Lyndon ramble on, even though they didn't have a clue what the man was talking about.

One Friday night we had a new member attend our discussion group. The newcomer was a bald, young, black man, about six feet tall with a muscular physique, wearing dark sunglasses. As was our custom, the moderator, a former mayor of Syracuse, invited the newcomer to introduce himself.

"I am the Messiah," he announced threateningly, "and I have come to save the world from Ronald Reagan and George Bush."

Something told me that this might not be the time to mention my dinners at the White House!

Most of the members in our discussion group stared at one another in disbelief. Then, we looked down at our shoes, at our hands, or anywhere except at each other or at the young man. All of us except Lyndon, that is. Lyndon was delighted to meet the fellow and quickly engaged him in conversation. Lyndon looked as if he finally had discovered someone in this prison who really understood him!

We later learned that the young man had been a law student at Berkeley and had actually broken into President Reagan's house in California, hoping to confront the president about how he was running the country. He had gotten as far as the Reagans' front door before Secret

Service agents apprehended him. Fortunately, the fellow did not attend our discussion group often; I'm not sure we could have handled the volatile mixture of Lyndon LaRouche and "the Messiah" in the same room for long.

Lyndon never left the political arena, not even while he was in prison. He ran for Congress in the 1990 Virginia elections . . . while he was still in prison! As part of his campaign, Lyndon's backers plastered the Virginia area with billboards and placards denouncing the president of the United States, not exactly a wise thing to do when you are in prison, awaiting an appeal of your case. Lyndon said he would have won that race had the election officials not tampered with the voting machines.

Some of Lyndon's ideas were quite interesting, especially his theories concerning the best ways to solve world hunger. His economic theories were fascinating too, as were some of his proposals to eliminate the national debt, but his ideas about colonizing Mars seemed a bit far-fetched to me. I never really knew whether Lyndon was serious about that one or not.

I was always respectful of Lyndon. I appreciated his quick wit and brilliant mind, even if I could not always understand him. However, many of the men who stopped by our room did not see Lyndon in the same light. One fellow who riled Lyndon was Rod Netherton, a wiry, extremely strong, karate expert. Rod was an airplane pilot, a sky diver, and a major marijuana smuggler.

Rod and Lyndon argued constantly. Regardless of the issue, we could be sure that Rod and Lyndon would be on opposite sides. Eventually Rod's incessant needling of Lyndon would be one of the major factors causing Lyndon to leave us and move down the hall to another cell, where he could have his own desk and a bottom bunk. Lyndon said he moved because of the constant parade of people coming to our cell. Tom said Lyndon moved because he needed the writing space from which he could mount his next presidential campaign.

Tom and I missed the daily intelligence reports and Lyndon's animated presence in our cell. Most of all we missed his colorful commentaries on everything from world events to what sort of efficiency measures should be instituted in the chow hall. Lyndon certainly livened things up. Fortunately, we still had the opportunity to enjoy his oratory at our weekly current-affairs meetings.

25

Buckingham, Colson, and Dershowitz

TOWARD THE END OF OCTOBER 1990, I RECEIVED A LETTER from Jamie Buckingham. At the time, Jamie, a pastor, was editor in chief of *Ministries* magazine, a columnist for *Charisma* (a leading Christian magazine), and had written more than forty books.

Enclosed with Jamie's letter to me was an article entitled "Praying for the Forgotten," which he was sending to me in advance of its publication in the December issue of *Charisma*. As I read Jamie's article, I was stunned by his bluntness and also by his kindness.

> I prayed for Jim while he was under attack by the press. I prayed for him during his trial. I lamented his sentence. Judge Robert Potter was harsh beyond reason. To sentence a nonviolent offender—of any kind— to 45 years in prison is not justice. In Jim's case it was cruelty, motivated, it seems, by vengeance against all enthusiastic Christians.
>
> The man who raped a 14-year-old girl, then hacked off her arms with an ax and left her staggering, naked and armless, along a dark road, received only seven years in prison. He now has resumed his normal life in a free world. . . . It is not right to give Jim Bakker a sentence seven times as severe as that given Al Capone. Bakker has been punished enough. He should be released.[1]

Jamie then went on to encourage his readers to pray for me and to write to me. I was deeply moved when I read the article. It was the first positive article I had seen about myself in over three years.

About the same time, I received a visit from Chuck Colson, former President Richard Nixon's famed "hatchet man" lawyer and special counsel who went to prison for obstruction of justice as a result of his role in Watergate. Shortly before going to prison, Chuck had become a Christian. Upon his release, he had founded Prison Fellowship Ministries, the largest prison ministry of its kind in America. Since then, Chuck had risen to become one of Christianity's most articulate spokesmen.

Chuck came to F.M.C. with an entourage. Chuck and I greeted each other in the visiting room, then sat down to talk.

Chuck had served seven months in a federal prison for his role in Watergate. Many had said at the time that the prison in which he had been incarcerated was a "country club" prison, but as Chuck emphatically stated, "If you were locked up at the Waldorf-Astoria, it would still be prison, because of your loss of freedom and being away from the ones you love."

Chuck encouraged me to fight my case through the appeals system, but to detach myself from it emotionally. "Take it one step at a time," he said. Chuck gave me a copy of his book *Loving God*, and assured me that he and his staff were available to help me any way possible while I was in prison. It seemed that they had just arrived and I was already waving good-bye to them as they were accompanied by the guards out the visiting room door.

I had been in prison for more than a year when, on October 30, 1990, my appeal was finally to be heard before the Fourth U.S. Circuit Court of Appeals in Richmond, Virginia. My team of attorneys presented part of my case, and Professor Alan Dershowitz presented the remainder to a panel of three judges. I was not required or permitted to attend the proceedings.

My lawyers contended that the trial judge failed to ensure that an impartial jury, untainted by publicity, heard the case. They also challenged Judge Potter's decision to disallow a five- to six-day break in the trial after I was released from my psychological evaluation at Butner Federal Prison. Also called into question were the judge's instructions to the jury before their deliberating my case, which said that they could convict me if they felt I had deceived people in raising money for PTL projects.

When it came to my sentencing, Alan Dershowitz hammered home the point that U.S. District Judge Robert Potter made an "incredible departure" from federal guidelines in sentencing me to forty-five years in prison. Alan argued that if my conviction was not overturned completely, at the very least I should be resentenced by another judge. Most important of all, however, was Alan Dershowitz's argument that Judge Potter had been biased by his own religious beliefs in sentencing me. Dershowitz reminded the appeals judges that moments before imposing the forty-five-year sentence, Judge Potter had said that "[Bakker] had no thought whatever about his victims, and those of us who do have a religion are ridiculed as being saps [by] money-grubbing preachers or priests."[2]

Deborah Smith, one of the U.S. Justice Department lawyers who had prosecuted the case, replied that Judge Potter's comment merely reflected overall testimony. "I don't think it at all reflects a personal bias on the part of the judge, but rather a reflection of what went on in that courtroom," Smith said.[3]

Alan Dershowitz did an outstanding job highlighting the errors in my case and in my sentencing. The same could not be said, however, of my Texas attorneys' attempt to contest the merits of the case. At one point they implied to the judges that I had not intended to defraud the PTL Partners, merely deceive them. My lawyer said. "It is not against the law in this context to deceive."[4] Of course, I had intended to do no such thing—defraud or deceive the PTL Partners! That was the last day the Texas firm worked as part of our legal team.

Now came the waiting game. This was not Judge Wapner making an arbitrary decision in a few moments of time after listening to the arguments on both sides. The appeals judges were permitted by law to take as long as necessary before rendering a decision and putting it in writing. Most appeals courts for cases such as mine took between four to six months before presenting their verdict.

In rendering their decision, the judges could decide in several possible ways: They could declare my trial a mistrial and throw out the case altogether; they could demand a new trial; they could reduce my sentence from the forty-five years to something less; or they could reduce my sentence to "time already served," and I would be free.

Tammy Faye rallied our friends to pray and petition lawmakers on my behalf. In a letter to me, she sounded almost exuberant,

> *Everyone* is praying for the appeal! I feel that God must move in our behalf. We have been faithful to Him during this thing, and I know He will not let us down. I believe, Jim, that we are on the brink of a miracle. So hold on a little longer, honey. This too shall pass. I love you! I miss you!

As for me, I was encouraged by the report that Alan Dershowitz had done well but discouraged that the remainder of the issues surrounding my trial were still blurred and distorted.

Chuck Colson wrote to me and said, "I've only discovered two kinds of inmates: . . . those who are still fighting their case and are miserable and . . . those who have accepted their lot, understand God has a purpose for their life and therefore are at peace and free."

I was beginning to understand. I did not feel free, but I was at peace.

CHAPTER

26

I Won't Be Home for Christmas

NOW THAT MY APPEAL HAD BEEN MADE AND WAS IN THE hands of the judges, I could do nothing but wait . . . and pray.

During this time I heard from a Florida man, Dr. Richard Arno, president of the National Christian Counselors Association. Dr. Arno felt compelled to send me information concerning their counseling course and the Temperament Analysis Profile, a psychological testing tool.

The course cost over $1,500, but Dr. Arno offered to send it to me free. I wrote back to Dr. Arno, telling him I would be interested.

I was fascinated when I began to study the course. From Dr. Arno's material I learned that temperament is the inborn part of a person that determines how he or she reacts to people, places, or things. Temperament pinpoints a person's perception of himself, determines how that person deals with the stresses and pressures of life, and shows a person's weaknesses and strengths.

Most temperament tests define four categories: Melancholy, Sanguine, Choleric, and Phlegmatic. Dr. Arno's test included a fifth category: Supine. Most people are a combination of temperaments rather than exclusively one or the other. Nevertheless, we usually lean toward one or two areas.

People who have a melancholy temperament often exhibit great intellectual abilities and are self-motivated, but they may also be withdrawn, moody, and living with a constant fear of rejection.

Sanguine temperaments are usually people oriented, open, and friendly individuals, but they may also be self-indulgent, rude, and superficial.

Cholerics tend to be well-organized people motivators who require a great deal of recognition, but they can also be dictatorial and controlling.

People with a phlegmatic temperament are often slow paced, calm, easygoing peacemakers, but they may also be self-contained, stubborn, uninvolved, and lacking in emotional response.

A supine is often a person who has a gentle spirit, is servant oriented and a people pleaser, but may also suffer from lack of self-esteem, loneliness, fear of rejection, and a victim mentality.

Like many people who study temperaments, I began to see myself, as well as my family members and friends, in the various characteristics. My temperament, I found, is a mixture of melancholy and supine.

Beyond the temperament material Dr. Arno's course provided valuable information about how to counsel people suffering all sorts of psychological and spiritual maladies, especially those suffering depression. Again, as I studied in preparation to help someone else, God was providing me with the precise information I would need to face what was happening and about to happen in my own life.

My family's second Thanksgiving in prison was tough to handle, but at least we knew what to expect. Pastor Phil Shaw was once again the great facilitator, picking them up at the airport, taking them to their hotel, and transporting them to the prison. It was wonderful to see my family members again. I could hardly believe how big Jamie was getting. I was so proud of my son.

Our good friends Faye and Ray LaForce from Canada had flown to Florida to accompany Tammy and Jamie to Minnesota. We discussed my appeal and the possibility of getting out of prison, and even the possibility of building or buying another retreat center where we could invite all the PTL Lifetime Partners to come and receive the benefits of the partnership they had anticipated at Heritage USA. One of the things I dreamed about in prison was how I could somehow restore to the PTL Lifetime Partners that which they had lost when PTL collapsed.

The following day, we were joined in the visitation room by our dear friends Dr. Basil Jackson and his wife Leila from Milwaukee and Dr. David Lewis and his wife from Springfield, Missouri. What a thrill it was for me to see these family friends.

The last time Dr. Jackson had seen me for any length of time, I had talked with him from a fetal position beneath the couch in Harold Bender's Charlotte law office. Dr. Jackson was delighted to see me adapting relatively well to prison life. At least I was standing upright—that was some improvement! The psychiatrist later expressed concern, however, that my imprisonment was beginning to take a heavy toll on Tammy and especially on Jamie.

As Tammy Faye and my other guests prepared to leave, my emotions began to get the better of me. We hugged and kissed and then waved good-bye. "Honey, I love you. Keep singing!" I called after Tammy Faye.

Tammy Faye called back, "I love you too. See you in a few weeks for Christmas!"

Not again. I was not looking forward to my second Christmas in prison.

Throughout the fall, I kept busy teaching the smoking cessation class. Each month, Tom and I started all over again with a new batch of inmates who wanted to quit smoking. We were just finishing our November class when the unit manager, Mr. Houston, told us that some of the inmates were complaining that Tom and I were not working hard enough since we had begun teaching the smoking cessation course. They were threatening to file discrimination charges. As a result, the unit manager informed us that if we wanted to continue to teach the class, that was fine, but we would also have to clean toilets on the weekends. Tom and I were assigned to toilets again.

The first week in December, I received some good news: My friend Franklin Graham, son of the Reverend Billy Graham, was coming to see me. Franklin and I had known each other for a number of years and had worked together on several projects dating back to the early 1980s. In 1980, Franklin joined Samaritan's Purse, a Christian relief and evangelism ministry that spreads the gospel by meeting the physical and spiritual needs of victims of war, famine, disease, and natural disasters. In 1982, Franklin was organizing an effort to help build an additional wing to Tenwek Hospital in western Kenya. The hospital was seriously overcrowded, often filled to 200 percent occupancy, with many patients sleeping on the floor.

When Franklin came on *PTL*, we talked at length about his work with Samaritan's Purse. Franklin began to tell me about the hospital in Tenwek and its over 200 percent occupancy.

"How does that work?" I asked. "One hundred percent is full. What does it mean to have a 200 percent-plus occupancy?"

"It means they have more than two patients to a bed." Franklin handed me a photograph that had not two people in one hospital bed, but three. I held the photo up so the cameras could get a shot to show the viewers, and I asked, "Franklin, what can I do to help?"

"Well, they need a new ward, and I'm trying to raise some money to have it built," Franklin replied.

"How much is it going to cost?" I asked.

Franklin Graham answered, "They think it's going to cost about four hundred thousand dollars."

I turned to the camera and said, "Everybody watching right now, I want you to send Franklin Graham one dollar. Send more if you want, but send him at least one dollar. Don't send it to me. Don't send it to PTL. Send it to Franklin Graham. Can we put Franklin's address on the screen?" I asked our technicians in the control room. Almost immediately, the address showed up near the bottom of millions of television screens.

I turned to our studio audience. "We're going to take an offering, and I want each of you to put in one dollar or more." Within minutes buckets were found to collect the offering. Every dollar went to Franklin Graham and Samaritan's Purse to help build the wing on that hospital in Kenya.

Two months after our spontaneous offering, I invited Franklin to return to *PTL* to give us a progress report.

"Money has come in from all over the country," Franklin told our viewers. "We received more than fifty-six thousand letters." Franklin reminded me that the hospital had needed four hundred thousand dollars to add the new wing. "And Jim, God provided through you and your partners more than we needed." Then Franklin Graham did something that nobody had ever done before on *PTL*. He reached into his pocket, pulled out a check, and handed it to me as he said, "We received a total of $409,000. Here is a check for $9,000. We want to give this back to PTL."

Franklin often reminded me that the interview on *PTL* had not only been the springboard to launch the new wing of the hospital, but it also made many people aware of Samaritan's Purse. Many of those people who sent in that first dollar have been some of the most faithful and generous benefactors of Samaritan's Purse over the years.

Franklin Graham was coming to see me, and it was not on the comfortable television set of *PTL*; it was in prison. I wasn't sure how he would react to me, but I could hardly wait to see my friend.

Franklin also agreed to speak in the prison chapel that evening. Tom Brandon and I were in the chapel early to help arrange the room when Franklin arrived with singers Dennis and Danny Agajanian. We walked toward each other and embraced. Franklin greeted me warmly, and all my fears concerning his acceptance of me melted away instantly. Dennis and Danny Agajanian greeted me with huge bear hugs. Dennis and Danny are extremely talented musicians who can play almost any instrument put before them. The brothers are both huge, rugged looking guys. I knew the inmates would love the Agajanians, and they did.

The brothers performed a blend of gospel, country, and bluegrass music, including a rip-roaring guitar rendition of "Dueling Banjos." The prisoners roared their approval. Following the Agajanians' music, Franklin Graham stood before the men and told them of his rebellion against being Billy and Ruth Graham's son and more importantly, his rebellion against God. The prison officials had informed Franklin prior to his visit that he was welcome to come on two conditions: that he did not acknowledge that he knew Jim Bakker and that he not have an invitation to accept Christ at the close of his talk. Franklin disregarded both conditions. From the podium, he publicly referred to me as his friend as he told the inmates how we met. Then at the close of his talk, he invited the inmates to commit their lives to Jesus Christ. Many of them did. Even my cellmate, Dr. Tom Brandon, said the night with Franklin Graham and the Agajanians was one of the best times of his life.

As Franklin and the Agajanians prepared to leave, I thanked them profusely for coming. "You will never know what your coming here means to these men . . . and especially to me."

Franklin Graham laid his big hand on my shoulder and said, "Jim, you stood with me when I was just starting out. You were my friend then and you are now. Anything you need, you can count on me."

No gift Franklin could have given me was greater than his affirming friendship.

That night, I began to realize what a gutsy thing Franklin had done by identifying himself with me, a disgraced television evangelist as far as the world was concerned, and a convicted felon. Of all the people whom I might have expected to allow their names to be linked with mine, I would never have thought that Franklin would have risked the Graham name. He had nothing to gain and everything to lose by identifying with me. I had been in prison for over a year now and had not heard a word from many of the people who were regularly seen on our television programs. Franklin demonstrated risky, genuine Christian love.

More and more, I understood why the Christmas season is one of the toughest times of the year for people in prison, so I especially appreciated the many kind cards and letters I received. I read and saved every one and sent them home in big boxes.

One letter was both encouraging and amusing. It came from Melvin M. Belli Sr., the old famous lawyer who was the first attorney who offered to represent me in the dark days of March 1987. I could almost hear Melvin's gravelly voice as I read his encouraging letter. The blustery lawyer had once referred to me as the "best damn Christian I know."

Another surprising letter came from Sonny Singer. More than forty years earlier he and I had been best buddies in Muskegon, Michigan, when we were between the ages of seven and twelve. Sonny was Jewish and knew of my deep love and concern for the nation of Israel, and although he and I were of different religious persuasions, his letter reverberated with tremendous faith. I was surprised that he expressed confidence in my early release from prison.

The Christmas card I received from my eighty-four-year-old dad nearly ripped my heart out. He cried for me almost every day and often told me: "I wish I could take your place, son." Daddy wrote:

> We know that your Christmas will not be like so many Christmases in days gone by, but God will be with you there. We are sure God will vindicate you soon. The jury is out now about the civil suit that some of the Lifetime Partners are supposed to have instigated. The best thing about this is that you are not guilty.
>
> I am feeling much better. Mother is okay, considering her age and all.

One of the cards that touched me most deeply during the holidays was from a woman I had never met. She wrote:

> In June of 1978 we went to PTL. My husband was not a believer and drank very much. But after watching you on TV he said we could go, although he did not believe. When we arrived at PTL, he was convinced the ministry was of the Lord. When we got back home, he chose to support your ministry financially. He told his friends, "I gave to the drinking places in this town for ten years and all I got was nothing. But these people are helping to change lives from a way that has no end but hell." He felt so strongly about your ministry, because you were real. I praise God for seeing a man coming home drunk change into a man in church with our two girls, praising God. My husband went to be with the Lord in 1981, but I want you to know, I am to this day so grateful for what your ministry did for our family.

That dear woman's card was one of the best Christmas presents I could have gotten that year.

Because I was receiving so much Christmas mail I wanted to send out some sort of Christmas greeting to the many people who had written to me. An inmate, who was a friend of mine, sketched a charcoal line drawing of me holding baby James during Tammy Sue's last visit. He was a true

207

artist and the drawing came out beautifully. I wrote a free-verse poem, describing my prison experiences to date. Tammy Faye and her staff reproduced the drawing on the front of a card with my poem inside, and they sent it out as a Christmas card from me. I had asked Tammy Faye to put my name on the computerized mailing list to receive one of the cards, since I had not seen the finished product. Just before Christmas, the card arrived at the prison. When the guard checking the mail saw a card *from* Jim Bakker *to* Jim Bakker, red flags popped up in his mind. *Something must be wrong here*, he must have thought. He turned the card over to the lieutenant's office. The prison official called me in to interrogate me.

I tried to explain to the official that Sam Houston had suggested having my wife send out the card from Florida. I explained that the card had been part of a computerized mailing, and my name and address were on the list, so I automatically received a card.

The officer stared back at me as though I were speaking a foreign language. "No, there must be more to it," he insisted. The officer demanded that I appear before the prison council. I was called in to give an account before the prison counselors, case managers, and other prison bigwigs.

I began to explain to this group in rudimentary terms how I received the card. This group of individuals worked every day with computers and other modern mailing equipment, and I had no sooner begun my defense than the entire roomful of people burst out laughing. When they realized the foolishness of the charges, they dropped them.

I told Tammy Faye that I preferred that she not come for Christmas that year. Of course I wanted to see my family, and Tammy had been trying to find inexpensive airline tickets, but the best she had been able to do was $515 each. I hated to see her spend that sort of money, plus several hundred dollars more for a hotel bill, when they did not have much money in the first place. Besides, I remembered how painful it had been for all of us last Christmas when my family had visited. I told Tammy, "The only gift I can give you this year is for you not to have to spend Christmas in prison again." My family reluctantly agreed to spend Christmas in Florida.

Since my family would not be coming for Christmas, Tom Brandon and I volunteered to serve at the Christmas dinner sponsored by the prison Jaycees for the inmates and their family members on Christmas Day. There was some question as to whether the prison officials would allow me to be involved in the Christmas dinner. The prison brass was adamant about me maintaining a low profile. I signed the volunteer list anyhow.

On Christmas Day, I walked over to the chow-hall door, lined up with the other volunteers, and waited to be allowed in to begin working. My name had made it onto the list of approved workers. We later discovered that the list of volunteers working at the Christmas dinner had not been reviewed by anyone in an upper-level position but had in fact been approved by an inmate working in one of the offices!

Once inside the chow hall, the volunteers separated into groups. Tom and our friend Richard were busboys. Others were to pass out the Christmas presents that the Jaycees were allowed to distribute to the children of the inmates. The job they gave me? Maitre d'.

My responsibility was to greet and help each family as they came through the serving line. This was probably the last job the prison officials would have wanted for me, since it meant that every single person coming in to eat that day would see Jim Bakker. "I can see the headlines now," Tom said, "Jim Bakker—The Official Host of Prison Christmas Dinner!" All the guys helping on the serving line broke up in laughter. I was having a ball, smiling at everyone coming in the chow hall, wishing them a Merry Christmas, pointing them in the direction of their utensils and food, and helping the elderly ladies with their food trays.

Late in the afternoon, the prison warden, other top officials, and Dr. Westrick came into the chow hall. When they saw me serving as host, their mouths dropped wide open, but nobody said a word. I greeted them as I had all the others, with a hearty welcome and a Merry Christmas.

I spent most of the remainder of Christmas Day in my bunk. Working with the Jaycees and serving the Christmas dinner to the inmates and their families had kept me too busy all day to become depressed over the fact that my own family was all the way across the nation. Then, as I lay in the dark, I missed my family terribly, and I could not prevent myself from sinking into despair.

The new year was about to begin, and I was a year older. Of course, one of the questions that occupied my thoughts frequently was, "How long, oh Lord? How long will I have to stay in prison?"

With my appeal now in the hands of the judges, Tammy Faye was hoping and praying for a speedy release. I was not quite so optimistic. One of us was about to be proved right.

27

Back in the Pits

JANUARY 1991 WAS THE BEGINNING OF ONE OF MY WORST downhill slides into one of the worst periods of depression I had known since coming to prison. Although I had encouraged my family to stay away at Christmas, I missed them horribly. It was the first Christmas of my life that I had not celebrated with my family. It was the first time I had not been with my family on my birthday. My emotions took a nosedive.

Adding to my depression was news that I had lost another legal battle. In 1987 the people who took over PTL and put it into bankruptcy hired a lawyer to instigate a multimillion-dollar class-action lawsuit against me, PTL builder Roe Messner, David Taggart, one of my top assistants at PTL, and our accounting firms of Laventhol & Howath and Deloitte, Haskins, & Sells. The suit alleged a conspiracy between PTL's builders, banks, accountants, and of course, me, to launder money and use it for our personal gain. It was a lawsuit seeking more than $575 million in damages. Even if the case would have had legitimate merit—which I felt it did not— I had no money anyway.

Most of the Lifetime Partners who expressed their sentiments to me wanted nothing to do with the lawsuit. They knew I had not defrauded them of anything, that their "Lifetime" gifts were just that—a gift or a donation to the PTL ministry. Many of the Partners were convinced that if I had been allowed to return to Heritage USA, they would have received everything they anticipated at PTL and much more. Hundreds of Partners wrote to U.S. District Judge James McMillan on my behalf. Many stated that they wanted their names to be withdrawn from the suit, because the suit did not represent their feelings toward PTL or toward me. As a PTL Lifetime Partner, if a person did not specifically write and ask to be removed from the civil litigation, he or she was automatically included.

Originally, those bringing the suit had hoped to win a large sum of money from our accounting firms or possibly from Roe Messner. When it became obvious that there was no misconduct on the part of our accountants or builders, one part after another of the case was dropped off the suit. In the end, the only defendant left was me. After more than three years of legal wrangling, a panel of judges decided that I was innocent of criminal charges, but guilty of civil charges of defrauding my Partners of $135 million. In other words, if I had any money, people would have been standing in line for it.

In prison, I was almost oblivious to what was going on in the world outside the razor-wire fences. My struggle was simply to get out of bed each morning and face another day. I could do nothing about the case, and I was trying my best just to keep my head above water emotionally. When I heard the news of the judges' decision, however, I was devastated. Beyond that, I wondered if the decision of the civil judges could adversely affect the decision of the appeals judges.

About this same time, because of budgetary restraints, the prison officials refused Tom's and my request for new films and other materials to help enhance the smoking cessation course. The juices that health experts felt were a physiological help to the guys as they were trying to stop smoking had also been refused.

Furthermore, when Tom and I had been reassigned to cleaning toilets as well as being allowed to work as teachers, Sam Houston had informed me that I had not been receiving "good time" for the months of work I had spent preparing for and teaching the class. Under the law, I was allowed to receive up to ten days per month—good time—for doing exemplary work and being a model prisoner. An inmate's good time could be deducted off his sentence. Good time is a prison's way of offering inmates an incentive to behave, especially for prisoners with long sentences such as mine. Now I learned I had worked from April to December and would receive not a single day's reduction of my sentence for the effort. It was discouraging.

My awful feelings of homesickness for my family, the disappointments concerning the smoking cessation course, and of course the blow delivered by the civil case verdict multiplied the effects of my depression. I did not want to do anything. I did not want to eat, drink, shave, or bathe. I began to allow myself to become more and more disheveled and unkempt, making little to no effort to clean up. I began to grow a beard, not because I

211

thought it would enhance my appearance, but because I no longer cared about my appearance. My clothes now went unpressed and often unwashed. I looked like a homeless person.

Tammy Faye wrote effusively throughout the months of January and early February, encouraging me that God was about to do something. Because I missed her so terribly, her letters—many of them written on lovely, feminine stationery—were bittersweet. For example, in January, she wrote: "I am just sitting here missing you. I wish you were here! I would give anything in the world if you could just walk in the door. But I know that one day soon that is going to happen. I could not live if I didn't believe that!"

In another letter, Tammy wrote: "I miss you so badly that sometimes I don't think that I can stand it another day. But I believe that this is about to come to an end. I expect *victory*! And I live in that expectancy! Every day! I am always saying and thinking, 'Next week Jim will be back home!' And I believe that."

In letter after letter, Tammy encouraged me, "Don't give up! We're on the brink of a miracle."

About that same time, I received an uplifting letter from Pat Boone.

Shirley and I have been your friends for years, and continue to be. As I hope you know, we defended you and Tammy everywhere, not faults or mistakes, but your hearts and accomplishments and desires to serve the Lord, which you did so admirably in so many ways. I just want you to know that Shirley and I still love you, are still your friends and brother and sister, and will always stand ready to help in any way we can. I'm sending you a song I wrote and produced, "The Fallen Giant."
Whenever I have sung it, and I have on a number of Christian television programs, I've always mentioned you by name and urge people to pray for you, and to stand by a wounded and fallen brother. Our hearts hurt especially for Tammy and the family, but no less for you. And we are confident that the Lord will not only see you through all this, but is still working everything together for our good, because we do love Him and are called according to His purpose!

In a letter I received from Tammy Faye near the end of January, she included a list on which members of our congregation in Florida wrote down their prayer requests, asking other members of the church to pray for them. On the last Sunday of January, there among all the requests on the list, in his own handwriting, was the name "Jay Bakker." Beside his

name in the prayer request column, Jamie had printed only: *My Dad.*
When I saw the unadorned prayer request of my boy, I burst into tears.

Once again, the Lord used ordinary circumstances to literally pull me
out of my bunk and back into the mainstream of life in prison.

I had maintained my association with the Growth Awareness
Development Association, the predominantly black group desegregated
only by Lyndon LaRouche and me. I have always had a great affinity
toward the black community, and for some reason, I have always been
accepted among most black people. As far back as the mid- to late 1960s,
when I was working at the Christian Broadcasting Network in
Portsmouth, Virginia, and doing *The Jim and Tammy Show*—our daily children's program, and *The 700 Club*, I had begun to invite members of the
black church community to appear on our programs. At that time most
churches were black or white; few congregations were integrated. But
Tammy and I wanted to minister to the whole community, not simply the
white segment of the Tidewater, Virginia, area. To our surprise, however,
we experienced great difficulty in getting black children to come on our
show. Finally, I contacted the pastor of one of the black churches and said,
"Pastor, we can't get black children to come on our show, and we want
them. Can you explain this to me?"

The pastor answered straightforwardly, "We have been told in so many
ways for so long that we are not wanted by the white community, not even
by the white churches, that we will not attempt to push our way in."

"But you are wanted on our program. Won't you please come?" After
about a year of calling and scheduling black churches to come and bring
their children to our show, black children finally began coming. At times
as many as 50 percent of the children on our program were black. Our
efforts had paid off.

While at CBN, I invited Doris Akers, who had written the classic song
"Sweet, Sweet Spirit," to come and lead a racially mixed choir on our live
television show. We never knew who was going to show up for the
rehearsals in those days, but amazingly, every night that Doris was there,
we had an even 50 percent mix of black and white singers. The same mix
held true the nights the choir sang on *The 700 Club*. Everyone involved felt
that God was giving us an obvious lesson in race relations. Some of the
best long-term benefits of the choir were the new friendships formed
between white and black people, who had previously been unaccustomed
to speaking to each other, let alone working together for the glory of God.

At Heritage USA, the black community was especially welcome, and
they knew that, and they came. Over the years, I had numerous black
guests on my programs. Pearl Bailey, E. V. Hill, Mahalia Jackson, Mr. T,

213

Kim Fields, Della Reese, Willa Dorsey, Rosey Grier, my beloved board member Dr. Evelyn Carter Spencer, Meadowlark Lemon, "Mother" Smith, Carlton Pearson, Clifton Davis, Marla Gibbs, Lillie Knauls, and many, many others graced our set. Tammy and I especially loved black gospel music. Some of our outstanding musical guests included the great Shirley Caesar, Andrae Crouch, Candi Staton, Jessie Dixon, and the legendary black songwriter Thomas A. Dorsey, who wrote "Precious Lord Take My Hand" and "There Will Be Peace in the Valley." I was also honored to have working with me black artists and ministers such as Derek Floyd, BeBe and CeCe Winans, Brenda Davis, Bob Bailey, Howard McCrary, Reverend Russell and Sandy Hosey, Pastor Hank and Emily Walker, and the host of the African *PTL* program, Benson Idahosa.

Race was never an impediment to my friendships. I had grown up in a racially mixed neighborhood in Michigan where blacks and whites mixed freely. Moreover, I always felt that if there was any place where people should be color blind, it was in the Church.

Because the guys had selected me as chairman of the religious activities committee, the responsibility to help secure an inspirational speaker for the Black History Banquet was passed to me. Because the stated goals of GADA were to improve the educational backgrounds of its members and to provide constructive leadership programs that would help the inmates return to their home communities as assets rather than liabilities, I naturally hoped to bring in a speaker who would bring both a practical and a spiritual dimension in his message.

One of the first names to come to mind was Dr. James E. ("Johnny") Johnson, the first black man ever to serve as the assistant secretary of the U.S. Navy. A former marine with a dynamic personality, a contagious smile, a quick wit, and a keen intelligence, Johnny Johnson is a man who inspires confidence. Johnny had once been a member of my board of directors in the early days at PTL, and I knew he was a dedicated Christian. In Johnny's stellar career, he had achieved over a hundred "firsts" for the black race. For instance, Johnny was the first black to become a commissioned warrant officer in the United States Marine Corps. He was also the first black to run for the U.S. Senate from California. He was the first black to be elected vice president of the Boy Scouts of America, and the list goes on and on.

When Johnny had agreed to come to the prison to speak at the GADA banquet, I was elated. To have a speaker of Johnny's caliber would be a treat indeed. Since I was the chairman of the committee that had been instrumental in helping our sponsor contact Johnny, I had been asked to introduce Johnny before he spoke. At the time, I had agreed. But by early

1991, I was wallowing in my own personal doldrums. I would not even have attended the GADA banquet, much less introduced the speaker, had it not been for my friend Johnny Johnson coming to speak. Once again, God was not going to allow me to waste away in my bunk. He used my friendship with Johnny and my prior commitment to force me back onto my feet.

On February 8, 1991, the evening of the GADA banquet, I shaved off my beard, showered, and put on fresh, clean, sharply pressed clothes for the first time in weeks. The banquet was scheduled to begin at 5:15 P.M., so after the 4:00 P.M. count had cleared, I walked across the compound to the chapel basement, to help set up the room and wait for my friend to arrive.

Johnny's plane was late that evening, so by the time he got to the chapel, the inmates and prison officials attending the banquet were already seated at their tables. As the person who was to introduce Johnny, I was seated at the table across from the guest of honor's table. When Johnny came in, he was seated at the head table, right next to the warden. Johnny nodded to me and flashed his trademark smile as he sat down.

When it came time for Johnny to speak, I got up and walked to the platform. The warden looked shocked to see me going to the podium, especially in light of the prison's efforts to maintain my low-profile status. I was not deliberately trying to violate the prison's wishes; I was merely fulfilling my obligation as chairman of the religious activities committee.

I was nervous as I stood behind the podium in front of the large room filled with people. I had spoken in front of our smoking cessation class, which was frightening enough, but this was a much larger group of people. I had not spoken before such a sizable group in several years. As I began introducing my friend Dr. Johnny Johnson, I relaxed a bit and started listing some of his many accomplishments. Soon, I was sharing stories and telling the banquet guests interesting tidbits about Johnny. The inmates were fascinated, but the longer my introduction went on, the more agitated the warden and prison officials looked. Although I was not reprimanded or punished in any way, I would not always be so lucky.

Finally, I finished my introduction, and Dr. Johnson bounded up the stairs to the podium. He made some kind remarks about me and then launched into his talk. In a matter of moments, the inmates were on the edge of their seats as he chronicled his rise from a poor, black family to the top of the military ladder. Throughout his speech, he interspersed stories that reached right inside the inmates' hearts.

Johnny told us about the death of his twenty-three-year-old son, Ken, who had died in the operating room during a relatively routine procedure in which the doctors failed to notice that oxygen was not getting to the young man's brain. Johnny's son had a cardiac arrest on the operating table. He remained alive, through the use of artificial life-support systems, for nearly two more weeks. As Ken's heartbeat slowed to an agonizing halt, Johnny leaned over his boy and whispered, "I'll meet you in heaven . . . I promise."

Johnny told us, "If you keep God ahead of all things, you will succeed." His idea of success related to one of his son's favorite sayings: "It isn't important what you do for yourself, because that will die with you. But what you do for others will live on afterward." When Johnny Johnson finished his speech, the inmates gave him a rousing round of applause. More than that, I knew that we had heard a message from God. I decided that I could not allow myself to hide in my bunk. If I had to live in prison every day for the rest of my life, I was going to make those days count.

CHAPTER

28

Good News

I WAS TEACHING THE SMOKING CESSATION COURSE ON the morning of February 12, 1991, when I heard a commotion at the door. Tom Brandon opened the door. "I'm sorry to interrupt you, Jim, but would you please come out in the hall for a minute?"

"Excuse me, please," I said to the class, as I followed Tom.

Out in the hall, I saw Rod Netherton and Tony, the president of the Jaycees. They were grinning as wide as their mouths would allow.

"All right, you guys," I said. "What's going on here?"

Rod suddenly blurted, "Your appeal has been granted!"

"What do you mean?" I stammered. "Come on, you guys. Don't joke with me." I looked at Tom Brandon. Tom was smiling and nodding his head.

I started to cry right there in the hallway.

"It's true! It's true!" my friends assured me. The guys did not know any of the details, but someone had seen the news on television.

Back in Florida, Tammy Faye was doing the housework when the telephone rang. She picked up the receiver and heard Tammy Sue's voice on the other end of the line, sobbing into the phone, "Mama, Mama! Have you heard the news about Daddy?"

"What is it?" Tammy Faye screamed into the phone.

"Mama, they have dropped Daddy's forty-five-year sentence! I just heard it on the news!"

217

Tammy Faye dropped the telephone and raced to the television to turn on the news. Sure enough, the reporters were still talking about the fact that my sentence had been overturned by the appeals court. As the full impact of the news set in on Tammy Faye, she realized that she had to get to Jamie at school before the media did. She said a hasty good-bye to Susie and quickly called the school officials to get Jamie for a very important call. When Jamie came on the line, Tammy Faye said, "Jamie, they have dropped the forty-five-year sentence against Daddy!"

Our fifteen-year-old son began to cry. "Are you sure, Mom? Are you sure? Oh, Jesus! Jesus! Thank You, Jesus!" Then the phone went dead.

A few minutes later, Tammy Faye's phone rang. It was Jamie. "Mom, I'm sorry I hung up on you," he said. "I was hyperventilating! I had to calm down so I could breathe. Now, Mom, please tell me about it again . . . *real slow*." Tammy reassured Jamie that the news was true, and that the reporters were saying it was possible that I might be freed immediately on bond while I awaited a new resentencing hearing. To my family members, the news meant one thing: I was coming home soon!

About the time Jamie hung up the telephone, I was on the phone from prison to Tammy Faye. "Tam! What is happening?"

Tammy told me what little information she had been able to gather from the television news reports. Suddenly, a call came over the prison loudspeaker system: "Inmate Bakker, report to the warden's office." I quickly said good-bye to Tammy and walked as fast as my legs would carry me toward the administrative offices.

The assistant warden explained to me what had happened. The good news was that the federal appeals court had thrown out my forty-five-year sentence. At that moment, I no longer had a prison sentence. The bad news was that the same court had upheld my original conviction on all twenty-four counts of wire fraud, mail fraud, and conspiracy charges for which I was imprisoned. I was to be returned to Charlotte, North Carolina, within the near future to be resentenced by a different federal judge. Since I had been allowed to be home on bail during the time between the original verdicts and the original sentencing, I would proba-bly be allowed to return home on bail while I awaited my resentencing. In the meantime, I needed to be ready to move out on a moment's notice.

I walked out of the assistant warden's office not knowing whether to laugh or cry. I had given up all hope that I would actually win my appeal and that the verdicts would be overturned. Attorney Allan Dershowitz had been quite blunt in informing me that the other attorneys involved in my appeal had botched their efforts. In fact, as I was later to learn, my attorneys had lost my appeal on every point except one: that Judge Robert Potter had improperly allowed his own religious prejudices to influence him in sentencing me. Specifically, the appeals court declared inappropriate Judge Potter's statement spoken during the sentencing, "Those of us who do have a religion are ridiculed as being saps from [by] money-grubbing preachers or priests." The opinion was reached by Judges J. Dickson Phillips Jr., John D. Butzner Jr., and Judge J. Harvie Wilkinson III who wrote:

> As the community's spokesperson, a judge can lecture a defendant as a lesson to that defendant and as a deterrent to others. If that were all that occurred here, the court would have been properly exercising its discretion, and we would be loathe to disturb what surely is an integral part of the sentencing process. Sentencing discretion, however, must be exercised within the boundaries of due process. . . . In this case, the trial judge exceeded those boundaries. Courts have held that sentences imposed on the basis of impermissible considerations, such as a defendant's race or national origin, violate due process. . . . While these cases focused on a defendant's characteristics, we believe that similar principles apply when a judge impermissibly takes his own religious characteristics into account in sentencing.
>
> Our Constitution, of course, does not require a person to surrender his or her religious beliefs upon the assumption of judicial office. Courts, however, cannot sanction sentencing procedures that create the perception of the bench as a pulpit from which judges announce their personal sense of religiosity and simultaneously punish defendants for offending it. Whether or not the trial judge has a religion is irrelevant for purposes of sentencing. Regrettably, we are left with the apprehension that the imposition of a lengthy prison term here may have reflected the fact that the court's own sense of religious propriety had somehow been betrayed. In this way, we believe that the trial court abused its discretion in sentencing Bakker. Consequently, the sentence is vacated and the case is remanded for resentencing. This resentencing will be carried out by a different district judge to ensure that the ends of due process are achieved.[1]

I called Tammy Faye again. This time I could barely contain my excitement. "Tam, it's true! I'm going to be resentenced. They just told me that I could be released from this prison on bail at any time."

Tammy screamed with joy through her tears.

We had no sooner hung up when one of my lawyers called Tammy to confirm the news. He told Tammy that a hearing would be held soon concerning the bond issue, but he saw no reason why the judge would deny bond and not allow me to be released until my resentencing. One of our good friends told Tammy Faye that he would gladly post the bond money, and my family began getting ready for me to come home.

Although my family, my friends, and I considered the vacating of my original sentence to be a victory, the resentencing itself held no guarantees that I would receive a lighter sentence. The same prosecutors who argued the original case were bent on asking the new judge for the identical sentence—forty-five years. Since they had won their case and the convictions had withstood the appeal, they must have felt confident that they could persuade the new judge that I deserved the same sentence. The new judge could uphold Judge Potter's sentence. On the other hand, he could reduce the sentence to "time served," and I would walk out of prison a free man. Or, he could cut the original sentence in half or thirds. We really had no idea how the judge would rule.

Nevertheless, my family and I were more excited about the possibilities of my release than ever before. Tammy Faye prepared a press release for the media in which she said, "My family and I are very grateful to the appeal court judges for their decision to drop the forty-five-year sentence given to my husband by Judge Potter. I just talked to my husband. Everyone is excited for him. I believe that before this is all over, my husband will be totally exonerated."

In Cambridge, Massachusetts, Alan Dershowitz was equally ebullient, commenting to the media, "Tammy says this is a great victory for Christians. I told her it was a Jew that did it, so let's call it a great victory for religious freedom in America. She agreed."[2]

Again, the "hurry up and wait" syndrome set in and was perhaps the most difficult part of the resentencing process. Harold Bender, one of my original lawyers on the case, filed a motion with the court asking that I be released on bail until the resentencing hearing could take place. A hearing would have to be held to determine whether I could be permitted to return home until my resentencing hearing.

The bond hearing took place in Charlotte, before Judge Graham Mullen, on March 1, 1991. Although I was not allowed to attend, Tammy Faye and my sister Donna drove from Orlando to attend the proceedings. The judge's decision whether to allow my release on bail hinged on two points: Was I a danger to the community, and was I a flight risk?

The prosecutors contended that I was a risk to the community because if I were let out on bail, I would begin soliciting money or Tammy Faye would do so in my name. Judge Mullen rejected this argument as unpersuasive. Next, the judge dealt with the matter of whether I might try to escape. My lawyers called as witnesses Tammy Sue; Eddie Knox, my former attorney and the former mayor of Charlotte; Reverend Douglas Pyle, a pastor at New Covenant Church in Orlando; and the psychologist with whom I was counseling in prison, Dr. Daniel Foster. All of the witnesses spoke confidently that they did not believe I would try to escape before my resentencing hearing. Dr. Foster, who had flown in from Rochester, spoke eloquently on my behalf, providing his opinion from a psychological perspective that I was not a flight risk.

When the witnesses had all been heard and cross-examined by the prosecutors, Judge Mullen dismissed the courtroom. On March 6, 1991, the day before Tammy Faye's birthday, Judge Mullen rendered his decision:

> While Dr. Foster no doubt is sincere, and even on sound professional grounds, in giving his opinion that the defendant is not a flight risk, this still falls short of meeting the defendant's heavy burden. The speculative nature of any psychological evaluation, combined with Mr. Bakker's previously demonstrated susceptibility to aberrant behavior in stressful situations, prevents this court from concluding that the defendant is clearly and convincingly not a flight risk . . .
>
> Accordingly, the defendant's motion for release pending resentencing is Denied.[6]

Denied! Tammy Faye was stunned. She had totally expected me to be released on bond. After all, I had been released on bond between October 6, 1989, when I had been found guilty and October 24, 1989, when I had been sentenced originally. And I had already spent over a year in prison and had been "a model inmate" with no negative marks against my record.

Tammy Faye burst into tears. Denied! I would not be sleeping in the same bed as my wife. I would not be able to hug my children every day. I would not be allowed to see my grandsons, one of whom I had yet to see. No amount of bond money would get me out of prison.

A brief trip to the assistant warden's office was how I found out that I would not be going home anytime soon. For some reason, I accepted the news in stride. The prison axiom, "You ain't got nothin' comin'," had been drilled into my head by my fellow inmates. I went back to my cell and unpacked my belongings.

I went to the phone to place my collect call to Tammy Faye. As soon as the operator put us through, Tammy asked, "Jim, are you okay?"

"I'm fine, Tam. I'm just numb."

For the next few minutes we tried to encourage each other. Our best attempts seemed futile, and before long, we hung up.

Just before we said good-bye, Tammy said, "I just don't know how many more shocks we are going to be able to stand."

Not many, as I was soon to find out.

CHAPTER

29

Burnout

ON APRIL 4, 1991, TAMMY FAYE AND SHIRLEY FULBRIGHT boarded a plane to Wichita, where Tammy was to do her first-ever ticketed gospel music concert.

Wichita was Roe Messner's hometown, and he was excited that Tammy had chosen to sing there. I had talked with Roe a few days before and had encouraged him to watch out for Tammy and to take care of her. Roe and his wife, Ruth Ann, visited with Tammy Faye and Shirley on the evening of April 4. Ruth Ann especially went out of her way to welcome Tammy Faye to Wichita. The following night, nearly six hundred people almost filled the theater to hear Tammy Faye sing and speak.

In Wichita, the Messners treated Tammy Faye like a queen. Ruth Ann hosted a lovely luncheon for Tammy with many of the leading women of the city. Then a number of the women piled into a limousine Ruth Ann had arranged, and the limo whisked the women off for a shopping spree. All in all, Roe and Ruth Ann Messner went to great lengths to provide Tammy with one of the nicest weekends she had known in a long time.

At first I was glad I had asked Roe to look out for Tammy. When Tammy sent me some of the photographs taken that weekend, I wasn't so sure. One photo bothered me particularly. It was a photo of Tammy and Roe, with Roe's arm around Tammy's waist, pulling her snugly toward him. I winced when I saw the picture, but I quickly put jealous thoughts aside. Tammy was my wife of thirty years . . . and Roe was my best friend.

One of the reasons I was able to not dwell on negative thoughts about my wife and best friend was because I was receiving a tremendous amount of spiritual insight from another book, *Spiritual Burnout* by Malcolm Smith.

As I read Malcolm's book, it was as though he had a computer printout of my innermost thoughts, describing what had happened to me during my last years at Heritage USA. In those days, I was not exaggerating when I told friends that by the end of the day, I had to literally tell my feet to lift up and take another step. I worked feverishly and constantly; I could do nothing less, because in my heart and mind, I felt I was doing it all for God.

Malcolm Smith placed a mirror in front of my face when he said: "The man or woman who does not reach for the top will never suffer from burnout; it is a condition found only among those who want the best."[1]

That was me! In my high school annual, I listed my future goal as "To do the best at everything I do." And I tried to. Malcolm Smith's book, however, helped me realize that although it was not wrong to want to do my best, I had developed an obsession with trying to do the best for God in an attempt to earn His favor. I never truly grasped the meaning of God's grace, which would have helped me understand that I already *had* God's favor; nothing I could possibly build or do for God would ever earn His favor because He had already bestowed it on me as an undeserved gift.

I did not like what I was beginning to realize. One of Malcolm's statements struck me right between the eyes: "The spiritually exhausted person . . . needs a completely new perspective on the way he thinks about life."[2]

I began to detect a pattern in what God was showing me through my prison experience and my newfound understanding of the words of Jesus. God was performing major surgery on my heart.

Smith's message drove home my responsibility to repent. I examined my heart. In truth, I *had* repented. I had poured out my heart to God, repenting of my sins and seeking His forgiveness.

I asked God to reveal any areas in which I still needed to repent, but I found that repentance was not the paramount issue on God's agenda for me. He was speaking to my heart about issues that went even beyond repentance.

God had been showing me that the reason He had allowed me to be imprisoned was not to punish me, nor was it so I could minister to other prisoners; I was in prison so I could know Him. Some people might find it ironic that a preacher who had spoken to millions of people about God needed to be sent to prison to renew a relationship with Him. But I am convinced there was no other way God could have gotten my attention. God wanted me to quit worshiping bricks and mortar, programs and talents, and get back to worshiping Him.

I discovered that I could go no farther until I confronted the matter of forgiving the people toward whom I harbored bitterness and resentment. Again, Malcolm Smith clarified the issue:

> Forgive those who have failed you, who were not there when you needed them the most. Forgive the gossips who carried the news of your exhaustion and problems to every believer in the vicinity. Forgive those leaders and elders who have hurt you with their words and actions. And forgive those who you thought were spiritual giants, but were found to have feet of clay and a set of weaknesses just like everyone else.[3]

Ouch! Malcolm, couldn't you mince at least a few words? The author went on: "We become the slave of the person we hate. . . . Unforgiveness hurts the unforgiver more than the unforgiven!"[4]

I had been so busy building Heritage USA—ostensibly for God—that I had lost my intimate relationship with Him.

A second area that came into focus was my relationship with Jamie Charles. Someone had sent a picture to me of four-year-old Jamie in Hawaii, sitting on the stage with several PTL band members, playing his little ukulele. As I put the picture up on the wall of my prison cell, I asked myself, *Where was I?*

Someone else sent me a picture that tore my heart apart. The picture showed me at one of the many building sites on which construction was being done at PTL. In the picture, I was standing with a bodyguard at my side, and in the background, looking on from a distance was my little boy, Jamie. When I saw the photograph, I literally wept in my cell. I was so intent on building Heritage USA that I missed my little boy growing up. I thought, *He was so cute! Why didn't I spend more time with him?*

Certainly, I had tried to be a good father to my son. Like any good dad, I had taken him places, done fun things with him, and tried to create special memories together with him. Yet somehow I had become so obsessed with "the work of God" and "saving the world" that I was oblivious to the longing look in my little boy's eyes that said, "I need my dad."

Instead of Dad, Jamie's constant companion was a PTL bodyguard. During the 1980s we had received several death threats, reported to us by our chief of security, Don Hardister. Although no attempts were successfully carried out against our family, an insane man once came to Heritage claiming that God told him he was supposed to rape and kill Tammy Sue. The man was apprehended and sent back to the asylum. We also received numerous bomb threats. Merited or not, we lived with a constant awareness of danger. Consequently, our children had bodyguards. While growing up, Jamie's closest friends were his adult bodyguards.

The bodyguards drove Jamie from place to place. They played with him while I was busy erecting another building. They picked him up after school. I hardly remembered Jamie Charles's childhood. He had just been born when we had started PTL in an old furniture store in Charlotte. Then we moved to a twenty-five-acre site we called Heritage Village, and our ministry began to take off, multiplying exponentially. Analysts from IBM Corporation estimated that we grew 7,000 percent over the next year and a half. We could barely keep up—things were happening so quickly. Before long, we were building Heritage USA. In the midst of the swirl of activity, I lost touch with my family, and especially with Jamie. I was not there when he needed me. I confused the *work* of God for God Himself.

I was wrong.

I am now convinced that God must come first in our lives, then our family, and *then* the work that we are doing for God. If our family crumbles while we are trying to serve God, we have missed our primary ministry. Yet that is exactly what I allowed to happen. It happened so subtly, while I was busy doing what I thought was important work for God.

My self-imposed responsibilities at Heritage USA were massive. I was the president of The Inspirational Television Network, seen on two hundred television stations and on over eight thousand cable systems. The television production center and the twenty-four-hour-a-day programming on our satellite system all came under my oversight. Of course, I served as executive producer and host of our daily flagship programs, variously named *The PTL Club*, *The Jim and Tammy Show*, and simply, *Jim Bakker*, seen live in all fifty states and in many foreign countries.

I was also the senior pastor of Heritage Village Church and Missionary Fellowship, with a congregation of several thousand people attending services each week. I preached at most of the Sunday morning services, unless I was out of town. As pastor, I was responsible for a staff of twenty-five assistant pastors, an active Sunday school program, and the usual fare of church ministry programs for all ages as well as special ministry needs, including weddings, funerals, baptisms, and communion services. We were not simply a television program. We were a bona fide church.

I also had spiritual oversight of all the other ministries at Heritage USA, including: New Vine Fellowship, a ministry to help alcoholics and drug addicts get free of their addictions and stay free; Heritage School of Evangelism, where we trained college-age young people in the techniques and methods of evangelism; Heritage Academy, a kindergarten through grade twelve Christian school; Heritage Day Care; The Heritage Preservation Society (formed to help preserve our religious heritage, such as the childhood home of Billy Graham, which was moved from Charlotte and restored at Heritage USA, with the help of Dr. Graham's brother,

Melvin); Fort Hope, a center where street people and former prisoners could find help, a home, job training, and spiritual development; Heritage House, a home for pregnant women; Tender Loving Care Adoption Agency, to help place babies in Christian homes; People That Love Centers, over nine hundred centers nationwide that provided free food and clothing and helped with job placement; Prison Ministry, placing Christian literature and Bibles in prisons; *Together* magazine, our full-color monthly magazine; Kevin's House, a home for disabled children; and The Upper Room Prayer Center, a replica of the Upper Room in which Jesus and His disciples ate the Last Supper before His crucifixion. The Upper Room was staffed twenty-four hours a day with pastors and a worldwide phone center for those seeking spiritual counseling and prayer.

In addition to these responsibilities, I was president of Heritage USA, the world's largest Christian retreat center. At the height of our efforts, our staff provided eighty-six religious services each week. According to PTL figures, more than six million visitors came through the gates at Heritage USA in 1986, the last full year I served as president. We had seven restaurants, three swimming pools, three trains, 3,336 lodging rooms and campsites built or being developed, Mainstreet USA shops and religious bookstore, a dinner theater where inspirational musicals and plays were performed with full orchestra, Heritage Island, a huge, $13 million, state-of-the-art water park staffed by seventy lifeguards per shift, and the Heritage Passion Play, a dramatic presentation of the life of Christ in a multimillion-dollar outdoor amphitheater. We also had time-share lodgings and a retirement village, which included single-family homes, high-rise condominiums, apartments, and duplexes, in various stages of construction.

Oh, yes, we also had a hotel. At the time of my resignation the five-hundred-room Heritage Grand was completed and the five-hundred-room Heritage Grand Towers was under construction and would have been completed within a few months. Besides all that, I was our chief fund-raiser, responsible to raise the money to keep it all going, which, in 1986, was almost $170 million.

It was little wonder that I burned out. I had allowed my attention to become centered on the packaging rather than on the Gift.

Now, as I sat in my prison cell, staring at the pictures of my boy who had gotten lost in all the buildings, I would have traded my entire life's work for just one full day that my boy and I could spend together, doing whatever Jamie wanted to do. My little boy was now a young man. I prayed that somehow, some way, I would have another chance to be a real father to my son. Although I could not have imagined it then, that time was soon to come.

227

30

"Big Doc"

IN THE EARLY PART OF 1991, I LEARNED THAT DR. TOM Brandon would soon be leaving Rochester prison. I was happy that Tom was getting out of prison, but I was sad to know that my best buddy was leaving.

On one occasion, as Tom and I were walking down the hall with our arms loaded with materials used for our class, a young guard approached us about only cleaning toilets on weekends. The guard persisted in questioning how Tom and I were allowed to spend our time studying instead of cleaning. He seemed intent upon getting us back to cleaning bathrooms full-time again.

Finally, Tom pulled his glasses down on his nose—he looked like Jerry Lewis in the 1960s movie *The Nutty Professor*—and peered at the guard's name tag. "What is your name, sir?" he asked and then read the guard's name aloud in a professorial tone of voice. "I will have Dr. Westrick call you and tell you what Jim and I do under her supervision."

When the guard heard Dr. Westrick's name, he started backing up, holding his hand over his name tag. "You don't know me!" he said. "We didn't have this conversation!"

Although Tom lost his license to practice medicine when he was incarcerated, he never ceased to care for people. One day, Tom was in the chow hall when he saw an inmate stretched out on the floor. A bite of cheeseburger had gotten stuck in his throat. As Tom approached the scene, besides choking, the man was beginning to go into a cardiac arrest.

Prison officials were attempting the Heimlich maneuver, but it was not working. Tom knew he was going to have to apply mouth-to-mouth resuscitation. He had only one question: *Does the man have AIDS?* As Tom jumped into the center of the chaos, the victim's body was already turning an ashen gray. The doctor in Tom took over, and as he wiped the vomit from the man's mouth and covered it with his own, he thought, *If I get AIDS, I get AIDS, but I have to try to save this man's life.* After several minutes of Tom's blowing air into the man, the choking man began breathing on his own again, and his life was spared. Tom sighed with relief when he later learned that the man did not have AIDS.

Since November, when Sam Houston had informed Tom and me that we would have to clean toilets on the weekends if we wanted to continue teaching our smoking cessation class during the week, we had spent every weekend, every holiday cleaning the rest rooms. Our lives revolved around shining porcelain bowls, mopping tile floors, and scouring shower stalls with our long-handled brushes.

Each day, the guards inspected our work, and regular monthly inspections were done as well. The inmate unit section with the cleanest facilities was permitted to line up first in the chow line, which amounted to about fifteen minutes earlier than the others. As such, it was a big deal that Tom and I kept the bathrooms as clean as possible.

That job was made more difficult on weekends because the inmates were in the unit. When we were doing the same job during the week, most of the men were out of the building at their respective jobs. On the weekends, however, many of the guys were "home." After trying several times to do my work on the weekend only to have other inmates tramp over the still-wet floors and flush the commodes that I was disinfecting, I inadvertently discovered a way to keep the other inmates out of the bathrooms until I had time to complete my cleaning.

One of the inmates tramped across my wet, freshly cleaned floor and was about to use one of the commodes in which I had just placed a dose of A-500 chemical cleaning agent. I usually allowed the disinfectant to sit in the toilet bowl for ten to fifteen minutes, causing the water to turn bright yellow. When one of the guys used the commode before I was done, I'd start over. This time, however, when the man saw the bright yellow water in the commode, he pointed and asked, "What's that?"

"Oh, that's the stuff the prison gives me to kill all the bacteria in our bathrooms," I said, adding nonchalantly, "including the AIDS virus."

When the man heard me say AIDS, he backed up immediately.

"AIDS virus! You go right ahead, Bakker. Don't let me bother you. I'll be back when you're done."

From that day on, anytime I wanted to keep the men from using the bathroom in which I was working, I would tell them I was disinfecting for viruses, including the AIDS virus. Inevitably, they would suddenly find the energy to make the short walk to the next bathroom down the corridor.

I had been working through the temperaments course provided by the National Christian Counselors Association (NCCA). Because I had been an ordained minister and had been counseling people for years, the NCCA gave me credit for my work in the field. So by completing this course of study, I would also have a professional counselor's license and the ability to administer and help interpret a wide variety of tests used in formal counseling situations. Part of my training required that I test and counsel a number of people, with the help of my instructors.

Tom Brandon volunteered to be one of my first guinea pigs. Shortly before Tom left F.M.C. Rochester, I administered a Temperament Analysis Profile to him. If completed honestly the short test is designed to reveal a person's true nature. Ordinarily, the results of a person's test were to be discussed over as much as a six-month counseling period. But since Tom was going to be transferred soon, he and I went over Tom's entire test in one night.

"It says here that you are an extreme introvert, a compulsive loner," I told Tom, "that you are a very private person, a homebody, someone who would rather stay home than go out and socialize."

"Well, I could have told you that." Tom laughed as he brushed off the comment. I could tell, though, that the description had hit home and that he was thinking about it seriously. "What else does it say?"

"Well, it says that you are very task oriented. That you relate well to tasks and systems, but you have little understanding of people."

"Hey, that's why I became a doctor!" Tom laughed.

"The report says that you are unwilling to allow anyone to control you. That you have low self-esteem, and that it is almost impossible to make you feel loved and accepted. It says here that you are an extremely lonely person." I stopped and looked up at Tom. He wasn't laughing now.

"Apparently, in an effort to lessen your loneliness, you are prone to undertake sexual sins. But the sexual relationships don't mean much to you." I knew this to be true. Tom had admitted to me that he had slept with over one thousand women over the course of his lifetime. He was not simply looking for love in all the wrong places, he was not looking for love at all. To him it was just sex, nothing more. He was not seeking affection. To him, physical touch had to lead to sex or else it was a waste of time. He didn't care about the women with whom he slept and he didn't want them to care about him. "The report says that your deep relationships are few and far between." I could not recall Tom having a visitor, and he rarely got personal letters. Most of his mail was magazines and medical journals.

"The report also says that you have a strong tendency to use alcohol and drugs to lessen the pain of living your everyday life." It was true. Tom had been an alcoholic. Part of the reason he was in prison related to his drinking problem. He slumped down on his bunk and stretched out, facing the ceiling. I was beginning to feel like a psychiatrist.

In one area after another, the test results seared into Tom's inner person. He was disturbed by the inside look at himself. He had never allowed anyone to know the things about himself that I was now reading.

We talked well into the night about the test, as well as the recommendations made by the National Christian Counselors Association concerning how Tom could use the information about himself. To Tom, the test was life-changing. It was as though he saw the real Tom for the first time.

A few days before Tom was transferred to a state prison, I wrote out a "prescription" for him from "Dr. Bakker." Since Tom was a medical doctor, I knew he would appreciate my effort to give him a "Prescription for Life." I included instructions for Tom to get married and maintain a monogamous relationship with only one woman; I encouraged him to attend regular Alcoholics Anonymous meetings; I cautioned him against ever taking another drink, because it would likely throw him right back into the destructive patterns of his past; I also instructed Tom that he was to read his Bible regularly and to find a good church he could attend, and to take care to maintain and develop his faith in Jesus Christ.

When Tom read the prescription, he smiled and nodded his head. I sensed that Tom truly appreciated that my concern for him stretched beyond the prison fence.

It was tough to say good-bye to Tom. He had been my cellmate, my coteacher, and my best friend in the Rochester prison. I was going to miss him badly. Toward the end of April we got word that Tom was going on the "Merry-go-round," one of the last trips an inmate takes around the prison compound, securing release signatures from each department head, including the inmate's unit manager, the chaplain, the inmate's day guard, as well as somebody from the recreation department. It was sort of a last check to make sure that the inmate did not have any work or forms to be completed before release, and a last good-bye to everyone too. It usually took an inmate all day to work his way around the "Merry-go-round."

On the Friday night before Tom left, we decided to have a going away party for him. Around 7:00 P.M., at a time when most of the prison officials except the guards were usually gone for the evening, we assembled in the

"Quiet Room," a twelve-by-twenty-foot room where the inmates played cards or went to read and study. The guys went all out and got our usual assortment of food including prison pizza and mop pails filled with ice and cans of soda pop. At least twenty-five guys showed up and were standing around talking, eating, and laughing when suddenly the door opened and in walked Sam Houston, the unit manager.

Instantly, silence enveloped the room. It was not against the rules to assemble in one place, but it was against the rules to eat in the card room. We had been caught.

Sam Houston instantly recognized what was going on. Had he wanted to be nasty, he could have had each of us thrown into the "hole" for being at the party. Instead, he walked slowly around the silent room and greeted each man by name, pausing an extra few moments to chat with Tom, the guest of honor. When he got back to the door, he addressed the room full of inmates.

"Carry on, gentlemen," he said with a hint of a smile. He turned around and walked out the door.

For a moment nobody said a word. One of the guys broke the silence by saying, "He's not such a bad guy after all." At that everyone cracked up and Tom's going-away party continued.

I have never liked good-byes. To this day, I am not good at them. Nevertheless, my friend Tony and I walked Tom over to the building through which all prisoners enter and leave the Federal Medical Center at Rochester. There he would go through the final strip search and change of clothes before exiting the prison and boarding the bus to "someplace else."

Just before we got to the R & D area, Tony and I stopped and embraced Tom. Men in prison do not usually touch, but when a fellow inmate is leaving, it is considered acceptable to give him a brief hug or a slap on the back. We said our good-byes. We did not prolong them.

Tom waved good-bye one more time and then stepped inside the door to R & D. I have never seen him since. Nor have I been allowed to talk with him because of parole regulations that prohibit fellow inmates from contacting each other for an extended period of time after they are released. The last I heard, Tom was going to AA meetings, rebuilding his life and his medical practice, and married. He has been actively involved in helping other alcoholics beat their addictions. I may never see him again, this side of heaven, but I will always be grateful to "Big Doc."

31

Partners for Life

A FEW WEEKS BEFORE TOM BRANDON WAS TRANSFERRED from F.M.C. Rochester, I had my progress review at the prison. Once again I was called before the review team, which included numerous prison officials, my counselors, and Sam Houston. Although everyone in the room knew that I was to be resentenced, it was obvious that I was still going to be calling Building Two my home for a while. My resentencing hearing had been delayed until May 31, 1991, over a month away.

The review team considered every aspect of my prison experience, including my work habits, mental and physical health, my volunteer activities, and my overall attitude. They reported that by my working "in toilets," and with other funds taken from my commissary account, I had been able to pay $1,050 toward the five-hundred-thousand-dollar fine imposed on me by Judge Potter when he had sentenced me in October 1989. The review also noted that my release date was October 15, 2034, but my projected release date was Tuesday, December 15, 2015. This included the thirteen days of "good time" I had earned. No matter how I looked at it, my report said that I was going to be in prison a very long time.

Despite the report, I was relatively upbeat. My request to be released on bail until the resentencing had been denied, but I still held on to hope that my resentencing might result in a reduction of the amount of time I would have to stay in prison. Tammy Faye had convinced Alan Dershowitz to stay on the case to handle my resentencing hearing even though Alan had readily admitted that he was an appellate lawyer and resentencing was not his area of expertise. Nevertheless, knowing that Alan was on the case gave me some hope.

More importantly, though, I had been immersing myself in the words of Jesus more and more. In addition to the Bible, I was also studying several books that I felt had been providentially sent to me.

I had read Malcolm Smith's book, *Spiritual Burnout*, over and over to the point that I could quote many passages of it almost verbatim. Another book, sent to me by the same woman in New York who had sent Malcolm's book, was also having a profound impact on me. *God Meant It for Good*, by R. T. Kendall, minister of Westminster Chapel in London, is a study in the life of Joseph. Although I didn't know it at the time, the book was destined to become a "manual" for me during the remainder of my prison years.

When Pastor Phil Shaw came to visit me in April, he noticed the change in my attitude and demeanor immediately. Phil later called Tammy Faye's office and talked to Shirley Fulbright. He told her that for the first time since he had known me, he saw hope in my eyes and in my spirit. He said the change was phenomenal and he attributed much of it to the book I was reading. Phil was right.

One day one of the inmates brought me a newspaper article that someone had sent him from the March 9, 1991, edition of the Chicago Tribune. The headline read: "PTL Materials Used as Textbook." The article described a college course at the College of Charleston, taught by Associate Professor Gary Tidwell, a former attorney with the U.S. Securities and Exchange Commission Division of Enforcement. The course studied the business practices at PTL, and on at least one occasion, students had even taken a field trip to visit Heritage USA after I had gone to prison. According to the article, students taking the course ostensibly were to "find and analyze 'red flags' in their PTL materials that are inconsistent with ethical business practices and that signal trouble ahead."[1]

Ordinarily I ignored most newspaper and magazine articles about me that crossed my path in prison. But for some reason, my interest was piqued. Perhaps because I was interested to see just how someone could develop an entire college course out of our business practices at Heritage USA, I read the article.

It laid out in bite-size, simple terms why I had been put in prison. As strange as it might seem, I had been asking myself and a few of my fellow inmates for just such an answer for nearly a year and a half.

"Why am I in prison?" I would ask my friends.

Usually they would laugh and make some sort of wisecrack.

"No, really," I said. "What crime did I commit? I want to hear your answer."

"Well, you know," my friends would say, "you . . . er, ah . . . well, you know, you stole all that money."

"What money? How much?" I asked.

"You know!" They insisted. "That $190 million you bilked those people out of. . . ."

"No, I do not know," I replied.

"Yeah, right," some of the guys would answer. One fellow said, "I'll bet you have that $190 million stashed away in a Swiss bank account."

Another fellow even wanted me to help set him up in business when he got out of prison, with the money I had supposedly stolen.

But those closest to me said, "What do you mean, you didn't steal all the money, Jim? Where did it go? If you didn't steal the money, what are you doing in here?"

When I read the Tribune article, for the first time since before my trial in 1989, I began to understand why, from the government's perspective, I was in prison. The article said it succinctly: "Overselling the hotel space and reneging on the lodging promises was at the core of Bakker's convictions in both a criminal fraud trial and a civil class action trial."[2]

For some reason, despite the five-week trial in 1989, I had never fully realized this before. Now, there it was right in front of me, in black and white: I was in prison for overbooking our lodging space at Heritage USA. Syndicated columnist and radio commentator Paul Harvey had first raised his eyebrows at this possibility in his article that ran in the Sunday papers less than two weeks prior to my sentencing. Harvey asked: "Are we really going to send Jimmy to prison for 120 years for overbooking his resort when hotel managers almost every day promise more rooms than they can provide? Airlines also almost every day overbook flights. Let's keep this in perspective."[3]

As I read the article about Professor Tidwell's course, I was appalled at the errors it included or implied. I pointed out several of the errors to one of my friends, and he encouraged me to write to the professor to help provide him with firsthand factual information for his course.

So on April 14, 1991, in my cell, late at night, I began drafting a letter to Professor Tidwell. I first asked the professor to identify what I did wrong. "What is my crime?" I asked him. "The article says I was tried, convicted, and sentenced for swindling my supporters. How much did I steal? (Give facts, dates, and amounts)" I then wrote about points of the article that weren't true.

Tidwell's students were apparently shown videotaped highlights of past *PTL* programming.

> The students hone in on those parts where Bakker gets down to business—such as segments where he announces a 25,000-person-limit on "lifetime partnerships" for the 500-room Grand Hotel; and later, a 30,000-limit on the 500-room tower addition. Both of those partnership plans guaranteed three nights free lodging every year for life.
>
> Despite those promised limits, court documents revealed that more than 68,000 partnerships were sold for the Grand Hotel. Another 63,000 were sold for the hotel's tower addition, which was never built as PTL went bankrupt.[4]

It was the last line of that statement that really got to me—reporting that the hotel's tower was never built, and implying that I had bankrupted PTL. The twenty-one-story Heritage Grand Tower *had* been built while I was still at PTL. The Tower was only about two to three months from opening when news of my sexual immorality with Jessica Hahn and subsequent resignation as president of PTL hit the press. The rooms in the Tower had already been carpeted through the tenth floor and had been wallpapered through the thirteenth floor. Most of the custom-designed furniture for the rooms had already been manufactured and was in local warehouses. Many of the hotel's accoutrements had already been purchased and were on site, ready to be installed as soon as the interior work was done on the Tower. Ironically, Professor Tidwell's own students would have had to have seen the Tower during their "field trip" to Heritage USA. To say that it had never been built was simply not true. I sent Professor Tidwell a photograph of the Tower as proof.

To his credit, at least Professor Tidwell encouraged his students to go tour Heritage USA for themselves. That was more than the jurors had been allowed when my original case had been tried.

What also bothered me was the implication in the article that I had taken PTL into bankruptcy. I wrote to Professor Tidwell, "PTL was not bankrupt when I left. Our debt-to-asset ratio was one-to-six on book value with no consideration for the appreciated value of the property." My estimation of the actual value of Heritage USA and The Inspirational Television Network was closer to $500 million, when the ministry and the eight thousand cable affiliates were fully functioning. When we purchased the property, we paid $1,200 to $1,500 per acre. By 1987 when I resigned, the least expensive land contiguous to the four square miles of Heritage USA was selling for $45,000 an acre.

I asked Professor Tidwell to supply the date that I put PTL into bankruptcy, which I knew, of course, was impossible for him to do. PTL had not filed for bankruptcy under my watch. It was several months into Jerry Falwell's leadership of PTL that the ministry was plunged into bankruptcy. Frankly, I would never have taken PTL into bankruptcy; I would have died before I put PTL into bankruptcy. More importantly, there was no need to be concerned about bankruptcy. In 1986, we had experienced one of our greatest years since beginning the ministry. Literally millions of people had visited Heritage USA that year, and although we had the financial pressures that any rapidly burgeoning company might have, we were having a banner year financially. We took in nearly $170 million in 1986. A large amount of money came in through our Lifetime Partnership programs. These were undesignated funds, money that was available to be used throughout the ministry, as it was needed. Although it seemed in my twenty-five years of pioneering Christian television, we were always playing financial catch-up, 1986 was by far the best year in our history and our fixed assets had a book value of over $140 million.

Professor Tidwell made much of:

A 1985 memo from Peter Bailey, chief financial officer for PTL, stating that while the ministry was generating a whopping $700,000 a week, its bills amounted to $1.2 million a week. The difference was made up by drawing from the "lifetime partners" accounts that were supposed to pay for building hotel rooms.[5]

Again, this reported another common misconception of PTL. Professor Tidwell's course looked for unethical business practices at PTL. Why then, I asked the professor,

. . . was I tried on memos, and not on audited financial statements? The Audited Financial Statement for fiscal year 1985 (May 1984 to May 1985), shows that the Ministry's income was $120 million for that year. . . . The 1985 fiscal year figures show average weekly income was approximately $2.4 million. That was twice the needed $1.2 million stated in the memo.

At PTL, we hired some of the best accounting firms in the U.S. We paid hundreds of thousands of dollars for their expertise. I personally instructed our accounting firms to make sure we were doing things exactly right. If there was a question of whether we were liable for a particular tax or not, or whether a certain item was a legitimate business expense or not, I encouraged our accounting firms to be stricter with us than necessary. I always told representatives of our "Big Eight" accounting firms, "I want our financial operations to be squeaky clean."

Concerning the government assertion that we had oversold lodging space at Heritage USA, and that I had willingly conspired with Reverend Richard Dortch to defraud the Lifetime Partners, I wrote to Professor Tidwell:

> When I gave the 25,000 Lifetime-Partner number for the five hundred-room Grand Hotel, it was true. We then added more lodging and camping facilities to the Lifetime Partner program. The growth and development of the Lifetime Membership program was shown and explained on our television program almost daily. The tapes will prove this.
>
> Here is a question of ethics I would like to ask you and your class. If Mr. Hilton said in 1982, "I am going to build a five-hundred-room hotel on this site; that is all the rooms there will be!" In 1984, business was so great he expanded the hotel. Should he go to prison for lying even though, in 1982, he firmly believed what he said was true?

It was well after midnight when I closed my letter to Professor Tidwell by saying,

> I take full responsibility for what happened to PTL and for my moral failure. I made many mistakes, but I did not conspire to defraud anyone and I am not guilty of any of the government charges. If I had read all the newspapers, and watched all the TV shows, or even looked on at my trial without knowing the other side of the story, I would have come to the same conclusion you have.

I signed my name to the letter, turned out the light, and crawled beneath the cover on my bunk. I didn't know if sending this information to a college professor whom I had never met would be of any value or not. When I awakened the next morning, I sent the letter. I also called Tammy Faye and had her send Professor Tidwell further information about PTL.

A few weeks later, I received a kind, cordial letter, dated April 29, 1991, from Professor Tidwell. He thanked me for my letter and my concern that his students be taught the truth and that his research be accurate. The professor assured me that he would incorporate the information I had given him into his lectures and the required reading material for his students.

Whether or not he did, I never knew. I later learned, however, that in 1993 Professor Tidwell published a book, *Anatomy of a Fraud: Inside the Finances of the PTL Ministries*, in which the erroneous information about which I had challenged him was presented as fact.

Regardless of what Professor Tidwell did with the information I supplied to him, my correspondence with him sparked a fire within me. I began to realize that much of the information I was giving Professor Tidwell had never been heard in a court of law. For a variety of reasons, none of which made sense to me, my original lawyers did little to contest the prosecutors' case against me. My lawyers spent most of their time trying to discredit the government witnesses and may have even succeeded had I not demanded that my lawyers "not hurt anybody."

Following their lead, my appeal lawyers, except for Alan Dershowitz, had simply tried to poke holes in the government's case against me. They did not base their arguments on information such as I gave to Professor Tidwell. Consequently, I had lost again. Now, it was too late to do anything about my appeal. The only recourse I had was to appeal to the Supreme Court, which was unlikely to hear the case. I had neither the money nor the will to pursue the appeal any farther.

I did, however, think that the information I had given to Professor Tidwell might be of value to Alan Dershowitz as he prepared for my resentencing hearing, now scheduled for the end of May. Over the next few weeks, I fired off several letters to Alan, bringing up points I thought might be helpful, information that I should have emphasized two years earlier.

First and foremost, I told him, I never "sold" Lifetime Partnerships at PTL. The fraud charges brought against me by the government and propagated by the press implied that I had been selling "time-shares." In my letter to Alan Dershowitz I quoted from several of our television program transcripts in which, from the early days of the Lifetime Partnership program, I emphatically told our viewers that Lifetime Partnerships were not time-shares.

> February 20, 1984: This is not in any way a time-share, so there are no fees. We don't guarantee anyone a particular room.
> February 28, 1984: There are no fees, no maintenance fees, no yearly fees—it is not time-share. You are saying, "Jim and Tammy, we want to be a part of your ministry.
>
> September 17, 1984: It is not time-share.

September 25, 1984: This is not time-share. You don't have a guaranteed time of the year. You come when you can book it in, and you have no fees to pay; there are no maintenance costs for you at all. . . This is a Christian ministry, we are a church, this is a religious organization, and we are here in fellowship together and that is what this is all about.

Similar statements could have been found hundreds of times on the voluminous videotapes of our programs housed in the PTL videotape library. As normal practice, we filed a videotape and a written chronicle for every program we produced. Unfortunately, none of these tapes or program logs, except those selected by the prosecution, were used in my trial. My lawyers did not access the PTL master-tape library at Heritage USA. They used only footage provided by the government in the "discovery room," a large suite of offices across from the courthouse, housing the portion of PTL financial records and videotapes that had been selected by the prosecutors for possible inclusion as evidence in the trial.

Another key point was that the monies sent in to PTL by the Lifetime Partners were not what the Internal Revenue Service calls "designated funds." The IRS is extremely stringent that money given to a nonprofit organization to be used for a specific, designated project must be used for that project, and that purpose alone. At PTL, we were careful to make sure that any money given to build a designated project was always used for building and operating that project. For example, if someone sent in fifty dollars to be used in our missions program in Africa, that money was used for missions in Africa. We did not put that money toward buying a television camera to be used in South Carolina. Had we done so, that would have been an improper use of designated funds.

On the other hand, money that was given to PTL, or any nonprofit organization in the U.S., that was not specifically designated to be used in a particular manner could be used as needed anywhere in the organization. The money received from the Lifetime Partnership fell into this category. Most of our building projects at PTL were not self-funded by designated monies, but rather were paid for out of the general fund.

As I explained to Alan Dershowitz in my letters, our brochures about the Lifetime Partnerships always included a statement such as: "This gift is for the worldwide ministry of PTL." Every receipt that we sent back to donors made it clear that their gifts were to be used wherever they were needed in the ministry. Over and over again, in our magazines, newsletters, and updates, we emphasized that when people gave to PTL, they were giving to the variety of ministries at Heritage USA.

On our live program aired February 22, 1984, I stated, "When you give this thousand-dollar gift . . . you are not just receiving a Lifetime Membership of four days and three nights at the Heritage Grand, [You are] helping us to build a conference center and a preaching center and a school and all the things that are going on here, reaching out in the prisons, reaching out with the People That Love Center, and the People That Love Home."

A few days later on February 28, 1984, I reiterated the message: "When you give, I want you to say to God, 'I am bringing my gifts to You. I am giving this thousand dollars in the name of Jesus. I am giving this Lifetime Membership because I want to go to all the world and preach the gospel to every creature. I want to be a part of the worldwide ministry of prayer. . . . I want to be a part of Your ministry of love that is reaching out to this generation, all of this scope of ministry, of the entire worldwide scope of PTL.' You are saying, 'I want to be a part of it and I want to sow a thousand-dollar seed.'" Clearly, from the inception of the Lifetime Partnership program, it was stated that the money given by the Partners was to be used for the overall ministry, not simply to build hotels and the other lodging places at Heritage USA.

Another area I clarified for Alan Dershowitz was the accusation that Tammy Faye and I had stolen $3.7 million from the ministry over a period of five years.

We never denied receiving this amount of money in salary, bonuses, and benefits over the five years. All of our financial remuneration, however, was voted on by the PTL Board of Directors and was duly noted in the board minutes. In most cases, I left the room while discussions of Tammy's or my financial picture were being held by our board. Had our board said, "Sorry, Jim, we just can't afford to pay you a penny this year," I would have worked at PTL for no salary at all. I never once got out of bed and thought, *I can't wait to get to work today! Am I ever going to make a haul!* Quite the contrary, I felt I was building something great for God and His people. I often suggested to the board that I did not need a pay raise. But board members always said, "You are worth it, Jim. Many sports stars, secular television personalities, and entertainers make much more than that!"

Whether that was true or not is debatable, but I know I worked very hard to build and maintain the ministry of PTL. If from no other standpoint than that of a fund-raiser, the board justified my income. During 1986, for example, I helped raise almost $170 million for the ministry. Had we hired a professional fund-raising organization to do the same and paid the normal going rate of 10 percent for such services, PTL would have paid $17 million in fees during one year alone. Of course, my responsibilities extended far beyond fund-raising, to the general oversight of the entire ministry, not to mention a daily television program that could be seen all over the U.S. and in various foreign countries.

Please understand: I do not want to justify the past. I am merely trying to share my mind-set at the time concerning what was happening. If I had it to do over again, I would not have allowed myself to receive the salary I did. It was a terrible mistake in judgment.

I know some will find this hard to believe, but I would have paid the board of directors for the privilege of being a part of the ministry at PTL.

For a three-year period, during which time the government would claim we were receiving exorbitant salaries, Tammy Faye and I donated almost 100 percent of the royalties earned from our many books, records, and tapes. Peter Bailey, PTL's vice president of finance, testified in court depositions given under oath that the estimated amount of our royalties during this time was $8 million. Richard Dortch attested to the same. They also confirmed under oath that these royalties went right into the PTL ministry, not Tammy's and my personal pockets. Beyond that, an album of Christian music, recorded by our daughter Tammy Sue, brought in another $1.6 million to the ministry in 1986. Tammy Sue was not on the PTL payroll and did receive $50,000 in royalties from that recording.

Legally, nothing required us to donate our royalties to PTL, but Tammy Faye and I felt that since our materials were publicized primarily on our television programs, it was only fair that the money should go to the ministry. I have had numerous advisers tell me since then that we would have been better off to have taken our royalties, as is normal practice, and taken less salary from the ministry. Apparently so.

While the prosecution painted me as a conniving, thieving charlatan, never letting up on the fact that Tammy and I received over $3.7 million in five years, Peter Bailey's and Richard Dortch's testimonies concerning the estimated income to the ministry from our books, tapes, and records were never used in my trial.

The prosecutor peppered members of PTL's Board of Directors on the witness stand with questions such as, "If you had known that PTL was bankrupt, would you have voted Jim and Tammy Bakker bonuses and raises?" Each board member answered emphatically, "No." Of course they would not have. But as I mentioned previously, PTL was not bankrupt at the time the remunerations were voted upon.

Similarly, the prosecutor asked each member of the board, "Did you vote for a $500,000 bonus for Jim Bakker?" One by one, the board members answered, "No." The implication was that I had stolen the $500,000. In fact, at the November 1986 meeting, the board *had* voted for various elements of a financial package that when added together totaled $500,000. Each part of the package had been voted on separately and had been recorded in the official minutes. The board had not, however, voted for a bonus in the same amount. The prosecutors omitted this detail, making it look as though I had stolen the money. My attorneys did not contest the point, despite the fact that I called it to their attention.

Nor did they ever call as a witness Shirley Fulbright, our executive assistant and the recording secretary of the PTL Board of Directors, who kept meticulous records of all PTL board meetings and other PTL activities. To this day, I wonder why neither side called Shirley as a witness. Shirley could easily have explained not only the bonuses and salaries, but she was also aware of all major decisions at PTL while the ministry was under my direction.

I was hoping that Alan Dershowitz could somehow use all this information in his preparation for my resentencing hearing. I also stressed to Alan what I considered to be one of the most important points in my case, in light of the insight I had received as a result of the Tidwell article—namely that we were building more than enough space at PTL to handle all of the Lifetime Partnerships.

The Lifetime Partnership program began in 1984, when we constructed the Heritage Grand Hotel. At that time, we decided to offer to anyone who donated one thousand dollars to the ministry four days and three nights of free lodging at the Grand every year as long as the donor or his or her spouse lived. The offer expired at the death of the donor. The Lifetime Partnerships were not transferable. Nor were they stock options in the hotel. They were simply a "gift" we offered to those who donated one thousand dollars to the ministry at that time.

When we first developed the idea, we felt that we would be wise to let the hotel pay for itself by allotting 50 percent of the five hundred rooms to paying guests and the other 50 percent would be available to the Lifetime Partners free on a first-come, first-served basis. We established the number of 25,000 Lifetime Partners as a feasible number needed to raise the money to build the hotel, while the income from the rooms reserved for regular paying guests would pay for the hotel's operating costs once it was constructed.

The ministry owned the entire hotel, and the 50 percent was a figure we imposed upon ourselves. When we initiated the plan, we were not legally required to set aside 50 percent of the rooms for paying guests and 50 percent for Lifetime Partners. We could just as easily have terminated our management contract and committed the entire hotel for use exclusively by the Lifetime Partners.

We expected a good response to the offer of Lifetime Partnerships, but we were overwhelmed. We quickly realized that our initial numbers were too small. The hotel was large all right, but even more people wanted partnerships than we had anticipated. The Grand Hotel was such a massive undertaking that it was hard to conceive that we would ever need more rooms in the near future. But as early as September of 1984, we had already exceeded our expectations. We recognized that we would have to change our Partnership program.

The first step we took was to include in the Partnership program the already built ninety-six-room Heritage Inn and add a bonus night for Lifetime Partners who chose to use that lovely facility. The twenty-one rooms located in the Lakeside Log Lodges were added to the Partnership program. We also added the 396 campsites located in the beautiful Fort Heritage Campgrounds. Lifetime Partners by the thousands chose to use their membership for ten nights, filling the campground with travel trailers, motor homes, and tents. To many of the avid campers, the extra seven free days at Heritage USA were a delightful bonus.

We immediately began designing and building other facilities, and all the while, the partners who had donated one thousand dollars to the original program were free to enjoy the benefits of it. Eventually the number of Lifetime Partners topped 150,000. Thousands of Lifetime Partners visited Heritage USA and stayed in the Heritage Grand Hotel four days and three nights each year free of charge. Others stayed in the Heritage Inn and Lodges for four days and four nights, while others enjoyed our campground for ten nights. Many of the Lifetime Partners were among our most generous contributors when offerings were received for various ministries at Heritage USA. In short, the Lifetime Partners believed in what we were doing, and they put their money where their hearts were.

So many reservations were coming in, we added scores of operators to our phone system. As the various lodging places were built at Heritage USA, the Lifetime Partners were informed of the changes and how they could use their free days of lodging in the new facilities. On our daily television program, by newsletter, and our monthly magazine, we constantly talked about our new building programs and how the Partners could adjust their visiting plans accordingly. In addition to the Grand Hotel, the ninety-six-room Heritage Inn, the twenty-one rooms in the Lakeside Lodges, the Fort Heritage Campground with 396 campsites, and 350 Wilderness Camping sites, we began building five hundred more family units in Bunkhouses, air-conditioned minisuite units that could sleep six people in a rustic decor at Farmland USA. Thirty-two rooms in two Bunkhouses were already completed by the end of 1986. And we were still building! As already mentioned, the Heritage Grand Tower was near completion and would add another five hundred rooms when construction was finished.

I want to make something clear: Our building program was interrupted in progress. While I was at PTL we never stopped building. We did not say, "Sorry, folks; that's all the space we're going to have." We were building as fast as our contractors could put up buildings. Three months before my unplanned departure, we had broken ground for The Crystal Palace, a new thirty-thousand-seat conference center, and the Grand Mansions, small hotels done in the same architectural style as the Grand Hotel. Eventually, I had hoped to develop a Crystal Palace Hotel as well. We had blueprints done and land cleared for at least seven other projects. Had I been allowed to continue, within two years I had planned for Heritage USA to have a minimum of 3,336 rooms and camping sites available to our Lifetime Partners. If these lodging facilities were used as we originally formulated—50 percent for paying guests and 50 percent for free use by the Lifetime Partners—we would have easily provided free lodging for 211,062 Lifetime Partners per year! One hundred percent of the campsites were available to the Lifetime Partners year-round. At 100 percent usage, our already built and planned lodging facilities could serve 356,147 Lifetime Partners each year.

Granted, it was difficult for partners to reserve space at busy times of the year, such as the Fourth of July or during the Christmas season when Heritage USA was transformed into "Christmas City," with 1.25 million lights, complete with pageants and special programs. The partners understood that, for the most part. Some protested, but of course anyone in the travel industry is well aware of this kind of seasonal problem.

The Lifetime Partners knew that everyone could not possibly book into the hotel or other accommodations on the same day. Most of the partners were willing to choose alternative dates. Some were not. Any partners who were disgruntled because they could not get space in our lodging facilities when they wanted, or were dissatisfied for any reason at all, were allowed to get a full refund of their donation. I personally had this policy put in effect, and it was implemented and overseen by Vice President of Hotel Operations, Charlotte Whiting. Were we happy to have partners request refunds? Certainly not. But while I was at Heritage USA, when refunds were requested, to the best of my knowledge, they were always given. Not only did we refund a Lifetime Partner's money if it was requested, we refunded *anybody's* donation if it was asked to be returned for any reason, as long as we had a record of the original contribution. Some of my top managers were not happy with this policy, and after my departure the policy was rescinded.

I can recall incidents in which we refunded money to someone who had given money over a period of time and he contacted us and said that he needed the money back because he was going to have an operation. We sent the money back. Others said they had lost their jobs and could use the money back. We sent it back. In at least one case, we sent money back to a grandchild of a PTL donor after the grandparent had died! The grandchild notified us that he wanted the money back, so we returned it.

To the best of my ability I had tried never to intentionally hurt anyone. If there was one group of people whom I would not want to hurt, it was the PTL Lifetime Partners. Sadly, I know I did hurt them by my moral failure and other unwise decisions and actions. I deeply apologize and ask their forgiveness. These were the people who believed in the dream I showed them. Many of them had such tremendous confidence in me and in what God was doing at Heritage USA that they were willing to contribute their money whether they ever got any free days of lodging or not. One partner and his wife had ninety Lifetime Partnerships! They are still some of my dearest friends to this day.

I would never have defrauded anyone intentionally, and I especially would have done everything in my power to avoid hurting the wonderful, godly group of people known as the PTL Lifetime Partners. In fact, for the first few years of my prison sentence, I awakened every day with one primary passion—to somehow restore the PTL Partners. When close friends would ask me in prison what they could pray for me about, I always answered, "Please pray that I can one day restore the PTL Partners." To me, the Lifetime Partners were just that—it was not simply a catchy phrase I used. I was committed to those people *for life*!

In prison, I was nearly as obsessed with finding a way to provide the Lifetime Partners all the benefits they deserved as I had been in building Heritage USA for them in the first place. I was willing to do anything to see them given their rightful place.

I had no idea how high a price I would ultimately pay in my efforts to see that obsession come to pass.

32

French Lick

ONE OF THE MOST DESTRUCTIVE THINGS THAT WAS DONE by the new regime after my resignation as president of PTL was choosing not to honor the Lifetime Partnerships. Over the years I had served at PTL, our mailing list had included more than a million people. Within this vast number, we had a core group of donors numbering nearly 600,000 people. Not all of these were regular contributors, but about 200,000 people sent donations of some amount each month. Nearly 160,000 of these people were Lifetime Partners. These were the people who made Heritage USA work. Most of these people were also the monthly financial mainstay of the ministry, and they gave their prayers and spiritual support as well.

I knew that when the Lifetime Partnerships were canceled, it was the death knell of the ministry. Had the leadership at that time not disenfranchised the Lifetime Partners but allowed them to continue coming to Heritage USA, I have no doubt those good people would have continued to support the ministry, whether Tammy Faye and I were there or not. In fact, literally tens of millions of dollars were raised for the ministry over the spring and summer of 1987, between the announcement of my resignation and the decision to take the ministry into bankruptcy. Who can forget the picture of Jerry Falwell going down the Heritage USA water slide dressed in a full suit? Ostensibly the money raised—and the reason for Falwell's slide—was to be used to complete the five-hundred-room Heritage Grand Towers and to pay PTL's bills, including money owed to contractor Roe Messner. The Tower's rooms were never completed and Roe Messner later told me that he never received a dime of that money.

Originally, Heritage USA was based on the idea of the old-time campground, where families used to go for rest and spiritual refreshment. I wanted a place where people could come for help, healing, and encouragement and enjoyment—basically a modern-day equivalent of the old camp meeting only with comfortable facilities rather than the dark, dank cabins and dormitories so many of us grew up with at church camps.

As a boy, I had worked side by side with the men, women, and children of our church family as we built our new sanctuary in Muskegon. I remember learning how to lay tile flooring in our church. I recalled hearing how my forefathers had built their first church, Creston Street Gospel Tabernacle. In the church minutes from back in the Depression era, the church secretary, my dear Aunt Maude, had written concerning the congregation, "They had a mind to work."

In my heart and mind, I believed that Christian people could do just about anything if they could work together. To me, what we were doing at PTL was like an old-fashioned barn raising, in which the people could be a part of the building process and share the benefits of it.

On our PTL television programs, I likened the Lifetime Partnership program to the time-honored custom of "buying a pew" in the local church. Church members contributed the money to pay for the seat, and in some cases, even had their names engraved on a small brass plate on the edge of the pew, but that did not mean the seat belonged only to them. They used the seating, but the pew belonged to the church. If a family moved to another location, they did not take their pew with them; it stayed in the church, to be used by others. If the original donors died or decided that for whatever reason they did not wish to attend that church any longer, their pew was not returned to them at their departure. Similarly, the PTL Lifetime Partners understood that the lodging space they had contributed toward building there was to be used by them and others.

During the months following my departure from PTL, tens of thousands of partners wrote letters of support and encouragement to me in care of PTL. I never received those letters and I would not have known that they existed had it not been for the loyalty of former PTL "readers." This was a staff of nearly fifty secretaries whose main job was to read the mammoth mounds of mail that arrived at Heritage USA daily. We had developed a system of reading the letters and passing them on up the line to various ministry or administrative personnel who would respond to each letter. We had an entire staff of people whose ministry was to counsel people seeking spiritual help by mail. Every letter that came to PTL was read and passed along to the appropriate person. No letters were ever simply scoured for money and then discarded.

After I resigned, it was announced on the *PTL* television programs—which were still on the air—that all mail sent to the ministry for members of my family or me would be forwarded to us. It was not. No letters sent to PTL in 1987 ever reached Tammy or me at our home in California. Instead, they were burned, buried, or otherwise discarded.

When our family returned to Tega Cay briefly in 1987, several friends who were still at Heritage USA brought stacks of Tammy Faye's records and my sermon tapes to the house and told us that there were literally truckloads of our mail and ministry materials being buried out by the original water tower at Heritage USA. Some of my most trusted maintenance men told me personally that they had been instructed to bury huge bags containing mail that was addressed to Tammy Faye and me. The same men told me that they were no longer allowed to go near the landfill where large volumes of mail and other materials were being burned under the watch of Pinkerton security guards. I was deeply grieved to hear all of this.

Living in California, watching events unfold at PTL on the television, I felt I had to do something to help restore the Partners. I was contacted by a man who owned hundreds of acres of beautiful property in the Palm Desert area of California. This man offered to help me build a "Heritage USA West." Heritage USA builder Roe Messner drew up the site plans and rough sketches and was ready to go to work.

Previously, I had been approached by one of the top hotel brokers and owners in the country. He had once served as the chief executive officer of one of the leading luxury hotel chains in the world. A limousine pulled up to our house one day, and the chauffeur got out and handed a letter over the wall to one of our security guards. In the letter, the man said he was Jewish but he had watched our television programs regularly. He asked for an appointment and we met for dinner. He offered to turn over to me the $100 million-plus property with no money down. The eventual price tag, however, was enormous. Beyond that, the hotel was located in one of the posh desert communities, and I did not think the residents of the area would appreciate my efforts to turn their leading luxury hotel into a Christian retreat center.

After several months, I moved our family back to the Charlotte area. Granted, I missed PTL and wanted to return to the ministry that I had poured so much of my life into building. Furthermore, by that time, I had come to a full realization that I had been deceived. Nevertheless, I can honestly say that my primary hope was to somehow restore to the Lifetime Partners that which I felt they deserved.

From July through September of 1988, I thought that I might be able to purchase Heritage USA. I had been working diligently trying to arrange financing with a group who purportedly represented a consortium of Greek shipping magnates. My offer to purchase PTL had no sooner been made public when I discovered that the money brokers with whom I had been dealing were a front for a colossal scam.

Tammy Faye, Jamie Charles, and I moved to Florida in 1988, and although I had given up hope of getting Heritage USA back, I never gave up hope of finding some way to restore the Lifetime Partners. I looked at several properties in Florida that friends had said might hold some potential for a new Partner Center. One such piece of property was at Rainbow Springs, once a beautiful tourist attraction before the new highways had passed it by. We also looked at another old, rather run-down hotel on Ormand Beach. Nothing seemed quite suitable.

Even in prison, I never lost sight of the dream to restore the Partners. An inmate named Bill had run a company that had purchased old hotel properties and turned them into retirement facilities. Each month, Bill received several hotel magazines and other publications and he allowed me to read them. I looked at Bill's hotel magazines the way some of the guys studied their hunting, fishing, or race-car magazines. I'd get excited every time I saw another property for sale that sounded as though it might be a suitable place for the PTL Partners.

One day during the early part of the summer of 1991, Bill excitedly approached me waving a full-color brochure. "You are going to be very interested in this!" he said with a broad smile.

The brochure described French Lick Springs, a resort in southern Indiana that was to be auctioned at 1:00 P.M. on August 1, 1991. The place was incredible! A huge, stately 485-room historic hotel—about the same size as the five-hundred-room Heritage Grand Hotel—was situated on 434 acres of land. An adjoining piece of property was also for sale, making the property only slightly smaller than Heritage USA. French Lick Springs boasted seven restaurants, sixty thousand square feet of convention space, a complete spa and health club, a bowling alley, eight indoor and outdoor tennis courts, an indoor swimming pool with a retractable dome, a ranch and stables housing thirty-two horses, with over thirty miles of riding trails, two eighteen-hole golf courses, one of which had been designed by Donald Ross, one of golf's premier course designers, and had hosted both the men's and women's PGA Championships.

Besides that, French Lick had its own old-fashioned steam locomotive that was owned and operated by the Indiana Railway Museum. The locomotive pulled authentic passenger cars on a ride of almost two hours through twenty miles of the Hoosier National Forest, through breathtaking limestone rock cuts, and the 2,200-foot Burton Tunnel, one of the longest railroad tunnels in the state. Uniformed crew members helped transport passengers back in time as they enjoyed the scenic train trip. All that, and I did not have to build a thing! It was already there.

In the 1920s and '30s the resort had reached its peak popularity when the mineral waters and casino of French Lick Springs had attracted a continuous bevy of America's rich and famous. Franklin D. Roosevelt had announced his candidacy for the presidency in the hotel's convention center in 1931. Gangster Al Capone gambled at the casino; actress Lana Turner, actor John Barrymore, composer Irving Berlin, the Vanderbilts, and President Harry Truman had all graced the guest lists at French Lick.

By 1991, however, the world had passed by French Lick Springs. People were not beating a path to southern Indiana to spend their vacation dollars. Instead, the once elegant resort center had experienced a steady decline, despite a $3 million renovation effort. Hotel insiders guessed that the property, estimated at more than $65 million, might sell for as little as $1 to $2 million.

For me, sitting in prison, the price tag on French Lick might just as easily have been $100 million. I had no money. But I had a great dream. I called Tammy and told her about French Lick. Then I called Roe.

Tammy Faye, Jamie, my sister Donna, and Roe Messner visited me in prison during the latter part of June, shortly after I had received the information about French Lick Springs. Pastor Phil Shaw and his wife, Faith, accompanied them. My excitement and enthusiasm were contagious. Soon we were all sitting in the prison visiting room, making plans about what we could do with the tremendous French Lick property.

"The auction is coming up in August," I said to Roe and Tammy. "Why don't you two and Jamie plan to take a trip to French Lick sometime in July to check out the property? Roe, you know what sort of structure we need. Tammy, see if you think the Partners would enjoy the facilities."

Tammy's eyes lit up. "Jamie doesn't really need to go," she said.

That was all Jamie needed to hear. "Dad, I don't really want to go," Jamie complained. "Can't I stay here with Pastor Shaw and his family?"

"Oh, I think you need to go with Mom and Roe," I replied. "Besides, it would be good to know what you think the resort will need to meet the needs of the partners' children."

"But I'd rather stay right here and spend the time with my friends." Jamie had been carrying on a long-distance romance with a young lady from Minnesota, so I was not surprised that he wanted to stay.

251

"Oh, you can come if you want or stay if you want," Tammy Faye spoke past me to Jamie.

"Good, I'll stay here," Jamie responded.

"I really think it would be a good idea for you to go along," I said to Jamie as I shifted uneasily in my seat.

"No, no. Jamie can stay here. Roe and I will go check out the resort and report back," Tammy Faye said breezily.

I caught Phil Shaw's eye ever so briefly. The gentle pastor did not say a word, but I could tell he disapproved of the arrangements. I tried once more to dissuade Tammy Faye from going alone with my best friend to French Lick Springs. I did not want to sound as though I didn't trust her, or Roe, yet at the same time, since she and I were such frequent fodder for tabloid rumor mills, it seemed extremely foolish to fuel the fire by having Tammy Faye and Roe seen together at French Lick.

Tammy Faye seemed to have read my mind. "Don't worry, honey," she said with a wave of her hand and a laugh. "We'll be discreet. I'll wear a disguise." We all broke up laughing at the thought of Tammy in disguise.

On July 7, 1991, Tammy Faye and Roe Messner checked into separate rooms at French Lick Springs. It was the first of many trips during which I later discovered they were booked in hotels in separate rooms. It was only a matter of time before the sparks began to fly.

As expected, Roe reported back to me that the French Lick Springs complex was a tremendous value. It needed $10 million to $15 million in refurbishing, but the structure was sound, and the layout was gorgeous. We began to make plans. Throughout the summer of 1991, I studied every detail of French Lick Springs's layout. Although I had never been there, I felt as though if I walked onto the property, I could almost give a guided tour of the complex. It was good therapy for me to focus on something besides prison and my resentencing. Of course, the upcoming resentencing, which had been postponed again, held out the hope of a possible lighter sentence and an earlier release date.

Roe found some investors in Canada who were willing to underwrite the purchase of French Lick Springs. Our plan was to purchase the property and have Tammy Faye do a television program from French Lick. We planned to restore the Lifetime Partners and allow them to use the free days of lodging they had been deprived of at Heritage USA.

We bandied about dozens of possible names for the new center and finally settled on "Heritage Springs International." I began making notes to call many of our friends and staff members who had helped us at Heritage USA, including Joyce and John Westheim. Joyce had a beautiful singing voice. John was a professional food-service manager. I hoped to invite

Joyce and John to join us at French Lick Springs, Joyce to sing and John to handle our food services. I also made a note to contact Charlotte Whiting, my former vice president of hotel management at Heritage USA, to help with the redecorating of the rooms. In addition, I planned to contact ministers such as Bob Gass and Mike Murdock, and seek a year's commitment from them to help get the ministry started. As we had done at Heritage USA, I wanted to have seminars and workshops featuring special Bible teachers, prayer meetings, and gospel music programs every day.

In prison, Bill and I began making lists of activities, management plans, marketing plans, and flowcharts of our new organizational structure. We were like little kids building sand castles on the beach, dreaming our best-case scenarios, hoping all the while that Tammy Faye and Roe might be able to pull off the real thing. Roe Messner and I designed plans for a new television studio to be constructed in the facilities of the hotel. I even dreamed up press announcements for Tammy to use at the appropriate time. Beyond that, Tammy and I began working on a letter we planned to send to our Partners. Heritage Springs International was about to happen. My dream that the Lifetime Partners would be restored was about to come true!

On August 1, 1991, Roe Messner attended the auction at French Lick Springs. He carried with him the $250,000 cashier's check required of all serious registered bidders. Unfortunately, the bids soon topped what Roe's Canadian backers had authorized him to spend, and Roe had to drop out of the auction. French Lick Springs was sold to Luther James, a Louisville, Kentucky, businessman, for $2.6 million.

Undaunted, Roe and Tammy arranged to meet with the Canadian financial backers at French Lick Springs. Roe had already met with the new owner of French Lick Springs and had convinced him to sell the complex, offering him a profit of $1 million. The new owner countered with a request for $1.5 million in profit, not a bad deal, considering the ink had barely dried on his check to purchase the property! When the Canadians toured the resort and saw the potential, they readily agreed to the purchase. While Tammy and Roe surged ahead with plans to put Tammy back on television from French Lick Springs, I had to focus my attention on the upcoming resentencing hearing, now scheduled for August 23, 1991.

33

Hope for Freedom

THROUGHOUT THE SUMMER OF 1991, I LEARNED MUCH concerning French Lick Springs, but I spent most of my free time continuing my study of the words of Jesus. As I read, dissected, and wrote down the recorded words of Christ, the study was raising serious questions in my mind concerning many of the things I had believed and taught while at PTL.

For instance, I had taught for years that Christianity was not a religion of "do's" and "don'ts." But when I began to closely examine the recorded words of Christ, I soon learned that much of what Jesus expected of me fell into the category of "Do this" or "Don't do that." Jesus was not encouraging legalism; He was simply instructing me how to live.

I concluded that about 75 percent of Jesus' statements were positive commands—He said, "Love God and one another"—and 25 percent were warnings against sin and negative conduct or attitudes—"Don't fear or worry." I discovered specific instructions in the words of Jesus, reduced them to an easily remembered rule, and wrote them out as a sort of guidebook for life. When taken at their face value, the words of Jesus explain clearly what a Christian is to do and not to do.

One of the most important principles I learned as I studied the words of Jesus was something I had read hundreds of times throughout my lifetime, yet had somehow never allowed to permeate my understanding. After Jesus had been fasting in the wilderness for forty days, Satan tempted Jesus to turn a stone into bread to satisfy His hunger. Jesus resisted the temptation and rebuked the devil by quoting Deuteronomy 8:3, saying, "It is written, 'Man shall not live by bread alone, but by every word that proceeds from the mouth of God'" (Matt. 4:4). I had read this passage, quoted it, and preached on it at PTL, but there in prison, suddenly for the first time, the word *every* practically leaped off the page toward me.

For years, I had taught that we are to guide our lives by the Word of God. I often spoke of *a* word of God, but amazingly I had missed the point of Jesus' statement. He was not saying that we are to live by one biblical principle; nor was He implying that it was okay to pick out our favorite verses from the Bible and make those our guiding lights. I began to realize that I had fallen into the trap of taking a verse here and a verse there and making the Bible say what I wanted, rather than what God wants.

Jesus was saying that we are to take the Scriptures as a whole rather than building our theologies on a particular verse or phrase that suits our needs. To accurately understand the Bible, we must study the moral principles established in the Old Testament as well as the New Testament. Certainly, as Christians we no longer live according to the letter of the Old Testament laws. We no longer sacrifice animals to come into God's presence, because Jesus became the ultimate sacrifice; He fulfilled the Old Testament laws and prophecies. Because of Jesus, we have the New Testament, the new covenant, which supersedes the old, but that does not mean we are to ignore the Old Testament.

On the other hand, I began to realize that since Jesus' life fulfilled the Old Testament, it was only possible to truly understand the Old Testament through the life of Christ. Where I found an Old Testament principle, I compared it to the words of Jesus. As it lined up with the life of Christ, I accepted it as a rule for my life. If something seemed not to coincide with Jesus, I studied further. Inevitably, I discovered that God's Word was consistent with itself from Genesis to Revelation.

This way of approaching the Scripture, looking at everything through the life and words of Jesus—as obvious as it may seem—completely revolutionized my understanding of the Bible. It also established a firm foundation upon which I could begin to build a new life.

My study of the words of Jesus challenged many of my ideas about theology, but Christ's words also gave me tremendous faith at a time when I sorely needed it. As my resentencing date grew nearer, I was concerned, but thanks to the encouragement I was receiving from the Bible, I prepared to go to Charlotte with a quiet confidence that God was in control of my life no matter what the judge decided about my sentence. Of course, I hoped for a sentence reduction or possibly even to be sentenced to "time served" and to walk out of that courtroom hand in hand with my family.

On the other hand, I was also aware that the prosecutors had not changed their attitude toward me one bit and would be pressing the judge to sentence me to a time equal to that which Judge Potter had meted out. Regardless, I was determined not to worry, but to trust God.

On August 19, 1991, I packed all my belongings into a duffel bag and took it to be inventoried by a prison officer. I would leave F.M.C. Rochester the way I came in, with only the clothes on my back. The only additional items I was allowed to carry with me were my legal papers regarding my court case. The good news was that at least I would be allowed to wear street clothes during the trip rather than a prison jumpsuit. The bad news was I would have to wear those same clothes throughout my transfers. Everything else must stay—my Bible and even my toothbrush had to stay behind when I went to Charlotte. Since there was a good possibility that I would not be returning to Rochester, all my personal belongings were to be stored until it was determined where I would be going next.

Most of my fellow inmates did not expect to ever see me again in prison. Consequently, the day before I left for my resentencing, a number of guys asked me if they could have a picture taken with me. I readily agreed, and we went over to the recreation building where the inmates turned in their tickets purchased at the commissary to the Jaycee member who was taking the pictures in front of the mural in the hall. Word had already gotten around that I was leaving and probably would not be back, so when other inmates saw me posing for pictures with their buddies, they too wanted a picture with me. Before the day was over, I posed for around 125 photographs with individual inmates.

I left Rochester the morning of Wednesday, August 21, wearing my favorite blue-and-white-striped shirt, black slacks, and leather boots, traveling by means of a small, private prison jet along with several other inmates and federal marshals. We flew to North Carolina, stopping once or twice for inmates to be removed from the jet, before finally arriving in Charlotte, where I was taken immediately to Mecklenburg County Jail. The guys at Rochester had warned me about county jails.

I took one look at my "home away from home," and I thought, *The guys back in Rochester didn't lie to me!* The cell was stark and small, obviously not meant for long-term occupancy. Two bunks hung off the wall, with the headboard almost touching the sliding door made of steel bars.

Almost everything about the county jail that night seemed to have a dirty feel to it. Even the bright orange jumpsuit I was given to wear seemed soiled. The blanket on the hard pillowless bunk smelled as though someone who had not washed in a long time had been sleeping on it. Despite

256

the dank aroma all around me, I was busy, writing furiously everything I thought my attorney Alan Dershowitz should tell the judge the next day. I needn't have bothered. Alan had his own plan in mind.

Harold Bender, my other lawyer, stopped by to see me shortly after my arrival at the county jail. Harold and I spoke briefly about what to expect in the resentencing hearing. Before leaving, he handed me a twenty-dollar bill to use to purchase snacks from the jail's small commissary shack.

I jumped back as though Harold had handed me a live rattlesnake. "I can't take that!" I cried. I had not touched paper money in several years.

Harold laughed aloud. "It's okay," he said. "You're allowed to have some money in a county jail."

"Are you sure?" I asked.

"I'm sure," Harold replied as he walked toward the door. "I'll see you in the morning. And be sure to shave."

Later that evening, Tammy Sue visited me in the county jail. She was not permitted to bring baby James or Jonathan Douglas, my new grand-child. During Tammy Sue's visit, we talked through a glass window. We could not touch. I had not seen her in a long time, and despite the cir-cumstances, I was still glad to see her face and hear her voice.

Earlier that day, Tammy Faye had landed in Charlotte and was accom-panied by Roe Messner. When Tammy arrived at the Adams Mark Hotel, she was met by numerous PTL Partners who called out, "You can make it, Tammy! Don't give up." For reasons unknown to me, the county jail offi-cials refused Tammy's request to visit with me that evening before the resentencing. She dropped off the clothing I was to wear in court the fol-lowing day and returned to her hotel.

On Thursday, August 22, I was awakened by a guard around 5:00 A.M. He handed me a small toiletry kit and instructed me to get cleaned up and ready to go to court. He opened the cell door and pointed to a shower stall across from my cell. I thanked him and headed toward the shower.

I opened the toiletry kit and looked inside. There was a bar of soap imprinted with the logo of the Heritage Grand Hotel. Once again the awful irony of my circumstances smacked me right in the face. Here I was only a few miles from the beautiful hotel and conference center, the con-struction of which I had personally overseen, but now I was climbing into a scuzzy shower stall in open view of other prisoners.

I was taken to where I was allowed to shave and was given my street clothes. I was told to get dressed and was then taken to another room where I was told to wait for a marshal to come to get me. There, I was placed in a tiny white holding cell with a high ceiling. I sat on the edge of the bench and stared at the wall in front of me, covered with foul graffiti and names of prisoners who had once occupied these quarters. Dried semen spotted the walls and the floor areas, where men had masturbated while waiting to be transferred to the courthouse. I was almost afraid to sit down for fear I might catch a disease. I glanced toward the top of the cell, where high on the wall, someone had gone to great effort to write in large letters: "It's a sad, sad, world." *Yes, it truly is*, I thought.

When the marshals finally came for me, I was cuffed, shackled, and transported in a prison van to the same federal courthouse in which I had been tried, convicted, and sentenced nearly two years previously. We drove down to same loading dock from which I had tried to wave good-bye following my sentencing by Judge Potter. As the marshals helped me from the van, I fought back fearful thoughts of what had happened on these grounds two years earlier, and tried to concentrate on the hope that perhaps this judge would view my case differently. I had heard that Judge Graham Mullen, the man who would preside over my hearing and make the decision regarding my sentence, was a strict judge but a fair one.

Once inside the courthouse, I was taken to another small holding cell, where I was given the suit of clothes Tammy Faye had brought from Florida for me. Tammy had chosen a sharp-looking, dark blue, pinstriped, double-breasted suit for me to wear during the resentencing trial. I felt the fine fabric between my fingers and rubbed it against my palms. I changed into the outfit and was ready when the marshal called for me.

I heard the small courtroom erupt in a commotion when I walked in the side door escorted by the marshal. As I walked across the room, the first sight to catch my attention was Tammy Faye sitting next to my best friend, Roe Messner. Both Tammy and Roe were nattily dressed, but Tammy Faye looked incredible! She wore a chic, tailored, close-fitting black dress with large white polka dots. A matching black-and-white leather bag was at her side. White, half-moon-shaped earrings decked her ears, while several gold bracelets and a watch, which I had given to her as a Christmas present years before, graced her left wrist. On her right wrist were several white plastic bangles. What I noticed most, however, was her hair and makeup. Gone were the simple, close-cropped curls and the massive amounts of mascara she had worn around me. Instead, her auburn-colored hair was long, big, and poofed. (I later found out that it was a wig.) Her makeup was much more subdued, and natural looking. In many ways, Tammy Faye looked like the girl I had married thirty years earlier. I had to tear my eyes from her as the marshal took me to my seat between my lawyers at the defense table, but not before I saw Roe slip his arm around Tammy Faye to comfort her.

Tammy Faye whispered from behind me, "Honey, I love you. You can make it!"

The courtroom had a surreal familiarity to it, almost as if I were reliving scenes from two years previously. It did not take long for the prosecutors to begin their relentless hammering away at my credibility once again. They presented the same videotape collage they had used during my trial. The tape was edited in an attempt to show that I had willfully deceived the Lifetime Partners by overextending the program beyond what the lodging facilities at Heritage USA could accommodate. They did not show a single instance of the literally hundreds of times I told our viewing audience that the Partnership program had expanded and that we were building more beautiful lodging facilities that would accommodate every one of our Lifetime Partners within a short period of time.

Hoping to get me off with time served, as a sort of unofficial plea bargain Alan Dershowitz suggested to Judge Mullen that he might release me and impose upon me a variety of probation restrictions, including a ban on me being on television for any length of time, and a barring of my involvement in any fund-raising activities. Dershowitz told the judge he would guarantee I would never again engage in the mixing of religion and money. Alan convincingly challenged the prosecutors' contention that I had defrauded people of $158 million, pointing out as the first government-appointed trustee had done two years earlier, that most of that money was right there invested in Heritage USA, just as it was supposed to be.

Judge Mullen ignored Alan's suggested bans and chose not to place any such restriction on me. By the end of the day, I felt as though my life had been dragged through a washing-machine wringer once again.

When Judge Mullen dismissed court for the day, the marshals quickly surrounded the defense table, ready to escort me back to Mecklenburg County Jail. Before they could usher me out, I leaned over the railing and kissed my daughter, Tammy Sue. Then I kissed my mother, whom I had not seen in nearly two years. Finally, I kissed Tammy Faye, and by that time, the marshals were at my side, insisting that I go with them.

We returned just as we had come, stopping long enough for me to change out of my suit into my street clothes, then back to the holding area where I changed out of my street clothes back into the same soiled jumpsuit I had worn the day before. I was placed back in the same filthy cell where I had spent the night.

Later that afternoon, when a guard offered the inmates a mop and scrub bucket to clean our cells, I put my Rochester cleaning expertise to good use. I not only mopped my own cell, I cleaned the common areas of the entire cell block. As usual, some of the guys chided, "Quit working so hard for the guards."

"Hey, we're staying here, not the guards. I'm not working for them; I'm working for us," I answered.

That night after supper, Tammy Faye and Roe Messner came to visit me. The officials at Mecklenburg County Jail were kind enough to allow us to use a vacant office for the visit rather than the jail's visiting room. The office was drab but private. A desk sat to one side of the room and several metal, institutional-looking chairs were arranged in front of it. A guard sat off to one side of the room, mercifully trying to be as inconspicuous as possible. Tammy Faye and Roe sat together on two of the chairs facing me.

The picture of my wife and best friend sitting together, with Tammy Faye making no effort to move closer to me after having been away from me for two years, impacted me powerfully. I had detected a cooling in our relationship in recent months, most notably during our daily telephone conversations. Where Tammy Faye had once talked freely for hours, now she was always in a hurry to get going. I knew she was busy. I never faulted her for having to break off our phone conversations to attend to the many details of her life. I recognized that I was in prison with nothing but time on my hands, but she was still on the outside trying to function as normally as possible. Before long, however, her indifference on the phone increased to the point where I could no longer fool myself into believing that she was simply overly busy. I'd seen these signs before.

Nevertheless, I was not prepared for Tammy Faye's blatant shifting of allegiance the night before my resentencing. As I looked at her and Roe, I could not deny the truth any longer.

My wife and my best friend were a couple.

I could see it in their eyes, the way they looked at each other. I could hear it in their voices, the way they talked to each other. They shared a camaraderie that is born only out of a close relationship. As I looked at the handsomely dressed man and woman sitting across from me, it was as though some unfamiliar *couple* had come to visit—Tammy with her crisp, stylish new look and Roe with every hair in place and his dapper clothes sharply pressed. I became increasingly aware of my own disheveled hair and the stinking, soiled jumpsuit in which I had cleaned the floors only a few hours earlier. We talked about the hearing, but I really did not hear what the couple was saying. We talked about French Lick Springs, but I could not get my mind off the *couple*. Fortunately, they did not stay long. I'm not sure how much more I could have taken. I never mentioned a word to either one of them concerning their relationship. I did not confront them in any way. We all went through the motions as though everything were simply normal.

Tammy Faye and I kissed in a perfunctory manner, totally devoid of passion on her part. Roe stood nearby, looking on.

And then she was gone.

My wife walked out of the room with my best friend, and the guard walked me back to my cell in silence. It was almost as though he was embarrassed for me.

The small courtroom in the federal courthouse was packed with spectators, mostly members of the media, when the marshals escorted me in. I had already been awake for hours, as we had gone through the identical routine in transferring me from the jail to the courthouse in downtown Charlotte. Prison procedures allow little room for variation.

Once again the prosecution attempted to shred my character in their closing arguments, encouraging the judge to reinstate the original forty-five-year sentence. To counter, Harold Bender pointed out that I had been a model prisoner since my incarceration, citing my work with the prison Jaycees and the various other groups of which I was a part. In what I'm sure was meant to be a positive image, Harold went on to tell the judge that I had also served on the prison's United Way fund-raising committee.

Ignoring Alan Dershowitz's plan to play down my fund-raising expertise, Harold rambled on in what I could only assume was meant to be a comment upon my exemplary community service in prison. "They raised, among the inmates, several thousand dollars," Harold told Judge Mullen. "It was *the* most successful United Way campaign they've ever had."

Thanks, Harold.

I glanced over at Alan Dershowitz while Harold was extolling my fund-raising capabilities. Alan's face looked as though he might explode. Had we not been dealing with my life, it might even have been funny.

At 10:22 A.M. Judge Mullen said, "Mr. Bakker, it is now your right to address the court on your own behalf. Do you have any remarks you wish to make on your own behalf, sir?"

Judge Mullen's politeness caught me off guard. I was not accustomed to being addressed as "Mr. Bakker" these days, let alone as "sir." I answered, "Yes, sir."

"All right, sir, you may," Judge Mullen replied.

I rose to my feet and began to speak. "Your Honor," I began, "I am deeply and seriously remorseful for my moral failure and for the hurt that I have caused so many people. I have failed so many people who trusted in me—my own church congregation, this community, my Partners, the church world as a whole, and myself and my God, and my dear family that I love so very, very much."

I recalled the message I had seen in the holding cell in Mecklenburg Jail, so I told the judge about it. "I looked up on the wall, and there was some writing and it said, 'This is a sad world.' And prison is a sad world. It's the land of the living dead for many. It's not just the strip searches and that kind of thing, it's the separation from your family, from your loved ones.

"I have a wife of thirty years who has stood with me through thick and thin, through an affair—a fifteen-minute affair that happened almost a decade ago—but she has stood with me and forgiven me, and I love her. We built Heritage USA together, even after our marriage had broken up and was put back together. I know even the bad times become good times as you look back in history, because you've stood together.

"I have a fifteen-year-old son who was ten years old when this happened. He's taller than I, and he needs a father. I need to be with my son. This will be [my] third Christmas in prison away from [my] family.

"I have a daughter and her husband here in this room. My daughter is the apple of my eye. She gave my wife and [me] two beautiful—" my voice cracked at the thought of Tammy Sue's children, and I had to pause before continuing. "She and her husband gave us two beautiful grandbabies, Jonathan and James. Jonathan is eleven months old. I have never seen him. I have never held him.

"I got to see my mother in the courtroom yesterday for the first time in two years. She just turned eighty-five. My dad will be eighty-five next month. I have failed my family, and I have asked their forgiveness."

Judge Mullen listened attentively to every word I spoke and his respect seemed to carry over to the spectators. I continued. I wanted to let the judge know that I never intended to hurt anyone or renege on any of the promises I made to my partners or to anyone else.

"Even though I planned to be honorable in all of my commitments, as leader of my church and family, I choose to accept full responsibility for the actions that I am now being sentenced for. I do not blame anyone else nor minimize my responsibility as the pastor and president of Heritage Church and Missionary Fellowship. . . .

"There's not been a day gone by that I have not grieved for the Partners and the Lifetime members who lost Heritage. Heritage USA did not belong to me; it belonged to the people who supported it. . . .

"I have asked God, and I don't have the answers, but I wish to God and pray to God that somehow they could be restored and I would do anything to do that and see that happen. . . .

"I have [said it] in the past, and I would say it again in front of this witness and this courtroom and Your Honor, I ask all that I have hurt to please forgive me. I have begged God for heavenly forgiveness, and I beg this court for human mercy. Thank you, Your Honor." I sat down. I had spoken for approximately five minutes. It would have taken hours to tell the judge everything I was feeling inside, but I felt that I had said enough.

Both the prosecution and the defense were allowed closing statements. In his final effort to influence Judge Mullen, Harold Bender suggested to the judge—as he had done to Judge Potter two years earlier—that he might consider "punishing" me by making me go back to Heritage USA at a minimum salary and "make good on my promises" and "make restitution." Harold latched on to a descriptive phrase used by the prosecutors and admitted that this idea might be akin to a "fox in the henhouse" approach, but it might work. Even reporters were scratching their heads.

Finally it was time for Judge Mullen's decision. "I am impressed with the fact that Mr. Bakker has made a remarkable adjustment to confinement," Judge Mullen began. "I could resentence Mr. Bakker under the new guidelines, but I choose not to do so." He then went on to explain the way he had divided the counts against me. At last he came to the sentence itself—five years, five years, five years, and three years. Judge Mullen had reduced my sentence to a total of eighteen years. As part of my original sentence, Judge Potter had fined me $500,000 in addition to the forty-five years in prison. Judge Mullen decided not to fine me at all.

The judge dismissed the court and it was done. *Eighteen years.* I was not going home. In fact, I would not be going home for a long, long time. I was going back to prison. I would be seventy years of age by the time my sentence was completed. The marshals were coming again.

I turned quickly to Tammy Sue, who was seated just behind me on the other side of the railing. I kissed her and said, "I love you, baby." I reached for Tammy Faye. I hugged her and kissed her good-bye.

I turned to my soon-to-be-eighty-five-year-old father and said, "Tell Mother I love her."

A marshal's voice boomed across the courtroom, "Let's clear the courtroom. It's over."

Tammy Faye slumped to her seat, sobbing and clutching a package of tissues. Roe put his arms around her, comforting her.

The exit routine seemed all too familiar.

Meanwhile, Tammy Faye was standing in front of the courthouse speaking to members of the media. "I'm understandably very sad today," she said. "I was hoping Jim would be able to come home sooner." She thanked the PTL Partners for their support, about fifty of whom were standing nearby wearing yellow ribbons. She concluded her remarks in chipper tones by reciting the "Serenity Prayer," which she had learned at the Betty Ford Center.

I sat dumbfounded in the back of the marshal's car as they whisked me back to the airport. The prison plane was waiting for me. Television crews followed my every move. I tenuously made my way up the steps to the small jet's doorway and ducked inside. Several other men were already seated in the jet. I shuffled to the first empty seat, sat down, and stared out the window. I'm not sure that I flinched a muscle during the entire trip back to Minnesota. It was a strange, sinking feeling as I reentered the gates of F.M.C. Rochester. Although I had been afraid to expect any positive results from my resentencing hearing, I guess deep down I had indeed entertained hope that I might walk out of that courthouse in Charlotte a free man. Now, as I was being processed through R & D, strip-searched again, and sent back to Building Two, my "home" for the past two years, the disappointment over my eighteen-year sentence hit me full force. Walking back into prison caused my stomach to churn.

Once I had cleared R & D, I was free to walk back across the compound toward Building Two. It was still light enough that many of the inmates were outside. A number of the guys came up to me and congratulated me.

"For what?" I asked.

"For your victory," someone replied. They had seen the reports on the news concerning my sentence reduction. I soon realized that they considered a reduction from forty-five to eighteen years a major victory.

I didn't feel like much of a winner. But I was about to discover that I was more of a winner than I had ever dreamed. It all began as I encountered the life of another imprisoned dreamer. . . .

CHAPTER

34

God Meant It for Good

BACK INSIDE THE GATES OF ROCHESTER FEDERAL MEDICAL
Center, I was more convinced than ever that I would not be released from
prison until God wanted me out, until I had learned whatever it was God
wanted me to learn through this experience.

My former cell was now occupied by two new men. As I walked
toward Building Two to be reassigned to another cell, my friend Rod
Netherton met me. "Jim, welcome back. Guess what! I put in a request to
have you move in with me, and Sam Houston approved it."

Rod was one of my best friends. I enjoyed his energy and enthusiasm
and I liked hanging around with him, but he was one of the last guys in
prison that I would have chosen as a cellmate. Our personalities were so
opposite. Rod was a world-champion sky diver, a drug smuggler who had
made his living parachuting out of airplanes. He was daring enough to land
planes in the middle of a South American jungle to pick up his next cache
of drugs. He was an outgoing, self-assured, confrontational sort of guy—
he had loved arguing with Lyndon LaRouche just for kicks.

I appreciated Rod looking out for me; had he not requested that I
room with him when I returned from Charlotte, most likely I would have
been placed in another four-man cell since no other two-man cells were
open at the time. More importantly, within a matter of months I would
learn that my rooming with Rod was no accident.

Back in the routine of prison, I once again plunged into activities to
deaden my disappointment. I started working out at the weight room

every day with Rod and enrolled in a college-credit computer course and a sociology course. I had never had the opportunity to complete my college education, and these classes fascinated and challenged me. I also began reading *God Meant It for Good,* by Dr. R. T. Kendall, a minister of London's famous Westminster Chapel. Along with the Bible, this book, which drew lessons from the life of the biblical character Joseph, became my handbook while in prison.

God instructed me about many areas of my life through this book, especially three key areas I had struggled with for years: self-pity and my desire to be vindicated, God's timing, and total forgiveness.

Both my worst critics and my strongest supporters have chided me concerning my propensity toward self-pity. Tammy Faye regarded my self-pity as one of my worst traits. Often when the press were beating me up, to escape the pressure I simply curled up and went to sleep. When problems arose at PTL with one of our building projects or one of our programs, rather than lashing out I withdrew into myself, becoming less and less accessible to others. To Tammy, this was a sign of weakness. Tammy handled her problems by letting the whole world know about them. If anyone was unsure of her mood, she gladly clarified it. If Tammy was hurting, she went shopping, to see a movie, or out to eat. Her motto was, "When the going gets tough, the tough go shopping."

Early on in my prison experience, self-pity frequently got the best of me. For example, one day during the first few weeks I was at Rochester, I was called to the warden's office. When I arrived, the warden had someone in his office, so I stood in the reception area while I waited. Pictures of the warden and all the assistant wardens covered the walls of the reception area, so to pass the time I began studying the faces of the various prison personnel so I might be able to recognize them when I saw them.

Out of one of the offices walked a tall man, a prison official of some sort, I was sure. He took one look at me and bellowed, "Bakker! What are you doing here?"

"I was called by the warden," I replied tentatively.

"Well, you can't stand here!" he said, referring to the small carpeted section of the reception area. "Go down the hall and wait," he ordered, pointing out the tile-blocked hall area about twenty feet away.

"Yes, sir," I answered. As I exited the reception area and headed down the hall, I felt like a schoolboy being told to go stand in the corner.

Just a few years before I had been comfortable standing with presidents in the White House. Now, my mind drifted back to late 1979 when I had been invited aboard *Air Force One.* I had been sitting in one of the powder-blue chairs near the doorway aboard the aircraft, along with

Johnny and June Carter Cash and other celebrity guests. When President Carter entered the compartment, I was the first person he saw. As he paused to greet me, he said softly, "Jim, I want you to come to my private suite in a few minutes." I nodded as the president moved around the small room shaking hands with each visitor. He came back to me. "Please come with me now."

I followed the president of the United States back to his private suite on *Air Force One*. When President Carter and I were alone in his quarters, we sat down to talk. It was obvious that he was under horrendous stress. The date was October 31, 1980; it was right before the presidential election, and American citizens were still being held hostage in Iran. After a while, President Carter asked me to pray for him. I was glad to oblige.

Now, however, it suddenly hit me that I was no longer good enough to stand on the cheap, all-weather carpet in the warden's reception area. I felt thoroughly degraded and self-pity poured over me like a flood.

As I studied the life of Joseph in Dr. Kendall's book, however, I began to see the folly of self-pity and recognize it for the first time in my life for what it really is—a sin. Dr. Kendall pulled no punches: "Self-pity wants sympathy." "We become absorbed with ourselves and our own feelings. We don't realize we are hurting people." "When a person is filled with self-pity, he is making no real progress." Kendall concluded, "I can safely say there is nothing at all good about self-pity."[1]

I had to come to grips with the fact that I might never truly be vindicated of the charges against me, but it no longer mattered. I knew the truth and those involved knew the truth, and more importantly, God knows the truth. If He chose to clear my name, I would be delighted. If not, I must not allow myself to slip into self-pity.

A second area in which Kendall's book spoke to me was regarding God's timing. I wanted God to move *now*. Frankly, I had believed that God was going to do something supernatural, or at least highly unusual, to keep me from going to prison in the first place. When He did not, I was shocked and shattered by what I considered to be God's abandonment of me. Again and again, I cried with the psalmist, "How long wilt thou forget me, O LORD? for ever?" (Ps. 13:1 KJV).

Through Kendall's book, however, I realized afresh that God had not abandoned me. He was shaping me into the man He wanted me to be. In His time, the rest of the story *would* unfold.

Kendall listed five ways we can know when God's time for us has come. "First, we know that God's time has arrived when we have come utterly to the end of our own strength. . . . This . . . comes hard to us. We don't like to think that we are utterly helpless."[2] It is human nature to want to manipulate people and events to our advantage.

I realized that I had done something similar by subtly believing that Alan Dershowitz and Judge Mullen might be my ticket out of prison. I had spent relatively little time in preparation for my resentencing because I had committed it entirely to God, but there was still a temptation to think that if Alan and I could convince the judge of my innocence, I might be able to walk out of that courthouse a free man. When Judge Mullen resentenced me to eighteen years in prison, I was reminded again that I was utterly powerless to orchestrate my release by mere human intelligence, persuasiveness, or personality. God's time had not yet come for me.

Second, "God's time has come when he does a work utterly outside ourselves." Kendall explained:

> When has God's time come? When something appears for which there is no natural explanation. . . . God delights to show the world that for which there is no known explanation. . . . As long as there is a natural or traditional explanation to something, men may well debate it. But when all explanations fail, God's time has come.[3]

A third indication that God's time is at hand "is when God works successfully at the precise point we have failed."[4]

Another sign that God is working in your situation is "when someone pleads your case (and knows all the facts) without your opening your mouth."[5]

Fifth, we know that God is working things out for us "when God reaches us where we are without any effort on our part."[6]

As I read Dr. Kendall's words, it was almost as if I was having a conversation with the author. "Are you in the equivalent of a dungeon at this moment?" Kendall asked.

"Yes!" I wrote in the margin of the book.

"Are you afraid that God does not see you?"

"Yes! That is my greatest fear."

Kendall's words were reassuring. "He does see you and he's come right now. All is in God's timing."[7]

Kendall's emphasis upon God's timing was a liberating concept. God knew exactly what I was going through. I slowly but surely began to believe that He could use this experience for good.

The third major area in which Dr. Kendall's book helped me was the matter of forgiveness. I had been actively trying to forgive everyone involved with the demise of PTL since the very public, scandalous days of

March 1987. Jesus emphatically stated, "For if you forgive men their trespasses, your heavenly Father will also forgive you. But if you do not forgive men their trespasses, neither will your Father forgive your trespasses"
(Matt. 6:14-15).

Dr. Kendall proposed five principles of total forgiveness: First, total
forgiveness is when we do not want anybody else to be hurt because of
what was done to us. [8]

Second: "Total forgiveness wants to make a person feel completely at
ease."[9]

Third: "Total forgiveness will not even allow the person to feel bad or
angry with himself. . . . When we really forgive another person, we want
them to feel good."[10]

Fourth: "Make it easy for that person to forgive himself; we do it in
such a way that it is obvious we really do forgive."[11] "Finally," says Dr.
Kendall, "total forgiveness is demonstrated when we keep someone's sin
hidden from the person who means the most to him."[12]

Kendall's pen continued to hit the bull's-eye of my heart:

> If you are a Christian, there will come a day—it may be soon—when the
> unexpected, the unthinkable happens to you. Your immediate question
> will be "God, why did you let this happen?" The temptation will be to let
> yourself be filled with bitterness, hatred, and desire for revenge. . .
> Sometimes, however, we are called upon to forgive people who refuse to
> acknowledge that they have even done anything wrong. And there are
> those who don't think they have done anything wrong. But you have to
> forgive them, too—they are the hardest people to forgive. . . . It is one
> thing to say, "I have forgiven him for what he did"—we can say it and
> think we mean it—but it is another thing to truly and totally forgive.[13]

I knew I had to forgive the prosecutors in my trial. I felt I must forgive
several of my own lawyers for their bungling of my case; and I had to forgive the judge for giving me a sentence of forty-five years. Beyond that, I
had to forgive the people who did not come to my aid—individuals who
could have actually stopped the madness but chose not to do so—as well
as church leaders and friends who I felt had abandoned me. I also had to
forgive my denomination, for defrocking me when I needed the church
more than ever.

In addition to forgiveness, Jesus also said, "Love your enemies, bless
those who curse you, do good to those who hate you, and pray for those
who spitefully use you and persecute you" (Matt. 5:44). Not only did I

have to forgive those people who had taken advantage of my sin, failures, and mistakes to orchestrate my downfall, I had to start praying for them!

I had a long list of people I began to pray for by name almost every day. When my cellmates were gone, I sat at my desk or on my bunk and prayed aloud for individuals, both friends and foes. In addition, I prayed every day that God would prolong the lives of my mother and father until I could get out of prison. I also prayed daily for my wife and children.

I knew that I had to pray for all the major players in the fall of PTL including Jessica Hahn, Jerry Falwell, Norman Roy Grutman, Jerry Nims, Reverend Dortch, Jimmy Swaggart, John Ankerberg, and many others. At first, I had awful difficulty praying that God would bless some of these individuals, but I tried my best.

I quickly found that this sort of prayer was impossible to fake. Perhaps it may have been possible to make a pretense of these prayers had I not been in prison, but in the isolation of my cell, where nobody could hear me, and nobody was paying any attention to me, the prayer either came from my heart or not at all. I confess, there were days when praying for my long list was too laborious for me. On other days, I simply hurried through my list of names, just to get it done. Some days, I merely read the list of names aloud to God, because that was the best prayer I could muster.

Some people with whom I corresponded concerning the need to forgive my enemies got angry at me and asked, "How can you forgive those people? I'm not going to forgive them! I will never forgive Jerry Falwell. I will never forgive Jimmy Swaggart."

I wrote back, "But we must forgive. We do not have any other options. If you or I harbor unforgiveness toward any of those individuals involved in the downfall of PTL, Christ will not forgive us."

I felt compelled to communicate my forgiveness to all the key players in the demise of PTL, whether they accepted it or not. I wrote, telephoned, or talked face-to-face with many of them. I received several letters asking me for forgiveness and apologizing for actions and statements that were made against me. Those were pleasant surprises.

Besides my own spiritual health, I recognized that I had to lead the way in forgiveness for my family. I did that by encouraging them to forgive the people who hurt them, including me. Looking back, I can now see that had I allowed bitterness and resentment to fester, I could have destroyed my own family.

During this time, I discovered something else: As I was forgiving those who in some way had been a part of my downfall, I had to confront my own culpability. For instance, as I prayed to forgive Jessica Hahn, I also began to realize that regardless of Jessica Hahn's attitude, I was responsible for my own actions. I cannot blame her or anyone else for my sin.

Similarly, as I expressed my forgiveness of Jerry Falwell and his questionable motives in taking over PTL, God reminded me that I can complain that I was hoodwinked until the day I die, but I cannot ignore the truth that *I allowed it to happen*. That was my responsibility, and I had to pray, "Dear God, please forgive me for disobeying You."

Dr. Kendall listed four proofs to know for sure that we have forgiven those who have hurt us. "The first is that you don't want the other person to be afraid."[14] I want all those men and women who spoke and acted against me to know that I harbor no resentment toward them. They have nothing to fear from me. If Christ can forgive me, I can forgive anyone.

According to Kendall, "The second way of knowing that you have really forgiven someone is that you refuse to take advantage of any superior position you might be in."[15] Joseph could have caused his brothers to cower in fear of him for the remainder of their lives, but he chose not to do so. Instead, when Joseph's brothers acknowledged their sin, Joseph replied, "You meant evil against me; but God meant it for good, in order to bring it about as it is this day, to save many people alive" (Gen. 50:20).

I am convinced that God did not send me to prison to punish me for my sins, even though I deserved it. God put me in prison so I could study His Word, get to know Him, and learn the meaning of forgiveness. Had I been seeking God daily, studying the Bible, and living by its principles all along as we built PTL and Heritage USA, I have no doubt that I would never have gone to prison. I would have seen the error of my ways reflected in God's Word, and I would have taken the appropriate corrective measures. But because I had allowed my relationship with God to grow cold and had ignored His Word, God put me in a position in which I had only two choices—either get right with God, or die.

"The third proof that you really have forgiven another person," says Dr. Kendall, "is that you bind up the wound so completely that you show that all that happened really was meant to be."[16] Joseph told his brothers, in essence, "This was meant to be." And he meant it. I feel the same way about what I have experienced.

> The final proof that you have really forgiven the other person is that you keep on forgiving them. . . . You know you really have forgiven and that it is not just a burst of emotional feeling because you keep on doing it. Total forgiveness holds two months later. Six months later. Two years later. Forever.[17]

That is the way God forgives us, that is the way He expects us to forgive each other, and that is the way I decided to forgive.

I wish I could say this was an easy process, but it was not. I found that I had to relearn the lessons on a frequent basis. While I knew that forgiveness was a matter of my will and required a choice, I also discovered that forgiveness was an ongoing process. I honestly forgave everyone involved with my ouster from PTL and I held no grudges. Yet from time to time, when an inmate brought another erroneous article to me or another attempt was made to vilify me in court, I found that I had to express my forgiveness again and again. Even in the writing of this book and reliving so many experiences I had tried to forget, once again, I have had to work through forgiving certain individuals.

I have anguished over how I could tell this story without violating the principles of forgiveness that have set me free, and without hurting anyone or dragging everyone back through events and circumstances that many besides myself have hoped to forget. Yet because so many of the events within these pages were played out before the public, I feel strongly that I have a responsibility to lead in publicly extending forgiveness and encouraging others to do the same. I believe asking for forgiveness and extending forgiveness are going to be integral parts of my life for as long as I live.

Through my study of forgiveness, God impressed upon me that I was not going to get out of prison until I had forgiven—from my heart, not simply in my mind—every last person who had said or done anything against me. Nevertheless, as the Minnesota summer turned colder, and the autumn chill began to set in, I would never have dreamed that two of the main objects of my forgiveness for the rest of my days would be my best friend and my wife.

CHAPTER

35

Tammy Faye

AS SOON AS WORD OF JUDGE MULLEN'S DECISION TO reduce my sentence from forty-five years to eighteen years hit the media, reactions came fast and furiously. Letters soon poured in to Tammy Faye in Florida and to me in prison. One letter that particularly piqued my interest was dated August 27, 1991, and was written on Liberty University stationery. It was from Mark DeMoss, the young public-relations director and administrative assistant to Jerry Falwell who had witnessed firsthand the events surrounding my pseudoresignation from PTL in March 1987 through Jerry Falwell's departure from PTL on October 8, 1987:

> As you may know, Dr. Falwell has publicly said many times that your
> 45-year sentence was outrageous, unreasonable, and unfair. When Judge
> Mullen reduced the sentence last week to 18 years, we issued a news
> release stating that the sentence was still excessive and that Dr. Falwell
> would have supported your release.

Another letter, also dated August 27, 1991, came from Owen Carr and was specifically addressed to Tammy Faye. Owen tried to console Tammy Faye concerning my resentencing: "Of course, eighteen years isn't as bad as forty-five, but it is still outrageous. There is no possible way to align this with 'justice.' Or to align it with what others are given who have committed crimes much worse than that with which they have charged Jim." Then he warned:

You have already been separated from Jim for a long time. And now, the prospects are that you will be away from him for an even longer time. There is bound to be a loneliness. You can't afford that. No one else can really take Jim's place—either in your home or in your heart. How you must long for his companionship. Just to be with him. Just to talk with him—when no one is watching or listening. Just to be held by him and to hold him.

Be very careful, Tammy. The devil will take advantage of this, and someone else may offer to provide "special attention." Even some preacher, who feels sorry for you, and wanting to empathize with you, may lead you into Satan's trap. Be very careful. Be alert. Be on guard. The Bible tells us, "We are not to be ignorant of his devices."

Unfortunately, even as Owen Carr was writing his words of admonition to Tammy Faye, she was already back at French Lick Springs . . . with Roe Messner. She and Roe were meeting with the Canadian financial backers to purchase the resort from the man who had bought it at the auction. The Canadian backers also offered to put up $500,000 to get Tammy Faye back on television. On August 28, Roe wrote to me in prison concerning his plan to get Tammy Faye on TV before Christmas.

It was good to see you in Charlotte. I was very disappointed in the new sentence. . . . We continue to pray every day that the Lord will give you the strength to carry on. Keep a positive attitude and don't let bitterness set in. I realize this is easy for me to say and probably hard for you to do. We have to believe that God is still in control.

. . . Who do you think we should hire or consult with to get the TV set up? Please give me any input you have on operating the hotel. I don't think I will have any trouble operating the hotel and overseeing the TV operation. . . . Tammy seems to be holding up pretty good. Do you have any suggestions on working with her?

A week or so later, I received another letter from Roe, informing me of further details that were being negotiated toward the purchase of the property. Roe wrote, "How are you doing, now that you are faced with such a long sentence? How are you spending your days? Is there anything you want me to do for you?" As he had begun doing more frequently in recent days, Roe signed his letter, "Your friend," and included a Scripture reference below his name. I could not bring myself to believe that my best friend was trying to steal my wife away from me.

I was struggling through another bout with despair myself. During one of my down days, a prison guard paged me and instructed me to report to the visiting room. I did not want to spend several hours talking to anyone. I had specifically requested that nobody be permitted to visit me.

I had just finished cleaning bathrooms and I was still dressed in my work clothes. I reeked of cleaning solutions, my hair was unkempt, and I had not bothered to shave in several days. I did not take time to wash before changing clothes.

Irritated and looking like I'd just crawled from under a rock, I made my way across the prison compound and into the visiting area.

My eyes scanned the visiting room to see who had the gall to intrude upon my self-imposed, depression-laden ban on visitors. Coming toward me was the apple of my eye, my daughter Tammy Sue . . . and she was holding in her arms a beautiful little baby boy—my grandson Jonathan Douglas, whom I had never before seen! Behind Tammy Sue and Jonathan were her husband Doug and baby James, who was now all of two and a half years old. I was never so happy to see my daghter in all my life!

Tammy Sue's and Doug's limited income had prevented them from making the trip to Minnesota for more than a year. It had been through the generous gift of our friends Faye and Ray LaForce that they could afford to make this trip.

For four glorious days, I was able to spend time with Tammy Sue, Doug, and my grandchildren. It was exhilarating to get to know little Jonathan; each day I cradled him gently in my arms until he fell asleep. Then James and I played together like we were old friends, which in a way we were. Although I had been in prison since the time of James's infancy, Tammy Sue had placed my picture on their refrigerator. Every day of my imprisonment, Tammy Sue pointed out my picture to baby James and said, "This is your grandpa, Paw-Paw Jim." By the time James finally "met" me, he was already well acquainted with me, thanks to a mother who loved her child and her dad enough to build a bridge between us.

James and I played with the old blocks stained by the thousands of little hands and teeth that had played with them and chewed on them in the visiting room. We built houses, boats, and anything our blocks could accommodate. When he tired of the blocks, I read stories to him from the well-worn children's books available in the visiting room.

Each day, our little family group ate sandwiches purchased from the visiting-room vending machines as we talked and talked. James, of course, had questions about everything. He realized that the prison was much bigger than his home. One day upon his arrival at the prison, James looked up and exclaimed to Tammy Sue, "Paw-Paw Jim has a *big* house!" Later when Tammy Sue related to me what James had said, I replied, "No, Paw-Paw Jim is *in* the big house!" We all laughed heartily. Only baby James could have brought me out of depression to laughter.

Near the end of October, Tammy Faye ministered in Louisiana at Metropolitan Christian Centre pastored by our friend Marvin Gorman. Reverend Gorman was so pleased he invited Tammy Faye to return to his church for a special Mother's Day service in May. Marvin wrote me a glowing letter, praising Tammy Faye and expressing appreciation for her ministry.

Tammy Faye was not quite so enthusiastic. Tammy wrote:

> Reverend Gorman's church went really well. But I thought it would leave me more satisfied than it did. I thought I would love the evange-listic field again . . . and I don't! I could never live that life again! I know that television is where I am supposed to be, and I guess I will never be happy in ministry again until I am back in my place, doing the thing I best know how to do. If that does not work, then I feel that I want to leave the ministry forever. There are other ways to serve the Lord.

The tone of Tammy's letter stunned me, but it did not surprise me. I could tell that she was changing.

Another bittersweet legal decision was rendered on November 4, 1991, by Judge William Thurmond Bishop, a U.S. bankruptcy judge in Columbia, South Carolina. Jerry Falwell had placed PTL into bankruptcy proceedings on June 12, 1987. At that time, the court appointed a trustee to oversee the property and all activities regarding PTL. On June 30, 1988, while I was still trying to find a way to buy or lease back Heritage USA, a small group of Lifetime Partners, represented by three private individuals, filed a suit before the Court against PTL's trustee, Mr. M.C. "Red" Benton. In their suit, the Lifetime Partners claimed that the PTL Lifetime Partners should receive priority in the disbursement of PTL's assets because they had paid a deposit of money and had not received the bene-fits they had expected. On October 25, 1988, the court made a decision allowing this small group of Partners to represent *all* Lifetime Partners, even though many Lifetime Partners showed little interest in the case.

After nearly three years of legal wranglings, Judge Bishop finally rendered his decision:

> Payments made by Lifetime Partners were not, in any sense of the word, deposits . . . In essence, the rights and responsibilities of individual Lifetime Partners and the Debtor were both fully operative and were being delivered and provided prior to the filing of the bankruptcy petition. . . . Further, the undisputed testimony of Plaintiff class representative . . . demonstrates that the Lifetime Partnership benefits were, in fact, delivered and provided before the commencement of the case.[1]

The court admitted that the PTL Lifetime Partners were in fact receiving all that they had been promised while I was president of PTL. The judge acknowledged the difficulties that Partners sometimes had in booking lodging space at Heritage USA during our peak seasons but did not consider that as a breach of our promises. Furthermore, he plainly acknowledged that the money donated by the Lifetime Partners was not meant to be "segregated" and used for construction purposes only.

The good news was that Judge Thurmond Bishop was saying that two of the basic premises on which I had been tried—that I had defrauded the Lifetime Partners by purposely overbooking our lodging space at Heritage, and using the money donated for projects other than construction—were false. The bad news was that I was still in prison serving eighteen years. It was at least a sort of moral victory. Finally, somebody in the legal system had said in essence, "Bakker did not defraud the PTL Lifetime Partners. That which had been promised to them was being delivered."

A few days after Judge Bishop's decision, on November 10, Reverend Richard Dortch was released from a halfway house in Florida, where he had been since June. He had served sixteen months at a minimum security prison at the Eglin Air Force Base federal prison after he made a deal with prosecutors to testify against me.

Although I was glad for Reverend Dortch, his release was yet another reminder that I was still looking at eighteen long years in prison. I had lost any hope of an early release and had resigned myself to my state. Nevertheless, when Tammy Faye, Jamie, and Donna arrived on November 22 for our Thanksgiving visit, I tried my best to put on a positive face, in spite of the fact that Roe Messner had accompanied my family to Minnesota.

Over the summer and fall of 1991, I had begun to suspect that something was going on between Tammy and Roe, but I refused to believe it. Where we had once spent hours talking by phone, now she was always in a hurry to end our conversations. She would tell me. "The girls from the ministry are coming to go out to lunch with me, and I have to get ready. I love you, bye!" Her excuses became more and more strained as the months wore on.

Regardless, I was delighted to see Tammy Faye. I had not been in the same room with her since the resentencing at Charlotte in August. Just to see her smiling face brightened my spirits.

We had our usual vending-machine Thanksgiving dinner and tried to pretend everything was normal. Nevertheless, Tammy Faye seemed to have difficulty looking me in the eyes. She appeared nervous. We had been married for over thirty years, so even in the awkward environment of the prison visiting area, it was impossible not to notice the difference in our relationship.

Tammy Faye, Jamie, and Donna visited each day from November 22 through December 2. Roe left over Thanksgiving. I assumed that he had gone home to spend the holiday with his wife.

After a few days of visiting, I could tell Tammy Faye was bored. She talked more to the wives of the inmates sitting near us in the visiting room. When she and I talked, she talked more about her excitement at going back on television at French Lick Springs than anything else. I knew the inactivity of our visits was tough for her; she was used to going, going, going all the time. No doubt it would have been difficuult for her to stay in one place for five or six hours each day under any circumstances, much less the growing coolness between us. On several days, I encouraged Tammy to leave the visting room a bit early. She was reluctant to go, but I could tell that it was useless for her to stay.

On the last day of Tammy Faye's visit, I was determined to reach out to my wife any way I could. I still loved her. I did not want to lose her, especially after all we had come through together. I was not about to allow thirty years of marriage to simply slip away without a fight.

I had taken extra care the night before to make sure my prison khakis were crisply pressed. I wanted to look my best for Tammy Faye. When I completed my check-in procedures, I looked for Tammy Faye's beaming face.

Today, however, her face looked less than radiant. The extra thick makeup she had applied could not conceal her somber look and her smile seemed forced. She seemed so detached. Her lips merely grazed mine as we kissed. I tried to hold her close to me for an extra moment as we had done on previous visits, but I could feel Tammy pulling away. "Jim Bakker, behave yourself. Do you want to get into trouble and be sent to the hole?" she scolded with a fake laugh. She whirled away from me, pulled out a chair, and sat down . . . on the opposite side of the table from me. Almost immediately she began telling me about all the things she needed to get done as soon as she got back to Florida.

I could hardly tear my eyes away from Tammy Faye for more than a moment, almost as if I was afraid she would disappear.

Toward the time when we knew we would soon hear the guard's voice calling "Wrap it up," Tammy Faye and I walked back to the rear visiting room, to the window near the vending-machine area. Normally at this time of day, the vending area was the closest thing we could find to some semblance of privacy, as most of the inmates and visitors congregated in the main room before the end of visitation time. With nobody around us, Tammy Faye and I stood in front of a soda pop machine, both of us facing the window as we had done on other occasions just to sense a moment of intimacy. It had been more than two years since I had slept with Tammy in our own bed, and every fiber of my being was straining to touch her and to be touched by her.

I knew I was taking a chance—but to me, it was worth the risk. I pressed my body against Tammy Faye's, placed my hands as inconspicuously as possible on her waist, and gently pulled her toward me. For a long delicious moment I basked in her warmth, as I allowed the heat of my body to intermingle with hers. She smelled so good. I wanted to kiss her and sweep her up in my arms and carry her away to some private place where we could be one once again. My body responded to her softness. I was lost in the moment. . . .

Suddenly, Tammy whirled around, took a step back, straightened her dress, and said icily, "Don't start something you can't finish."

I stood there aghast. I was so stunned I could not even respond. I mumbled something about it must be time to go, and we went back to where Jamie and Donna were waiting for Tammy Faye. We all said hasty good-byes, Donna's and Jamie's eyes filled with tears. Tammy's eyes were dry.

My head and heart were still reeling as I watched them go out the door. That was the last time I ever touched Tammy Faye Bakker.

36

Billy Graham

TAMMY FAYE'S THANKSGIVING VISIT HAD LEFT ME discouraged and depressed. On top of that, shortly before Christmas, I started coming down with the flu. For some reason, the heat in my end of Building Two was not functioning correctly. At night, the brick walls in our cells felt like the inside of a refrigerator. To keep warm, I put on both of my jogging suits and piled on as many extra covers as Rod Netherton and I had been able to borrow. I still froze. In the morning, I could hardly move my fingers. I had developed arthritis in my hands, and the cold caused my knuckles to become stiff.

One cold morning, a week or so before Christmas, I finished cleaning and returned to my cell. Still in my work clothes I climbed onto my bunk and pulled a blanket over the top of me, trying to get warm. My nose was running, my head was pounding, my body ached; all the symptoms of the flu were catching up with me. I felt miserable. I had just shut my eyes when I heard a guard's voice echoing in the hall over the prison paging system, "Inmate Bakker! Report to two-one guard station."

"Oh, no," I moaned as I rolled off my bunk. *What now?*

I walked down the hall to the guard station. There I saw a familiar-looking box containing an artificial Christmas tree and the same sort of scrawny Christmas tree ornaments I had used to decorate the Christmas tree the year before . . . and the year before that.

"Bakker, take these ornaments and go put up the Christmas tree and decorate it. There's an electrical outlet across the hall from the Coke machines," the guard said.

I carried the box back up the hallway toward the spot where the Christmas tree was placed each year. It was like the rerun of a bad movie. *The third year in a row*, I thought. *Is this just a coincidence or is it some kind of cruel trick that the guards are making me decorate a tree that nobody wanted to see— not even me.*

The prison officials were not oblivious to the antipathy with which most inmates regarded Christmas. Consequently, the prison offered numerous activities to help prisoners make it through the holiday season.

One night my friend Tony asked me to go with him to hear a singing group comprised of senior citizens, the group known as "Young at Heart." I reluctantly agreed. Sure enough, like most choral groups who performed at the prison during the Christmas season, the senior citizens had in their repertoire the classic, "I'll Be Home for Christmas," which they sang with deep emotion. As the dear golden-agers sang their hearts out, they little realized that they were tearing the hearts out of the inmates. Many inmates simply couldn't take it and they walked out of the concert.

In over two years, I had not violated the prison officials' mandate that I refrain from being involved in any position of spiritual leadership. The only time I attended chapel functions had been when special guest speakers or singers came to the prison.

So I was shocked when the chaplain approached me and asked if I would be willing to read the Christmas story from the Bible during the ecumenical Christmas Eve service to be held that night. I agreed to do it.

Christmas Day was relatively uneventful. I tried to eat the traditional Christmas dinner, but I didn't have much of an appetite. The flu was definitely catching up with me now, so I was glad for a day off work, just to rest. I stayed in bed most of the day, getting up only for the prison's mandatory 4:00 P.M. count and to call my family. I talked briefly with each of my family members. Tammy Faye acted as though her rebuff of my affection only a few weeks before had never happened. She told me that basically it had been a good Christmas. I was glad I had encouraged the family to stay at home this year.

On January 2, 1992, I "celebrated" my fifty-second birthday in self-imposed exile, talking to as few people as possible. Tammy Faye spent the day in Des Moines, Iowa, having her teeth worked on by Dr. Jim Boltz, a friend of ours who had done much of our dental work over the years. I later learned that Roe Messner accompanied her for her dental trip.

A deep sadness plagued my heart and mind. Nevertheless, I got up each morning and went to work, but as soon as I finished cleaning the bathrooms and halls, I returned to my cell, closed the door and crawled back onto my bunk, still wearing my work clothes.

On the day I had the worst fever, I lay in my bunk, trying to "sweat it out." Suddenly, my cell door opened and a guard appeared in the doorway. "Bakker, come with me," he commanded.

I groaned and rolled out of bed. I had not showered or shaved yet that day. I knew I looked awful, but I was too sick to care. I did not even bother to comb my hair; I simply ran my fingers though the increasingly thin strands and left it at that. I started to put on my good tennis shoes and stopped short. I had no idea why the guard wanted me. *Maybe he wants me to clean up a mess somewhere or help push the trash carts over to the dumpster*, I thought. I had two pairs of tennis shoes in prison, one pair I wore while I cleaned the rest rooms, and the other I wore to exercise, walk the track, or during after-work hours. The old tennis shoes I wore mopping and cleaning rest rooms were torn and filthy. I decided to put them on.

I reported to the guard, wearing my work clothes and work shoes. He looked at me strangely, but he simply told me to sit down and wait.

Another guard came over to me. "Get your coat," he said. I walked back to my cell, retrieved my green army overcoat with its bright orange lining, and returned to the guard station.

"Let's go," the guard said. We walked out of Building Two into the bitterly cold air, toward the front of the prison compound. It eventually became clear that we were going to the warden's office.

The guard and I entered the building. I noticed a number of people buzzing around a doorway. *Something is up*, I thought.

A high-level prison official approached me and whispered, "Somebody is here to see you, Bakker. Do you want to see him?"

"See who?" I asked, honestly surprised. I was expecting no visitors.

"Hasn't anyone told you who it is?" the official asked.

"No, sir," I responded.

"Why, Billy Graham is here to see you!" the prison official gushed.

"Billy Graham?" I repeated. "He's here? To see me?" I looked down at my shoes. The gaping holes in them stared back at me.

"You do want to see him, don't you?" the official asked.

For a fraction of a second, I almost said no out of sheer embarrassment. The last time I had seen Billy Graham face-to-face had been when he had appeared on *PTL*. Billy's opening line to Tammy Faye and me that day had been, "You feel just like family, you have been in our home so much." On that day, I had been dressed in one of my best suits of clothes, with every hair in place. Now, I was in rumpled prison khakis, totally disheveled. How could I allow the great Dr. Billy Graham to see me like this?

But then I thought, *Billy Graham has come here . . . to this place . . . to see me.* There was no way I was going to refuse his visit.

"Yes, I would like to see him," I replied. I took off my old green overcoat and tried to straighten my hair. It was no use. I took a breath and walked into the warden's conference room where Dr. Graham was waiting along with Dr. Westrick and other prison officials.

As I walked through the door, Billy Graham turned toward me and opened his arms wide. Immediately, I felt his total acceptance and love. I wanted to run into his arms like a little boy would run into his daddy's arms. I had not seen such compassionate eyes in a long time.

We stepped toward each other and embraced. "Hello, Jim," he said in his rich Carolina accent. "How are you?"

"Hello, Dr. Graham. I'm sorry you have to see me like this." Billy Graham simply waved my apology away.

We sat down beside each other at the conference table and began to talk. The room was still swirling with people, but I felt as though Dr. Graham and I were in our own separate world. We talked quietly but freely. He told me that he was glad to be able to see me. "I wanted to come sooner," he said almost apologetically.

His wife, Ruth, was in Mayo Clinic for some tests, which is why they were in Minnesota in the first place. He told me Ruth was especially insistent that he come to visit me. "She sends her greetings and her love."

Billy Graham asked about my family and about my life in prison. He seemed genuinely concerned, so I shared with him some of the good points and the bad.

He then told me about his most recent overseas crusade and how God had done such great things there. He was clearly pleased that so many people had accepted Christ. He noted that satellite television had extended the crusade coverage to the four corners of the world.

I told him about Dr. Ruth Westrick. "This woman is the Mother Teresa of the prison system," I told Dr. Graham. I told him of Dr. Westrick's compassion to the inmates, and about the dignity she had given me. I got the feeling I was not telling Billy anything he did not already know.

Before he left, Billy Graham offered to pray with me, and as he began, the activity in the room instantly ceased. Time seemed suspended during Dr. Graham's visit, so I have no idea how long he stayed. Probably not long, but I will never forget that the man who had just been voted one of the most influential men in the world and who has ministered to millions of people took time out of his busy schedule to come minister to one prisoner. Amid my depression, flu, filth, and hopelessness, Billy Graham had come. I felt as though Jesus Himself had come to visit me.

CHAPTER

37

Dad, Mom Is Leaving You!

ALTHOUGH I DID NOT KNOW IT JUST THEN, BILLY GRAHAM'S visit was providentially timed. God must have known that I was going to need an extra boost in my spirit to make it through the next difficult days.

As excited as I was about his visit, the next news I received was even better. Jamie had turned sixteen years of age on December 18, and he wanted to come to the prison to see me! Jamie had visited me several times previously, but never by himself. Now that he was sixteen, prison rules allowed him to visit me alone, without being accompanied by another adult. I could hardly wait to see my boy.

The first thing I noticed when I saw Jamie was that my *boy* was now a man. Almost overnight, it seemed, he had grown up. In many ways, Jamie was much more worldly wise at sixteen years of age than I was at fifty-two.

The collapse of PTL after the public exposure of my moral failure had wreaked havoc in thousands of people's lives. Godly, dedicated men and women who had moved to Heritage USA to be a part of the ministry were suddenly jobless and spiritually disillusioned. I believe nobody suffered more than my own son, Jamie Charles.

Jamie had just turned eleven when the PTL scandals hit the news. Granted, his life at Heritage USA had been anything but normal. Nevertheless, Jamie had grown up in a comfortable home with the love and nurture of caring Christians all around him. Even when Tammy Faye and I had been preoccupied, Jamie still had Tammy's parents and mine living at

Heritage, schoolmates and teachers from Heritage Academy, and hundreds of PTL staff members who loved him and doted over him.

Suddenly, after March 1987, Jamie had nobody. Tammy Faye and I were trying to keep our lives together, Tammy Sue had run off and gotten married, and most of Jamie's closest friends, including his bodyguard buddies, had been encouraged to have no further contact with him.

Our family moved to Florida just as Jamie moved into his teenage years. Besides struggling with all the cruel things teens say to each other, Jamie also had to deal with tabloid scandal sheets shredding what little respectability our family had left. At a time when most teenage boys crave acceptance at almost any cost, Jamie was treated like a leper. After I went to prison, a large student sitting in the back of the classroom accused me of having homosexual relationships in prison. Jamie went ballistic. He leaped to his feet and began picking up the desks between him and the boy in the back of the room. One by one, Jamie heaved the desks out of his way. When he reached the boy, Jamie shoved him up against the classroom window. Jamie later confessed that he had intended to punch the boy literally through the window, but his teacher stopped him. Later Jamie chased the boy all the way to the school bus, fighting his way through several of the kid's larger friends and screaming, "I'll kill you!"

By the time Jamie was fourteen, he was already smoking cigarettes and drinking beer with his friends. At fifteen years of age, he was smoking marijuana and had experimented several times with LSD. During the summer of 1990, I could tell that something was wrong with Jamie when he came to the prison to see me. His face was drawn and gaunt, and his eyes had a hollow look. He later confessed to me that he and some friends had been drinking and using LSD at the Kahler Hotel all week long while he had been in town along with Tammy Faye to visit me. The boys partied well into the night. The next morning, Jamie was an emotional basket case when he came to see me. He seemed disoriented much of the time. I told Tammy Faye that I feared Jamie was on some sort of drugs. I would have been horrified had I really known what my son was doing.

About that same time, Jamie became sexually active. By the summer of 1991, at the age of fifteen, he was deeply embroiled in a bona fide love affair with a young woman named Suzanne, a first-year college student. She was his first true love. He was so in love that he hardly paid any attention to what was developing between Tammy Faye and Roe.

Jamie's first clue that something wasn't quite right came one night when he and Suzanne were at our home in Florida. Tammy Faye had been gone for several hours and had come home late. She rang the doorbell. Jamie answered the door. "Mom! What's wrong?" he asked her.

"Well, um, I locked my keys in the car at the grocery store, where I had gone to walk around for a while. . . ."

Jamie was suspicious but didn't say anything at the time.

Another night toward the end of 1991, Jamie and Suzanne were eating dinner at our home when Tammy Faye came home upset. She told Jamie and Suzanne, "An article is coming out in one of the rag mags that says Roe and I are having an affair. I just want you to know that it's not true. It's just a bunch of garbage."

Jamie made light of Tammy's comment. "Man, those people will write anything, won't they?"

Early in January 1992, Jamie and Suzanne broke up, by mutual consent. They had been together almost constantly for more than a year. Jamie later confided to me that breaking up with Suzanne was one of the most devastating moments in his young life. Tammy Faye was absorbed in running the church in Florida, while trying to get everything together at French Lick Springs to purchase the resort and go back on television. Without Suzanne, Jamie's emotional props were knocked out from beneath him. Jamie plunged into a deep depression.

He repeatedly told Tammy Faye, "I have to talk to Dad. I need my dad! I want to go see Dad."

"All right," Tammy Faye said. "Roe says he will be glad to fly up there with you so you can go see your dad."

"Great, let's make the reservations," Jamie answered.

On Friday, January 17, Jamie and Roe flew to Rochester. Early Saturday morning, Roe and Jamie left the Kahler Hotel for F.M.C. Rochester. As they started to get into the car, Roe handed the keys to Jamie, and said, "You drive, Jamie."

"Me?" Jamie replied. "I don't drive yet, Roe."

"That's okay," Roe answered. "Go ahead. I'll teach you."

It was a cold, winter, Minnesota morning and the ground was covered with snow and ice.

"I'm afraid I might mess up the car if I drive," Jamie said.

"Oh, you'll do fine," Roe replied.

Jamie had never driven a car before, but fortunately, he negotiated the icy roads safely and arrived at the prison without incident.

As soon as I saw Jamie, I recognized that he was deeply depressed. It wasn't long before he began to bare his soul concerning his breakup with Suzanne. Jamie told me how lonely he felt without her, and I could honestly empathize with my son. As I looked at him, I couldn't get over how much he resembled me when I had been his age.

287

"Jamie, when I was in high school, I was always a loner," I told him. "I was active in school programs, but deep inside, I was lonely."

"Really, Dad? You felt that way?"

I went on to tell Jamie how much I now missed Tammy Faye, and how lonely I was for her. Jamie looked back at me with an understanding that far surpassed his years.

The longer we talked, the more open we both became with each other. He spoke straightforwardly of his involvement with drugs, alcohol, and sex. I told him candidly of the events leading up to my tryst with Jessica Hahn. I tried to explain to him again how I had lost PTL. We talked for hours, we laughed a lot, we cried a bit, and for the first time in his sixteen years, Jamie and I spent one entire day alone together. The irony was not lost upon me that it took me going to prison before I could spend the day with my son, giving him my undivided attention.

No subject was off-limits that day. Whatever Jamie wanted to talk about was fine with me. We talked at length about his relationship with Suzanne. We talked about Jamie growing up to be a man. I told him that I was concerned about how thin he looked. Jamie countered by telling me how he always felt self-conscious about being pudgy as a little boy. We both laughed as Jamie recalled how as a child he used to wander the grounds of Heritage USA and well-meaning people would feed him anything he wanted, ice cream, candy, soda pop, whatever.

"You know it's true, Dad," he said laughing, "You're the one who hung the sign around my neck that said, 'Please don't feed me!'"

"I never did such a thing!" I poked Jamie as we both laughed.

Throughout the day, I did my best to listen to Jamie more than I advised him. I was careful not to condemn him about anything but attempted to remain open. It was the father-son talk we should have had five or six years previously.

Toward the end of the day, Jamie and I were laughing about something when suddenly, he said, "Hey, Dad! What do you think about that rag-mag article that is supposed to be coming out, saying that Mom and Roe are having an affair? Isn't that crazy?" Instantly my mood turned somber. I said, "What do you think?"

Jamie stopped in the middle of a laugh and sat up straight in his chair.

"What do you mean, Dad? You don't think it's true, do you?" Jamie asked.

I looked down at the table for a moment. Finally, I said quietly, "Jamie, I think it is true. I think your mother is seeing Roe."

Jamie was horrified. "No, Dad; it's not true. Mom would tell me. She's always been honest with me. Mom hates lying."

"Jamie, Jamie, Jamie . . ." I said.

"Dad, it's not true. Mom would not lie to me. Dad, I swear, it is *not* true!"

Jamie was so adamant that Tammy Faye and Roe were not seeing each other, it was almost reassuring to me.

Jamie and I let the subject drop and moved on to other things. By the time Jamie was ready to leave, our spirits had risen once again.

"I'll be back tomorrow, Dad," Jamie said.

"Great!" I answered. "What time do you think you'll be coming?"

"I'll be here first thing in the morning, as soon as they open the doors!" Jamie answered.

"Don't you want to sleep in a little bit?"

"Oh, no, Dad. I want to spend as much time as I can with you."

"Okay. I'll be waiting. I'm not going anywhere." Jamie and I both grinned.

Just before Jamie left the visiting room, he turned to me and said something I will never forget. "Dad, this has been the best day of my life. All my life I have wanted to have you all to myself for a whole day."

I nodded my head and hugged my son. No words were possible. No words were necessary.

Jamie went through the prison exit procedures, and then waited outside for Roe to pick him up. Once again, Roe insisted Jamie drive the car.

Jamie was hungry since he had not eaten an actual meal all day long, so he said, "Roe, do you want to grab a bite to eat in the hotel restaurant?"

"Sure."

As Jamie and Roe were eating dinner, they talked about me. Jamie's mind was in turmoil. Finally, Jamie looked across the table and said, "You know what's crazy? My dad said today that he thinks that my mom might be leaving him. . . ."

Roe swallowed his food and gulped hard. "Well, Jamie, I'm afraid to say that it is true."

Jamie later said he felt at that moment as though someone had just shot him with a shotgun at close range and splattered him against the back of the chair. Jamie reached into his pocket, pulled out a cigarette, lit it, took a deep drag, and blew the smoke in Roe's direction.

"Really?" Jamie said. "And Dad thinks it might be because of you."

"Well, Jamie, there is some truth to that. If, ah . . . well, er, if your mother, ah . . . if your mother leaves your father, um, I have . . . I have some interest in her."

"Some interest?"

"Why, yes, Jamie. I would like to ask your mother to marry me."

Jaime took a deep puff on the cigarette, looked squarely in Roe Messner's eyes, and asked point-blank, "Are you sleeping with my mother?"

Roe stammered, "Um, er . . . ah, of course not, Jamie. But I would want to marry your mother. . . . "

Jamie slammed his fist down on the table and jumped to his feet. Instinctively, Roe flinched backwards. Jamie stormed out of the restaurant.

That night, Jamie did not sleep. He paced back and forth in his hotel room, smoking one cigarette after another. "I've got to tell Dad," he kept saying over and over to himself. "I've got to tell Dad . . . but how? How does a son tell his dad that his wife is leaving him to marry his best friend?"

The next morning, true to his word, Jamie was one of the first visitors into the prison. He had driven to the prison with Roe in silence.

I entered the visiting room in an exuberant mood, expecting to pick up with my son where we had left off yesterday. But from the moment I saw Jamie in the prison visiting area that day, I could tell something was wrong. His eyes had shadows under them, and he looked as though he had been crying. I checked in with the guard and quickly went to where Jamie was sitting. He saw me approaching and stood to meet me. Jamie hugged me and held on to me tightly.

"Hi, Dad," he said softly.

"Jamie, what's wrong?" I asked. He had been so up when he left the prison less than eighteen hours earlier. Jamie sat down in a heap and I noticed the tears beginning to form in his eyes.

"Dad, promise me that you'll never leave me. . . ."

"Leave you? Jamie, of course I'll never leave you."

Jamie was adamant. "Dad! Just promise that you will never leave me!"

"What on earth is wrong?" I asked.

Jamie looked up with a pained look in his eyes and leaned forward in the chair. "Dad! Mom's leaving you!"

My entire body went numb. My greatest fear had come to realization. My wife of nearly thirty-one years was leaving me.

Jamie started to sob. Other visitors stared at us. We didn't care.

For the longest time—I have no idea how long—both Jamie and I sat, grieving, yet speaking not a word to each other.

Finally, I asked, "How do you know?"

Slowly, Jamie poured out the story of his conversation with Roe the night before. He told me that Roe denied he and Tammy Faye were having an affair but admitted that she was planning to leave me and that Roe was waiting with open arms. He was planning to leave his wife, Ruth Ann, and their four children, and marry Tammy Faye.

Neither Jamie Charles nor I spoke much the remainder of the day. We spent over six hours, the entire visiting period, bonded together in our mutual distress. What a contrast to yesterday when Jamie and I had talked nonstop for six hours, ending with Jamie exclaiming, "Dad, this has been the best day of my life!"

How could we go from the best day in my sixteen-year-old son's life to the worst day in his life—and in mine—all within twenty-four hours?

"Visiting hours are over," the guard called. "Wrap it up!"

My handsome son—now a young man in more ways than I had ever hoped he would be at sixteen years of age—hugged me tightly. With tears in his eyes, he said, "Good-bye, Dad. I'll be back soon."

"Good-bye, son." I started to say, "Take care of your mother," as I had done on so many occasions before, but the words would not come. "Stay close to Jesus," I said instead. The words sounded hollow as Jamie nodded his head and turned away toward the door.

My emotions were numb. I walked to the strip-search area and mechanically pulled off my khakis. The guard went through the normal routine. Eventually, I put on my clothes and moved in the direction of my building. As I walked across the compound, I felt no emotion at all.

Later, as the full realization wrapped its clammy fingers around my heart, I wrote in my journal:

> I only live because I do not die . . . My God, my God, have mercy on me! My heart cannot stand the pain.
>
> A projector keeps running movies on my imagination's screen— moving pictures of my wife making passionate love with her new lover . . . in our bed . . . laughing, having fun. The projector will not shut off. It runs when I lay down on my bed; if I get up to go to the bathroom, the film is still running.

I had to go on with the normal routine of prison life. One night, while standing and looking in the commissary window, I felt as though I was about to explode with grief.

I put on my robe and made my way down the hall to the shower room. The small cubicle was the only private area open to me. I stepped inside the shower stall and pulled the curtain. The moment I closed the curtain and turned on the water, I began weeping uncontrollably. I cried so hard I thought I was going to vomit. I could not stop.

My wife of more than thirty years was leaving me.

I wept . . . and wept . . . and wept. . . .

38

War of Words

"MAYBE YOU SHOULD PUT ON A SEAT BELT" JAMIE SAID TO Roe as they drove toward the Minneapolis airport. With one hand on the steering wheel and the other holding a cigarette, Jamie looked over at Roe, took a long drag from the umpteenth cigarette he had smoked that day, and blew the smoke in Roe's direction.

"Oh, that's all right, son. I don't need to wear a seat belt," Roe replied.

Jamie's eyes burned into Roe as he said, "Don't ever call me 'son.'"

Jamie later confided to me that the thought kept going through his mind that all he had to do was to crash Roe's side of the car into a wall and he could take care of Roe once and for all. Jamie had never hurt anyone in his life, but at that point he was barely in control of his emotions.

Jamie then boarded a jet and flew across the country, seated next to the man with whom he was now convinced his mom was having an affair.

In Orlando, Tammy Faye and Shirley Fulbright met Jamie and Roe at the airport. All four of them piled into the same car. "How was your flight?" Tammy gushed.

"Fine," Jamie replied.

"Are you doing okay?" she asked him.

"No," Jamie again replied angrily.

"Are you upset?"

"Yes!"

Roe was returning to our home with them. It so angered Jamie that he went into his bedroom, tossed his clothes into a suitcase, and moved out.

On the way out the door, Jamie turned to Tammy Faye and said, "I'm leaving. I'm going to live with one of my friends. I'm mad at you and don't want to talk to you right now. I can't believe you did this to Dad. He's sitting there in prison, and you've done this to him. You make me sick!"

Tammy Faye tried to defend her actions by saying, "Well, Jamie, there are a lot of things that you don't understand. . . ." Jamie cut her off mid-sentence and walked out of our family home.

Back in prison, my life plunged into a dark abyss. I flipped back and forth between anger and overwhelming love for Tammy Faye.

On January 21, Tammy Faye mailed an urgent letter to me. No doubt she was alarmed over Jamie's visit and that her involvement with Roe had been exposed. She wrote:

> Please call me. We need to talk! I am so sorry for what happened when Jamie was there with you. Jim, I wouldn't hurt you for anything in the world. I am not planning on rushing into anything! I am so confused, and hurting so bad, and so mixed up about life. Please don't shut me out! I feel so far away from you, and sometimes feel as if I hardly know you anymore, and it is sure hard to "feel married" when you have been apart for such a long time. I am so lonesome.
>
> I hate prison so bad, and lawyers, and courts. I get really sick to my tummy when I have to be involved with any of it anymore.
>
> Please try not to worry. I am not going to do anything fast or foolish. I just need some time to sort out life. I have to rethink so many things, the ministry, Christians, TV, I just don't know what to do in life anymore. I want to get out of the ministry so bad, yet what can Tammy Bakker do except what she knows? Who would hire me? I keep trying to have faith, yet I pray and there is no answer. . . . I don't want to travel and do meetings; I am called to TV and that mountain will not move in my direction one bit. I blame you and yet I don't blame you. I am so confused, I just sometimes want out of everything. Even life! I know that you feel that way, too. So please, Jim, give me time. Please pray for me. I won't do anything fast.

As I read Tammy Faye's letter, I was amazed at how easily I began to feel sorry for her—and she was the one who was walking away from our marriage. Her letter made me feel as though it was my fault that she had fallen in love with Roe Messner.

293

When I called Tammy Faye, I did not have to broach the subject. Though she tried to deny that anything was going on between her and Roe, gradually she realized that I knew much more than she had thought. She never came out and said, "Yes, I'm having an affair with your best friend," but she did confirm the fact that she was leaving me. She said she just couldn't take any more. I knew that our marriage was over.

I began pouring my feelings into letters. I fired off a letter to Tammy Faye, beginning what would become like a series of missiles sent screaming back and forth between Minnesota and Florida. I readily admit I resorted to my old friends of self-pity, guilt, manipulation, and others in my attempts to bring Tammy back to me. I tried pouring out my love to her. I tried explaining psychological principles and temperament needs I had learned about in my studies with the National Association of Christian Counselors. I tried preaching at her, reminding her of scriptural principles. I reminded her of ministry, telling her what a great job she had done, hoping to evoke a desire within her to do even more. When all else failed, I reminded Tammy Faye of our two wonderful children and the impact her actions might have on them. In one of my first letters I wrote:

> The last days have been filled with the deepest pain I have ever experienced. I want to scream out from the depths of my soul a primal sound that I cannot express with words.
>
> After the massive betrayal by those I loved and trusted at PTL, and the media hate . . . and then being thrown into prison to die a little each day, I thought there could be no more pain inflicted on me. . . .
>
> Please do not come to see me. I cannot stand the hurt of hearing you say again, "Jim, I don't love you any more." Those words at Waikiki are burnt in my brain. I live with the knowledge, as you said to the group in Palmdale, "I never loved Jim." [Tammy had confessed this to the Palmdale team of counselors when she and I had sought help after our marital stress in 1980.]
>
> I would fight for you, but I know you don't love me and perhaps, as you said, you never did. You have tried to get free of me for a long time.
>
> I cannot look into those blue eyes I fell in love with so hard thirty-some years ago and see only cold pity coming back. I cannot take any more pain.

I don't want you and Roe to try to explain how, "We didn't plan for this to happen; we just fell in love." I knew for a long time you did not love me when you pulled back from my kisses and would refuse even to touch my hand or leg. There is no human touch in this prison, and I was dying for your touch, but you were touching someone else . . .

Even though for many months, I knew you were meeting Roe around the country, I kept hoping it was not true. It just could not happen with the man I trusted most, my last, best friend. It is like the last act of a bad movie. I understand your loneliness and pain, and I can't really blame you, but I am so sorry for all the people who believed in us and defended us. My heart also aches for our children, but they are strong, and with God's help, they will make it. Please, for their sake, let's be kind and not feed the hate through a messy divorce.

I still love you and always will! From the day I first met you, I have been in love with you only. I know I have failed you and made many mistakes. I have been a fool and a simpleton.

My dream was your nightmare.

Sleep does not come to me much in these last few days. Visions of you and Roe making love I will admit have made me jealous and lustful. My thoughts return to the night I first made love to you in our little third-floor walk-up apartment. I have relived all the good and the bad times, especially all the hours we spent together. The birth of Tammy Sue and how happy we were, and how I wanted to have a boy and how I could not be there for his birth. What a fool I was.

As I was looking at the cards I had picked out for Valentine's Day for you, I realized that this would be the first Valentine's Day I will not give you a card in thirty-two years. Remember our first Valentine's Day, I sent you a heart candy box and roses to your room? Do you remember the white poodle with the purple bow? I'm rambling on like a sentimental slob. . . .

But I have to face reality. (1) You are in love with someone else. (2) You are not in love with me, and perhaps never have been. (3) You are unhappy. (4) You don't want to do the work we felt called to do anymore. (5) You have someone to support you and take care of you. (6) You have tried to leave me for many years. (7) I am in prison.

The list could go on, but I will close. As much as I love you, I won't try to convince you to stay with me. I know it is too late for that anyway. Be happy; stay as close to the children as possible. Don't give up on God.

My next letter, was to my "best friend," Roe Messner.

Tammy Faye is the love of my life. She is the only one I have been in love with for thirty-two years. She was my best friend and lover, and, of course, the mother of my children.

You were the one last friend I thought I could trust—with my life, and my wife—a man of real integrity.

I can almost hear you saying, "But Jim, we did not plan for this to happen." Roe, we are not sixteen anymore. We know when to back away from the fire. Tammy has a great need for love and affection, and during this time of separation was very vulnerable to anyone who would take advantage of her loneliness and pain. I'm sorry she has to bear the added pain of the media saying she is an evil woman stealing another woman's husband, while her own husband is in prison.

If you were going to betray me and my trust, why did you have to flaunt it from coast to coast, even in front of my children. . . . I knew it was going on for a long time, but I just didn't want to believe it of you. . . .

As I told Tam, it's like the ending of a bad movie for me. My wife of thirty-two years rides off into the sunset with my best friend. What a conclusion to six years of hell! . . .

Several days later, I wrote Roe again. Roe never answered my letters. A few days later, I received a letter from Tammy Faye in response to my letter to her. At 3:14 A.M., she wrote:

I have cried my false eyelashes off and my tummy hurts so bad my whole body feels sick. I have read and reread your letter—the last one you say you will ever write me. Sissy and Doug and the kids and I spent the day today at Disney World.

As I read Tammy's comments, I realized afresh how differently she and I faced pressure points in our lives these days. When something bad happened to me, I would retreat to a bed or couch, curl up, and either try to figure a way out of the mess or anesthetize myself with sleep. When something awful happened to Tammy Faye—such as her husband finding out that she was leaving him—she went to Disney World! Even at Disney World, however, Tammy Faye could not escape the obvious:

Jim, every time I look at a music box I think of you. Every time I see a giraffe, every time I go to a theme park, I always think of your building Heritage USA. Every time I look into the eyes of our kids and grand-kids, I see you mostly, and a tiny bit of me. Jim, everything in life reminds me of you and me together. Jim, I would not hurt you for any-thing in the world. Please believe that! My heart has ached for you until I think it finally just broke! I could not live in hurt anymore. . . I lived and relived that horrible day they took you away over and over and over. I think there is only so much pain a human mind can take and then something happens.

I feel as if my whole existence was torn away from me—every-thing familiar; everything comfortable; everything warm; my home—I loved Tega Cay; my job—I loved our work; my securi-ty—you, whom I loved. I was left by myself in a strange town, a strange house, left to raise a teenage boy, support us both, plus Sissy and the children, try to keep a ministry together that I was not called to—I am not a pastor! I have never been so lonely in my whole life, have never felt so raw and so scared, and so absolutely friendless.

I entered a terrifying world of lawyers, courts, judges, trials, juries, handcuffs, news media, prison, debts—a horrible world of betrayed friendships, betrayal by Christian leaders, watching the singers I trained for TV now doing their own TV shows on Christian television, while I sit at home and cry and hope like some pitiful little kid that someone will help me to get back on the air.

Somehow she conveniently seemed to forget that my sending her to French Lick Springs with Roe was to explore the possibility of purchasing the property and getting her back on television. Even as she wrote to me, she and Roe were still committed to going ahead with the original plan to get Tammy Faye back on the air. Her letter continued:

Jim, I'm so tired of feeling lonely, pitiful, so full of hurt and near hate at what has happened to you and me. I find myself screaming, "If only Jim wouldn't have given PTL away! If only! If only he would have listened to my begging him, 'Please, Jim! Don't give up your place on the Board of Directors.'"

I'm afraid that if you and I stay together, I will only make you miserable. I would resent all the hard work of building everything back up again. And I don't think my health would even take trying to make it to the top again. My blood pressure is so high. My heart is doing strange things. My whole left side goes totally numb. My nerves are so bad, Jim! My body just sort of takes over and there is nothing I can do to control it. I must find some peace—somewhere! I am so disappointed in Christians—and yes, even in God. I really love God and always will, but. . . . I feel I just need to get out of the ministry for everyone's sake! I need to get away from the public eye! But that is my problem.

Jim, don't ever put yourself down! You are a great man! You are handsome, talented, kind, and so good! You're really too good. Your heart wants to "save the world," wants to make everything wonderful for everyone—and that is just how it should be. But that is you, Jim. It is too heavy a burden for my heart and health to carry anymore. You are going to make it—again. I know you are. You might not if you have to carry me and all my hurts and disappointments. Please try to understand what is going on inside of me. Jamie and I are going to California for counseling. I pray that it will help me.

I, too, hate to let down all of our faithful partners. I feel I have disappointed and let down the whole world. I am so sorry, so very sorry.

Love,
Tam "Still your wife"

P.S. I wanted to touch you in prison, but you told me it wasn't allowed. And it's awfully hard to kiss too long with 100 people watching you. Now I've got to try to stop crying and try to go to sleep.

Tammy Faye had once again succeeded in making me hurt for her. I wrote back to her:

Today I took all the pictures of you down off the corkboard in my prison cell. So many of the pictures were of you and the children and you and the grandbabies. It is hard to tuck those pictures in a shoe box and say a final good-bye. I've loved you so desperately for three decades and I can't just cut off my love.

I'm so hurt that you could throw me away with such an ease and cold heart. You talk about your pain and hurt and how you want to be happy. How I worked to make you happy! I felt we had something that no other couple had going for them, a special bond. Most all wives of inmates leave their husbands if they are in prison for two years or more, but I thought we would beat the odds. Jim and Tammy were going to make it; they are not average America. We are children of the most high God.

Tonight was my final exam for my computer course. It was so hard to concentrate on the test. I fought off thoughts of you and Roe making love. Later I tried to watch a movie on TV, but every girl in the movie made me think of you. . . .

How does love turn to hate? I'm told my great love for you will go away. Some even say I will be happier than ever with a new life. God is the only one who can take my love for you from my heart.

Our lawyer said you and Roe talk every day by phone and spend much time in conversation. I'm so jealous how he has taken my place in every way. Oh, how I needed someone to talk to and love me. How I longed for your touch, your voice, your encouraging words, just to hear you say, "I love you." I feel like a chain saw has cut us apart. Jim and Tammy were one flesh. Now you and Roe are one flesh—how that hurts me! I'm going to try to sleep in my narrow bunk and fight off visions of you and Roe making love in our king-size bed. What hell is wrought in our minds.

> Good night, my love,
> Jim

Thinking that perhaps I had shut the door too soon on Tammy's and my relationship, a few days later I wrote to her again:

. . . I feel I owe you, after thirty-two years, an explanation why I'm giving you a divorce. I realize that I have been obsessed with you all these years, to the point I know now that I smothered you. My love for you is so great that I didn't think I could live without you. Even your outrageous traits made life exciting. I worshipped you and wanted to please you, sometimes putting you before God in my life.

As I said before, I have been in love with you and you only since the day I met you. I tried to give you lots of love and all the good things of life, giving you what you wanted, or at least, needed the most.

Since Jamie told me you were leaving me, my life has been hell. I have eaten and slept very little. I hate myself that I have such a hard time giving you up. I do get the picture, but my heart won't stop loving you—there's that stubbornness in me that you hate so much.

I don't want your pity or platitudes. Even though I deeply want you to love me, I'm not trying to win you back. I did that before. I have faced the fact you just don't love me. My mistakes and sin lost our life's work and material possessions. I have not been the spiritual covering for you that I should have been and I left you open to Satan's attacks. I am so sorry I was not the spiritual leader in our home. There is not much left of me and believe me, you made the right decision. I don't like Jim Bakker, either.

I can hear you say, "There he goes, feeling sorry for himself," and you're right! I had it all and lost it. No longer can I live in the pain I brought on myself, perhaps freeing you will help ease my hell. I see how you were like a little bird I tried to keep and protect, but the little bird wanted to fly and be free.

You are free. You can check with our lawyer on signing the final divorce papers.

On February 16, Tammy responded to my letters.

I have started so many letters to you and they are all wrong. I wish that we were somewhere we could just talk this thing out. Letters leave so many unanswered questions.

First of all, you have given me *everything* a woman could ever want. Fine homes, fine cars, beautiful jewelry, more clothes than most women will have in a lifetime; I have traveled to lots of wonderful places, eaten at the best restaurants. I have had maids, beautiful offices; I have had fame and fortune, plus a very powerful man to love me. Two wonderful children—I have had it all! God and you have certainly been good to this gal from International Falls, MN. The oldest of eight kids, outdoor bathroom and all—sounds like a Cinderella story, doesn't it? And perhaps it was.

Her letter then quickly changed in tone:

You have once again succeeded in making me feel like an ungrateful wretch! No, a sinful, ungrateful wretch! I feel like I don't deserve to even live. I am letting Jim Bakker (who is in prison for something he didn't even do) down; I am letting down two kids; I am letting down our partners (who have been so faithful to us); I am letting down God who has taken such good care of me since you have been gone. I feel lower than low! I would commit suicide but that "just ain't my style!" I'm too chicken to do that. . . .

Jim, I am not ungrateful to you or to God. In fact, I really do feel as if I have lived a "fairy tale life." I love God more than anything in this world, and am so grateful to Him for all He has done for me. But somewhere, something went wrong. I cannot even tell you what it is or was. I know you are going to say that the only time things went wrong for me was when I sinned by getting too close to other men. But *why* did I feel I needed that closeness? You were always there for me. I don't know! I wish I did. My heart hurts until I can hardly breathe. I feel so ungrateful, so unworthy. But that still doesn't stop the awful hurt inside of me. I don't have any tears left to cry. I feel numb.

I don't want to hurt anybody, especially you and God. But something has been missing for years that even prayer won't fill. Believe me, I have prayed and cried out to God until I had no strength left.

The thought of going back into our whirlwind life sends me into a "panic attack." It really does, Jim. Trying to start all over again in TV, going from church to church preaching to a lot of Christians that were so cruel to us, raising money just to hear people condemn us for the car we drive, the house we live in, or the clothes we wear. You know that I have *never* enjoyed sitting in church; I have never been able to even bear the thought of being a pastor's wife. I'm tired, Jim. I need a rest from it all. My mind hurts. . . .

Then Tammy Faye launched into a part of her letter that was most devastating to me. She compared Roe Messner and me:

About Roe—No, he isn't the "knight in shining armor" that you talk about. He is a very simple man. In many ways, he is a lot like you. He is kind, gentle, and even giving. You are all those things. He is tall and lanky and casual, where you are short, well-built, and very elegant. You are both very hard-working men.

Roe is grass roots—baseball, football, golf. You are not really grass roots—you are artistic, creative, a genius. Roe is very even— you are very moody. Roe golfs out his problems; you sleep out your problems. Neither is wrong. Roe and you are almost in the same condition financially since he has had to file bankruptcy. He is no longer a wealthy man.

"Then, why, Tam?" you ask.

301

I don't know, Jim. Except when I think of Roe, I think of peace. When I think of you, I think "high energy, big, no stopping."
Roe is not better—just different.
It's a different time of life for me, Jim. I have changed so much. I think I have reverted back to "that little girl from International Falls" again. That little girl just doesn't fit into the mold you want to make anymore. Maybe she never did. . . .

Tammy then picked up on a statement I had made in a previous letter, encouraging her to go ahead with a divorce. Actually, I had hoped to shock her into reality. Unfortunately, my attempt backfired:

You are urging me to go ahead with the divorce. You put it, "Quit cutting me up a little piece at a time. Get it over with."
Jim, I will do that for you if that is what you really want. I don't mean to drag it out. I don't want to hurt you any more than you are already hurting. I would never do that! I was going to wait till the end of the year, and leave the ministry and move to California. But I will file right away if you want me to. I will not remarry right away. I want some time. Roe also realizes the importance of taking time. I want to wait at least a year. . . .
Your letters have helped me a lot, Jim. You make a great teacher, and, needless to say, you're still quite a preacher! Please know that *I have counted the cost.* I will probably be "the world's most hated woman"! But they make fun of me as it is, so it could not get too much worse. They have called me everything they can call me— and that was before I was guilty of anything.
You will always have a very special place in my heart, Jim. I have not forgotten the good times; I have wonderful memories. Everything I look at, you gave to me. I remember the time and place.
And I cry!

Tammy Faye sent me a copy of a letter she planned to send to our friends and the partners who had supported us in our ministry in Florida. Tammy wrote:

I am experiencing many emotions as I write to you today. Great sadness . . . fear of your rejection . . . and relief that I am able to be totally honest with you. It is a letter that I have needed to write for a long time. I do not expect your understanding, but please try not to react cruelly. Cruelty cannot help anyone nor can it change any situation.

Jim and I are getting a divorce. I can almost hear you gasping . . . saying, "It's not possible! How could they get a divorce with Jim in prison? How is this going to affect the Christian world?"

First of all, I am not being forced to write this letter. *I have chosen to do so!* I feel that, for too long, you have had to get your information from TV and newspaper articles that contained just bits of the truth . . . the rest of the story just figments of someone's overactive imagination. . . .

Jim and I were married very young. I was eighteen and he was twenty-one. Our marriage started out as everyone else's . . . full of excitement and dreams for the future. God had placed a calling on our lives and we were determined to win the world for Jesus!

But somewhere along the way, we got our priorities mixed up. God's order for things is God first, husband or wife second, children third, then comes ministry or whatever job you do. Over the years, God was always first in our lives, but somehow ministry became second, our partners and Heritage USA third, and our family followed.

For years, I have been pretending that everything is all right . . . when in fact I hurt all the time. I cannot pretend anymore. Pretending becomes too hard on the physical body. I have been suffering with high blood pressure, anemia, asthma, hyperventilation— all the doctors tell me—related to stress and severe nervous strain.

Jim and I have had marriage counseling many times. We even separated at one time in an attempt to work things out between us. We have never kept our marriage problems secret from you. As you know, the marriage workshops at PTL were started as a result of our own hurts. I have spent the last few weeks once again in Christian counseling and through that counseling have made this decision.

I still love the Lord with all my heart. *Nothing will ever change that!* God's calling is still a fire that burns within me. . . .

Jim and I will always remain friends. We are still in constant communication. We both remain open to God, and to whatever His will is for our lives. I have decided to complete the divorce proceedings before he gets out of prison. I feel that having been apart for over two years anyway, the hurt will be less this way. Neither one of us can take much more hurt.

I want to say thank you from the bottom of my heart for the love you have shown to me these last two years. You have helped me build a beautiful ministry. Tammy Sue, our daughter, will be taking my place at New Covenant Church.

Please pray for our dedicated staff as they make this difficult transition, and please continue to support Tammy Sue as she endeavors to keep the ministry alive until Jim gets home from prison. More than anything else in the world, I desire to have a strong foundation for Jim to build on when he gets home.

All I have ever wanted to be is a Mom and someday a Grandma . . . I am now both. My dreams have been fulfilled. I am Tammy Sue's and Jamie's Mom, and James' and Jonathan's Grandma. God has been so good.

When I read Tammy Faye's last letter to me and her letter to our partners, I was decimated, yet I continued to try to win her heart. This time I tried a different tact:

After reading your last letter and your letter to the partners, I realize that you know what you are doing and that you know right from wrong. I think, as you said in your letter, that I thought of you as that little girl from International Falls who I needed to protect and save from her own decisions, when in fact, you are a grown fifty-year-old woman who is capable of making her own decisions and living with the consequences. . . .

You said in your letter: "That little girl just doesn't fit into the mold you want to make anymore." Tam, no one has ever been able to fit you into any mold. I did not try to fit you into my mold. You were called of God the same way I was called. I always let you do your own thing. When I met you . . . you said everyone was always trying to change you. You wrote a book, *I Gotta Be Me*. If you are ever going to be happy, you must get to know the real Tammy Faye and deal with her. You have an inborn need to control others, and according to your temperament chart, you are unwilling to allow anyone to control you. Just as you said, one of my traits is moodiness.

You keep talking about how no one cares for you and how mean the press and everyone is to you, that you get no respect. Tam, you are very wrong. You have probably reached the highest level of respect and love you have ever had from the public. I'm sending you an article using you as an example of a woman who "stood by her man." Of late, you have been portrayed as a beautiful

woman, with a soft, classy look. Whoever is telling you otherwise—
even if it is you—is wrong. . . .

You said, "Maybe you never did fit my mold," and maybe you
were never called of God but followed my calling. Maybe I am
your April fool after all. Forgive me for saying that, but it's how
angry I feel when you talk like marrying me was the great tragedy
of your life. I don't take rejection very well, you know! We had a
very full and exciting life.

I felt that I was beginning to get in touch with many areas of my life
just about the time Tammy Faye decided to leave. I knew that if we
could just weather this storm, I would be a much better husband, a
much better man, a much better person. I hinted at that to Tammy in
my letter:

I am still wearing my wedding ring. It will be hard to take it off. But I
have been doing better each week, and I'm much stronger than I have
ever been. Dr. Foster said there was a part of me that did not grow up
because of something that happened to me as a child. . . .
I will try not to preach to you anymore.

Tammy's next letter was paradoxically upbeat:

Hello Mr. B,
And how are you doing today? I always try to picture your life there
and what you are doing. I know that it is so hard to get up every day
and face it. I'm at home and at times can hardly face another day. But at
least I can go to a shopping center, and get my mind off things by walking, and getting away from people. . . .

About what I am planning to do. I am not going to rush into
anything, Jim. I would like to give myself a year if you don't insist
on "pushing me." What is another year in light of what we have
already been through? It looks like things are going to be fine
here at the ministry, in spite of the "rag" magazines. I have
received some of the nicest letters I have ever received. I want to
keep the ministry strong for you so you will have a solid foundation to rebuild on . . . so far, nothing has changed with the ministry.

Hang in there, Jim. Remember, "It's not over till it's over."

305

When I read Tammy's letter in its entirety, I was livid. I could not believe that she wanted to continue on in the ministry, while her loyalties were so divided. On February 17, I wrote back:

Your letter has put me in a state of shock. I can't comprehend what you want! You told me and the children you were in love and planned to marry. You told me on the phone you and Roe were going to live in Dallas. You were angry when I stopped the divorce [by refusing to sign the divorce papers] and said that you would have to be the one to file. You said you hated the church and were not called to pastor and be a pastor's wife and preach the Gospel and would not help me rebuild a TV ministry.

Now, you want to keep the church for a year. It looks like you want to make this delay so Roe Messner can hold his business together and get his divorce and then you can divorce me and walk away from the ministry and let it crumble.

Tam, you keep playing me for a fool. You have trampled on my deep love for you. While in prison, I longed to talk to you on the telephone, my arms ached to hold you. Out of thousands I received, the only letter I looked for was the pink envelope from you. The saddest day of my life was Valentine's Day when, for the first time in thirty-two years, I didn't receive a Valentine from you. I am sure you and Roe exchanged loving Valentines.

For the last year, I needed your love and support and you were in the arms of Roe Messner. Now you want to keep up a front with me until Roe is ready to receive you and has his ducks in a row. You make me feel like a piece of dung. You have been more of a wife to Roe Messner than to me. I can't understand why he will not support you. You have been paying for his travel and hotel rooms and rental cars. If you were my lover and I was a free man, I would take care of you like a queen. . . .

I was shocked to find how you and Roe were together almost everywhere you traveled for the last nine months and even spend-ing many days together in our own home. You and he flew to California for the Women's meeting November 11 to 16. I am sure you enjoyed visiting San Francisco while you were there. Even when you cut your record, you had adjoining rooms in Tennessee. Of course, I know you were together on trips to French Lick.

Then the wonderful fun-filled acts in Las Vegas. Then, we don't want to forget the romantic and happy days at the Kahler Hotel in Rochester while you and your lover were visiting Prisoner

07407-058. And, of course, there was Thanksgiving at the Kahler. We must not forget the trip to Charlotte while the lovebirds went to see "poor Jim" at the county jail, dressed in his orange Pierre Cardin prison jumpsuit, and then back to French Lick for some more fun. Then the one that hurt the most was my birthday celebration you and Roe had in Des Moines at the Marriott, with lots of room service.

Once I got all that venom out of my system, I went back to the issue of Tammy staying on as a minister at the church in Florida:

Tam, you said I am "pushing you." . . . You tell me you want out of our marriage and the church, and I give you what you ask for and then you say I am pushing you!

Tam, you have not said, "Jim, forgive me," or "I am sorry"; only, "Just let me stay on at the church." You act like you don't care about me or my feelings. There is not a man on earth who would put up with his wife and former best friend living like they are married while he looks on. *You have misjudged my undying love for you as weakness!* It is time for you to do what you plan to do and not play me for the fool anymore. . . .

How can you live with Roe in adultery and pastor the church, making believe you love me to the partners and to the public? Tam, you have some decisions to make. You can't have it both ways. Just remember, because you feel the anointing of God when you sing or preach does not mean that God has stamped His approval on what you are doing. God says His callings are not without repentance. That means, once He gives the gift, He does not take it back. Think of the preachers we have known that have preached the Gospel under the anointing of the Holy Spirit and lived an ungodly life. "Not every one that saith unto me, Lord, Lord, shall enter into the kingdom of heaven; but he that doeth the will of my Father which is in heaven."

You are deciding if you are willing to pay the price to serve God or not. You can leave Jim Bakker and go to heaven, if you live a godly life. But if you can rationalize that what you and Roe are doing is not sin, you are in a fearful state. My sin or Roe's wife's sin does not justify more sin and what you and Roe are doing. You have the biggest decision of your life to make and I or no one else can make it for you. Tammy Faye, are you going to serve God or the devil?

307

Tam, for God's sake, read the Word and pray. You need to be where the Word is taught and be around godly people. I am afraid you are out from under God's covering. Sin opens the door for Satan to have a heyday. You also stepped out from beneath my covering as your husband. I have been fasting and praying for the last several days that God would not let you make an eternal mistake and go to hell.

If you know without a shadow of a doubt you have made up your mind to marry Roe and you know that is what you want and it is God's perfect will for you, then call Jim Toms and sign the divorce papers today. Don't play with my love by saying, "It's not over till it's over" if you know full well you and Roe plan to be married. Love in a marriage is commitment. You can't be committed to two men. If you are committed and pledged to Roe, then be honest with me and sign the divorce papers today and walk away. If you want to give up Roe and stay with me, then get on an airplane and come and see me and tell me so. But, after that, I will not put up with one phone call or meeting between you and Roe.

You said you received some of the nicest letters. Tam, I am receiving the same kind of letters. Almost everyone is saying how much Tammy Faye loves me and how wonderful she is to have stood by her man. I think if only they knew every time I read them it is like a knife going through me. Jim and Tammy are no more. My heart is broken Oh, how I loved you. . . .

I have committed you to God.

It is your decision.

Thinking that perhaps I had been too hard on Tammy Faye in my previous letter, the following week, I sent Tammy another letter, outlining what I felt were the only acceptable conditions for her to stay associated with the ministry in Florida.

I dared to suggest a course of action to her which I now realize was dogmatic, and yes . . . an attempt to get Tammy Faye to do what I felt was right. I began once again by reminding her of her own temperament:

Actually, I am asking you to consider two alternatives: One is to help meet my needs, and the other to do what you will and simply walk away.

If you want to stay, I need:

You to seek God and read your Bible every day, at least a chapter each day, reading through the entire New Testament.

The main sanctuary of Heritage Village Church and the location for nightly camp meetings. Also located in this complex of buildings were seminar and Sunday School rooms, a nursery, day-care, and a K-12 school. This building was nicknamed the "Big Barn Auditorium."

My associate pastor, Richard Dortch, joins me in serving Holy Communion to our congregation.

(following page) The beautiful, state-of-the-art 1,500 seat television studio where Tammy and I originated our daily programs. Often, over 2,000 people packed this studio while several thousand more watched on closed-circuit, big-screen TV in the Big Barn Auditorium.

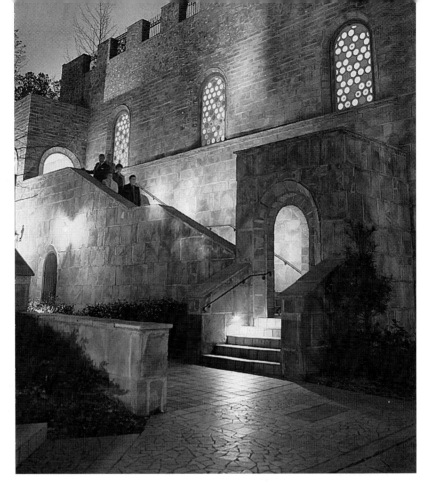

On July 4, 1982, we dedicated to God what I consider the nerve center and very heartbeat of our ministry, the Upper Room. Modeled after the historic Upper Room in Jerusalem, this prayer center never closed. Pastors and phone counselors were stationed there 24 hours a day.

Prayer and communion service being held in the Upper Room.

Camp meetings, gospel "sings" and teaching seminars were held 365 days a year at Heritage USA. Eighty-six religious services were conducted each week.

The family center served as a hub for Heritage USA youth activities: basketball, roller skating, pizza parlor, and worship, music, and teaching activities.

One of the greatest passion plays in America was presented in the beautiful outdoor setting of the Jerusalem amphitheater.

Live music and singing were performed daily on Main Street Heritage USA and in the fellowship lobby. During the summer months, musical presentations were performed throughout the park, including the lakeside amphitheater.

In July of 1984, we opened the beautiful Heritage House for expectant mothers who chose birth rather than abortion. A 24-hour hotline for women in critical pregnancy situations and the Tender Loving Care Adoption Agency were also formed around the same time.

Our ministry developed a nationwide network of nearly 1,000 People That Love Centers to help feed, clothe, and provide furniture, counseling, and employment assistance to people in their time of need. This outreach touched nearly 10 million people a year.

The childhood home of Dr. Billy Graham was slated for destruction to make way for a building complex. PTL friends and partners moved the house piece by piece to Heritage USA and furnished it in the same style of the period as when Billy Graham was a boy. One of our goals at Heritage USA was to preserve our spiritual heritage for future generations.

Kevin's House, built to accommodate severely disabled children in a homelike setting.

On January 2, 1987, in one of my last official duties at Heritage USA, I broke ground for our new church and conference center which, when completed, would have seated 30,000 people.

Old Jerusalem Village was just one of the new facilities already on the drawing board for a future lodging and ministry center at Heritage USA.

One of the happiest days of my life, shortly before I entered prison, was when Tammy Sue presented me with my first grandchild and namesake, Baby James.

I debated long and hard before including this picture in my book. This is one of the lowest moments of my life—a time during my trial when I suffered a nervous breakdown and was put into what I call an "insane asylum" inside the prison at Butner, NC.

This picture is the only possession I was able to somehow take with me into almost every prison to which I was assigned. There were times when simply looking at this picture of my grandbaby gave me the will to hold on just a little longer.

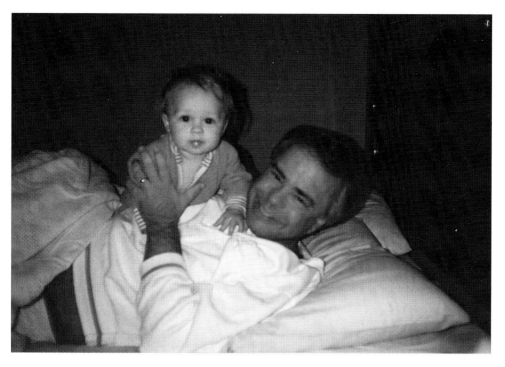

My last night of freedom for almost 5 years. This picture was taken the night before Judge Potter sentenced me to 45 years in prison. I took care of Baby James throughout the night, giving him bottles. It was a joy to be with him.

Being led in chains from the courthouse to begin my 45-year sentence.

The first Christmas we "celebrated" in prison. This picture was taken on Christmas Eve of 1989. Pictured with Tammy and me are my sister Donna, Tammy Sue's husband Doug, Tammy Sue, Baby James, and my son Jamie Charles.

April 1, 1990: Our first wedding anniversary in prison.

Two of my best friends in the world, Rev. Phil Shaw and Rev. Paul Olson, who visited me in prison every chance they got.

My parents holding the vase that I had poured and painted for them while in prison.

Jamie Charles had just turned 16, and was able to visit me by myself for the first time. As he started to leave, he declared, "Dad, this has been the best day of my life." This picture was taken that day.

A scene from prison that I had scribbled down on a piece of paper.

It was always a happy day when Baby James came to see me in prison. One day, as he walked in with his mother, he exclaimed, "Paw Paw Jim has a big house!"

What a thrill it was after two years to finally see my parents again.

(far right) In the deepest days of despair and despondency, even shaving became a difficult task.

While I was in prison it seemed as if my son grew up overnight. One day when he walked in, it felt as if I was looking at myself 30 years before. Pictured here, I am preaching during my Bible College days, and Jamie Charles is standing on the platform of our church in Orlando.

What a wonderful day when James Blackwood came to the Jesup prison and brought his quartet to perform a gospel concert on the prison's loading dock. The prison guard even allowed me to visit with them on their bus, though he had to accompany me.

Franklin Graham not only visited me in prison, but he ministered in our chapel programs, bringing with him Dennis and Danny Agajanian.

At the end of my prison experience, the chaplain allowed Tammy Sue to come and sing in the chapel service. It was the first time I had heard her sing in almost 5 years. We both cried.

One of my favorite gospel singers and old friend, Candi Staton Sussewell, came to the Jesup prison and ministered in concert to an enthusiastic and receptive house.

Professor Jim Albert from Drake University rallied to my cause and provided valuable legal insight and encouragement.

Inmate and former Pastor Larry Wright became my best friend in the Jesup prison. He was like a pastor to the entire compound, conducting a Bible study each morning at 5:30, evening Bible studies and church on Sunday night.

On my brief furlough from prison. I visited my father in the hospital after he fell and broke his hip.

Jamie Charles and I visited with Uncle Henry and Aunt Susan while on a 48-hour furlough to visit my ailing father. Years before Uncle Henry had vowed to keep his Christmas tree up until I was released from prison.

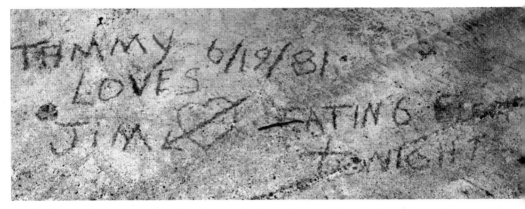

On the way back to the Jesup prison from my furlough, Jamie and I stopped at the spot where our home in Tega Cay had burned to the ground. We shared a sad moment as he brushed the sand from what was once the floor of our garage. There, etched in the concrete, was a message Tammy Faye had written almost a decade and a half before. It read, "Tammy loves Jim. Eating fish tonight."

This is the painting I did in my cell the night that our Tega Cay house burned to the ground.

The living room of our Tega Cay home, where we raised our children. I watched from a prison television as this home burned to the ground.

Another of life's happiest moments was photographed here. This shot was taken just moments after my release from prison. Jamie Charles likes to call this photo "the flight to freedom."

Being fingerprinted as I was admitted into the halfway house at the Salvation Army in Asheville, NC.

This was a welcome sight as my family greeted me just hours after my release from prison.

Flinchum Photography ®

A happy reunion in the North Carolina mountains with my parents, my sister Donna and my brother Norman. My nearly 90-year-old parents and I rejoiced that God had answered our prayers that they would live to see me walk out of prison.

Most of this book was written in a small rented farmhouse, surrounded by the beautiful mountains of North Carolina. The farmhouse was a place of solitude and refuge for me as I continued to seek the will of God for this next chapter of my life. This picture was taken in my barn.

Accompanying Aunt Susan to the memorial service for her husband and my friend, Uncle Henry. This was my first sermon following my release from prison.

For you not to call or receive calls from Roe Messner or see him or any other lovers . . . no contact.

For you and me to talk every day or night on the telephone.

For you to get good regular Christian counseling, at least two times per week.

For you to let me help you understand yourself and your temperament traits.

For you to write me every day.

For you to come to see me often.

For you to be faithful to the church and the partnership and spend regular time working at the office.

For you to be faithful to me as long as we are married.

You to face the fact your inborn personality traits make you demand to be in control and that you will ask God to help you turn control to Him. (Actually, you are not in control. Your temperament is controlling you to do the opposite of what anyone tells you to do, making you in reality not to be in control.)

I want you to work on your anger and temper, which you use to control people, and ask God to help you surrender your will to Him.

For you to love and demonstrate love to our children and grandchildren and spend much time with them.

For you to sign the divorce papers. I will not sign them if you live up to this agreement.

Or, you can walk now.

Tam, I love you dearly, but this roller coaster you are on and putting everyone around you on must come to a stop. As I said before, your conflict is because you are trying to live two lives and it just will not work. Even the law allows for only one husband at a time. Your life and future is in your own hands. If you will endeavor to find out what makes you tick, you will become at peace with yourself, and you will understand and be able to deal with your feelings with God's help. Then, you will like and forgive yourself.

When will you stop running? Before you crash, I hope.

After this letter, all I can say is that it was probably a good thing I was already in prison for my own protection—from Tammy Faye. Since she was too far away to wring my neck, she wrote a scathing response. Tammy Faye came out swinging: "There are two words that came to my mind when I read your last letter. They were: 'Pompous Ass!'"

Tammy quickly got more specific in her letter:

You tell me to quit putting the people around me through so much.
You forget the horrible emotional roller coaster they put me on for
months when they all were fighting and hating each other so bad that I
was going to close down the ministry. I nearly lost my mind, if you
remember. So please don't tell me I must make a decision "for their
sake."

You tell me it's time for me to "meet your needs." How easily
you forget the last two years of hell you have put me through.
Telling you every day, "You can make it," "Don't give up," "Trust in
God," "The people love you." Sometimes I have nearly lost my
mind trying to keep you from losing yours. I have followed you
around this country from prison to prison; I have faced TV cameras and news media in your defense; I have faced ridicule and hate
and embarrassment defending what you did or did not do at PTL. I
have had to do it alone! I have had to stand by and watch as the
whole country has made fun of *me* because of *you!* I not only have
had to hold you up but your children and the partners! I have
raised thousands of dollars to pay lawyers, have held *your* ministry
together so you would have something to come back to. I have
cried until I had no more tears to cry. And you did not hear me
complain or have a temper tantrum over any of it! I have tried to
live trusting the Lord, and believing in you . . . So don't give me all
this "bull" about "meeting your needs"! That is the ultimate put-
down! When is someone going to care about *my* needs? You sure
haven't.

So let's cut all the psychological crap and get down to where
the rubber meets the road.

Don't tell me about "controlling mechanisms"! You have used
controlling mechanisms on me for years. But instead of temper—
which is at least an honest emotion—you have used "Oh, poor me,
feel sorry for me" control. "Nobody loves me. Nobody appreciates
me." These are controlling mechanisms in my way of thinking.
Even Sister Fern Olson picked up on that years ago. She told you
that you have a way of "making people feel sorry for you so that
they wanted to help you." She said for you never to take advantage
of that.

And who are you to tell *me* to read the Bible every day and
pray? There were months while you were in prison that I bet you
never once opened the Bible or said a word of prayer. Besides, you

cannot *demand* that anyone read the Bible and pray, Jim. That is too personal of a thing. That is between God and me, not you, me, and God.

You said that I had to "write you every day." "Talk on the phone to you every day." What in the world do you think I have been doing for the last two years? I have been paying $800 a month phone bills for some reason. So don't give me that crap!

I will *not* go to Christian counseling twice a week! I have been through more than any Christian counselor that I know. I could counsel *them!* I will not waste the money on it. Besides, you didn't like or agree with the advice the last Christian counselor in California gave me. You said that what she said did not agree with the Word. And that she was wrong! That little visit cost me $1,400 for her and $2,000 in airline tickets!

You said that I had to "come to see you often." I have come as often as I could possibly afford. I spend at least $2,000 a trip. Where do you think that comes from, Jim? Do you think money grows on the palm trees here in Florida? Plus, you want me to pay to send Tammy Sue and Doug and the kids, and your sister, which I have done time and time again. I think I have done pretty good. Give me some *credit*!

You asked me to be faithful to the church and partnership. Why in the world do you think that our church is full, and our partners are still writing and supporting *you*? Because I have been unfaithful to them?

There are two things I can do in your ten commandment list. I can stop seeing Roe, and I can sign the divorce papers.

I would have thought you would be happy for me to wait six months if indeed you care about me as much as you say you do. I will keep the church together and write the monthly letters, and take care of Jamie and his household. I will talk with you on the phone and I will write to you, but *not* every day on either account. I will visit you as often as the money allows.

You cannot ask more of me than that. You have absolutely no right to!

I am not promising *anything* in our personal relationship. We need to just take one day at a time and see what happens. If you are not happy with things, then *you* can sign the divorce papers.

As I read Tammy Faye's response to my last two letters—especially my "ten commandment letter," as she referred to it, I realized there was no way she was going to agree to all of my demands, and I probably knew that when I wrote the letter. I was trying to get her to react to me . . . and she did. I knew that for all intents and purposes I had already lost her.

Within days after Tammy had mailed her rebuke to me, I received a beautiful greeting card from her, apologizing for her last letter. The reality was, however, that I owed her an apology for being so arrogant.

Tammy's birthday, March 7, was approaching. I decided to send her one last birthday card. In it I wrote:

One last Happy Birthday—I hope the card does not offend you.

As I read Richard Dortch's book, I realized that even he had not caught the vision of what I was building. I had a dream in my head and I saw Heritage USA complete and beautiful. While I was building on this dream, all he saw, and now I realize, all you and others saw, was a driven man building something that looked helter-skelter. I understand your feelings of not wanting to go through that again. Neither do I. I had wild faith that Heritage USA was of God and He would bring me through.

Science says that many people cannot see pictures in their minds like others can, so don't feel badly that you could not see my dream. I look at a blueprint and see a completed building; you see lines on a paper.

I was a driven man with a dream and a burden to raise the money to build it. I want to apologize for the hurt and pain I caused you by my intensity and immaturity. . . . I have come to believe God's will is not to build His kingdom on earth, but in heaven. He does not want us to worship buildings or fall in love with places or things. He wants us to fall in love with Him.

The French Lick project helped put you and Roe together and when it fell apart I realized it was not of God. My dream was that Roe and I would rebuild or restore Heritage together, but of course, Roe and I can never work together again. God has closed the door and I believe He is telling me I will not be doing much building. God has restored my first love of soul-winning and I have fallen in love with Jesus and I feel His presence, like we used to. . . .

I'm sure you will be leaving for California any day now. So if this is the last correspondence I have with you, please forgive me for all the hurts. I loved you and wanted to make you happy. I will always remember our life together.

Finally, I had come to grips with Tammy's feelings toward Heritage USA and my obsession to build it. I had resigned myself to the fact that Tammy Faye was leaving me. Nevertheless, that did not make the finality of the divorce any easier when it came the following week.

39

The Dreaded Day

FRIDAY, THE THIRTEENTH OF MARCH, 1992, DAWNED A COLD, crisp Minnesota morning. It was a normal day in prison, and I arose as usual to clean the toilets and hallways. Everything was the same, yet in a way, I knew that from this day forward, everything would be different. I was unusually hyper, aware that a drama was being played out in a Florida courthouse that morning that would change my life as much or more than anything I had experienced in the past five years. Tammy Faye had decided to proceed with our divorce.

A few days previously, I had been paged to report to the unit manager's office. Sam Houston, who had been in charge of my building when I had first arrived at Rochester, had been transferred. A new unit manager, Doug Brendle, was now in charge, a man whom I did not know well.

Earlier that week, I had received a phone call from Tammy's and my lawyer, Jim Toms, informing me that the preliminary divorce papers would be arriving at the prison and that I would have to sign them. Nevertheless, when the call came to report to Mr. Brendle's office, it felt as though clammy, cold hands began to wrap around my heart.

I walked into the unit manager's office. A prison staff member was already there, ready to notarize the papers.

"Sit down, Bakker," Brendle commanded, as he began spreading some papers in front of me. Technically, the papers were an "acceptance of service" stating the terms of the divorce. I took time to read the divorce papers before signing. In essence, the papers confirmed that I was not contesting the divorce. Nor were there any property considerations involved. I had already agreed to give Tammy Faye any of our belongings—what was left of them—that she wanted. Anything that she did not want was to be placed into storage. Tammy Faye was to receive legal custody of our sixteen-year-old son, Jamie Charles. The most devastating part of dealing with the divorce document was seeing the bold, flowing signature of Tammy Faye Bakker on the paper. I could no longer live in denial. Tammy Faye had signed the papers, declaring the dissolution of our marriage.

The entire process was so cold, stark and clinical. How could it be that with a few strokes of a pen a vibrant relationship would come to an end? I knew that the marriage was basically over long before this point, but there was still something horribly final about seeing the papers in front of me. I had hoped that at some point—Tammy Faye would have backed off from the divorce. She handn't. It was over.

I signed my name. The deed was done. A relationship that I had shared for over thirty-one years was severed in a moment.

No doubt the officers in the unit manager's office had witnessed such proceedings many times previously, but today they seemed unusually aware of my grief. I later learned that for several days before and after this day, the guards and prison officials were watching me more closely than usual out of concern that I might attempt to commit suicide.

As the clerk notarized the papers and gathered them together to be sent back to Jim Toms, Brendle sat back in his chair.

"I know a little bit about what you're feeling, Bakker," he said more kindly than usual. "I went through a heartrending divorce myself."

I never established the same sort of relationship with Doug Brendle that I had with Sam Houston, but I will always appreciate the man's willingness to be vulnerable at a moment when I needed him to.

On Friday the thirteenth, Tammy Faye and Shirley Fulbright left Orlando about 4:30 A.M. to make the four-hour drive to Tallahassee. There they met Jim Toms at the office of B. K. Roberts, a former judge and a highly respected lawyer who was a friend of ours, and who had agreed to be Tammy Faye's counsel in the divorce proceedings. I had already signed papers giving Jim Toms authority to represent me. After meeting briefly with Roberts, the group traveled to the Tallahassee courthouse where Hal S. McClamma, a judge who was a friend of B. K. Roberts, perfunctorily went through the divorce papers.

Judge McClamma signed the dissolution papers and ordered the proceedings to be filed the same day. Ordinarily, before a divorce became final, a waiting period of several weeks was required under Florida law. To avoid any unnecessary publicity, however, the waiting period was waived in our case. By midday on March 13, 1992, Tammy Faye and I were legally divorced. After nearly thirty-one years of marriage, the final dissolution of our union had taken less than twenty minutes.

Following the judge's decision, Tammy Faye, Shirley, and Jim went out to lunch with Justice Roberts. At lunch, Tammy Faye expressed her pleasure that the proceedings had gone so smoothly and quickly. Tammy Faye concluded that because she had received a peaceful arrangement, it was an indication of God's favor. In reality, Judge Roberts's longtime friendships in Tallahassee had expedited matters.

Earlier that morning I had gone to my regularly scheduled counseling session with Dr. Daniel Foster. I had developed a deep trust in Dr. Foster since coming to Rochester.

"There is an appropriate and necessary amount of grieving that must be done for every loss, Jim," Dr. Foster told me. "You have suffered a major loss and you must now grieve the loss of your wife. Don't fight against it. If you do not avoid the grieving process, it can be speeded up considerably. On the other hand, by not grieving, it can lead to a low-grade depression that can last for many years."

"But Dr. Foster, I think I can handle it. This has been a long time in coming."

"Jim, I give you permission to grieve," Dr. Foster reiterated quietly and calmly. "You cannot short-circuit the grieving process. The more deeply you grieve now, the sooner you will recover. No significant healing can take place as long as you refuse to ignore reality. Tammy Faye is gone. You are divorced. That relationship is dead."

"Then what should I do?"

"Be kind to yourself," Dr. Foster answered. "Do your work; take part in your classes; enjoy your hobbies, but don't overload yourself right now.

"Let me encourage you to explore the full implications of your loss, even though it might mean the intensifying of your depression for a while. That's okay. It will facilitate the grieving process. The more effectively you experience the low times, the quicker you'll get better. Let's keep talking about the pain. We won't try to run away from it. Nor will we move through it too quickly. These are important days for you, and I will walk alongside you each step of the way.

"Face the reality of your loss, Jim. Tammy Faye is gone," Dr. Foster said again. "Let her go."

"But Dr. Foster. . . ."

"Grieve, Jim," Dr. Foster said compassionately but firmly. "It is all right for you to cry. It is very important when men or women experience significant loss that they have a good cry. I understand the danger of being vulnerable in prison, but you must cry. I give you permission to cry."

Dr. Foster's tone softened even further. "God has provided you with the resources you will need to heal emotionally, but you must do your part too. Grieve, Jim. Grieve."

Five days after our divorce, Roe Messner filed to divorce Ruth Ann, his wife of thirty-six years.

Almost immediately the word of Tammy's and my divorce hit the airwaves. All afternoon friends dropped by my cell to console me and offer their condolences. Many of the inmates had suffered through a divorce themselves since coming to prison. Statistics suggest that there is an over 80-percent possibility that a couple will divorce if the husband goes to prison for two years or more. My friends knew what I was feeling.

One of my friends was a large, gray-haired Italian man named Dominic, who lived in the cell across the hall from Rod Netherton and me. Dominic was a kind, grandfatherly sort of man in his late sixties or early seventies. The constant twinkle in his eyes and quick smile caused most inmates to wonder about the rampant prison rumors that Dominic had at one time been a prominent member of the Mafia.

As soon as news of my divorce circulated inside our cell block, Dominic came across the hall to cheer me up. Several other guys were already there. Dominic voiced the sentiments of many of the inmates as he tried to comfort me, "You should be really happy, Jim. You're a free man now. When you walk out of this place, you'll be free as a bird!"

"Yeah, just think of all the women who will be chasing after you once you get out of here!" one of the guys exclaimed.

I didn't want to be free. The only woman I wanted would soon be on her way to California to start a new life with my former best friend. I appreciated my friends' efforts to lift my spirits, but I was inconsolable. I was glad when they all left and I could be alone with my thoughts again.

That night, however, one of the fellows who worked in the prison bakery baked a cake and brought it to my cell.

"It's your divorce cake," he told me. "It's sort of a tradition around here that when anyone gets divorced, we have a cake." Before I knew it, my cell was crowded with guys, laughing, joking, and relating their own awful divorce stories. It was a strange but wonderful camaraderie.

Despite the encouragement of my friends and the emotional fatigue I was feeling from the stress of the day, I slept very little that night. I was up at the crack of dawn on Saturday morning. In the flurry of activity and the nightmare of Tammy's and my divorce, I had almost forgotten that a good friend of mine was coming to speak for a special Saturday morning event at the prison chapel. I can see that Dave Roever's visit was providentially planned.

It was a bitterly cold morning as I made my way across the prison compound to the basement meeting room of the chapel. Given a choice I would have spent the entire day on my bunk in my cell. The only reason I was going out one day after Tammy's and my divorce was because Dave Roever was an old friend who had appeared on *PTL* programs many times. Dave was a Vietnam veteran who had had half his face blown off by a grenade in Nam and had spoken at Rochester before. As he stood in our prison chapel that morning, Dave's face was still a mass of scars, but for the first time since I had known him, I didn't really notice his disfigurement. All I saw was love in the eyes of my precious friend. Dave and I threw our arms around each other and hugged—not exactly a familiar sight in prison—and the moment he saw me, Dave began to cry. Few sights in life are more heartrending than Dave Roever crying. I struggled to hold back my own tears as Dave and I embraced. Almost immediately my friend began ministering to me, encouraging me, and comforting me. I knew I had to excuse myself before I lost my composure. I told Dave that I would be right back, and I hurried into the rest room to hide my tears from the sight of my fellow inmates.

When I returned, the program was about to begin. Dave's message that morning was about scars. "Many of us are more scarred on the inside than on the outside," Dave said.

Dave went on to relate how people who stood by his bed after his tragedy would say things such as, "I know how you feel." Yet they had never had their face half ripped away by a grenade or their body burnt beyond recognition by a fireball. It is only the person who has experienced the scars who can truly say, "I know how you feel," and mean it.

Dave's message spoke to me. It had been eight weeks since I had first learned that Tammy Faye was leaving me. I had counseled other men that divorce was sometimes more painful than death; now I was experiencing the truth of my own words. Never again would anyone be able to say to me, "You don't know how I feel."

As Dave continued to pour out his heart, I noticed some words written on a chalkboard behind his head. Even as Dave was speaking, the words on the chalkboard seemed to shout at me, "Life is 10 percent what happens to you and 90 percent how you react to what happens to you!"

For the next few days following Dave's visit, I continued to ponder the message of the words on the chalkboard. I determined in my heart and mind that the message was true, but experientially I was still trapped in a cavern of grief.

Although Dr. Foster had encouraged me to let go of Tammy Faye, I kept seeing her everywhere. As I did, I slid into a pit of despair.

I didn't want to do anything. I didn't want to get out of bed. I didn't care to eat, but Dominic, my Italian friend from across the hall, brought food for me that he had made in the hall microwave.

"Jim, you must eat," he would say in his grandfatherly way, as he slipped some of his special spaghetti or other pasta in front of my face.

At the close of the day, I tried to write in my journal. The words came slowly:

Today the pain of loneliness began to descend upon me like a dense fog as denial turned into a sad reality. My heart is breaking; it aches like an unbearable weight is crushing my chest. I can feel my heart—it is as if a meat hook has been plunged into it. Each day it feels like more weight is being added to that hook. The feelings of total rejection are taking over. My teenage bride, the love of my life, has just walked away. Each day brings new feelings—feelings of love, hate, anger swing like a pendulum in a grandfather's clock from day to day, digging the hole of depression deeper and deeper.

Another night I wrote:

Today memories of thirty-one years will not stop coming—our wedding, our first apartment, ministering together in churches, on television, putting our house together, having and raising our babies, all the years of making love—the good and the bad times blend together in my brain. It was our time, our history, and it was like our marriage was being ripped apart by a chain saw.

Of all the miracles I now see that God performed for me while I was in prison, the temporary transformation of my cellmate Rod Netherton remains the most amazing to me to this day. Rod was a fascinating fellow, a persuasive motivator, and a good man. He could also be horrendously stubborn and demanding.

I had begun working out, exercising regularly and lifting weights in the recreation building. Rod was a fitness fanatic, so before long, he and I were working out together. Rod was a taskmaster when it came to lifting weights. He would drill me as I went through my regimen. "Watch me!" he shouted as I lifted weights. "Keep your eyes on me."

319

During my first year at Rochester, Rod had grown as a Christian. But, he was still a choleric, controlling type of person.

When I first learned about Tammy Faye leaving me, I lapsed into depression, but my condition did not take God by surprise. Months before it all happened, He had already prepared someone to counsel me and minister to me—my cellmate Rod Netherton.

Night after night, for a period of sixty days, Rod Netherton sat on a chair at the foot of my bed and ministered to me. Amazingly, throughout that entire period of time, Rod was a changed personality. My normally confrontational cellmate was transformed into a gentle, compassionate counselor. Beyond that, he espoused wisdom far beyond his years or learning. It was as though the Holy Spirit was speaking directly through the man. I had never before heard such wisdom coming from a man, nor have I since. It was so out of character for him, I could hardly believe my ears. But I savored every syllable that came out of Rod's mouth. Rod prayed with me and for me. It was as though God knew that I needed intensive care on a daily basis, so He had prepared my cellmate in advance to be the vessel through which He could minister to me.

Perhaps the most fascinating part of this experience came at the end of the sixty-day period. Abruptly, without any warning, Rod changed back into his normal temperament, and he never again exhibited the same gentleness toward me for as long as we lived together in prison.

40

Pulling Out of Depression

I DID NOT SUDDENLY STOP GRIEVING OVER TAMMY FAYE after the divorce. I am not "over" the divorce to this day.

Yet life goes on . . . even in prison.

Looking back, I can now see how God used numerous people, events, and circumstances to help me through those difficult days. Rod Netherton and Dr. Foster were invaluable in their willingness to talk with me. Dr. Westrick called me to her office shortly after hearing about the divorce and welcomed me to come to her office any time I simply needed to talk. Sam Houston also went out of his way to encourage me after he learned of Tammy's and my divorce.

I had lost my ministry, my life's work, my home, almost all of my material possessions including my life's savings and retirement accounts, my reputation, and most of all, I had lost my freedom. Now, added to that, I had lost my wife. No wonder the counselors were concerned that I might try to put an end to it all.

Yet God kept giving me a reason to take one more step.

Prior to the divorce I had been taking a Bible course offered by North Central Bible College's Correspondence Institute. The course was on the book of Acts. I took my first test on March 7, Tammy Faye's birthday. Despite the fact that my mind was distracted, I scored 99 percent, answering seventy-four of seventy-five questions correctly.

In the midst of my doldrums, I received a surprise letter from Richard Dortch, who had been released from prison in November of 1991.

Reverend Dortch had gone to prison for the same charges that had been pressed against me: mail fraud, wire fraud, and conspiracy to commit fraud. Dortch, however, had made a plea bargain with the prosecution and in return for pleading guilty and testifying against me, was sentenced to eight years in prison, of which he served less than two at a minimum security facility. I, on the other hand, had pleaded not guilty and was originally sentenced to forty-five years in prison. I had not heard from Reverend Dortch since 1987, so I was quite interested in what he had to say:

> You are in our thoughts so often. Mildred and I know where your heart and intents are. Our respect for you as a brother in Christ [is] unchanged. Both of us have been so pulled from every direction that we will need time to work through our differences and resolve our conflicts. That will come in due season. . . .

As I read Reverend Dortch's letter, I could not help wondering what "differences" and "conflicts" he meant. While I had served at Heritage USA, I had never known of any differences or conflicts that needed to be resolved between us. It was not until the subterfuge that went on at PTL in March and April 1987 and the events that followed that Richard Dortch and I took separate paths. His letter continued:

> I remember you telling me on one occasion that people forget what they read, get it mixed up, and things lose their punch after time. We have seen that demonstrated in the past few weeks. People are already asking, "Richard, what is it you did?"
>
> I'm sure you have heard that I have written a book. It came out last week. I am sure many will give you their opinion of it, but please wait until you have read it *all* yourself. I know you will not agree with some things, but the book is about what I believe to be the truth. What I have written about you is not written to offend, but to give my honest view of what I have been through. . . .
>
> I'll be in touch,

True to his word, Richard Dortch was in touch soon; I received a request from him to visit me in prison.

Actually, I looked forward to seeing Reverend Dortch if the prison system would allow it—I had several important questions I wanted to ask him personally and privately—although I recognized that our meeting might be a bit awkward. When I walked into the visiting room, the first thing I noticed was how much he had aged in the few years since I had last seen him—but then, so had I. Prison will do that to a person. Reverend Dortch, however, had been sick while in prison, and he now looked gaunt, tired, and worn.

We embraced each other and sat down to talk. Phil Shaw, who had helped facilitate Reverend Dortch's visit, stayed nearby as I had requested. Reverend Dortch and I talked freely about the one thing we had in common lately—prison life. We compared stories of prison food, clothing, and prison terms that neither of us had ever heard before being thrust into the prison culture. We laughed a bit, which eased the tension.

We talked about Tammy Faye, and Reverend Dortch told me that he had met with her in an attempt to talk her out of the divorce. She had treated him with respect, but she remained determined to proceed.

We also talked about our last years at PTL. We both agreed that we had made a mistake in trying to beat *The Charlotte Observer* at its own game. Reverend Dortch smiled when I reminded him that someone had warned us, "Never get in a battle with someone who buys ink by the barrel." Rather than trying to defend and justify ourselves to the press, we should have answered their questions as simply and as forthrightly as possible and kept our focus on the work that God had given us to do.

We talked about Jerry Falwell's role in the demise of PTL, and the duplicity of the man who supposedly came in to help us. Reverend Dortch knew full well now that he had been deceived by the men from Lynchburg. I admitted to Reverend Dortch that Jerry Falwell would have had no inroad if the Hahn incident had not occurred.

As the conversation went on, I decided to go ahead and confront Reverend Dortch as to why he pleaded guilty to crimes we did not commit. He told me that he had not testified against me, but that he answered the prosecutors' questions as honestly as he could. He said that he never confessed to any crime, although he did confess to offering Lifetime Partnerships on our PTL television programs and by mail. Since he had done so with me, the charge of conspiracy was included, as well. Reverend Dortch insisted that he did not consider any of these things to be a crime. I listened thoughtfully as Reverend Dortch explained his position to me. I understood that he had decided to plead guilty because his lawyers had advised him that his case would probably go better for him.

I looked Reverend Dortch right in the eye and asked him whether he thought that I had conspired with him to commit any crime. Reverend Dortch did not flinch. He answered, "Absolutely not."

I made the statement personal. "I did not commit a crime, nor did I conspire with you to commit a crime."

Reverend Dortch agreed wholeheartedly.

The visit was bittersweet. I was glad to hear that Reverend Dortch had not believed that he or I was guilty of the government charges. Yet, like the conclusions of the bankruptcy judge in November 1991, it did nothing to ease the pain of being in prison. If anything, it served only to increase it.

Reverend Dortch's visit also reminded me of how much I missed the people who had been a part of our programs at PTL. Maybe that's why I was especially delighted to learn that three special friends were coming to visit me on April 27, from three separate parts of the country. Jerry Barnard, a pastor from California, Mike Murdock, a singer-songwriter-evangelist from Texas, and James Blackwood, the outstanding tenor for the world-famous Blackwood Brothers Quartet from Memphis, were all coming to F.M.C. Rochester on the same day. All three of the men had appeared on *PTL* programs numerous times. None of the three men knew that the others were coming.

Phil Shaw accompanied the men to the visiting room. It was still chilly in Minnesota but the sun was shining and it was a beautiful day, so we decided to take our plastic chairs outside to the "visiting yard." The visiting yard was actually a bleak cement area just off the main visitation building; it was about the size of a small backyard, surrounded by a narrow strip of grass upon which inmates and their visitors were not permitted to sit.

The five of us huddled in the sunshine to keep warm. We talked and laughed and reminisced about better days at PTL. Suddenly I had an idea. *Wouldn't it be tremendous if these guys could sing a song?* The prison officials frowned upon anything that hinted at what they considered excessive noise, but since we were outside, and because there were only a few people in the visiting yard, I could not resist asking these great singers to sing me a song. It had been *so* long since I had heard a gospel song, it was worth going to the hole for, if necessary.

"Would you guys sing something?" I asked. "You'd have to sing quietly, but I would love to hear a song or two."

"What do you want to hear?" Jerry asked.

Jerry was known throughout the world for his rendition of the song "It's Real." I asked him to sing that song.

Jerry began singing softly, "It's real! It's real! I know it's real!" His voice began to get louder as he sang the chorus again. My heart welled with joy. I didn't care how many guards heard the singing. It was worth it!

Next, James Blackwood began singing the old hymn "The Eastern Gate." James tried his best, but he just does not know how to sing softly. As the legendary tenor got wound up on the chorus, singing, "I'll meet you in the morning, just inside the eastern gate," I thought that at any minute we might all be transported to heaven.

Then Mike Murdock softly began to sing "You Can Make It." There they were again—those familiar words that kept coming back to me throughout my prison experience. Mike sang a verse and chorus of the song. Then, he began singing another song that he had written and that Tammy had recorded, "God Is Not Through Blessing You." As Mike sang, the lyrics sounded as though he was describing my life:

> A man lost every dime to his name,
> His best friends even said he was through.
> But God said, "Job, your best days are just ahead,
> 'Cause I'm not through blessing you."
>
> God's not through blessing you,
> God's not through blessing you.
> Never give up; what He said He will do;
> God's not through blessing you.
>
> Have you ever prayed for something, day after day,
> And nothing happened?
> Have you ever asked God for a miracle
>   and it seemed the answer would never come?
> That very moment, that very second,
>   you might feel like letting go, quitting,
> You may not realize it, friend,
>   but you might just be a moment from your miracle.
> Don't quit, don't let go,
> 'Cause God's not through blessing you.

Mike went back to the chorus, only this time as he sang, he substituted the words:

> God's not through *using* you,
> God's not through *using* you.
> Never give up;
> What He said He will do;
> God's not through using you.[1]

The faces of all five of us—grown men—glistened with tears. I had felt for so long that God had abandoned me. Then slowly but surely as I studied the Scriptures I began to sense His hand was still upon my life. The words of men who had so boldly and absolutely proclaimed that I was through, that I would never preach again, that the "Bakker ministry is done," still rankled in my mind. Now, it was as though God had sent a special trio of singers to remind me that He had not given up on me.

One of my great joys during my twenty-five years on television had been to present to the world talented singers and gifted speakers. Now, as the beautiful voices transformed the prison visiting yard into an outdoor amphitheater, it seemed so unfair for me to be having this heartwarming, inspirational "concert" in private. I felt guilty having these great singers all to myself. I made a mental note that when singers and speakers wanted to come to visit me, I was going to try my best to encourage them to minister to the entire prison population as well.

To me, it was a turning point. From that day forward, I began to pull out of my spiritual tailspin.

One night after chow time I turned to my athletic cellmate, and asked, "Rod, would you teach me how to catch a ball?"

Rod did not laugh. He merely waited for me to explain.

"My father was always too busy to teach me how to play ball," I told him. "I always wanted to learn, but I was too afraid to risk it. Even at family reunions when I was a child, there was always a softball game, but I was embarrassed. I didn't know how to throw or catch."

"You never played ball as a kid?" Rod asked in disbelief.

"No, I was always too afraid."

"Okay, come on," Rod replied. "It's getting dark out, so we won't have much time tonight, but let's get started."

We went over to the outdoor recreation area and checked out a softball and two mitts.

"First, you need to know a few things," Rod began explaining in his usual instructor's manner. "The key to catching a ball is that you must keep your eye on the ball. Got that?" Rod moved the ball around in a circle in front of my face.

Rod went on to explain the rudiments of how to use a baseball glove. I wasn't even sure which hand to put it on! It was as though he was teaching a six year old. We went to a less populated area of the recreation field.

Rod began by tossing the ball to me from only a few feet away. At first, I had difficulty coordinating my glove and hand movements, but after a bit more instruction from Rod, I began to get the hang of it.

Inch by inch, Rod began to move back farther and farther. I was afraid if Rod went back too far, I would not be able to catch the ball. Rod, however, kept moving back, throwing the ball harder . . . and I caught every one! At fifty-two years of age, in prison, I learned how to play catch for the very first time.

Next Rod taught me how to throw the ball overhand so it could fly a long distance. "You throw like a girl," Rod told me. I knew he was trying to help me. He taught me how to stand, how to move forward when I threw the ball, bringing the ball straight down over my shoulder to get the maximum thrust on the ball.

He began throwing the ball high in the air—I was scared stiff that it was going to come down and smack me right in the face—but I caught it. Again and again we threw the ball back and forth. I could do it!

Rod and I played catch until the sun disappeared. My hand turned red from the ball smacking into the glove, but I didn't care. I was playing ball. Finally, the guard called out that it was time to get back inside before dark. We checked our gloves and ball back in and returned to our cell.

I was euphoric. I thought, *I could have been doing this all my life!*

Rod eventually taught me how to swing a bat and the basic rules of baseball. I didn't feel confident enough yet to enter into the prison ball games. I enjoyed going to the games and watching, sitting on the sidelines, dreaming of the day that I might be good enough to play on such a team.

CHAPTER

41

The Hole

I KEPT BUSY DURING THE SUMMER MONTHS, OFTEN working out with Rod at the "iron pile," the stack of dead weights outside near the recreation field. With Rod's help and the coaching of a bunch of other guys, I was getting myself into better physical shape than I had ever been in my life. Besides lifting weights, I walked several miles around and around the track that surrounded the soccer field. Physically, my strength and stamina were returning; spiritually, I was studying the Scriptures. Emotionally, I was beginning to accept the truth that Tammy Faye was gone.

In addition to my other activities, once each week, members of the local Toastmasters group in the Rochester area held a class in the prison for those who wished to learn how to speak better in public. Although I had spoken to millions of people on television, I was still nervous about standing in front of a group of people to talk. Especially since coming to prison, I had lost my confidence as a communicator. My brain seemed so damaged from my experience over the past several years, I sometimes had difficulty even putting a sentence together.

I had much to gain by attending the weekly Toastmasters meetings. The organization was comprised of a supportive group of men and women who volunteered their time to work with the inmates. Most of the Toastmasters from the outside were gregarious, intelligent individuals, some of whom actually made their livings as professional speakers. Each week they taught the inmates how to write a good speech and deliver it.

We had numerous paper handouts in the class, often exchanging agendas, "table talks," speech topics, critiques, and notes with the other members of the group. A prison guard stood nearby, watching everything.

Well, almost everything.

One evening, several months after my divorce had been finalized, I attended the Toastmasters meeting as usual. We were especially active in passing papers around our group that night, so nobody thought much about it when an attractive woman who helped regularly with the class passed me a piece of paper. I started to read it but then stopped short when I realized that the woman wasn't critiquing my speech topic; she was writing a personal note to me! I folded the piece of paper and stashed it in my pocket. I smiled at the woman and she smiled back at me. I turned my attention to the person who was presenting a talk and tried to avoid prolonged eye contact with the woman for the remainder of the class.

Later that night, after I had returned to my cell, I took out the woman's note, unfolded it, and read it by the light of my small bed light. It was a good thing the room was dark other than my reading light because I'm sure I must have blushed as I read the complimentary note.

A few days later, the woman sent me a greeting card in the mail, again effusively complimenting everything from my appearance to my intelligence to my speaking ability. I purchased a nice card at the Vietnam Veterans' card sale and sent it to her, thanking her for her kind words and letting her know how much they meant to me. I had not heard such glowing sentiments directed toward me in a long, long time, and I lapped up her words like a thirsty man in the desert.

The next week I received another letter in the mail, this time including a photograph of my new friend. I pinned the woman's picture onto my corkboard in my cell, placing the woman's picture in clear sight with my family photos and spiritual reminders.

Having the woman's photo on my corkboard was not in itself a breach of prison rules. Guys had all sorts of photos plastered on boards. But having a picture of a prison volunteer worker was considered inappropriate, although I didn't know that at the time. It wasn't long before somebody saw the picture on my board and turned me in for breaking the rules.

Within days after I had put the woman's picture on my corkboard, a high-ranking female guard stopped me in the hallway one afternoon.

"Hold it, Bakker," she commanded. "Do you have a picture of a woman in your wallet?"

Wallet? What wallet? I wondered. *Inmates aren't allowed to have wallets.* "No, I don't have a picture in my wallet. I don't even have a wallet."

"Do you have any pictures on your corkboard?"

"Well, sure," I answered.

"I want to see them right now," the officer said.

"Sure, okay," I replied, confused but unconcerned.

The officer walked over to my corkboard, and without asking about any of the other individuals in photos on my corkboard, the officer pointed to my Toastmasters friend and asked, "Who is that?"

I knew immediately that I had been set up by a snitch.

"That is Denise Jones," I replied.

"Is she a family member?"

"No, she is a volunteer at the Toastmasters meetings."

"Well, you are not allowed to have that picture. Give it to me." The officer wasn't entertaining any questions. "Come with me, Bakker. You're going to the hole. Leave your things here. You won't be needing them."

The hole? Not the hole!

I had been in prison since October 1989 and had meticulously avoided doing anything that might get me thrown into solitary confinement. Memories of the hole at Butner Federal Prison still haunted my mind. The last place on earth I wanted to go was to the hole. It was the prison within the prison. The hole was located in a section of the building directly behind Rod's and my cell. Inmates often came into our cell to yell out our window across the chasm to their friends who were serving time in the hole. I had heard firsthand of the loneliness, monotony, and the sheer maddening impact of the hole.

The guard escorted me back down the hall in the direction of the entrance to the hole. As we passed other inmates, I whispered to anyone I knew even vaguely, "Get Dr. Foster. I'm going to the hole! Please, get hold of Dr. Foster." What upset me the most about going to the hole—besides the awful feeling of being incarcerated in solitary confinement—was the fact that my children were coming to visit the following day. I had turned the corner and pulled out of my deep depression. I had really been looking forward to having a wonderful time with my children.

Now, I was going to the hole.

The female guard escorted me as far as the entrance to the hole, where another guard opened the door and I stepped inside a "security chamber." The heavy door closed and locked behind me, with the same awful sucking sound as all the prison cells at Rochester. Once I was inside the security lock, the guard inside the cell block on the other side of the chamber unlocked the next door and I stepped into the cell block known as "the hole." The guard slammed the door shut behind me, locking it instantly.

As soon as I stepped inside the cell block, the guard put me through a strip search and took away my clothes. He issued me a rumpled jumpsuit and pointed me toward a solitary confinement cell on the left side of a row of solitary cells. The guard unlocked the cell, and I walked inside. The door slammed behind me, seeming to pull all the air out of the room.

I looked around. The cell reminded me of a tomb. In the back of the room was a window out of which I could see my regular cell in the wing across the way.

I walked over to the cement slab cot, sat down, stared toward the tiny window in the cell door, and waited . . . and waited. I knew that nobody got out of the hole quickly, not without going through a trial-type hearing before the unit manager and other prison officials. That usually took time. Meanwhile, there was nothing to do but wait.

I had been in the hole for two or three hours and had already begun to feel the walls closing in on me when suddenly I saw a guard's face in the window of my cell door. The guard opened the door and said coldly, "Okay, Bakker. Let's go."

Someone had gotten a message to Dr. Foster, late Friday afternoon. It was a miracle of almost biblical proportions that he was able to investigate the reason for my punishment and have it overruled on Friday afternoon, right before many of the senior officials went home.

Bless you, Dr. Foster! I thought as the guard expedited my release and sent me back into the general prison population. Or perhaps it was Dr. Westrick or some other unseen benefactor, but I was sure glad to be out of there. The guard on duty on my floor gave me a large, army-green duffel bag that contained my belongings, all of which had been thoroughly searched while I was in the hole. I walked back to my regular cell and began to put my things back in their usual locations. All of my pictures had to be remounted on my cork bulletin board as well. One picture was conspicuously absent from my photo montage.

I wanted to find my friends and let them know that I had been released. When some of the guys who had been in prison for a long period of time saw me walk into the chow hall, they could hardly believe their eyes.

"Nobody gets out of the hole that fast!" they said with genuine astonishment.

Tammy Sue and Jamie arrived the following day. Our visit truly was one of the best we had in Rochester. Perhaps I especially appreciated the visit because I was so grateful to be out of the hole and back in the familiar confines of my cell. Had I known what horror was coming, however, I might have opted for the safety and security of solitary confinement.

42

My Worst Nightmare

IN PRISON, MOST INMATES KNOW THAT IF THEY DO NOT make a conscious effort to exercise, they will soon become lethargic and overweight. An inactive lifestyle will quickly take a toll on a person's body in any environment, but especially in prison, where inmates have nothing to look forward to but the passing of time. Beyond the physical benefits of exercise, there was a sort of unwritten respect for the inmates who exuded a tough, macho image. In that area, my cellmate Rod was concerned for my well-being. He said, "Jim, you walk like a girl. You have to walk tough in prison, or somebody is going to try to take advantage of you."

I knew Rod was right. I have always walked with a short step, sort of like a bandy rooster, so I have always walked quickly. I'd never had a macho image. As a teenager, one of the bullies in our school teased me that I walked like a "fairy."

Apparently, my walk was one of the first things people noticed about me in prison. Dr. Foster later admitted his concern upon my arrival because I looked vulnerable when I walked. Added to my overall timid demeanor, Dr. Foster feared I would be a sitting duck for predators if I did not present a tougher look. Most of my friends in prison realized the same thing. Some of my black buddies tried to teach me how to walk with "soul." "You gotta get loose, Jim," they'd tell me.

Rod taught me some rudiments of boxing. He also taught me some basic techniques of street fighting, how to use my fingers to poke an aggressor in the eyes, and how to leverage my weight to turn my body into a battering ram if I were attacked.

Rod helped design a regimen for me, using free weights at the indoor workout room. On nice days we exercised outdoors at the iron pile. Rod also developed a vigorous regimen of exercises for toning my body on the days I was not working out with free weights.

One afternoon I finished my cleaning work early, so I got permission from the guard to go out to the iron pile to work out. Most of the other guys were at work so I was relatively alone at the pile. I went about my usual weightlifting routine, quickly becoming immersed in my regimen.

I was sitting down, doing arm curls. Although I was always on alert in prison, I was concentrating so intensely on my weight lifting I barely noticed when a new inmate sat down on another workout bench a few feet away from me. When I did finally look in his direction, I saw that the man's steel-blue eyes were fixed on me, not a good situation in prison.

I did not recognize the man, so he must have been recently transferred to Rochester. He was a husky man of muscular build, in his midtwenties I guessed, and I was no match for this fellow. I continued doing my arm curls as he continued to stare at me unflinchingly, even now that I had taken notice of him. I became acutely apprehensive.

Suddenly, the stranger blurted, "Why does God hate me?"

His words caught me off guard. I looked up at the man and realized that the same eyes that had been so cold only moments before were now two of the saddest eyes I had ever seen.

"God doesn't hate you," I replied. "God loves you."

The man introduced himself as Craig and we struck up a conversation. He told me his wife had moved in with another man and he no longer knew where she and his four-year-old daughter were living. He felt totally abandoned by his family, friends, and even by God. He could only conclude that God hated him, that God was trying to get even with him.

As we talked, I explained to him that God was not trying to get even with him for doing wrong things. God had already gotten even for our sins by sacrificing His own Son, Jesus, on the cross. Then I told him about some Scripture passages that had helped me deal with my own sense of being abandoned in prison. I quoted Hebrews 12:6, "For whom the Lord loveth he chasteneth [punishes], and scourgeth every son whom he receiveth" (KJV).

I then surprised Craig by asking, "Are you a bastard?"

"No, I'm not a bastard," Craig retorted.

I really shocked Craig when I continued by quoting verse eight of the same chapter: "But if ye be without chastisement, whereof all are partakers, then are ye bastards, and not sons." I explained to Craig that God might be trying to get his attention by allowing him to come to prison, and that whomever God loves, He disciplines, not to hurt us, but to help us. The same words I was telling Craig, I needed to be reminded of myself.

In fact, I was beginning to wonder if some of my former "feel good" messages that I had preached, teaching that Christians could have a pain-free, problem-free life if we only believed, might be wrong. Had I been encouraging Christians to give birth to spiritual "bastards" rather than legitimate children of God? The Bible clearly teaches that it is the trial of our faith that God uses to refine us and to bring us forth as "pure gold," yet I had been encouraging a theology that avoided any trials. I went so far as to refuse to have guests on our *PTL* television programs whose problems did not have a happy ending. Our programming took on a "Pollyanna" tone, leaving people with the unrealistic impression that Christians did not have to struggle, or at least they lived "happily ever after" if they did encounter troubles.

In prison, however, I was coming to grips with the fact that everyone is battling with something in their lives. I was reminded again and again of a T. H. Thompson quote that I had read in Tim Hansel's book, "Be kind. Remember that everyone you meet is fighting a hard battle." I was being hit in the face with the fact that much of what I had been teaching at PTL had given the impression that unless Christians were extremely successful, they were living a second-class spiritual life. It crushed me as I realized that millions of people might be feeling that God does not love them because they have not been able to attain a happy-go-lucky, pain-free existence.

Over the next few weeks, my new friend frequently worked out with me or played catch with me when Rod wasn't available. Craig and I also walked the track together, and he poured his heart out to me as we walked. He listened intently as I told him how God had been helping me and would help him too. With heavy conviction, I shared with him one of the verses that had been so meaningful to me in my life, "That the trial of your faith, being much more precious than of gold that perisheth, though it be tried with fire, might be found unto praise and honor and glory at the appearing of Jesus Christ" (1 Peter 1:7 KJV). I suggested to Craig that even prison had to work out for his good someday, somehow.

Craig began reading *The Living Bible*, a modern paraphrase of the Scripture; he started praying and seeking God's help and direction. In the months that followed, I saw a new peace and faith coming into his life.

Eventually Craig's wife wrote to him saying that she had broken up with her lover, and she wanted to know if it would be okay for her and their daughter to visit him. Craig was ecstatic. When Craig's wife and daughter came to see him in prison, I "happened" to be in the visiting room that day. Craig's darling little girl would not let go of her daddy. At that moment, Craig had no doubt that God really loved him.

Chris was another inmate I became friends with at the iron pile. I was working out one day when a strong, athletic looking young man asked me to be his workout partner. After a few weeks of exercising together, I found out that Chris was actually a former national championship bodybuilder.

What I did not know at the time was that my new friend was also a snitch. Chris had cancer caused by the steroids he had used in his body-building career. He had been given an extremely long prison sentence for his large-scale drug dealing, and in an attempt to get his sentence reduced, Chris had agreed to return to his home area to testify against the drug dealers he had once bossed. When a photograph of Chris and an article about him hit the newspapers, it also hit the prison. The word was out on Chris. His former friends wanted him dead.

One day Anton, another one of my workout buddies, spoke quietly and seriously. "Do you know who that guy you're working out with is?"

"Yeah, I sure do. He's a championship bodybuilder," I answered.

"Well, stay away from him," Anton warned. "Don't hang around with him. He's a snitch and he's coming down."

"What? Why? What do you mean, 'he's coming down'?"

"He's coming *down*, Jim," Anton repeated angrily. "Stay away from him! If you're near him when he comes down you're gonna come down too. Do you understand?" I felt that Anton was just blowing smoke, but he sure was angry.

I had no special place in my heart for snitches. Nevertheless, Chris was my friend. I felt that I should keep working out with him.

I tried to explain my position to Anton. "You see, Anton, I am a Christian. I have to do what I think Jesus would do. And He would be a friend to everyone. I gave my word to Chris. I said I would be his friend, just as much as I'm your friend."

Anton trounced away in a huff. For several months, he refused to speak to me.

Providentially, just as the word got out that Chris was coming down, he was called out again "on writ" to testify.

I believed that God had protected me in the situation with Chris. But my confidence was about to be severely tested.

As I mentioned previously, the positive aspect about cleaning toilets in prison was that I was often able to complete my work early in the day and then, before the other inmates returned to their cells, have the time left to study the Bible or write. The relatively quiet afternoons were extremely conducive to concentrated study and writing. Often I became so absorbed in what I was doing, I was oblivious to the sights and sounds around me.

On one such afternoon, when my cellmate Rod was out of the building, as were most of the other inmates, I was busy studying and writing letters in my cell when suddenly I glanced up, and to my horror, I saw a huge man standing right next to me.

Already shocked that someone had been able to enter my "space" without me hearing the door, I was terrified when I saw that the man had unzipped his fly and was exposing himself. "You want this, don't you," he growled, leering at me.

I was terrified, but I sat stoically, not making a move. I knew the only way I could possibly rebuff him was to be equally gruff.

"No!" I growled back, doing my best to sound surly and authoritative. "Get out of here before I call the guards!"

I turned back toward my work and kept my eyes straight ahead toward my desk. I dared not move. The man could easily have killed me; he could have snapped my neck in a moment. But God gave me courage and an unusual power to my words.

The man taunted me again, "You know you want this."

Then as quickly and as quietly as he had entered the room, he whirled around and left, pulling up his zipper as he went.

I sat there quaking in the chair. I had heard horror stories of attacks in prison, and for the first few months at Rochester, I avoided eye contact with other inmates unless absolutely necessary. I did not know whom I could trust, if anybody. Books and movies give the impression that everyone in prison is either a predator or a victim. In truth, some inmates do engage in homosexual contacts, especially those who have been incarcerated without conjugal visits for a long period of time. After being in prison for more than two and a half years, however, I had not had any incidents in which another inmate had tried to attack me. Aside from a death threat by an insane inmate, and a few threatening comments by another inmate, I had not experienced any real trouble from anybody.

Then out of the silence came a huge man with evil intentions.

A few days later, once again during the midafternoon when Rod was out of the room, I was lying atop my bunk sleeping. I had been out walking the track after work and had come in to take a nap before all the other inmates returned from their work duties. I was wearing a T-shirt and a pair of tennis shorts. With my back to the door and my face to the wall, I had just fallen into a comfortable sleep when I was abruptly awakened by hands groping inside the backside of my shorts. The man was back!

As he rammed his fingers toward my rectum, I twirled on the bed, pulling my body away from him, screaming at the top of my lungs, "Get out of here! Get out! I'm going to call the officers."

The giant man glared at me but backed off when I screamed. Like a dangerous wounded bear, he hunkered toward the door, glowering at me one more time before leaving.

I fell back on my bunk and stared at the bunk above me. Undoubtedly, had I not responded so vociferously, the person who had sent me the letter early in my prison experience expressing the hope that I would be raped by the biggest black man in prison would have gotten his wish. I knew I had to do something about this situation, but what?

Toward the end of my next session with Dr. Foster, I tentatively brought up the subject of the recent assault. Dr. Foster maintained his usual cool, professional demeanor, but I could tell he was agitated by the news. He asked me if I knew the name of the man and I told him that I did not. I wasn't lying. I had a general idea what section the man lived in, but I didn't know him.

"Jim, the prison system has rules that say you cannot perpetrate a crime on another inmate and remain in that same prison. If you will tell me his name, I will have the man transferred for your safety."

Again I told Dr. Foster that I didn't know the name of the perpetrator. He then asked me to describe the man in detail and provide as much information about him as possible, but I refused. I knew how other inmates regarded snitches—on the same level as child molesters—and in most prisons snitches didn't last too long.

What I did not know at the time was that Dr. Foster was understating his concern. Dr. Foster had been around the prison system long enough to know the true dangers. Many years later, Dr. Foster explained to me why he had been so concerned. First, the man had entered my cell, my *space*, uninvited. That was a prison taboo. Second, he had put his hands on me in an intimate way. Contrary to popular movie grist, most inmates do not touch in prison. Dr. Foster emphasized that fear of being labeled a homosexual is so high that most inmates do not touch at all unless they are actually intimate with each other. Bad enough that the man had made an overt sexual pass at me, but the fact that I had rejected him would most likely cause him to kill me to prevent news of my rebuff from circulating in the prison and "ruining his reputation." Third, the man was black and I was white. Although the prison officials attempt to maintain good racial relations, racial tension exists in most prisons, just as it does in much of society. Many ethnic groups in prison form gangs. I don't know if my attacker was a gang member. But if he was and word got out that I had stood up to him, Dr. Foster knew that it was not unlikely that I could meet some tragic "accident."

Although I appreciated Dr. Foster's concerns, I knew that if I snitched on my attacker, he would probably be shipped to a tougher prison. But I would not be forgotten by his fellow gang members.

Consequently, as Dr. Foster continued to press me for the name or description of the man who had crossed the line, I just as adamantly refused to snitch. It was one of the moments in my life where I felt I had to grow up and be a man, regardless of the consequences to me.

In the meantime, the man stalked me any time he saw me, hovering nearby when I was working out at the iron pile or walking across the compound. He never said a word, but he was always there, lurking in a place where he was certain that I saw him, just glaring at me, taunting me by his perpetual presence.

One day, a friend and I were working out at the iron pile and, as usual, my attacker soon showed up. He made no effort to lift weights or do any exercises; he simply stood off to the side and stared at me. Seeing him hovering, as if waiting for the best opportunity to strike at me, had a different effect on me that day. Ordinarily, I was frightened when I saw the man stalking me, but for some reason, on this day I became extremely angry instead. So incensed was I that this man could dominate my life to such an extent, I exploded with anger.

I had not told anyone except Rod and Dr. Foster about the attacker, but I was so enraged at the moment, I broke my self-imposed code of silence and blurted out, "He won't leave me alone!" My friend knew immediately what I meant and guessed what was going on; I didn't have to tell him the details. He waved his hand as if shooing away a mosquito and picked up a heavy free weight. "No problem, Jim," my friend said as he lifted the weight high above his head. "I'll get rid of him for you."

I nearly dropped the dumbbell I was holding. "No! No way! Don't you ever do anything like that. Don't! God will take care of me."

My buddy, a bear of a man himself, laughed aloud as he dropped the weight to the ground. "Okay, okay. Take it easy," he said with another laugh. "I was just trying to help."

I later committed the matter of my safety to God. I knew I was no match for the attacker if he really came after me. There was little I could do to defend myself and no place in prison to hide. If he wanted me, sooner or later, I'd be dead meat. On the other hand, I knew that God could protect me if He chose to do so.

Dr. Foster finally realized that I was not going to back down and tell. "If you are not going to let me help you," he sighed, "at least do something to protect yourself."

"Like what?" I asked.

"Take the lock off your locker at night—or any time you are in your cell alone—and put it inside a heavy sock. Keep it with you under your pillow as you sleep. If the predator attempts to attack you again, use the lock and sock and whale the tar out of him. Hard. Don't worry, you probably won't kill him, but you might be able to frighten him away."

I was shocked that Dr. Foster was actually suggesting that I beat another man with a combination lock. Only then did I begin to realize the seriousness of my situation. Yet I couldn't bring myself to take the precaution Dr. Foster suggested. I felt that if God could not or would not take care of me, then He had a different plan in mind. I slept soundly each night and left the combination lock on the locker.

My prayer life improved dramatically, however.

Within three weeks, the man who had accosted me was transferred to another prison. As far as I know, Dr. Foster had nothing to do with the man's transfer. To this day, I have never revealed the name of the man who attacked me and I never will. I believe, however, that God knew his name and decided that he needed a new address.

The attack in prison served to focus my attention on an issue that I had never been willing to deal with. This was, after all, not the first time I had been violated by a person of the same sex.

CHAPTER

43

My Darkest Secret

DR. DANIEL FOSTER WAS ALMOST AS RELIEVED AS I WAS that the man who had attacked me had been transferred. We talked at length concerning my feelings about the situation. The sense of being violated was something that Dr. Foster and I had already been discussing for more than a year. I gradually came to feel that I could trust him.

I wanted to tell Dr. Foster my darkest secret. He didn't push me any further or faster than I was ready to go, and he respectfully backed off once he sensed that I wasn't ready to continue. We skirted the issue for some time.

Finally, one cold morning, as I sat huddled in my big, heavy overcoat in the large easy chair in Dr. Foster's office, I decided I would open up to him. He listened patiently. The story was not easy to tell.

I was born prematurely and was placed in an incubator. While I was in the incubator, the heel of my right foot was severely burnt on a heating element, prolonging my hospital stay. Even after the doctor allowed me to come home, I was small enough to fit into a shoe box. Mom and Dad didn't allow my brothers and sister to even breathe on me as I lay in the bassinet. A gauze material perpetually covered the bassinet during the first months of my life.

Consequently, during my first crucial months as a baby, I never experienced my family members' touch. My family was not overly expressive of affection anyhow, and I was deprived of what little touch and affection my parents and siblings were accustomed to giving.

As I grew older, my stern, Dutch family members were comfortable with hello and good-bye hugs, but little more than that. Our parents were kind, loving, and committed to the family, but affection was not one of their stronger points. Consequently, during my preteen years, although I didn't know it, I was starved for physical touch and attention.

One Sunday night after church, when I was around eleven years of age, I was standing on the front porch of our church, along with a number of other children and adults who had congregated outside after the service to talk. Russell White (not his real name), a young man in our congregation in his late twenties or early thirties, approached me and cheerfully asked, "Hey, Jim, how would you like to go with me over to the drive-in for a hamburger? I'm kind of hungry, aren't you?"

Of course I was hungry, but I was even more awed that this adult would want me, an eleven-year-old boy, to accompany him to the burger shop. I had heard people say—when they thought they were out of my earshot—that I was mature for my age. I would never have guessed, however, that an adult man would invite me to go someplace with him. My dad worked hard as a tool and die maker. In addition he worked other part-time jobs selling everything from lightning rods to storm windows to baby cribs in his efforts to support our family; he rarely had the time or energy to take us kids out for hamburgers or anything else.

"Sure, you bet!" I said. "But I better ask my mother and father if it's okay first." I darted through the crowd and located my parents. I asked permission to go with the family friend. They knew Russell because he and his family were longtime attendees of our church and he was a friend of my brother and sister, so Mother and Dad readily consented.

I felt so big sitting in the front seat of Russell's car, like I was one of the "big guys." I sat up as straight as possible so I could wave good-bye to my friends as Russell and I pulled out of the church parking lot.

Russell took me to the drive-in restaurant, bought me whatever I wanted to eat, and gave me his undivided attention. I felt special.

It was almost 10:00 P.M. by the time we finished eating. Russell pulled out onto the highway. I thought it slightly strange that he did not turn the vehicle in the direction of my house. *Maybe Russell has to stop for gas or something*, I thought. But I could see the gas gauge, and it was on full.

"Where are we going, Russell?" I asked.

"Oh, I just thought you might like to take a little ride," he answered pleasantly. As soon as the car cleared the city limits, Russell reached across the seat and placed his hand on my leg. Even through the heavy material of my new Levi's, Russell's hand seemed to sear into my skin.

"I hear you are a big man," said Russell as he slid his hand up my thigh. He smiled at me in the darkness.

I was apprehensive about what was happening, so I didn't answer Russell, but I was extremely aware of where his hand was resting.

As an eleven-year-old boy, I had no prior sexual contact. I hadn't kissed a girl yet at my young age. Like most preadolescent boys, I was, however, becoming increasingly self-conscious about my rapidly maturing body.

Not long before, my mother had given me a booklet designed for Christian boys to inform them about sex. I had no other knowledge about sexual matters; our family did not discuss sex. From reading the book, however, I learned that babies somehow came from sperm.

Once as a pubescent child, I had touched my genitals to the point that a small amount of semen was emitted from my penis. I was horrified! I thought that I had done something really bad. I wanted to put the semen back in me, I was so afraid! That was the extent of my sexual information and my sexual experience before going to the drive-in with Russell.

Russell drove the car onto a deserted dirt road. Other than the beam from the car's headlights, no other lights could be seen anywhere. I was scared, but Russell was so friendly and kind, he allayed my concerns about his probing fingers. When Russell pulled off the road, turned off the car's ignition, and unzipped my jeans, I was alarmed. But as Russell kept talking to me about how great I was, I thought, *So this is what having a buddy is all about! This must be what the big guys do.*

Russell continued to reassure me that what he was doing was okay. Maybe he could tell that I was nervous, so he kept telling me that everything was fine. Carefully but deliberately, he reached inside my underwear and put his hand on me. I was frightened at first, but Russell was not being mean to me, so I assumed that what he was doing was okay.

(Parents, please never assume that your children know what is right or wrong when it comes to "good touches and bad touches"—especially if you do not talk to them honestly and frankly about the subject of sex.)

Russell then unzipped his pants and instructed me to do to him what he was doing to me.

"No!" I said, "I'm too scared. It's dirty."

"Oh, don't be afraid. It's okay, I'm clean. I just took a bath," Russell said kindly. He never raised his voice to me or was mean to me in any way. He simply told me how special I was. Many people assume that child molesters beat their victims into submitting to their desires. I am convinced the exact opposite is true in most cases. The molester gives the child the love, attention, self-esteem, or kindness that the child may not be getting from his or her family or friends. That's what Russell did to me.

He did not force me to do anything, but he kept pressuring me gently until I did everything he wanted me to do. When it was over, he drove me home and dropped me off. I went inside the house and went to bed. I did not talk to anyone about what had happened to me. I had no desire to tell anyone, nor would I have known how to explain what had happened to me. Instead, I kept the secret hidden deep within me.

Over the next few years, Russell was a frequent figure in my life. Often he took me out after church, ostensibly for a hamburger, but usually for much more. Sometimes he took me to isolated construction sites; at other times we simply stopped along the road somewhere. Occasionally, my parents naively permitted me to mow the lawn at Russell's house. Russell took advantage of those opportunities. He took me up to his bedroom and molested me. He did not have to purchase my cooperation with candy or gifts, as many child molesters do. I allowed Russell to do whatever he wanted to do to me and I tried to comply with his requests because he lavished attention and caring touches upon me. I realized from the first that something was wrong, but my deep need for attention was being met. I felt ashamed, but who could I talk to about such a thing?

Soon I became interested in girls and enjoyed an extremely active dating life throughout junior high and high school. I saw Russell less and less, and eventually he faded from the scene, but for nearly forty years, I would live in fear that what he had done to me would one day be discovered.

I wanted to have sex with some of the girls I dated in high school, but in the 1950s, most girls did not have sex before marriage, and most boys respected the young woman's wishes. Certainly some teenagers were having premarital sex, but it was not a socially accepted practice, and unmarried mothers were frowned upon. Furthermore, as I came into a genuine relationship with Jesus Christ during my late high school years, I learned that God intended marriage to be a sacred covenant between a husband and a wife. According to the Bible, all sex outside of marriage is sin.

Knowing the truth from God's Word did not keep me from being tempted sexually. I experienced all the usual sexual temptations that teenagers encountered. I spent many evenings parking down at the lake necking and "petting" with my dates. If I dated the same young woman for any length of time, the relationship took on sexual overtones. Nevertheless, because the message of the Bible was beginning to take hold in my heart, I knew there were lines I could not cross. For the most part, I was able to restrain expressions of sexual intimacy until Tammy Faye and I married and established a loving, vibrant sexual relationship.

For years I thought that what had happened between Russell and me had been my fault. I wondered, *Did I invite Russell's actions? Could I have avoided them?* After all, Russell hadn't held a gun to my head or threatened me with bodily harm if I didn't do things with him sexually. As a child, I had willingly consented to his attention, so perhaps there was a part of me that was not heterosexual, but homosexual. In my worst moments, when I experienced rejection or severe criticism of almost any kind, the ghosts swarmed through my thoughts.

Those ghosts were never very far from the television studio sets upon which I had spent most of my career. Especially frightening were the worries that someday, someone was going to stand up in one of our PTL audiences, and announce, "I know something about you, Jim Bakker."

At times I wondered if maybe someday God Himself would require me to stand up and reveal what had happened to me as a child to our studio audience and to the world. Stranger things had happened on our sets as we tried to spontaneously and immediately obey the Holy Spirit's directions.

Worse yet, what if I shared with the world what had happened to me as a child and nobody believed me? In the 1970s and '80s our society rarely discussed child abuse. Child molestation and its long-term effects have only recently become topics of magazine articles and talk shows. When Heritage USA was booming and our PTL programs were garnering their best Arbitron ratings, I felt that to reveal my secret past to our audience would be the kiss of death. So I held the secret inside.

I certainly couldn't reveal the details of my past to the church at large, or to other pastors, or to my denominational leaders. At that point in our Christian history, the impression was given—and had to be perpetuated at all costs—that things such as child molestation did not happen in "nice" Christian families and churches. It was easier for the church to pretend these things didn't happen than to deal honestly with broken lives.

Consequently, for over forty years, I lived with the fear of exposure. I never told a soul about what had happened to me as a child and how it had impacted my sexual identity. I had hinted at the subject with Vi Azvedo, head of our pastoral counseling ministry at PTL, but could never bring myself to discuss such a sensitive subject with her. Vi was a good friend and a counselor, but she was also part of my staff.

I didn't even tell Tammy Faye. I was afraid she might reject me if she ever found out about the molestation. Looking back, I now think she could have handled it. At the time, however, I dared not risk her rejection, so I lived every day in fear that somehow, some way, some day, she would find out.

Perhaps it took going to prison and losing everything I had ever held dear for me to finally muster the courage to tell someone about my past. Dr. Foster was the first person to whom I chose to reveal my true self.

Dr. Foster exhibited no signs of surprise at my revelations. Quite the contrary. Because of his dealings with cases of molestation, he had suspected that something such as what I told him had been a part of my past. He said that incidents of child molestation were much more common than most people think and that I was not some sort of freak for having experienced it. He did, however, tell me that because of the molestation, it was likely that a part of me had never truly grown up emotionally. Part of my emotional growth was stalled as a little eleven-year-old boy.

As Dr. Foster and I began to deal with what had happened to me, one of the first things he did was to help me understand that I had not brought the attentions and perverted actions of Russell upon myself. I had not gone after Russell in any way, trying to seduce him. He pursued me and, unfortunately, the relationship scarred me for life.

Throughout the years of 1991 and 1992, Dr. Foster and I walked together through almost every aspect of my life. One day after we had been working through many of the effects my childhood experiences had had upon my adult life, I could no longer avoid the one question that had haunted me throughout my life. I looked Dr. Foster straight in the eyes and asked, "Am I gay?"

Dr. Foster did not blink. "No, Jim. You are not a homosexual."

I sat back in my chair, relieved at last to hear someone whom I trusted, a professional in his field, tell me that my fears were unfounded. Dr. Foster confirmed to me that I am heterosexual, an avid heterosexual. He jokingly said, "No man can love women as much as you do and be a homosexual. It is obvious you're not gay."

Dr. Foster pointed out that I was the perfect victim for a child molester. I was compliant, responsive to the requests and demands of adults, shy, not too likely to talk, especially reluctant to talk in a group setting, and yet I had good social skills. I could keep up appearances; I could maintain a public persona even when I was falling apart internally.

Dr. Foster and I discussed how my situation was tragically replicated in the lives of many pastors and missionaries, who know how to present a persona that is perfectly appropriate for the public, but they try to maintain that same persona in private and it is impossible to do so.

Dr. Foster noted that some of the most hurting people he has had to deal with over the years in his profession have been pastors and pastors' wives. Just because they can speak well, wear nice clothes, and present a positive image in public doesn't mean they have it all together in their private lives.

Part of the reason is that when they realize they have a problem, there is no one they feel they can turn to, nobody with whom they can share their innermost thoughts and fears. In the past, career-wise, it has not been safe or expedient for ministers or their family members to seek help for personal problems. By sharing my experience, I hope that aspect of the ministry will change for some people.

In time, Dr. Foster and I went on to discuss how my sexual identity had been confused by my childhood experiences. Dr. Foster told me that I was not alone, that sadly millions of men secretly worry that they might be gay or have homosexual tendencies because of something that happened as a child or as a teenager. In some cases, men may seek to compensate for and overcome this fear by being excessively rough, tough, and macho. Dr. Foster and I also discussed my fear of exposure at PTL and throughout my life. I admitted to him that, perhaps because of my simple upbringing, or possibly because of my experience with Russell, I had always felt like something of an impostor. I feared that someday I would be exposed, because like many successful men, I had a fear that I really wasn't good enough to be where I was, especially at the top of the Christian world.

I determined in prison that I was going to start believing what I had always preached, that "God loves you, He really does." I had to forgive Russell for his actions and I had to forgive myself for mine. I can say with confidence that I am not now, nor have I ever been a homosexual. But don't expect to hear me lashing out at gay men and women. I never railed at homosexuals in my past ministry, and I am certainly not going to start doing so now. I understand some of the hurt and pain they are going through. I want always to express Christ's love and compassion.

As for me, I am free. I no longer have to fear exposure. I was well on my way to facing reality when I was able to sit down in the prison visiting room with Tammy Sue and Jamie Charles and tell them the entire story of being molested as a child. They accepted it much better than I expected.

God was truly changing me. But the next change surprised even me.

44

What Went Wrong at PTL?

HAVING FINALLY RESOLVED SOME OF THE ISSUES THAT HAD dogged me all of my life, I should not have been surprised when God began to really bear down on me in prison. I had nothing left to cling to other than God Himself—which was exactly what He wanted.

I realized that I had to let go of Tammy Faye as well. I still loved her and would have taken her back in a moment, but I had to face the fact that she was no longer my wife and would most likely soon be the wife of someone else. It hurt me to do so, but finally, many weeks after the divorce, I took off my wedding ring and mailed it to my son, Jamie Charles.

After Tammy Faye moved to California following our divorce, Jamie moved from Orlando to St. Petersburg. The move was difficult for Jamie; he had to leave what little security in life he had, but with Tammy Faye gone, our church doors closed, and my daughter moving her ministry offices to Largo, there was little reason for Jamie to stay in Orlando.

Our friends Bob and Molly D'Andrea gave Jamie an apartment in which to live, right next door to their home. Bob was the president of the Christian Television Network, based in Largo, Florida. Ironically, it was a telethon at Bob's flagship station, WCLF Channel 22, that took me to Clearwater in 1980, where I met Jessica Hahn. If anyone in Christian television had a right to be angry with me, it was Bob D'Andrea. Instead, Bob gave my boy a home while I was in prison. Not only did he give Jamie a place to live, he also gave Jamie a job.

Many of my friends who wrote to me during this time expressed the belief that God had something more for me. My friends had much more faith in that regard than I had. C. M. Ward, for example, wrote to me, "It won't be long until you are circulating again. We know in our hearts that things are going to look up for you. Keep the faith!"

I often wondered if I had any future. Was I out of the ministry for good? Had I sinned so badly that God had replaced me, never to use my life for His glory again? I was not concerned about ever having a megaministry. I no longer desired to be the head of anything, but as a Christian, grateful for what Jesus had done for me and the forgiveness that God had given to me, I wanted to give my life back to Him in some sort of service. Was there something else God wanted to do in my life?

I had been studying the words of Jesus, as I sought the answer from God concerning the questions that rankled in my heart and mind, He directed me to the words of Jesus, specifically, Matthew 7:15. The verse read, "Beware of false prophets, who come to you in sheep's clothing."

What was this? *False prophets*? I had always assumed that false prophets would come blatantly preaching antichristian messages, the Beast-of-Revelation type of messages, and we Christians would recognize them, stand up, and shout, "Aha! That is a false prophet!" Here, however, God was showing me that the false prophets were more likely to appear innocuously, that they would look and sound like sheep in the Father's fold, but actually they are ravaging wolves.

The Scripture said, "You will know them by their fruits" (Matt. 7:16). For most of my Christian life I had evaluated other believers and especially myself according to our *works*. It suddenly hit me that God was not all that impressed with our works; He wants to see spiritual fruit in our lives. I began to understand that spiritual fruit did not merely mean bringing in a harvest of converts to Christianity, as important as evangelism is to God. The Lord was showing me that He was more concerned with the character of our lives rather than what we could do for Him. I remembered the Scripture, "But the fruit of the Spirit is love, joy, peace, longsuffering, kindness, goodness, faithfulness, gentleness, self-control. Against such there is no law" (Gal. 5:22).

God was showing me that I should not try to evaluate anyone on the basis of their actions, words, works, or abilities, but only by their spiritual fruit. One of the worst mistakes I made during my tenure at PTL was that I became enamored by men and women who had talent, gifts, and abilities. I stood in awe of great preachers, teachers, singers, and musicians, often knowing that some of them were not living according to the standards of the Bible . . . but they had such talents! I was aware that sometimes at PTL we had people on our programs or on our staff who were living with willful sin in their lives. I knew it, and I winked at it because of their gifts.

One of the things I did not fully understand was that it is possible to preach about God, play an instrument or sing for God, and even perform miracles in His name, yet be totally out of step with Him in our personal lives.

As I continued studying Matthew 7, my eyes began to open. Jesus repeated the concept of recognizing true men and women of God by their fruits, and then He drove home the message even more emphatically.

> Not everyone who says to Me, "Lord, Lord," shall enter the kingdom of heaven, but he who does the will of My Father in heaven. Many will say to Me in that day, "Lord, Lord, have we not prophesied in Your name, cast out demons in Your name, and done many wonders in Your name?" And then I will declare to them, "I never knew you; depart from Me, you who practice lawlessness!" (vv. 21-23)

I thought, *That doesn't make sense. How could Jesus not know them? The Bible says He knows when a sparrow falls to a ground, and how many hairs are on our heads. If somebody was casting out devils in Jesus' name, surely He would know him, wouldn't He? How could Jesus not know someone who was a prophet? Or someone who was performing great miracles in His name?*

I was puzzled. Certainly I had read this passage before, but I had always applied it to people who did not really regard the Bible as authoritative. As I read the passage carefully, I noticed that the people to whom Jesus was referring had legitimate gifts. They really did prophesy, not only speaking forth the truth of God's Word, but declaring predictive prophecies as well. They actually did cast out demons; they did perform mighty miracles. They did "many wonders," all in the name of Jesus (v. 22). I looked up that phrase in the Greek and I discovered that the root word for the phrase was *dunamis,* which in various forms can mean, "power, powerful, able, capable, miraculous, abundance, a worker of miracles, strong, or mighty." It is the root from which we get our words *dynamic* and *dynamite.*

As I reread the passage with that understanding, I realized that Jesus was describing people who would say to Him, "Jesus, we did powerful things in Your name. We had dynamite choirs. I was a dynamic preacher. We built wonderful buildings in Your name. We did wonderful works, all in Your name."

Yet Jesus said that He did not know them!

The point was not lost on me that we had done all those things at PTL. We had dynamic singers and musicians. We hosted some of the greatest preachers in the world. And yes, we built a great television network and a fabulous Christian retreat center. Beyond that, we had some miracle workers at PTL who astounded me with their supernatural gifts. The horrifying thought struck me, *Could it be possible that after all we had done at PTL, that our buildings, programs, and ministers were not what God wanted from us?*

I had to find out. What did Jesus mean, He did not *know* those gifted people who had done such great exploits in His name? Once again, I went back to the original language of the New Testament and began looking up the various words for *know* that are used.

In Matthew 7:23, the word translated as "know" comes from the Greek word *ginosko*. It is the same word that is used in Luke 1:34, when Mary was first informed by the angel that she was to conceive and give birth to a child. Mary innocently replied, "How shall this be, seeing I know not a man?" (KJV). Mary was saying, "I have never been intimate with a man."

I found that in other places in the New Testament, a different word is used for *know*. For instance, on the night before Jesus was crucified, Peter, one of His inner circle of friends, denied three times that he knew Jesus. Peter's most vehement denial can be found in Matthew 26:74: "Then began he to curse and to swear, saying, 'I do not know the Man!' Immediately a rooster crowed."

The word for *know* used here, *eido,* is a different word than the one Mary used to describe an intimate relationship . . . and the word Jesus used to describe the lack of such an intimate relationship between Himself and the miracle workers in Matthew 7:22-23.

Jesus was saying, "Yes, these people did wonderful works in my name, but I never knew them. I never had an intimate relationship with them; they never had an intimate relationship with Me!"

During my years at PTL. I had gotten so busy trying to do something great for God and for His people, I totally missed the point. Instead of fostering an intimate relationship with Him, I loved the spectacular, the supernatural, the signs and wonders.

For instance, when I heard a great song on one of our programs, I was prone to think, *My! What an anointing of God!* Now, I realize that sometimes it was God's anointing, but oftentimes it was not. I loved music, and still do; music can be a tremendous tool to help us praise and worship God. Music itself, however, is a neutral element. Some people can go to a Broadway show or a rock concert and be moved equally as much as I was at PTL by a great performance.

Similarly, I thought that because a man or woman had a spiritual gift, he or she must be close to Jesus. At PTL, we sometimes went bonkers over the ministries of individuals who I knew were not in a right relationship with God. With some I wondered if they had an intimate relationship with Jesus. With others I wondered if they had any relationship with Jesus at all! But because they had a healing ministry, or a gift of discerning spirits, or were gifted in "a word of knowledge," which was often expressed by an ability to look into people's lives and accurately describe certain circumstances, I thought that these ministers must be of God. Now I am not so sure about some; others I am positive were not.

Because I was so enamored with talented people and laid such emphasis upon the ability to perform, I now realize that I was setting people up, preconditioning them to accept an Antichrist who will be able to perform great miracles.

Jesus became upset with people who were always looking for another sign, another miracle to prove who He was. Jesus said, "Unless you people see signs and wonders, you will by no means believe" (John 4:48). He wants us to believe in Him for Himself, not simply for the miraculous, wonderful things He can do.

At PTL, I was always looking for a new spiritual sensation, a new truth, a new revelation, preaching a gospel "of stuff," when all the time, I was missing one of the most basic truths of all: Jesus wants us to have an intimate relationship with Him.

Not that we did not emphasize Jesus at PTL. We did! And millions of lives were impacted as a result. That's the good news.

The bad news is that because we were trying to do so much in our own energy the attention often got sidetracked from Jesus and placed on human achievements. Back in the early days of Heritage USA, for example, when we were trying to complete The Barn auditorium, we ran out of money. That in itself was nothing new; we were always running out of money at PTL because we were always starting some new project or ministry. This time, however, the financial crisis severely threatened the viability of our entire ministry. Construction stopped cold for nearly a year.

When we finally were able to complete the facility, thanks to the sacrificial financial giving of the PTL viewing audience and the dedicated people working with me, we wanted to mark the event by having a parade, a time of celebration and thanksgiving unto God. Complete with people singing praises to God and waving palm branches, we marched from the entrance of Heritage USA all the way to The Barn, which was at the back of the property. We promised God that we would hold this parade each year to remind us of the great miracle He did in rescuing Heritage USA. Each year, the parade got a little bigger and more grandiose. After a few attempts at having the celebration at various times of the year, we eventually declared

July Fourth as the official "birthday" of Heritage USA and turned the parade into a colossal birthday party.

What started out as a simple celebration honoring Jesus soon degenerated into a parade of floats, with Christian celebrities and preachers riding in convertibles. The renowned concert pianist Dino Kartsonakis was perched upon a float shaped like a grand piano while riding down the street. Tammy Faye and I rode on a float waving to a crowd of onlookers as we basked in their love and adulation. Our final parade was the most elaborate of all, an "Electric Light Parade," with all the floats lit up with thousands of lights powered by portable generators. The Electric Light Parade opened the 1986 edition of Christmas City, so we had "Uncle Henry" and "Aunt Susan" Harrison dressed up as Santa and Mrs. Claus and riding a sleigh pulled by reindeer on a float. The celebration went on all day, culminating in an extravagant fireworks display over the waters of Lake Heritage at night.

What happened? As with so many things done under my leadership at PTL, we started out with the best of intentions and somehow got sidetracked onto a path of pride, arrogance, and indulgence. If a little celebration was a blessing, just think how pleasing it would be to God to have a *huge* party. That was wrong, and I was wrong for allowing it to happen.

Another area where I went wrong at PTL was the balance between faith and works, and my understanding of what sort of "works" were truly pleasing to God.

Throughout my ministry, I thought that hard work was of God, and that I was proving my faith by my hard work. At PTL, I believed that by constructing large buildings, a great television network, and other marvelous, big programs and far-reaching ministries, I was showing my faith through my works. All the while, I sincerely believed I was working for God.

During my first few years in prison, I wrestled with the question, *What went wrong at PTL?* I understood that my sin had opened the door to attack, but I could not comprehend why God did not merely remove me and allow the ministry to carry on unabated. So many good things were happening at Heritage USA, so many lives were being positively changed, why did it have to come to an end?

I knew God had given me the vision to build a Christian retreat center, a place where people could gather to relax, vacation, and be refreshed physically and spiritually. During my boyhood in Michigan, I often attended a camp in which the services were held in an old, wooden tabernacle with a sawdust floor. The lodging facilities were little more than rustic, stuffy cabins with lumpy, stained mattresses. Indoor plumbing or bathroom fixtures were rare at most of the camps I attended as a youth. For recreation, we played in the large, vacant field when it was not being used as a parking lot, or we went swimming in the chilly waters of the lake or the muddy waters of the old swimming holes. Neither option was too inviting.

Attendance at camp meetings began to dwindle during my lifetime. I believed at least part of the decline could be attributed to the facilities, not the message being preached there. I recognized that the drab, outmoded campgrounds I had attended as a child would no longer appeal to a generation accustomed to vacationing at clean hotels and theme parks and other recreational centers, a generation to whom "roughing it" meant the hotel had only an outdoor pool. Consequently, I felt that God birthed within me a vision to build what I called a twenty-first-century, total-living community modeled on the old-time camp meetings, but where the entire family could come and enjoy both a beautiful park and plentiful opportunities for spiritual growth.

I designed the buildings and worked with the architects and contractors; I walked the land and laid out the roads, parks, sidewalks, water towers and water lines, underground electrical lines, fiber-optic phone lines, and other community facilities. I oversaw every aspect of the building of the four-square-mile Christian retreat center.

Tammy Faye and I personally picked out many of the furnishings for the Partner Center, which included the Heritage Grand Hotel. We attended auctions, estate sales, and flea markets, searching for just the right "period" pieces for the shops and stores at Heritage USA. I personally selected much of the wallpaper, furniture, drapes, pictures for the walls, lighting fixtures, and hardware for most of the lodging facilities at Heritage USA.

In addition to overseeing the construction of Heritage USA, I also had the primary responsibility to raise the funds to pay for it. Most of what we built prior to my departure in 1987 was built debt-free, paid for by the contributions of the *PTL* viewing audience.

I was consumed with building Heritage USA. When evangelist James Robison preached a week of "camp meeting" services—ours were now held in the air-conditioned and carpeted Barn auditorium—he confronted me about my "mistress": "Jim, you are committing fornication with brick and mortar."

Although I responded politely to James's face, I resented his remark. I was working night and day just to keep everything at Heritage USA afloat. I thought angrily, *Who is he to come here and tell me something such as that?*

The day before our highly touted, $13-million water park was to open, we discovered a problem that caused the wave pool to tug the sand from the beach area back into the pool. The sand had to go. The contractors told me that they could move in heavy equipment to move the sand, but doing so would most likely crush some of the concrete pool edges, thus delaying our announced and heavily publicized grand opening the following day. I decided to dig the sand out by hand.

Some staff members and PTL Partners volunteered to help, so I dispatched several of them to go find shovels. Knowing that every minute counted, I began digging out the sand with my bare hands. Was I obsessed?

When the workers returned with shovels, we shoveled by hand literally tons of dirt, cleaning out the pool and removing the sand from the area. We worked long into the night, but we did it. The pool was ready to open the following day. At the opening ceremonies, I could hardly walk, I was so sore from shoveling sand the previous night.

Besides being obsessed with building Heritage USA, I was also fanatical in my efforts to maintain it and keep everything running smoothly. I carried a microcassette tape recorder with me most everywhere I went, so when I spotted things that needed attention—light bulbs that were burned out, trash that needed picked up, a pothole in the road—I recorded the reminder and had my executive secretary transcribe my comments and notify the appropriate departments. When I went on trial in 1989, some of the transcripts of my taped comments were used to show what an "overbearing dictator" I was in managing PTL. The truth is, I wanted every detail to be right; I wanted our partners, many of whom planned all year long for the time when they could come to Heritage USA, to receive the best attention and service we could possibly provide.

Oftentimes I was so busy building Heritage USA, I ignored or purposely attempted to avoid the very people for whom Heritage USA existed. "Oh, Jim, can I talk to you?" someone would call out as I hurried from one project to another. "Can I get a picture taken with you?" someone else requested. I was glad to meet and talk with the many visitors who came to PTL every year, but at times when I was stressed and stretched to the limits, I became easily irritated by the interruptions. On several occasions, I resorted to wearing a disguise simply so I could move around the grounds with a minimum of delays. Often exasperated at my inability to get everything done that I had hoped, I sometimes complained, "Don't these people realize that I am building this place for *them*?"

Perhaps one of the worst mistakes I made at PTL was to ignore the spiritual health and nourishment of my coworkers. When we first started at PTL, we had prayer every day and staff meetings every week. Eventually we backed off to meeting once a month or so. I asked everyone to attend, if possible, for a time of Bible study, prayer, praise, and worship. We literally pulled as many of our people as possible off the grounds for an afternoon time together in which we could focus on the Lord. The meetings were designed to last an hour or an hour and a half, but sometimes, when the Holy Spirit moved mightily in our midst, the meetings extended twice that time and longer. We didn't care. God was there, and His presence in the place was the most important part of what we all did.

Our staff members were paid during the time they attended the meetings. As our payroll reached a peak of nearly $30 million and three thousand employees, my financial advisors repeatedly reminded me that it was costing us between $250,000 and $300,000 in wages and salaries while our people were listening to a sermon or praising the Lord at the staff meeting. I foolishly agreed to limit the number and frequency of our staff meetings, and as PTL grew, the meetings became fewer and further apart. Granted, with a twenty-four-hour-a-day, seven-day-a-week operation, it was becoming increasingly difficult to pull all our people together at one time anyhow. We did encourage our department heads to open each day with prayer. Nevertheless, by eliminating the spiritual focus, we were making a subtle statement that money was more important than ministry. Slowly but surely that attitude began to pervade much of the leadership of PTL during the mid 1980s. I should not have let that happen.

One night in prison, I had a dream in which I saw many of our PTL Partners at a huge, sumptuous banquet back at Heritage USA. Large tables were overflowing with all sorts of food, some of the best food in the world. The people were feasting and having a tremendous time, and a seemingly endless supply of food was always available for them. One of my staff members approached me and begged, "Jim, we're hungry too."

In my dream, I reached into my back pocket, took out my wallet, and I placed it between two pieces of bread. I handed the "sandwich" to the staff member and said, "Here, let them eat this."

When I awakened from the dream, I felt that God was rebuking me for not providing spiritual nourishment for our staff. Looking back, it was easy to rationalize that we had a spiritual smorgasbord available at PTL if our employees wanted to avail themselves of it. In truth, however, so many of our employees worked so hard trying to meet the many needs of our ministry, they had little time or energy left for attending services. Some staff members were so burned out from the constant drain of ministering to others, like me, they were becoming dangerously dry in their own spiritual lives.

I always felt that Heritage USA was merely the box in which we packaged the gospel, a big box, a beautiful box, but just a box, nonetheless.

Unfortunately, the box began to get more attention than the gift inside. Eventually, we spent so much time, energy, and money trying to build a bigger, better box, we neglected the priceless gift of Jesus Christ. If I could somehow be transported back in time to PTL in the 1980s, I would keep my attention off the physical, material plant, the place known as Heritage USA, and keep my eyes on Jesus.

About the same time that I was coming to grips with the message of the Scriptures and how far away from it I had been at PTL, my pen pal Jim Dickinson from St. Paul, Minnesota, who wrote to me almost every week and often sent me challenging books at Rochester F.M.C., sent me *Life Together* by Dietrich Bonhoeffer, a pastor in Germany. Because Bonhoeffer dared to buck Hitler's system, the theologian was thrown into a Nazi concentration camp, where he died.

When I read Bonhoeffer's words, they seemed to leap off the pages at me. Written in 1938, two years before I was born, Bonhoeffer wrote:

> Innumerable times a whole Christian community has broken down because it has sprung from a wish dream. The serious Christian, set down for the first time in a Christian community, is likely to bring with him a very definite idea of what Christian life together should be and to try to realize it. But God's grace speedily shatters such dreams. . . . God will not permit us to live even for a brief period in a dream world. He does not abandon us to those rapturous experiences and lofty moods that come over us like a dream. God is not a God of the emotions but the God of truth. . . . A community which cannot bear and cannot survive such a crisis, which insists upon keeping its illusion when it should be shattered, permanently loses in that moment the promise of Christian community. Sooner or later it will collapse. . . . He who loves his dream of a community more than the Christian community itself becomes a destroyer of the latter, even though his personal intention may be ever so honest and earnest and sacrificial.[1]

Ouch! I did not like to think of myself as the destroyer of the very community I had hoped to build because of my love for my dream. But the message got worse before it got better: "God hates visionary dreaming; it makes the dreamer proud and pretentious."[2]

My friends and admirers had been telling me for years that I was a visionary, a dreamer of great dreams. I saw myself that way and considered my visionary dreaming to be one of my better qualities. As Bonhoeffer's words sank into my heart, mind, and spirit, I was suddenly more deeply grieved than ever before that Heritage USA, my dream, had been the cause of so much infighting, hurt, and shame in the Body of Christ. I never intended it to be so. My dream turned into a nightmare. The world watched as Christian leaders fought over who would get "the box." Fellow believers betrayed one another in their efforts at gamesmanship. Money and buildings were more important than obedience to God's Word and reaching the souls of men and women with the gospel. When the world looked and saw PTL, they saw Christians, a relatively small number of Christians to be sure, at their worst . . . and that included me.

We had so much going for us. People were meeting Jesus at Heritage USA. Lives were truly changed. Marriages were restored and healed. Unborn babies were saved, and unmarried mothers were supported as they began a new quality of life. The gospel was broadcasted daily around the world. Witnesses to the transforming power of Jesus Christ were trained to reach the world with the gospel. We had so great an opportunity . . . and we lost it, because we got our eyes on the box rather than keeping our attention on Jesus.

My dream was that Heritage USA might be a modern-day City of Refuge, a place where hurting people could find the help and healing they needed, a place of refreshment and encouragement.

45

Rule 35

THE PHRASE "TIME FLIES" IS SELDOM HEARD IN PRISON. NOR did I ever hear an inmate nonchalantly say something such as, "It seems like it was just yesterday that I came to this place!" On the contrary, time in prison seems to stand still, life becomes drudgery; it is interminable, and it is intended to be so. Although I cannot say that the time passed quickly, for me, the summer of 1992 was filled with activity.

Jamie, Tammy Sue, Doug, and the grandchildren came to visit me on the Fourth of July, just in time for the annual Inmates' Families Picnic. I was so excited to see them! Unfortunately, the Minnesota summer suddenly turned cold and the temperature plummeted to near freezing. The prison officials rolled out huge laundry carts filled with coats and allowed inmates' family members to borrow the old, green army coats to help stay warm during the gathering in the prison yard. My family and I felt a strange but wonderful sense of comradeship as we huddled together, all of us dressed in our prison-issued jackets.

As we packed back into the visiting room, the guard called out, "Visiting time is over!" He ordered the visitors to one side of the room, near the outside door, and all the inmates to the other side, near the door that lead back into the heart of the prison. As I was standing with a group of prisoners, I looked down, and there was little three-year-old James, making his way through a crowd of inmates, with his hands outstretched to me. I picked him up, and he said, "Paw Paw Jim, I lovvvvvvve youuuu-uuu!" He gave me a big kiss.

I said, "James, I love you too!" I put him down and James left the forbidden zone and ran back to his mom.

One of the best and worst days of the summer was August 10, the day my mother and father first visited me in the Minnesota prison. Along with my sister, Donna, Mother and Dad had made the long, arduous trip from Fort Mill, South Carolina, to Rochester by automobile.

Mother and Daddy still lived at Heritage USA in the house Tammy Faye and I had purchased for them. Living there among so many memories was a bittersweet experience for them. Nobody grieved any more deeply at my ouster from PTL than my parents, especially my dad. He often said, "I wish I could take your place in prison, Jim. I would do it." Long after Tammy Faye and I were gone, every direction my mother and father looked, they saw something that reminded them of what once was. I can't even imagine the pain they endured as PTL went through its traumatic changes. On the other hand, because my parents had remained living at Heritage USA, they had a group of godly friends and neighbors around them.

At eighty-six years of age, my mother was especially feeble; I wasn't sure she could handle a cross-country trip by car. Daddy, though much more spry than Mother, was also only a month away from being eighty-six years old, and was beginning to show it.

Overshadowing their visit was the awareness that this could well be the last time I would ever see my parents this side of heaven. Even if I was able to get paroled after twelve years, my parents would be close to one hundred years of age before I could get back to see them at home.

When I walked into the visiting room, Mother and Father were sitting at one of the low tables waiting for me. I signed in and quickly went to them. My mother was desperately trying to hold back her tears. "I promised myself that I wasn't going to do that," she said.

I turned to embrace my dear dad. I know it must have been extremely hard for him to see me in prison.

Later that day, my family and I ate the usual visiting-room dinner, procured from the vending machines in the back of the room. Mother and Dad didn't seem to mind. We were together; that's all that mattered to them. We had our pictures taken by the Jaycees cameraman, then went back to our table to talk some more. I didn't want the day to end. I hated to see my mother and father leave, driving all the way back to Charlotte.

Before my mother and father ever reached their home, I received bad news. Kevin Whittum, the adopted son of my cousins, David and Ione Whittum, had died. Kevin was twenty-three years old when he died; he was the victim of a lifelong brittle-bone disease, that prevented him from walking and stunted his growth. He had to be carried, moved on a gurney or in a wheelchair everywhere he went.

I met with Kevin in 1986 when, at seventeen, he had already lived sixteen years longer than the doctors ever expected. At the time, he and his family lived in Michigan. Kevin and I talked about Kevin's dream, to provide housing for other handicapped children like himself.

Kevin's faith in God and his upbeat, positive attitude despite his severe handicap so inspired all of us at PTL that we caught his vision. Before long, we were making plans to build a facility to house special children, severely handicapped children that most adoptive parents would not want or for one reason or another were ill-equipped to handle. I went on the air and presented the plan to our *PTL* viewers. Kevin's parents agreed to move to Heritage USA and run the home. David and Ione had been in pastoral ministry with the Assemblies of God, and they obviously had a heart for this type of ministry. Over the years, they had taken in, cared for, and helped raise more than twenty-five foster children.

We dubbed the project "Kevin's House." The viewers responded by pouring in enough money to build, furnish, and operate a 13,000-square-foot, thirty-six-room Victorian home in which Kevin and the disabled children could live. Roe Messner and his construction crews outdid themselves, working with a sense of mission and passion, night and day. They finished the house from start to finish in only thirty-two days!

The home was fully functional for handicapped and disabled children. We had installed handicapped-equipped bathrooms, ramps, and railings. In the fall and winter of 1986, after the home was occupied, a dispute arose about the building codes. We already had secured licenses for the residence to operate as a group home, so I was surprised when the problem occurred. Regardless, had I been given enough time, I would have rectified anything necessary to comply with the local codes. Unfortunately, I was not able to help resolve the problem as I was in California with Tammy Faye while she worked to get free of her drug addiction. By the time I got back to PTL, Jerry Falwell and his new leadership board were in charge of Kevin's House. They decided to close it.

In late 1987, after the Falwell regime had departed the scene, a judge ordered Kevin and his family to be evicted. The Whittums were reluctant to leave, and fortunately nobody forced them to go. They stayed until 1989 before returning to Michigan, when Heritage USA for all intents and purposes shut down until the Malaysian businessmen reopened it June 27, 1992, two weeks before Kevin's death. The new owners turned the home into a bed-and-breakfast.

When I learned of Kevin's death, I was deeply moved. He had been such a courageous little guy. The world had lost a true hero.

I was equally shaken and totally surprised when Kevin's mom, Ione, died within three months of Kevin's death. She had poured out her life for her son and others like him. She was sixty-one years of age at her death.

Death seemed intent upon knocking on my family's door during 1992. That same year, Tammy Faye's mom, Mrs. Rachel Grover, was found dead in her home at Heritage USA. At seventy-three years of age, she was still a vibrant woman right up to the day she died. She was believed to have died from a heart attack or a stroke. Tammy Faye was shocked at her mom's death. I wrote her a letter, conveying my sincere sorrow. She wrote back kindly and gratefully.

Throughout the summer, one of the things weighing heavily on my mind was my upcoming "Rule 35" sentence-reduction hearing before U.S. District Judge Graham Mullen in Charlotte. The hearing had been postponed several times, creating even more interest in the case and stress for me. Everyone seemed to have an opinion. Even Billy Graham weighed in when questioned about my eighteen-year sentence in an interview with The Charlotte Observer. Dr. Graham said, "I thought that was an awfully heavy sentence for that when you see people like [Michael] Milken and [Ivan] Boesky and people in that area getting lighter sentences."[1]

One man who had a strong opinion about my case was a man I had never met before. James A. Albert was a professor of law at Drake University in Des Moines, Iowa, a graduate of Notre Dame Law School, and an Episcopalian. Professor Albert was never a "Jim Bakker fan," nor did he share my religious beliefs.

James Albert was a legal educator who had served on Drake's faculty for twelve years, teaching broadcast law. He had been voted Professor of the Year three times at Drake and had been selected as the outstanding law professor in the nation by the Delta Theta Phi International Law Fraternity. He was also an outstanding, active lawyer, specializing in cases dealing with administrative law and broadcast law. In the previous sixteen years before meeting me, he had read and briefed every wire fraud case.

In August 1991, as my lawyers were preparing for the initial resentencing hearing before Judge Mullen, after Judge Potter's sentence had been thrown out, Jim Albert wrote me a letter. In his letter, he explained that he had read a twenty-five-page article in the April 23, 1990, edition of The New Yorker, which had extensively analyzed my trial and conviction on federal fraud and conspiracy charges. The article piqued Professor Albert's interest. He was convinced that from all that he had read, I had not received a fair trial. Wire-fraud cases and broadcast law, he said, are more complicated than most normal trial lawyers assume. Professor Albert did not criticize the lawyers who had handled my initial defense, but he strongly hinted that they may have been working in an area outside their expertise. Perhaps, he offered, he could be of help—free of charge—to my legal team as they prepared for my resentencing hearing. Professor Albert told me right up front that his motive for offering was twofold: one, that he felt an injustice had been done in that I had been tried more on my religious beliefs than on facts; and two, he hoped to one day write a magazine article on what he found as he explored the case.

I was excited by Jim Albert's credentials and his awareness of my case. I wrote back and told him I would welcome any help he could give us.

Jim Albert traveled to Minnesota at his own expense to talk with me about my case. I answered all of his questions concerning the original trial as best as I could recall. For the first time, I felt that somebody was asking all the right questions. Besides his own exhaustive research into my case, Professor Albert incorporated the help of volunteers from his classes to search out information and comparisons of other cases similar to mine. After Professor Albert had met and talked with me, he asked his classes, "How many of you would be interested in volunteering to help do the research on Jim Bakker's case?" To Professor Albert's surprise, the number of volunteers totaled almost 100 percent of his students. For more than a year, my case became their pet research project.

Professor Albert read all eleven volumes of the court transcripts of my original trial. Each volume had over five hundred pages. He became convinced that I had been wrongfully convicted, and he could prove it.

As I thought of Jim Albert's unsolicited interest in my case and his commitment to seeing the truth revealed, I could not help but be reminded of R. T. Kendall's poignant words about how we will know when God's time for working in our lives has come: "When someone pleads your case (and knows all the facts) without your opening your mouth."[2]

On October 1, 1992, I notified Harold Bender that I had officially asked Jim Albert to be an uncompensated member of our legal team as they prepared for the Rule 35 hearing. For the next six weeks, Professor Albert worked closely with my lawyers, Harold Bender and Jim Toms. He and his students represented a wealth of research into not only my case, but every other wire-fraud case in American history. When the Rule 35 hearing came, we would be prepared.

In the meantime, my family sent out a letter to our friends, asking them to write to the judge and appeal for mercy. Hundreds of letters poured in to Judge Mullen's office.

The list of everyday folks as well as Christian leaders who were concerned enough to write to Judge Mullen read like an edition of *Who's Who*—Chuck Colson, president of Prison Fellowship; gospel singer James Blackwood; psychiatrist Dr. Basil Jackson; Jim Henry, pastor of First Baptist Church in Orlando; John Hagee, pastor of Cornerstone Church in San Antonio; Bishop Alfred A. Owens Jr.; Gregory C. Tibbetts, family law attorney; Carlton R. Reichert, attorney-at-law; author and speaker Judson Cornwall; James Brumbaugh, mayor of Astatula, Florida; Jimmy Dolan, pastor of Argo Presbyterian Church in Springville, Alabama; Charles Roundtree, principal of Palnez Academy in Plant City, Florida; evangelists Charles and Frances Hunter; Pastor Tommy Reid of Orchard Park, New York; Bishop Earl Paulk of Decatur, Georgia; Oral and Richard Roberts; Billy James Hargis, author and evangelist; Sid Kleiner, southeast coordinator of B'nai B'rith Jewish Prisoner Services; Don Argue, president of the National Association of Evangelicals; famed lawyer Melvin Belli; Dan Betzer, *Revivaltime* radio speaker; actor Pat Boone; author Harold Bredesen; evangelist Philip Cameron; Glen Cole, executive presbyter, southwest region of the Assemblies of God; author and minister Kenneth Copeland; Karl Strader, pastor of Carpenter's Home Church in Lakeland, Florida; evangelist James Robison; Clarence St. John, district superintendent of the Minnesota District Council of the Assemblies of God; Bill Swad, Chevrolet auto dealer; Cecil Todd of Revival Fires Ministries; David Mainse, host of *100 Huntley Street* television program; George Otis, president of High Adventure Broadcasting; Dr. James McKeever, noted Bible teacher; Dr. John Osteen, pastor of Lakewood Church in Houston; Charles Morgan, attorney-at-law and husband of noted author Marabel Morgan; Gerald Derstine of Christian Retreat Center; Jamie Buckingham, editor in chief of *Ministries*; Bob D'Andrea, president of the Christian Television Network; Loren Cunningham, president of Youth With a Mission. Almost all of my friends who visited me in prison wrote to Judge Mullen, including my daughter, Tammy Sue. I myself wrote, pleading with Judge Mullen to be merciful in his decision. I reiterated to the judge that "I made many mistakes, but I never conspired or intended to defraud anyone. I take full responsibility for all my actions and for all that has transpired under my leadership of (Heritage USA)." I could do nothing else but wait. The rest was up to God.

On November 16, U.S. District Judge Graham Mullen and the lawyers arguing my Rule 35 case finally convened in Charlotte. Judge Mullen was the same judge who had reduced my original sentence from forty-five years to eighteen years. That was both good news and bad news. For the judge to lower the sentence further might be interpreted by some as the judge saying, "I made a mistake when I first decided this case." Or if he reduced the sentence, such an action might be interpreted as being "soft on crime," and no judge in the mid-1990s wanted that reputation.

On the positive side, Judge Mullen had been compassionate enough to reduce the sentence once; he might be willing to reduce it further. I certainly hoped so. Beyond that, the decision to grant a sentence-reduction hearing was at the judge's discretion. Relatively few cases ever get heard, and the simple fact that Judge Mullen had agreed to hear my case was cause for hope. My hope was tempered, however, by the prison adage "You ain't got nothin' comin'," combined with my own realization that I was not going to get out of prison one day before God so directed. Consequently, although I was excited that the decision was going to be made, my expectations were not running wild.

As with my initial appeal, I did not attend the hearing. I remained imprisoned at Rochester while the lawyers duked it out in Charlotte. The testimony opened with my lawyers calling to the witness stand Dr. Daniel Foster. Like Professor James A. Albert, Dr. Foster had read the transcripts of my trial and knew the details better than I. Again, I was reminded of R. T. Kendall's claim that you will know God's time has come when somebody else pleads your cause, somebody who knows all the facts.

When asked to describe my conduct, Dr. Foster replied,

> . . . In the course of the three years that I've known Mr. Bakker, I've seen him make substantive progress just in terms of coming to terms with his loss, but also coming to terms with bigger life issues. I've seen a quiet and substantive maturation process. . . . His work reports have been good to outstanding on a consistent basis, and he's received extra-good bonus pay for his work as an orderly, also with the smoking-cessation program. Since his assignment at F.M.C. Rochester, Mr. Bakker has been primarily cleaning the bathrooms in the work cadre. . . . He's taken the task seriously in the sense of he receives outstanding work reports with a lot of humility. He's been patient, hasn't complained or asked for a job change. Typically, we don't keep people in that particular position for more than three to four months. For whatever reason, Mr. Bakker has been sustained in it now for three years.[3]

Dr. Foster went on to list the various activities in which I had busied myself in prison and emphasized that I had not requested or expected any special treatment. He then answered several questions relating to Tammy Faye's and my divorce and my concern for the effects upon Jamie.

The prosecuting attorneys made much of the fact that I was not the only inmate to suffer a divorce while in prison, that in truth, most prisoners get divorced if they are incarcerated for any length of time. The implication was, "Who does Bakker think he is to ask for mercy? Everyone who goes to prison should expect his or her family to dissolve."

Next the prosecutors pressed Dr. Foster to tell them whether I had ever admitted that I had knowingly defrauded the PTL Lifetime Partners. Although I had explained to Dr. Foster that I had not defrauded anyone, he wisely deferred to the judge for a decision about the confidentiality of our conversations. The judge decided that Dr. Foster did not have to discuss privileged information between a doctor and his patient. At that, the prosecutors were no longer interested in hearing from Dr. Foster.

The next witness was Jamie, the only family member to testify at the hearing. Tammy Sue and my parents were in the courtroom, but the lawyers did not invite them to testify.

Even the prosecutors admitted that Jamie's testimony was heartrending. Jamie confessed that he was lonely and angry. "I have never hurt so bad before," he said. Jamie told the court that he talked to me by phone each day, and that I wrote to him nearly every day. Because of his dyslexia, Jamie admitted that he was embarrassed to write to me.

"Do you need your father?" Harold Bender asked.

"More than anything I've ever needed in my whole, entire life."

"Do you love your father?"

"More than anybody in the whole, wide world. He's my best friend."

The prosecutors had no questions for Jamie.

As the final witness, my lawyers called Benjamin J. Malcolm, an expert on the U.S. Parole Commission. Since 1984, Ben had operated a private consulting agency to attorneys and inmates concerning parole issues.

Ben Malcolm gave a strong testimony that said in essence: If the judge did not reduce my sentence, it was doubtful that the commission would grant parole. Under my present eighteen-year sentence, I would not even be eligible for parole until I had served six years, which even with the time off for good behavior, the "good time" I had earned, would not be before August 30, 1995. In Ben's expert opinion, because of the amount of money in my case, he felt parole would be refused no matter what. Basically, Ben Malcolm was saying that if the judge wouldn't let me out of prison earlier, I would be there for the full extent of my sentence, which, considering time reduced for good behavior, would still be at least twelve years.

Ben compared my case to that of Ivan Boesky and Michael Milken, both of whom were convicted of white-collar crime and received much shorter sentences than mine. The prosecution countered that the reason the two men whose crimes involved far more money received sentences that were much lighter than mine was because they "cooperated" and pled guilty to their crimes. I had pled not guilty, and had never admitted to committing a crime. Attorney Deborah Smith complained that my "lack of cooperation" cost the government a sixteen-month investigation that could have been completed in one month. The prosecution also cautioned the judge to keep in mind that Jamie Charles's testimony was an attempt to play upon the sympathy of the court.

In his closing arguments, Harold Bender suggested to the judge that he put me on probation for five years and order me to serve no fewer than one thousand hours of community service.

In his closing arguments, attorney Jerry Miller contended that the PTL Lifetime Partners were victims who would never get a penny of their money back. Mr. Miller conveniently failed to mention that in bankruptcy court on November 4, 1991—over a year earlier—Judge Thurmond Bishop had ruled that the Lifetime Partnerships "were being delivered and provided," that the money given to PTL by the Lifetime Partners was considered a gift, and that the partners were not eligible to be reimbursed. Nor did he mention that most of the Partners had given their contributions to further the Lord's work and did not ask for their gifts to be returned.

In her closing words, Attorney Smith lamented that if Judge Mullen reduced my sentence further it would be sending a wrong message and would create "a tremendous problem for law enforcement" because I was asking for the same sort of leniency granted to Boesky and Milken, who had admitted their guilt, yet I had the audacity to walk out of the courtroom and announce that I was innocent. Attorney Smith also presented a thinly veiled accusation of insincerity on my part when I said that I accepted full responsibility for my moral failure and the wrong priorities at PTL.

At the conclusion of the proceedings, the judge gave the lawyers on both sides permission to submit twenty-five pages of written material within two weeks. He promised to then render his decision expeditiously.

On Tuesday, December 22, I heard a guard calling my name at the door of my cell, "Bakker, you're wanted in the Warden's office."

By the time I stepped into the reception area of the Warden's office, my stomach was turning flip-flops. "Have you heard?" the Warden's secretary asked.

"Heard what?" I asked tentatively.

"The judge has reduced your sentence," the secretary told me. "We don't know what it all means yet."

Just then the assistant to the warden called me into his office. He told me that members of the press had been calling, saying that my sentence had been reduced. The courthouse in Charlotte would be faxing the paperwork any time now, as soon as all the figures were fed into the computer and the calculations were made concerning my new sentence and release date and the actual dates I would be eligible for parole.

I sat there dumbfounded. Release date? Parole? Those were foreign concepts. My heart was pounding, my palms were sweating as I waited to hear the news. Could freedom be near?

At exactly 3:22 P.M., on December 22, 1992, the prison computer determined that, "James O. Bakker, 07407-058, was eligible for parole as of April 29, 1992.

That was eight months ago! Judge Graham Mullen had cut my sentence from eighteen years to eight years, saying that he felt that the eighteen-year sentence was "unduly harsh." The judge's decision made me eligible for parole immediately!

Parole! I might be going home! I might be getting out of prison! My lawyer estimated that the parole commission would not hear my case for three more months, but three months seemed as though they were a moment compared to forty-five years or even eighteen years.

Being eligible for parole did not automatically guarantee that the parole board would grant it. But surely the parole board would concur with the wisdom of the appeals judges who had thrown out my original sentence; surely they would accept the decision of Judge Mullen who had reduced the sentence twice. Surely, they would allow me out of prison on parole! Or would they?

CHAPTER

46

A Taste of Freedom

I APPLIED FOR PAROLE AS SOON AS I COULD AFTER HEARING the news of Judge Mullen's decision. The parole board that would decide my case came to the prison quarterly and usually spent about three days there, reviewing potential parole cases. After interviewing the inmates under consideration for parole, the board then made a decision whether to recommend parole to the regional board, which had the authority to release an inmate. I had no idea how long everything was going to take, but I recognized that I had to keep busy because I would still be living in prison for a while. I was about to find out how long "a while" could be!

Even before Judge Mullen's decision, I had been keeping busy getting ready for my fourth Christmas in prison. I wanted to make this a special Christmas for my family, especially since it would be the first Christmas following Tammy Faye's and my divorce. I had saved a little money in my commissary account and planned to purchase a few small Christmas presents for my family members. It would be the first time I could actually buy them Christmas presents since 1988.

Pastor Phil Shaw helped me select my Christmas gifts by collecting all sorts of mail-order catalogs and sending them to me in prison. When I settled on the items from the catalogs, I withdrew the money from my commissary and sent it to Jamie so he could arrange to have the gifts sent to Tammy Sue's home. It was such fun to be able to feel like a real person again at Christmas. It felt especially good to be able to give again. Contrary to popular belief, I have always enjoyed giving more than getting.

Phil also helped me in putting together a special "prison Christmas card" that I could send out to all the many people who had written to me in prison. I wanted to make up our own card with a picture of Canadian geese on the front. Those geese had special meaning to me.

Shortly after arriving at F.M.C. Rochester in 1989, one day I had been walking across the prison compound, when suddenly I heard a loud honking sound in the air. I looked up and to my surprise, I saw thousands of large, loudly honking Canadian geese. Each one looked as though it might weigh as much as twenty pounds, with wingspans of four to six feet. I could not believe my eyes.

As the geese drew closer their honking grew louder. When the entire flock could be seen, it was almost as though someone had thrown a huge canopy over the prison. When I asked someone about the geese, they told me that the birds fly over the prison almost every single day. The prison, I was told, was in a direct line between the field where the geese fed and the warm waters of Silver Lake, which, because of a power plant located there, doesn't freeze even in the coldest of winters.

A few weeks later, in the midst of a blizzard, I was making my way across the compound through the snow. I closed my parka tightly and pulled its hood over my face, leaving only a small slit for my eyes to be exposed to the elements. Suddenly, I heard the geese honking high in the sky above me as they traveled their daily route. It was snowing and the wind was blowing so hard that I couldn't understand how the birds could stay aflight.

I looked up, peeking through my parka's opening, as I clutched the hood around my face. The sight was so awesome, I let go of my parka and let the hood fly off my head. The sight of the birds against the gray sky dashed with a driving white snow nearly took my breath away.

At that moment, standing in the middle of a prison compound, completely surrounded by razor-wire fence, I felt incredibly free.

Over the next several years, I studied and learned much about my fine, feathered friends. I discovered the reason why geese fly in a V formation. By flying together in a V they lift up each other by creating an upward air current through the movement of their wings, each bird getting 71 percent greater flying range than if it flew on its own. The flock actually flies in the shape of one great bird. I thought instantly of the people in the Church: How much more we could accomplish if we mobilized and helped each other.

When the warm weather finally came to Minnesota, I noticed three geese had landed in our compound near the dining hall. The inmates instantly adopted them. Each day, some of the inmates saved scraps of food and smuggled it out to feed the geese. Soon we realized that the reason the trio had left the flock for the "security" of the prison compound was that the mother goose had laid eggs in a nest next to the chow hall door. I wondered, *Why three geese? Why not just the expecting goose and the nervous daddy gandy?* Then I read that if one goose is hurt or wounded, two geese fall out of formation and follow the hurting goose to the ground. The two geese stay with their fellow goose until he or she can fly again. In Tim Hansel's book *Through the Wilderness of Loneliness*, he commented, "If people knew we would stand by them like that in the church, they would push down the walls to get in."[1]

Every day, eight hundred prisoners lined up for "mainline" and watched over this new life experience being played out before their eyes. When the goslings were born, with their soft, downy coverings, they were the pride of the prison. Almost everyone felt a sense of ownership of the goslings, as an attitude of parental protectiveness filled the compound concerning the geese. On some days, the inmates brought out enough food for the new family to feed a whole flock. One inmate built a tiny pond with a piece of plastic next to the nest so the baby geese could swim. The concern and compassion the "hardened criminals" showed to those creatures was amazing and is incompatible with the image most people have of inmates.

The new family of geese might have become permanent pets at the prison, but eventually the order was given to the guards to shoo the baby geese out of the prison yard, where they were snatched up and eaten by the huge hawks that constantly hovered near the prison. The following day, the three adult geese came back to what they had obviously believed to be a safe place. The geese were wrong. Their babies were gone, victims of a prison system that seemed intent on sucking out all vestiges of life, rather than revitalizing what life is there.

Throughout my stay at F.M.C. Rochester, I continued to study and learn from the geese. Often, spiritual principles came alive to me. As I read about the geese, I thought, *What a beautiful picture of what the family of God should be like! We should be helping each other, watching out for one another, rather than seeking an opportunity to better ourselves at someone else's expense.*

For my 1992 Christmas card, Phil Shaw secured the services of a photographer who captured the geese on film while they basked in the warm waters of Silver Lake on a cold but sunny day. The ground and trees were all decked in ice and snow against a deep blue sky background. It was perfect. Phil sent me a copy of the photo, and I laid out the artwork in prison, picking out the type. Phil arranged the printing, addressing, and mailing of the cards with Tammy Sue and Shirley Fulbright. Numerous people over the years have commented to me how deeply meaningful that 1992 Christmas card was to them. You can imagine how much it meant to me.

As Christmas grew closer, I talked by telephone with Tammy Sue almost every day, helping her plan the party for Jamie's seventeenth birthday on December 18 and discussing the many details concerning her planned visit to Rochester for Christmas. I was really excited to see Tammy Sue and her family.

Tammy Faye flew in from California for Jamie's party; she spent four days with the children and got to enjoy an early Christmas with two-year-old Jonathan and three-year-old James. I had purchased small Christmas presents for everyone else in the family, so it only made sense to me that I should purchase a present for Tammy Faye too. I had ordered her a leopard-patterned, lightweight jacket. It had that "Tammy Faye" look, but it was a far cry from some of the more luxurious coats I had bought her in the past.

That same week, a nasty cold spell locked onto the Minnesota weather map. The windchill factor reached thirty-six degrees below zero. I hated to think of the children standing outside in such cold weather, waiting in the visitors' lines to get in to see me, so I reluctantly called Tammy Sue and told her that I thought it might be best if they stayed home for Christmas. I tried to mask my disappointment as best I could, but Tammy Sue understood. Since she and the family were planning on coming to Rochester for Christmas, she had allowed the boys to open some of their Christmas presents early with their "Mama Faye," as the children refer to Tammy Faye.

Tammy Sue described to me how her boys opened the presents I had purchased for them through the catalogs. I had given them some wooden building blocks, similar to the kind we had in the prison visitation room—only without the dirt and the teeth marks. Tammy Sue told me in detail about what the boys were building with the blocks and how they loved to stack them up and knock them over, just as James and I had done in prison. They also loved the wooden train I had given them. I was thrilled.

I telephoned Tammy Sue and Jamie on Christmas Day. Tammy Sue answered the phone, and immediately I could tell that something was wrong. "Grandpa Bakker has been in a wreck and he is in serious condition."

Instantly, my first response was, *Oh, God! Please don't let Dad die! Not yet. Not now!* My mother and father had prayed every day for the past three years that they would live to see me free from prison.

Tammy Sue was tearful but she remained calm as she told me, "His pelvic bone is broken and he is bleeding internally. He's been transferred

371

from one hospital to another one that has a trauma center. His car was totaled. Grandmother is okay."

I asked Tammy Sue and Jamie to go to the hospital to be with Grandpa and Grandma Bakker. Tammy Sue agreed and said that my brother, Norman, was already there as well. As soon as I hung up the phone, I tried calling the hospital where my dad had been taken, but the hospital would not accept my collect call. I called my attorney Jim Toms, and asked if he could find out any details about my dad's condition. Jim promised that he would get back to me as soon as he knew anything for certain.

I tried to find Doug Brendle, our unit manager, to let him know that I was waiting to hear from the hospital or from my lawyer about my father's condition. The guard on duty suggested that perhaps Brendle was in the chow hall or the visiting area, helping out for the Christmas dinner. In my concern over Dad, I had forgotten that it was Christmas Day, the most hectic day of the year in prison. Besides that, since many inmates want to make Christmas calls, inmates must line up to use the pay phones and must limit their calls to fifteen minutes in length. I rotated in the phone lines, calling family and friends, trying to find out about my father's condition.

Finally Brendle came down the hall. He came right to me and said, "I heard your father has been in an accident."

"Yes, sir. That's correct." I filled in the details for him as best as I could with what I knew of the situation back home.

"Come up to my office. You can call the hospital from there."

I thanked him and gladly followed Brendle upstairs to his office and called the hospital direct.

When I finally got the doctor on the phone, he explained to me that my dad's blood count was dropping and that they would do another test at 6:00 P.M. If the count continued to drop, they would give him blood and perhaps operate. The doctor then talked to Brendle and recommended that I come home immediately, if possible. I later learned that the doctor's own father had died recently from a similar set of medical circumstances.

Doug Brendle placed an urgent call to the warden. They talked for a few minutes, while I waited, wondering, *What is going on?*

When Brendle turned his attention back to me, he spoke matter-of-factly but compassionately. "We are going to try to get you home to see your dad. The warden is working on clearance from Washington, D.C., right now. We can't promise anything, but we will try."

I was flabbergasted. *Home! To see my dad! And my mother! Home!* I tried to temper my emotions. I had been in prison long enough now to know better than to ever get my hopes up.

Brendle instructed me to return to my cell and said he would contact me as soon as he heard anything, one way or the other.

About midnight on Christmas night, Brendle gave me the news. "Your trip is approved," he said. "You'll be going home in the next two days to see your father. That's as soon as we can get you there." He explained how it was possible for me to get out on leave. "Because of your sentence reduction this past week, the warden is giving you a new inmate classification. You will be able to travel, without handcuffs and legcuffs."

I was going home to see my dad! It was to be a one-day-only trip, to see my dad in the hospital, then straight back to prison in the same day. The cost of the trip for both Mr. Brendle and me would come out of my commissary account.

I was dressed in street clothes as Brendle and I met to begin our trip by car from the prison to the Minneapolis airport. We were to travel by commercial airline to Charlotte rather than the prison transportation system. Just walking out the front gate of the prison without wearing handcuffs was a thrill. Once in the car, I was fascinated to see the scenery of the countryside surrounding the city of Rochester. I had arrived at Rochester in the middle of a snowstorm in a daze, so I had never really seen much. As I looked around now, the frozen, snow-covered Minnesota rolling hills and lakes looked wonderfully refreshing. Cold, perhaps, but free!

Walking through the airport without restraint was my next tiny taste of freedom. Did it ever feel great! On the plane, I was nearly overwhelmed by a simple question from a flight attendant. "What would you like to drink?" she asked pleasantly.

I could hardly make up my mind. There were so many choices. For three years in prison, I had been told what to do, when and where to do it, and for how long. Finally, I ordered apple juice. When the flight attendant brought breakfast, I ate every bite. Airline food was delicious compared to prison food.

A police car was waiting on the tarmac when we landed. We exited the plane quickly and hustled into the back seat of the waiting car. I had so many mixed emotions about Charlotte. I had spent some of the best years of my life there, and some of the worst. The officer driving the car to the hospital was friendly and talkative, which helped take my mind off the past. He told me that crime in Charlotte had shot up significantly since I had been gone. I wasn't quite sure if he was joking or being serious.

When we arrived at the hospital, we were ushered upstairs by a security guard, and I was allowed to go into the intensive care unit to see my father. Even with all the tubes in him and monitors attached to his body, my father was a sight for sore eyes! My mother was sitting by his bedside as I entered the room. Dad was in good spirits, despite his banged-up body. A few minutes later, Tammy Sue and Jamie arrived. My brother, Norman, came in shortly thereafter. What a family reunion we had at my father's bedside! Tammy Sue told me that the grandbabies were in the waiting room. I couldn't wait to hug those precious little boys. It was a special moment when I got to see my grandbabies, in the hospital or not. What fun we had. I read them a story from their new sound-effects storybook they had received for Christmas.

The head nurse arrived bearing good news. The internal bleeding had stopped and my father was to be transferred to another room in the trauma ward, a room in which the whole family could be together, even the children. My dad's condition seemed to improve just from seeing everyone around him.

Tammy Sue's husband, Doug, and Jamie went out and bought food for everyone—Kentucky Fried Chicken and Pizza Hut pizza. When they brought it into the room, it looked like a king's banquet to me. Real food. It's one of the things prisoners dream about. Tammy Sue later said that I looked like a starving man! I was holding a piece of chicken in one hand and a piece of pizza in the other.

For six wonderful, fantastic hours we were a family once again, even though one of us was injured. Actually, we were a family, plus one. Doug Brendle sat outside the hospital-room door the entire time. He tried to remain inconspicuous, that is, until someone suggested that we take some family photographs of the occasion. "No pictures!" Brendle ordered. I assumed he was worried about publicity.

It was heartwrenching to say good-bye. We all hugged, and the family members prayed for me to be released on parole so we could be back together again soon. Jamie Charles did not want to let go of me. He sobbed as if his heart was breaking. "Dad, I need you," he said again and again. Tears streamed down Tammy Sue's face as well. All the good-byes in prison were tough, but this one was the worst. Maybe it was because I had actually been back home rather than the family coming to see me in prison. This was a tantalizing taste of what *could be* if I did not have to go back to prison. As I walked out of the hospital into the chilly Charlotte night, I felt as though it had all been a dream—a good dream, to be sure, in many ways, but nonetheless a dream.

By the time Mr. Brendle and I arrived at our gate, a terrible ice storm was turning Charlotte's roads into a giant skating rink. We were told that our plane had not yet even left Washington, D.C., and would be more than an hour behind schedule. The airline allowed us to wait in a pilots' lounge to avoid a potential scene in public. We waited . . . and waited . . . and waited.

After about three hours, Brendle decided he was going to rent a vehicle and drive me to the nearest federal prison, where I would spend the night. A stickler for prison rules and routines, Brendle was committed to making sure I slept that night in a federal prison—any federal prison at this point. It had been a long day for him. No doubt he just wanted to sleep someplace where he didn't have to worry about watching over me. Unfortunately, the closest federal facility was three hours away . . . in Butner. Just the thought of going back to that hellhole sent shivers up my spine.

Getting to Butner was no easy chore, either. Brendle rented a jeep-type vehicle hoping to get better traction on the icy roads, but when the weather turns nasty in the South, traction is irrelevant, especially in an ice storm. Most southern states are ill-equipped to deal with an arctic blast such as we were having that night. It was the type of night when most people didn't even want to let the dog out, let alone drive three hours. But Brendle was not most people. We headed toward Butner, inching along at times over the treacherous roads.

When at last we pulled into the prison at Butner, I had to force myself to get out of the vehicle. Even at that late hour, coming into the prison with a unit manager from another major federal facility, I was strip searched. I was processed quickly and put in a solitary-confinement cell—the hole, the same sort of cell I had been in during my first experience at Butner. Fortunately, I was not put among the insane inmates again.

The following morning, Brendle and I boarded a flight—also to be paid for from my commissary account—from Raleigh-Durham Airport to Charlotte, where we connected to a nonstop flight back to Minneapolis. By 5:00 P.M. that afternoon, I was back in prison at F.M.C. Rochester. The inmates there welcomed me back as though I had been on vacation. Several of my friends said that they had seen me on television newscasts. Most of my buddies were more interested in hearing how my dad was doing than anything else. They seemed genuinely concerned.

This was the second time that I had been outside of prison for a few days, the first time to go to my resentencing trial, and now to visit my dad at the hospital. Reentering the Rochester prison this time, however, I had less of a feeling that I was coming "home." I had tasted freedom, and I longed for the day that I would walk out the front gates at F.M.C. Rochester and never have to come back.

47

The Last Appeal

I WAS TO MEET WITH TWO PAROLE-COMMISSION EXAMINERS on Maundy Thursday, April 8, 1993, at 8:00 A.M. Dressed in my best prison khakis and accompanied by my lawyers, Jim Toms and Harold Bender, and parole expert Ben Malcolm, I walked across the compound to a room in the chapel building to meet with the examiners. I knew that if I wanted out of prison early, this was the first group of people I would have to convince that I was worthy to be set free. I was confident, upbeat, and hopeful, but extremely nervous.

I walked in and met the examiners, two large men, one black and one white, both dressed in business suits. They greeted us cordially and instructed us to sit down. My lawyers and I sat on one side of a conference table and the two men sat on the other. Stacks of inmates' files sat on the conference table in a heap. These commission examiners went from prison to prison, listening to story after story.

I would be given about half an hour to make my case. The examiners would then decide whether it was worth recommending me for parole or not. If they responded positively, the case would be referred to the regional office where the decision to grant parole or not would be made. If they reacted negatively, I would have to reapply.

The examiners wasted no time in questioning me. I answered their questions and had the opportunity to present any statements or new evidence in my case that might help them in their decision. I presented the actual lodging records of the Heritage Grand Hotel, documents that showed that the Grand Hotel had space available to accommodate Lifetime Partners during most of the year except during our peak occupancy periods such as the Fourth of July and Christmas. These documents had not been presented in my original trial or in any of my resentencing hearings.

Thomas Sima, a student at University of North Carolina at Chapel Hill, was working as a law clerk for my lawyer, Jim Toms. Jim regarded Thomas as one of the brightest young clerks he had ever employed. Thomas Sima searched the PTL class-action suit files of Leventhol & Horwath, PTL's former accounting firm. Looking for anything that might be of help to me there in the files, Thomas discovered the hotel lodging records for the entire Heritage USA complex, including the much-disputed Heritage Grand Hotel. Thanks to Thomas, for the first time in my case, I was able to present clear, easily understandable, verifiable information.

My lawyer Jim Toms made a few brief statements on my behalf, followed by Ben Malcolm's presentation regarding the options the parole board might have in my case. The examiners didn't rush us. After about fifty minutes, the examiners asked my representatives and me to leave the room while they deliberated. In a few minutes, they called me back and said, "We are going to recommend that you be released this December, which is the maximum sentence under the federal guidelines for your case."

I wanted to stand up and shout "Hallelujah!" Instead I smiled and said, "Thank you very much."

The black examiner looked me right in the eyes and said to me, "I believe you're innocent."

I thanked him. I was so excited. I might be getting out of prison soon!

Later, when I was alone with my representatives, Ben Malcolm told me, "Jim, in all my years in dealing with parole boards, I have never heard an examiner tell an inmate that he thought he was innocent."

The examiners sent their recommendation to the U.S. parole commission in Kansas City, the regional commission that had jurisdiction over my case. In most cases, an inmate who was recommended for parole was notified of the Regional Commission's decision within twenty-one days.

Real hope that I might be getting out of prison never was any higher than the days following the hearing with the parole examiners. I felt confident too because Ben Malcolm had prepared a masterful summary of my case for the regional commissioner, prior to the hearing, using the government's own printed material on my case:

From 1984 to 1987, Bakker and other officials solicited lifetime partners to fund the construction of facilities at "Heritage USA." In return for their gift, partners were promised lodging based on the availability of space.

The Preliminary Sentencing Information (PSI) indicates that PTL received a total of $172 million as a result of the sale of 152,903 fully paid lodging partnerships. The PSI also states that $64.9 million was spent on construction at Heritage. The remainder of the funds went to cover operating expenses at PTL. The record also states that more than $4 million was paid in bonuses to Bakker and Codefendant Richard Dortch. Of this amount, Bakker received $2,780,000 spread over a four-year period. His wife Tammy received $685,000 and Codefendant Dortch $550,000. In addition, Codefendant Dortch paid $275,000 into a trust fund to be paid to Jessica Hahn to prevent her from publicly accusing Bakker of sexual misconduct. Of this amount, she (Hahn) received only $20,000.

To clarify Jim Bakker's total remuneration from 1984 to 1987, inclusive, the PSI lists a total on his tax returns for $4,321,496. These were joint returns for Bakker and his wife and include salary and bonuses for both of them. Therefore the total, spread over a four-year period, averages out to $1,080,374 for both Bakker and his wife. It should be noted that approximately 60 percent of their taxable income was paid to the government as income taxes. It should be further noted that Bakker was not a greedy person who tried to steal from PTL; instead, he and his wife made large contributions to PTL. Codefendant and Chief Elder Richard Dortch testified that Jim Bakker and his wife assigned their royalties for tapes, books, LP's, etc. to PTL.

According to the record (PSI), it appears that the salary and bonuses paid to Bakker since 1984 were not fraudulently received. Salaries and bonuses were approved by the Board of Directors. What the record does not allow for is a retroactive compensation for all the very lean years from 1974 to 1984 when he received no bonuses and a very small salary.

One of the major allegations against Heritage USA and Bakker was that they oversold, that there were no vacancies and that this constituted a fraud. At the outset, the plan in the Grand Hotel was to set aside 50 percent of the rooms to Lifetime Partners and 50 percent to the general public. Lifetime Partners would make a donation of $1,000 in return for an annual stay of 4 days and 3 nights for the rest of their natural lives. Documentation clearly shows that there was always space at the Grand Hotel and the Heritage Inn, with the exception of July and August, 1985. There were a total of 125,191 vacancies during the years of 1985, '86, and '87.

Finally, it has been alleged that the Lifetime Partners *purchased* for $1,000 four days and three nights for the rest of their lives. Nothing could be further from the truth. For the sake of argument, a well-to-do parishioner or church member could contribute $1,000 a month or more. Does the parishioner purchase part of the establishment? Absolutely not! This is a gift, no different from the gift of the Lifetime Partners. The average age of the Lifetime Partners was approximately 50 years. Given a conservative life span of 20 years, a Partner would be entitled to a total of 80 days and sixty nights lodging at Heritage USA. This averages out to approximately $16 per night. Where in America can you get that kind of bargain? Even so, during the trial held in the Federal Court of the Western District of North Carolina, numerous Lifetime Partners testified that they considered the $1,000 paid as a gift to the ministry and nothing else.

Unlike most frauds in which the defendants designed a scheme to solicit large sums of money and intended to defraud the public, Bakker did not intend to defraud the Lifetime Partners. It appears that his intentions were good, as stated by the Probation Officer on page 13 of the PSI. Therefore it is my opinion that the offense behavior is a Category Five because the fraud is more than $200,000 and the appropriate guidelines (before granting parole) should be 24 to 36 months (in prison). . . . By the time Bakker has his hearing in April 1993, he will have been incarcerated approximately 43 months. It is recommended that he be paroled after service of 45 months, on June 10, 1993.[1]

Most of my friends in prison believed as Ben Malcolm that I would be released before the summer of 1993. Even the warden seemed to think that I would soon be gone. "Hi, short-timer," he quipped, when he passed me on the compound.

My case manager at Rochester too told me that because of my clean prison record, she thought I might be released to a halfway house for six months.

Jim Toms cautioned me about getting overanxious. Because mine was a high-profile case, it would probably be sent on to Washington, D.C., for a ruling by the full U.S. parole commission. Most likely that would take a minimum of sixty days for the commission to make a decision.

Jim was right. On May 3, I was called to the warden's office. I should have known that the news was bad, because everyone who talked with me around the office was somber. Robert McFadden, executive assistant to the warden, broke the bad news to me that the regional office of the U.S. parole commission had disagreed with the decision of the parole board and had sent the case on to Washington. The news was disappointing.

On May 11, the United States parole commission handed down their decision concerning my case:

Parole Denied.

The national commission determined that I must serve every day of my sentence until it expired. The commission denied parole on the basis that the amount of money involved in the case was in excess of $1 million, which made it a Category Six offense. They accepted as fact the figure of at least $130 million in fraud and therefore said that my case was more than one hundred times the cutoff amount which would have made the offensive behavior a Category Five offense. Parole guidelines suggested an offender serve between forty and fifty-two months for a Category Six offense. I had already been in prison for more than forty-three months. The parole commission wanted me to serve all fifty-two months before they would consider letting me out on parole.

Beyond that, the board wrote in their explanation of why they had turned down my request for parole: "You abused the trust implied by your chosen profession and the fact that you were a highly respected public figure."

Friends and family members who had anticipated my impending release were floored by the news. One letter that particularly ministered to me came from Dr. R. T. Kendall, minister at Westminster Chapel, in London, England and author of the book that had so profoundly touched my life in prison, *God Meant It for Good*. I had written to Dr. Kendall, thanking him for his book and the deep meaning it had helped me find in my prison experience. When Dr. Kendall heard that my parole had been denied, he wrote to encourage me:

> It is my own view that when Joseph was not allowed to be released
> from prison . . . it was then he really began to get to know God in an
> intimate manner. I predict you are going to find this to be true. I
> believe that the best is ahead for you at the spiritual level. God wants to
> know you at a level of intimacy that you have never before experienced
> and that is what is in store for you next.

The shock of being turned down by the U.S. parole commission sent me reeling. Jim Toms and Ben Malcolm, however, were not going to allow me to stay down for the count. I was permitted to appeal the U.S. parole commission's decision, but time was of the essence. The appeal must be filed within thirty days. To make the case for the appeal, I had to present the facts as best I could and answer the same questions the examiners had asked me, only with the disadvantage of not being able to appear in person.

Phil Shaw and Jamie, who had come to visit me and was staying with Phil's family, flew into action. Together with Shirley Fulbright in Florida and Jim Toms in North Carolina, we began to gather materials to present to the commission. We included pictures of Heritage USA to prove that we had, in fact, built the lodging facilities we had announced. I even had a friend take pictures of the almost-completed twenty-one-story Grand Tower and the two completed bunkhouses to prove they existed. We found brochures and newsletters describing the Lifetime Partnerships, all clearly stating that the donations were intended for use by all the ministries and operations of Heritage USA, not simply for construction costs.

We also showed examples of the various changes in the Lifetime Partner program. We included a chart to show that if we chose to use 100 percent of our facilities, once constructed, we would soon have room for 356,147 Lifetime Partners. At the time of my resignation, we had only 152,903 Lifetime Partnerships. In other words, had we been able to finish the projects that were under construction or in blueprint stages at the beginning of 1987, we would have had more than twice as much space as needed to accommodate all the Lifetime Partners on any given day. Using the information procured by Thomas Sima, Jim Toms's law clerk, we provided charts showing that we had 125,091 vacancies at the Heritage Grand Hotel and Heritage Inn during the years 1985 through 1987.

I attempted to explain to the parole commission how our original Lifetime Partnership program expanded with the full knowledge of those people involved. I told them we began in January 1984 to build a Partner lodging center at Heritage USA. This new project became the Heritage Grand Hotel. We offered a "Lifetime Partnership" to anyone who donated $1,000 to the ministry of PTL. As a way of saying thank you for their gift, the Lifetime Partners received four days and three nights free lodging at the Hotel every year for life. I had said on television and in mailings sent out to our mailing list that only twenty-five thousand of these Partnerships were available. Once they were gone, we would close the offer.

We didn't. We kept on receiving more Lifetime Partners and simply changed our original lodging offer by adding to the program other already built properties such as the ninety-six-room Heritage Inn and the Fort Heritage camping facilities to accommodate them. This brought the Partner total to 69,142. All the while, we were expanding every facet of Heritage USA and the ministries that flowed out of there. The crowds kept coming, and soon I announced the second expansion of the Lifetime Partnership program. We began building the twenty-one-story, five hundred-room Heritage Grand Towers, which was nearing completion at the time I foolishly resigned from PTL in March 1987.

The reason I was accused of fraud, I explained to the parole commission, was because by 1987, we had more than 150,000 Lifetime Partners. The government's case against us said that there was no way we could accommodate all those people and that we did not intend to do so, but were merely pocketing the money. It was like being stopped in the middle of building a house and being told, "You never really planned to build it!"

I also tried to answer some of the most pervasive questions, such as: "Who gave the money to PTL and where did it all go?" Contrary to the impression given by the prosecutors and subsequently trumpeted in the media, PTL did not receive a major portion of our donations from little old ladies. According to Dr. Patricia Kyle of FacFind, Inc., a marketing research company PTL hired to tell us about the demographics of our support base, the most frequent contributors to PTL were between the ages of twenty-six and thirty-five. The *least* frequent contributors were senior citizens over sixty-five years of age. The majority who became Lifetime Partners were of above-average incomes. Overall, visitors to Heritage USA had higher income levels than the national averages. Forty-one percent of the contributors to PTL had at least two years of college education.

Where did the money go?

William Robinson was the first government-appointed trustee of Heritage USA after Jerry Falwell took it into bankruptcy. It was William Robinson's responsibility to inventory everything at Heritage. Later, he stated on television "that the numbers show us that the money that came in basically is here at Heritage or has been used to support the projects that are here at Heritage over the past five or six years."[2]

I now felt that I had taken too large a salary during my final years at PTL and had allowed some of the top people on our staff, such as Reverend Dortch, to receive salaries that were unwise for a ministry to pay. Because of the rocket-like speed of our growth, we made many mistakes. We sometimes spent money unwisely. Nevertheless, apart from the money spent on payroll, TV airtime, and missions, the bulk of the money contributed to PTL was right there on the property.

The financial figures I included in this section of my appeal all came from certified audits done by the highly respected "Big Eight" auditing firms who handled PTL's accounting for the years 1984 through 1986. Unfortunately, the figures provided by the auditors were never introduced in my original trial. It is understandable why the prosecutors did not focus on the audits as evidence. What puzzled me, both then and now, is why my own lawyers didn't present the audited figures to counteract the implied accusations of mismanagement of funds. When I asked my lawyers that question, they replied that we did not have enough money for outside research work to be done on my case. The lawyers used the same excuse when I asked them to subpoena videotapes of the television programs I had done while at PTL. The tapes, which are still in existence today, would have established my case because I specifically and emphatically stated two things: I repeatedly announced when the Lifetime Partnership programs were changing, so nobody could say we were trying to deceive them, and I repeatedly reminded the viewers that even though they were able to stay at Heritage USA in return for their financial gift, they were not purchasing time-shares by becoming Lifetime Partners. They were donating the money to the ministry to be used wherever it was needed.

Shirley Fulbright and Jim Toms sent some books and brochures from which I cut pictures with my prison-purchased, blunt-edged, mustache scissors and pasted them onto separate pages. Again and again, I pasted in the question: "Where did the money go?" and then tried to show a photo of some aspect of Heritage USA, with the amount it cost to build and maintain it. For instance, using the auditors' figures only from the years 1984 to 1987, the years during which we had implemented the Lifetime Partnership programs, I listed and illustrated with photos:

$171 million to build and equip Heritage USA between 1984 and 1987 (many structural parts of Heritage USA had already been built before that time period).

$35 million for general operating expenses.

$13 million to build Heritage Island (the famous water slide and giant swimming area).

$22 million for food, retail shops, and lodging costs besides the Grand Hotel and the Grand Towers.

$1 million for the Passion Play presented in the amphitheater nightly during the summer months.

$17 million to pay interest on loans, accounting fees, and legal fees.

$91 million to pay for television time to stations that aired our program and broadcasting on our own satellite broadcasting system.

$101 million for wages and salaries. In 1987, we employed approximately 2,400 people and had a $25-million payroll.

$17 million for Bibles and books.

$15 million for printing and postage.

$21 million for real estate development. This was the area in which we were building houses and condominiums for the people who wanted to live at Heritage USA all year long.

$1 million per year to put on our annual Christmas City display.

$15 million for maintenance and utilities. This included water towers, wells, sewage treatment plants, phone systems, electric power, roads, landscaping, maintenance, and warehousing. These things are often taken for granted by the average visitor to a public place, but the costs are gigantic.

We also included in the appeal copies of the court record showing the shocking disparity between what the government said I had built at PTL and the projects for which I had actually overseen the construction. The government had contended, "Bakker used relatively few of the funds solicited from the partners to construct promised facilities. In fact, of the proposed Heritage Village facilities, only the Grand Hotel and one bunkhouse were actually completed."[3]

Few of the funds! Only two buildings! Anyone who had ever come within camera range of Heritage USA could have disproved that statement. Yet it went uncontested in my trial and my appeal. In truth, during the time I was president of PTL, we built over one hundred buildings! Granted, many of them were not lodging facilities, but the impression given by the prosecutors was that I had used millions of dollars on my own lavish lifestyle while the people who donated money to PTL were being ripped off because we did not build what we said we were going to construct.

Even while Tammy Faye and I were in California attending the Betty Ford program, construction continued at Heritage USA. Had I not resigned in March 1987, we would have continued to build according to our master plan that I had shared with the community leaders of Fort Mill in January of that year. God had always helped me through the most desperate financial situations in the past, so I had no reason to doubt that, with His help, we would make it even then. The Bible says, "Now faith is the substance of things hoped for, the evidence of things not seen" (Heb. 11:1 KJV). The government and the media dealt in hard facts and figures, however, and they were convinced that PTL had been tottering on the precipice, ready for a great financial fall, even before my resignation. To those of us who had worked in Christian ministry, it was just normal, everyday life.

All of this information and much more we put into the 144-page appeal to the parole commission. Phil Shaw then had the pages copied and bound together in plastic binders. Jamie Charles and a group of volunteers put together fifty color copies and hundreds of black-and-white copies of the appeal and sent them to significant pastors and Christian leaders who might be willing to write to the parole commission on my behalf. We also prepared five sets of the material for the national commissioners.

384

Jamie spent hours every day calling Christian leaders all across the country—at Phil Shaw's expense—asking high-profile Christians to send a letter to the commissioner. The responses were mixed, but many pastors and leaders readily agreed to write and to help any way they could.

The call that most surprised Jamie was to Jimmy Swaggart. Jimmy and I had never been close friends before the disclosure of his or my moral failures, nor were we close friends afterwards. We had corresponded twice by mail, however, in 1992. Jimmy's letters were encouraging, yet noncommittal. Jimmy continued to deny that he had had anything to do with my demise at PTL. Jamie always had a love and respect for Jimmy Swaggart as a man of God. Much of that had been eroded by the events of the past few years, but Jamie decided to call Swaggart anyhow and ask him to help.

Jamie reached a secretary, and after he had identified himself and given the purpose for his call, Jimmy Swaggart came on the line.

"Well, hello, Jay," Jimmy's big voice boomed into the phone. "What can I do for you?"

Jamie explained that he was calling pastors, television preachers, and other Christian leaders in an attempt to generate support for me at my upcoming parole hearing.

"How can I help?" Jimmy asked without Jamie having to ask.

Not expecting Jimmy Swaggart to be so cooperative, Jamie stumbled around for a moment before suggesting, "Well, you could put the address of the parole commission on the screen during your TV program and encourage people to write on Dad's behalf."

"All right, I'll do it," Jimmy answered. "I've always felt that your dad's sentence was grossly unfair." Jimmy and Jamie talked for a while longer and Jamie asked Jimmy Swaggart to forgive him for the hard feelings he had held toward the man since 1987. It was the beginning of changes in my son's heart.

Another of Jamie's life-changing phone calls was to Mark DeMoss, Jerry Falwell's young associate. Since I had first met Mark at the Maxim's Hotel in March 1987, he had continued to work with Jerry Falwell, serving as his administrative assistant and director of public relations until August 1991, when he moved to Atlanta and established his own public relations firm.

In May, Mark had mentioned to Jim Toms that he would be willing to contact some nationally known Christian leaders, requesting a letter of support to be sent to the parole commission in my support. Jim had encouraged the idea but had not pursued Mark's suggestion.

In mid-June Mark DeMoss traveled to Des Moines, Iowa, to meet with Jamie, Phil Shaw, and Jim Albert, the law professor from Drake

University. They spent five hours together, and Jamie tore into Mark, telling him in no uncertain terms how he felt about the coup that Mark had been a part of that eventually led to my imprisonment. Mark listened graciously to Jamie's tirade. He did not attempt to dispute Jamie's accusations or defend his former boss's actions or motives. Mark merely listened and let Jamie know that he wanted to be his friend. During the meeting and again afterward, Mark mentioned that he would be glad to encourage some high-profile national Christian leaders to write to the parole commission on my behalf. On his own accord, Mark stuck his neck out for me.

More than three thousand letters poured into the parole commission in Washington. Meanwhile, Mark DeMoss collected letters from numerous well-known Christians. Some of the people who wrote on my behalf had done so before. Pat Boone wrote another kind letter, as did Charles Colson.

Other letters came from several unexpected sources. The letter that surprised me the most came from none other than Reverend Jerry Falwell. Jerry had expressed on several occasions that he had felt my forty-five-year sentence and the reduced sentences were unduly excessive and unreasonable. Jerry passed on those sentiments to the parole commission.

Similar concerns were addressed by members of the legal community. David A. Funk, professor of law at Indiana University School of Law, wrote to the U.S. parole commission, "In my view, for what it is worth, the conviction and imprisonment of this man truly does constitute the greatest American miscarriage of justice of the twentieth century."

Of all the letters written to the parole commission, nobody understood the case better than Professor Jim Albert of Drake University Law School. He had studied my case for more than a year, had read every page of the transcripts of my trial, and had made notes throughout that raised points he felt should have been addressed or could have caused a mistrial. Most gratifying to me, Jim Albert was convinced beyond a doubt of my innocence, not on the basis of my personality, spirituality, or past positions, but on the sole basis of the evidence and the facts. Although he had not been a supporter of PTL, he became convinced that the case was not only an insult to me but to people of faith in general.

Jim began his letter by relating some of his formidable credentials, and he explained how he came to be involved in my case, then went on:

> What I have learned about that trial prompts several questions about its conduct. The transcript is clear that the trial judge allowed the prosecution to belittle some of Mr. Bakker's key witnesses, including Arnold Santjer, whose evangelical religious beliefs were mocked and ridiculed by the prosecutors in the presence of the jury. It appears that in that

way the focus of the trial was wrongly shifted from the question of fraud to the reasonableness and acceptability of Mr. Bakker's religious beliefs. The government's major emphasis on Bakker's lifestyle, with testimony the first day ranging from jewelry purchases and cars to Jessica Hahn, belies the prosecutors' often stated explanation that this was a garden variety fraud case. I don't think it was tried as one—they kept beating the jury over the head with testimony and evidence of the elegance of Bakker's lifestyle. The strategy was obviously effective, but I think they got an inordinate number of bumps and plenty of free mileage toward the fraud counts with that kind of red meat for the jury. It surely doesn't read like a fraud case.

I have interviewed Mr. Santjer at length and was staggered by what he told me. Not only did the jury laugh and giggle when the prosecutor belittled his statement that God had made it possible for him to earn the money that he did in his life (he was asked whether God had signed his paychecks, if that was indeed the case and the prosecutor smirked and the jury erupted in laughter), but I have now talked to two people who were in that courtroom during Mr. Santjer's testimony who have told me that while Mr. Santjer was testifying Judge Potter sat shaking his head with his fingers in his ears. One focus of my article is the signals that the Judge was sending to the jury and the permissiveness of the Judge allowing the prosecutors to humiliate Mr. Bakker's witnesses and belittle their religious beliefs. It could credibly be argued that, as a result, Mr. Bakker was denied a fair trial. I have researched the narrow question of prosecutorial misconduct which takes that exact form, *vis* belittling the religious beliefs of witnesses and found rock solid authority for the proposition that such conduct violates the constitutional fair trial right of an accused. *United States v. Ballard*, 322 U.S. 78 (1944); *Munn v. Algee*, 924 F.2d 568 (5th Cir. 1991).

I wish that these points had been raised on appeal, but they were not. Based on the case law that I have cited, I think they would have been most relevant on the appeal of the case and would have justified the Fourth Circuit overturning the conviction. I present these facts to you, then, as new information which in your discretion may warrant a parole at this time.

Jim Bakker was probably careless and inattentive to matters financial, relying on others, but I haven't seen any persuasive evidence of intent. He was a man of the cloth, one whose whole life was his religion. He preached an optimistic, miracle-filled and abundant evangelism that admittedly inspired millions of people. I think that a person like that operates on a completely different plane than most of us in the sense that he believed in miracles and in the Holy Spirit moving him to raise money and to build a Christian retreat and vacation center at Heritage USA. His broadcasts were always spontaneous and, in a sense, stream of consciousness outpourings by he and his wife as they were moved on the air to talk optimistically about all that they were doing and planning to do. I have read the transcripts and, for the life of me, I can't see the intent to defraud in them. I have also seen the fund-raising brochures and the solicitations mailed to the PTL contributors and each of those solicitations contains a very plain legend that the monies received would be used for any of the ministry's purposes. And, I have read the November 6, 1991 decision of United States Bankruptcy Judge William Thurmond Bishop which concluded that the premise upon which the government convicted Jim Bakker in that courtroom in Charlotte was simply invalid. As you know, Judge Bishop found that "[i]t was not contemplated that Lifetime Partners would be entitled to a specific hotel room, condominium, or unit on the premises nor more importantly, were Lifetime Partners promised availability of rooms or any other benefits for the use of their partnership." He also found that "the benefits of the Lifetime Partner memberships were being delivered and provided" by Mr. Bakker.

I would submit that the analysis of these same facts provided by Judge Bishop also constitutes the kind of new information which would justify a parole. The consideration given by Judge Bishop certainly stands in sharp contrast to the hostility which Judge Potter openly displayed toward Mr. Bakker, his witnesses and their religious beliefs in the presence of the jury in the fraud trial and in sharp contrast to the atmosphere that prevailed in that courtroom when jurors were laughing out loud at the sincere and honest answers concerning the religious beliefs of Mr. Bakker's witnesses.

I also strongly disagree with the position taken and representations made by the prosecutors in their May 3, 1991 sentencing memorandum and the affidavit of John Brugger which is attached to it to the effect that the unbelievable forty-five year sentence imposed was appropriate for the crime for which Jim Bakker was convicted. Mr. Brugger makes reference to the sentence imposed on Michael Milken as an example of the strict punishment justified in these cases. Of course, Milken is now free and I've got a file two inches thick of wire fraud and securities fraud opinions where the fraud perpetrated was far more serious than that proved in Jim Bakker's case and the sentences imposed significantly less severe. Particularly, people in these cases are simply not incarcerated for eighteen or forty-five years. That is even more true given the lack of intent to defraud on Mr. Bakker's part and the purposes for which he was raising that money. It was certainly not to defraud those contributors. If he had intended to do that, he would not have built a five star hotel and furnished each room as elegantly as he did. Each room was fancier than the nicest hotel I've ever stayed in. Bakker chose the furnishings himself. If he really was raising this money to defraud his contributors and "rip them off," it seems to me he would have built a less elegant hotel and decorated it more cheaply given the premise that he knew he was overselling and the contributors wouldn't ever see or use those rooms.

I honestly believe that Mr. Bakker's trial was tainted in the ways I've suggested. The *New Yorker* concluded that, as well, Mr. Bakker was not provided a vigorous defense. Jurors that magazines interviewed were quoted as saying that they were waiting to hear Jim Bakker's side of it and his defense to the charges but that it never came. That is a provocative aspect of this, too and one that I find coalesced with Mr. Bakker's own lack of any appreciation of his true legal exposure in the case. Whether it was a fair fight or whether an attorney more experienced in defending public figures charged with crimes could have successfully defended him is something that haunts me.

Please allow me to share some of my impressions of Mr. Bakker as they relate to the fairness in allowing him to be released from prison now. He has obviously been pulling himself up by his bootstraps from that sinkhole that was the national humiliation of being convicted and shackled and ridiculed on television sets in tens of millions of homes. He is taking college courses in prison through a community college there in Rochester and a Bible College in the Twin Cities. He is becoming computer literate. His correspondence to me has been intelligent, positive and insightful. He has really pulled his life together and I think stands as a model prisoner.

I have spent several days over the past twelve months with Mr. Bakker in Rochester. I have been struck by his repentance, his introspection and his forgiving and nonmalicious outlook on life. He has certainly been broken. Everything he owned has been taken away. His wife has left him. And he is attempting to raise, as a single parent, his son who has remained in Florida and who is very close to his dad. His son happens to be dyslexic, as is my own son and I know something about how important it is on a day-to-day basis for a child with a learning disability to have the nurturing and support that only a parent can provide. And Mr. Bakker is doing it from prison, but that child is having trouble getting through high school and is now in a computer therapy program. I would simply urge that some compassion be shown for that child which would allow him to be reunited with his father and permit him to receive the daily parenting that is necessary for someone like him with a mental disability to cope in this world.

I honestly believe that to release him would not only recognize all that he has done to deserve it, but would provide you an opportunity of historic dimension to reflect the compassion and forgiveness which [have] always defined this country.

Even more importantly, I believe a wrong has been done here and that it should be righted. The trial was turned into a referendum on whether that jury thought the religious beliefs of Mr. Bakker and his followers were acceptable. To have voted to acquit after the focus of that trial was thus shifted would have required a juror to embrace those evangelical beliefs. And that is why I am so troubled by that trial. If the framers intended nothing else by the First Amendment, it was to prohibit that type of inquiry in a court of law in this country. Jim Bakker's religious beliefs were put on trial.

I could see other benefits to society in releasing Mr. Bakker. The new Jim Bakker, down but now rehabilitated, preaching a message of forgiveness and compassion himself, could be a boost to this country. Frankly, in the context of all the gloom and doom I see on television today, the euphoria and optimism of Jim Bakker's programs would be refreshing again. I would think that he could be a powerful role model with a message of hope and belief in God even when a person is at the very bottom in their life.

He is not vindictive in any way, shape or form and I am sure would not use his freedom to seek vengeance from those who toppled him. He would not be looking back, he would be looking forward. He is not a hateful man. There does not appear to be a mean streak in him and I certainly can't see him abusing his freedom by attacking his accusers or the system that I think failed.

I am a believer in the system. If I were not, I couldn't send hundreds of law students each year into it. And I believe that, at some point, justice will be done in Jim Bakker's case. I hope that you are the ones to do it and I thank you for considering these comments.

Sincerely,
James A. Albert
Professor of Law
Drake University Law School
Michael G. Galligan Law Firm, P.C.

Professor Albert sent me a copy of his letter to the parole commission and I included it in my appeal. If they had not read it previously, they had another opportunity to do so as they considered my case. I could not help remembering R. T. Kendall's words once again, "This is another sign that God's time has come: when someone pleads your case (and knows all the facts) without your opening your mouth."[4]

Thank you, Professor Albert. Thank you, R. T. Kendall. Thank You, God!

Certainly I wanted to be set free. More than ever, though, I felt that my case was completely in the hands of God. He had raised up Professor Albert to plead my case; if God wanted me to be free now, the commission could not prevent it. On the other hand, if God had more for me to learn in prison, the best-argued case to the parole commission would not win my freedom. As Chuck Colson had advised me during his visit with me in prison, I had fought my case, but I had to let go of it.

On Tuesday, July 27, 1993, *Los Angeles Times Syndicate* writer Cal Thomas made my parole the topic of his column. Cal had been a close associate of Jerry Falwell and the Moral Majority during my tenure at PTL. That's why I was surprised when Thomas wrote:

> But perhaps Bakker should never have been sentenced to prison. He was a nonviolent, nondangerous offender and there are already too many of them being warehoused expensively in federal and state institutions. They take up space that could be used for those who are serious threats to the public. In fact, because of overcrowding, the truly dangerous get out early, often serving just a fraction of their sentences. Restitution and community service for Jim Bakker and for many white-collar criminals would be far preferable to several years in prison. . . . [5]

The same day Cal's article first appeared on newsstands across the country, the U.S. parole commission was meeting in Washington and deciding my case. They must not have deliberated long; the response came almost immediately.

391

Knowing that my freedom from incarceration had already been decided by a higher court did not lessen the blow when it came.

Parole denied.

On July 27, 1993, the national commissioners rejected my appeal and affirmed their previous decision in its entirety. I was to stay in prison the maximum length of time the law allowed for my sentence and for an inmate with my exemplary record in prison.

Basically, the parole commission was saying, "We believe that you never intended to build enough lodging space for all the Lifetime Partners." The Commission's report continued:

> You claim that no promise was ever made that the entire donations solicited would be used other than for your ministry. This is correct. You conclude that the donors were therefore not victims of any fraudulent misrepresentation. The Commission disagrees. The fraudulent misrepresentation was that (a) the hotel and other forms of lodging would actually be constructed in the near future and (b) there would be free lodging for each "partnership" on a reasonably available basis. Therefore, you were not free to abandon your hotel construction projects while continuing to solicit (and to receive) money on the strength of the promised "partnerships." Over $100 million was solicited for construction projects such as $74 million for the Towers Hotel which were never completed. Your scheme was criminally fraudulent because you kept soliciting money with promises of free lodging long after you knew that your operating costs made construction of those lodgings impossible.[6]

I began to wonder if the commission even read my appeal. In full-color photographs, I had pointed out to the commission that not only were we going to construct the Tower, we had done so! The twenty-one story building was there! As long as I was president of PTL, construction was continuing on not only the Tower, but numerous other projects as well. The Tower was only weeks away from being completed and stands at Heritage USA to this day.

All of our charts, explanations, and pictures were for naught. These people wanted me to stay in prison . . . apparently God did too.

48

I Was Wrong

DURING MY TIME AT F.M.C. ROCHESTER, I OBSERVED something that it seemed to me had gotten nearly every inmate into trouble. It was something insidious, pervasive, something that I too had tried to cover and push aside in my own life—the love of money. The underlying reason why some of the bankers, Wall Street businessmen, doctors, and others are in prison is because of something they did to get more money. I realized that of the 60 percent of inmates who are in prison because of drug-related crimes, most are not there because of an addiction to drugs; they are there because of an addiction to the drug of money. It was their insatiable desire for more money that led them to selling drugs in the first place, not a desire to ruin someone else's life by getting him or her hooked. Unimpeded, that lust for money carries the potential to destroy both the buyer and the seller.

About the time of my parole hearing, I completed my study of all the words of Jesus in the New Testament. To my surprise, after months of studying Jesus, I concluded that He did not have one good thing to say about money.

As the true impact of Jesus' words regarding money impacted my heart and mind, I became physically nauseated. I was wrong. I was wrong! Wrong in my lifestyle, certainly, but even more fundamentally, wrong in my understanding of the Bible's true message. Not only was I wrong, but I was teaching the opposite of what Jesus had said. That is what broke my heart; when I came to the awareness that I had actually been contradicting Christ, I was horrified.

For years I had embraced and espoused a gospel that some skeptics had branded as a "prosperity gospel." I didn't mind the label; on the contrary, I was proud of it. "You're absolutely right!" I'd say to critics and friends alike. "I preach it and live it! I believe in a God who wants to bless His people. Look at all the rich saints in the Old Testament. And the New Testament clearly says that above all, God wants us to prosper even as our souls prosper. If your soul is prospering, you should be prospering materially as well!"

I even got to the point where I was teaching people at PTL, "Don't pray, 'God, Your will be done,' when you're praying for health or wealth. You already know it is God's will for you to have those things! To ask God to confirm His will when He has already told you what His will is in a matter is an insult to God. It is as though you don't really believe that He is as good as His Word. Instead of praying 'Thy will be done' when you want a new car, just claim it. Pray specifically and tell God what kind you want. Be sure to specify what options and what color you want too."

Such arrogance! Such foolishness! Such sin! The Bible says we are not to presume upon God, but we should say, "If the Lord wills, we shall live and do this or that" (James 4:15).

I may not always have been so blatant about it, but I often preached a prosperity message at Heritage USA and on our *PTL* television programs. But when I began to study the Scriptures in depth while in prison, something I am embarrassed and ashamed to admit that I rarely took time to do at PTL, I was very distressed at what I discovered.

I realized that for years I helped propagate an impostor, not a true gospel, but a gospel that stated "God wants you to be rich!" Christians are children of God, "King's kids," as I often put it. And shouldn't the King's kids have the best this world had to offer?

The more I studied the Bible, however, I had to admit that the prosperity message did not line up with the tenor of Scripture. My heart was crushed to think that I led so many people astray. I was appalled that I could have been so wrong, and I was deeply grateful that God had not struck me dead as a false prophet!

How could I have taught and even written books on the subject of "how to get rich" when Jesus spoke so clearly about the dangers of earthly riches? One of the statements of Jesus that kept echoing in my head and heart was in the parable of the sower, where Jesus said that "the cares of this world, the deceitfulness of riches, and the desires for other things entering in choke the word, and it becomes unfruitful" (Mark 4:19). *The deceitfulness of riches.* The more I thought about it, the more I had to admit that I had fallen into that snare. I had allowed the quest for material possessions and the deceitfulness of riches and the lusts for other things to choke the Word of God in my own life and in the lives of my family members and coworkers. As PTL grew larger and our ministry more widespread, I had a financial tiger by the tail, and just coming up with enough money to meet the daily budgets dominated my thoughts and my time.

In prison, I decided to dig into the Scriptures further to see what else Jesus had to say about money. I noticed that He said,

> Do not store up for yourself treasures on earth, where moth and rust destroy, and where thieves break in and steal. But store up for yourselves treasures in heaven, where moth and rust do not destroy, and where thieves do not break in and steal. For where your treasure is, there your heart will be also. (Matt. 6:19-21 NIV)

Another Scripture that seared into my heart was Matthew 6:24, "No one can serve two masters. Either he will hate the one and love the other, or he will be devoted to the one and despise the other. You cannot serve both God and Money" (NIV). In that same passage, I discovered that God's priorities were much different from what mine had been.

Jesus said,

> Therefore I tell you, do not worry about your life, what you will eat or drink; or about your body, what you will wear. Is not life more important than food, and the body more important than clothes? . . .
>
> So do not worry, saying, "What shall we eat?" or "What shall we drink?" or "What shall we wear?" For the pagans run after all these things and your heavenly Father knows that you need them. But seek first his kingdom and his righteousness, and all these things will be given to you as well. (Matt. 6:25, 31-33 NIV)

Other teachings of Jesus scored direct hits upon my heart, as well:

"But woe to you who are rich, / for you have already received your comfort" (Luke 6:24 NIV).

"Then Jesus said to his disciples, 'If anyone would come after me, he must deny himself and take up his cross and follow me'" (Matt. 16:24 NIV). This verse dramatically illustrated the stark contrast between what Jesus taught and what I had been teaching. I had taught that Christians could have the best of both worlds, the best that this world had to offer and heaven too. Jesus said, "Deny yourself."

Jesus taught, "How hard it is for the rich to enter the kingdom of God! Indeed, it is easier for a camel to go through the eye of a needle than for a rich man to enter the kingdom of God" (Luke 18:24 NIV). Unwittingly, I had tried to explain this verse away with the help of modern scholarship. I had taught people that the "eye of the needle" of which Jesus spoke was a low arch in the Holy Land. Supposedly, a camel carrying a heavy load had to get down on its knees to slip through the "eye of the needle." This was the explanation that I had heard from other prosperity teachers whom I admired and respected, so I simply passed on their explanation as fact without really examining the verse carefully, especially in the original Greek. Nor had I consulted any Bible dictionaries or encyclopedias.

In prison, however, when I took time to study the meaning of Jesus' words in the original Greek language, I discovered that Jesus was not talking about camels walking on their knees at all. The word He used was one commonly used to describe a *sewing needle*, not an archway. The verse meant exactly what it said: It may not be impossible for a rich man to enter heaven, but apart from a miracle of God, he doesn't stand a chance!

The more I studied, the more I had to face the awful truth: I had been preaching false doctrine for years and hadn't even known it! At PTL I had been doing just the opposite of Jesus' words by teaching people to fall in love with money. Jesus never equated His blessings with material things, but I had done just that. I had laid so much emphasis upon material things, I was subtly encouraging people to put their hearts into things, rather than into Jesus.

Was Heritage USA of God? I believe it was; I believe the original concept was His and that He planted it in my heart. But as I said before, Heritage USA—with all its facilities and buildings—was the box, the package. The box was meant to enhance people's appreciation of the true gift, Jesus Christ, but before long, many people began to worship the box . . . and I allowed them to do so; no, I encouraged them to do so by what I was teaching and by the manner in which I was living. I lived the prosperity message I was preaching. I should have taught people to fall in love with Jesus rather than the trappings.

Sadly, long after I left Heritage USA, some people still wanted to worship the box. Others compromised their values trying to be the boss of the box, and still others nearly sold their souls in attempt to get . . . what? The box? So many people tried to save the box, saying they wanted to save the ministry, but I have never heard a building preach a sermon or a box reach out and help a hurting person. How sad. The box is empty without Jesus.

I began to share some of the things I was learning with several of the Christian inmates with whom I often discussed the Bible. I was stunned by their responses. Rather than being excited that I had finally come to a knowledge of the truth, they were aghast that I was denying what they considered to be sound spiritual principles taught by sincere men and women of God.

"I was sincere about what I taught too," I told them, "but I was sincerely wrong. Just because somebody repeats something often or loudly does not make it true. The big question is: 'What does the Word of God say?'"

To their credit, the guys replied, "Well, what *does* the Word say?" In response, we looked up verse after verse as I pointed out to them what Jesus had to say about money. The guys accepted Jesus' words as authoritative, but then they developed a bad case of the "Yes, buts."

"Yes, but doesn't Jesus also say that He came that we might have an abundant life?" asked David, an inmate whose background was steeped in the prosperity message. We turned to John 10:10 and read, "I am come that they might have life and that they might have it more abundantly" (KJV). It was a wonderful statement by Jesus Himself, so I could easily see how David had related it to material prosperity. As we looked up the words in a Greek-English dictionary, however, we found that the Greek word for "life" used in this verse was *zoe*, a word indicating "life in the spirit and soul" rather than the word *bios*, which is used to refer to physical, material life. Of the two words, *zoe* is usually considered the more noble, higher word. Basically, Jesus was saying, "I want you to have an abundant life in the spirit, which is My highest and best for you."

"Hey, that verse doesn't have anything to do with material prosperity," David said, as the light turned on in his heart and mind. "If abundant life meant having houses, cars, riches, parties, and entertainment, then I guess the world is experiencing abundant life. Yet we have more hatred, disease, and pain than ever."

"Not only that," piped up Jorge, a Spanish guy with a big smile who had walked into my cell and was leaning up against the bunks as he watched David and me searching through the Bible reference books, "but if you're figurin' how much God loves you by how much money you have or what kind of car you drive, or how big a house you live in, what happens when all that stuff is gone?" Jorge had hit the nail right on the head.

The next night after work, David and Jorge were back. David had talked to his Christian girlfriend on the telephone that afternoon and she had told him, "Of course God wants us to prosper, David. You know the Bible even says so in 3 John, verse two."

I knew the verse well. It had been my favorite "prosperity verse" for years; it was the premier New Testament verse upon which I had built my prosperity message and lifestyle. The verse reads: "Beloved, I wish above all things that thou mayest prosper and be in health, even as thy soul prospereth" (KJV).

I had preached on this verse for most of my ministry. It said exactly what I believed—that God wanted His people to prosper, and by that, I interpreted it to mean prosper financially and materially, in other words, to get rich. Again, I never really examined the true meaning of the text, nor did I ever seriously consider why this verse, on the surface anyhow, seemed to contradict so much of what the New Testament said in other places. I simply pulled this verse out of context and took it to the bank—literally!

"First of all, let's look at this verse, David," I said. "We have to take the whole counsel of God's Word, just like Jesus says in Matthew 4:4, 'Man shall not live by bread alone, but by *every* word that proceedeth out of the mouth of God.'" We began going through the verse, word by word, deciphering the meaning from the Greek with the help of a few Bible reference books someone had sent me. I didn't tell David that I had been tearing this verse apart for nearly two years and trying to find where it fit with the message of Jesus.

It did not fit. No matter how hard I tried to make my former interpretation of 3 John 2 consistent with the words of Jesus, the verse as I had understood it simply did not make sense. How could John be saying, "above all things, I want you to prosper"? First, David and I looked up the meaning of the word *prosper* in a dictionary. The various forms of the word all had one common meaning: "to increase in wealth."

"David, tell me something," I said pausing and pointing to the Bible. "Jesus said that our number one concern was to love God supremely; after that we are to love our neighbors as ourselves. Why, then, would John say that 'above all' I should have wealth?"

"I don't know, Jim," David replied. "What do you think?"

I ignored David's question and asked him another. "Do you think God wants you to have money above your soul's salvation?"

"No. Of course not!"

We looked up the meaning of the word *prosper*. We found the word translated "prosper" in the King James Version of the Bible came from a Greek word, *euodoo*, which is made up of two Greek root words, *eu*, which means "good," and *hodos*, which means "road, or route, a progress, or journey." We did not find a single reference in the Greek to money, riches, or material gain from the word translated *prosper* in the King James Version.

The apostle John, the writer, was saying simply, "I wish you a good, safe and healthy journey throughout your life, even as your soul has a good and safe journey to heaven."

John was not saying "Above everything else, I want you to get rich. Above everything, you should prosper and make money." That is not even implied in the true meaning of the verse. Yet I had based much of my philosophy at PTL and even before that on this one verse that I had totally misunderstood!

David reluctantly agreed that to base a prosperity doctrine on this verse would be shaky indeed, but he was not yet ready to abandon his belief in the prosperity message with which he had been indoctrinated. He took some of the notes from our study sessions and wrote to several leading "prosperity preachers," some of whom were close friends of mine. Day after day, David was back, armed with more books sent to him by prosperity teachers.

"Jim, look at this!" David said as he pointed to a passage in the Old Testament. "Look here. It says right here that God has given us the power to get wealth. Now, why would God give us that power, if He didn't expect us to use it?"

I looked at the passage to which David was pointing. I wasn't surprised to see that he had been referred by some of my friends to Deuteronomy 8:18. I had used the verse myself in countless messages and appeals for money. The verse reads, "But thou shalt remember the LORD thy God: for it is he that giveth thee power to get wealth, that he may establish his covenant which he swore unto thy fathers, as it is this day" (KJV).

At first glance, the verse did seem to support the idea that God is the one who gives us the power to get rich. When David and I read the verse in context with the entire passage of Deuteronomy 8:1-18, however, it took on a different meaning. We realized that what God is actually saying to His people in this passage is, "When I bring you out of Egypt into the Promised Land and you are enjoying the blessings I have given to you, don't think that you have been successful in your own strength. Don't say that it is your own power, that you did all this yourself." The Lord then warns His people to remember that He is the one who deserves the glory. All God was saying was, "When you get into the Promised Land, don't forget who brought you there and gave to you everything that you have."

I admit, in the past I had used this verse to make it sound as though it was God's will to make everyone wealthy and if any of His people were poor, it was probably due to lack of faith or not applying the biblical "formulas" correctly. That was an improper interpretation of the passage. Yes, it is God who gives us the power to receive all that we have, but to assume that He wants all His people to be wealthy based on this Scripture is an illegitimate extension of that truth.

As David and I studied the Scriptures concerning material wealth, he became convinced that the Bible does not teach that God wants us to be rich in material possessions. "But Jim, doesn't God want to bless His people?" David asked.

"Of course He does," I replied, "but we don't have to twist the Scriptures into saying something they don't mean. There are plenty of passages in the Bible that tell us that God will provide for us, and as we honor Him by using the resources that He gives us for His glory, He will continue to pour out even greater blessings upon us."

God has promised to bless those people who put Him first in their lives. That principle has never changed. I still believe that God blesses His people and will meet their needs. The sin is falling in love with and seeking after money and material things. He doesn't want us to equate mere money with godliness. In fact, the apostle Paul said that "If any man teach otherwise, and consent not to wholesome words, even the words of our Lord Jesus Christ, and to the doctrine which is according to godliness . . . supposing that gain is godliness: from such withdraw thyself. But godliness with contentment is great gain" (1 Tim. 6:3, 5-6 KJV).

For the first time, I began to really understand what Paul meant when he wrote,

> But they that will be rich [which I discovered meant: "they that want to be rich"] fall into temptation and a snare, and into many foolish and hurtful lusts, which drown men in destruction and perdition. For the love of money is the root of all evil: which while some coveted after, they have erred from the faith, and pierced themselves through with many sorrows. But thou, O man of God, flee these things; and follow after righteousness, godliness, faith, love, patience, meekness. (1 Tim. 6:9-11 KJV)

For years I had glossed over that passage of Scripture. I ignored it, made excuses for it, or tried to explain it away. I refused to accept the obvious interpretation. I now see that the message was right there all the time, so plain that even a child could see it and understand it. I was wrong.

I had influenced so many people to accept a "prosperity message," I now felt that I had a responsibility to tell my friends what I had been learning from my studies of the Bible. I wrote a straightforward letter and sent it to some of the people who had written to me in prison. I told of the verses I had used improperly and what I had discovered by studying the true meaning of those verses. I apologized for preaching a gospel that emphasized earthly prosperity rather than spiritual riches. I wrote, "I ask all who have sat under my ministry to forgive me for preaching a gospel emphasizing earthly prosperity. Jesus said, 'Do not lay up for yourselves treasures on earth.' He wants us to be in love with only Him."

> Many today believe that the evidence of God's blessing on them is a new car, a house, a good job, etc. But that is far from the truth of God's Word. If that be the case, then gambling casino owners, drug kingpins and movie stars are blessed of God. Jesus did not teach riches were a sign of God's blessings. In fact, Jesus said, "It is hard for a rich man to enter the Kingdom of Heaven." And He talked about the "deceitfulness of riches. . . ." There is no way, if you take the whole counsel of God's Word, that you can equate riches or material things as a sign of God's blessing.
>
> If we equate earthly possessions and earthly relationships with God's favor, what are we to tell the billions of those living in poverty, or what do you do if depression hits, or what do you say to those who lose a loved one? Many "in name only" Christians would curse God if they lost all of their material possessions.

The Charlotte Observer got a copy of my letter and ran portions of it on the front page under the headline: "Ministry of Prosperity Was Mistake, Bakker Tells Friends." Other publications picked up on the story, and ran excerpts of the letter as well.

Some people were appalled that I—a person they considered as a primary propagator of the prosperity message in the twentieth century—had disavowed my former teaching. Others who wrote to me were delighted that I had "finally seen the light."

Some people saw the reversal of my position on prosperity theology as self-serving, as an attempt to curry favor with the judicial system. Others were concerned that just as I had gone overboard on the prosperity message previously, I was now going overboard on a message of austerity and self-sacrifice as a result of my prison experience.

Frankly, I was not greatly concerned with what the critics or the skeptics had to say about my speaking out against the prosperity message. I knew what God had clearly shown me from His Word. I had studied every word of Jesus over a period of two years, and I was convinced that the prosperity message was at best an aberration and at worst "another gospel" contrary to the gospel of Jesus Christ.

I had accepted Jesus as my Savior and with my lips I had called Him "Lord," but in my heart and lifestyle, I now realized that He was not the

Lord of my life; I was. As I came to grips with Jesus' words in Matthew 7:21, however, I was shattered. Jesus said, "Not every one that saith unto me, Lord, Lord, shall enter into the kingdom of heaven; but he that doeth the will of my Father which is in heaven" (KJV). Jesus was saying, "You can sound religious; you can do great works in My name; you can even preach the gospel, cast out devils, and do wonderful things—ostensibly for God—and still miss heaven."

Although I was committed to following Jesus, I wanted to do it my way rather than His; I had given my life to Him, but I was still in control of it. I had attempted to compartmentalize my relationship with Him, giving Him control of certain parts of me, yet not surrendering to His absolute Lordship.

In prison, I came to the end of Jim Bakker. God was teaching me that I must "die" daily and that the process would continue for the remainder of my life. The more I studied the Word of God, the more I realized that I have so much further to go . . . but I have made a start.

I truly believe that one of the reasons God allowed me to go to prison was to learn this. Only then was I ready to leave F.M.C. Rochester.

CHAPTER

49

Diesel Therapy

THE LAST YEAR THAT I WAS IN F.M.C. ROCHESTER, WINTER
lasted nine months. It was so cold. And dark. It seemed as though the sun
rarely came out all winter long. Throughout my prison sentence, I had
resigned myself to going wherever I was ordered to go, and I did so without appealing to any prison officials and only occasionally appealing to
God to transfer me to another environment. During the cold winter of
1993, however, I began praying, "Oh, God, please let me go someplace
where the sun is shining and it's warm."

At my next meeting before the prison review committee, I requested
to be transferred to a prison camp in a warmer location and, more importantly, a location closer to my children and my aging parents. It was normal procedure and within my rights to request such a transfer now that my
sentence had been cut to eight years. I had heard that the minimum-security prison camp at Eglin Air Force Base in Florida was as good as the
prison system gets. The prison review team promised to process my
request but made no promises.

My heart was warmed by a letter I received from a group of ministers
known as "Shepherds of Charlotte." The group was comprised of pastors
from various denominations who met together with the purpose of praying for each other, encouraging one another, and working together to
spread the gospel in Charlotte. It was before this group of pastors and
church workers that I had first taken public responsibility for my sin and

the hurt my actions had inflicted on the Body of Christ. The meeting took place in 1988 and few members of the press decided it merited reporting.

The Shepherds of Charlotte letter resonated with love and compassion. The group expressed their joy that my sentence had been reduced and assured me that I would be accepted and welcomed by them if or when I returned to the Charlotte area. The letter was signed by seventeen pastors who were members of the Shepherds of Charlotte. I was sincerely moved that my brothers in ministry would welcome me so openly.

Franklin Graham had been keeping up on my condition in prison and had written me several times. Three weeks before the Commission rejected my appeal, Franklin wrote:

> Jim, let me just say that one of these days you will be released. I don't know what the terms will be, but I would like to invite you to join me on an overseas trip to see what God is doing through Samaritan's Purse. I would love to take you to Kenya to see Tenwek Hospital, a work that you have had a vital role in. I think it would bless your heart and give you great encouragement. Please be thinking about this.
>
> Your friend,
> Franklin Graham

Once again, Franklin had amazed me with his kindness toward me and his acceptance of me.

Around that same time, I received some wonderful news! I was being transferred to a minimum-security facility work camp in Jesup, a small town about sixty-five miles southwest of Savannah. The bad news was that I was being transferred to Jesup by way of El Reno, the most feared facility in the entire prison system. That meant I was going to have "diesel therapy."

"Diesel therapy" was the name the inmates used to describe the prison system's method of transferring prisoners from one location to another when there was no hurry involved in moving them, or, as the inmates assumed, when the prison officials wanted to get even with an inmate. Rather than sending the inmate on a direct flight to the location to which he was to be transferred, as had been done to me when I was returned to Charlotte for my resentencing, the inmates believed that the prison officials purposely routed the inmate the long way to his destination, with layovers at various federal prisons or county jails along the way. On such trips the inmate may start out traveling by plane but usually ended up traveling by bus. Thus the name: diesel therapy.

Diesel therapy usually took a dramatic toll on the inmates. I had personally known and seen inmates who had been called to testify in court (or "go out on writ") and had been given diesel therapy as they traveled to and from their destinations. Oftentimes a strong and robust, emotionally stable inmate returned as an emaciated basket case. One of the worst parts about diesel therapy is that the inmates are not told where they are going, how long they will be there, or when they will return. It's almost impossible for family members to keep track of their loved one who is on diesel therapy. I wondered if at times it was not difficult for the prison system itself to keep track of its travelers on diesel therapy. Inmates only half-joked that some of their friends are still out there . . . somewhere . . . lost in the system. Several inmates told me they knew of prisoners whose testimonies were potentially damaging to politicians, so the inmates were kept on diesel therapy until the days of the election campaign were over.

The most frightening parts of diesel therapy are the stopovers—often at one of America's large, maximum-security prisons. In these facilities, the inmate on diesel therapy is often thrown in with hard-core prisoners. Just the names of certain prisons around the country sent shivers through the average inmate, prisons such as Terre Haute, Lewisburg, Atlanta penitentiary, and worst of all—El Reno.

I had heard many hellish accounts of what inmates had encountered at El Reno. Several guys told me how they had to sleep side by side with hundreds of men on cots in a large common room that looked like an old train station. Many of the windows were broken out, so the birds would fly freely inside the building and hover overhead, defecating on the inmates below day and night.

Cockroaches at El Reno were notorious. One inmate told me that he slept with cotton in his ears and his mouth covered, because the roaches would crawl in a guy's ears or in his mouth while he was sleeping.

Even though a prison official assured me that I would not be put in with murderers or violent criminals, for the next several weeks, fear and uncertainty mounted in my heart. I was delighted to be going somewhere, anywhere. But the thought of diesel therapy terrified me.

It may not have been necessary for me to have gone on diesel therapy. Because of my reduced sentence, I had a new prisoner status known as "out-custody," which allowed me to travel by conventional means, by myself or in the company of a federal officer. It was possible to have a federal marshal accompany me and fly directly to the major airport nearest the facility to which I was being transferred. Such special transfers were permitted, but the expenses for both the inmate and the marshal had to be paid by the prisoner. I didn't have much money left in my commissary account, but I figured a direct flight was worth the price, no matter what the cost.

Consequently, when I found out that my transfer had been granted and that I was probably heading to Jesup, I mentioned my concerns to Jim Toms. Jim immediately contacted the prison in Rochester to see if we could arrange for a marshal-accompanied transfer.

Jim ran into a stone wall with the official who was in charge of my travel arrangements. When Jim suggested that he was concerned for my safety as a high-profile prisoner, the official retorted, "I've transferred thousands of inmates. I know how to transfer people. I have never lost an inmate yet!" As my lawyer persisted in trying to arrange for a direct transfer, the prison official became irate. His position solidified further with every call from my lawyer. No doubt part of his consternation resulted from the fact that my lawyer was already trying to arrange transfer details and the official had not yet even informed me that I was in fact being transferred!

When the official confronted me about it and confirmed my fears, he angrily answered, "Well, if you're afraid to be transferred through the normal prison procedures, you're not ready to go to a camp yet! Don't worry. You won't be in with any violent criminals such as murderers or rapists. The prison system keeps the various types of inmates separated."

I knew then, I was definitely going on diesel therapy.

Just before the Fourth of July weekend, I got the official word—I was moving out. I packed everything I owned into a large green duffel bag and took it to the mail room to be inventoried and shipped to my destination. I kept only the clothes on my back—my prison khakis, my glasses, and my inventory sheet.

I made my rounds, saying good-bye on Sunday. Somebody suggested taking a few pictures and I readily agreed. We went over to the recreation building and had the Jaycees photographer snap some shots.

That Sunday night, I posed for literally dozens of pictures with the guys, because we all knew that I would be leaving at any time. I then gathered as many of my friends as I could for a group picture. When I got back to my cell, guys were still dropping by to say good-bye. Several men were laughing and talking in my cell and outside the door when Dominic, my Italian friend from across the hall, came in to say good-bye. Dominic had brought me food he had made especially during the time when Tammy Faye left me. He may have been a tough man at one time—I never asked about his past—but the grandfatherly man I knew who lived across the hall was a deeply caring human being. Dominic told me, "Jim, you've served your time with more dignity than any man I have ever seen." Dominic hugged me good-bye and then, right there in front of the other inmates, tears began to form in the eyes of this tough man. He turned away and quickly left my cell.

I didn't sleep much the night before I was to leave F.M.C. Rochester. A guard came to my cell in the wee hours of Tuesday morning and ordered me to get dressed. I started to put my prison khakis over my underwear and I had to laugh. The undershorts I was wearing were the exact same shorts I had been wearing the day the marshals brought me in to the prison.

When I got to R & D, I was strip searched one last time. The guard made me take off my underwear and toss them into a bin. It was the end of the line for those shorts. The guard handed me a pair of mint-green jockey shorts. Most of the prison-issued shorts were dark army-green or white, but I had never seen any articles of inmate clothing that were mint green. The color of those underwear, however, would soon take on extreme significance to me.

I was only one of a group of men being transferred that day. We were given the usual prison travel clothes. The guards put the usual handcuffs, leg irons, and chains on us. A few of the nicer guards said good-bye. The guard who put my leg irons on did not fasten them tightly around my ankles. At first I thought that was a blessing, but I soon discovered it was the opposite. Every time I took a step, the irons rubbed up and down. By the time I got to Georgia, my ankles and feet were bruised.

Once our handcuffs were fastened to the chains around our waists, the other transferees and I were marched out to the compound and ordered to stand in a straight line. There, bound in shackles, I got my last look at F.M.C. Rochester. I had seen so many other guys chained and lined up, ready to go out the gate. Now, at last, it was my turn.

I stared into the morning darkness with mixed emotions. I was exhilarated that I was finally going somewhere, I knew not where.

At the Rochester airport, a large plane was waiting for us on the tarmac. The inside of the plane looked similar to any other commercial jet airliner, except that all the passengers were dressed alike, we were all chained, and there were no flight attendants. In their places were government marshals, stationed throughout the plane.

The aircraft began to taxi toward the runway. Looking around at the chained passengers, it suddenly hit me, *If this plane crashes, we don't stand a chance. There would be no survivors, only a mangled mess of charred, chained corpses.* As the large plane lumbered down the runway, I prayed that God would keep the old bucket of bolts in the air. I tried to keep from thinking about the stories I had heard about how poorly these prison planes were maintained.

Once airborne, the big bird's landing gears pulled up and the pilot banked the plane hard to the west. *That's an odd way to go to Georgia*, I thought.

Throughout the day, the plane made several stops at other prison towns, dropping off inmates and picking up others. I didn't move out of my seat, not even to go to the bathroom. Late that afternoon, the plane landed in some flatlands and the marshal called my name to get off.

"Where are we?" I asked the man next to me.

The man looked at me as if I had just stabbed him with a knife. He answered in an anguished tone, "El Reno."

We did the bus routine in reverse, this time as the shotgun-wielding marshals loaded us onto a prison bus. After what seemed like a forty- to sixty-minute ride, the bus pulled up in front of a huge, old building.

El Reno Penitentiary.

I stared out the wire-mesh bus windows at what looked to be a dilapidated Dracula's Castle. True to what I had heard, numerous windows were broken out of the higher sections of the building, and sure enough, I saw birds going in and out of the windows.

Outside in the parking area, prison buses were lined up in front of the bus on which I was sitting. I couldn't tell how many buses were ahead of ours, but there were enough to make the lot look like a bus stop at a busy tourist attraction from hell. We sat chained in the bus for more than two hours, waiting for our turn to unload at the processing area.

When it was our turn to unload, we were marched to a concrete pad alongside the barbed razor wire and made to stand, still chained, facing Dracula's Castle. I thought, *Are they trying to impress upon us the horror of this place?* It was as though they wanted to psych us out. Whatever the reason, I was beginning to realize that I was going to get the full "diesel" treatment.

After another count, we were herded inside to a narrow bull pen holding cell with backless benches along the sides. Inmates from many prisons around the country were jammed together in that room; another bull pen crammed with hot, sweaty inmates was next to the one in which I was placed. Perhaps as many as two hundred men were confined in those cramped bull pens. The noise was intense. Everyone was talking at the same time.

I sat down on one of the benches. The man sitting next to me began to talk wildly. First of all, he told me that he was Martin Luther. Then he told me that he was Joan of Arc. Suddenly, with a dark, dead, glassy look in his eyes, he leaped to his feet and, still chained, jumped up onto the bench, yelling at me, telling me that he was Satan. I thought sure that at any moment he was going to pull his chains over my head and choke me to death.

This is where I will die, I thought seriously. I thought for sure that I would be raped, beaten, and killed before this night was over. Thankfully, some of the other inmates got the deranged man to calm down. One inmate then told me that "Satan" had tried to kill a large number of people by locking up a skating rink with the people inside, then setting it on fire. Encouraged by the demented man's outbursts, some of the inmates from the Terre Haute prison began telling "war stories" about some of their experiences in that facility. The more I listened, the more convinced I became that it would be only the goodness of God if I were still alive in the morning.

The middle door clanged open and the guard ordered us to file out to have our chains removed. The guards then ordered us to take off all our clothes and toss them in the bins, all except our undershorts. I became extremely aware of the mint green undershorts I was wearing. We were then herded into another long, narrow bull pen. Backless benches lined the sides of the pen as well as the middle. Another identical bull pen was alongside ours.

"Hey, Bakker," I heard a rough voice call my name from behind me. I turned around to see a man holding out his inventory sheet and the small pencil used for filling out medical records and other forms in the bull pen. "How about an autograph?" he asked.

I gladly signed the man's paper. As soon as I signed one inventory sheet, another was thrust in front of me. "Yeah, me too. Will you sign one for me?" I signed the paper. In a matter of minutes, I was signing autographs like a home run slugger at a ballpark. Guys in the bull pen next to ours began rolling their inventory sheets up into tight, pencil-thin tubes and passing them through the wire mesh so I could sign them. A large group gathered around me and began asking questions while I signed the autographs. They wanted to know all about the many things they had read in the newspapers and rag magazines. Some of the guys even wanted to know where they could get Bibles and other Christian books.

All of a sudden, the picture of me sitting in my underwear signing autographs hit me and I started laughing out loud. There I was, scared to death, thinking this might be my last night on earth in this cramped dungeon with a couple hundred guys, sitting there in my mint-green underwear, talking and signing autographs!

More hours went by and brown-bag lunches, comprised of an apple and prison "mystery meat" sandwiches, were passed out to all the inmates.

I ate my apple, but I thought of a better use for my sandwich. I decided to trade it for "protection."

"Satan" had been moved to the bench across from me. The man next to me was a big, friendly black man from Terre Haute. He had been telling me awful stories about some of the things he had seen in prison. He told me about a young man who had been raped by twenty-two guys and left to die during a movie in the recreation room. He told me about the guys who had rats for pets. And he told me about the way men were stabbed on the way to chow by somebody slamming a "shiv," a makeshift knife, into the inmate's back as he was pressed against the other inmates trying to enter the chow hall. His horror stories weren't exactly calming my nerves.

My mind thought back to the prison official in Rochester who had promised, "Oh, don't worry, Jim. You won't be in with any violent prisoners."

Because I was a "high-profile" prisoner, it was not out of the question that somebody might be tempted to attack me just for the publicity that would surely follow. I was getting along rather well with the big guy from Terre Haute, so I decided to ask him straight out, "Would you sort of watch out for me tonight? I'll give you my lunch if you'll be my bodyguard. If we get placed in that big room with all the cots side by side, will you see to it that nobody rapes or kills me?"

My big friend threw back his shoulders and replied, "I sure will!" He pointed to some of his friends from Terre Haute and said, "And they'll watch out for you too. Nothin' is gonna happen to you tonight."

I knew the guy could be a con and that he might be lying to me through his teeth, but I believed him and trusted him.

We sat with our clothes off in those bull pens hour after hour, waiting to be processed. I was the only man in the crowded room who was wearing mint-green underwear. Guys from various prisons had different colors of underwear; some had army green, some had light brown, but only one man had mint-green underwear—Jim Bakker.

After several hours, we were told to line up and march to an inspection area. Huge racks of prison clothing, separated by size, lined the back wall. We were ordered to strip naked and the guards began strip searching entire lines of inmates at one time.

When it was my turn, the guard who was inspecting me said in an extremely sarcastic tone of voice, "Where did you get those green panties?"

I had been up most of the night before and it had already been a long day. In the roughest, gruffest voice I could muster, I answered, "They issued them to me at Rochester."

The guard shrugged and grabbed a bundle of clothes and tossed it to me. My new clothes were nearly twice my size. I had to hold my pants up with my hand as I walked. Next stop was a window where a man asked me, "Have you testified against anybody?"

"No, I haven't," I replied.

"Do you want to go into isolation?" he asked matter-of-factly.

"That's up to you," I answered.

The man looked at me a moment. "I think we better put you in solitary," he said.

Considering the rooming possibilities in that place, I was delighted to have a private room for the night—a cell with no birds overhead—even if it was in the hole. A full eight hours after I had arrived at El Reno, I was taken to a cell. It was well past midnight. I was dead tired.

I had not been in my cell much more than an hour, lying on the bunk, still wide awake, when a guard came to the door. "Get dressed. You're leaving." He gave me a brown paper bag. In it was a hard-boiled egg and some bread. I tried to eat it, but I had no appetite. The food was unappetizing and I was nervous.

I couldn't believe it, but it was true. It was about 2:00 A.M. Along with two bull pens full of inmates, I was brought out of my cell and we reversed the procedure we had just gone through coming into the prison.

Back through the lines we went. We gave them our prison clothes back. Another strip search. The guards gave us new traveling clothes, back to the bull pens, another long wait, and from there, the guards prodded our only half-conscious bodies back toward another prison bus.

By 7:00 A.M., we were back in the buses, ready to head toward the airport. The bus radio, tuned to a local rock 'n' roll morning show, was blaring. As we were waiting to depart for the airport, the disk jockey announced, "Guess whose birthday it is today? Why, it's Jessica Hahn's birthday!"

There I was, cuffed and chained, along with a busload of inmates, and the morning guys on the radio were going through an entire Jessica Hahn and Jim Bakker routine. I wanted to crawl under a bus seat and hide. Fortunately, everybody was too tired to make jokes or harass me, but I couldn't help thinking, *How much more?*

At last the bus pulled out, drowning out the sound of the morning show. We traveled all the way back to the airport, at least a forty-minute ride. When we arrived at the "Con Air" prison plane, however, we were not permitted to board. We sat in the buses on the tarmac for a long time. I could tell something was wrong. I had been around enough planes in my lifetime that just by watching the flurry of activity on the ground around the plane, it was obvious that there was some sort of mechanical problem. Con Air had broken down. I watched as a tow unit pulled the big bird back into the hanger. After sitting there for what seemed like hours, the decision was made. The buses turned around and headed back over the same roads we had just traveled. We were going *back* to El Reno!

We went through the entire laborious process once again, doing the exact routine we had done the day before.

This time, I received clothes that fit. Nevertheless, it was nearly noon before I was finally assigned to a cell. I had not slept for two full days. Nor had I gone to the bathroom that entire time.

The guards decided to put me into a cell block with other prisoners in transit, so I was taken to a blood-red, basement cell. Even the bars were red. In the cell block were some tough looking guys and others who looked more like businessmen than hardened criminals. I was assigned a top bunk in the first cell in the unit.

For the next several days, the red cell block was my home. One night, an older man was put into our unit. I didn't recognize him, but by the way the other inmates deferred to him it was obvious that he was fairly famous. Men gathered around him outside my cell, much as they had surrounded me when I first arrived. Soon the man was telling his story.

Apparently, he had been involved in a well-known standoff between government law officers and some sort of dissident group. As he related the story to the inmates, it was so fascinating, I slipped down from my bunk and joined the circle of guys standing around him. He told how the agents had shot his wife and how he had run to his pickup truck, dove inside, pulled a gun, and shot and killed a government agent. I didn't know anything about his story, but the other men seemed very familiar with it, asking him details.

Right in the middle of the man's story, he suddenly stopped cold. He stared at me for a moment then burst out, "Why, you're Jim Bakker! How are you?" He got so excited, he forgot to tell the rest of his story. He said he was overwhelmed at meeting me, "Why, my mother watched your TV show. She just loves you!" he gushed.

I had now been housed in the end cell of that cell block for several days. During that time I rarely went outside or to the chow hall. Some of the guys brought back items of fruit or bread for me, and that was the only food I ate at El Reno.

A few days later, a doctor came to examine me. Jim Toms had contacted the prison and asked the officials to check on me to see if I was okay, because nobody was hearing from me. While the doctor examined me, he asked me some personal questions about my physical and mental well-being.

"Come to think of it, I haven't gone to the bathroom since I left Minnesota," I told him. I had not eaten much and I had drunk only a little in several days.

"You what?" the doctor exclaimed. "You need to get some food and water into you right away."

I told him that I didn't want to go to the chow hall and I was not able to drink the water, but he was adamant. Reluctantly, I went to the chow hall and ate a meal.

Whether it was a coincidence or the doctor recommended that I move to a different environment, I never discovered. The next day, however, an officer came to my basement cell and said, "Get your stuff together, Bakker. You're going next door."

"Next door?"

"That's right, next door. There's a prison camp right across the way. Because you're a minimum-out status, you can be over there." My minimum-out status meant I could be outside the walls of prison without chains on. The officer led me out of El Reno penitentiary, past the maze of walls and barbed razor wire.

When we stepped out into the sunshine, I hesitated. I noticed the guards in the gun towers brandishing their weapons. I suddenly realized that I was outside the prison and I didn't have any chains on me, and I was terrified. I expected to be gunned down at any second.

"Come on," the guard ordered me firmly but kindly.

"Are you sure?" I asked tentatively.

The guard was on his radiophone talking with somebody. "I'm sure," he replied with a slight smile. "But the minute you get over there, change your clothes. If they see you out here without me calling them," he nodded toward the gun towers, "you're gonna be shot. The clothes you're wearing mean you're supposed to be inside the walls of the main prison."

The guard ushered two other men and me past Dracula's Castle, past the broken windows, the horrible, ugly walls and across a driveway. I couldn't believe it. I thought, *Any minute now, several guards are going to come and tackle me*, as I had seen them do to erring inmates at Rochester. Worse yet, I might be gunned down.

Nothing happened. We walked over to a fairly new-looking prison camp with modern buildings, well-manicured grass, and basketball courts . . . all with no walls or electrified fences.

Once we made it to the camp, the guards inside took me to a laundry room and got me some clothes, a dark-blue shirt and pants. They took me to a cell, which was a four-man, open-door, cubelike room. Three guys were already in the cell and they welcomed me like a long-lost brother—which in a way I was, because all three men in that cell were Christians. One fellow had worked at the Assemblies of God headquarters at one time in his life. I never ceased to be amazed at whom I met in prison . . . some of the nicest people!

"What am I supposed to do here?" I asked the guys.

"You can do whatever you want," one man replied, with a slight laugh.

"But there are no fences, no walls. Where can I go?"

"Well, that road over there is Old Route 66. You can't go over there," the man said with a twinkle in his eye. The other men in the cell laughed out loud. "And don't cross that road down the opposite direction. Other than that, you can go pretty much where you please. I wouldn't go back over to the big house, though, if I were you." Everyone laughed again.

I was shocked. I could not get over the fact that yesterday I was in the closest thing to hell I had ever seen and now, here I was, looking out over the flat, wide open expanses of Oklahoma terrain. More than that, to think that somebody actually trusted me to walk around outside with no razor wire to define my parameters. It was overwhelming. Before I stepped out into the yard, I once again asked an inmate, "Are you sure it's okay for me to walk out there?"

"I remember that feeling," the inmate said with a laugh. He then patiently reviewed with me the legal limits within which I could walk.

It was still daylight, so I went outside and just walked around. I noticed that it was almost hot, but I didn't mind. I thought back to the many times when I had felt so cold and so cooped up in Minnesota and I had prayed, "Oh, God, please let me go someplace warm. Let me go where I can see some land, some fields and trees. Let me go someplace where I can see forever."

Now as I looked out across the Oklahoma plains, I realized that God had answered my prayer. I continued walking and looking and the plains kept spreading out further in front of me. It seemed as though they had no ending. I felt the tears begin to trickle down my face, and I prayed, "Oh, thank You, God, for bringing me to a place where I can see forever."

That evening I went to chow with my new Christian buddies. There I got a real surprise. The inmates were allowed to eat with silverware—real metal flatware, not the plastic stuff. At first, I couldn't bring myself to touch it. Finally I picked up the knife and fork. Like a little child, I clanged them together to see if they were real. The guys roared with laughter, but they all understood.

On Sunday morning, I went to chapel. It was a wonderful service and such a great time of Christian fellowship. For a few moments, I almost forgot I was in prison. Later that night, however, I received a graphic reminder. A female officer called me into her office and informed me bluntly that there had been a threat on my life.

"Do you want to go back to the penitentiary to spend the night?" she asked. "We can put you in solitary confinement and you'll be much safer there, much more protected."

"No, thank you," I answered. "If I can, I'd rather stay right here." I did not want to give up my newfound sense of freedom.

"Okay, fine," she replied. "But if you get any notes on your bed, or a threat of any kind, let us know immediately." She dismissed me and I went back to my cell. I told my cellmates and they all promised to keep an eye out for any signs of trouble. My awesome sense of joy at being free overrode any fear of being killed. After two or three days of relishing this tantalizing taste of freedom and the encouragement of a strong Christian group of guys, I received word that it was time to move on.

I had to go back through the processing systems at the "big house" at El Reno. Once again, it was an all-night ordeal, just getting ready to go. Strip searches, clothes changes, chains, the long bus trip back to the airport and finally boarding the plane to the next stop in the twilight zone. When Con Air landed this time, I was in Atlanta.

The Atlanta Federal Penitentiary was an old, huge, complex. Our prison bus pulled up and we unloaded at the front door. Shackled once again, we were led up a long set of stairs, into one of the most feared prison facilities in America. For most of the day after processing, I was by myself in a large holding cell where female prisoners passed by. When they recognized me, some of the women were very friendly. Some were lewd. I was glad when a guard finally came and moved me into a cell block.

An inmate told me that the cell block in which I was being housed had once been occupied by Al Capone. My cell was a very old, six-man cell, with high ceilings in which the pipes were exposed and looked as though they were ready to fall right out of the ceiling. The whole place looked dingy.

In my cell block, I met a man who had once been a banker in Charlotte. He recognized me and we struck up a conversation. He told me there was another former Charlotte resident in our cell block—the very man who had been outside the courthouse during my trial, making fun of me. The man had written and recorded a song about Jim and Tammy and PTL and had been hawking it on the lawn of the courthouse.

When the songwriter saw me in Atlanta Penitentiary, he came right up to me. We had never officially been introduced during the trial days, and now he was shocked to actually meet me in prison. He apologized to me for what he had done and he asked me to forgive him.

I told him, "Of course I forgive you. I don't have any animosity toward you whatsoever." I then went on to explain to him some of the things God had shown me during my time in prison, especially that I had to forgive everyone involved in those hurtful last days of PTL, and that included the street vendors outside my trial.

Later, I heard that the man felt that God had purposely allowed our paths to cross in prison so he could make amends. The man went on to become a Bible study leader in prison.

After several days it was moving time again. The final session of diesel therapy was from Atlanta to Jesup, Georgia, my new home away from home. We ended up driving all the way to Jesup, a distance of about two hundred forty miles in one of the bumpy prison buses. At one point, we were bouncing along a road when the bus passed a church. I saw the name of the church and had an instant panic attack. The church was of the same denomination as the man who more than any other, in my mind, had been responsible for orchestrating the fall of PTL and my eventual imprisonment. My adrenalin shot up. Never before in my life had I looked at a church with fear in my heart.

As I slowly regained my composure, I began to think about what had just happened. I have a feeling that I am not the only person who had ever felt that way about the church.

Like El Reno, Jesup has both a large major penitentiary and a prison camp on the premises. After several hours in the big house, a group of inmates and I were led to another bus for the short ride to the prison camp.

I boarded the rickety old bus and took a seat and looked idly toward the driver as we began to pull out. To my amazement, the driver was an inmate. And there were no guards on this bus. And no fences around the prison camp. What kind of place was this Camp Jesup? After a two-week journey on Diesel Therapy to get there, I was about to find out.

CHAPTER

50

"Camp Jesus"

IT WAS OBVIOUS THAT JESUP WAS A DIFFERENT SORT OF camp; we were met by a congenial officer with a deep Southern accent. He told us where to go to get our issuance of new clothing, the dark-blue outfits like the sort I had worn in the El Reno camp.

I stumbled down the sidewalk, physically and emotionally exhausted. All I wanted to do was get to a bunk and fall asleep.

Just then I was met by a group of inmates standing in front of me. Everyone was welcoming me with outstretched hands, all talking excitedly at one time, volunteering to help me get my clothes, pointing out the laundry room, and being extremely helpful. I wasn't used to this sort of reception in prison. I was overwhelmed by their friendliness and appreciated it immensely, but I was exhausted and wanted to sleep. Nevertheless, I tried my best to be friendly in return.

"Hi, Jim! I'm Larry Wright," said a big, friendly looking fellow as he stuck out his hand. Larry had sandy hair, just beginning to gray; he wore eyeglasses and a contagious smile. "We've brought you a few things that you might need until your own items arrive," he said as he handed me a bag of toiletries, shower shoes, stamps, and a small New Testament. "We're part of the Christian brothers here at Jesup," Larry nodded toward the other guys who were also smiling and nodding, most of whom I had already met and shaken hands with, "and we're available to help you any way we can. Is there anything you need right now?" Larry asked.

"No, no. I'm fine," I replied.

"What you probably need most right now is some sleep," Larry offered knowingly. "Why don't you get some rest? We'll check on you later."

"Thank you," I answered. I had never before seen a Christian welcoming committee in prison! I later found out that they were not doing anything for me that they were not doing for almost every new inmate at Jesup. The Christians there were putting their faith into a tangible meeting of needs.

Soon I was on my way to a cell block, which at Jesup was not really comprised of cells at all, but cubicles enclosed by painted cement-block walls about half the distance between the floor and ceiling, about the height of the partitions in a business office. The room housing about sixty men was open above the cubicles. No doors or bars slammed shut in the Jesup cell block, because there were none.

I stopped in the bathroom before I went on to my bunk. When I caught a glimpse of my reflection in the mirror, I was shocked. I hardly recognized myself! I looked like I had aged twenty years.

I went to bed and slept for nearly three days, getting up only for orientation information and count. I had not yet been assigned a work duty. Truthfully I just wanted to lie in my bunk and sleep the days away.

But the body of believers at Jesup was not about to let that happen. True to Larry's word, the men kept a close watch on me. After they allowed me to rest, they began to pull me out of my bed.

Chuck, a small, wiry guy and one of the Christian brothers, kept nagging and cajoling me like a little bull dog. "Go away, Chuck. I'm tired. I just want to sleep," I told him over and over.

"You've slept enough. It's time to get up and on with your life. Come on, there's a service over in the chapel. We can go together."

"Oh, Chuck, I don't want to go to chapel. I just want to stay here and sleep. You go ahead and you can tell me about it later."

After I had spent the majority of several days in bed and had not attended any Bible study or chapel programs, Chuck was exasperated. "Are you backslidden?" Chuck asked me bluntly.

"Okay, Chuck, okay. I'll go."

Smiling, Chuck extended a hand. "Good, it's about time."

And it was time, time for me to begin functioning as a human being again, time for spiritual nourishment, and time to get back to work. One of the female officials had given me a work assignment—picking up the cigarette butts in the yard.

When I first was called to see the attractive, young black woman who was designated as my "counselor," I was not prepared for her behavior. She started yelling at me. I later learned that she yelled at everybody, but she caught me off guard when one of the first things she said to me was, "Bakker, don't ask for a furlough, 'cause you're not gettin' one."

A furlough? I didn't know it was possible to earn a short furlough from prison camp. I was used to a medium-security prison, from which furloughs could only be granted for unusual circumstances, such as my father's accident. What the woman was basically saying to me was, "Don't ask for any special treatment around here, because you are not going to get any!"

Camp Jesup itself was well kept, clean, and had beautiful landscaping, including South Georgia palm trees, lots of flowers and green grass. The complex was located in a swampy area, and since there were no fences around the minimum security camp, the guards incorporated the natural elements as part of our orientation. "Don't go across that field, because the swamp over there is filled with poisonous snakes and alligators," they warned. "Even the grass beyond the field might be dangerous because of the brown recluse spiders. If you get bitten by one of them, get help fast. Otherwise, your flesh will rot right to the bone." I didn't know whether they were exaggerating or not, but I had no intention of finding out.

The best part of Jesup's location was that it was much closer to my parents and halfway between Tammy Sue's home and where Jamie was living.

Of course, I wanted to be out of prison completely. Looking back, however, I now believe God knew that I was not yet ready to go back out into the world. I needed a sort of decompression time. I needed to be emotionally healed and spiritually strengthened. God was not going to allow me to live in burnout as I had done at PTL. He was not going to allow me to stand up in front of a group of people and do a spiritual routine, as I had sometimes done at PTL. For that I was wrong. I beg the forgiveness of anyone who may have been hurt by that.

In Jesup prison, God began to show me what true ministry is all about—people caring for one another, teaching the Word, devouring the Bible. As a result, every week, more men—some of them so-called hardened criminals—came to trust Jesus Christ as their Savior and Lord. I needed to learn more of how the true Body of Christ is meant to function. So God sent me to Camp Jesus, er, Camp Jesup.

The body of Christian believers at Jesup prison was the strongest example of the functioning Body of Christ I have ever seen anywhere. The Christian men in that prison held Bible studies, prayer meetings, or other services almost every night. I soon started getting up at 5:00 A.M. so I could get to morning prayer and Bible study at 5:30. Some of the guys were getting up at 3:00 A.M. to pray for the 5:30 Bible study group!

Larry Wright, I quickly discovered, was one of the godliest guys I had ever met. A former Wesleyan pastor, Larry's ministry on the "outside" fell apart when his wife left him. Not only did he lose his wife, he lost his church and his ordination because of his marriage failure.

Since Larry Wright felt cast off by his church, he put his formidable gifts to work making money. He found that he was good at it. So good that he built a multimillion dollar corporation. He got in some sort of business trouble and was sentenced to prison. There in prison, Larry Wright found that he did not have to be in a church to be a minister of Christ's love and compassion. He began reaching out to inmates with the love of the Lord, teaching them the Bible and pointing them to Jesus Christ.

One of the main characteristics of the Christians at Jesup was that the guys cared for each other in godly, practical ways. For instance, when one of the men received a "Dear John" letter from his wife or girlfriend and wanted to curl up on his bunk and die, the brothers at Jesup would not allow him to do it. They pulled him out of his bunk and said, "Come on, we're going out to walk the track," or, "We're going to Bible study and you're coming too. We're not going to let you roll up in your self-pity and die. We are your brothers and we are going to take care of you, even when you don't care enough to take care of yourself."

I strongly disliked picking up cigarette butts as my work duty. It wasn't the work I minded—that part was easy. It was the location. Because of my notoriety, I felt uncomfortable working out in front of the prison complex where everyone could see me. When an opening among the orderlies occurred, I volunteered to switch jobs. Guess what my new job was?

Back in the toilets again.

As I got to know Larry Wright better, he and I began to meet each day around lunchtime. As we ate lunch, we studied the Bible. We went from Genesis to Revelation. We were like two little kids who had just discovered candy. "Oh, look at that!" one of us would say as we found a new insight from the Bible. It was wonderful to rediscover that "Look what I found!" attitude about the Bible. Larry and I also shared our deepest questions, pains, and joys. It was great to have a friend I could trust.

In the afternoons, I worked out with weights regularly, much as I had at Rochester. I had committed myself to a completely low-fat diet after seeing all the grease and fat in the food in prison, so with the combination of diet and exercise, I was more physically fit than ever, though some of my friends on the outside worried that I was getting too thin.

Many evenings at 6:30 P.M., I went to some sort of church service. After being discouraged from attending the chapel programs during my early years at Rochester, I felt like I was feasting at a spiritual smorgasbord now that I was at Jesup.

The Jesup chapel services were so popular, we had more inmates wanting to attend chapel than the library could handle. Interest in the things of the Lord was so high among the inmates that instead of referring to our camp as Camp Jesup, we soon began using the term Camp *Jesus*.

In addition to the many services and Bible studies conducted at the camp, Larry Wright and I did a great deal of biblically based counseling. The inmates had so many questions and were so in need of direction, Larry and I could have spent twenty-four hours a day counseling if we would not have had other responsibilities at the prison camp. To expand his counseling abilities, Larry took the same course as the one I had taken from the National Christian Counseling Association. Consequently, we always had a backlog of men waiting to be tested and advised concerning their temperaments and spiritual opportunities. Tammy Sue's ministry paid for all the testing and sent in hundreds of Bibles and encouraging Christian books to the Jesup prison. The inmates latched onto the literature within minutes of its arrival. No matter how many Bibles and books we received, we always needed more because new inmates were arriving constantly and many were becoming new Christians.

Not everything about Camp Jesup seemed like an old-time camp meeting. Besides the big house looming across the road in the background, there were still plenty of other reminders that this was prison, not a spiritual party. One night I will never forget was the night the federal authorities raided their own prisons and rounded up the Cuban inmates.

In the middle of the night, suddenly the doors of Camp Jesup burst open and in swarmed an army of prison guards. They went to every cell where prisoners of Cuban descent were sleeping, woke them up, chained them, and moved them out toward the road where a line of prison buses was waiting. Men screamed out, "I didn't do anything. Please! Why are you taking me? Where am I going? I didn't do anything!"

My heart ached for them. It was like a bad dream. For me it was reminiscent of when the federal marshals had seized me in the middle of my trial. Worse still, it was something one could imagine happening in a Russian gulag, but not in a "civilized" prison camp in America. Rumor had it that on the same night, Cuban prisoners all over the country were being singled out and transferred to someplace in Louisiana to await deportation. Some of the men who were rounded up at Jesup were members of our Christian fellowship. Many of them we never heard from again.

On another occasion, I woke up between 4:00 and 5:00 A.M. and got out of bed to go to the bathroom. As I walked up the corridor toward the bathroom, I noticed several guards in the bathroom doorway. That struck me as unusual, especially since the guards didn't use the same bathrooms as the inmates. Then I saw the blood.

A pool of blood stretched at least five feet across the bathroom floor. It looked as though someone had thrown a bucket full of blood onto the floor and then let it spread. The blood must have been there for some time. While some parts of it were still red, much of it looked as though it had already begun coagulating with what looked like grotesque blueberries jutting up here and there throughout the pool of blood.

The guards were talking quietly about the scene when I realized that it was going to be my job to clean up this mess! Sure enough, one of the guards nodded to me and said, "Better go get your cleaning materials."

I went back to my cell and put on some clothes, then went to the mop closet and gathered my bucket, cleaning agents, and a new pair of rubber gloves. I had to use a hose to get all the blood off the floor, the black and blue chunks turning bright red as the water splashed on them. I hosed the blood down the drain, scrubbed the floor, and disinfected everything in the bathroom. It took me until 6:30 A.M. just to get the place cleaned up. The entire time I was working, I thought, *Somebody must be dying. A person can't lose that much blood and survive without medical attention.*

As soon as I was done, I went to one of the officers and said, "Somebody's dying in here."

"Yeah, I know. We're all dyin' a little bit more every day in here," he answered sarcastically.

I went to one of the women who worked in the counselor's office and told her the story. She seemed concerned, but she didn't do anything.

I went to two other guards and said, "An inmate is dying in this prison, somewhere." I told them about the blood and said, "You can't lose that much blood and not be dying. Somebody in here is bleeding to death."

"Oh, don't worry about it," one of the guards responded carelessly. "If he doesn't stand up for count, we'll know he's dead." Count was still six hours away!

The insensitivity of the guards and my sense of utter helplessness to do anything to assist a fellow human being nearly drove me crazy. Sure enough, at the midday count, in a cubicle not far from my own, a young man did not stand up for the count. He remained in bed as the guards called his name. When the guards pulled the covers off him, they discovered he was covered with blood. The wall next to his bunk was spattered with blood. They stood him up and his blood-soaked clothing clung to his body.

"Get him into the shower and get him dressed," a guard commanded.

I couldn't believe that they were going to try to clean him up before dealing with the situation. Eventually, the boy was taken to the hospital. We were told that the young man was going to be okay, but the prison rumor mill reported his death. Regardless, he never returned to Jesup.

Most of the guards at Jesup were kind, compassionate human beings. Others were sometimes less than that.

One day I was going through my normal routine when over the prison paging system I heard, "Attention on the compound and in the housing units: Jim Bakker, report to the administration building." As I made my way across the compound to the administration building, I didn't know what to expect. Once inside, I learned that it had been the senior chaplain, David Morton, who had paged me. The chaplain dropped a bombshell on me that day. "The Reverend Jerry Falwell has requested permission to visit you," he told me.

Falwell! Visit me? What does he want with me?

I had prayed much about Jerry Falwell long before this day. I had asked God's forgiveness for my mistakes and sins and I had received His forgiveness. I did not want to open any old wounds. I had extended forgiveness to Jerry Falwell in my heart and had even written him a letter telling him so and asking for his forgiveness. Wasn't that enough?

I asked the chaplain for some time to think and pray about Reverend Falwell's request. I went back to the cell block and found Larry Wright. I explained the situation to Larry, and we prayed for quite a while. When we were done, there was no question about what I should do. Larry and I both felt that the only right and biblical alternative I had was to meet with Reverend Falwell. I told the chaplain that I agreed to the visit. For me to be convinced I should meet face-to-face with Jerry Falwell was one thing; for my kids to be convinced of the same was something else. I wasn't sure how they would respond to the idea. After all, in their minds, Jerry Falwell had not only stolen our ministry but had thrown them out of their home, me into prison, and them into impossible circumstances.

When I broached the subject by telephone to Tammy Sue, I was surprised she was elated.

"I think it's the right thing to do, Dad," she told me.

Telling Jamie Charles would not be so easy. Of all my family members, Jamie seemed to be carrying the deepest scars from the wounds inflicted by the takeover of PTL in 1987. Jamie was only eleven years old when he was uprooted from every bit of security he had known. Not to mention the pain, embarrassment, and teasing he endured when I went to prison. In his young mind, nearly all the major hurts he had experienced in his life were directly or indirectly attributable to one man—Jerry Falwell. It is impossible to overstate the bitterness and resentment Jamie felt.

I knew Jamie could better handle the news of the planned visit if I were to tell him face-to-face rather than over the telephone. Jamie was scheduled to visit me the Friday before Falwell's visit, so I decided to wait until then to break the news to him. Unfortunately, it didn't work out that way.

Just before his scheduled visit to me, Jamie contacted my lawyer's office to see if there were any new developments he could tell me about. When my lawyer mentioned the Falwell meeting, Jamie felt betrayed and angry that such a meeting could be arranged without his knowledge. More than that, he was afraid for me. Jamie felt sure that Jerry Falwell was going to try to hurt me in some way. He begged me not to go through with it. "When you come to see me on Friday, we'll talk about this," I promised.

On Friday morning when I walked into the visitors' area, I could tell Jamie was distraught. He was visibly shaken. We spent the day together and we talked a great deal about the planned Falwell meeting. "Dad, please! Don't do it!" Jamie begged. "Don't trust him. He will destroy you." Nothing I said could calm Jamie's fears.

The next morning, Jamie was back at 8:30. He had not changed his mind overnight. That day I was able to bring my Bible into the visiting area and Jamie and I went through the Bible, talking about forgiveness. When we came to Matthew 6:15, "If you do not forgive men their trespasses, neither will your Father forgive your trespasses," I knew we had found a key. I realized that God wanted Jamie to be involved in the healing process that was going on between Jerry Falwell and me.

Finally, an idea hit me. I said, "Jamie, would you like to meet with Jerry Falwell before I do and see how you feel about our meeting together?"

Without a moment of hesitation, Jamie said, "Yes, I would."

I told him, "I'll make a deal with you. If you go meet with Falwell and you don't feel that I should meet with him, then I won't do it. But if after meeting with Reverend Falwell, you feel that it is right, then you come with him and bring him back here to meet with me." Jamie agreed.

Jerry Falwell was in Jacksonville, Florida, that night, preaching at a large Baptist church. He was planning to come see me the next day at the conclusion of the series of services there. I contacted Jim Toms and asked him to arrange a meeting between Jamie and Jerry for the following evening after the service. Jim took it from there.

The next day, Mr. Toms picked up Jamie and the two of them left for Jacksonville. As he departed, I prayed, "God, if You want this meeting to take place, then You're going to have to work in that boy's heart."

What happened next surprised even me!

CHAPTER

51

Reunion

EVEN THOUGH WE HAVE FORGIVEN A PERSON IN OUR heart, sometimes it helps to put a face with the person we forgive. That is what I needed to do with Jerry Falwell. Although I had forgiven him time and again in my heart for what I considered to be his deceit in getting me to resign and turn PTL over to him, I still needed to express it to him in person.

Our family advocate, Jim Toms, and Jamie traveled to Jacksonville and arrived in time for the evening service at the church where Jerry Falwell had been speaking. Another man was preaching that night, so when Jerry entered the sanctuary accompanied by Mark DeMoss, he walked to a reserved seat on the front row . . . right in front of Jamie. Jamie later admitted that his anger toward Jerry Falwell surged to the surface and was almost uncontrollable. There was Falwell sitting within inches, and with his back to Jamie! For a moment, Jamie thought, *If I were that kind of guy, I could reach my hands around his neck and strangle him!* Jamie blinked hard and tried to drive the nasty thoughts out of his mind.

When Jerry Falwell was introduced from the podium that night, many people in the audience jumped to their feet, giving him a standing ovation. Jamie remained seated.

Jamie went back to his hotel room and waited for a call from Mark DeMoss, indicating it was time to meet with Jerry. Jamie and Jim Toms waited for several hours in their room and Jerry Falwell never showed up.

Around midnight, the telephone rang. It was Mark DeMoss, and he informed Jamie that Jerry Falwell was tired and would meet with Jamie the following morning. Jamie was livid. He felt sure that Falwell was trying to play a game with him. Mark DeMoss assured him that was not the case, but that Jerry had been preaching all weekend and was simply tired. He invited Jamie to his room so the two young men could talk. Jamie went to Mark's room, where he poured out his heart to Mark.

Mark listened as Jamie emphasized that Jerry Falwell had acquired the leadership of PTL through less-than-honorable means and that he knew what had happened in the fall of PTL. He told Mark, "I feel that Jerry Falwell's influence is a major part of why my dad is in prison right now."

Mark contested a few details, but he didn't attempt to change Jamie's mind about anything. He and Jamie talked for quite a while and parted amicably.

About 8:30 A.M. the following day, Mark called Jamie and said that Jerry was ready to meet. With Jim Toms at his side, Jamie marched into Jerry Falwell's hotel suite. Jerry Falwell immediately rose to greet them.

"Well, hello, Jamie. I'm glad to meet you," Reverend Falwell said, extending his hand.

Jamie shook Jerry's hand, but he did not reciprocate niceties.

They opened the meeting with prayer. Jim Toms initiated the discussion, saying, "We wanted to meet today because Jamie has some concerns and wanted to check things out before Reverend Falwell sees his father."

Mark DeMoss responded, looking at Jamie, "Yes, this is why we want to see your dad. . . ."

Meanwhile Jerry Falwell and my son sat across the table from each other, not saying a word.

Finally, Jamie blurted, "Just why do you want to see my dad?"

"Well, Jamie, I just want to visit him to see how he is doing."

"Okay. Well, Jerry, I just want to let you know that you are a life-changer. You changed my life. And I want to let you know how you did it."

Jamie proceeded to tell Jerry Falwell how he had cried when our family was kicked out of the Tega Cay house where he had spent most of his life. Jamie told him how it hurt to hear Jerry Falwell call his father a homosexual on national television. Jamie was extremely blunt. He challenged Reverend Falwell saying, "You can't deny it. I saw and heard you do it. I have it on video. If you'd like to see it, I'll send you a copy."

Jerry Falwell remained quiet and simply let Jamie erupt. Jamie went on to remind Reverend Falwell of what he already knew. "My parents are divorced, my dad's in prison, all sorts of bad things have happened. . . . " Jamie told Falwell about his own bouts with drinking and drugs.

After Jamie's outpouring he shifted gears in his inimitable, rapid-fire way. "I want you to know that I forgive you for what you have done to my family. And I want you to forgive me for hating you for so long."

Jerry Falwell chose his words carefully. "Well, Jamie. I thank you for forgiving me. Forgive me for anything I might have done, or you think I might have done. There are some things that you don't understand."

Jamie took a deep breath and let it out slowly. Those were not the words he had come to hear. Yet he suddenly realized that as much as he would like to have heard Jerry Falwell admit his manipulation of the events of 1987 that eventually culminated in me going to prison in 1989, Jamie suddenly felt liberated in his own soul having extended forgiveness to Falwell and asking for Jerry's forgiveness.

Jamie responded, "Well, like I said, you are a life-changer. You have changed my life again. Now I can go on being a free man, because I don't hate you anymore."

Jamie and Jerry Falwell talked for nearly an hour and a half. At the close of their session, Jamie and Jim Toms asked to be excused and went into the interior room of the suite to discuss what should happen next.

"What do you think?" Jim asked Jamie. "How do you feel about it? Do you think your dad should meet with him?"

Jamie responded, "Yes, I think they should meet." Jamie later said that his sole reason was the sense of peace he had experienced in his own heart after talking with Reverend Falwell and extending forgiveness personally. "Dad must experience what I have experienced."

Meanwhile, I had been anxiously waiting to hear from someone whether the visit was on or off. I fully intended to abide by my promise to Jamie, that if he did not feel right about Reverend Falwell and me meeting in person, I would forgo the visit.

At last, around noon, I heard my name over the prison P.A. system, calling me to the administration building. When I walked into the building, I saw Jerry Falwell, a man whom I had not seen in person in more than seven years, standing next to my son. Jamie looked as though a heavy weight had been removed from his shoulders. I hugged my son, and then Jerry Falwell and I embraced. I had been a bit nervous about seeing him. After all, at one time. I felt Jerry Falwell was the most evil man I had ever met. All that, however, was in the past. Now, I was not fearful or hateful; I had already dealt with that when I had studied *God Meant It for Good*. I was tense due to the circumstances, but as I embraced Jerry Falwell, I felt no animosity or resentment. At that moment, I knew that God had done His work in my life.

The prison chaplain took Jerry Falwell and me back to his office. Out of earshot from the others, both Jerry and I seemed to sense the awkwardness. The last time we had sat in a room together, we had discussed his helping the leadership of PTL for a period of thirty to ninety days, after which I would return to my previous position. Jerry had since repeatedly and publicly disavowed those details of our conversation.

Now, as we sat together in a room again, it would have been easy to dredge up all the sordid mess from the past. I was not even tempted to do so, and apparently, Jerry had no desire to relive the past either. Instead, I asked Jerry Falwell to forgive me for the hateful statements I had made about him. Jerry asked me to forgive him as well though he was not specific. He stayed for about twenty minutes to half an hour and then said that he must be on his way to his speaking engagement. We prayed together, said our good-byes, embraced again, and he was gone.

Nevertheless, I couldn't help wondering why Jerry Falwell had really come to see me. Was Jerry more concerned about the future than he was over the past? Was this the last act in a play that began in Palm Springs in March 1987? Our conversation was relatively low-key, mundane, and uneventful, but perhaps more was going on than either Jerry or I was aware.

I will never know for sure why Jerry Falwell got involved in my life. God knows, and He will judge all of our words and deeds. But I have settled the matter in my heart, that regardless of Jerry's motives or anyone else's involvement, God used the circumstances of losing PTL to bring me to a place of genuine brokenness, repentance, and surrender for the first time in a long, long time. It hurt. And the losses my family and I have endured have been many and irreplaceable, but in the light of eternity, it will be worth it.

Jamie was allowed to see me for a few minutes while the Falwell group said their good-byes to the prison personnel. Jamie was euphoric about the way things had turned out. He quickly briefed me on his meeting with Jerry Falwell and told me that he and Jim Toms would be flying to the place where Jerry was speaking that night.

As I watched my son walk away that afternoon, I felt at that moment, my "little boy" was more of a man than I had ever been. He had confronted his worst fears and had turned what he had perceived to be a grizzly bear into a human teddy bear. This visit had not been for me only, but for my son. God had done a miracle that day, but it was not in bringing Jerry Falwell and Jim Bakker together; it was the healing of Jamie's heart.

Perhaps it was a little easier for me to deal with forgiveness issues concerning Jerry Falwell, because a few weeks earlier, I had been grappling with even more difficult issues of forgiveness. My former wife, Tammy Faye, and my former best friend, Roe Messner, were married.

Tammy Faye had written a letter to Tammy Sue and Jamie informing our children that she was planning to marry Roe on October 3, 1993. I had heard several rumors, but it was still a shock when someone came into my cell at Jesup and showed me a copy of *People* magazine with Tammy Faye on the arm of Roe. She was wearing a white wedding dress, and she and Roe were smiling contentedly at one another.

It hurt deeply for me to read about Tammy and Roe's marriage. It pierced my heart every time I saw a picture of my wife of more than thirty years kissing another man. Thanks to Larry Wright and many other inmates who had been through the pain of divorce, I was able to maintain my balance. As a true Body of Christ, they were there for me in my time of need. They cared for me all through the aftermath of my former wife's marriage to Roe Messner. They prayed with me and for me. And they encouraged me to forgive her.

Forgiveness is rarely a one-time deal, especially for something like divorce. I soon discovered that I had to deal with the issue of forgiving Tammy and Roe every time it came up and every time I saw another photograph of the two of them. Yet God had seared into my heart and mind the Scripture, "And when you stand praying, if you hold anything against anyone, forgive him, so that your Father in heaven may forgive you your sins" (Mark 11:25-26 NIV).

It was easier for me to forgive Tammy Faye than Roe. I was still in love with Tammy Faye. Roe was a different matter. He was the man who had stolen my wife. When Roe betrayed my trust, it was as though he had stabbed me in the back.

Nevertheless, I knew that I couldn't avoid forgiving Roe. Even if I could somehow circumvent the many Scriptures on forgiveness—which I did not attempt to do—I couldn't get away from Jesus' command to "Love your enemies, bless those who curse you, do good to those who hate you, and pray for those who spitefully use you and persecute you" (Matt. 5:44). Whether I regarded Roe as a friend or an enemy, I was locked into forgiving him and praying for him.

At one time, Roe and I shared dreams of building the greatest Christian center the world had ever seen. When I learned that he and Tammy were seeing each other while I was in prison, I wrote to him and told him that he and I would never lay another brick in another building together. Amazingly, though, during those difficult days at Jesup and afterward, I forgave Roe so completely that if in the future God instructed us to build something else together, I could do it. I don't plan on building anything else with Roe, but I am free enough to do it.

Looking back, I can now see I should never have placed him in the position of trying to care for Tammy Faye while I was in prison. Yes, they must take responsibility for their own actions, but I should have trusted God more and a man less when it came to taking care of my wife. I thought friendship superseded wisdom and common sense, and I was wrong.

Of course, I had to forgive Tammy Faye as well. I do not want to give the impression that forgiveness came easily. It did not, but it did come. At this writing, Tammy Faye and I have no contact except through our children, but I harbor no resentment or animosity toward her. At times, my heart grieves for her. I understand the pain and loneliness she suffered during those early prison years better than I once did, and I hurt for her.

Almost every week, I receive mail from well-meaning people who are praying that Tammy Faye and I will someday be remarried. I appreciate their kind and loving words. But both Tammy Faye and I must move on with our lives. She remains the mother of my children, and that is reason alone to always love and honor her. I truly want God's best for Tammy Faye and Roe. I pray that God's will may be done in all our lives.

52

Return to Heritage

THE FIRST WEEK IN APRIL 1994, MY EIGHTY-EIGHT-YEAR-OLD father fell down while he was working in his garage. He was in severe pain, but he hobbled back into the house and sat down in his favorite recliner. He sat there all night, barely moving a muscle. By morning, my father's pain was so intense, he and my mother had no choice but to call an ambulance to take him to the hospital. After a quick X ray, the doctors gave Dad the bad news—he had broken his hip. And to think he had sat up all night on it!

Because of my parents' advanced ages, the prison officials kindly allowed me a thirty-hour furlough to go see my dad in Charlotte. Jim Toms and Jamie came to meet me at Jesup on Saturday, April 10. Before I left the compound, my counselor warned me that I must be back by 8:00 P.M. Sunday night, or I would be considered an escapee. I assured the counselor that I would be back on time.

Although I was concerned for my father's well-being, it was an exciting moment when I walked out of that prison without shackles and handcuffs and chains. I felt like a real human being.

I met Jamie Charles and Jim Toms out front, and together we piled in an old, dilapidated car, borrowed from the manager of the local airstrip, for the short trip from the prison to the tiny airport. Jamie had just gotten his driver's license a few days earlier. The old former police vehicle had more power than the car Jamie had learned how to drive, and when Jamie tramped down on the gas, we took off like a jet! I thought, *Oh, no. Only two minutes out of prison and we're already breaking the speed limit.* Jamie quickly got the car under control and smiled at me. He was so proud to be driving his dad away from prison. I was proud of him too, and thrilled to be free, riding in what Jim Toms called our "getaway car."

We boarded the small plane for our trip to the Carolinas, and as we lifted off the runway, I looked down at my prison home below. From this vantage point, it looked like a well-kept college campus.

Jamie had brought along one of his blue denim shirts and a pair of pants he borrowed from a friend. I changed out of my prison blues in the back seat of the airplane. The fit wasn't the greatest, but after wearing prison jumpsuits, anything seemed stylish to me.

The airplane landed near Greenville, South Carolina, where Jim had left his car. We were anxious to get to the hospital, but Jim Toms insisted that everyone would feel better if we stopped to get something to eat. We pulled into a lovely Italian restaurant. It had been nearly five years since I had last eaten in a restaurant.

When we walked in, the hostess said they were no longer serving lunch, and the restaurant would not be open for dinner until after 5:00 P.M. Since Mr. Toms had eaten at this restaurant many times and he knew both the owner and the chef, Jim asked if he could speak with one of them. Jim talked briefly with the restaurant owner, who then came out and ushered us to a beautiful table in the center of his charming dining room. Since his regular serving hours were over, we had the restaurant to ourselves.

As I looked around the dining room, I was struck by the sheer beauty of it. The table was set with real china, placed perfectly upon a clean, starched, white linen tablecloth and Williamsburg-blue linen napkins.

A strange fear suddenly came over me. I worried that I might not be able to remember proper etiquette and table manners. Often in the Jesup Prison chow hall, our food would be simply heaped onto our trays, especially on days when bowls were in short supply.

I was in culture shock. Instead of an inmate yelling for me to hurry up and finish so he could clean up and get out of there, a fresh-faced waitress dressed in a crisp, clean uniform stood waiting to take my order. I almost lost my composure when she asked me kindly, "What would you like?" I could feel the tears welling up in my eyes. I was out of my element, and try as I might, I could not remember the simplest of social graces that had once been such a natural part of my everyday existence. I sat frozen.

The congenial restaurant owner, a tough, former football coach, sat next to me and realized I was having difficulty readjusting to life outside of prison. He quickly said, "Let's pray." He reached out his hands and we formed a prayer circle around the table as he called on God. Then, noticing that I could not make up my mind as I looked over the mouthwatering selections on the menu, the kind restaurateur said, "I'll have the chef prepare a little of everything for you." The chef made each of us an Italian platter, with veal, chicken, spaghetti, and even the owner's special home-made Italian sausage. Each of the delectable dishes was doused in rich Italian tomato sauce, some of the best I have ever tasted.

"I could get used to this," I quipped to the group around the table.

After the meal, we loaded back into the car and drove to the hospital in Charlotte. At the hospital, we found my mother sitting at my father's bedside. My dad was still groggy from some pain medicine, but he was thrilled to see us. The doctors had just operated and placed a pin in his broken hip. The prognosis looked good. After we had visited for a while, I could tell both my mother and father were getting tired, so we decided to go home.

My mother and father still lived in their home at Heritage USA. Jamie and I were to spend the night at my mother's place while Jim Toms was going to check in at the Heritage Grand Hotel. As we drove onto the grounds of Heritage USA, I had a queasy feeling in my stomach. I had not been back at Heritage since 1988. It still looked the same, yet it seemed a lifetime ago that I had been here.

The first residents to greet us were Uncle Henry and Aunt Susan Harrison. Henry had been my cohost on our television programs for many years, but now he was unable to walk and had to get around on a motorized cart. He and Aunt Susie had church in their home on the hillside location that I had personally selected for them a number of years ago.

Uncle Henry and Aunt Susan insisted that we come in and see their Christmas tree.

Christmas tree? What are they doing with a Christmas tree in their house during the second week of April? I wondered.

Sure enough, inside their home was a fully decorated Christmas tree. Uncle Henry explained to me that he had made a commitment that he was not going to take down the Christmas tree until I was released from prison. It had been up for several years now, and it still looked stunning. Henry turned on the tree lights and ran them through their beautiful displays of flashing colors and patterns.

Sensing my emotional exhaustion, Aunt Susan suggested that I lay down on Uncle Henry's big recliner bed. We talked and laughed, and I rubbed the tummy of their dog. It was like old times except we were all much older, sadder, and hopefully wiser. Aunt Susan woke Grandma Ruthie, a sweet, old woman who had volunteered her services at PTL for years, and who now lived with Uncle Henry and Aunt Susan. Grandma Ruthie had written to me faithfully while I was in prison.

"Look who's here!" Aunt Susan said as she gently nudged Grandma Ruthie awake. "Somebody has come to see you," she said.

When Grandma Ruthie opened her eyes and saw me, she looked as though she had seen a ghost! When she finally realized it was me, she relaxed and said, "I can die now. You're home."

"Oh, no, Grandma Ruthie," I told her, as I leaned over and kissed her. "We need you around here a lot longer."

I was glad to have been able to spend a few minutes with these dear folks. As difficult as the past years had been on them, I was grateful that God had blessed them with a good life and many friends who still lived at Heritage USA.

As we drove down the gently winding road that led to the Heritage Grand Hotel, where Jim Toms was going to spend the night, it was like traveling back in a time machine for me. As difficult as it may be for some people to believe, at times in prison I actually wondered if Heritage USA was all a dream. But as I caught my first glimpse of the Heritage Grand, I realized that it was no mirage after all. It had been six years since I had seen the Grand, but now the memories of it all, from blueprint stage to seeing every brick put in place, to the madcap dash to open it on time, and the many celebrations we held there, all came flooding back to me.

Jamie drove right up to the front of the hotel, under the canopy. No doubt, had I been driving or giving directions, I would have chosen a side entrance. Not Jamie. It was right up front or nothing. Jim Toms went inside to check into the hotel, and Jamie and I remained in the car. As we sat silently for a few moments, my mind replayed scenes in which thousands of people had gone through those front doors to one of the many functions we had held inside the hotel or in the Grand Ballroom. I thought back to the grand opening. Who would have guessed that this hotel would be the crux of the court case that would send me to prison? The pathos of it all swept over me as we sat in front of the hotel.

"Come on, Dad," Jamie was saying. "Let's go inside."

"Oh, no, Jamie. We can't do that."

"Come on! It's past midnight and there aren't many people around. Besides, I've really wanted to see it. Come on, Dad. It will be fun."

Fun?

Finally I consented and Jamie and I stepped inside the hotel. Only a few people were milling around, and nobody seemed to pay much attention to us as we walked past the front desk, around the corner, and down the hall toward the shopping area known as "Main Street," an indoor street lined with Victorian shops, all decorated in a turn-of-the-century motif. Main Street was nearly deserted at that hour, but its soft blue ceiling created a beautiful sense of warmth and serenity even now.

My mind raced back to Tammy Faye's and my twenty-fifth anniversary, as our family walked together down that cobblestone street, the band playing, the old-fashioned street lights lit, the twinkle lights sparkling in the trees, confetti flying, and people shouting words of love and encouragement. Now, on this night, Jamie and I walked down the deserted streets alone, the sound of our shoes echoing through the long corridor.

Because it was so late, all the stores in Main Street were closed, but Jamie insisted that we walk the length of the street and on around to the Grand Ballroom, the spacious hall where so many great Christian artists and speakers had once graced the stage.

"Jamie, let's go home." It had been a long, emotion-packed day already. I was tired, and the memories were too vivid. I felt that at any moment I was going to explode from trying to hold in my emotions. Jamie, however, was energized by it all. We got in the car and circled past the famous water park, the log chalets, and Heritage Inn. We drove by the tennis courts, Olympic-sized pool, and the recreation complex. Past hundreds of campsites, then down to The Barn auditorium and television studios. We drove near the Upper Room, the twenty-four-hour-a-day center for prayer and counseling that I had initiated after driving the streets of Charlotte looking for an open church in which to pray one night in the midst of Tammy Faye's and my problems. As Jamie and I passed by, I wondered if there were any ministers available at this hour in the Upper Room. We came upon the great amphitheater looming like a large abandoned castle in the darkness. At one time, thousands of people praised God in the amphitheater as their hearts were warmed by the Passion Play, depicting the life, death, and resurrection of Christ. Now, the amphitheater cast an eerie shadow across the grassy knoll.

Out past the Youth Center we drove; Jamie wanted to see it all. Even in the dark, I knew every bend in the road, and each turn brought back wonderful yet heartrending memories.

After what must have been an hour or more, Jamie and I made our way back to the residential area of Heritage USA. That night, I slept in my dad's bed, the first real bed I had slept on in a long time. I slept like a baby.

The next morning, I had my first bath in almost five years. Prisons have shower stalls only, so baths were a "luxury" I sorely missed. I now had a new appreciation for even the simplest of life's pleasures.

As I was shaving with my dad's razor that morning, I heard a knock on the bathroom door. I opened it and there was Jamie, standing, smiling at me. "Dad, that was the best night of sleep I have had in several years, just knowing that you were in the house with me."

"Thank you, son," I replied. Jamie stood in the doorway and watched me shave, as he had done so many times as a little boy. "It's neat to see you shave again, Dad." Jamie said.

My mother seemed more like her usual spry self that morning. She seemed physically revived by the fact that we were home with her. She wanted us to eat breakfast at her home, but I had promised Tammy Sue's family that we would have breakfast with them, even though she was still in Russia on a missions trip. I was sorry to have missed my daughter, but I was not going to miss a chance to see my grandbabies.

The time went so quickly; the clock simply refused to slow down. I knew that we had to hurry. Hopefully I would have other opportunities to visit with my family in the near future, but if I returned to Jesup after 8:00 P.M., it might be many years before I saw them again.

"Hurry, Jamie," I said. "We have to get going."

When we arrived at the hospital on Sunday, Dad was feeling much better. His room was filled with dear friends from our former church congregation at Heritage. While we chatted, a nurse brought Dad a tray of food for his lunch, which I fed to him like a little child, just as my dad had done for me as a little boy. Now it was my turn.

There was still one important stop I wanted to make before leaving.

We drove out to Tega Cay, the sight of our home that had burned to the ground while I was in prison. Nothing could have prepared me for the shock of seeing the charred remains of what had once been our home. Very little was left, only a cement slab on the hillside overlooking the lake and the beautiful, old-fashioned lampposts that had once lined the driveway in front of our home. The glass in the lamps nearest the house was partially melted in a grotesque pattern.

Jamie and I roamed around to what had once been the back of the house. As I gazed at the patio, my thoughts drifted back to so many good times at that house. Sunday afternoons were always special times for us. After I had preached at the morning worship service at The Barn, I came home and started cooking up the burgers.

We never knew how many people we would be having for lunch on Sundays. Everyone was always welcome at our home for Sunday afternoon burgers. And were they ever good! I always made the burgers extra big and thick. Tammy's specialty was her brown-sugar baked beans. We called them "Tammy Beans."

When we had more time, I loved to fry up a huge batch of seafood for the family and friends who dropped by—shrimp, scallops, flounder, oysters, and my famous homemade battered onion rings. For a moment, I was back there. I could smell the fish frying. I could hear the laughter of family and friends gathered around the table. Each batch of fish I delivered to the table disappeared as fast as I could fry it. . . .

Jamie's voice jolted me out of my daydream. "Dad! Dad, come here, quick! Look what I found!" I looked over to where Jamie was standing on the concrete slab where our garage had once stood. The garage was one of the first parts of that house that we renovated. Shortly after we bought the place, the garage began threatening to fall down. When we rebuilt it, we put in a concrete floor and eventually tiled it over so the kids could also use the garage as a playroom when the cars were not inside. The blaze that had burnt up the house also destroyed the garage, including the tile that had once covered the cement. Now that the asphalt tile had been burnt off, Jamie had discovered some scrawlings in the concrete. I brushed the dirt off the writing, revealing Tammy Sue's childlike signature. Jamie brushed away more debris and discovered his name written in the concrete as well. I could see some more writing, and as I pushed the sand off the concrete, I read the words, "Tammy loves Jim. We're eating fish tonight." The date of June 19, 1981, was scratched above a heart with an arrow through it.

Both Jamie and I stood there speechless. Time had been frozen in that concrete. The memories of what once was enveloped us. It was almost as if we were looking at a tombstone, only in this case, the tombstone marked the passing of the Bakker family as it once was.

Jamie and I reluctantly pulled ourselves away from the remnants of our former home and climbed the hill to where Jim Toms was waiting in the car. We jumped into the vehicle and Jim drove as fast as we dared all the way back to Jesup, Georgia. We arrived with just twenty minutes to spare.

53

Released!

KNOWING THAT I WAS A CANDIDATE FOR A GOOD-BEHAVIOR release to a halfway house, my lawyer and friend, Jim Toms, studied the latest prison requirements regarding my case to ascertain how such a release might be expedited. He discovered there were some basic requirements that were necessary before the prison system would even consider allowing me out of Jesup. I had to have a place to live, preferably with a family member. I needed to have a job waiting for me before I left the prison compound. I needed to have the potential to get my driver's license and to have access to a car in order to get back and forth to work. If an inmate could prove that he had realistic opportunities outside of prison, the odds of receiving a release to a halfway house increased immensely. Jim Toms began working toward that end.

Around the same time, Franklin Graham came to visit and to conduct a chapel service at Jesup. During his visit, Franklin again invited me to go along with him to help oversee the construction of two more hospitals in Africa. I told him that I would consider going but that I would like for Jamie to be able to go along, partially because I felt Jamie would greatly enjoy the experience, but also because Jamie had been waiting for me to get out of prison for so long, I didn't want to run off on another building project soon after being released. Franklin expressed certainty that Jamie could accompany me to Africa, and that Tammy Sue could visit me and minister through her music as well.

In April 1994, Franklin wrote a series of letters formally extending the invitation to work with his organization in their medical relief efforts. In essence, Franklin guaranteed me employment, if the prison system saw fit to release me to a halfway house. Jim Toms checked into the halfway houses around Boone, North Carolina, where Franklin's ministry was headquartered. Although most halfway houses in the U.S. were full, there was space available at the Salvation Army in Asheville, about an hour-and-a-half drive from Boone.

Franklin offered to pay for a place for me to live along with Jamie, and to provide an automobile for me to use. He put his name on the line and sent all the necessary information to my lawyers, who presented it to the prison officials in charge of granting the halfway-house releases.

It was beginning to look as though I might be able to serve the last part of my sentence in the halfway house after all! Yet I was troubled by something. I did not want Franklin to feel obligated to pay me back for a small kindness I had extended to him years ago. Moreover, I did not want to give the impression that I was trying to slip into the good graces of the public, and especially the Christian community, on the coattails of the Grahams' good name. I recognized that the Graham family name was one of the most respected in the country, and mine was one of the most disrespected.

During Franklin's next visit to Jesup I pulled him aside to a lawyer's room where we could talk about it. "Franklin, you don't need me," I told him. "More importantly, my baggage could hurt you. I could be a real detriment to you. If people find out that you are associating with me, it could hurt your reputation or that of your family. You don't want to identify with me. You don't need my baggage."

Franklin looked slightly offended. "Jim!" he said, "you're my *friend*." I will never forget the way Franklin Graham said that word: "friend."

Franklin said, "You helped me when very few people wanted to have anything to do with me at the beginning. The people who began supporting me at your encouragement are still the foundation of our ministry's support today. You were my friend then, and you're my friend now."

Then Franklin Graham flashed his trademark grin and with his eyes twinkling, he said, "Besides, if anyone doesn't like it, I'm ready for a fight!"

In late June, I began to hear rumors that most inmates in Jesup could serve the last six months of their sentences in halfway houses. I was thrilled to think that I might soon be released to a less-restrictive environment. The rumors were confirmed by an unusual source. A man whom I had never met, Terry Inman, a prominent Assemblies of God pastor from California, traveled all the way across the country with a special message he felt that God had laid upon his heart. Pastor Inman quoted Isaiah 40:1-2, "Comfort ye, comfort ye my people, saith your God. Speak ye comfortably to Jerusalem, and cry unto her, that her warfare is accomplished, that her iniquity is pardoned: for she hath received of the LORD's hand double for all her sins" (KJV).

Pastor Inman explained to me that God had sent him to tell me that the work that God had wanted to do in me had been accomplished, that I had received double for my sins, and that I would be released. I was humbled and awed by Pastor Inman's words. They resonated in my heart, but I had a hard time accepting his message.

Nevertheless, I began to prepare for my exit.

Around 3:00 A.M., on Friday, July 1, 1994, a guard awakened me in my cell. "Bakker, it's time," the guard said.

Those were some of the sweetest words I had ever heard.

My release to a halfway house at the Salvation Army in Asheville, North Carolina, had been granted.

Finally, it was my turn to go on the merry-go-round! You'll remember the "merry-go-round" was the term inmates used to describe the mandatory process by which prisoners are released. Before getting out of prison, the inmate must go around to each prison department head and have him or her sign off, saying that it was okay for the inmate to be released and that there were no outstanding responsibilities undone. It usually took most of a day to make the rounds, but I had never heard an inmate complain about it. This was the day every inmate longed for!

The media received word of my imminent release and began gathering a full day ahead of time. A slew of press people set up camp in front of the gates to the Jesup prison camp. Television remote trucks lined the road outside of the prison. Mr. Harris, the camp administrator, called me to his office late Thursday afternoon. He expressed his concern about the circuslike atmosphere outside the prison compound. To avoid the media hassles, the prison officials at Jesup decided to process me out in the middle of the night. I didn't mind a bit.

At about 4:00 A.M., I walked out of Jesup prison camp, wearing the clothes my family had sent to me. I got in a car driven by a female prison official, and we drove out the back gate of the prison while the throng of media people snoozed out front. I sat in the front seat. I was not cuffed, shackled, or chained. Along the way to Savannah, the woman offered me a stick of gum. I accepted it as a first token of my freedom. Inmates are not permitted to have any gum at all in prison. The taste of freedom was in my mouth!

440

In Savannah, I was met by Jamie Charles and Jim Toms. Meeting in the airport in the middle of the night made for an extremely surreal reunion. Jamie was sporting a goatee and a mustache. Before we caught the flight, however, he ran into the rest room and shaved it off. He seemed to sense that the images of this morning were going to be indelibly impressed upon our minds, not to mention newspapers and magazines all over the country, so he didn't wish to risk making a fashion statement he might regret in years to come. That's my boy, always cognizant of the big picture.

We hugged and hugged and did not want to let each other go. This was the day we had dreamed about, prayed for, and longed for. We kept saying, "I feel like I'm dreaming!"

Jamie, Jim, and I flew to Atlanta and boarded an Atlantic Southwest Airlines flight that would take us directly to Asheville. I took the window seat and Jamie sat in the aisle seat to shield me from other passengers. We had escaped relatively unnoticed. The only picture taken on the plane that morning was by Jim Toms, who took a picture of Jamie and me, a picture I treasure to this day.

We arrived in Asheville at 10:35 A.M. We waited until everyone else got off before we exited the small aircraft. A white automobile, arranged by Jim Toms, was waiting for us on the tarmac. A few well-wishers who had somehow heard of our arrival were on the other side of the fence surrounding the tarmac, and I waved to them as I bounded toward the car. I was nervous, and I wasn't sure how they would respond to me, so I was elated when they waved back enthusiastically with warm smiles on their faces. I felt so good, I wanted to wave to everyone at that point!

We drove the short distance from the Asheville airport to the Salvation Army halfway house and arrived there shortly after 11:00 A.M. A larger crowd of well-wishers was there, as well as a throng of reporters and photographers. I knew we had only limited time, because I had to report to the halfway house by noon, but I wanted to take just a few minutes to greet the well-wishers and make a statement for the press. I felt great! I was fit and tanned from walking the track in the Georgia sunshine. I was dressed casually in a black shirt and trousers and a charcoal-gray sports jacket.

One of the reporters shouted, "Jim are you happy to be here?"

I smiled broadly and said, "I'm glad to be here. I'm excited to be anywhere!" *Anywhere outside of prison*, I could have added but didn't.

I gave a prepared statement, and I greeted a few members of the press and the small group of people who had gathered to welcome me home. Jim Toms answered a few more technical questions about my release, and then I went inside to report and be fingerprinted.

The Salvation Army halfway house was a split-level, brick building that accommodated anywhere from ten to sixteen men at one time. I was to be housed with five other men. There were no guards, bars, or razor-wire fences. During the days, I was permitted to leave early in the morning to go to work, then required to return each night to sleep at the halfway house. I could eat my meals at the Salvation Army house, or I could buy my own elsewhere. I was to do my own laundry, ironing, and keep my room orderly and clean. After over four and a half years of cleaning experience in prison, I did not anticipate that as being a problem. Although I was still considered a prisoner of the federal government, a percentage of my income went toward paying for my lodging at the halfway house until my full release date in December.

Lt. Colonel David Holtz and his staff of Salvation Army officers were some of the kindest, most compassionate people I could have hoped to meet at that juncture. They did not judge me in any way, they simply loved me and cared for me, and helped me make the transition back into the mainstream of community life.

In one of the multitude of ironies connected to my case, just two blocks down the street from the halfway house was the office of Jerry Miller, one of the federal prosecutors who had tried my case in court and had represented the government in all the subsequent hearings concerning the criminal charges.

The same week that one of the national news magazines ran the story of my release from prison to the halfway house—on the same page, in the same story—the magazine ran the news of Norman Roy Grutman's death. Mr. Grutman had been the lawyer who had accompanied Jerry Falwell to Palm Springs in March 1987 to inform me that *The Charlotte Observer* was going to expose my adulterous encounter with Jessica Hahn. The Saturday before I was released to the halfway house, Norman Roy Grutman succumbed to liver cancer. He was sixty-three years of age.[1]

True to his word, Franklin Graham paid the rent on a home in the town of Etowah, a small mountain town about thirty minutes from Asheville, where I could stay with Jamie when I was not at the halfway house. Ruby and Roy Morgan literally moved out of their mountain home and lived in their motor home so we would have a place of privacy and tranquility. Franklin also gave me a car to use during my first six months out of prison—a nice station wagon too, not a jalopy. Everything that Franklin had said he would do, he did.

That first afternoon when Jamie and I rode up the mountain to the Etowah house, I could hardly believe my eyes. To be able to enjoy the natural beauty of God's creation, unfettered, unguarded, was mind-boggling. But the best part was yet to come: When Jamie and I pulled in to the house, there were Tammy Sue, Doug, and James and Jonathan. They were holding a large sign they had painted that read, "Welcome home Dad! We love you! July 1, 1994." What a joyous reunion we had!

On Saturday, one of Franklin Graham's assistants took me to a store so I could pick up some items I might need in order to go to church on Sunday morning. We went into a drugstore and I was struck by how bright and cheerful the store was. I had grown accustomed to shopping at the commissaries in prison, looking through a glass at a limited selection of products in a locked room on the other side of a window. Now, all the vibrant colors of packages danced before my eyes. I stepped tentatively down the aisles, taking in the wonder of it all. At one point I stopped and looked around to make sure nobody was listening. Franklin's assistant stopped with me and asked, "Is anything wrong, Jim?"

I whispered quietly as I pointed to the items on the shelf, "Man, somebody could steal this stuff!"

The assistant convulsed in laughter. "Yes, I guess they could," he said. When we left the store, he asked me where I would like to eat.

I told him, "I'd really like some seafood. It's been a long time since I've had any of that."

He took me to a Red Lobster restaurant, and as soon as the waitress brought the menu, I knew I was in trouble. The menu was so big! And there were so many selections. I read the menu again and again and I simply could not make up my mind. There were just too many choices. Eventually, I ordered a seafood platter with a little bit of everything on it. Wow! Was it ever great to be out!

I rose early on Sunday morning to get ready for church. I felt somewhat nervous about attending a formal church service outside of prison. I had many concerns: How would people react to seeing *me* in their sanctuary? Would I be a distraction from the worship service? Would the pastor want me in the congregation? I did not want to cause any trouble.

Nevertheless, I had promised Franklin's mother, Ruth Graham, that I would attend the Sunday morning worship service with her and her family at the Montreat Presbyterian Church. Franklin was to be the guest speaker at the 10:45 A.M. service.

The beautiful stone church was already nearly full when I arrived. I was ushered back to the office of the pastor, Dr. Calvin Thielman, to meet with him and Franklin before the service. The pastor was extremely kind and gracious. He assured me that I was welcome in the church and told me that he had been a lifelong friend of the Graham family. One of Franklin's staff members ushered me to the row where they had saved a seat for me . . . with the Graham family. The Graham family, with all the children and grandchildren, filled up nearly two rows of the sanctuary.

By the time the organist finished playing the prelude on the stately pipe organ, the church was packed with people. Just before the invocation, Ruth Graham walked down the aisle and sat down right next to me.

The introductory hymn that morning was "Christ Has Set Us Free." When Franklin got up to preach, one of the first things he did was present me to the congregation. He told them the story of Tenwek Hospital and how he had come to know me. When he introduced me as his friend to his sophisticated home congregation, the audience applauded and I lost control of my emotions. Tears streamed down my face as I sat with the congregation and the members of one of the most respected families in America applauding all around me. I spent most of Franklin's sermon trying to regain my composure. Only forty-eight hours previously I was in prison, Inmate 07407-058, and now I was in the beautiful Montreat church with Ruth Graham and her family.

After the service, I climbed into Franklin Graham's pickup to drive to his parents' home. Fortunately, he had removed the guns from his gun rack—federal felons are not allowed to be in the same vehicle with a gun.

By the time we arrived at "the cabin," as the Grahams refer to their lovely, old, log mountain home, Ruth and Franklin's wife, Jane Austin, and the children had already arrived. Ruth had prepared dinner for us. We enjoyed a wonderful, casual dinner together. I felt as though I was sitting in the midst of a family reunion. We talked and laughed just as any family might during the Sunday afternoon meal. We talked a great deal about one of Ruth's favorite subjects, as well—how we could better get Bibles to inmates and their families.

During the course of our conversation, Ruth asked me a question that required an address. I reached into my back pocket and pulled out a paper envelope in which I kept my addresses and cash. I had not owned a wallet for over four and a half years—prisoners are not allowed to have wallets.

As I fumbled through the envelope looking for the address, Ruth Graham watched me quizzically. "Don't you have a wallet, Jim?"

"This is my wallet," I replied pointing to the envelope. Right then it seemed natural to me to have a paper envelope as a wallet.

Ruth got up and left the room. In a few minutes she returned carrying one of Billy Graham's wallets. "Here is a brand-new wallet Billy has never used. I want you to have it," she said.

I still carry that wallet to this day.

Before I left that afternoon, Ruth Graham insisted upon sitting down and writing a thank you letter that she asked me to carry with me to Darlene Thompson, the woman who was in charge of the Salvation Army halfway house. In the letter, Ruth wrote thanking the directors of the halfway house for being good to me. She also thanked them for allowing me to come and spend the day with the Graham family.

Over the years, I have met literally thousands of wonderful Christian men and women and families. I have never met anyone more humble, gracious, and, in a word, "real," than Ruth Graham and the members of her marvelous family.

During my first few weeks out of prison, I went to several meetings with Franklin Graham and his staff members to get a better understanding of the work of Samaritan's Purse. I was amazed by what I saw. Many people ballyhoo about the good work they do. Franklin and his staff just do it.

I met with some of the staff and the doctors who were supplying medical help overseas. I met with the head of the overseas hospitals. I attended Samaritan's Purse planning meetings at "The Cove," the Billy Graham Conference Center. With every person I talked to, I came away impressed and convinced that it was truly Christianity in action.

Franklin and the staff of Samaritan's Purse have huge warehouses, filled with everything from medical supplies to hospital tools. The buildings were stocked with baby beds and anything else that might be necessary to meet the needs of diseased and dying people in Third World countries. As I toured the facilities in one location, I saw workers rebuilding X-ray machines and other technical medical equipment to be used on the mission field. On another floor, I saw their staff working on a worldwide communications system to create faster and better lines of communication with missions all over the world in times of need or crisis. Samaritan's Purse is an awesome ministry, a massive undertaking, and without a hint of ostentation. Franklin and his coworkers simply go about their work in a quiet but effective manner, saving and changing lives around the world.

It seems to me that wherever there is a crisis of human need, Franklin is there. On a moment's notice he hops in his small plane, which he enjoys flying himself, landing in the most war-torn, disease-ridden areas of the world, to see how he and his organization can help.

As impressed as I was with Franklin's work, I was not able to go to Africa with him at that time. The government was reluctant to let me leave the country, having just been released from prison. More importantly, I was not emotionally ready to help anyone yet. Tears came easily and frequently. I needed to get acclimated to a semblance of normal living again.

I had grown spiritually by leaps and bounds while in prison, but I needed time to learn how to function in polite society again. Beyond that, my family needed me to be home; I had been gone for such a long time. As much as I enjoyed working with Franklin Graham and was disappointed that I could not help in Africa yet, I felt it was part of God's plan that I stay home for the time being.

So I worked part-time for my attorney, Jim Toms. I prepared lunches for Jim's clients, buying all the ingredients at the local grocery store, cooking the meals, and serving the clients. One of my favorite jobs was painting the front of Jim's law office, wearing old, paint-spattered clothes and a baseball cap as I worked. Besides getting to work outside in the fresh air, it was fun to watch the reaction of people as they went by on the street. Their facial expressions said, "Is that Jim Bakker covered with paint on that ladder? Naaahhhh!"

54

Back From the Grave

WITHIN A FEW DAYS OF BEING OUT OF PRISON I RECEIVED several job offers, dozens of interview requests, and invitations for speaking engagements. I accepted none at that time. I kept busy and out of the public eye. As much as possible, I stayed at the mountain house in Etowah, which was a wonderful time of rest and refuge for me, but terribly boring for Jamie.

Jamie slept on a pull-out couch in the den on the lower level of the house. He loved his room with the pool table, a fifties jukebox, and the walls covered with Coca Cola memorabilia, but he eventually tired of doing little besides watching television and playing songs on the jukebox.

Jamie soon told me the isolation of being out in the middle of nowhere was causing him to go stir-crazy. He had lived for the day that I got out of prison. Now that I was actually out of prison, I wanted to live quietly in the mountains and rebond with my son and rebuild our lives. Jamie, on the other hand, wanted to visit his former friends in Charlotte, some of whom I feared were not a positive influence on him.

Like Jamie, I too had dreamed of the day we could be together. When things did not automatically work out the way we had hoped, I felt that I was failing him as a father again. I knew I had failed him when he was a boy, and the last thing I wanted to do now was to fail him again when as a young man, he needed my love, acceptance, and guidance. I knew he needed more than just being around me. Jamie needed to be with friends his own age as well. He also needed desperately to catch up on the education he missed while I was in prison.

Furthermore, because the mountain house had only one actual bedroom, and that with French doors, we had little privacy for Tammy Sue and her family members when they came to visit. Besides, Jamie, Tammy Sue, and I had lived very separate lives for the past four and a half years, intersecting with each other only for a few days every so often in prison, in a stressful, artificial setting. We all had our own image of the family that we used be, back in the glory years of Heritage USA, and we all wanted that image of "family" to return. But the heart of our family, Tammy Faye, was missing. We all missed Tammy Faye's presence in our family.

Tougher to admit, we were not functioning well as a family before the fall of PTL. Tammy Sue hit me with that truth one day when I was lamenting the good old days of family life. "Dad, get a grip," she said in her down-to-earth manner. "We *never* really were a family. We all were doing our own things. We came out of our rooms for meals and then went back to doing our own things."

When I stopped to think of it, Tammy Sue was right. If we were going to rebond as a family, it would have to be almost like starting from scratch.

Consequently, we did not know how to react to one another. After praying so hard and so long, and having such lofty expectations of what it would be like if I could just get out of prison, we were all somewhat disappointed when reality poked holes in our illusions of perfection.

About that time, Dr. Raymond Meadors, a former professor at Heritage School of Evangelism, told me about a wonderful program that his children were attending at the First Assemblies of God Church in Phoenix, a church pastored by my longtime friend Tommy Barnett. The group was known as "Master's Commission" and was having spectacular results, especially with the children of missionaries, pastors, and other teenagers who had grown up in the glass house of some ministry.

I immediately called Lloyd Zigler, the leader of Master's Commission, and explained to him that Jamie and I were having some difficulties. I explained that Jamie had had some drug problems as well as difficulties resulting from a learning disability. The leader assured me that Jamie would be welcome at Master's Commission.

Shortly after that, I talked with Tommy Barnett by phone. He too assured me that Jamie would be welcome there. He extended an invitation for Jamie to stay with his family or live in the school apartments if he decided to be a part of the group. I told Jamie about the idea. At first, Jamie recoiled at the thought of leaving me so soon after I had gotten out of prison. When I realized how Jamie felt, I suggested that he go visit for a week, "just to check it out."

Jamie agreed to go to Phoenix. When he arrived, he soon discovered a special branch ministry directed by Mike Wall, a former member of Master's Commission. Jamie wanted to do something to take the gospel to some of the fringe elements of the youth culture, for instance, the skateboard crowd with whom he identified and participated. Consequently, he easily related to Mike Wall, who dressed more like a rock musician than a youth pastor. Mike had a passion to minister to the youth of his generation, "alternative" kids, punk rockers, hippies, grungers, and other nonconformist youth. Mike told Jamie about a new youth ministry he was just forming. The group was to be called "Revolution." Jamie joined on the spot. Mike trained Jamie for five months, studying the Bible together and preparing to take the gospel to a new generation.

In addition, Jamie sat under the ministry of Tommy Barnett, who powerfully impacted him. The entire experience helped change and deepen Jamie's spiritual life. During that time, my boy was transformed into a youth minister who began helping other kids solve their problems by introducing them to Christ. My little boy had become a man of God.

Shortly after Jamie left for Phoenix, I moved to the Bennett Farm, a small, secluded farm outside Hendersonville, North Carolina, about forty minutes from Asheville. The farm, with its rolling hills, apple trees, old barn, and wonderful view of the mountains, was a perfect spot for gently easing back into normal society. It was quiet, peaceful, and restorative. The farm was located between a large cattle pasture on one side and a cemetery on the other, so my neighbors were no bother, except for those few times when the cattle got out.

The owners of the farm gave me a credit card from Lowe's, a building-supply company, to purchase items to use in fixing up the place. I threw myself into turning the stark white walls of the house—which reminded me of the blandness of prison—into a warm, cozy home. I painted my bedroom a deep forest green and decorated one of the guest rooms in a deep mauve motif. I called it the Tammy Sue Room. The other bedroom I painted dark navy blue and called it the Jamie Charles Room. I hung family photographs in each room; many of the photos came from the children's childhood bedrooms.

One day as I was working on the house, I realized that I had no bath towels or shower curtain in my guest bathroom. I decided to take some of the money I had earned from working and go shopping. I went to J. C. Penney's department store and found a wallpaper border, a shower curtain, and a set of mauve towels and facial cloths that matched. The woman who

449

checked me out at the counter was extremely kind, but shortly thereafter, another clerk at the store did an interview on the local television station in which she expressed the sentiment that I should not even be allowed to buy towels! I realized then that not everyone was glad that I was out of prison and living in the area.

Most people, however, in the Hendersonville area were extremely kind to me. I often took my grandchildren to the old main-street drug-store, which has an old-fashioned soda fountain and a player piano. My grandsons loved hearing the old songs, many of which I hadn't heard since I was a little boy. We drank cherry-ice-cream sodas and plunked quarters into the old player piano and sang along with the songs. Nobody ever bothered us. On the contrary, most of the people of the town were almost always supportive and friendly. In fact, the day following the woman's protest on TV, as I was going into a Wal-Mart store, an elderly gentleman expressed to me, "I wish they would just leave you alone. You have already gone through enough."

A few days later, something happened that totally overshadowed the J.C. Penney clerk's judgment. I had looked everywhere in Hendersonville to find drapes within my price range that would match my living room. Finding nothing suitable, I decided to drive to the Asheville Montgomery Ward. Slightly nervous about being out of my small-town environment, I made my way to the "big city" store's drapery depart-ment, where I found what seemed like hundreds of drapes and curtains from which to choose. As I ambled from one aisle to the next, my eyes fell upon the exact pattern and fabric I was looking for. As I checked the price tag, out of the corner of my eye I saw a rotund black lady looking at me intently from the doorway leading to the stockroom. My heart began to race and I prayed, "Oh, God. Please don't let me have an unpleasant confrontation."

The woman was making a beeline right for me! When she was within an arm's length, she said, "Aren't you Jim Bakker?"

I looked down at the floor and said, "Yes."

She said, "I knew it! I knew it!" She turned her head back toward the stockroom doorway and exclaimed loudly, "I told you it was him!"

At that, an entire lineup of clerks rushed out of the stockroom as the first lady said, "Do you mind if I give you a hug? I have always loved your ministry so much!"

I was in no position to argue. Anyway, I was in need of a hug.

She threw her arms around me and squeezed tightly. One by one, each of the other salesclerks lined up to give me a hug. It was like God was expressing His love toward me through these people in the drapery department of Montgomery Ward.

I got the draperies, hooks, and a whole lot more!

When Tammy Faye and I divorced, we struck an extremely simple settlement. Through our lawyers, I told her to take whatever she wanted, and I'd take anything that she didn't want and have it placed in storage. Tammy Faye left behind quite a large amount of household items and pictures, as well as several roomfuls of our old furniture. When I first moved to the farm, I spent many of my early days there playing Mr. Fix-It, cleaning, painting, wallpapering. Finally, I was ready for the items in storage.

To my delight, when everything was unloaded from the U-Haul truck, I discovered that I had enough furniture to completely furnish the one-story house. Coming out of prison, I had nothing with me except my clothes and a few belongings, yet I had three beds in storage, a dining-room table and chairs, some living-room furniture, and perhaps best of all, my desk that Tammy had bought back for me at one of the PTL auctions. I had dishes, a full set of silverware, and some cooking utensils. The only problem was that I had several pans that I'm sure Tammy Faye had the lids for and several lids for which she probably had the pans.

Along with the furniture, I found box after box of old, family photographs. At first it hurt me that Tammy had left behind so many memories of our life, but as I opened one box after another filled with framed photos and other trinkets, I was grateful that Tammy had left them for me. In the boxes, I found photographs from every stage of our life and ministry, dating back to some of our childhood pictures, to the early days at CBN, TBN, and PTL, to pictures with Presidents Carter and Reagan. I found dozens of framed photos of Tammy and me with various celebrities who had graced our *PTL* sets. I also found a huge painting done by a Disney artist, depicting the existing Heritage USA and some of the ideas I had only dreamed about. The artist titled the work "The Dream Never Ends."

I found so many pictures that I decided to turn my living room, dining area, and hallway into a family gallery. Any area on the walls above the chair rail was open game for picture hanging. It took me days to hang all the pictures, but each one was a special memory.

When I finished hanging all the photographs, it was as though my whole life was hanging there on the walls. I walked through each part of the house, gazing at the walls and remembering. Then I broke down and sobbed and sobbed and sobbed. Since then, several people have asked me, "Why would you put up pictures that include your former wife?" For me, it was good therapy. By not trying to hide the photos of the woman who had been such an important part of my life for so long, I was facing the reality that she was gone. The pictures became part of my healing process.

A further help in my healing was doing the outdoor, day-to-day work on the farm. I had large fields to mow, fences to mend, and other maintenance matters. It was great therapy for me simply to be out puttering around in my flower and vegetable garden.

When my grandsons came to visit, we decided what the farm really needed was a tree house. We started with only one plank placed across several branches of a large mulberry tree. When I was growing up, an old mulberry tree at my school produced big, black mulberries and I used to love to pick and eat them. Now, as an adult, I felt that God had given me another mulberry tree to enjoy, this time with my grandsons.

We kept adding boards to make the floor of the tree house. Before long, I was involved in another major building project, along with my two grandsons, ages four and six at the time. I put a window and door in the tree house. I shingled the roof. Soon we added a slide, which created a fun, quick exit from the structure. After that, we added a set of swings. In hardly any time at all, the tree house was almost bigger than the tree in which it was perched. When some of my friends and family members saw the project, they jokingly said, "Yep, that's a Jim Bakker tree house!"

On December 1, 1994, I was officially released from the halfway house. People who don't understand the American legal system and dichotomy between the way sentences are handed out compared to the amount of time served thought that I was getting out early. Not so. I had served the mandatory amount of time normally served by an inmate with an eight-year sentence, under old law. Granted, at any point, had I been a problem prisoner, the system could have kept me in prison and made me serve every day of the sentence I was given. That, however, would have been unusual treatment for an inmate who was not considered to be incorrigible. Under old law, it is extremely rare that someone's sentence and time served are identical. Basically, I was treated normally by the system, no better and no worse.

To be declared free at last meant an enormous amount to me. Practically speaking, however, it did not greatly change my day-to-day routine, other than the fact that I no longer had to pay the halfway house part of my earnings, and I no longer had to report to the Salvation Army. I could live in my own rented home, without having to check in with anyone except my parole officer, Glen Alexander. Technically, my prison sentence did not expire until April 18, 1997. Until that time, I was to be accountable to the parole officer, who checked in on me regularly and often unexpectedly at the farm.

At the Eighteenth Annual Pastors and Leaders Conference to be held at Phoenix First Assembly in early February, Pastor Tommy Barnett asked Jamie to give a testimony of what God had done in his life. Each year, Tommy has what he calls a "Parade of Ministries," in which each of the church's more than 180 ministry groups presents a review of their ministry and key testimonies. Jamie's testimony was to be part of the presentation by the alternative youth ministry, Revolution.

Tommy wrote to me, informing me of the special conference and the Parade of Ministries. He said he hadn't mentioned to Jamie that he was contacting me, but since this was going to be Jamie's first public testimony, the pastor thought I might like to attend. At first, I declined Pastor Barnett's kind invitation. I told him that the media had not ceased to be interested in me since my release from prison, plus I did not want to hurt his church by my being there.

A few days after I sent my answer, Tommy called me by telephone to personally invite me to attend the service. "We won't tell anybody you are coming," he said. "Not even Jamie. You won't have to deal with the press. I know Jamie would love for you to be here."

"I don't know, Tommy," I replied, still hesitant.

"Jim, anybody has a right to hear his boy give his first testimony."

I decided to go.

The night of the Parade of Ministries, I was as nervous as I had ever been at the opening of a new facility at Heritage USA or the launching of a new television program. And I didn't even have to do anything but sit in the audience, as inconspicuously as possible! Jamie was not aware that I was there. For an hour and a half, thousands of people marched, sang, and testified about Jesus. It was overwhelming. The church had ministries to everyone, from children to the aged, from AIDS patients to street people to nursing homes, and on and on. At one point, the "Bikers' Ministry" rode right across the platform on their motorcycles. Many of them reminded me of men with whom I had been incarcerated.

"And now for our last ministry," Tommy Barnett announced. My heart began to beat more rapidly. The pastor had saved my son's testimony to the very end. When the youth group Revolution was introduced by a wild music video featuring teenage skateboarders, my heart was in my throat. I could hardly breathe. I strained to see my son as the group bounded onto the stage. I almost did not recognize Jamie. His black hair was cut short and dyed blonde, and he had grown back his goatee.

Jamie's best friend and the director of Revolution, Mike Wall, spoke with deep concern and compassion for young people. After that, Pastor Barnett introduced Jamie as Jay Bakker, the name he had been using for some time, partly to establish his own identity, separate and distinct from being known as Jamie Bakker, son of Jim and Tammy Faye Bakker and PTL infamy. Most people in the auditorium and even in the local church and ministry group with which Jamie worked did not know Jamie was my son.

Jamie took a deep breath, "I want to tell you why Revolution is important to me. My dad got out of prison a few months ago. . . ."

"Jim Bakker," Pastor Barnett whispered in Jamie's ear, encouraging him to tell the audience who his dad was.

"Jim Bakker is my dad. Jim and Tammy Faye Bakker are my parents. . . ."

The crowd erupted in applause and a standing ovation that never seemed to end. Surprised and shaken, Jamie broke down sobbing. Tommy Barnett put his arms around Jamie and comforted him. The crowd continued to applaud. When the people finally sat down, Jamie attempted to continue through his sobs, "You don't know how much that means to me. . . ."

Or me either. The entire crowd of more than seven thousand people continued applauding all around me. One man shouted out, "We love you, Jamie!" I was one of the few people in the room not on my feet. I was slumped forward in my chair, my face in my hands. I simply could not handle this marvelous outpouring of love expressed toward my son, and indirectly toward me. I had thought that people hated my family and me, but these people were applauding at the mention of our name! It was humbling that God's people cared that much.

Jamie fought through his tears to give his testimony. "I was living right up until the time my dad got out of prison—well, I was living wrong a little before that—but then when dad was getting out, I figured I better take a summer off and party a little. I had had drug problems before, and I started getting into some stuff that I shouldn't have been. My dad and I began to have some problems."

Jamie continued, "My dad is the greatest person in the world, and I love him to death. He said, 'I want you to go to Master's Commission.' That's where I met Mike Wall. God had given me a dream before, and Mike was living that dream and allowed me to be a part of that dream, a place where my generation can fit in, where we're not judged because of the color of our hair or because of an earring.

"I also would like to talk about some things I went through in my past," said Jamie. "When my dad lost Heritage USA and PTL, it hurt me . . . bad. There weren't a lot of people who stood by us, not a lot of ministers, not a lot of preachers. . . . There were a few great people who stood by . . . but it was hard. Then two years later, my dad went to prison. He was in prison for four and a half years. That's serious. Then my mom and dad got a divorce." The ache of Jamie's soul caused his face to contort.

"You all know this, I guess it's been in the media and everything, and everybody has been in our business." Jamie paused. "I found out there is a way to make it, people. . . . " The crowd broke into applause once again.

Jamie said, "You might remember a song from my parents. . . . They used to say on their show, 'you can make it.' We used to say that by faith, but now we say it by experience." The crowd erupted again.

Jamie went on to encourage the churches represented at the conference to care for their pastors. "People, there are hurting pastors out there— some of you are here and you don't have churches because your churches have been taken away from you. Church, we have got to start healing people. We've got to stop playing games with each other. It's important. It almost destroyed my life. It put my dad in prison for four and a half years. But the only way to do that is with a personal relationship with Jesus Christ. So if you know of a hurting pastor, show him the love of Jesus Christ. Have a love relationship with Jesus Christ. Thank you."

The crowd broke into another standing ovation. Loud whistles filled the air as well as applause, cheers, and praises to God. Standing as part of the audience, I could barely contain my own emotions.

Pastor Barnett brought the room to order and put his arm around Jamie. When the room was quiet, the pastor told Jamie and the congregation about his and my correspondence and my reluctance to come to Phoenix, for fear of being an embarrassment to the church or to Jamie. Tommy Barnett then told the congregation what he had told me, "Any man has a right to hear his son's testimony!"

Then Tommy Barnett announced, "Jim's here tonight!" Jamie's face expressed his surprise and elation. The audience burst into wild applause. "Come on, Jim!" Pastor Barnett encouraged me through the bedlam. "Come on down here and give your boy a hug!"

As I was moving toward the front of the auditorium, I could feel the thousands of eyes on me. I hurried to the platform, but I had only one sight in my focus—my son standing on the platform, tears streaming down his face.

Tommy Barnett was ecstatic. He said to Jamie and the crowd, "You didn't know he was going to be here!" The crowd was still on its feet, cheering louder than any audience I had ever heard. The people kept clapping and clapping!

When I reached the platform, I went straight to Jamie. I wrapped my arms around him and we wept on each other's shoulders while the congregation continued to praise God and cheer. It was truly one of the most moving moments of my entire life.

As the audience continued to applaud, I whispered in Jamie's ear, "I'm scared to death!"

Jamie said, "I am too!"

When I finally let go of Jamie, I went to Mike Wall, who was standing on the platform behind Tommy Barnett. I threw my arms around Mike and said, "Thank you for loving my son."

Again the room erupted in thunderous applause. Next I hugged Pastor Barnett and thanked him, weeping uncontrollably the entire time. The congregation cheered each step.

As the noise subsided, a loud voice called out of the crowd, "We love you, Jim!" Someone else shouted, "We love you, Jay!" Others picked up the call and the crowd applauded even more. "Say a few words," Tommy Barnett said, nodding toward the microphone. The audience picked up on the pastor's words. "Say a few words, Jim!"

I honestly did not know what to say. Beyond that, as I looked out into the bright lights and the sea of faces, I was not certain that my mind could form real words into actual sentences, or that my mouth and tongue would cooperate in speaking them aloud.

At last, my emotions running rampant, I mustered five words: "I'm proud of my boy." Once again the audience responded with applause.

I took a breath, tried to maintain some sort of composure, and started to speak slowly, "This is my first . . . public . . . appearance . . . in six years."

The audience exploded. I looked around and saw some of the bikers, a rough-looking bunch still on stage.

"Boy, am I glad these bikers are up here," I said. "I feel right at home. This is my group!" One of the bikers burst out of the crowd on stage and hugged me, as the crowd went wild again.

I began to share from my heart with the people in that audience. "I have sat with the presidents of the United States of America. I have flown on Air Force One. I have sat with the most famous people in all the world. I built parks for the young people to enjoy. But I want to tell you people something. I want to tell you pastors something. I had to go to prison for this boy to spend the first day with me in his lifetime." I went on to tell the crowd about the day, shortly after Jamie's sixteenth birthday, when he came to prison by himself. "After we had spent the day together, he said, 'Dad, this is the best day of my whole life. I've spent my whole life trying to get your attention. I wanted just to spend one day with you and have you to myself.'" Knowing that there were many busy pastors in the audience, I felt compelled to tell the group, "Preachers, don't go around the world and win the world and lose your own kids." The crowd broke into another long round of applause.

Holding onto Jamie, I told the group, "This boy at four and five—I put his pictures up in prison—he was the cutest little boy that ever walked the face of the earth." Jamie looked embarrassed. The crowd crowed with delight. "But I was too busy," I confessed. "I missed it. Somebody sent me a picture of me building Heritage, and there in the background following me was this little boy. All he wanted was his dad."

I finished with: "Tonight . . . I have seen a church with the love of God in action. A church that says, 'We're not going to hurt the hurting anymore. We're going to love them!' Thank you for your love." The room thundered with applause once again. Pastor Barnett stepped quickly to the microphone and asked those who wanted to pray to come to the front of the auditorium. Hundreds did. Many pastors came and poured their hearts out to God. One pastor knelt down beside Jamie and me and told me through his tears, "Jim, it has been a long time since I have spent any time with my boy. I'm not even going to stay for the remainder of the conference. I'm going home right now to spend some time with my son."

It was well past midnight when I finally crawled into bed. My heart was rejoicing in what God had done for Jamie . . . and for me.

I had planned to stay in Phoenix for about two weeks to enjoy some time with Jamie and to really have some good father-son time. But then I got the phone call.

Uncle Henry Harrison, my longtime friend and sidekick on our *PTL* television programs, had died of complications caused by muscular dystrophy, and his wife, Aunt Susan, had contacted Tammy Sue to ask for me to come back to Heritage USA to preach the funeral. When Jamie heard the news of Henry's death, he was shocked and saddened. He was disappointed that I would have to return east so soon, but he understood.

I grieved deeply at the loss of my friend Henry. We had worked together in Christian television for years, dating back to the fledgling days of the Christian Broadcasting Network. Henry had come to visit me on the farm in Hendersonville shortly after my release from prison. He could barely move his body, except for his hands, but despite his declining health, Henry was still so positive, so upbeat. Henry said, as he had so many times before, that he would see Jim Bakker preach again at Heritage USA.

On January 21, 1995, I attended a party in Fort Mill in honor of Henry's sixty-seventh birthday. Once again, Henry reminded me that he would see me preach again at Heritage USA. Two weeks later, Henry went to be with the Lord.

Immediately after learning of Henry's death I placed a call to Aunt Susan. When she came on the line, she sounded very sad, but I could tell her faith in God was still strong. She told me that Henry had been bedridden almost since his birthday party two weeks earlier. He had been having dreams of heaven, that he was running through heaven.

As we talked, Aunt Susan emphatically requested that I speak at Henry's memorial service that was to be held on Sunday. Although I recognized that my presence at Henry's funeral might be awkward, I couldn't refuse Aunt Susan. I told her that I would be there.

As soon as I disconnected with Aunt Susan, I was back on my phone calling Jim Toms. Aunt Susan had said that their plans were to have the service on the grounds of Heritage USA. I wanted Jim to check on whether the new owners would allow me to speak there. I needn't have worried. The owners graciously consented to my preaching Henry's memorial service; they kindly offered to open any facilities we needed at no charge. Eventually it was decided that to facilitate the anticipated crowd, the service should be held in The Barn . . . the place where I had regularly preached to our local congregation and guests on Sunday mornings all through my years at PTL.

Bob and Debby Gass accompanied me to the Radisson Grand Resort—the place I knew as Heritage USA. At some point after PTL was sold, the new owners had put a facade sign over the old Heritage USA sign at the entrance way. A few days before Henry's memorial service, an automobile had crashed into the base of the structure. The Radisson Grand Resort facade had fallen down and had not yet been replaced. The original sign was showing plain as day. As I drove in, I could not help noticing the name on the sign: *Heritage USA*. I thought of Henry's words that were now sounding more and more prophetic, "I will see Jim Bakker preach at *Heritage USA*."

I checked in at the Heritage Grand Hotel, the place that held such wonderful memories for me, yet had also been the foundation of the case that put me in prison. The management arranged complimentary lodging for me in one of the most beautiful suites in the hotel, the Maude Aimee Humbard Suite, named after the wife of the famous preacher Rex Humbard. I had this suite decorated with special care due to my friendship with the Humbards. It was the only suite in the hotel in which I had installed pure-white carpet, because that suited Maude Aimee's tastes. I was surprised how beautiful the suite still looked. I took off my shoes and walked barefoot on the beautiful white carpet. It felt slightly damp; the management must have just recently cleaned it.

Later that evening, I dined with Mr. Kok Yin Khet, the president of the New Heritage USA. Mr. Khet was so kind, warm, and gracious to me. He took me to a Chinese restaurant, did all the ordering, and personally served the meal to me. I presented my host with a copy of a book of poems, the same collection I planned to give to Aunt Susan after using it in the memorial service the next day. During the course of the evening, I thanked Mr. Khet again and again for maintaining Heritage USA so well, and especially for keeping it all together as I believed God had intended rather than selling off parcels of land, which would have been an easy and lucrative thing to do. It was a very pleasant evening for me, but the tension of speaking at Heritage USA the following day was weighing heavily upon me.

The service was held Sunday afternoon, February 12, 1995. Aunt Susan and I arrived, riding in the funeral car to The Barn. No local news cameras or reporters with cameras were permitted inside where the ceremony was to take place, so we anticipated that there might be a group of media people outside. Although we wanted an atmosphere of celebration and praise to permeate the ceremony, we did not want the service to be a media event. This was Henry's day.

I was particularly concerned with how people in the audience might react to me. This was, after all, my first officially announced return to Heritage USA. Many people's jobs had been lost and lives had been uprooted when I toppled from the pinnacle of PTL. More than a few, especially those who had been among the higher ranks at PTL, could not find jobs in the area after the fall. Ostensibly they were overqualified, but most of those who later told me their stories probably had grounds for winnable job discrimination suits, not being hired simply because they had once been employed at PTL.

Now as I entered The Barn, supporting Aunt Susan on my arm, I could see in my peripheral vision that the building was packed. I walked in and sat down with Aunt Susan on the front row.

Stepping back into that auditorium was an emotional experience for me. I had preached here so many times before. This was the church I had pioneered, the pulpit behind which I had stood so many times before. What amazed me most, perhaps, was that the platform looked almost the same as it had the last time I had preached there in 1986. The stage looked just as I had left it, with royal-blue carpet and a white pulpit set against a deep-red, Austrian-pleated stage curtain. According to those who had seen it, the platform had not looked that way a mere twenty-four hours earlier. When the Inspirational Network had been sold off, the purchaser stripped from the building the state-of-the-art audio and video equipment, worth hundreds of thousands of dollars.

The announcement that Henry's memorial service was to be held in The Barn drew our former crew members together like a magnet. Even our former ushers gathered to help. They reset the platform and the auditorium seating. The new owners of Heritage USA even had my former dressing room repainted. Lee Mowry and Don Kendrick brought in their own audio equipment and put together a professional sound system on the spot. Our former staff moved in plants and set up columns and all the things that people would have seen had they tuned in to one of our live programs broadcast from The Barn in the mid-'80s. The former crew members did it without anyone even asking, free of charge. They simply came together to make things right for Uncle Henry. When Tammy Sue walked into that building late Saturday night, she couldn't believe her eyes. As she looked around the huge Barn auditorium, everywhere she turned she saw former team members. Tammy Sue was overwhelmed at seeing all these people with whom she had grown up on the set. It was like stepping back in time. She simply stood there and wept at the sight.

The memorial service itself was a celebration of Uncle Henry's homecoming. The service lasted well over two hours. Although everyone in the room would miss him dearly, we all had perfect confidence that Henry was in heaven with Jesus. Bob and Jeannie Johnson, two of my longtime singers and staff members at PTL, kept things moving. Bob introduced Tammy Sue to sing and without any fanfare—as I had asked him to do— he said simply, "After Tammy Sue sings, her father will bring the message."

The first song Tammy Sue sang was "When Jesus Passes By." I had never heard the song before, but to me, it was the perfect selection. Tammy Sue had come to Jesup and had sung for the inmates in the chapel program, but to hear her sing at Henry's funeral was the fulfillment of a dream for me. Many times while in prison, I had dreamed of a day when Tammy Sue might sing on the same program at which I was preaching.

Yet preaching seemed such a remote possibility for me. Feelings of total worthlessness often overwhelmed me. I was out of prison, but I couldn't get prison out of me. I just didn't know what I was supposed to do with the rest of my life. Yet deep inside, I had a dream of one day preaching again, with Tammy Sue singing. Who could have guessed that it would have been Uncle Henry who pulled us all together?

When Tammy Sue concluded her second song, as planned, there was no introduction of me. I stepped up to the pulpit in my home church for the first time in nearly a decade. The auditorium was full and the huge crowd rose to greet me with a thunderous ovation. I was shocked! I had never before seen a standing ovation at a funeral, but then, this was not just any funeral. This was homecoming day, for Henry . . . and for me.

The people wouldn't stop clapping. I felt dizzy from the waves of love that washed over me from the audience. I grabbed the edges of the pulpit to steady myself from swaying backwards. Gradually I felt more confident and stepped away from the pulpit to wave at friends. Inside, my stomach was churning. I figured I might as well level with the audience. "I'm scared to death and I'm going to tell you that. . . . This is my first time in the pulpit in many, many, many years."

"We love you, Jim!" someone shouted.

As I looked at the crowd, it was like looking at a high school yearbook, only the living pictures in front of me represented segments of my life. Sitting at the front of the auditorium were my mother and father. I had prayed so many times that my parents would live long enough to see me get out of prison. To have them hear me preach again at Heritage USA was more than I could even imagine! I said, "All these faces, I can hardly stand it." I told the crowd, "I've got my whole life in front of me."

As I continued to look around the room and saw so many friends who were still serving God after surviving all that had happened at PTL, I was reminded afresh of God's promise, "I will never leave you or forsake you." The promise was not for me alone; it was for these people too. The faith of many in this room had been severely tried, and they had come through the refining fire as pure gold. They had not gotten bitter; they had become more loving, more kind, more Christlike. PTL was not a group of buildings; it was the people of God, in whom God was working. They truly were the People That Love, the people who, no matter what, have continued to Praise the Lord.

Slowly, and with deep emotion, I began to read the Twenty-third Psalm: "The LORD is my shepherd; I shall not want. . . . Yea, though I walk through the valley of the shadow of death, I will fear no evil. . . . Thou preparest a table before me in the presence of mine enemies."

I once thought that God had abandoned me. I thought that my days of ministering for the Lord were done. I thought that I would never preach again.

I was wrong.

Epilogue

ON JULY 22, 1996, SHORTLY AFTER JIM BAKKER HAD COMPLETED the writing of this book, a federal jury ruled that PTL was not selling securities by offering Lifetime Partnerships at Heritage USA. The jury's ruling thus affirms what Jim Bakker has contended from the first day he was indicted and throughout this volume.

The Publishers

Notes

Chapter 1
1. Karen Garloch and Nancy Webb, "A Sign in the Sky? Some People Saw It," *The Charlotte Observer*, Wednesday, 25 October 1989.

Chapter 2
1. *The Saturday Evening Post*, 1 September 1980.

Chapter 4
1. Richard Dortch, *Integrity* (Green Forest, AR: New Leaf Press, 1992), 15, 80-81.
2. Ibid., 87-89. Also Charles E. Shepard, *Forgiven* (New York: Atlantic Monthly Press, 1989), 284-86.
3. Shepard, *Forgiven*, 277, 284.
4. John Stewart, *Holy War* (Enid, OK: Fireside Publishing and Communications, 1987), 75.
5. Ibid.
6. Shepard, *Forgiven*, 306.
7. Dortch, *Integrity*, 139.
8. Stewart, *Holy War*, 75.
9. Dortch, *Integrity*, 139.
10. Ibid.
11. Swaggart's fax is reprinted in its entirety in Dortch, *Integrity*, 140-41 and Shepard, *Forgiven*, 495-96.
12. Dortch, *Integrity*, 142.
13. Ibid.
14. Ibid., 149.

Chapter 5
1. Shepard, *Forgiven*, 500-501.

Chapter 6
1. David Margolick, *The New York Times*, 28 June 1994; B, 15.
2. Dortch, *Integrity*, 155.
3. Ibid., 185, 188.
4. Ibid., 39.
5. Ibid., 159.
6. Ibid., 160.

Chapter 7
1. Jim Bakker files.
2. Shepard, *Forgiven*, 512.
3. Ibid., 514.

4. *Nightline*, ABC-TV, 20 March 1987.
5. Stewart, *Holy War*, 83; *Nightline*, 24 March 1987.
6. Jim Bakker's files. Also, Shepard, *Forgiven*.
7. Shepard, *Forgiven*, 536.
8. Bob Gray, audio transcript, 26 April 1987.
9. Jerry Falwell, news conference, Cocoa Beach, FL, 25 March 1987, broadcast by CNN.
10. Jerry Falwell, news conference, 28 April 1987, broadcast by CNN.
11. Jerry Falwell, news conference, 27 May 1987, broadcast by CNN.
12. Jerry Falwell, news conference, 8 October 1987, broadcast by CNN.

Chapter 8
1. Basil Jackson, *Headline News*, 31 August 1989, CNN.
2. Kevin M. Denny, "Jimmy, Where Were We?" *The Charlotte Observer*, 29 October 1989, B, 1, 4.

Chapter 9
1. Gary L. Wright, Charles E. Shepard, and Elizabeth Leland, "Jim Bakker May Be Back in Court Today," *The Charlotte Observer*, 6 September 1989; A, 1.
2. June Preston, "Bakker Ruled Competent; Trial Resumes," *United Press International*, 6 September 1989.

Chapter 14
1. Mike Murdock, "You Can Make It." Copyright 1979. Win-Way Products, Inc. P.O. Box 99, Dallas, TX 75221. All rights reserved. Used by permission.

Chapter 17
1. Tim Funk, "It's the PTL Movie," *The Charlotte Observer*, 11 March 1990, F, 7.
2. Mike Adkins, "Don't Give Up on the Brink of a Miracle." Copyright 1985. All rights reserved. Used by permission.

Chapter 19
1. June Preston, "One Thing's for Sure—Bakker's Alibi Is Solid," *United Press International*, 10 March 1990.

Chapter 22
1. As quoted in Tim Hansel, *Through the Wilderness of Loneliness* (Elgin, IL: David C. Cook Publishing Co., 1991), 23.
2. Ibid., 26.
3. Ibid., 29.
4. Ibid., 141.

Chapter 23
1. Gary L. Wright, "Bidders Lining Up for PTL Retreat, TV Ministry," *The Charlotte Observer*, 15 November 1989.

Chapter 25
1. Jamie Buckingham, "Praying for the Forgotten," *Charisma*, December 1990, 122.
2. *United States of America v. James O. Bakker*, United States Court of Appeals for the Fourth Circuit; Case No. 89-5687; 925 F2nd Series, 740.
3. Ibid.
4. Ibid.

Chapter 28
1. *United States of America v. James O. Bakker*, Court Document: 925 Federal Reporter, 2d Series, 740-41.
2. Linda Marx, "Jim and Tammy Faye Bakker Cry Hallelujah at the Chance His Prison Term Will Be Cut," *People*, 4 March 1991, 41.
3. Court Document Number C-CR-88-205, filed March 6, 1991, U.S. District Court W. District of N.C.

Chapter 29
1. Malcolm Smith, *Spiritual Burnout* (Tulsa, OK; Honor Books, Harrison House, 1988), 11.
2. Ibid., 113.
3. Ibid., 174.
4. Ibid., 181.

Chapter 31
1. "PTL Materials Used as Textbook," *The Chicago Tribune*, 9 March 1991; D, 4.
2. Ibid.
3. Paul Harvey, "Did Bakker's Victims Have a Choice?" *Delaware County Sunday Times*, 15 October 1989, 24.
4. "PTL Materials Used as Textbook," *The Chicago Tribune*.
5. Ibid.

Chapter 34
1. R.T. Kendall, *God Meant It for Good* (Charlotte, NC: Morningstar Publications, 1988), 152-53.
2. Ibid., 83.
3. Ibid., 85.
4. Ibid.
5. Ibid., 86.
6. Ibid., 87.
7. Ibid., 83-87, adapted.
8. Ibid., 192.
9. Ibid.
10. Ibid., 193.
11. Ibid.
12. Ibid., 194.
13. Ibid., 247, 249.

465

14. Ibid., 250.
15. Ibid.
16. Ibid., 251-52.
17. Ibid., 252.

Chapter 35
1. *Lifetime Partners of PTL v. M. Joseph Allman*, Successor Trustee for the Debtor, Heritage Village Church and Missionary Fellowship, Inc. a/k/a PTL, Case No. 87-01956; United States Bankruptcy Court for the District of South Carolina, 6 November 1991, 17-18.

Chapter 40
1. Mike Murdock, "God Is Not Through Blessing You." Copyright 1981. Win-Way Productions, Inc. All rights reserved. Used by permission.

Chapter 44
1. Dietrich Bonhoeffer, *Life Together* (New York: Harper & Row Publishers, 1954), 26-29.
2. Ibid.

Chapter 45
1. Ken Garfield, "Graham's New Journey: Reflecting on His Part," *The Charlotte Observer*, 16 August 1992.
2. Kendall, *God Meant It for Good*, 86.
3. *United States v. James O. Bakker;* Docket No. 88-CR-00205-01, 6-9. Official court transcripts of Rule 35 Hearing, November 16, 1992; Barbara K. Peterson, Official Court Reporter, U.S. District Court, Charlotte, NC, 6-9.

Chapter 46
1. Hansel, *Through the Wilderness of Loneliness*, 103.

Chapter 47
1. Ben Malcolm's written presentation to the U.S. Parole Commission, Kansas City Regional Office, April 1993.
2. *PTL*, 24 June 1987.
3. *United States v. James O. Bakker;* 925 F2d Federal Reporter, 731.
4. Kendall, *God Meant It for Good*, 86.
5. Cal Thomas, "Let Jim Bakker Go," *Los Angeles Times Syndicate*, 27 July 1993.
6. Notice of Action of Appeal; U.S. Dept. of Justice; U.S. Parole Commission, Chevy Chase, MD 20815, 27 July 1993.

Chapter 53
1. David Margolick, "Obituaries," *The New York Times*, 28 June 1994, B, 15.